UVF

In memory of my grandparents,
May and Jackie Graham

UVF
BEHIND
THE MASK

AARON EDWARDS

MERRION
PRESS

First published in 2017 by
Merrion Press
10 George's Street
Newbridge
Co. Kildare
Ireland
www.merrionpress.ie

© 2017, Aaron Edwards

978-1-78537-087-8 (Paper)
978-1-78537-088-5 (Kindle)
978-1-78537-106-6 (Epub)
978-1-78537-125-7 (PDF)

British Library Cataloguing in Publication Data
An entry can be found on request

Library of Congress Cataloging in Publication Data
An entry can be found on request

Interior design by www.jminfotechindia.com
Typeset in Minion Pro 11/14 pt

Cover design by www.phoenix-graphicdesign.com
Cover front: © Extramural Activity, 2014
Cover back: © private collection

Printed by ScandBook AB, Sweden

'All I maintain is that on this earth there are pestilences and there are victims, and it's up to us, so far as possible, not to join forces with the pestilences.'

Albert Camus, *The Plague* (1947)

'We have been the silent witnesses of evil deeds.'

Dietrich Bonhoeffer, *After Ten Years* (1953)

Aaron Edwards has been a Senior Lecturer in Defence and International Affairs at the Royal Military Academy Sandhurst since 2008. He is the author of several books, including *Mad Mitch's Tribal Law: Aden and the End of Empire* (2014) and *War: A Beginner's Guide* (2017). His work has featured in the *Irish Times, Belfast Telegraph, Belfast Newsletter* and *Irish News*.

'I have no doubt that in time to come, this new book by Aaron Edwards will be seen as the definitive history of the loyalist paramilitary grouping known as the Ulster Volunteer Force.'

Hugh Jordan, *Sunday World*

'The Ulster Volunteer Force can legitimately claim to have played an important role in the defeat of the Provisional IRA through its use of extreme violence, at times similar to what we have witnessed from ISIS. Aaron Edwards' work is easily the best account of this little known but possibly most successful terror group of the Northern Ireland Troubles.'

Jim Cusack, *Irish Independent*

CONTENTS

Author's Note   ix

Dramatis Personae   x

Acknowledgements   xiii

Foreword   xvii

Preface   xix

    Prologue. The Two Billys   1

1. The Bishop   9

2. 'Hell Slap it into Them'   23

3. Liquidating the Enemy   40

4. The Beginning of the End   55

5. Talking and Killing   69

6. Regimental Loyalty   82

7. The Shankill and its Butchers   97

8. 'That Bastard Murphy'   118

9. A Million Miles from Home   137

10. An Atmosphere of Pure History   151

11. At the Bottom of the Well   166

12. Compromise or Conflict   181

13. The Kitchen Cabinet   201

14. In the Hands of Philistines   217

15. Their only Crime was Loyalty   239

16. An Intense and Loyal Following 255

17. 'You're Either With Us or Against Us' 270

18. Family, in a Sicilian Sense 285

19. Decommissioning the Mindsets 307

20. The Praetorian Guard 321

Epilogue. The Sealed Knot 335

Endnotes 345

Abbreviations 385

UVF Structure 388

Chronology 390

Bibliography 394

Index 403

AUTHOR'S NOTE

Given the nature of the events described in this book it has been necessary for ethical, legal and security reasons to anonymise several of the interviewees who have assisted me. The major armed conflict in Northern Ireland may have subsided but the threat of violence has not gone away. Various journalists and academics – and those who have talked to them – have discovered, to their personal and professional cost, the consequences of engaging in research on paramilitary violence. By their very nature, the acts committed by these groups were illegal, whether that is accepted in some quarters, or not. And in liberal democracies, like the United Kingdom, law enforcement agencies have a duty to investigate whenever there are reasonable grounds for suspecting that a crime has been committed. As a series of proscribed acts, terrorism remains unlawful. With no statute of limitations on murder, and no mechanism for 'dealing with the past', people involved in these acts are still liable to be prosecuted in ongoing or future investigations.

I would like to thank those journalists, academics, police officers, solicitors and other legal professionals who took the time to explain the law to me and to discuss the many pitfalls of researching political violence in Northern Ireland. As I have consistently said in public, it is vital that when historians interview eyewitnesses – and perhaps even participants – to the events under scrutiny, we ensure we first do no harm. To that end, I made it clear to my interviewees that they must not incriminate themselves or others (unless allegations made were against those now deceased) in specified unlawful acts. My aim, however, is to narrate the most accurate story possible despite these limitations.

DRAMATIS PERSONAE

John Bingham Born in 1953, Bingham joined the UVF sometime in the early 1970s. He was assassinated by the Provisional IRA at his home on 14 September 1986 in disputed circumstances. Bingham was the commander of the 1st Belfast Battalion of the UVF when he died.

'The Craftsman' Born in the late 1940s, he is believed to have served as the UVF's second-in-command and Director of Operations. Rumoured to have joined the organisation on Easter Tuesday 1966, he became a founding member of the UVF's C Company in the Shankill, subsequently rising to the Brigade Staff in the late 1970s. He led the UVF's talks with the Irish government in the early 1990s.

David Ervine Born in 1953, Ervine joined the East Belfast UVF in 1972. He was arrested and imprisoned for the possession of explosives in 1974. After his release from prison in 1980, he became a shopkeeper and joined the PUP, running, unsuccessfully, for the Belfast Pottinger ward on the city council in 1985. He subsequently became the party's spokesperson and later its leader. Ervine was elected to the Northern Ireland Forum in 1997 and the Northern Ireland Assembly in 1998, serving as an MLA for East Belfast until his death in January 2007.

Billy Greer Born in 1943, Greer joined the UVF in 1968. He became the commander of the East Antrim UVF in the mid-1970s. When the East Antrim and North Belfast battalions of the UVF were merged in the 1990s, he became deputy to Rab Warnock until 2004 when he resigned his position. He was elected to the University Ward of Newtownabbey Borough Council in 1997, serving until 2001. He died in July 2006.

Gary Haggarty Born in 1970, he allegedly joined the UVF in the early 1990s and rose to prominence within its North Belfast Battalion. He took over command of the East Antrim and North Belfast UVF in 2004, replacing Rab Warnock. He was arrested in 2010 for the murder of John Harbinson in 1997 and became an assisting offender. At the time of writing, his trial for terrorist-related offences is still pending.

Jim Hanna Born in 1948, Hanna was a leading member of the UVF's Brigade Staff when he was killed in April 1974. Reports suggested that he was the group's Director of Operations or its Chief of Staff. He was also rumoured to have worked for British Intelligence, which would explain why his name never appeared on the organisation's official Roll of Honour when it was issued in 2006.

Billy Hutchinson Born in 1957, Hutchinson was a member of the UVF's C Company in West Belfast when he was arrested and imprisoned for his role in a double murder. Inside Long Kesh he became close to Gusty Spence, holding the appointment of Adjutant. Upon his release, Hutchinson became involved with the cross-community group SICDP (later Interaction Belfast) on the Upper Springfield Road. He later worked for the Mount Vernon Community Association. He was an MLA from 1998 until 2003 and a City Councillor from 1997 until 2005. He became PUP leader in 2011 and was re-elected to Belfast City Council in 2014.

Trevor King Born in 1953, King joined the UVF at sixteen. Aged eighteen, he took part in the 'Battle of Springmartin' estate in 1972. A legend within the UVF, he took over as commander of the UVF's 1st Belfast Battalion after the assassination of John Bingham in 1986, overseeing the complete restructuring of the Belfast military teams in the late 1980s and early 1990s. Known as 'Kingo' to his friends, he was shot by the INLA on 16 June 1994 and died just over three weeks later.

Frenchie Marchant Born in 1948, Marchant was a leading member of the UVF's 1st Belfast Battalion on the Shankill Road. Implicated in the supergrass trials of the early 1980s, he was assassinated by the INLA on 28 April 1987 as he stood outside the PUP offices on the Shankill Road.

William Irvine Mitchell Born in 1939, Mitchell was part of the conspiracy which gave birth to the modern UVF. A member of TARA in the late 1960s, he later joined the UVF and became the commander of its East Antrim Battalion in 1970. Mitchell was appointed to the UVF's Brigade Staff in the mid-1970s. Arrested and imprisoned for his role in the killing of two UDA members, Mitchell served fourteen years in prison. He was released in 1990 and subsequently became involved in the PUP. A leading strategist for the PUP, he died in July 2006.

Lenny Murphy Born in 1952, he was a prominent member of the West Belfast UVF. A commander in the organisation's notorious Brown Bear 'team', he was implicated in dozens of murders and attempted murders in the first half of the 1970s and in the months after his release from a six-year spell in prison in 1982. He was assassinated by the Provisional IRA in November of the same year.

Hugh Smyth Smyth was born in 1941. A long-time member of the Orange Order, he became a spokesperson for the UVF in the 1970s and was a founding member of the PUP in 1977–8. He served for forty-one years on Belfast City Council. He became the city's Deputy Lord Mayor in 1983 and 1993, and was eventually appointed Lord Mayor in 1994–5. Awarded an OBE for his services to the community in 1996, he died in May 2012.

Gusty Spence Born in 1933, Spence joined the Royal Ulster Rifles in the mid-1950s, seeing action in Cyprus during the EOKA Emergency. He was sworn into the UVF in 1965 and led its Shankill unit until his arrest in 1966. He escaped briefly in 1972 and went on the run, helping to restructure the organisation. He was released from prison in 1984, becoming involved with the PUP until his retirement from politics in the late 1990s. He died in September 2011.

'The Pipe' is believed to have joined the UVF in the late 1960s. Born sometime in the late 1940s, he joined the UVF in the late 1960s. He is believed to have risen to the position of UVF military commander and, subsequently, took over as its Chief of Staff in the mid-1970s. An articulate and tough individual, he has been a key architect of the UVF's long transition from war to peace.

Rab Warnock Born in 1948, Warnock joined the UVF in the 1970s and was imprisoned in Long Kesh in the middle of that decade. A tough and streetwise individual, he was the Officer Commanding of Compound 19 in Long Kesh. Sometime after his release from prison, he rose up the ranks to become the overall commander of the East Antrim and North Belfast UVF. He died in December 2012.

Billy Wright Born in 1960, Wright joined the Mid Ulster UVF in 1975 and was imprisoned for terrorist-related offences in 1977. After his release in the early 1980s, he underwent a brief conversion to Christianity. By the late 1980s he had risen to prominence to assume overall command of the Mid Ulster UVF when its long-serving commander, Robin Jackson, stepped down. Wright was assassinated by the INLA in the Maze Prison in December 1997.

ACKNOWLEDGEMENTS

This has been the most challenging book I have ever written. It has had a long gestation, stretching back over three decades to when I first became aware that I was growing up in an environment that was, by all accounts, deeply unusual. I was born in Belfast in 1980 and grew up in the predominantly working-class areas of Rathcoole and Carnmoney in Newtownabbey on the outskirts of North Belfast. It is a part of Northern Ireland that acts as an intersection between the sprawling urban streets of the region's capital, Belfast, and the vast undulating rural Glens of Antrim. It is also somewhere deeply intertwined with the history of the modern Ulster Volunteer Force (UVF). In the 1960s, UVF units based in Carrickfergus, Glengormley and Rathcoole carried out a series of sectarian attacks in conjunction with another UVF unit on the Shankill. This form of militant loyalism soon spread throughout the province. As it grew, the organisation became more centralised and structured along British Army lines across five 'brigade' areas: Belfast, East Antrim, Mid Ulster, North Antrim, and Londonderry and North West Ulster. Each of these areas was sub-divided into 'battalions', 'companies' and 'platoons', though in reality each of these sub-units was split into welfare 'teams' and military 'teams'.

At the time of writing, most of those structures are still in place and, despite the hard work of some genuinely progressive people, show little sign of withering away on their own. In fact, the most recent evidence suggests that a 'Praetorian Guard' has been formed to maintain the old adage of a 'pike in the thatch'. One only hopes that the record provided in this book will highlight the wrong turns taken by loyalists in the past, before more young people ruin their lives by travelling the futile road of paramilitary violence.

Several people have made the process of researching and writing much easier than expected. The person who originally suggested that I write the book was the former UVF Brigade Staff officer turned PUP strategist Billy Mitchell. At a meeting in Monkstown in October 2005 he asked me: 'When are you going to write the history of the UVF?' He paused for a moment, grinned, then continued: 'Cos you'll have to do it before these guys [indicating the group's senior leadership] and others, like me, pass on.' I told Billy then that I would undertake the project. 'Ah,' he said, 'but it needs to be told warts and all.' I hope that this book has fulfilled the objective which Billy first handed down to me, as difficult and dangerous as it has been for me to do so. The story I narrate will not please everyone, but hopefully it has prized open a pitch-black past and exposed it to a little more light than heat.

Billy was a close friend and mentor as I worked with him and others to try and bring the UVF, in his memorable phrase, 'out of the jungle', and along the path of conflict transformation, from war to peace. Without his support and advice between 2001 and his tragic death in July 2006, I would not have had the confidence to assist in this ambitious project. From the moment I first encountered Billy when he gave an oration at Derry Hill in Rathcoole in November 2000, until a few weeks before his death when I sat in his company with community representatives, leading UVF members and a handful of 'critical friends' to address the legacy of the violent conflict, I knew Billy was a sincere individual who wanted to right the wrongs he and others had committed in the past. It was said of Billy by his friend Liam Maskey that not only did he 'walk the walk' but that he demanded others 'walk with him'. I always found that to be true.

Ben Forde, the policeman who began a dialogue with Billy and other former paramilitaries in the 1980s, told me that he believed strongly that 'God had a plan' and that he 'used me and Billy – and now you – to bring this message to the world'. While I would not claim the same reserve of spiritual faith that these two gentlemen drew upon in truly dark times, I would like to think that everything happens for a reason. With that in mind, I would like to acknowledge Ben's assistance in accessing his collection of correspondence with Billy, which shed new light on our mutual friend's prison experience. In the years that I knew him, the 1980s always seemed like something of a 'black box' as far as Billy Mitchell was concerned. He rarely talked about it. Therefore, it was imperative that I spoke to those who knew Billy well in those years. I spoke to Ian Major and Kenny McClinton at length about their interactions with Billy in the 1980s and 1990s. Without their perspectives, I would have been unable to offer a more rounded picture of Billy's intellectual development from conflict to peace.

For obvious legal and security reasons, I cannot name the numerous individuals who assisted me with my research. However, it is unlikely that this book could ever have been written in such detail without their help. As with my other research and writing in the past, the ability to undertake this kind of work in an honest way would not have been possible without the trust placed in me by many loyalists, including those belonging to the UVF, at all levels. I would like to acknowledge the cooperation of the UVF leadership who responded to my questions over the years. I only hope that I have represented their views fairly.

Writers and researchers around the world have always relied upon individuals who are prepared to assist them by going the extra mile and putting themselves at considerable risk. This book was no different. Apart from the assistance afforded by the late Billy Mitchell in the last years of his life, I benefited enormously from the assistance of 'Matthew'. Without his help, this book would not have been possible. I would like to pay tribute to the risks he has taken to ensure I gained a balanced insight into the UVF.

Someone I can publicly acknowledge for the trust he placed in me is the leader of the PUP, Billy Hutchinson, who has given me incredible insights into progressive loyalism over the sixteen years I have known him. Billy's encouragement during some very difficult periods in the research prevented me from throwing in the towel. Similarly, my friend Dawn Purvis recalled her extensive work alongside David Ervine and gave me an unparalleled glimpse into the PUP's relationship with the UVF. Tom Roberts at EPIC had also been helpful and supportive. None of these people bears any responsibility for my analysis.

Other individuals who opened doors and sat with me for hours as I wrote, spoke and interviewed people since 2001 include Gusty Spence, Jim McDonald, Billy McCaughey, Billy Greer, Bobby Gourley, David Ervine and Hugh Smyth, all of whom are no longer with us. I am fortunate in having known these people personally and, importantly, to have been able to revisit other people's memories of them and their interactions with me many years ago. Thanks also to Johnny Adair, Liz Bingham, Robert Niblock and Clifford Peeples, as well as a range of interviewees – some are named and others are not – who have taken the time to talk to me over very many years.

Others who have helped enormously include Stephen Bloomer, a close friend and confidant, Dr Sean Brennan, Dr Paddy Hoey, Dr Martin McCleery and Dr Connal Parr. Without their support, this project would have floundered in its later stages. Prof. Arthur Aughey, Prof. Lord Bew, Joe Bowers, Glenn Bradley, Ian Cobain, Prof. Richard English, Harry Donaghy, Nigel Gardiner, John Greer, Phil Hamilton, Prof. Tom Hennessey, Hugh Jordan, Joe Law (sadly missed by his friends and comrades), Prof. Jim McAuley, Lyra McKee, Brendan Mackin, Les Mitchell, Dr Gareth

Mulvenna, Dr Tony Novosel (and his late wife, Alice, also sadly missed by us all), Niall O'Murchu, Prof. Henry Patterson, Derek Poole, Dr Richard Reed, Dr Andrew Sanders, Prof. Jon Tonge, Iain Turner, Prof. Graham Walker and Ian S. Wood all helped to clarify my thinking on a range of matters. As ever, Malachi O'Doherty has been an outstanding source of ideas and inspiration.

I must also thank my colleagues at the Royal Military Academy Sandhurst for supporting my continuing research on Northern Ireland. Tim Bean, Dr Christopher Duffy, Dr Ed Flint, Lieutenant Colonel (Ret'd) Peter McCutcheon MBE, Sean McKnight, Dr Martin Smith, Simon Taylor and Alan Ward were always on hand, while Colonel (Ret'd) David Benest OBE has challenged my thinking on the military and strategic dimensions of the 'troubles'.

Thanks also to the hard work of the team at Merrion Press. My publisher Conor Graham has been astounding in his support of this project and my editor Fiona Dunne has kept me right when I began to veer off the beaten track. It was Lisa Hyde who first encouraged me to submit the proposal to Merrion and I want to thank her for doing so. The advice given by John Greer at Reavey & Company in Belfast has helped put my mind at ease on some of the more challenging legal aspects of a book like this.

I feel it is important at this stage to state that I am solely responsible for the analysis presented in this book.

In closing, I would like to put on record the enormous support from my family over the years – my mother and father, Barbara and Jim; my brother and sister, Ryan and Stephanie; and the wider Edwards and Graham clans – who all helped sustain me throughout some very challenging times indeed. This book would just not be possible without their forbearance. I am also indebted to the love and direction provided by my late grandparents, May and Jackie Graham, who kept us all safe during the troubles. This book is dedicated to their memory. As my grandfather was fond of telling me, 'Always be a good listener.' I hope this is reflected in the book you now hold in your hands.

FOREWORD

BY MARTIN DILLON

Sometimes when I begin reading a book, I sense that I was wise to have opened it. This was the case with *UVF: Behind the Mask* by Aaron Edwards. From the first chapter I was persuaded that he has a genuine grasp of a very complex topic at the heart of the 'troubles', namely the significant political and violent roles of the highly secretive Ulster Volunteer Force.

With an eye for detail and an intimate knowledge of political nuances at work in Northern Ireland's tribal environment, he succeeds in unpacking the genesis of the UVF. He takes his reader on a journey to a genuine understanding of an organisation that created an aura of mystery while its members engaged in organised crime and terror, often displaying a propensity for the most grotesque violence, especially in the multiple killings by the Shankill Butchers. Aaron Edwards weaves his personal knowledge and experiences of having grown up in Belfast into his explanations about the origins of the separateness of the two communities and the violence they inflicted on each other.

Like any good historian, he strips his findings back to basics for the reader, making expert use of the eyes and memories of witnesses. He offers a fine analysis of the inherited prejudices, fears and dreams of his subjects. He skilfully avoids the trap of succumbing to oral history distortions of the past. Instead, he confronts head-on the UVF's adoration of the cult of the gunman, its glorification of violence, and its tendency to manufacture history while often ignoring facts.

Always remaining true to the data and to his sources, Aaron Edwards questions the truthfulness of sources, while maintaining his focus on the broader context and parameters of the conflict and its impact on society as a whole. His research skills are impressive in his outlines of the re-emergence of the UVF against the fast-evolving landscape of protest, tribalism, sectarianism, paranoia and fear in 1960s Northern Ireland. He cleverly navigates a path through the violence emanating from both communities, displaying an intimate knowledge of the shorthand for the political machinations of all the players. He also explains the ways the UVF often denied its role in terror and how it came to realise that making peace came with a cost to its unity and existence.

Great historians are good storytellers and Aaron Edwards belongs in this class. His account of the modern UVF's history is told without embellishment. Facts are carefully woven into the troubles' historical tapestry. He is aware that UVF supporters will not see the UVF as he does. For them, it will always be the last line of defence in a loyalist community that continues to embrace a siege mentality on an island with unresolved divisions and a violent past. *UVF: Behind The Mask* is an excellent addition to the written history of the troubles.

Martin Dillon,
California, May 2017

PREFACE

For much of the afternoon of Tuesday, 11 September 2001, I was engrossed in conversation with veteran members of the Ulster Volunteer Force (UVF), an illegal Northern Ireland-based terrorist group responsible for hundreds of deaths and thousands of injuries during the 'troubles'. We were meeting in a neatly refurbished working man's social club, which served as the powerbase of the organisation's East Antrim Battalion, situated in Monkstown, a working-class estate on the outskirts of North Belfast. As we sat discussing the finer points of English premiership football and horse racing, we were suddenly interrupted by news from one of the bar stewards that two planes had crashed into the World Trade Center in New York. I vividly remember standing transfixed as the images were beamed onto the club's huge projection screen. The irony was not lost on me as I watched these events unfold on the other side of the Atlantic. Mass-casualty terrorism was unleashing its devastating killing potential across the most iconic skyline in the world while I sat quietly and comfortably opposite men who had probably been responsible for sustaining one of the longest-running campaigns of terror in British history.

The new UVF was reconstituted in 1965 as a preemptive defence mechanism against a perceived Irish Republican Army (IRA) threat, though its main purpose was as an instrument to put pressure on the ruling Unionist Party that was seen as weak on Irish republicanism and far too liberal in its views on northern Catholics and the Republic of Ireland. In a world of half-truths and paranoia, the reality was somewhat different, of course. The IRA would remain moribund until the outbreak of serious intercommunal violence between Protestants and Catholics in August 1969. While Al-Qaeda could now claim to have killed more innocent people in one day than any other terrorist organisation in history, the UVF could certainly claim the dubious title of being one of the world's oldest and most resilient terrorist groups, which, on 11 September 2001, was still very much in existence.

The UVF has cast a long, dark shadow over life in Northern Ireland. During the troubles it killed 564 people, mostly Catholic civilians, and injured thousands more Protestants and Catholics between its first killing in 1966 and its most recent in 2010. Its violence – like that perpetrated by the

IRA and its nearest rivals in the loyalist Ulster Defence Association (UDA) – has left behind a bloody legacy of almost 4,000 deaths and ten times as many injuries in a relatively small region of only 1.8 million people. Yet the physical and psychological scars on Northern Irish society are apparent to anyone who has taken the trouble to look. Had the same violence been unleashed on the population of Great Britain, the proportional numbers killed would have stood at 100,000, and, if it happened in the United States, the losses would have peaked somewhere in the region of the astronomically high figure of 1 million.

Today, most people think that Northern Ireland is at peace. After all, a 'peace process' was indeed begun in the early 1990s, culminating in the signing of the Belfast Agreement in 1998 and the establishment of power-sharing institutions a decade later. Crucially, it is important that we acknowledge the limitations of this process. For one thing, it has not completely ended the conflict and removed the causes which gave rise to it in the first place. Almost twenty years on from the peace accord brokered between Unionist and Nationalist politicians, loyalist and republican terrorist groups are still in existence. What is more, they have shown a willingness to become involved in civil disturbances, intimidation, threats, physical violence, particularly within their own communities, and even murder, whenever the situation demands it.

For this reason, you will find much of what you read here shocking. It is a story of young men (and occasionally young women) who turned to violence, some in the heat of the moment and others in more premeditated circumstances. At the time and since, many of these individuals would give their motives for doing so as indicative of wanting to 'hit back', to 'defend their country' or to 'return the serve' against Irish republicans. Others, less troubled by the trappings of patriotism, engaged in violence because of the promise of power, money, and the status it gave them in the deprived working-class communities where they try to carve out lives for themselves and their families. No matter what the motive, the collective sum of all parts of this violence was to contribute to the continuation of the Northern Ireland conflict from its outbreak in the 1960s – via the intense violence of the 1970s, 1980s and 1990s – to the present day. There were other motives, of course, and this book is aimed at uncovering what they were.

★★★

As a professional historian, I draw inspiration from the advice passed on to future generations of writers by one of the twentieth century's most influential historians, the French intellectual and resistance fighter Marc Bloch. Bloch was a man of action as well as a man of letters and – as a direct consequence – paid the ultimate price for his activism when he was captured, imprisoned and subsequently machine-gunned to death by the Nazis in occupied France as the Allies invaded to liberate his country in June 1944. Bloch believed history to be the study of both the dead and the living. In a line that would become synonymous with his approach to the past, he wrote, 'As soon as we admit that a mental or emotional reaction is not self-explanatory, we are forced in turn, whenever such a reaction occurs, to make a real effort to discover the reasons for it. In a word, in history, as elsewhere, the causes cannot be assumed. They are to be looked for ...'[1]

One of my motivations was to uncover the real causes of the 'mental or emotional' reactions that lead people to engage in violence. This has necessitated adopting the time-honoured historical approach of assembling evidence and scrutinising it as rigorously as possible, while placing it in its proper context. In pursuing a forensic examination of the causes and consequences of individual and collective actions, it has been necessary to recognise that the past is as hotly contested as the present and, without sounding too cynical, as the future may well be in this deeply divided society. In ethnic conflicts, like Northern Ireland, rival groups rarely agree on much, except on who they do not like. The past is an important adhesive in binding these prejudices together and giving them a meaning that, in marginalised and deprived communities, acts as an accelerant on an open fire.

Interestingly, most of those who write about Northern Ireland's troubled past do so in a way that removes human agency from the violence. To deny that the people responsible for some of the most horrific killings of the twentieth century were ordinary men and women, with human frailties and with choices, is to sanitise the past according to the political logic of the present. I realise that my approach will not be welcomed by many who were caught up in the events narrated here. However, the findings are accurate and based on evidence, including interviews with people who were intimately involved in UVF activity, from the origins of the troubles to the present day.

The book also takes inspiration from the important work by Canadian liberal journalist and politician Michael Ignatieff, who informs us that when investigating these sorts of conflicts, 'The very fact of being an outsider discredits rather than reinforces one's legitimacy. For there is always a truth that can be known only by those on the inside.'[2] It has, therefore, been necessary to adopt an approach acknowledging that I am 'already native' in this setting, by the objective fact that I was 'born of this island', to paraphrase the late, great Ulster poet John Hewitt, and having lived alongside people who feature prominently in this story. Unlike numerous academics who refuse to admit that their background colours their analysis, my identity has facilitated access where others are unlikely or unwilling to tread.

★★★

I have been watching the UVF at close quarters for over two decades – even longer if we include the fact that I am from the working-class community where it has traditionally recruited its foot soldiers. However, I must make it absolutely clear that I am not a supporter or an apologist of this organisation. I refuse to seriously entertain the conceited view that ordinary working-class people who live 'cheek by jowl' with terrorist organisations (for that is what they are – they use terror to spread fear in a political context) are either necessarily sympathetic or supportive of, or complicit in, the actions of these people.[3] Often, people are forced to live with the presence of armed groups because the state has failed to retain the monopoly over the legitimate use of force. In many respects it appears, on the surface at least, that the state has ceded authority to these malign non-state actors in some of the country's most marginalised neighbourhoods.[4]

This book challenges the misguided view that people who join terrorist groups are all 'willing executioners', driven wholly by structural forces or cultures that give them no other choice than to become involved in violence. All human beings are endowed with a degree of free will and must choose to become involved in the enterprise of murder, or not. In much of what you read here, the motives of paramilitaries are directly attributable to a range of micro factors: peer pressure, the internal structures by which the UVF enforced discipline, or by a deep-seated hunger for revenge, all of which propel people into action just as readily as macro factors like intolerance, ideology or, as has become a fashionable explanation in certain circles, a conspiracy of 'collusion' with representatives of the British state and its Security Forces. The truth is much more complicated than the propagandists would have us believe.[5]

Whether we choose to accept it, or not, the actions of a few violent men (and women) in committing some of the worst atrocities of the troubles continue to affect the society and politics of this part of the world. That cannot be a good thing. Yet regardless of my own personal beliefs, there seems to me to be an urgent need to strip back the parochial language used to describe this phenomenon – of militancy within predominantly marginalised and deprived working-class communities – to instead ask serious questions about why, how, and with what consequences, members of the UVF felt the need to take the lives of other human beings in the way that they did.

Therefore, I am interested in depicting the violent acts perpetrated by these individuals not only according to their primary motivations but also in terms of their secondary motivations and, ultimately, tertiary motivations, which make sense only within the wider political context in which they are committed. The truth is that this is a complex story. To say that religion was always the motivating factor is empirically wrong and cannot be supported by the evidence. The fact remains that not all UVF killings were motivated by a 'pro-British, anti-republican' ideology either. Many members were blissfully unaware of British or Irish history and politics. Very few had a sophisticated understanding of Ulster unionism or Protestantism, never mind Catholicism, Irish republicanism or nationalism. The fact is that some of the UVF's murders were a direct result of umbrage being taken by an acquaintance so as to save face, as a consequence of simply 'looking for a taig', personal grudges against a particular person who happened to be a nationalist or republican in political belief, the 'thrill of the kill', and because the protagonists would have become murderers even if the political conflict did not give meaning to their actions. To suggest otherwise is to abdicate responsibility for assessing the myriad causes and consequences of violent conflict in this divided society and risks foregoing the opportunity to identify and ameliorate what terrorism experts call 'root causes'.

***

In order to explain the actions of the UVF it has also been necessary to look at other illegal armed groupings like the UDA/Ulster Freedom Fighters, Irish National Liberation Army and the Provisional IRA, as well as those of the legal British State Security Forces. This is important, for without examining the phenomenon of political violence more broadly it is difficult to explain why the UVF members did what they did. Understandably, these are questions that have been asked of other armed groupings around the world and are questions I am just as likely to ask in my own teaching on Hamas, Hezbollah, ETA, the Islamic State in Iraq and al-Sham (ISIS, known by the Arabs as Daesh) and even Al-Qaeda. Yet one would be forgiven for thinking that what has happened in Northern Ireland is *sui generis*, a preposterous assumption that has hampered much analysis of political violence there.

In this respect, I am more interested in the generic features of the UVF as a militant group – how it recruited, trained and organised, the disciplinary system of control exerted over its volunteers, its command structures, how it operated when carrying out its 'counter-terrorist campaign against violent nationalism' and everyone else, and, perhaps, most controversially of all, the forensic details of its acts of violence. It is my intention to look behind the mask of UVF terror to paint as accurate and comprehensive a picture as it is possible to give of a ruthless, organised and determined armed group.

It is my belief that the violence recorded in this book is not the only past we can attribute to the wider working-class Protestant community. In fact, for those of us who have lived with the oppressive reality of paramilitarism in our communities, there is an urgency to address the underlying conditions that give rise to these groups if we are ever to eradicate them from our midst. A good place to start – for all of us in Northern Ireland, Great Britain and Ireland – would be in resolving to adhere to the principle that what happened in the troubles should never be allowed to happen again. Only when this level of maturity and honesty is reached can we hope to transform the situation we have found ourselves living in beyond the violence that has for so long plagued our lives.

Prologue

THE TWO BILLYS

'Only the dead are safe; only the dead have seen the end of war'

George Santayana, *Soliloquies in England and Later Soliloquies*.[1]

The blistering warmth of the summer's day made sitting indoors uncomfortable; probably one of the reasons why people had started to mill around in the shade. As the funeral cortège passed by, throngs of burly men joined the ranks of the mourners. Six neatly turned out pall-bearers sporting black trousers, white shirts and skinny black ties clasped arms as they shouldered the pristine oak coffin, which had been carefully dressed with the familiar paramilitary trappings of the purple-coloured Ulster Volunteer Force (UVF) flag, coal-black beret and shiny brown leather gloves. Progressive Unionist Party (PUP) leader David Ervine brushed past me, as he barged into the swollen ranks of paramilitary types, young and old, many of whom fell back into line briskly, with little fuss.

A sea of grimacing, solemn faces pushed silently into the light breeze as the sound of semi-marching feet trudged along keeping time to a lone piper's lament. As the medieval noise of the pipes gathered to a crescendo, the mourners congregated outside the tiny Baptist church. Standing proud at the foot of the railway bridge, the poky little church was the focal point of the exclusively Protestant working-class housing estate overshadowed by Carnmoney Hill, a commanding, undulating feature that presides over everyday life in this part of Northern Ireland.

The funeral on this occasion was for prominent loyalist Billy Greer, who had been a leading member of the outlawed UVF and a former PUP councillor on Newtownabbey Borough Council. Greer was a popular figure, a larger-than-life character held in high esteem by his fellow councillors and by a legion of supporters in the local community. During his tenure on the local authority he had even met Prince Charles, on one of his many visits to the area; a photo of Billy bowing to the heir to the throne still hangs in the social club he chaired for over a generation. Greer lived in Monkstown all his life except, of course, for the time he spent incarcerated for UVF membership, in the compounds of Long Kesh in the 1970s. Those close to Greer admired how he had worked tirelessly for those who resided in this fiercely working-class housing estate. As a consequence of the PUP's effective voting management, he was elected in University Ward in 1997 with 448 First Preferences votes.[2] Greer was a strong believer in the community spirit that lay at the heart of the UVF's support base in areas like this across Northern Ireland. Consequently, Monkstown was synonymous with Billy Greer and the UVF; it would now turn out *en mass* to give him a good send-off.

On the day of Greer's funeral, I was enrolled as chauffeur to three UVF veterans. It was a glum occasion. As such, the car was loaded up with an eclectic mix of former gunmen and auxiliaries who counted Greer as one of their 'team', a comrade from 'the old days'. As the men spoke they seemed to have captured their memories of their friend in a bubble of surreptitious remembrance. They painted a picture of a world inhabited by 'goodies' and 'badies', and they, they assured me, were firmly on the 'right side'. 'Ulster', the men were at pains to tell me, 'had then been under threat from militant republicans', and this presaged first vigilantism, and then a military response. It meant that everyone needed to pull together for the good of the community; for the good of their country. It was also a time when almost everyone was armed and connected to one or other of the alphabetic spaghetti bowl of paramilitary organisations sprouting foot soldiers across the province. Northern Ireland became awash with weapons, blood and death during these years. Popularly known as 'the troubles', violence and murder had exploded onto the streets in the spring and summer of 1966, when the UVF perpetrated a handful of attacks across Belfast, Rathcoole and Carrickfergus.

Forty years almost to the day when the first UVF killings rocked Northern Ireland, the organisation was still in existence. There was nothing to indicate otherwise, in that it had murdered over thirty-two people since its 1994 ceasefire – almost all of them, bizarrely, from the Protestant community they claimed to be defending. Although the violence from all sides had wound down significantly, loyalists, it seemed, were stuck in a time warp; biding their time, and waiting for any excuse to return to war.

Over 3,700 men, women and children had tragically lost their lives over thirty years of political violence. And although the Provisional IRA murdered around 1,800 people before calling a halt to its campaign in 2005, the UVF contributed significantly to the overall body count, killing somewhere in the region of 564 people and injuring many more.[3] Its founding members claimed at the time that it had originally been formed to oppose the perceived threat posed by the IRA, though they later admitted that the UVF was really a tool of political intrigue utilised by a handful of faceless right-wing unionist politicians. The irony that the UVF pre-dated the Provisional IRA and had now outlasted its old foe was not lost on me, as I watched the organisation bury one of its leading lights on that piping hot summer's day.

As I edged my way into the crowd, which had by now assembled according to their importance inside the organisation's hierarchy, I searched for a friendly face. Even though I had been born and reared in the area, and was known by those connected to the organisation for my voluntary work on a UVF-endorsed conflict transformation process aimed at its disarmament and eventual departure from the 'stage', I was a non-member – a civilian – and therefore counted very much as an outsider, at least in public.

The more senior UVF veterans, all men in their 50s, 60s and 70s, sharply drawn frowns and rugged faces, sloped in behind the family circle of their fallen comrade. All the top brass had turned out – from the leader of the organisation, the so-called Chief-of-Staff, known to his close confidants as 'The Pipe', through to his headquarters staff and a sprinkling of local commanders from across the province. There seemed to be more chiefs than Indians in attendance. All of them dressed in smart suits and sensible shoes, even if some of them insisted on the addition of not-so-sensible white socks. The sweet smell of cheap deodorant and aftershave wafted through the air, as beads of sweat dripped beneath the arms of the stockier members of the crowd. They had now formed up, ready to see off their fallen comrade.

By now the piper's lament had been drowned out by the sobbing of Greer's wife, family and close friends, all of whom were now emotionally gathered round the coffin as it paused under the mural painting of the iconic charge of the 36th (Ulster) Division at Thiepval Wood in the first Battle of the Somme on 1 July 1916. Billy had prided himself on the upkeep of the mural, and it would become a shrine to him when he died.

Militarists led politicos, with many of the latter having worked with the dead loyalist when he was the chairman of the PUP's East Antrim

Constituency Association, the UVF's political associates. A member of the UVF since 1968, he was a commander of the group's powerful East Antrim Battalion from the mid-1970s until it amalgamated with North Belfast in the mid-1990s. Prior to its amalgamation with North Belfast, Billy Greer was asked by the UVF leadership to join the PUP talks team in the mid-1990s as a means of selling the loyalist ceasefire to the organisation's rank-and-file. Greer inhabited a place within the UVF that – in equivalent terms – was reserved only for the likes of Bobby Storey in the republican movement. In other words, Greer was a key grassroots figure, a man of stature and influence, the proverbial 'UVF man's UVF man', that ranks of volunteers looked up to and followed out of a mixture of fear and adulation. When Billy Greer attended the multi-party talks in 1997/98, he was not attending as a PUP member *per se* but as the UVF Brigade Staff's plenipotentiary.

When he died, Billy was no longer the deputy commander of the UVF's East Antrim and North Belfast brigade. He had tendered his resignation to 'The Pipe' over the activities of some of his colleagues on the local command group who had gone against Brigade Staff policy. Following an internal investigation, Billy, his brigadier and long-time friend sixty-year-old Rab Warnock, and their team were replaced by a relatively unknown UVF man called Gary Haggarty. It was a choice that would have huge repercussions for the organisation as it sought to dismantle its paramilitary structures over the next decade.

That Greer was held in such high esteem meant that few people questioned why the organisation had not taken more stringent action against the leadership around Warnock, especially in light of the seriousness of the allegations levelled against them. He still remained chairman of the local social club, an indefatigable presence who dominated working-class life in the district, just as prominently as the Napoleon's Nose feature jutting out of Belfast's Cave Hill Mountain, which could be seen some way in the distance towering above the city. Billy knew everybody and everybody knew Billy. Nothing, except death it seemed, could remove him from the place he called his home for over half a century. Greer had been the quintessential community activist, frequently interviewed by local newspapers, whether it was about his campaign of dispensing free personal alarms for the elderly or urging the removal of unsightly paramilitary murals in Newtownabbey.

It was his positive contribution to returning this place to some semblance of normality that left people aghast when they learned of the extent of the actions of the area's UVF leadership. I had heard that some of these men had joined the UVF for political reasons, while others were there to line their own pockets. Greer had been in the former category. He had joined the UVF at the very beginning, prior to the outbreak of the troubles, and he would later rise to prominence in the 1970s, when the IRA began its armed campaign. Now, three decades later, he had fallen on his sword for the men around him. In the two years after he was replaced, Billy became a different man. He stopped drinking and, though he was still the life and soul of the company he kept, he had become isolated inside the organisation he loved.

On the day of his funeral, though, he was just another fallen comrade. The UVF had put its internal squabbles aside and forged a united front. A clear signal was being sent out. Whatever had happened in the past had now been consigned to the dustbin of history, of relevance only to the naysayers who had a vested interest in derailing the accomplishments of the UVF's internal consultation process. The strife wracking the inner circles of the UVF died with Billy Greer, or so it seemed on this occasion. In time, a different story would emerge, one more complicated than people realised. It would leave little doubt in some people's minds that Greer's departure from the leadership of the East Antrim UVF was seen by some as a cynical attempt to reverse the UVF's decision to move towards a permanent disengagement from political violence.

★★★

Seven days after Billy Greer died, another former UVF leader passed away. His name was Billy Mitchell. At one time he had also commanded the East Antrim UVF and, subsequently, became a member of the group's ruling Brigade Staff. Like Greer, I knew Billy Mitchell very well. He had been a mentor to me as we worked together on peace-building projects in the divided communities across Belfast and East Antrim in the last years of his life. If Billy Greer imbibed the UVF's militaristic ethos throughout his entire life, Billy Mitchell embodied the political dynamism of a far-reaching catharsis that took him on a personal odyssey from militarist to politico.

'How could you not like Billy,' said 'The Craftsman', said to be one of the top two most senior UVF Brigade Staff officers. Like Mitchell, The Craftsman became involved in militant loyalism sometime in 1966 in the belief that the IRA were about to launch an armed coup to take over the government of Northern Ireland and subsume it into an all-island republic. It was astonishing to think that in the same year Beatlemania was sweeping the world, when Carnaby Street represented a new departure in British culture and when the world was changing dramatically amidst a Cold War, old shibboleths were returning with great vigour in Northern Ireland. Mitchell's route to embracing extremist views began when he came under the spell of Reverend Ian Paisley, a fundamentalist Protestant preacher, though he had already been indoctrinated into loyalism by way of other, less prominent, religious extremists who belonged to the Flute Band he joined in his early twenties. Born in Ballyduff in 1940, Billy's father died soon afterwards and the family went to live with his mother's parents on the Hightown Road, close to Belfast's Cave Hill. By 1974 Mitchell was on the UVF's Brigade Staff, the only non-Shankill man ever to have served in that capacity. 'I couldn't tell you what role he played on Brigade Staff,' The Craftsman told me. 'I remember Billy turned up to a Brigade Staff meeting in the 1970s in his overalls. I think he worked [as a truck driver] at the time. He had the air of a country man about him.' It is likely that Mitchell served as the organisation's Director of Operations, following the death of Jim Hanna in April 1974. That he commanded one of the most active units inside the UVF meant he had a foot in both the Shankill and East Antrim.

When Mitchell was arrested by the Security Forces in Carrickfergus in March 1976, he had ring binders full of information used by the UVF for targeting. He told detectives that there was an innocent explanation for the material found in his possession. The truth was that he was double-hatted as the UVF's Director of Intelligence at the time, responsible for targeting his organisation's enemies, wherever they were to be found. Unbeknown to the CID detectives who questioned him, they had arguably the UVF's most important leader in their custody. Here was the organisation's top strategist, its chief scribe and its quintessential man of action. It is rare for guerrilla or terrorist organisations to have men who possess both the military aptitude and the political astuteness in their ranks. It is even rarer for them to be concentrated in one person.

During his long period of incarceration between 1976 and 1990, Mitchell spent his time wrestling with his conscience and attempting to unravel the puzzle of what had propelled him into the ranks of the UVF. After a few years, he would come to reject his paramilitary past, commit himself to Christianity and give up his coveted Special Category Status to enter the newly constructed H Blocks as a Conforming Prisoner in the early 1980s. There was little Billy conformed to. He had been a senior UVF commander who had been responsible for leading the organisation through its darkest years, when it was responsible for murdering several hundred people, thirty-three of whom were killed in a single day in bomb attacks on Dublin and Monaghan. He had even talked to the highest-ranking members of both wings of the Official and Provisional IRAs. It was part of the UVF's twin track of 'talking and killing' he told me thirty years after those turbulent events. Yet, by 1979, he had given all of that up.

When he emerged from prison in 1990, Billy dedicated himself to rebuilding the communities the UVF had helped to shatter with their violence. He was committed to this and, as one of his friends would remark in his funeral oration, not only did he 'walk the walk but he demanded that people walked with him'. This was the Billy Mitchell I knew. The man who could in one room bring together sworn enemies from across a deeply divided community. IRA members, UVF members, Irish National Liberation Army (INLA) members, even some from the so-called dissident hinterland – all had come into contact with him in his years as a peacebuilder. It is little wonder, therefore, that as people gathered to pay their final respects to Billy Mitchell at his funeral service, they represented the broad spectrum of Northern Irish society.

As we look back on its fifty-year history, we see that the history of the UVF is a very rich and complicated one. It is at its heart a story of ordinary men like the two Billys, Greer and Mitchell, who became involved in paramilitary activity for a variety of reasons. They both rose to prominence through their ability to get the men and women under their command to do things they wouldn't have otherwise done. Yet, their stories also demonstrate why some individuals remain involved in militarism, while others go against the grain and ask serious questions of what had brought them to the point where they advocated, planned and participated in violent acts.

This book charts the shifting contours in Ulster loyalism, and explains how and why men like these came to make the choices they did and what the consequences were for the world around them.

1

THE BISHOP

'In such cases, where law and justice fail him, the Ulster Protestant will infallibly take his own measures for his protection. He is built that way. His resolution and his courage are unshakeable. He has all the unflinching determination of his border ancestors and by a question of principle he will stand to his last gasp.'

Lord Ernest Hamilton, *The Soul of Ulster*, 1917.[1]

It was a stormy night in mid-November 1965. Snow was forecast, as gale-force winds continually battered Northern Ireland. A car carrying four men steadily made its way from the Shankill Road in Belfast, south-west via the towns of Lisburn, Moira, Lurgan and Dungannon to the outskirts of the rural County Tyrone village of Pomeroy, some eighteen miles from the Irish border. It was a long and slow journey, as the roads got increasingly narrower and the bad weather made it difficult to navigate as the driver turned off the main A-road out of Dungannon. While Pomeroy was overwhelmingly Roman Catholic in religious composition in the mid-1960s, it had a long association with Protestant militancy that stretched back to the late eighteenth century. The Orange Order was formed not far away at the Diamond near Portadown, in 1795. It had been established at a time of great uncertainty. Revolution abroad, sectarianism at home and debates over constitutional issues and the fear of invasion brought the Order together.[2] It was also a time when militia-based organisations flourished, with the predominantly Presbyterian United Irishmen raised a few years earlier to agitate for religious freedom for Catholics and dissenters. Both organisations had a resemblance to earlier, agrarian-based secret societies, like the Peep O' Day Boys and their rivals, the Defenders.

As the antagonism between these revolutionary and counter-revolutionary groups developed, the United Irishmen became imbibed with a culture of popular radicalism common in Britain and America at the time. Meanwhile, Orangeism became more aggressively anti-Catholic and reactionary. Opposing social and political outlooks soon triggered conflict between both organisations. To Protestant vengeance groups, 'the entire Catholic population became defined as the enemy'.[3] Portadown, in North Armagh, was the epicentre of the trouble and would remain so for the next two centuries.

As the carload of Belfast men made their way along the rolling countryside, with its narrow country lanes, prominent hedgerows and wide-open emerald green fields, they passed workers' cottages and farms scattered along the side of the roads. This was farming country and, on the surface at least, places like Pomeroy appeared all but immune from the modernisation programme gripping Northern Ireland in the 1960s.[4] Some Protestants, in fact, harboured a deep-seated feeling of bitterness, anger and fear as the winds of change blew through their land. What would they usher in, other than the creeping hand of Irish nationalism, which had always aspired to gain a foothold in their beloved Ulster? To the more militant-minded Protestants, change of any kind pointed towards dark days ahead for their homeland.

The terrible weather conditions on that November night in many ways matched the foreboding that had been percolating down to the Protestant grassroots who resided in the surrounding rural hamlets of Cappagh, Carrickmore and The Rock. Chief amongst these was the feeling that the Unionist government at Stormont was far too liberal and soft on those who, hardliners believed, were dedicated to the destruction of the Northern Ireland state. Evidence of this existential threat came in the form of a summit a year earlier between the Northern Ireland Prime Minister Terence O'Neill and the Irish Taoiseach Seán Lemass. The meeting was held in private, but did not escape the prying eyes of a thirty-nine-year-old lay preacher Ian Paisley, the rabble-rousing leader of the Free Presbyterian Church, a fundamentalist Christian sect formed in 1951. Born in Armagh in 1926, another citadel of Orangeism, Paisley burst onto the scene in the late 1950s when he formed Ulster Protestant Action (UPA), a sectarian-based organisation that lobbied against unemployment within the majority Protestant population.[5]

By 1964, Paisley was threatening to lead a Protestant mob to the offices of Irish Republican election candidate and Irish Republican Army (IRA) leader Liam McMillan in West Belfast. McMillan had placed an Irish tricolour in the window of his office on Divis Street. It caused uproar amongst Protestant extremists in the neighbouring areas. In a bid to quieten tensions, the RUC intervened in the dispute and removed the flag. When it appeared back in the window a short time afterwards, Paisley brought a Protestant mob back onto the streets, provoking a three-night riot with local Catholics and the police.

Paisley had always made sectarianism the leitmotif of his political protests. Apart from agitating on exclusively Protestant issues, he opposed attempts by the Roman Catholic Church to reach out to other Christian denominations in a spirit of harmony. Paisley and his followers found ecumenicalism abhorrent and, as a result, set themselves against it just as firmly as they had done the rapprochement between the two governments north and south of the border. Underpinning this acrimony was an undercurrent of violence, a spectre that continually haunted politics and society in this part of the world. Paisley warned that the IRA, which had dumped arms in 1962 after its six-year border campaign fizzled out, was still waiting in the wings. McMillan's defiance in West Belfast proved as much, Paisley told his supporters, despite IRA guns having fallen silent amidst widespread apathy from the northern nationalist community.[6] With the approach of the fiftieth anniversary of the failed Easter 1916 rebellion against British rule in Dublin, further impetus was given to militant Protestants who feared the 'unholy alliance' between the Irish government, Roman Catholic Church and the IRA.

A propensity for regular elections in Northern Ireland – there were seventeen local government, Stormont and Westminster parliamentary elections between 1945 and 1965 – gave Paisley the opportunity to test his paranoid claims on the voting public. Something was stirring amongst Ulster Protestants, and Paisley erroneously tapped into it. He was fast becoming the midwife in the rebirth of a noxious strain of militancy that was prepared to take the law into its own hands. By doing so, millenarian Protestant fundamentalists who identified with Paisley saw themselves as a bulwark against greater encroachment of British liberal democratic norms on their state. Paisleyites, as they soon became known, departed from this inclusive form of liberal unionism, preferring to hold fast to the belief that Northern Ireland should govern only on behalf of one section of its divided population. For these extremists, Northern Ireland was truly a 'Protestant state for a Protestant people'. The faith-based ideology expounded by Paisley blended an extreme loyalty to the Crown with a narrow and exclusive interpretation of Ulster unionism and, above all, a rabid hatred for all things Roman Catholic.

By the mid-1960s, Paisley had attained cult-like status. His stirring speeches whipped his wide array of followers into a frenzy, and helped galvanise street protests. On one level, his oratory was certainly effective in winning over adherents, but his 'swift rise to prominence occurred because fertile ground awaited the seeds of his bigotry'.[7] He was an effective speaker, but he acted principally as a lightning rod for angst, frustration and fear amongst the Protestant working class.

***

The car carrying the Belfast men pulled off the minor B-road and followed a country lane towards a series of farm buildings, including a large barn. Outside, hurricane lamps swung violently in the wind. Men mingled in small knots. Some smoked cigarettes, while others avoided being drawn into small talk by looking at their feet. Those gathered outside only averted their eyes into the darker recesses of the surrounding undulating landscape when they spotted the car carrying the Belfast men approaching. As the vehicle pulled up next to the barn, the driver let the engine idle for a few moments before finally switching it off. The doors flung open to reveal the five visitors. They climbed out of the car with bearing and purpose. The Belfast men were greeted by an organiser, who had been expecting them. They exchanged pleasantries before being shown inside to the poorly lit barn. Shadows disappeared into the ambient light of the lamps which dangled from high wooden beams.

About forty men had gathered from different parts of the country on land owned by a prominent family in the area. The men stood side by side as they were brought to attention by a former British Army colonel and told to raise their right hand as they were sworn into a newly rejuvenated grouping, which was to become known as the Ulster Volunteer Force (UVF), tracing its lineage back to the paramilitary organisation formed in the early twentieth century.[8] While the objective of the old UVF was to oppose the British policy of Home Rule for Ireland by 'any means necessary', this new UVF was raised to oppose 'an assumed threat'[9] from physical force republicanism. In reality this new private army was formed by elements within the right wing of the Unionist Party as part of a wider conspiracy to oppose O'Neill's liberal unionist agenda.[10]

These were desperate times, said the faceless men presiding over the secret ceremony, and they called for desperate measures. The visitors from Belfast readily agreed. Some of them had seen the dangers posed by subversive movements in far-flung colonial outposts, like Cyprus; others were led to believe they were joining an underground organisation, preparing for a doomsday scenario in which armed republicans would be fielded in an attempt to seize control of the local state and impose upon them an island-wide Irish republic.[11]

***

A few weeks before the swearing in ceremony in Pomeroy, the Honorary Secretary of the East and Mid Tyrone Unionist Association had written a gloomy letter to the Minister of Home Affairs, Brian McConnell, to inform him of some worrying developments. At their last meeting, reported the party functionary, a motion had been unanimously passed pleading with those 'responsible for the peace of our beloved Province' to 'take immediate and appropriate action to ensure that peace will prevail during this dangerous period'. Local party members were people who took a 'serious view ... of the fact that preparations are in hand, by our political enemies, to have large scale celebrations on the fiftieth anniversary of the Easter Rising of 1916.' Republicans were not only content to commemorate the past violent deeds of their ancestors, warned the East and Mid Tyrone Unionist Association. They were also intent on spreading fear by intimidating Protestants living along the border with an irredentist neighbour next door. 'We fear that these celebrations could disturb the present peaceful state of Northern Ireland and lead to grave breaches of the peace,' wrote the Honorary Secretary.[12] Something had to be done, he urged, and fast.

What compounded frustrations amongst Protestants in his part of Mid Ulster was the political dominance of the old Nationalist Party, which had returned Austin Currie in the 1964 Westminster election. To those living in the Mid Ulster area there could be no compromise with nationalism wherever it reared its head, whether politically or culturally. A handful of members of the Orange Order, including several who wore the uniform of the Ulster Special Constabulary (USC, known popularly as the 'B-Specials'), an auxiliary force to the Royal Ulster Constabulary (RUC), met in secret to plan for the worst. They were determined to step into the breach, should O'Neill's government prove unwilling or unable to confront what these hardliners suspected was a direct threat to their security. Matters soon came to a head when local newspapers reported that up to 30,000 people planned to gather in Pomeroy for the town's Easter Rising parade.

A few miles north of Pomeroy, in Magherfelt, nine prominent unionists from the area, who also held overlapping members of the Orange Order and, in some cases, the B-Specials, paid a visit to the local RUC commander for the area. They warned of 'strong intervention by loyalists' if republicans were permitted to hold a commemorative parade in a local centre known as the Loup, which would 'probably result in the use of firearms' if it was to go ahead. After he showed them out, the police chief reported to RUC Headquarters that he was 'convinced beyond all doubt' that the men were 'prepared, if necessary, to use sufficient physical force in order to prevent these celebrations taking place'.[13] An undercover Crime Special Department (later renamed Special Branch) detective attending a local election meeting in South Derry also reported how republicans wished to hold a protest in a 'peaceful and orderly manner' but that if they were given any trouble would 'give all the trouble that would be needed'. Applause and loud cheers greeted these defiant words.[14] Tensions between both communities ran exceptionally high.

At Stormont, McConnell's replacement at the Ministry of Home Affairs, Bill Craig, was busy poring over more detailed intelligence reports from the RUC about the steps they were taking to tighten up the security situation. Craig promised Inspector General Sir Albert Kennedy the fullest co-operation and support from the government as they moved to preserve law and order. The Minister informed Parliament that he had authorised the mobilisation of the B-Specials as a necessary precaution, 'to deal with the threatened IRA outbreak which constituted a very serious threat to the peace of this Province'.[15] Briefings provided by intelligence chiefs in London, far removed from Mid Ulster, concluded that 3,000 IRA members were armed and poised to take action.[16] Such alarmism within security circles was now matched by Paisleyites, who stoked fears amongst grassroots Protestants of an imminent armed attack by republicans.[17]

Not far from Stormont on the Ravenhill Road, Paisley was busy playing to a packed congregation in his church, the Martyrs Memorial. 'England had always been weak in the face of Roman Catholic onslaughts and now rebels were dictating the policies of the country', he told his flock, many of whom were thrown into hysterics by his booming, uncompromising rhetoric. 'Free Presbyterians had been branded extremists', he said, 'in a way that left them with few options to register their grievances.' This only encouraged them to amplify their chorus of disapproval, argued Paisley. The more republicans and the unionist government played up to one another, the more extreme Free Presbyterians would become. 'My fellow ministers and I are united in denouncing the action of the Northern Ireland government in allowing celebrations of the Easter Rebellion to take place', Paisley told them. Concluding his remarks, the Free Presbyterian leader vowed to continue to 'protest in the strongest possible manner'.[18]

When the report of the sermon by the RUC's Crime Special Department eventually landed on Craig's desk, it left him in no doubt that Paisley was planning to heighten tensions, though few knew what form his plan would take. Less than forty-eight hours after Paisley's dire warnings, UVF members sworn in at Pomeroy were taking to the streets armed with pistols. They fired shots at the home of the Stormont Unionist MP for the area, Johnny McQuade, in an attempt to create the impression that the IRA had awoken from its self-imposed slumber. The feigned attack at McQuade's home was by no means an isolated incident and there was soon a close correlation between the escalation of Paisley's rhetoric and the actions of the UVF.[19]

Two days after the attack on McQuade's house, twenty-five-year-old Noel Doherty, a member of Paisley's church, was busy in his printer's shop, composing an intemperate letter to Bill Craig. Doherty was born in Cuba Street on the Newtownards Road on 26 December 1940 and attended Beechfield Elementary School. In 1956, aged fifteen, he left school and joined the Free Presbyterian church. By 1965, Doherty had set up the Puritan Printing Company with Paisley, publishing their fortnightly *Protestant Telegraph*. He was mesmerised by the clergyman he affectionately dubbed 'The Bishop'. Under Paisley's tutelage, Doherty contested the 1964 Belfast Corporation election as a Protestant Unionist party candidate. Although he failed to win a seat, the experience left him enthralled by the gravitational pull of radical, fringe politics. By April 1966, Doherty had established the Ulster Constitution Defence Committee (UCDC), a vehicle for rejuvenating Paisley's flagging electoral fortunes.[20]

As he worked late into the night at his printer's shop, Doherty allowed his frustration with the liberal unionist agenda to spill out of his pen and onto every page of every letter he drafted to Stormont officials. His correspondence grew in volume, especially those letters personally addressed to Bill Craig. They typically elicited the same tawdry answer from his Private Secretary, who informed Doherty that he 'should rest assured that the Minister would read the correspondence'. The evasiveness of the Stormont bureaucrats infuriated the East Belfast man. These were wily men who worked for even wilier politicians, he believed. Doherty knew instinctively, from the moment he opened the official-looking envelopes, that his letters were going unread. Much to his chagrin, the government was showing no sign of taking the dire warnings of 'the bishop' seriously. The young East Belfast man resolved to make them listen. 'My chairman,' Doherty began his latest diatribe, 'had certain plans for Easter about which he wanted to tell the Minister but, as the Minister would not see him, he must be held responsible for the consequences.'[21]

Doherty signed off the letter just as sharply as he had started it. This obstinacy by the government officials would not do. He would up the ante to force them all to pay attention to the chorus of Free Presbyterian criticism. By now his plans for forming a secretive, illegally armed unit within the UCDC, known as the Ulster Protestant Volunteers (UPV), were at an advanced stage.

★★★

'I've called for the gelignite', said the man with black curly hair and a long fringe. James Frederick Marshall, a forty-six-year-old quarryman from Bond Hill, Derrycrew, in Loughgall, was expecting the stranger. He had earlier been informed by his friend, twenty-nine-year-old Jim Murdock, a machinist by trade who lived at Grange Lower, Portadown, that someone would call to his home to collect the explosives 'for a job in Belfast'. Marshall had carefully secreted them in an outbuilding on his farm, situated in rolling countryside just over seven miles due west of Portadown. The man with the curly hair who called to his door that evening was not alone. In the farmyard behind him sat a white Hillman Imp car with three other men in the vehicle. The car engine ticked over while the two men spoke in hushed tones about the secret work they were engaged in. Marshall led his visitor to the outhouse, where he encountered another man, who stood motionless with his hat pulled tightly down over the tip of his nose to disguise his face. Marshall was not alarmed by the presence of the strangers. Deep down he knew they were all brothers in a struggle that relied upon the strictest of secrecy and trust. They were, after all, his kith and kin.

Some weeks earlier, Marshall had been invited to join the UCDC[22] following a meeting with two of Paisley's key lieutenants, Noel Doherty and his twenty-six-year-old acquaintance Billy Mitchell, at Murdock's home on 21 April 1966. As staunch Protestants and committed Paisleyites, the Loughgall men were eager to do their bit for their country. They were bound together with these men from Belfast by their extreme views and through their overlapping memberships of the Orange Order and the B-Specials. Their position was simple: in the event of any police or B-Specials being shot, 'reprisals might be taken against the IRA'.[23] Although aware that their actions would place them outside the law, these men were guided by a single-minded commitment to defend Ulster by any means necessary. Doherty provided the men with that opportunity, when he recruited them into the ranks of a highly clandestine cellular group within the existing ranks of the UPV. It may have been devised as a 'loose association', but it pulled in people from across the province who believed in the efficacy of armed resistance against 'known enemies'. They were a force within a force, and the nucleus of an ultra-right-wing conspiracy that now ran through the veins of Protestant Ulster.

This was not the first time Doherty and Mitchell had met the Loughgall men. Both men had previously travelled down to Loughgall in a car driven by none other than Ian Paisley himself. Doherty later recalled how:

> He was going to a meeting in Armagh and offered to pick us up on the way back. During this meeting I met a man called Winters, [and also] Marshall and Murdock. There was [sic] other people present whose names are unknown to me. The meeting took place in Murdock's house, and I learned at the meeting that arms could be supplied. These men were of the opinion that IRA monuments and IRA leaders could be shot. While I agreed to a certain extent on blowing up monuments, never could I sanction the taking of life. After the meeting was over, Mitchell and myself travelled home in Mr Paisley's car. Mr Paisley is a friend through his church of Mr Murdock and entered the house and waited on us drinking tea. I would state here that Mr Paisley knew nothing of the discussion that had taken place.[24]

In Doherty's mind, it was vital to keep Paisley in play as a 'figurehead', but not to involve him in the intimate detail of the 'job underneath him'.[25]

After returning to Belfast with Doherty and Paisley, Mitchell, the key link-man between the UPV and UVF, met with twenty-eight-year-old Geordie Bigger. Mitchell wanted to discuss with Bigger, believed to be the main organiser for the group, the transportation of explosives to Belfast from Loughgall. Bigger, a tyre process worker by trade, lived with his wife and children in a modest three-bedroom house in Queen's Park, Glengormley, a solidly working-class area on the northern outskirts of Belfast. He had a reputation as a hard man, though he also had a predilection for talking when he should have been listening. Nevertheless, his willingness to obtain explosives for a 'big job' made him just the sort of character the UPV and UVF needed in their ranks. The meeting between Bigger and Mitchell was a low-key affair, but it would prove to have profound repercussions for the course of Northern Irish history.

Later, Doherty said Bigger and his thirty-one-year-old friend and colleague Dessie Reid contacted him at his mother's home in Cuba Street. He claimed he did not recognise the two men at first, though after speaking to someone about Bigger – in all probability Billy Mitchell – Doherty travelled to Queen's Park to 'make sure who he was'. Once he reached Bigger's home, the men entered into a fairly lucid discussion centring on the acquisition of explosives. At this point, Doherty promised to introduce them to the quarryman, Jim Marshall. It was arranged that Doherty would accompany Bigger to Portadown, where they would collect the illicit cargo. In the meantime, Bigger had acquired a pistol, a Webley revolver, which he brandished in the company of the men who were now meeting on an almost nightly basis.[26] The conspiracy against O'Neill was now beginning to take on a much more serious form.

Ten miles north of Glengormley, in Carrickfergus, forty-five-year-old bricklayer Hugh McClean of Larne Road in the town was presenting himself as another willing volunteer in the cause. Carrick has long been a place etched in the Ulster Protestant psyche. It was the hallowed ground where William of Orange first set foot in Ireland before marching south to fight the forces of King James II, at the celebrated Battle of the Boyne in 1690. Now, Carrick would play host to a smaller and more clandestine army of men who were prepared to carry out armed actions in a very different, less conventional, way than their hero King Billy. Although the rumoured IRA assault on the Northern Ireland state had failed to materialise, McClean nonetheless remained convinced that the threat had not gone away. He wholeheartedly believed Paisley's dire warnings, and saw violence as the only way to respond. As an ex-serviceman, McClean knew his way around weapons and explosives. McClean's contact from Glengormley, Dessie Reid, soon paid him a visit to inform him that Bigger was organising volunteer groups. He asked McClean if he would like to join their ranks. McClean said he would and, crucially, that he knew of others who were prepared to step forward and be counted. One of those he proposed for membership was his neighbour and close friend, twenty-two-year-old William Blakely.

Willie Blakely was a well-regarded young man who served as an apprentice for the Electricity Board for Northern Ireland. To his friends, Blakely was a 'very capable and dependable tradesman' who 'worked in closest harmony' with his colleagues, including his foreman, a devout Roman Catholic who held the young Blakely in high regard. 'We always found him to be strictly honest and trustworthy,' the foreman later said of him.[27] There were no outward signs that Blakely had become involved in militant Protestantism. He had apparently been 'very popular with his workmates, both Protestant and Catholic alike'.[28] Beneath the affable exterior, though, the truth was more complicated. Within a short space of time, Blakely found himself involved in a conspiracy he was neither prepared for, nor fully understood.

Events now moved quickly. After the meeting between Reid and McClean, the Carrick men travelled to Bigger's house to join the group. When they arrived, Bigger denied the existence of a group in Glengormley and, he told them, they would have to establish one of their own in Carrick. It is likely that Bigger wanted to keep the Glengormley group under his direct control and, having picked up on McClean's military bearing, saw him as a challenge to his own authority as a member of the Shankill UVF. Disappointed, albeit undeterred, the Carrick men returned along the coast to their homes in the picturesque seaside town.

A couple of days later, Reid again called on McClean to tell him that he had made contact with another group in Armagh. Meanwhile, Bigger travelled forty miles south to Loughgall with Doherty, where they met Marshall. They vowed to return a week later to collect the explosives.[29] On their next visit, Reid, Bigger and McClean collected two sweet jars with twenty-seven sticks of gelignite, six detonators and a length of fuse wire. The men carried them to the car, placed them in the boot and then drove back to Glengormley, where Bigger held them overnight. The next day they took them to an old disused house on the Hightown Road where they 'planked them'.[30]

The reason why the men had to move the explosives so quickly after depositing them in Bigger's home was probably a direct result of the Glengormley man's penchant for alcohol. 'I was really drunk that night as Dessy was driving his car,' he later admitted. 'Well whatever talk went on as far as I know the transaction was made. Anyway as I told you I was drunk, when I woke up in my own house I saw the gelignite at my feet. There was [sic] two glass bottles of it – about ten pounds. I put it out in the back yard to protect my family. The first thing next morning I took it up to that a farmyard, which I think belonged to Montgomery at one time. That's where it stayed and it has remained.'[31] McClean denied that the men had ever intended to use the explosives. 'We never used any of the gelignite up to that date but we were thinking of blowing up the Monument to St. Patrick in Downpatrick,' he said. 'In fact, we went to Downpatrick and inspected it. About two weeks later we joined the Shankill Road volunteers and we never got around to the monument.'[32] It is impossible to really know why the men opted not to use the explosives they had brought up from Loughgall. It could have been due to the lack of leadership in directing the conspiracy, or that the men had simply been incapable of developing a plan beyond 'big talk'. For the moment, they resolved to concentrate their efforts on shooting at the homes of those they considered to be their 'enemies'.

Over the coming weeks, the men began to meet more frequently, and their conversations would turn to talk about using their newly acquired guns and explosives. At the same time, Doherty was fast becoming disillusioned by Bigger's increasingly erratic behaviour and sought to distance himself from his co-conspirators. 'This was the start of my breaking away from this group,' he later confessed. 'I believe that when men start handling arms their intention is to kill. These men were intent on killing IRA leaders as reprisals. This was the last contact I had with this group as I did not agree with taking life.' In his role as a B-Special, Doherty had considerably more experience of handling weapons than most of the other men involved in the conspiracy. 'As a member of the USC seeing firearms in the hands of men who could not handle them really frightened me,' he would later admit.[33]

At this time, volunteer groups had begun to spring up in other parts of the province too, testament, perhaps, to Doherty's skills as an organiser. The conspiracy now extended from the Shankill, Ligoniel, Willowfield and St Annes in Belfast south to Lisburn and deep into the rural Protestant heartlands of Portadown and Pomeroy, and beyond to Iveagh and Kilkeel.[34] The conspiracy's tentacles were spreading far and wide, as more and more disaffected working-class Protestants found a sense of belonging in its ranks.

★★★

On the Shankill Road, the men of the newly formed volunteer unit, known locally as the UVF, had other things on their minds, and the destruction of nationalist memorials was not one of them. These men, ten of them in total, most of whom were ex-servicemen,[35] were on the lookout for a live target, one that would send out an altogether more amplified message that a new, more militant organisation had formed to defend the Protestant community.

The leader of this group was thirty-three-year-old Augustus Andrew Spence, one of the men who had travelled to Pomeroy to be sworn into the newly reconstituted UVF. A former soldier with service in the Royal Ulster Rifles, 'Gusty' Spence had seen action on counter-insurgency operations in Cyprus in the late 1950s. Although he was first and foremost a hard man, with few qualms about killing for what he considered to be the loyalist cause, he was also a reasonably competent tactician of terror, who had watched and learned from EOKA, the Greek nationalist terrorist group he had encountered at close quarters in the Eastern Mediterranean. Spence knew, as Colonel George Grivas who commanded EOKA had known, that armed propaganda helped spread fear amongst the people and that could have a far greater political effect disproportionate to the real size of the threat the group actually posed.

Spence had initially been approached to join the UVF by two people, one of whom was a Unionist Party politician.[36] It has been alleged that the RUC's Crime Special Department was so 'anxious to uncover links between the UVF and any so-called respectable politicians opposed to the O'Neill government' that they harboured 'suspicions regarding a number of well-known figures within unionism'. Amongst those suspected of – but never directly implicated in – some kind of involvement in the conspiracy were thirty-seven-year-old James Kilfedder (the Unionist Party MP for West Belfast), thirty-six-year-old Desmond Boal (a Stormont Unionist MP for Shankill and close adviser to Ian Paisley) and fifty-four-year-old Johnny McQuade (a former dock worker who had just won the Stormont seat for Woodvale).[37] A key linkman between these Unionist Party politicians and militant Protestants was Billy Spence, Gusty's brother, who had served as Kilfedder's election agent in the 1964 and 1966 Westminster elections.

The friendship between Kilfedder and Boal had its origins in the close bond they had forged as schoolboys. Both men attended Portora Royal School in Enniskillen, a private institution founded in 1608 during the reign of James I.[38] Portora, like so many other independent schools, prided itself on turning out young men fit to lead their country in some of the most sought-after positions in middle-class society. As a result, Kilfedder and Boal were brought up on a staple diet of tales of intrigue and adventure in the service of Britain, at a time when it still controlled a quarter of the world's population. Both men even followed their hero Sir Edward Carson in becoming barristers after a spell at Trinity College in Dublin. But it was in their concerted opposition to the liberal policies of Terence O'Neill that Kilfedder and Boal truly excelled. They might not have been fully aware of it at the time, but they were helping to create a political climate that gave birth to an extremist form of Ulster loyalism.

Although it has never been proven who exactly recruited Spence and the others into the UVF, the faceless men responsible had inadvertently created a Frankenstein's monster they could neither hope to lead nor control – as events would soon prove.

2

HELL SLAP IT INTO THEM

Shots were fired of plenty, some say even twenty,
Were fired that warm June night in Malvern Street,
Three taigs lay on the ground, and a fourth was wisely bound,
From a fate the others thought they'd never meet.

Anon, *Ambush* (1966)

Conway Bar, West Belfast, Evening, 27 May 1966

'I am going to get it tonight. I'm going to get a hiding,' said the heavyset man sat at the bar. John Patrick Scullion, a twenty-eight-year-old labourer from Oranmore Street in Belfast, was out for a few drinks on a Friday evening after work. He was employed at the textile machine manufacturers James Mackie and Sons on the Springfield Road. It was said of Scullion that he was a man of intemperate habits. Described by his workmates as a 'good comrade', he was a popular figure on the factory floor. A large man of eighteen stone, Scullion had earlier dressed in a smart dark suit, white shirt and sensible tie when he decided to pay a visit to his local bar near the bottom of the Springfield Road. As he sank pint after pint of Double X Guinness, Scullion would become increasingly distraught. The landlord of the pub, Frank Kelly, knew Scullion well, and was keenly aware that he could be prone to bouts of paranoid delusion the more alcohol he drank. Kelly later recalled how Scullion would frequently talk about how he expected to die before his thirtieth birthday.

As Kelly called last orders at the bar, Scullion rose from the stool he had been perched on for much of the evening, staggered across to the toilets to relieve himself, before leaving for the home he shared with his aunt Alice. Minutes later, he was spotted by eyewitnesses stumbling in a southerly direction, down the Springfield Road, then hanging a left along an entry near the junction of Falls Road and Clonard Street.

As Scullion made his way onto Clonard Street, he burst into song, drawing the attention of a small number of people still out and about. It wasn't long before he tripped and fell over. Watching him hit the road with a hefty thump, four local men rushed over to help him up. A local police officer on the beat also caught a glimpse of Scullion as he fell. He had even contemplated arresting him on the charge of being drunk and disorderly, though resisted the temptation and, reassuring himself that Scullion would continue on his way, let the matter drop. A few moments later Scullion turned from Clonard Street onto Oranmore Street, where he was spotted by two young girls. It was 11:30 p.m. when the girls registered the drunk man shuffling across the street. Seconds later, they heard two loud bangs pierce the still, night air. One of the girls thought it was the sound of gunfire, while the other believed it was a car backfiring in the direction of Oranmore Street. As they ventured along the pavement, a car came racing out of Oranmore Street, before turning left into Clonard Gardens and then right into Waterville Street, a few yards from Bombay Street. The vehicle accelerated onto Cupar Way and slipped away into the heart of the Shankill. Moments later, it vanished. As the car passed the girls, they recalled how the occupants stared straight at them, their faces those of strangers. Inside the vehicle were several young men, one of whom had blonde hair.

Oblivious to the injuries he had sustained by the gunshots, John Scullion continued on home. As he reached the front door, he paused for a moment while he fumbled in his pockets for his keys. After finding the right key, he thrust it into the lock. He staggered into the hall and slammed the door behind him. A few minutes later he slouched into an armchair in the living room noisily exhaling breath as he did so. His aunt, who had been asleep upstairs, woke to the sounds of her nephew's groans. Just as Alice Scullion came to her bedroom door, she was met by John who had forced himself upstairs, before collapsing at her feet. 'When he left me after tea, John was in good form', she later said. 'He was not injured in any way.' Realising her nephew had indeed been injured in some way, she promptly telephoned an ambulance and John was rushed to the Royal Victoria Hospital, a short distance from his home. Two weeks later John Patrick Scullion died from the wounds he received that night; wounds which doctors mistakenly attributed to him having been stabbed in an altercation. The reality had been much more serious. John Scullion had been deliberately shot by an organisation calling itself the UVF.

It would not be long before the UVF was stalking the streets again. On Sunday, 5 June 1966, James Doherty, a middle-aged lorry driver, was sleeping at home in Abbotts Drive when his son-in-law John McChrystal called, to see him about an incident that had happened just before dawn.

When both men arrived to McChrystal's home at Innis Avenue in Rathcoole estate, they found that the living room window had been shattered by what appeared to be a gunshot. As the bullet entered his home, it narrowly missed McChrystal's head, striking the wall above the settee where he was resting.[1] McChrystal was a machinist at a local industrial plant who, some loyalists alleged, had expressed republican sympathies.[2]

★★★

Most UVF members in 1966 were working men in their late teens, 20s and 30s. Only a tiny number, like Hugh McClean, were older. They were typically recruited on the basis of their reputations as hard men. Some were singled out for their service history. The added bonus of having experienced military men in the ranks, Spence believed, meant that they could handle themselves and handle weapons, if armed conflict with republicans ever broke out. The reality was that few of them had ever fired a shot in anger. As a consequence, it was usually personal grievances, mixed with hefty doses of alcohol, which played a key role in their decision to target specific individuals. In many cases, it gave them much-needed 'Dutch courage' to pull the trigger on fellow human beings.[3] The fact that the gunman who pulled the trigger in the drive-by shooting of John Scullion aimed low at his target is evidence of the difficulty most UVF men at this time had in killing, and probably explains why the vast majority of attacks where on property, not people. This single factor would prove crucial for RUC detectives investigating subsequent UVF attacks.

Despite Spence and several others having been sworn in by high-powered faceless men, instructions from the top of the chain of command appeared to be in short supply. Essentially, the new UVF became self-tasking insofar as Spence acted as the officer in command, who selected targets and authorised action against those suspected of being 'republicans' or holding 'republican sympathies'. In most cases, Spence and the Shankill UVF were manufacturing these enemies out of their own paranoia, which made them see an IRA man under every bed. The reality of the situation was somewhat different, but it did not deter the UVF from declaring war on the IRA and its enemies on 21 May 1966. They were 'heavily armed Protestants dedicated to this cause' read the statement they released to the press.[4]

In order to give the organisation a semblance of military bearing, Spence revised the oath he had taken at Pomeroy. New recruits were now to give an undertaking that they would never 'betray a comrade or give any information to whomsoever which could prove detrimental to my Cause'. Furthermore, they had to pledge: 'if I fail in my obligations I shall truly deserve the just deserts befalling me'.[5] For Spence, the UVF was a 'very secretive' organisation; everything was 'on a kind of need-to-know basis'.[6] Harry Johnston, a twenty-six-year-old electrician's mate from Argyll Street on the Shankill, recalled the circumstances leading to his own swearing-in ceremony at the time:

> I joined the Ulster Volunteer Force. It was in the Standard Bar on the Shankill Road. Gusty Spence asked me to join on Monday, 13 June, and he informed me that he was a member. Spence asked me to join in the presence of Harry Millar and Sammy Robinson. Spence told me that this was an organisation to protect Ulster and Protestants. I agreed to join and, by arrangement, I went to a meeting of the Ulster Volunteer Force in an upstairs room of the Standard Bar, Shankill Road, at about 8 p.m. on 16th June 1966. Those present were Augustus Spence, Rocky Burns, Eddie McCullough, William Johnston [unreadable] and a man called 'Bertie' from about Berlin Street. McCullough, William Johnston, Bertie and myself were sworn in by Spence, and we took an oath to protect Ulster and Protestants against the IRA and *Cumann na hBan*. The object of the Ulster Volunteer Force was to keep the IRA in their place and they were classed as our enemies.[7]

To reinforce the seriousness of the oath they were taking, Spence slapped each of the recruits on the face and pinched their thumbs. 'You will have to sign this oath in your own blood,' he barked at them. 5/- was the weekly subscription, or 'dues', which members were forced to pay, and would be used to buy arms. In all, the initiation lasted for an hour and a half, and included a general talk about the organisation and its aims. The group next met in the Standard Bar a few days later on Saturday 18 June. 'We talked in general and the affairs of the UVF were not discussed,' Johnston said. The UVF would also meet regularly in the Standard Bar every Thursday night. Spence told the manager that they were forming a social club to send money to loyalists in Glasgow. All the men would then socialise together until closing time.

Those men who formed the nucleus of the Shankill Road UVF at the time were also office bearers and members of the Orange Order's Prince

Albert Lodge, which sat in the Whiterock area. The Orange Order remained strong in places like the Shankill. Lodge meetings were an occasion to meet like-minded people.[8] One of those men who spent time in the company of Spence and the others was twenty-five-year-old Hughie Smyth.

Smyth grew up in a working-class home on the Shankill Road. His father, Jimmy, worked in McGladdery's and Parkview, two brickworks in West Belfast. Like most working-class men who worked as labourers, his shifts were long. For twelve hours a day, five days a week and then seven hours on a Saturday, Jimmy worked tirelessly to put food on the table for his family. When work was scarce, the local pawn shop became a regular haunt. A life-long supporter of the Northern Ireland Labour Party (NILP), Jimmy drilled into his family a sense of pride in work. His favourite motto was 'In order to better ourselves we must rise ourselves.' At elections, Jimmy Smyth would often comment that all a politician needed to do to get elected on the Shankill was to 'traipse a donkey in a union jack up the Road and people would vote for it'. There was some truth to this well-worn adage. Unionist Party politicians in the area had been regularly re-elected without much opposition, save from the occasional breakthrough coming from Independent Unionists or NILP politicians.

Jimmy Smyth would frequently express his frustration at what he believed was an unfair system, which made all working-class unionists third-class citizens. It was a view of politics that would greatly influence his son, Hugh, a committed Christian who would go on to become a respected Sunday School teacher in the neighbouring Mayo Street Mission Hall. Hugh carried his strong, faith-based beliefs into the Orange Order and Royal Black Preceptory, where he met several men who were to become the UVF's leading lights, including Gusty and Eddie Spence, Dessie Balmer Snr, Norman Sayers, Harry Stockman Snr and Jim McDonald. Stockman and McDonald were also members of the NILP. In joining the UVF, these men found an avenue by which to hit back at the establishment, 'as well as the IRA threat'.[9]

***

Belfast City Centre, Daytime, 16 June 1966

A medieval crescendo of flute band music carried far and wide along the Shankill Road as Ian Paisley headed a large parade, which was steadily making its way to the Ulster Hall in Belfast city centre. Heading up the Shankill Road from the Peter's Hill direction was Willie Blakely, who was accompanied by twenty-one-year-old Leslie Porter, a dumper driver from Beltoy Road in Kilroot. Porter had expressed keen interest in joining the UVF in the days leading up to the parade, and was anxious to become involved in their activities. Blakely and Porter had arranged to meet Gusty Spence in the Standard Bar on the Shankill. They were told to come armed, and so brought with them an automatic handgun and a Smith and Wesson revolver. Not long after they had arrived at the bar, Spence summoned Blakely and Porter to the toilets to examine Porter's gun. After clearing it by ejecting the magazine, Spence handed the weapon back and left the bar to join the parade. The two East Antrim men remained in the bar and carried on drinking as the bands marched past.

As the final columns of the parade disappeared down the Shankill, Blakely and Porter joined the last of the marchers as they made their way towards the city centre. There they met Geordie Bigger, who was intoxicated. He became giddy with excitement at the prospect of handling Porter's revolver. The East Antrim man became somewhat uneasy by the prospect of having to produce the pistol in broad daylight and, at first, refused. Bigger continued to badger him until Porter gave in and invited him over to a dark corner, where the gun was produced. Bigger promptly snatched it from him, unclipped the chamber and loaded three bullets into it. 'I'm getting off side,' Porter told both men. Blakely asked Porter to carry his automatic in his holster, which he did. The three men then headed to a pub on May Street, passing on the opportunity to attend the Paisley speech. Once the rally had finished and men began to disperse from the hall, the three UVF men left the pub and joined with others from their unit on the march back up the Shankill Road.

'On the way up there was five of us; that was myself, Reid, McClean, Porter and Blakely,' Bigger said later in a confusing recollection of the events of that day. 'We got up the Shankill allright [sic]. We broke off at Crimea Street and I got the gun off Porter. I know Porter had a gun but I can't remember what way the talk about it came round.' It seemed that the men had hastily hatched a plan to attack premises in Crimea Street that, they alleged, 'was doing business with tinkers and the like'. Bigger now had Blakely's automatic handgun, or, 'at least I was told afterwards by Dezzy [sic] Reid that was what it was'. Once they got to the 'wee electrical shop' Bigger fired one shot at the rear door and, he claimed, Blakely then fired two shots. 'The gun Blakely had was a small one. I kept my gun and after the next morning I took it down to Des Reid at his home. What he did with it I do not know. After we fired the shots I went up Meenan Street. I ran. I don't know what way Blakely ran ...'[10]

A couple of days later, with this initiation ritual over, McClean informed Porter that he had been accepted as a member of Shankill UVF, and that both men were to be officially sworn in. Porter said that the ceremony had taken place in a house on the Shankill. Also in attendance was McClean, Spence, Frank Curry and his wife Cassie, who was Spence's sister, and one other man. 'Robinson, Reid, Blakely and myself were then brought into the back kitchen,' Porter recalled. 'I was there, together with Blakely, Reid and McClean, [and we were] sworn in as members of the Ulster Volunteer Force. This was done by Spence. After this, Spence produced my 45 Smith and Wesson revolver and asked me if he could hold on to it. I told him that he could keep it. He then asked me if he could keep the revolver, and I said that he could. That was the last I seen of it.'[11]

A few days later, on 20 June, Alexander McClean, a young joiner from Carrick, was at home watching television with his daughter. The curtains and blinds were open, though the living room was in darkness. Only the flickering of the light from the TV could be seen outside. McClean was startled by a loud bang before seeing the whole front room window of his house come flying into the room. He panicked, jumped up and ran outside onto the street to see what had caused the window to shatter. The streets were empty. He couldn't see anything out of the ordinary.[12] In the shadows, though, someone, somewhere bore a grudge for something. McClean went back inside and began to clear the glass. He heeded the warning. The UVF in East Antrim had carried out its first attack. They were gearing up for many more.

***

Watson's Bar, Malvern Street, Shankill, 2 a.m., 26 June 1966

The noise of the crash and whistle of the bands echoed around the streets of West Belfast as Orangemen made their way from the Shankill Road, along Workman Avenue and onto the Springfield Road. The annual Whiterock parade would later become one of the most contentious in Northern Ireland, but in 1966 it would pass by predominantly Catholic houses without so much as a murmur from the residents. Later that evening the men returned from the centre of Belfast, some a little worse for wear with drink. Gusty Spence and other members of the Shankill UVF decided to call into Watson's Bar after they broke from the parade. They spent the whole evening drinking, which had, by now, become a predictable pattern of behaviour for the gang.

As the moon rose high in the night sky four young friends made their way up from where they worked at the International Hotel in the city centre to Watson's Bar on the Lower Shankill, one of the few bars that stayed open after licensing hours. It was 1 a.m. Having consumed a fair amount of alcohol, Spence returned to the bar for more, where he caught a glimpse of the four young men entering the premises. When he returned to the table, he told the men in his company what he had seen, namely that 'four IRA men' had entered the premises. Spence left after a decision had been made to fetch a sack of guns from his sister Cassie's house. Within an hour the UVF men had taken up firing positions on the corner of Ariel Street and Malvern Street. As eighteen-year-old Peter Ward and his three friends exited the bar, they were shot at by the UVF men. Three of the young friends were wounded, two seriously. Peter Ward tragically died at the scene, after being shot through the heart.[13] It was a cruel sectarian act brought about as a direct result of Spence's unit being unable to kill a well-known republican, Leo Martin, who lived in the Falls Road area. Frustrated by their failure, the UVF men resorted to Spence's base philosophy of 'If you can't get an IRA man, get a Taig.'[14]

Robert Williamson, one of the UVF men involved in the shooting, later explained how events unfolded that night:

> I went around to Watson's Bar. I had a Luger gun in a shoulder holster with me. It was loaded with six rounds of small calibre ammunition. I think it was .79 ammunition. I joined two comrades, who I don't want to name. I was told that there was [sic] four IRA men in the bar. There was [sic] instructions given by one of my comrades to scare them. I took up a position at the corner of Malvern Street and Ariel Street. My comrades took up their own positions. The four IRA men came out of Watson's Bar through the Ariel Street door. I moved out towards the centre of the road. I drew my gun and fired towards the men, but low. Everybody was told to fire low. I mean my comrades. My gun jammed twice and I had to 'cock' it, and a round was ejected each time. That's how I know that I fired four rounds. We all ran down

Longford Street and made our way to a certain place where we all put our guns in a sack. I went home after that. This was not a deliberate attack, it happened on the spare [*sic*] of the moment. I think that the one who got away had a gun on him. We did not know that these IRA men were going to be in Watson's Bar that night.[15]

In the twilight of the night, one local boy living across from Watson's Bar witnessed the aftermath of the shooting. As he looked out of his bedroom window, he could see the body of one young man, Peter Ward, slouched against the wall of the bar. He had been shot in the chest. His white shirt was plastered in blood. Nobody in the area witnessed the actual killing, only its aftermath.[16]

The Stormont government reacted swiftly to the Malvern Street shootings, promptly proscribing the UVF under the Civil Authorities (Special Powers) (Northern Ireland) Act (1922), where it was to remain alongside the IRA as an unlawful organisation. Speaking in a rare debate on Northern Ireland at Westminster, Prime Minister Harold Wilson reassured his fellow MPs, who were concerned with the security implications of the Queen's proposed visit. 'With regard to this organisation,' Wilson told the House, 'I do not think that the hon. Member overstated the position in the words he used; it is a quasi-Fascist organisation masquerading behind a clerical cloak.'[17] Following hot on the heels of Prime Minister Gerry Fitt, a Republican Labour MP who won a seat at Westminster a few weeks earlier, made his first determined breach of the convention that prohibited discussion of Northern Ireland affairs in the chamber. He asked Wilson if he was 'further aware that there are Unionist extremists and murder gangs operating in the streets of Northern Ireland?' Demanding that Whitehall 'take action and not the Government of Northern Ireland,'[18] he was interrupted by heckling from Unionist parliamentarians. The Speaker of the House then took steps to censor Fitt. The debate ended abruptly.

At the Stormont Parliament on the same day, Fitt's Republican Labour colleague, Harry Diamond MP, told those in the Belfast chamber that the attacks were not the work of an 'isolated crackpot' but a resolute armed conspiracy against Roman Catholics. Diamond illustrated his point by highlighting an incident in which police discovered that a bullet had been fired through the back window of a house on the Glen Road in West Belfast, something that had received 'no publicity' but was duly noted in the minds of Roman Catholic residents in the area.[19]

Before panic could set in further, the perpetrators, including Spence, were quickly apprehended by the RUC and charged with Ward's murder. Detective Sergeant Robert Agar, based at Leopold Street, interviewed the men for several hours but couldn't get them to admit their respective roles. In an interview with Spence, the Shankill man remained deeply evasive. 'Was Hugh McClean, or a man named Porter from Carrickfergus, in your company last Saturday night?' asked the detective. 'I don't know anyone named Hugh McClean, and I don't know Porter,' Spence told him flatly.[20] Despite Spence's ardent refusal to give details, some of the other men did begin to break after further, much harsher, questioning, and after threats were allegedly made against them by the detectives.[21] According to McClean, Detective Constable Leo McBrien told him, 'Once your name is in the paper, the IRA will shoot you and your family.' McClean also reported that Detective Constable Robert Crockett had struck him on the side of the head with a rolled-up sheaf of paper. Both detectives denied making the remarks, that they had coerced a confession out of him or that they had said 'Give us Spence and you can get out.' Curiously, the only evidence the detectives had against Spence and his co-accused were 'verbal' statements, supposedly made to the police, which the witnesses refused to repeat in court. McClean later denied making the statement,[22] confirmed by the fact that he was admitted into what became the UVF wing at Crumlin Road gaol.

While McClean was being questioned, the RUC had arrested Dessie Reid. He broke after only a short spell in interrogation, and voluntarily took Detective Constable George Thompson to a place known as Cherry's farm in Ballyboag in Mallusk, where the UVF had secreted the two glass sweet jars of gelignite in an outhouse. Beside the jars, Reid showed Detective Constable Thompson six detonators wrapped in cotton wool and a length of fuse.[23] Once the RUC officers obtained further evidence of the type and calibre of weapons used in the attacks from their suspects, their forensics team worked to link spent cases to several shooting incidents, including one in Carrickfergus and another found in the doorway of 2A Oranmore Street.[24] They were found to be a match for the same gun, a .455 calibre Webley revolver. It did not take detectives long to piece together the conspiracy, involving men from Belfast, Glengormley, Carrickfergus and Loughgall.

The suspects rounded up by the RUC were quickly charged. After spending the summer on remand, they appeared in court on 5 September

1966. As Billy Millar, Geordie McCullough and Gusty Spence stood solemnly in the dock awaiting news of their fate, the presiding judge, Lord Chief Justice MacDermott, took his seat. Looking across at the three defendants, he read out the charges against them, which included the murders of John Scullion and Peter Ward. The judge told them he believed they had committed these acts 'in the course or furtherance of a dangerous conspiracy and, or alternatively, or, in the course of furtherance of the activities of an association or organisation which is an unlawful association'.[25] Sentencing each of the men to at least twenty years' imprisonment, Lord MacDermott said the murder of Peter Ward had been especially 'brutal, cowardly and cold-blooded'.[26]

As the wives of the defendants wept openly in the courtroom, one of them collapsed and had to be helped from the public gallery.[27] Wracked with emotion, all three men did their best to look composed as they stood to attention, facing the judge. In chorus they replied 'No Sir' to the charges. With the exception of Spence, all of the men who appeared in the dock had broken under interrogation.

This was not the first time Spence had found himself in court. Eighteen months earlier, he had been working for the Post Office in Belfast when, on 11 March 1965, he was arrested and charged with the offence of 'Obtaining money by false pretences contrary to Section 32(1) of the Larceny Act, 1916'. It transpired that Spence had claimed overtime that, it was alleged by his employers, he did not undertake. Twelve separate charges – relating to falsified overtime claims for each month between 27 October 1963 and 4 November 1964 – were put to the court.[28] The Post Office Investigating Officer put the allegation to Spence, who claimed that, 'Any overtime that I have claimed on the forms P1. 21B has been performed, and if you think otherwise you will have to prove it.'[29] When questioned under caution, Spence told the investigating officer Detective Constable Leonard V. McConaghy at Queen Street RUC Station that he had 'nothing to say to all the charges at this particular time'.[30] He had been released on bail, but was later recalled and convicted of theft.

As Spence and the other UVF men began their lengthy prison sentences in Crumlin Road prison, the police released a statement to reassure the wider community that the threat of IRA violence had vastly diminished. The Easter Rising jubilee commemorations, which the IRA hoped would stimulate recruiting and draw more youths into the ranks, 'fell far short of expectations' an RUC spokesmen told the *Belfast Telegraph*. 'In the few months before the celebrations there was a slight rise in recruiting, but interest since has waned. It is known that there is a swing towards a much more cultural approach, and that the militants are having a poor show.'[31] Militant Protestants, like Spence, were now being exposed as having manufactured enemies out of the unfounded paranoia that had temporarily gripped the darker recesses of the Ulster Protestant psyche.

That an armed republican campaign had not materialised did not deter UVF supporters from believing that the imprisoned men had been right to take the actions they had taken. As he languished in his Victorian-era prison cell, one UVF member composed a poem called 'The Man in the Soft Black Hat' to celebrate the murder of Peter Ward:

> The Peelers came and the ambulance too and took the three men away, 'Three taigs they were' said ould Liza Jane, 'and one of them's dead they say.' 'I don't know what they were doing up here, especially the Shankill Road,' 'Hell slap it into them,' big Joe declared, 'You'd think they wouldn't have knowed.'[32]

Such sentiment played straight into the hands of Protestant extremist opinion on the Shankill, and in other places throughout Northern Ireland. If the IRA threat did not exist, they would continue to manufacture it.

★★★

The incarceration of the UVF's 'leading lights' in 1966 may have decapitated the organisation, but the genie of violent sectarianism was now well and truly out of the bottle. The liberal unionist editor of the *Belfast Telegraph*, Jack Sayers, a close ally of Prime Minister Terence O'Neill, warned of the growing 'dangers of Paisleyism', which he found 'are not only that it provokes communal strife, but that the belief in its leader's "fundamentalism", in politics as well as religion, colours as much as half of the working class backbone of unionism.'[33] For his part, Paisley refused to acknowledge the consequences of his rampantly sectarian sermons and speeches, with Spence's co-accused Hugh McClean, admitting under interrogation that he was 'terribly sorry I ever heard of that man Paisley or decided to follow him'.[34]

Unlike Doherty, Billy Mitchell stayed the course with Paisleyism. If the 'bishop' warned of dangerous times ahead, then that was something the Protestant people should take as gospel. Privately, though, he began to harbour some doubts. 'Despite all the rhetoric I never consciously felt that there was going to be this all-out war where loyalists and republicans would be in the field fighting,' he later said. 'We always assumed that if there was [going to be] anything like that ... it would be the B-Specials and the police [who] would have dealt with it ... But, at that time, Paisley was whipping us up into believing it.'

For Mitchell, dangers did lie ahead, but he wasn't quite sure what they were. 'The object of our wrath was more O'Neill and liberal unionism than it was the republicans, because, being honest with you, we wouldn't have known an IRA man from a man on the moon,' Mitchell said. 'Most of the big rallies we attended, all the rhetoric of Paisley at that time – ok the IRA came into it – but the main object of his attention was O'Neill and liberal unionists, ecumenical clergy ... So, I never consciously felt to myself that we would be lining up with guns to go and fight the IRA. The object seemed to bring O'Neill down, and to establish a strong government that would deal with any threat.'[35]

The imprisonment of leading UVF men did little to take the wind out of the sails of the challenge now underway against O'Neill, nor did it stop the growth of the organisation. In late 1966, the UVF had 'a nucleus of about thirty men on the Shankill Road', though the more rural parts of the organisation became moribund.[36]

O'Neill was facing a conflict on two fronts. From the Protestant grassroots who were angered by the Stormont government's refusal to ban Easter Rising parades, and by Catholics who remained unconvinced at the pace of reform O'Neill had put in motion. It was the latter who took to the streets, first, by forming the Northern Ireland Civil Rights Association (NICRA) in January 1967. This protest movement had its roots in the agitation of a husband and wife team, Con and Patricia McCloskey, from Dungannon who had been highlighting discriminatory policies by the local unionist-dominated council since 1963. The Campaign for Social Justice gained considerable support amongst the backbenchers of the British Labour Party and soon a Campaign for Democracy in Ulster was formed which gave political backing to NICRA. On 5 October 1968, a civil rights march was met by heavy-handedness from the RUC and B-Specials in Londonderry. Northern Ireland was moving closer to the precipice of major civil unrest.

As a means of upping the ante, the UVF and its allies in the UPV stood-to again, deciding to bomb a number of key installations around the province. Two explosions on 30 March and 21 April 1969 destroyed water and electricity sub-stations in Castlereagh, Belfast, and at the Silent Valley reservoir in the Mourne Mountains, County Down. The bomb attacks were designed to exaggerate the threat posed by the IRA and, hopefully, to bring down O'Neill.[37] In response, O'Neill mobilised the B-Specials to protect key installations. By then it was too late. O'Neill looked weak. The UVF–UPV plot worked, with even O'Neill coming to believe that the UVF had 'literally bombed me out of office'.[38] He resigned as Prime Minister on 28 April.

UVF subversion was not without its dangers. One volunteer, Thomas McDowell, was found badly burned on 19 October, having been electrocuted by 5,600 volts as he attempted to fit a bomb to a hydroelectric power station near Ballyshannon in County Donegal. McDowell had been pulverised by the extremity of the electric charges surging through his body; succumbing to his wounds in hospital two days later. A committed Paisleyite, McDowell was a close associate of Billy Mitchell. Mitchell later explained his thinking at this time:

> In the years leading up to the outbreak of civil unrest, which erupted in August 1969, I had come to believe that the Ulster Protestant had a traditional and unalienable right to resist 'by any means under God' the supposed enemies of our Ulster heritage and distinctive protestant way of life; and I felt that my views on this were adequately confirmed by the public and private pronouncements of many 'pillars of society' and by 'men of the cloth'. The much-loved phrase – 'by all means under God' – was simply a synonym for 'by force of arms' but with the added thought that God himself would approve of such action. In the early days of the troubles, and for several years before, threats of armed resistance together with a 'holy war' philosophy was put across in religious phraseology, in traditional slogans linked to the old 1912-UVF, and in sermons based on the warfare of the Old Testament. [Sermons which could be taken literally or figuratively – whichever way you wanted to take them].[39]

For Mitchell, the piety of religious fundamentalism fused with his new-found militant mindset:

> It was this carefully insinuated idea that the Ulster Protestant was a modern-day Israelite and the Irish Roman Catholic was a modern-day

Philistine that gave me, and many more like me, the firm conviction that force of arms was legitimate in the struggle for Ulster's continued existence as a Protestant state for a Protestant people. The only real difference between the battle plans and weaponry of the Old Testament Israelites and the Ulster Protestants being that of modern technology and military strategy.[40]

With the political situation now descending into anarchy by late 1969, Mitchell quickly drifted into the ranks of TARA, a religious fundamentalist group led by the aggressive homosexual and paedophile William McGrath.

Hence, when the Troubles finally did escalate into open-street warfare I was a natural candidate for paramilitarism, and quickly joined TARA [an Orange Order based group] and, later, the Ulster Volunteer Force. It is interesting to note that the TARA leadership opened and closed their meetings with prayer and had other religious trappings, and that most of them claimed to be evangelical Christians. Another interesting point – they were mainly from the middle-class strata of society, or, at least, from the upper working class. 'Could these cultured and respectable folk be wrong?' I wondered. I always answered in the negative. 'No, of course not. They were only following our traditional Protestant way of resisting the enemy'. My brief experience of TARA reinforced my belief in the legitimate right of Protestants to use violence.[41]

As TARA became more of a 'talking shop', than a conservative armed group, Mitchell sought refuge alongside like-minded individuals, many of whom had decided to leave and join the ranks of the Shankill UVF.

The tragic irony of UVF violence was that it actually prompted republicans to rejuvenate the IRA to defend the Catholic community against militant loyalist attacks. One of the IRA's new recruits was Tommy Gorman, who would later rise to prominence in its ranks. He recalled how intercommunal rioting intensified in August 1969, and prompted the return of the IRA, which:

… was in a pretty bad state. I think in Divis Street that night [in 1969] there were a couple of short arms and a sub-machine gun. But … at that time it was moribund. And it was in the influx of new recruits and all these older people who had been retired and had gone out back to their farms or something and had suddenly reappeared again and gave us some sort of structure.[42]

There has been some dispute amongst republicans, academics and journalists over the exact size of the IRA in the 1960s. Estimates vary from 30–120 members in Belfast.[43] In early April 1966, Scotland Yard intelligence reports placed the numbers at 1,000, which would explain why the RUC's Crime Special Branch believed they were facing a concerted subversive campaign. In reality, the IRA only had 1,039 members in the Republic, 251 of whom were Border Campaign veterans. Around 300 members were concentrated in Dublin.[44]

★★★

More than anything else, UVF activity between 1966 and 1969 fed intercommunal fears and whipped up emotional reactions from hardline republicans and their supporters. The IRA may have remained somewhat inert in this period, but unionists believed that it had been plotting subversion and the appearance of the NICRA marches served to confirm as much in the minds of hardline unionists at the time.

Roy Garland was one of those who believed the dire warnings. Garland was second-in-command of TARA at the time. 'I mean, you didn't know what to make of some of this stuff,' he said. 'There was talk of a coming doomsday situation and "You're going to have to defend Ulster." And the politicians, the sort of moderate accommodating politicians, were prepared to "sell out" so we would have to defend Ulster.' Garland, like Mitchell, believed that the 'doomsday situation' was just around the corner. Paisley's predictions were coming true. 'I went to Paisley's church and so on – but I didn't find him inspiring,' said Garland. 'The whole leadership of TARA though did. But … to me he wasn't an inspiring person. He didn't inflame me with zeal or anything. But it was just the idea.' The idea, as Garland, put it, was like an unquenchable thirst, which the fall of O'Neill in April 1969 did little to satisfy.

By the summer of 1969 violence became more organised and widespread. 'James Chichester-Clark at one stage said it was an insurrection, referring to republicans on the Falls Road, and others talked in that sort of terminology, and if they were saying it, [we said] "look, well, obviously it's true".' For

Garland and other Protestant extremists, the UVF and TARA were hardline groupings with only one objective – defending their beloved Ulster from all enemies, from wherever they came. 'That was centrally important from where I was coming from. Coming from the sort of religious background ... that can't be underestimated. There were doubts in your mind about things.' Garland believed that his faith was being 'sold out'.[45] Recognising an easy way to get hold of arms, the UVF under Samuel 'Bo' McClelland, began to infiltrate TARA. 'When TARA came along,' reported *Irish Times* journalist David McKittrick, 'these men eagerly seized the opportunity for organised action again, but it was not long before they became restive. The main reasons for this disquiet were the religious fanaticism of the TARA leadership and the organisation's reluctance to engage in "procurement activities" – a common euphemism for robberies.'[46]

In McClelland and the UVF, Billy Mitchell saw great promise. When he was given the opportunity, Mitchell jumped ship and, along with other UVF men, took 'much of the equipment with them', later to be interpreted by informed observers as the UVF's strategy all along.[47] Roy Garland admitted that the real reason why McClelland ordered his men to leave TARA was triggered 'when evidence was received ... of McGrath's homosexual abuse of young men, along with rumours of his reliability'.[48] It has been said that McClelland was so infuriated by McGrath's transgressions that he burnt the TARA membership book, which included the names of many of his own men.[49] Among this cadre of UVF men, what McKittrick called the 'tougher and brighter element in the seceding group', was Mitchell. The UVF would allow him to fulfil his deep-seated desire to fight by force of arms for God and Ulster.

3

LIQUIDATING THE ENEMY

'WE ARE LOYALISTS, WE ARE QUEEN'S MEN. Our enemies are the forces of Romanism and Communism, which must be destroyed.'

UVF Recruiting Circular (1971)[1]

Belfast, the capital city of Northern Ireland, grew from a small market town in the seventeenth century to become one of the major hubs for trade and industry in the British Empire by the late nineteenth century. One hundred years later its twin staple industries of shipbuilding and textile manufacturing had been joined by another, aeronautical engineering, which employed several thousand people, primarily in the east of the city. The large yellow cranes of Samson and Goliath at Harland and Wolff Shipyard, symbols of Belfast's industrial heritage, towered high above the skyline, but were becoming increasingly exposed to the push and pull of global capitalism, now in the process of transferring its centre of gravity from North America and Western Europe to markets in the Far East. Belfast relied disproportionately on a sizeable subvention from the British taxpayer to keep its heavy industries afloat, its public services running efficiently and its social security and welfare payments pouring in amidst this transformation in its economic fortunes. At the dawn of the seventh decade of the twentieth century, this once dominant industrial city was beginning to decline.

Although Belfast had a reasonably healthy economic base when the troubles broke out in the late 1960s, it was a system which overlay a sectarian distribution of jobs. The workforce in the staple industries was divided between the majority Protestant and the minority Catholic communities. Up until 1972, such division was not always reflected in political terms, along unionist–nationalist lines on the shop floor. Sectarianism had waxed and waned since the formation of the local state in the early 1920s. By the late 1950s and early 1960s most working-class people were more interested in earning a crust and providing for their families than they were in the constitutional question. As a direct consequence, a third political labour tradition began to flourish, going on to command 100,000 votes in both the 1964 and 1970 Westminster elections.[2]

Higher rates of employment and the availability of disposable income may have ensured the dampening of sectarian tensions, but it wasn't the only reason. Paddy Devlin, a Northern Ireland Labour Party (NILP) politician who represented the Falls constituency in the Northern Ireland Parliament at Stormont in East Belfast, observed that for 'the first time in forty years there was a spirit of compromise in the air. People from the two communities were more prepared than ever to live together in harmony, and the old shibboleths that had for so long been sources of division were being closely questioned.'[3] There was nothing inevitable about the outbreak of the troubles and, with the exception of a residual amount of loyalist and republican militancy, all signs pointed towards a relatively settled population. Even those who came from areas that would later become staunchly republican, like West Belfast, acknowledged how, in the 1960s, they were 'conditioned towards accepting Northern Ireland and playing a part in it, rather than towards resisting it or begrudging it'.[4]

With the escalation of intercommunal tensions in 1969, people began to pull apart more noticeably. In the inner-city slums of Belfast, residential segregation gave birth to a patchwork quilt of sharp sectarian division between Catholics and Protestants. Street corners suddenly demarcated rigid psychological and territorial boundaries, as communities intersected along increasingly fraught tribal lines. Housing estates became the exclusive preserve of one side, or the other. Built in the 1950s, Rathcoole, on the outskirts of North Belfast, grew exponentially as sectarian confrontation escalated. Those Protestants displaced from their homes in Ballymurphy, Suffolk and other areas of Belfast flooded the estate as it became more and more Protestant in religious composition. As a direct consequence, Catholics began to move out into the areas vacated by Protestants in increasing numbers. Some of those individuals forcibly ejected from their childhood homes in Rathcoole, such as Bobby Sands, Freddie Scappaticci and Jim Gibney, left with embittered memories of sectarian intimidation. Like others, who also subsequently joined paramilitary organisations, they would point to their direct experience of intimidation and threats as a principal motivating factor in explaining their drift towards political violence.[5]

By the early 1970s, the garish pebble-dashed council houses in these new estates on the periphery of Belfast enveloped the tiny red-brick terrace houses of the old city. Both would sit in stark contrast alongside larger, more imposing, bungalows and semi-detached homes of the greater Belfast area. The commanding, undulating glens of Antrim, sat flush against Belfast Lough, where the Irish Sea disappeared into the Lagan River Valley. On the surface, the arteries of trade and industry gave Northern Ireland the appearance of a modern, outward-looking society. To the people who lived in increasingly ghettoised areas though, a different story was emerging, as the air became chokingly thick with the nauseating waft of bigotry and intolerance. It was amidst Belfast's changing demographics that sectarian violence was reborn.

***

Shankill Road, West Belfast, Evening, 4 December 1971

Christmas decorations began to spring up along the Shankill Road as people prepared for the festive season. There was a chill in the air, but the weather was more wet and windy than wintry. Robert James Campbell, known as Jimmy to his friends, joined the UVF in the summer of 1971. On 4 December, he was summoned to a meeting with his superior officer in a bar off the Shankill Road, where he was told to accompany two other men on an operation and not to return until 'the job' was done. Accepting the task without knowing the full picture of what he was about to become involved in, as many other UVF men did at the time, Campbell walked outside and climbed into the back seat of a car. He sat quietly as the driver moved off towards the city centre. After a few moments, he broke the silence by informing his companions that they were 'going to do a bar in North Queen Street'. The full significance of the task which lay before them had still not sunk in by the time the men reached their intended target, just under a mile from where their journey began.

As they sat in the vehicle alongside the pavement opposite McGurk's Bar, the men caught a glimpse of the silhouettes of patrons moving around inside the premises. Men and women were busy enjoying themselves. The party was in full swing. Outside, the UVF men watched their prey. Calmly, deliberately, they checked every move, noted every outbreak of laughter, registered the happy revelry going on inside. Allowing the engine to tick over for a few minutes, the driver slowly slipped the car into gear and drove off around the block, before returning to the street, this time pulling up just outside the side door of the bar. One of the men picked up a taped parcel at his feet and climbed out of the car. He walked with purpose across to the bar door, before slipping inside to deposit his device in the narrow hallway. 'That's it', he shouted as he hurriedly returned to the car. The men drove off down a side street and onto York Street. The driver accelerated, not too sharply, for he didn't want to draw the attention of any passing Army patrols. As the UVF men rounded the corner a huge explosion sent their pulses racing. As calmly as he could, the driver pulled up at the kerbside and turned off the ignition. The doors opened and the men got out, making their way towards Donegal Street, where they were collected by another vehicle and driven the short distance to an Orange Hall on the Shankill.

Campbell was first to appear from the vehicle, walking inside the hall to the small bar where he reported back to the man who had sent him out on the bombing mission only half an hour earlier.[6] His commander appeared pleased with the result. The two men enjoyed a drink together before calling it a night.[7] Both men rounded off the evening with mixed emotions. In the eyes of the UVF commander, a blow had been struck against the enemy. Campbell was much more sanguine. He took no pleasure from his actions that evening, or on any other. He was later described by Gusty Spence as someone who was 'non-sectarian, someone who not only worked happily alongside Catholics, but associated with them through his membership of the Grosvenor Homing Pigeon Society', which was situated off the Falls Road. Campbell had joined the UVF in the aftermath of sectarian rioting in Penrith Street, near Dover Street, on the Shankill.[8] A few months later he was participating in the first major armed attack by the UVF. At one time, Campbell had glimpsed the humanity in the faces of his Catholic work colleagues. That empathy now evaporated with every new job he was handed down by his UVF superiors.

★★★

When the dust settled from the explosion at McGurk's bar, local people ran to the scene to see if they could help the injured. They were greeted by the horrific cries for help from their friends and neighbours, who had been pulverised in the bomb attack. When it exploded, the device ripped through the two-storey building, causing it to collapse in on itself. Panic spread, as people desperately picked through the rubble to rescue survivors. Body parts peppered the debris, some still smouldering from the intense heat of the explosion. This was a slaughter of innocent people, out for a drink in their local pub. They now lay dead, their bodies mangled by the callous acts of members of another community. It transpired that fifteen people had been killed in the attack, and another thirteen injured.[9] Shortly afterwards, a caller to the Belfast newsroom claimed that the 'Empire Loyalists' group had carried out the attack. In reality it was the UVF, which, in 1971, killed seventeen people. All but two of their victims died in this single atrocity.

Although RUC and British Army intelligence on Protestant armed groups at this time was limited, they were subsequently able to intern two loyalists for terrorist offences, including the bombing of McGurk's bar. However, it was the Unionist government's spread of disinformation about the explosion being the result of an IRA 'own goal', which led to a botched handling of the case.[10] That bias crept into the follow-up police investigation had even deadlier consequences, for it was the UVF, not the IRA, which had already honed its bomb-making skills at the time, the only loyalist organisation to have this capability.[11] Consequently, more death and destruction would follow unchecked.

The warning signs that the Security Forces were ignoring the threat posed by loyalist paramilitaries to civilians were apparent many months earlier. Paddy Devlin, a local Stormont MP, had been handed a secret military intelligence dossier from a constituent, who had picked it up after it was dropped by an army officer in Andersonstown. Devlin found its contents 'so hair-raising and inaccurate' that he felt compelled to raise the matter at Stormont. Importantly, Devlin believed that the document exposed the Army's 'partiality ... for there was little mention of the UVF or any other loyalist paramilitary organisations, even though they accounted for a significant proportion of violence at this time.'[12]

That said, for anyone reading the newspapers or listening to news bulletins in the closing months of 1971, the McGurk's Bar massacre was undoubtedly part of a broader pattern of tit-for-tat attacks on pubs in Protestant and Catholic areas across Belfast. Patrons only narrowly escaped with their lives in an IRA attack on the Bluebell Bar, in the Protestant area of Sandy Row on 20 September. Two Protestant men, sixty-year-old Alexander Andrews and thirty-eight-year-old Ernest Bates, weren't so lucky when an IRA bomb exploded in the Four Step Inn in the Protestant Sandy Row area on 29 September. Retaliation came just over a week later, with the UDA's bombing of the Fiddler's House Bar on the Falls Road on 9 October, which killed a forty-five-year-old Protestant, Winifred Maxwell. Some weeks after the attack, the IRA bombed the Red Lion Pub on the Ormeau Road on 2 November, which led to the deaths of three Protestants.[13] A further attack on the Toddle Inn in York Street on 9 November heralded a new low in the armed conflict. By targeting McGurk's Bar, the UVF was sending a message to republicans that any further attacks in the Shankill would meet with stiff opposition from loyalists.

In their targeting of premises frequented by civilians, paramilitary organisations on both sides were demonstrating a flagrant disregard for their communities, who were by now bearing the brunt of the violence. Predictably, the UVF attack on McGurk's Bar invited swift retaliation from the IRA, which bombed the Balmoral Furniture Company on a busy Saturday on the Shankill Road a week later. Four civilians were killed instantly, including a seventeen-month-old baby and a two-year-old child. If the UVF had been seeking to increase the safety of Protestants by its actions, it failed miserably. More carnage was to follow as young people flocked to join paramilitary groupings.

★★★

Violence now escalated quickly across Northern Ireland. The reintroduction of internment without trial for terrorist suspects on 9 August 1971 was a strategic blunder, serving as a 'recruiting sergeant' for the IRA.[14] Although the policy failed to decapitate the Provisional IRA, whose leaders had escaped the clutches of the Security Forces, it was based on reasonably good intelligence provided by RUC Special Branch. The military, which had been given the task of rounding up suspects, had a poor intelligence organisation and, consequently, relied disproportionately on the RUC, despite it having assumed responsibility for overseeing security policy at the operational level.[15] Senior army commanders at their headquarters in Lisburn grew more and more concerned at the escalation of violence, and this made them prone to knee-jerk reactions.

The urgency to curtail disorder was felt most acutely in Londonderry, the second major city in Northern Ireland. On 28 January 1972, the RUC's senior officer there attended a Security Forces planning meeting in the city that had been convened to deal with the possibility of a mass protest march by civil rights campaigners in defiance of a government ban.[16] Although the RUC and army were jointly responsible for security in the city, the Army was to take the lead in dealing with the march when it took place on 30 January 1972. On the day, as anticipated, protestors defied the ban and left the Creggan estate for the Guildhall in the city centre. The military responded with aggressive tactics aimed at halting the march as it passed through the nationalist Bogside area. Poor tactical leadership by the commanding officer of the 1st Battalion, the Parachute Regiment, Lieutenant Colonel Derek Wilford, led to him failing to comply with an order issued by his superior officer, Brigadier Pat MacLellan, and deploying a company of his soldiers into the Bogside area where they opened fire on protestors.[17] Thirteen people were massacred, and another died of his wounds two weeks later. The day became known as 'Bloody Sunday' and it transformed the political and military situation in Northern Ireland.

Meanwhile, in London, at the very highest levels, senior civil servants at the Ministry of Defence (MoD) began to scope out contingency plans for a united Ireland in the event that civil war broke out in the province. The Deputy Under Secretary of State at the MoD, Pat Nairne, sat down to write a letter to Sir Stewart Crawford at the FCO about what he judged to be 'an extremely remote contingency'.[18] Both men nonetheless gave serious thought to the unlikely sequences of events, should the worst happen, with the MoD tasking several staff officers to assess the effects it would have for defence. 'The need no longer to garrison Ulster, nor to provide for its reinforcement would reduce overstretch in the army and increase the credibility of GB's contribution to NATO', wrote Nairne. 'On the other hand the probable loss of the five Irish regiments and the Ulster TAVR, and the reduction (perhaps loss) of the Irish recruiting intake would be of major concern to the army. It would be necessary to replace much, possibly all, of this loss within GB [Great Britain].'[19] A full inventory of Britain's national security assets was subsequently compiled and quietly filed away.

Across from the MoD building, in Number 10 Downing Street, Prime Minister Ted Heath was facing a major fall out from the shootings on Bloody Sunday. Huge protests got underway in Dublin, where the British Embassy was promptly burnt to the ground by demonstrators. Across the world, international opinion now shifted to London's handling of the security situation in Northern Ireland. Much would depend on what the British government did next.

★★★

Dublin, 13 March 1972

A few months before Bloody Sunday, in September 1971, Ted Heath had reached out to the leader of the Labour Opposition, Harold Wilson, to see if he could use his influence with the SDLP to ensure they participated in talks aimed at reshaping the political future of Northern Ireland.[20] In the wake of Bloody Sunday, Wilson sought to extend his remit to try and persuade the IRA to resist the urge to use the massacre in Derry as a justification for a renewed campaign. He made contact with an Irish Labour Party TD, Dr John O'Connell, to scope out the opportunities of getting a message to the IRA leadership. O'Connell, a respected Dublin physician, sounded them out and reported back to Wilson that they wished to meet him. Losing no time, Wilson flew to Dublin for secret talks, accompanied by his chief spokesman on Northern Ireland, Merlyn Rees, and Labour's Chief Press Secretary Joe Haines.[21]

The leaders Wilson had come to meet were the Provo top brass, Dáithí Ó Conaill, John Kelly and Joe Cahill. Ó Conaill was the Provo's lead spokesman. A tough character, he had risen to prominence with the IRA in the 1950s, and remained so. He began the meeting by reiterating the IRA's position, which appeared, at first glance, more flexible than it had been only a year earlier. Wilson's own position had also softened, he told the IRA delegation. In a speech he gave in November 1971, the former Prime Minister set out his 15 Point Plan for Irish unity. 'I said fifteen years. The way your friends are going on it will be a longer period. If it could be cut down to eight or ten years I would be delighted,' he informed the IRA leaders. Wilson's naïvety was clearly getting the better of him. He believed that he could persuade the IRA to abandon its violence, if the British government set out a concrete timetable for withdrawal. Wilson was also convinced that he could also persuade the Provos to turn to the SDLP for political guidance. The IRA rebuffed the idea of striking a deal with the SDLP. There was no love lost between them and SDLP figures like Gerry Fitt and Paddy Devlin, they said. The IRA commanders told Wilson that they believed the SDLP had lost touch with its support base. Happy to have the IRA defend them in 1969 against loyalist attacks, the SDLP leadership now came to utterly reject the violence. The IRA delegation nevertheless maintained the façade that they hadn't the authority to speak on behalf of the rest of the army. They could, however, sound out the Labour leader on his own position, and report back.

Veteran Belfast IRA leader Joe Cahill, who had served a prison sentence for his role in the murder of an RUC officer in the 1940s, then proceeded to reiterate the IRA's three demands of the British government. First, he informed the Labour Party delegation, the British Army should withdraw to its barracks. Second, Stormont should be prorogued. Lastly, Cahill demanded that the British announce a total amnesty for all of its political prisoners. 'The three demands,' Cahill told Wilson emphatically, 'cannot be watered down.'

It was clear from the meeting between Wilson and the IRA leadership that they wanted the British government to get tough with the Unionist regime at Stormont, which had begun to stoke fears of a 'Protestant backlash' in the event of security powers being taken out of its hands.[22] Republicans were concerned about what that would mean for ordinary Catholics as much as for themselves. Unionist leaders were becoming more and more unpredictable, a sentiment echoed in the public speeches of most republicans at the time. Malachy McGurran, the press officer for the Republican Clubs, had been the first to publicly inquire whether Bill Craig's Vanguard movement might embark on 'a campaign of selective assassinations and bombings in Northern Ireland, with the possibility of certain activity in the border counties'. A day before the meeting between Wilson and the Provo leadership, IRA Chief of Staff, Sean MacStiofain, claimed that guns were being imported by Protestant extremists without much difficulty.[23] Ironically, the Provisionals had also imported large numbers of weapons themselves, principally from the United States,[24] and in the preceding twelve months were responsible for several hundred shootings and bombings.

Curiously, rather than find a way to disarm loyalist and republican armed groups, Wilson chose the path of least resistance. The biggest single issue for him at the meeting with the Provisional chiefs was the presence of 112,000 legally held guns, the vast majority to be found in the hands of law-abiding Protestants. Rees shared his leader's concerns, believing that the prospect of civil war was not far off. To head it off at the pass, the IRA needed to be talked down and the loyalists disarmed. Both Wilson and Rees were of the view that the Protestants were behaving unpredictably, telling the IRA leaders they were terrified 'that there would be massive atrocities and attempts to charge the IRA account with what came from Orange sources'.[25] British opposition politicians, it seemed from this meeting, were happy to agree with the Provos that Protestant extremists were the main source of the violence. Ironically, this was not reflected in the higher echelons of the

Stormont and London administrations, in large part because they may not have wanted to fight a war on two fronts. Despite having intelligence on loyalists, the British government was not to act on it until February 1973, when the first loyalists were interned.[26]

In giving the fullest consideration to the Provisional IRA's three demands, Wilson told the leadership that he felt the British Army should be deployed in a defensive, peacekeeping role, an impossibility now that IRA gunmen insisted on engaging them in intense gun battles on the streets. Running in parallel with this plan, Wilson said that Protestants would be relieved of their legally held guns. The British would also simultaneously move against loyalist paramilitaries, thereby creating breathing space for negotiation between the British government and the IRA. On the question of suspending Stormont, Wilson believed that Heath was close to doing so anyway, regardless of the opposition from within the unionist community. The IRA would get their wish. With regard to the IRA's third demand for a total amnesty for political prisoners, Wilson was considerably more guarded. 'No British Government could accept point three after Aldershot,' he told the stony-faced IRA leaders. 'I would not accept it, nor would any British Government,' he said flatly. Ó Conaill was quick to respond. 'Not even after Bloody Sunday?' he inquired. Wilson did not appreciate being interrupted. 'No. An amnesty comes at the end of a political settlement. Makarios, Kenyatta ... the amnesty followed the political settlement. I do not think this is out (indicating the IRA document). I would put three and two on the agenda of all-party negotiations. At the end of the day, an amnesty is on. At an appropriate point I will send a message through John O'Connell and say, "For God's sake, give us a truce".'

In closing the secret talks, Rees addressed the IRA leaders directly. 'What we want out of the Government are internment and security. The question is this: What can all of us do to get it out of the Government?'[27]

When news of Wilson's clandestine talks with IRA leaders leaked, the Labour leader came under a barrage of criticism. He remained undeterred. His personal view was that it was the right thing to do. By engaging in these exploratory talks, Wilson misjudged the threat posed by Protestant paramilitaries who were showing little sign of halting their violence.

Support for a united Ireland was not only confined to the opposition benches. On the day that Wilson met with the IRA in Dublin, Foreign Secretary Alec Douglas-Home wrote a letter to Prime Minister Ted Heath in which he professed his dislike for the option of imposing Direct Rule on Northern Ireland, 'because I do not believe they are like the Scots or Welsh and I doubt if they ever will be'. For Douglas-Home, the 'real British interest would I think be served best by pushing them towards a united Ireland rather than tying them closer to the United Kingdom'. He copied the letter to other senior Cabinet ministers, including the Defence Secretary, Chancellor of the Exchequer, Lord President of the Council and the Cabinet Secretary.[28]

At the highest reaches of power, loyalists had become friendless. Caught between a duplicitous British government on the one hand and their enemies in the IRA on the other, the UVF leadership resolved to carry on its campaign until such times as their republican enemies were bowed.

★★★

Ravenhill Road, East Belfast, Evening, 13 March 1972

A few hours after Harold Wilson concluded his talks with the IRA, loyalist paramilitaries were on the streets once again stalking their prey.[29] Nineteen-year-old Patrick McCrory was at home with his mother, getting ready to go out to meet some friends. He was in good spirits as he washed and dressed himself, pulling on his brand-new rust-coloured Canada jumper and slipping on his smart black shoes. His routine was interrupted by the sound of the doorbell ringing. Thinking it was one of his friends, he trundled downstairs, stopping to pick up his jacket from the living room as he went, closing the living room door behind him. 'I heard a loud crack,' his mother later told police. It quickly dawned on Patrick, as he answered the door, that the caller was a gunman and not a friend. As he turned to run back into the house, a bullet was discharged from the pistol, hitting Patrick on his right shoulder blade and leaving his body by his left jaw bone. Understandably, the shot startled Patrick, sending him falling backwards. He managed to regain his balance for a few seconds before staggering into a dressing table in the hallway, knocking over an ornament with a loud crash in the meantime. The young man who had appeared from the shadows to fire the fatal shot at Patrick McCrory was Frankie Curry, a young volunteer belonging to the Red Hand Commando (RHC), which had aligned itself to the UVF. Curry was a year younger than his victim when he pulled the trigger.[30]

In a state of shock, Patrick stumbled into the living room holding his neck, desperately trying to stem the flow of blood now seeping from the open wound. He managed to make his way to the kitchen where he picked up a facecloth. 'What happened son?' asked his mother, as fear gripped her. 'A gang,' replied Patrick, before fainting. As he fell to the floor, Patrick's mother ran out onto the street to raise the alarm. 'Phone an ambulance! Phone an ambulance!' she cried out. Lights flickered on in other homes in the street, as the McCrorys' neighbours appeared at their front doors to see what the commotion was about. The first people to arrive on the scene found Mrs McCrory in a hysterical state. 'Patrick has been shot,' she told them as she went into shock. When the ambulance arrived, the paramedics found Patrick lying face down on the living room floor where he had collapsed from his wounds. 'Don't worry Mum, I'm alright,' he told his mother, as he was lifted out on a stretcher from his home. A few minutes later, Patrick began to complain of not being able to breathe properly. As the ambulance screamed its way from one side of the River Lagan to the other, the paramedics fought desperately to save Patrick's life. It was no good. Before they had even reached the Royal Victoria Hospital, Patrick suffered cardiac arrest and died a short time later.

In the days and weeks after the death of Patrick McCrory, growing resentment was being reported across Protestant areas of Belfast. Bill Craig, who was by now leader of a self-styled, right-wing organisation known as Ulster Vanguard, held a rally in Belfast's Ormeau Park, attended by up to 100,000 people. 'We must build up a dossier of the men and the women who are a menace to this country,' he told those gathered on 18 March, 'because if and when the politicians fail us, it may be our job to liquidate the enemy'. Loud cheers went up from the crowd.[31]

Less than forty-eight hours after Craig's dire warning, the IRA detonated a car bomb without warning on Lower Donegal Street, killing four Protestant civilians, two RUC officers and an off-duty UDR man, and injuring a further nineteen people. Paranoia gripped huge sections of the Protestant working class. The suspicions many of them harboured of British politicians brokering secret deals with the IRA became rife. Craig's words of warning gained further traction when the Heath government prorogued the Stormont Parliament on 24 March 1972. 'The Shankill Road and Sandy Row, probably the strongest loyalist areas, have remained outwardly calm,' reported Times journalist Robert Fisk, 'but plans have been made for a campaign of civil disobedience similar to that by the civil rights movement.'[32] Even moderate Protestants seethed with anger. Loyalist paramilitary groups mobilised their members to take part in a planned two-day strike.

The biggest and most powerful of the loyalist groups that had attended Craig's Ormeau rally was the Ulster Defence Association (UDA). Originally established in the Woodvale area of West Belfast, likeminded vigilantes soon formed larger associations in East Belfast, East Antrim and Londonderry. By January 1972, the UDA had come together under the control of a thirteen-member 'Security Council', with Charles Harding-Smith, Tommy Herron and Jim Anderson taking up leading positions. The UDA was first and foremost a mass movement, 'democratic to a degree, recognising merit in men's abilities to fight, or organise or commit offences for which they could expect long terms of imprisonment'.[33] Like the UVF, the UDA's membership was fiercely working-class, but its paramilitary activities were initially limited in the sense that it orientated principally around defence and street disturbances.[34] As the organisation grew in size, it began to structure itself along British Army lines – into platoons, companies and, eventually, brigades. UDA leaders were usually elected on the basis of tough reputations as hard men in local areas, others if they had prior military training. In Rathcoole, the South East Antrim's power base, leaders were elected by free vote.[35]

The UDA opposed any constitutional weakening of Northern Ireland's position within the United Kingdom, and initially led opposition to attempts to undermine the Stormont government.[36] Like it had done on 20 March, the UDA led its men to another huge Vanguard rally outside Belfast City Hall on 27 March, attended by around 10,000 people. Craig denounced as 'traitors' anyone who willingly sided with the British government's policy of suspending the local Parliament. In perhaps the most visible sign of a rightward shift towards talk of independence for Ulster, a young man scaled the front façade of the City Hall and tore down the Union Jack that fluttered in the breeze, unmolested, all year round. A few moments later he raised the red, white and gold Ulster Flag emblazoned with a red hand in its centre. The crowd roared with approval.[37]

Despite the fiery rhetoric of a handful of unionist politicians, the Security Forces had little, if any, intelligence to suggest that this Protestant disaffection would translate into a much more concerted armed campaign. However, the army did believe that there was 'increasing evidence that extreme Protestant organisations are trying to procure arms, but no evidence so far that any large quantity has been successfully delivered'. Security Forces commanders were of the view that Protestant resentment would manifest itself in 'more low level, largely uncoordinated incidents of a sectarian nature'.[38] By spring, military commanders were looking eagerly to moderate politicians and a nascent peace movement to take the 'sting out of the tail' of the violence before it worsened any further. Until such times as such violence dissipated, soldiers would remain locked in intense gun battles with the IRA in Belfast, Derry and elsewhere.

While the IRA remained active in terms of shooting incidents, it struggled to perfect its bomb-making capability. The Abercorn Restaurant bomb attack on 4 March 1972, which killed two young women and injured 130 others, was the high point of its bombing campaign. In seeking to complement the sniping activity of its volunteers, it sought to school more of its members in the deadly ingenuity of constructing home-made devices, colloquially known as 'Co-Op mix', because of how easily accessible the ingredients were in local shops. But it came with a heavy price. The IRA lost four members in a premature bomb blast in the Clonard area of West Belfast in early March, three members in Bawnmore, North Belfast, a few weeks later and another eight members in Short Strand, East Belfast, at the end of May. Some of those killed were Catholic civilians, who had merely been at home relaxing, as the bombers tinkered with their explosives in so-called 'safe houses'. Nevertheless, the IRA's strategy of targeting army mobile and foot patrols soon paid off when, in June 1972, the group killed sixteen soldiers over a four-week period.

By July 1972, the armed conflict had taken on a deadlier form in Belfast, as loyalists and republicans carried out a sectarian tit-for-tat murder spree across the north and west of the city. Civilians were the principal casualties in this mini-war of attrition. The UDA abducted, beat and shot two men at the beginning of the month. The next day the Provisional IRA killed two Protestants who had mistakenly crossed into a Catholic area after a night out in the same way. The UDA were quick to retaliate by abducting and killing two Catholics the same day. On 3 July, the UVF abducted, beat and shot John Patrick O'Hanlon. Police discovered his body with a hood over his head and his hands and ankles tied with a bootlace, which was a ritual performed by terror gangs on both sides before they shot their victims at point-blank range in the head. O'Hanlon lived in the lower Crumlin Road area, and had gone out late at night to buy chips from a local cafe. Seven months earlier, John O'Hanlon was one of those who scrambled to help victims of the UVF bombing of McGurk's bar. He had even pulled the owner's son, John McGurk, from the rubble, thereby saving his life.[39] It was one of many dark twists of fate in the close-knit killing grounds of the troubles.

A few days later the Provos abducted and killed a Protestant, David Andrews, in North Belfast. In the south of the city they kidnapped another Protestant civilian, who did manage to escape before being killed, and they also murdered a UDA member who strayed into a Catholic area. On 9 July, the Provisionals abducted and shot three friends on a night out, one of whom, a Catholic, was serving as a Staff Sergeant in the Territorial Army. In retaliation, the UDA murdered two Catholics on 11 July, one of whom was a fourteen-year-old boy. IRA members responded by abducting a Protestant civilian, torturing him and shooting him in the head at point-blank range. He was found with a pillowcase over his head. In the remaining days of the month, the UDA abducted and killed Catholic civilians on five other occasions. All the victims were killed in the same way. At the end of the month, a fifty-seven-year-old Protestant lorry driver, William McAfee, was also abducted, probably by the same gang. He had his hands tied with cord, a hood placed over him and had been shot twice in the back of the head. It was believed that the UDA had mistaken him for a Catholic.[40]

According to the logic of local circumstances, the violence pulsated uncontrollably despite British government attempts to take the sting out of the IRA's tail by suspending unionist rule at Stormont. Worse was to follow.

4

THE BEGINNING OF THE END

'Anarchy will not defeat anarchy. Lawlessness will not defeat lawlessness. The only way in which this movement can be put down is by the Forces of the Crown, who must be supported by all law-abiding citizens in the duty that lies before them.'

Ian Paisley, speaking at Westminster on 24 July 1972.[1]

Oxford Street Bus Station, Belfast City Centre, 2:45 p.m., Friday, 21 July 1972

The depot manager of Oxford Street bus station heard the crash and thud of the bombs as he sat in his office. One explosion nearby shook the building and sent shards of glass flying inside. 'Due to the bomb on the bridge going off some of my staff in the general office were in hysterics, so I calmed them down and then left the office to see if there was any more damage to the offices,' he later recalled. It was about then that his telephone started ringing. 'A caller from the Ulsterbus head office rang the Oxford Street bus station general office saying that a bomb had been left in a car outside the station.' Two soldiers came in and asked if he could identify the car. A few minutes later the depot manager took the soldiers outside to a Morris 1100 car. Curiously, he noticed that it had one of the company's official passes on it, a sign perhaps of how well-organised the attacks were that day. Just as the depot manager put his hand on the vehicle, a bomb inside the vehicle exploded. 'I was thrown up into the canopy outside the offices and when I fell one of the steel beams pinned me down,' he told the police. 'I was conscious and knew that I was badly injured and a lot of my clothes were blown off. I saw a fire starting in the rubble near me and tried to get closer. There was smoke and dust everywhere and someone eventually pulled me clear.'[2]

A few moments earlier, thirty-nine-year-old Tommy Killops, fifteen-year-old Billy Crothers and eighteen-year-old Billy Irvine were searching the yard for suspicious vehicles. They too were caught in the explosion, their bodies were incinerated by the blast. Thirty-two-year-old soldier Stephen Cooper, who had arrived on the scene with his patrol, was also killed after dismounting from his vehicle. The warning that was passed to the depot manager was completely inadequate and received too late to evacuate the premises. It was the same story throughout the city as the IRA blitzed key infrastructural targets.

Nineteen-year-old David Ervine was sat in the top lounge bar of Clancy's Tavern on the corner of the Albertbridge Road and Castlereagh Road across the Lagan in East Belfast when the explosions started. He was enjoying a quiet pint with some friends at the time. Glancing out across the city, he could see the puffs of smoke rising over the Belfast skyline, as one bomb after another detonated before his eyes. 'I think it was the beginning of the end,' he recalled. 'It was so brutal, so raw.' The day would go down in infamy as 'Bloody Friday'. Resolving then to 'hit back', the young Ervine took up a 'long-standing invitation' to join the UVF.[3] It was in this context that scores of young men began to flock to loyalist paramilitary groups, many of whom later recalled that Bloody Friday had pushed them 'off the fence', thinking that 'the best means of defence was attack'.[4]

The noise of the explosions carried far and wide across Belfast. A group of children playing on waste ground overlooking the city in the Turf Lodge estate watched on in disbelief as the puffs of smoke went up. 'We thought the world was going to end', one of them recalled. Down below, the children could see the city centre, knowing it was packed with shoppers.[5] Men, women and children strolling happily through its streets, basking in the beautiful sunshine, were soon running in blind panic and screaming for their lives as the buildings around them shook with the sheer force of the bomb blasts. RTÉ journalist, Kevin Myers, was standing on top of one of the tallest buildings in Belfast. 'Smoke rose from almost a score of spiralling columns. The city was a bedlam of sirens, of loosened sheets of glass exploding on the ground,' he wrote in his memoirs, 'and most of all, of the wailing and the shrieking of the maimed and the hysterical, rising above the streets in a chorus of atonal dementia.'[6]

Remarkably, for the ferocity of the attack, only eleven people were killed and a further 130 were injured in the IRA's indiscriminate terrorist attacks on the city centre that day. Some twenty-two bombs were detonated within a one-mile radius. 'The figures,' wrote Myers, 'do not begin to capture the horror of that long-lost era. Nothing can.'[7] What did stick in the minds of most people who watched the drama unfold on television screens across the world were the pictures of firemen shovelling bits of bodies into bin bags. It was imagery that became seared in memory of the teenage David Ervine.

UVF leaders now faced a dilemma in the wake of Bloody Friday. On the one hand, they were swamped by the influx of new members, many of whom, like Ervine, were eager to 'hit back' at the IRA. On the other hand, several influential community leaders, such as West Belfast Methodist minister and NILP activist Reverend John Stewart, were trying to wean the UVF away from violence and towards politics. Billy Mitchell, who led the powerful East Antrim UVF, was one of those senior UVF commanders who regularly met with Stewart. He said that Stewart 'encouraged them to think in terms of bread and butter politics as well as the constitutional issue'.[8] This was a crucial development, especially since other NILP activists, like Jim McDonald, had now entered the ranks of the welfare component of the UVF and were keen to develop its political awareness.[9] Stewart believed that the UVF should 'respond to republicanism through non-violence and dialogue'.[10] It was to be a case of too much too soon, as the UVF faced internal calls from younger members to respond in kind to republicanism. Despite his failure to persuade the UVF to unilaterally halt its violent campaign, he was able to plant the seeds that would later re-emerge in a political form as the UVF sought to establish a class-based challenge to the Unionist Party, VUPP and DUP.

In response to the devastating bomb attacks on Belfast on Bloody Friday, British politicians in Whitehall ordered the army to retake so-called 'no-go' areas, which had been established primarily in republican areas. They were determined to smash the power the IRA had now come to hold over some communities. It was in these areas that people turned a blind eye through loyalty, fear and intimidation by paramilitary organisations. It was in these communities that terrorist bomb-makers could operate with impunity in constructing their instruments of destruction, where they could train their members and where they could plan for their renewed offences. London was not prepared to allow this to go unchallenged. Launched on 31 July, the army's Operation Motorman, one of its biggest surges of troops since the ill-fated Suez intervention in 1956, successfully dismantled no-go areas and reasserted British government control over nationalist areas. Though government officials hoped for the best, loyalists confirmed their greatest fears, using the Security Forces' offensive against the IRA as an excuse to lay firm roots in areas where loyalist paramilitaries held sway.It would draw the police and army closer towards conflict with Protestant armed groups, particularly with the UVF.

On 16 September 1972, twenty-six-year-old UVF activist, Sinclair Johnston, was shot in a confrontation between loyalists and the Security Forces during a riot at St John's Place in Larne. Newspaper reports at the time described Johnston as a UVF sergeant working in the intelligence section of the organisation. On the day of his funeral, over 3,000 mourners turned out to pay their respects. 'The first unit behind the coffins were the girls dressed in white,' recalled Billy Mitchell, Johnston's superior officer at the time. 'Then the unit of the Command Staff in full black uniform and then civilians behind – although many of them would have been UVF. It would have been the first public showing of the UVF on parade.'[11] Ranks of volunteers dressed in black leather jackets, Sam Brown belts, cap comforters and sporting dark glasses followed in military fashion behind the cortège.

Minutes before Johnston's remains were interred, a colour party of three gunmen emerged to fire a volley of shots above the coffin. The carefully stage-managed event announced the UVF to the world, in a way that the Vanguard rallies had done for the UDA.

★★★

Glenvarlock Street, East Belfast, Afternoon, 28 September 1972

It was mid-afternoon when a young man with long curly black hair and blue eyes called at the door of thirty-two-year-old Ted Pavis, an unemployed paint sprayer, who lived with his parents in the east of the city. Ted rose early at 8 a.m. and spent the morning lazing around his parents' house, when his father came home from the local shops where he had gambled some of his wages in the bookmakers. It was a normal routine for thousands of working-class men across the city at the time. Meanwhile, Ted's mother was busy in the kitchen, peeling the spuds for her son and husband, leaving late morning to go to the shops to pick up some butter for their tea. The smell of cooking wafted through the family home as Mrs Pavis left the kitchen to answer a knock on the front door. When she opened the door, she saw a young man standing there. 'Would you come in a minute?' she inquired, inviting him in. As he crossed the threshold of the family home, Mrs Pavis called out to Ted to let him know he had a visitor.

Ted had been looking out of the living room window at the time and spotted the caller, someone who he had been expecting. 'Thanks ma,' he said, as his visitor entered the living room.

'Here's a fellow who has come to borrow the mini bus,' he added.

'Sure we have no mini bus.'

The young man with the long curly hair sat down on the sofa and made himself at home, unimpressed by the attempt to fob him off. Ted fidgeted, then turned to his father. 'How long is that old van of ours away?' he asked. 'It's been away a long time,' replied his father. The man looked over to Ted's father, noticing a small dog resting under the table. 'That's a brave lump of a dog you've got,' he said. 'It's not a bad un,' Ted's father responded, as he folded his newspaper in half and placed it in front of him. As he rose from the kitchen table, Ted's father walked into the hall, where he slipped on his shoes and lifted the dog lead from a coat hanger. A few minutes later he had gone, leaving the house by the back door. As Ted's father walked down the side entry and onto the street, he caught a glimpse of another young man sitting astride a red Honda motorcycle. He had a helmet on and the engine was still running. He thought nothing of it as he carried on walking down the street until he neared the main Castlereagh Road.

A few minutes later, the young man with the long curly hair got up and made his excuses to leave. As he did so, he approached Pavis and put his arm around him, before walking with him down the hallway towards the front door. Ted had no sooner opened the door than the other young man pulled out a pistol from his waistband, shooting Pavis at point-blank range. Ted's mother was busying herself in the kitchen when she heard the shot. 'I looked out of the inside front door and saw Ted lying in the hallway near the doorstep,' she later told detectives.

The young man with curly hair lost no time in running out of the house and climbing onto the back of the motorcycle. 'Come on, get out of here quick,' he shouted to his accomplice as they made good their escape. Ted's father was halfway up Glenvarlock Street when he heard the shot ring out. 'I then heard squealing so I ran up the road to [redacted] where I saw of the body of Ted lying in the hall. There was an awful mess of blood and I knew Ted had been shot,' he said.

In his statement to the police, Ted's father described the suspect as being 'twenty-five years to thirty years, 5'6" or 7", well built, dark longish hair with long sidelocks, swarthy complexion or unshaven, thick lips, wearing a black leather shorty jacket which seemed to have a belt on it'. Ted's mother also gave a very similar description of the main suspect, who, she said, was 'approximately thirty years, 5'5"–5'6", black curly bushy hair with long side locks, scruffy appearance, very thick lips, he was wearing a black coloured motor cycle type coat with a belt'.[12] Ted's father also gave a further description of the man driving the motorcycle, who he recalled was 'twenty years, 5'3" or 4", light build, good-looking and tidy appearance, light or gingery hair, shortish, wearing a light coloured jacket'.[13]

It was not immediately obvious why Pavis had been shot, though it soon emerged that word had been passed to him during an earlier spell in prison that he 'would be out, but you wouldn't be back'.[14] The UVF leadership, journalists believed, had ordered Pavis' killing because they suspected that he had been selling guns to the IRA.[15]

It took several months for the police to establish who was responsible for the killing. Eventually their inquiries led them to two young men, Hugh Leonard Murphy, a twenty-year-old lorry driver, and John Mervyn Connor, a nineteen-year-old apprentice motor mechanic. Both were arrested and charged with the murder of Ted Pavis on 25 January 1973. Connor refused to reveal the name of his accomplice in the first round of questioning. After a follow-up interrogation, he gave a full statement to police about the incident:

> I now want to tell you who done the shooting over in Glenvarlock Street, it was [Lenny Murphy] who comes from Percy Street and who you have in custody at the present. On the day we went over to Pavis's house I did not know what [Murphy] wanted to see him about. When they were talking outside I was fiddling about with the bike to keep it going and I did not see [Murphy] produce a gun, but I heard the shot and saw Pavis slump to the ground. [Murphy] ran over and got on the back of the bike. He put his arms around my waist and I noticed a gun in his right hand, pointing up in the air. [Murphy] took the gun away from my waist when he stopped at the bottom of the entry.[16]

The RUC also established that, when the two men returned to the Shankill, Murphy ordered Connor to torch the motorcycle and hide the weapons they had taken on the job with them.

An associate of Murphy and Connor, who was not involved in the killing, said that after killing Pavis, he was travelling in a car along the Shankill Road with both men. 'The car hit a pigeon, or something like that,' the man recalled, 'and Mervyn Connor stopped the car. He got out and Murphy wasn't far behind. Mervyn picked up the pigeon but Murphy just snatched it out of his hand and twisted its neck. I knew then that he was not a person you should ever cross. He was just cold. The way he spoke about the murder of Ted Pavis was not something you would expect. I've heard guys in hysterics, hitting the drink, crying after they've done a murder. The way Murphy talked about the murder was just not normal.'[17]

Despite his best attempts to cover his tracks, Murphy and Connor were remanded in custody and transferred to the remand wing of Crumlin Road Prison.

★★★

Conlon's Bar, Belfast City Centre, 9 p.m., Saturday, 28 September 1972

John J. Conlon's Bar in Francis Street, Smithfield, was alive with the sounds of revellers enjoying themselves. Twenty-one-year-old James 'Jimmy' Gillen and twenty-four-year-old Patrick McKee, two young unemployed men from Ballymurphy, had come down into the city centre for a night out with friends. The group sat perched on a long bench in front of the window of the pub, watching *Saturday Variety* on the TV along with other customers. Laughter filled the air, and the alcohol kept flowing. There were up to thirteen people in the bar at the time. At around 9:05 p.m. an old man with a dog walked into the bar. No sooner had he ordered a drink than an explosion ripped through the building, collapsing the front wall. Patrick McKee was killed outright. His friend, Jimmy Gillen, died two weeks later from the injuries sustained in the blast. 'I do not remember hearing a bang or explosion and just felt myself spinning and I was buried below a lot of rubble,' an eyewitness told police. 'I was pulled out into the street to the corner of the markets and a soldier bandaged my head and an ambulance brought me to hospital.'[18] The survivor who gave the statement had been sitting beside Jimmy Gillen when the bomb went off. His injuries included a fractured skull, deafness, shock and concussion. Moments before the explosion, a policeman had been passing the Conlon's on a routine patrol.

He became suspicious of the vehicle parked across the street from the bar. His partner halted the patrol car and the officer got out to investigate. As he closed in on the suspicious vehicle, he smelt something unusual and immediately realised it was a bomb. As the officer turned around to relay his discovery to his partner, the bomb exploded, sending him flying over his vehicle.[19] This was one of a number of car bombings by the UVF at the time.

Despite having now perfected its bomb-making skills, the UVF was chronically short of weapons. On 23 October the Mid Ulster UVF staged a massive raid of the local UDR barracks. Armed men overpowered the sentry and gained access to the armoury, where they stole 85 SLRs, 21 SMGs, 1,300 rounds of ammunition, flares and flak jackets. Those who gained access to the camp knew exactly where to find the weapons.[20] Most of the weapons, however, were later recovered. The UVF would continue to seek out other avenues, especially as its ranks began to swell further. A satellite organisation had also been formed in 1972 by William 'Plum' Smith, Winston Rea and twenty-year-old Stevie McCrea. On Halloween night, 1973, McCrea, a young gunman belonging to the Red Hand Commando (RHC), shot and killed seventeen-year-old James 'Jiffy' Kerr on the Lisburn Road in Belfast. A police officer standing nearby heard the fatal shots. When he arrived, he found McCrea stood over the body of a man. He tried to escape, but was later caught red-handed with a Webley revolver stuck in his waistband. When asked why he targeted Kerr, McCrea said it was 'because he was a fenian bastard'. It seems that Kerr's close association with IRA man John Rooney sealed his fate in the eyes of the RHC, though he was never claimed by the Provisionals as a member.[21] McCrea was later charged with murder and sentenced to sixteen years in prison.

★★★

HMP Crumlin Road, Belfast, 7:30 p.m., 11 February 1973

The sound of a loud siren pierced the cold wintry air that seemed to envelope Crumlin Road Prison that evening. It was a sound familiar to people who lived locally and usually signalled an attempted escape. Moments earlier, two UVF prisoners, Lenny Murphy and Ronald Waller, had sawn off the bars of the window of cell number 21 in C2 wing before throwing a rope over the thick Victorian-era walls. Cell chairs with rope tied around them had been used as grappling hooks. A prison officer walking past on a routine patrol below was startled when he saw two legs dangling from the cell window.[22] As he shone the torch up on the wall he shouted, 'Don't bother, lads', hoping the prisoners would give up and crawl back the way they came. He was surprised when a voice shouted back for him to 'keep quiet', which was followed by an appeal to his community spirit. 'You are a Shankill Road man like ourselves', whispered Murphy. Without hesitation, the officer retorted with a curt, 'No chance'. A few moments later Murphy jumped down and turned to face the prison officer. Both men eyeballed one another in a brief Mexican standoff before the prison officer felt something sharp being thrust into his stomach, causing him to double over in pain. As he did so, he tried desperately to use his radio. 'Yankee Two …' No sooner had the words rolled off the officer's tongue than Waller moved to grab him. 'For fuck's sake keep quiet', he said in a hushed voice. There was a brief struggle as the prisoners tried to grab the radio receiver off the officer. He resisted, and was kicked in the balls. As he fell to the ground, a loud siren warbled into action. Realising their chances of escaping had been dramatically reduced, the men beat a hasty retreat back up the rope into their cell. They were going nowhere.

Nine weeks later, as prisoners enjoyed a musical concert in C Wing, Murphy was putting a new and more daring escape plan into operation. Sometime on 24 April, he visited Mervyn Connor, his accomplice from the Pavis murder, for a chat. The two men had since been separated to prevent them from getting their story straight and, in the meantime, Connor had taken the opportunity to give evidence to detectives who visited him that Murphy had killed Ted Pavis. What happened next is unclear, but it appears that either Murphy slipped a vial of cyanide into Connor's drink or forced his mouth open and poured it down his throat before clamping his jaws shut and holding them closed, until Connor swallowed the poison. As the afternoon wore on, Connor complained to his cell mate of feeling unwell and lay down on his bunk. He even skipped his tea in the canteen. At 6:20 p.m. Connor roused himself from his cell and approached a prison warden patrolling the landing to ask for hot water. It was the last time anyone saw him alive. Twenty minutes later his cell mate returned from the concert to find Connor lying prostrate on his bed face up, his mouth full of bloody foam. The floor around him was soaking wet with urine. Relaxing music played on the radio in the background but the scene was one of utter chaos. Connor's right arm and leg were dangling off the bed and his other leg was outstretched where he had undergone spasms from a nasty, violent death. A prison officer on the wing quickly entered the cell to administer first aid when the alarm was raised. He managed to get a faint pulse. Connor had been revived momentarily, turned violently before vomiting onto the floor. A doctor from the Mater Hospital was called and, when he arrived a few minutes later, applied external cardio massage and administered oxygen. Connor was unresponsive, then, suddenly, his pupils dilated and his heartbeat became even fainter. Despite the best efforts of the doctor, Mervyn Connor was pronounced dead at 7:30 p.m.[23]

Like other prisoners facing long days in the Crum, Mervyn Connor had suffered from bouts of depression. Initially, it was thought that he had committed suicide. A note addressed to the prison governor and discovered on the small desk in his cell, supported this theory. It read:

> To whom it may concern,
>
> During my time in prison I have done nothing but think about what I have done to the fellow called [name redacted] I have told lies and made false statements against him. I would not have done this only for the pressure the police put on me most of all [name redacted]
>
> So I can not live with this on my mind
>
> I hope you will understand
>
> [name redacted]

In a short, unremarkable report on the incident, the prison authorities noted how, 'During the previous couple of days Mervyn took a craze for drawing crosses on sheets of paper.' The prisoner who had shared a cell with him for three weeks said that Connor had never said anything against the police. He seemed fine, and his request for some letter writing paper gave nobody any cause for concern.

C Wing had originally housed the execution chamber. Now it would become synonymous with Lenny Murphy's ruthlessness, and form part of the urban legend surrounding his reputation inside the UVF.

Mervyn Connor had joined the UVF in 1972. Originally from the Shankill Road, he was a labourer by trade. Apart from a surgical procedure for a hernia when he was eighteen, Connor was in good health when he died. Psychologically, he was also fit and healthy, which aroused suspicions about the apparent suicide note. So devastated by their son's death were his parents that police believed they would be willing to testify at his inquest later that year about his state of mind. When they were shown the alleged suicide note, Mrs Connor said that she did 'not think' her son 'was telling the truth' in it. 'He had written a statement which implicated another prisoner in being guilty of murder. The name of the other prisoner is the name mentioned in Exhibit C1.' Detectives attempting to investigate the death said they had 'run into a wall of silence when questioning prisoners in the jail'.[24]

It did not take the pathologist long to identify the cause of Connor's death, concluding that the young man had been poisoned with cyanide. The autopsy revealed that he had significant levels of the substance in his blood and organs and that this was a result of it having been ingested orally. Normally an amount of 50–300 milligrams was needed to kill an adult male but in Connor's case it was inordinately high, at 450 milligrams. The only way that that could have possibly been administered was if his mouth had been held open and the poison forced down his throat. Even though the poisoning of Mervyn Connor had been witnessed on the wing, most of the eyewitnesses placed themselves at the scene of the concert – it would have been risky giving evidence against Murphy.

At his trial between 18–20 June 1973, Lenny Murphy was acquitted of killing Ted Pavis by the jury. Having observed several murder trials before from the public gallery, he knew how to play the system.[25] Without incriminating evidence from his co-accused, who he had killed, he was convinced that the trial would collapse. Murphy walked free from the Crumlin Road Courthouse opposite the prison. His taste of freedom lasted only a few minutes, after which RUC officers re-arrested him under the Special Powers Act.[26]

***

During his several months at large in July–October 1972, Gusty Spence had reorganised the UVF more formally along British Army lines, with three battalion areas established in Belfast, East Antrim and Mid Ulster. In turn, units equating to geographic areas where established in roughly company size of 100–200 men each. Although these companies were further divided into platoons of 20–30 men, the welfare component continued to dominate.

The military 'teams' were much smaller, and numbered up to a dozen or so men. With more men in the non-combatant ranks of the organisation, the ruling Brigade Staff began to think about ways to put them to good use in support of military activities. By the middle of 1973, this included approving political activity. Billy Hutchinson, a young YCV member who was particularly active on the Shankill Road at the time, remembered how this played out:

> I think what you have to do is you have to look at the UVF structure in terms of who occupied the five command positions on Brigade Staff and, at any given time, whoever was in charge, it would have been a minority view in terms of the politics, whether it be left-wing or right-wing, actually dictated what happened on the streets. In '73 you would have had a more left-wing sort of regime. I remember in '73, they called a ceasefire to try and allow the whole thing of the power-sharing executive at Stormont to actually formulate a government. Now, what brought that down was a number of things. But the UVF did ... try and allow ... politics to actually grow. All those things came about because of the politics of the leadership of the UVF.[27]

For much of 1973, there was a feeling within the UVF that a turn towards politics meant 'going soft'. Several prolific gunmen in the Shankill UVF believed that force, not politics, was the only thing their enemy understood. In leadership terms, this was a period of 'great flux' for the UVF.[28] The carnage unleashed on 'Bloody Friday' still weighed heavily in the minds of the UVF's newest recruits a year after the events of that day. They were determined to hit back, even if they had no idea why they were doing so.

In late 1973, a Mini Cooper made its way through Belfast city centre with five men onboard. They were all packed tightly into the car. The three men in the rear passenger seats sat with a large gas canister bomb at their feet. They were loyalist paramilitaries from the UVF on their way to mount an attack on a Catholic bar, when they were promptly halted at an army checkpoint. The soldiers at the checkpoint raised their rifles, pulling them tightly into their shoulders as they took up firing positions. At great personal risk, an NCO stepped forward and put out his hand, indicating to the driver to stop. He then ordered the men out of the vehicle, and radioed for RUC backup. 'Rucksac required at my location. Over,' he spoke clearly into the transmitter. A few minutes later two RUC officers arrived at the scene, greeted by a fairly typical sight of terrorist suspects spread-eagled against a wall, with the soldiers training their rifles on the men. One of the policemen ordered one of the young suspects to turn around to face him. As he did so, the suspect whispered something to him. 'What's that,' asked the stern-looking police officer. 'Here mate,' the man repeated. 'You distract the army and we'll make a run for it.' The policeman stared back at him with a sense of amusement. 'The young loyalist really believed I was on his side,' said the officer. 'Right,' answered the RUC man. 'I've a better idea. I'll distract the army, you make a run for it, and I'll shoot you.' The loyalist was confused. A member of *his* police force was talking about shooting *him*. It didn't make sense. 'Sure we're all on the same side,' said the loyalist. 'No we're not,' replied the officer, a Protestant. 'I'm law and order. You're a law breaker.'

The young loyalist's confusion was shared by many other working-class Protestants who were by now feeling marginalised. British politicians had spoken to the IRA on two separate occasions in March and July 1972, the army seemed to be tolerating IRA patrols, even after Operation Motorman, and the police were now turning against loyalists. Young men flocking to paramilitary groups began to feel out of sorts with the world. In their anger and frustration, they responded by wrecking their own areas. 'Most of the major public order disturbances I was involved in then were in Protestant areas,' recalled a former RUC officer based in Whiteabbey at the time. 'It was just stupid. I often asked them did they not think it was stupid to wreck their own areas? They never offered me an answer.'[29] In lieu of answers on why they were doing what they were doing, loyalist paramilitary groups continued to swell with disaffected young men like these.

In political terms, unionism was divided. The Ulster Unionist Party had been dealt a body blow by the transference of powers to Whitehall. A Northern Ireland Office had been established in London and at Stormont, which would administer British rule directly. The new Secretary of State, William Whitelaw, held talks in October and November 1973 aimed at resolving the continuing crisis. A conference was called in at the Civil Service college at Sunningdale in December to plot a course for Northern Ireland's constitutional future, which would lead to an Agreement to establish a powersharing executive at Stormont. For many moderate unionists, led by Brian Faulkner, a cross-community government, with strong representation from the SDLP, was just about tolerable. But what they couldn't accept was the greater say that Dublin would have in their own internal affairs.[30]

The UDA's 'supreme commander', Andy Tyrie, and other paramilitary chiefs believed that a power-sharing executive with a 'Council of Ireland' attached to it would leave Protestants further exposed. What terrified Tyrie was what he saw as the effectiveness of SDLP Ministers, and the relative inexperience of their Unionist counterparts. So, he set about conspiring with Glen Barr, a UDA spokesman from the Waterside area of Londonderry, and trade unionist Harry Murray from Belfast, to set up a coordinating committee for what was to emerge as the Ulster Workers' Council (UWC). Its first meeting was held in the Seagoe Hotel in Portadown, in December 1973. Tyrie was right to be sceptical. Ulster loyalism was not served well by its politicians. Brian Faulkner had failed to carry the majority of his party with him, while Bill Craig talked tough in large fascistic rallies in Ormeau Park about the need to 'liquidate the enemy'. In truth, like his main political rival Ian Paisley, Craig liked to hedge his bets.

On 28 February 1974, a Westminster election was held that would remove the Conservative Party from power, and replace it with Harold Wilson's Labour Party, the man who had talked to the IRA in March 1972. By now political events had shifted. The major political concerns in mainland UK were primarily economic ones, with the miners' strike carrying Labour into Downing Street. In Northern Ireland, leading shop stewards in Ulster's industrial heartland of Belfast watched with considerable interest. Could a similar tactic be used to bring attention to their opposition to the Sunningdale Agreement, and its proposal to give the Dublin government a say in the constitutional affairs of a region of the United Kingdom? Loyalist paramilitaries and Protestant trade unionists certainly believed it was possible, and so they formed the UWC. However, it was the UDA and not the UVF that would remain at the forefront of these political developments in the Spring of 1974. UVF spokesman Ken Gibson and two other members of the RHC were certainly sitting around the table with the others who made up the thirteen-man UWC coordinating committee. It met at UDA headquarters in East Belfast, and is perhaps the reason why the UVF continued to equivocate on the plans for strike action. Gibson would later say that they were merely there as 'observers', which led Andy Tyrie to believe that UVF support for a strike was 'still only conditional'.[31]

5

TALKING AND KILLING

From Portadown to Shankill Road,
From Larne to Drumahoe,
Where volunteers do organise,
Says he, 'You'll find Big Jim,'
Says he, 'You'll find Big Jim.'

UVF Poem (1974)

Loyalist Club, Shankill Road, Belfast, 31 March 1974

The 'Royals' pop group were on stage performing a few of their well-known cover songs as part of the weekly Sunday night cabaret show. The Loyalist Club was fairly crowded. Downstairs, it was standing room only for most of the evening. There were another fifty people in the upstairs lounge, where club stewards served hamburgers from a small kitchen to those anxious to line their stomach after a few hours of heavy drinking. Bar staff hurriedly pulled draught pints of Guinness as men and women mingled at the bar. Some were impatient, and had been waiting a while to be served. 'Twenty Embassy please mate,' said the tall man with red hair, as he joked with the barman.[1] Twenty-seven-year-old Jim Hanna, nicknamed 'red setter', was a married man with one child. He was a self-employed heating and plumbing engineer, and part-time bar steward. He was also the UVF's Director of Operations, making him responsible for targeting the group's enemies. Hanna had arrived at the club shortly after 7:30 p.m. in the company of a female friend.[2]

Hanna spent most of the evening in the club chatting to people and enjoying a few drinks. At midnight, Hanna and his female friend left the Loyalist Club through the gates of the delivery yard towards Jim's car, a fawn-coloured Morris Marina 1.8 saloon, which he left parked under a street light outside St Michael's Church in Mansfield Street. 'We walked to Jim's car and he unlocked the doors,' his friend recalled. 'I got into the car into the front passenger seat and Jim got into the driver's seat. Just as soon as we got into the car, the driver's door was opened and I heard a number of bangs. Jim slumped over me. I thought immediately it was shots and I curled up in the car. After Jim slumped over me the shooting continued, and I was shot on the top of both legs. I did not see who fired the shots and I did not see any other person at the car. The way Jim fell across me obstructed my view.'[3]

Hanna was shot in the chest and abdomen by two men armed with a pair of Walther 9mm pistols. One of the men opened the driver's side door before both gunmen emptied their magazines into their victim. Twelve rounds were fired in total, hitting Hanna nine times in the chest and torso. Journalists later claimed that he was shot point blank in the head, which was not the case.[4] The gunmen blended back into the shadows from where they had come to kill Jim Hanna.

Having heard the shots and the woman's screams, up to a dozen local people rushed over to the vehicle to see if they could help. A doorman from the club lifted Jim Hanna's lifeless body out of the vehicle and carried the victim back into the club where a bar steward telephoned an ambulance. The attack had taken place in a dimly lit street when most residents had retired to bed for the night. The doctor who examined Hanna on his arrival at the casualty department of the Royal Victoria Hospital pronounced him dead at 12:40 a.m. In his post-mortem, pathologist Dr John Press found twenty-one entrance and exit wounds in Hanna's body, right arm and right thigh.[5] It had all the hallmarks of a deliberate, planned assassination that was devoid of mercy. By opting to shoot their victim at such close range, the gunmen made sure he would not survive the attack. Hanna had to go, they reasoned, and this was the most effective way to ensure that it happened. Nothing had arisen in the club that night to indicate that Hanna was in any immediate danger. He had not found himself entangled in any heated arguments, nor did he have any visible enemies. His murder remained a mystery to many people on the Shankill.

The assassination didn't come as a surprise to some of those in the UVF's inner circles, for Hanna had courted controversy in recent months by soft-pedalling on calls from the rank and file to further escalate the organisation's terror campaign. As the group's overall military commander, this was an unfathomable position for Hanna to adopt, the group's younger hardliners believed.

It later emerged that Jim Hanna had also met with an Official IRA leader in the Europa Hotel in central Belfast, widely regarded in the 1970s as the 'most bombed hotel in Europe'. Robert Fisk of the London *Times*, who first broke the story, claimed that the UVF and Official IRA shared common ground on the political front, and wished to see an end to sectarian killing.[6] Internal discord ensued, with one hooded UVF leader promptly emerging from the shadows to quash rumours of any talks. 'We need a political front to counter the propaganda of the Provisional alliance, the British government and the Faulkner–Fine Gael Pact,' the UVF spokesman told those journalists gathered at a hastily convened press conference. When questioned about his organisation's position on a united Ireland, the UVF leader reiterated the group's total opposition to any moves in this direction.[7] The UVF followed up an impromptu media appearance with a written statement, carried in its journal *Combat*, denying that it had ever 'at any time discussed political or military policy with either the Official or Provisional Wings of the Irish Republican Movement'. For the UVF, 'Irish Republicanism and Ulster patriotism are poles apart and can never come together in common policy decisions.'[8]

The truth was that Hanna had been one of two senior UVF Brigade Staff members who had also met secretly with the Provisional IRA in Lough Sheelin in County Cavan. The other person who had attended the meeting was Billy Mitchell, the commander of the powerful UVF battalion in East Antrim. The meetings had been brokered by journalist, Kevin Myers. There to meet the two UVF men were Dáithí Ó Conaill and Brian Keenan. 'Keenan was militarily the most important man in the IRA, then and over the coming decades. His presence made this a very high-powered delegation indeed,' recalled Myers. It was to be the first and only meeting between these sworn enemies. In Mitchell's eyes, 'we genuinely wanted a political voice. The very fact that the UVF had met with the Officials and the Provos at the highest level indicates that they wanted to think about bringing the conflict to an end. Unfortunately, it was too much too soon,' he later admitted.[9]

Although it was something of an open secret that Jim Hanna had 'friends in military intelligence' at the time,[10] the reality was that if he was also an agent he was almost certainly working to put the UVF out of business. After his death, Fisk suggested that because of his moderate tendencies, Hanna may have strongly opposed a plan hatched by UVF hardliners to bomb Irish towns south of the border.[11] Hanna's liberal outlook, combined with reports that he had met with both wings of the IRA, provided the excuse Young Turks within UVF ranks needed to justify his execution. Hanna's wife was in no doubt who had killed her husband, 'You know Billy Marchant?' she asked Myers. 'Well, Marchant killed Jim.'[12]

At the time, the UVF strongly rejected the rumours it had played any role in Hanna's death. 'The Ulster Volunteer Force Brigade Headquarters Staff view with contempt the erroneous suggestions made by the Security Forces against the UVF regarding the murder of Mr James Hanna at Mansfield Street on Sunday evening 31st March 1974,' read a statement issued by the organisation after his death. The denial was designed to refute rumours that Hanna had been executed after an internal 'Court of Inquiry' found he had compromised weapons and explosives in the same place where he had died. In signing off, the UVF vowed to bring his killers to justice. In reality, the UVF Brigade Staff was under repeated internal strain, ever since it announced its ceasefire on 18 November 1973. By eliminating Hanna, UVF hardliners believed they were removing the final obstacle for a return to their organisation's military campaign. These men were soon disappointed when, a few days later, the Secretary of State for Northern Ireland, Merlyn Rees, de-proscribed the UVF and Provisional IRA.[13] The UVF Brigade Staff's flirtation with politics, rather than militarism, appeared to be working.

★★★

Dublin City centre, Evening, Friday 17 May 1974

Thirty-five-year-old Ann O'Neill was out shopping with her family when the first car bomb exploded at 5:28 p.m. in Parnell Street. It killed her husband Edward outright, and badly injured her son, Edward Junior, who was hit by flying shrapnel. So severe were young Edward's injuries that the surgeon who performed skin grafts on his face could see the bridge of his nose protruding through what was left of his skin. His face had literally been blown off by the force of the blast, and shards of metal and glass had become lodged deep in his tiny body. One young girl was decapitated by flying debris. It was impossible for either the emergency services or the other civilians who went to her aid to know who she was. Eleven people were killed, including two infant children. Elsewhere in the city, on Talbot Street, another bomb exploded at 5:30 p.m., killing thirteen people, one of whom had been pregnant.' At the same time, a third bomb exploded in South Leinster Street, killing two women. The bombs had exploded with such force that the blasts had knocked people over like skittles. Men, women and children were thrown along streets, into doorways and against walls like rag dolls. A mother walking her baby in a pram was thrown violently into the air. People screamed in sheer terror. Shock set in, and some people were literally frozen to the spot. Twenty-six people were killed in Dublin, and another 253 injured. It was the worst terrorist atrocity in the city since the Anglo-Irish War of Independence. Just over two hours later, in Monaghan, some seventy miles away, another car bomb detonated outside a Protestant-owned pub, killing seven people.

That the bombs were placed with such military precision immediately raised questions over who could have perpetrated the attacks.[14] No group admitted responsibility at the time, though the finger of blame was pointed at loyalist paramilitaries. It was not long before allegations of 'collusion' between the terrorists and British state agencies were raised. They were based largely on the public confession of John Weir, who was jailed for his part in atrocities perpetrated by the so-called 'Glennane Gang', a group of part-time and reserve RUC officers who, in their guise as UVF members, murdered dozens of people in the Mid Ulster area.[15]

It has since been established by an Irish government inquiry into the bombings that the UVF was responsible, and that its members from Belfast and Mid Ulster carried out the – fastidiously planned and well-executed operation. 'The loyalist groups who carried out the bombings in Dublin were capable of doing so without help from any section of the security forces in Northern Ireland,' wrote the judge who led the inquiry, 'though this does not rule out the involvement of individual RUC, UDR or British Army members. The Monaghan bombing in particular bears all the hallmarks of a standard loyalist operation, and required no assistance.'[16] In line with the UVF's own explanation for the attacks, it was believed by the Irish government that the farm used by the UVF members who carried out the attacks was central to the planning and preparation of the bombs. 'It is also likely that members of the UDR and RUC either participated in, or were aware of those preparations,' read the report.[17] Yet, despite the close involvement of some Security Forces personnel who moonlighted as terrorists, the inquiry into the Dublin and Monaghan bombings concluded:

> Ultimately, a finding that there was collusion between the perpetrators and the authorities in Northern Ireland is a matter of inference. On some occasions an inference is irresistible or can be drawn as a matter

of probability. Here, it is the view of the inquiry that this inference is not sufficiently strong. It does not follow even as a matter of probability. Unless further information comes to hand, such involvement must remain a suspicion. *It is not proven.*[18]

The carnage unleashed by the UVF on unsuspecting shoppers in Dublin and revellers in Monaghan was not the first time, nor the last, that the group would turn its sights south of the border. Reflecting on the rationale for sending the carnage to the Irish Republic, one Brigade Staff officer at the time observed how, people in the south were 'being very blasé about their attitude towards republicans – they weren't getting extradited, they weren't being actively pursued into the Republic, we saw it as they were getting a free hand to do what they wanted … And well, we just wanted to let them know what it feels like. That was it.'[19]

The Dublin and Monaghan bombings were the tip of the iceberg as far as UVF attacks were concerned. The vast majority of the devices were well-constructed, expertly transported and planted, and in a considerable number of cases they demonstrated advanced bomb-making skills. The UVF certainly had such men in its ranks, with a few of them having seen action in Britain's post-war conflicts, such as Palestine, Korea, Malaya, Cyprus and Aden.[20] Some of these men had been NCOs in the British Armed Forces, and were extremely adept at leading men on operations, handling explosives and other weapons of war. Like those in the Provisional IRA at the time, one or two of these UVF men had even demonstrated a deadly ingenuity by turning under-the-counter products – the so-called 'Co-Op mix' – into what we would today call Improvised Explosive Devices. Organisationally, of course, the UVF had been involved in constructing bombs from as early as 1966. By 1974 they had perfected their bomb-making techniques. Although the Provisionals had also made great strides in their own bomb-making prowess, they hadn't the same kind of pedigree of well-trained volunteers in their ranks that the UVF could call upon. It was little wonder that the UVF could explode more bombs than their IRA rivals in 1971 and unleash a wave of death and destruction on Irish streets, north and south of the border.[21] Until the mid-1970s, the UVF preferred to take most of its recruits from the ranks of disgruntled ex-servicemen. This cadre of individuals not only possessed intimate knowledge of weapons and explosives, but were also adept at passing that knowledge on by way of training and advising others.

Another way in which the UVF acquired such military experience was by infiltrating the ranks of the British Army. One such individual was Geordie, a young volunteer who hailed from the Oldpark Road area of North Belfast. He said that in the early 1970s, 'there was no formal training' for UVF members. In order to acquire such skills and drills, he claimed he was ordered to infiltrate the Territorial Army (TA) by 'Big Sam' McCorkindale, the UVF's commander in West Belfast. 'Big Sam' certainly had prior military experience, having served in the ranks of the British Army. Geordie alleges that, as a result of his infiltration, he spent hours cleaning weapons in military armouries. 'We cleaned millions of them; from SLRs to Sterling sub-machine guns to GPMGs,' he said. He also claimed that, in one incident in the 1970s, he and several other UVF men tried to smuggle guns into the province. In one run, the men were able to conceal a cache of weapons inside their military vehicles, which were then returned to Belfast after a weekend exercise. Searches by the Royal Military Police turned up hundreds of stolen weapons hidden in the side-panelling of huge water tankers.[22]

The UVF's infiltration of British military ranks also extended to the newly formed UDR, the British Army's largest infantry regiment, which was based permanently in Northern Ireland.[23] Many of these men led 'double lives'. Geordie remembers how, at one UVF meeting in the early to mid-1970s, almost all the men present held dual membership of the UVF and British Army. Two were UDR Sergeants, one was a UDR Corporal, and two other men were in the TA. It was then that the army moved swiftly to eradicate dual membership – leaving these men on borrowed time. Billy Mitchell, a leading member of UVF Brigade Staff at the time, justified such infiltration on the following basis. 'It is part and parcel of human nature. Anyone who believes that it did not happen, or that it should not have happened, is naïve in the extreme,' he later wrote. 'There are a number of valid reasons why loyalists would want to join elements of the local Security Forces – intelligence gathering and military training being among them.'[24]

Up until its de-proscription a few weeks before the Dublin and Monaghan bombings, the UVF had been a highly secretive organisation, which people were only invited to join. It vetted its members rigorously and styled itself as a 'counter-terrorist force', established to oppose 'violent nationalism'. In an early issue of *Combat* magazine, the UVF said its objectives were to:

(a) Watch over, promote and protect the Protestant liberties, culture and traditional way of life of the Ulster people.
(b) Work for the physical defence of the loyalist community in the face of armed aggression and terrorist activity.
(c) Train, equip and discipline a dedicated body of Ulster patriots capable of implementing (a) and (b) above.[25]

The UVF claimed that the vast majority of decisions it took were 'of a military nature', directed towards 'producing an efficient military reaction against the terrorist programme of the Provisional Republican Alliance and its various political and cultural front organisations'. Billy Mitchell went on to elaborate:

> Primarily the UVF saw itself as a military machine. The term which fits although wasn't used at this time was 'defensive retaliation' but very often it was 'get your retaliation in first', [such as] defence of working-class areas, retaliation for republican activities. UVF Brigade Staff at that time employed this twin track approach. It was never going to follow the Stickies and go for politics alone. It was always going to be both approaches. It was useful to engage with the NIO. It was useful to engage with political parties, useful to try and get people elected, as they did with Hugh Smyth and in Carrick with Hugh Burton. [However], the main campaign was a military one.[26]

The UVF argued that this policy was 'legitimate, essential and rewarding', making the organisation 'a force to be reckoned with by our enemies'.[27]

Such familiarity with weapons and explosives gave the UVF a greater killing potential, but it came at a price. Geordie recalled attending a UVF training session in the Shankill, where he and other volunteers were invited to pack tubes full of explosives and attach a fuse. The bombs were crude and volatile, with volunteers nicknaming them 'candy sticks'. 'They were very unstable,' Geordie revealed. 'The place looked like Switzerland, as the fertilizer was stacked high in the warehouse.' So blissfully unaware were some of the men to the dangers of handling explosives that he remembers seeing 'one guy coming to the door of the warehouse with a fag in his mouth'. The amateurish nature of the operation meant that volunteers were sometimes killed by their own bombs.[28]

What made it difficult for the UVF to maintain a high tempo of operations at this time was that the vast majority of its members began their terrorist career in their spare time. Some men worked as office clerks, others as painters and decorators, engineers and even carpenters. Geordie worked as an office clerk by day and acted as a 'wheel man' for the UVF by night, which involved stealing cars for UVF operations. His platoon commander then was a young John Bingham, who would later rise to become the UVF's military commander in West Belfast. According to Geordie, there was little thought given to thorough planning inside the UVF at this time. From deciding on the spot to go out and 'shoot a taig', to neglecting to change the plates on stolen cars, UVF teams took a blasé approach to their military operations. In one particular incident in the 1970s, Geordie recounted the circumstances that led a UVF team to drive a van into republican West Belfast loaded with two gunmen in the back. Dressed head to toe in boiler suits, masked and armed with sub-machine guns, the men believed they had been tasked with killing two republicans. The plan was simple. They were to drive up to the street corner where the targets had been spotted on a regular basis, slam on the brakes alongside them and the gunmen in the back of the vehicle would kick open the doors and shoot the two men dead. When they got to the scene, the UVF men kicked on the doors but they failed to open. The intended targets, hearing the commotion inside the van, ran off. The UVF team, dazed, confused and anxious to get away, ditched the van and reported back to their commander. 'It was a farce,' Geordie said, 'The doors were not locked, yet they couldn't open them. Such was the way many of these operations went.'

The UVF's botched operations in the mid-1970s certainly pointed to the lack of forward planning and even bordered on recklessness, but they also highlighted the autonomy that individual members and teams had in targeting Catholic civilians with no connection to physical force republicanism.[29] In some cases, this was due to a lack of specific intelligence on IRA members; at other times, Catholic civilians were deliberately targeted. Although Gusty Spence had set himself firmly against indiscriminate attacks on Catholic civilians, it appeared that some UVF volunteers were still prepared to adhere to his earlier dictum that, 'If you can't get an IRA man, get a Taig.'[30]

★★★

Antrim Road, North Belfast, Night, Saturday, 12 October 1974

Seventeen-year-old Ciaran Murphy spent the day drinking Guinness with his best friend Seamus Larkin in several bars in North Street in Belfast city centre. He looked old for his age, standing tall at 6'1". At the time, Ciaran sported an afro hairstyle that made him look like the Irish singer-songwriter Gilbert O'Sullivan. He was the youngest in a family of six children, three boys and three girls, and lived at the family home in Ardoyne with his mother Kathleen. His father, John, had passed away in 1967. Ciaran worked for G Plan Central Heating, a firm that gave him a small company van for his own personal use. He was spotted around the area on a frequent basis, often stopping to offer lifts to local people. Ciaran was a friendly lad, a young man full of boundless energy and of the hopes and dreams of many teenagers at the time. He had ambitions but loved to stay grounded by socialising with friends and family.

As evening passed into night in that cold October night, Ciaran and his friends made their way back to Seamus' house, where they were picked up by another friend, Patrick Mulholland. All three travelled to the Saunders Club in Elmfield Street, arriving promptly at 7:30 p.m. It didn't take them long to get into the swing of things in the club. Ciaran drank gin and tonic all evening. At 11:45 p.m., the three friends left to go home. Even though he had been drinking all day, Ciaran volunteered to drive so they could pick up takeaway food on their way back to Ardoyne. As they drew up behind some parked cars at the Wei Ping Chinese restaurant on the Antrim Road (known locally as 'Provie Charlies'), Ciaran misjudged the distance and touched the back bumper of the rear car. Slightly shaken by the experience, he got out of the car and told his two companions that he couldn't drive anymore. Before they could protest further, Ciaran walked off on his own, picking up some chips before making his way home to Ardoyne along the Cliftonville Road.

After a few minutes, Ciaran noticed a beige-coloured Ford Corsair drive past him. Inside were three UVF men. The car crawled along at a slow pace. The three men inside joked to one another about the drunk teenager they spotted on the other side of the Street. 'Look at that idiot, let's stop him and see who he is,' shouted one of the men. The driver made a sharp U-turn in the road, before pulling up alongside the young man. Ciaran ignored them and carried on walking. He was drunk and staggered along eating his chips. 'Do you want a lift then mate?' the men in the car inquired. 'Dead on, dead on,' he replied, and one man opened the door. Realising in a split second the danger he was now in, Ciaran quickly changed his mind. Before he could protest any further, he was grabbed from behind and bundled into the back seat of the car. At that moment he dropped his chips, which spilt across the pavement. Two of the men sat either side of Ciaran holding him down. He tried to break free but his attempts to do so were futile. The men had no intention of letting their captive go.

After driving a short distance to the 42 Club in the Silverstream area, the leader of the gang, a young man, got out of the car and strolled inside. In a loud voice he proclaimed, 'We've got a taig.' Upon hearing the young man's boast, a senior UVF man threw him out of the club, believing he was drunk. Taking umbrage at the slight, the young UVF man returned to the car and ordered the driver to take them to the home of a UDA man, an infamous paramilitary who was nicknamed 'the window-cleaner' for his tendency to murder people while out cleaning windows in West Belfast. The four men then travelled to Tyndale Community Centre. There, Ciaran was badly beaten, and had his watch, money, driving licence and rings taken from him. The men then stabbed him repeatedly with a small bladed knife. He fought back, holding up his hands as he tried to deflect the thrusting blows away from his body. Ciaran was beaten again before being dragged out to the car. Meanwhile, 'the window cleaner' had retrieved a Luger pistol from a nearby weapons cache.

The men took Ciaran to a quarry overlooking the city, where they lifted him out of the vehicle, making him take off his jacket to stand in the freezing cold. A pistol was thrust into his back and he was ordered to walk forward into the darkness. Ciaran was then told to kneel down. The men gathered around their prey, swopping like vultures. The young Ardoyne man was again punched and kicked. His knuckles were red raw as he tried desperately to shield himself as the blows rained down on his thin frame. He cried, probably for his mother, knowing that he had nowhere to go. The men made him pick himself up and kneel down facing away from them. One of the men cocked his pistol, then shot Ciaran in the back four times. His body slumped to the ground. On his way out of the quarry, one of the gang scrawled his nickname, 'The Pope', on the road.[31] An employee of the quarry, Leonard Stewart, discovered Ciaran's body at 8:30 a.m.

It was a few hours before Ciaran's family were told of the horrifying news of his death. His twenty-year-old brother, Patrick, was at his home when his mother came to visit him at lunchtime, having returned home from Mass to discover her youngest son was missing. 'When I saw her, before she even said anything, I think I knew something was wrong, and knew he was dead,' Patrick recalled. After a brief visit to the Army Barracks in Flax Street, Patrick and a few friends were told that a body had been discovered matching Ciaran's description and that they should go immediately to Musgrave Street RUC Station. There they were met by a CID officer, Detective Constable Jonty Brown, who took them to Laganbank Morgue to identify the body. When Patrick walked into the room he spotted three bodies on trollies to the left and one body on the right. Before the sheet was pulled back, he knew instinctively that it was his brother, his black frizzy hair was sticking out from under the white death shroud the mortuary staff had placed over his body.

The police detectives investigating the murder later traced the weapon used to kill Ciaran to two other shooting incidents, an armed robbery, a murder and an attempted murder. It was a weapon held and used by the UDA. On this occasion, though, it was used by members of the UVF to murder Ciaran Murphy, an innocent young man, killed for no other reason than that he was a Catholic.[32] In 1977 the RUC charged one man with involvement in the attack. He pleaded guilty to Ciaran's murder at Belfast City Commission on 11 September 1978 and was sentenced to life imprisonment.[33] Drunk and vulnerable, his death would come to signify the deep visceral hatred harboured by many loyalist paramilitaries at the time.

Ciaran Murphy would not be the only young man murdered by the UVF that year. Up until that point, he was the sixty-fourth victim of the organisation. Seventy men, women and children would lose their lives at the hands of UVF members in 1974. Twenty had been shot, the remainder had died in bomb explosions, including the Dublin and Monaghan atrocities. The average age of the UVF's victims that year was thirty-eight. The oldest victim was an eighty-year-old caught up in the Dublin bombings, and the youngest an unborn baby and her one-year-old sister, in the same incident. Although the vast majority of victims were Catholic civilians, French, German and Italian tourists were also killed by the organisation, at a time when it was apparently observing a ceasefire.

★★★

The slaughter of Catholic civilians was not the only thing running through the minds of UVF and RHC volunteers. Inside Long Kesh, loyalists attached to both organisations were engaging in political thinking. A ten-point plan for peace was even put forward, which called for the continued lowering of the army's profile, reduction of military footprint, strategy of non-violence, release of prisoners, an amnesty and, of course, de-proscription.[34] One of its key architects of the plan was RHC volunteer 'Plum' Smith. It was his belief that the proposal 'built on or reiterated ideas that the RHC and UVF had put forward earlier'. There was an acceptance that paramilitaries on both sides 'had acted for political reasons'.[35]

In January 1975, the UVF and UDA took separate, albeit complimentary, decisions to talk to British government officials. Up first was thirty-four-year-old Andy Tyrie, the UDA's Supreme Commander, who led several delegations to meet James Allan, a British official working out of Laneside in North Down. Much of the UDA's demands of the government revolved around the welfare of their prisoners, especially in Long Kesh. Accompanying Tyrie on these occasions were fellow members of the organisation's ruling Inner Council, including Hugh McVeigh, the thirty-six-year-old UDA commander from East Belfast, who represented the organisation on prison-related matters. As soon as the UDA delegates left Laneside, the UVF were shown in to meet Allan. On the afternoon of 27 January 1975, the UVF delegation consisted of political spokesman Ken Gibson, their prisoners' representative Jim McDonald and Brigade Staff officers Billy Mitchell, Jackie 'Nigger' Irvine and Eddy Kearns.[36] The mood surrounding the meetings was not good. Both loyalist groupings were involved in a violent feud that would lead to several of their men losing their lives as the year progressed.

6

REGIMENTAL LOYALTY

'The UVF was not formed to deal with interfaces, it was formed because they believed there was a sell-out, there was a rebellion which had to be stopped, whether you were from the Shankill or East Antrim you had the one enemy – the IRA, indeed the nationalist community as most UVF volunteers didn't distinguish between the IRA and those they fought for.'

Billy Mitchell, UVF Brigade Staff Officer in 1975[1]

Newington Avenue, North Belfast, 7 April 1975

The large furniture removal truck rattled along the narrow North Belfast street, before coming to a sharp halt, throwing the occupants in the front cab forward in their seats. In big bold letters along the side was written Gillespie and Wilson, a furniture company based on the Upper Newtownards Road in East Belfast. The men on board were making their routine deliveries of carpets and bedding to customers on the other side of Belfast Lough. The driver – a tall, older man – applied the handbrake before switching off the engine and taking out the keys. The doors of the cab were flung open as the driver and his young helper, much shorter than his colleague, jumped out and walked to the back of the truck.[2] They opened the roll-up door a couple of feet before they were surprised by the sound of footsteps behind them, followed by a guttural voice. 'Get your fucking hands up.' Without much hesitation, they raised their hands and turned around, to be greeted by a group of armed men. The delivery driver and his young helper were promptly frog-marched to a waiting car, where they were bundled in and driven a few miles north of the city to be interrogated. Nobody would ever see or hear from the two men again.[3]

The next day, a Monkstown man, twenty-nine-year-old Norman Cooke, received a knock on his door by another man who asked Cooke to accompany him to a two-door Vauxhall Viva car parked outside his house.

Inside the vehicle were two other men. All four men drove down onto the Shore Road and along the coast road to Carrickfergus where they headed towards Whitehead, before heading towards the Gobbins in Islandmagee, a breathtakingly beautiful, if incredibly isolated, spot overlooking the County Antrim coast. As they neared their destination, Cooke turned around in his seat when he noticed a blue transit minibus following them closely behind. Its headlights burned brightly, dazzling him. He averted his eyes, turning to the man sat next to him to ask what was going on. He was told he 'would find out later'. A short time later the car and van slowed down, pulling into a lay-by. Two men in the front of the minibus got out and walked around to open its rear doors. 'I then seen them taking two men out of the back of the van,' said Cooke. 'These two men were walked from the van across the Gobbins Road, they then got over a fence and into a field by the two men who had been in the front of the van. I did not know who the men were who were in the back of the van, but one was a young man and one was an older man.' Cooke emerged from the car with the other men and followed them across the road, climbing down from the fence. 'As I was walking I heard two shots,' he recalled, adding, 'I didn't know what was happening. I just turned round and ran towards the car, two other fellows ran out behind me. As I was running I heard two more shots.' Cooke said he was 'sickened' by what he had witnessed, and claimed to have entered 'a state of shock at what had taken place'. He maintained his innocence when questioned by police about the episode, making it clear that he 'didn't know that the men were going to get shot'.[4]

The truth of what had actually transpired was shocking. Sometime on 7 April, the second-in-command of the Islandmagee UVF was called to a meeting with his Officer Commanding, thirty-one-year-old unemployed fitter Sydney Corr, in the Brown Trout pub in Carrickfergus. Also in attendance was the military commander of the Carrick UVF, thirty-one-year-old George (Geordie) Anthony and his second-in-command.[5] They were accompanied by the commander of the area's Special Services Unit, thirty-five-year-old Geordie Sloan. It appears that another man was also in attendance along with UVF Brigade Staff member Billy Mitchell who had travelled all the way from Belfast to arrange the execution of two UDA men who were earlier abducted in North Belfast. 'You go along with them too,' Anthony allegedly told his second-in-command and Sloan, as they accompanied Corr and another UVF man[6] to dig a hole in a secluded part of the countryside. The hole they dug was roughly five-foot long by five-foot wide and four-foot deep. Corr claimed that he was only told that it was for 'stuff coming from Tiger's Bay', which he took to mean weapons and ammunition.[7] It would seem that most of the volunteers were not fully aware of what was about to transpire.

Later that evening, the two UDA men were transferred to a minibus used by the UVF to take families on prison visits to Long Kesh. As the welfare minibus passed through Carrick, it continued on in the direction of the coast road towards Whitehead, where it picked up speed on Cable Road before turning right onto the Larne Road and towards Ballycarry. It caught up with a car, which it followed to the Gobbins, where both vehicles stopped. As the men got out they could hear the tide lapping against the shore down below. It was in this picturesque part of East Antrim that they had brought their captives to their place of execution.

Billy Mitchell followed two of the UVF men down a path on the other side of the road, to the secluded spot where his underlings had prepared a shallow grave. He was closely followed by Sloan, who was frogmarching the older man. Another man held Douglas by the shoulder so that he couldn't make a run for it. Both of the prisoners had their hands tightly bound behind their backs. 'Go ahead, you'll be alright,' the UVF man told the younger man. Out of the side, another UVF member quickly ran over to the youth and grabbed him by the neck, putting a gun to the back of his head. The boy groaned as the man pulled the trigger. His lifeless body collapsed onto the ground in a crumpled heap next to the hole in the ground. 'You nearly got me there,' snapped the man who had held Douglas, before losing his balance and falling over. Panicking, he hurriedly picked himself up and ran off back up to the road. As he made good his escape, the unknown gunman took a few steps over to the older man, levelling his pistol at him, he pulled the trigger at point-blank range. Sloan, who had been gripping the older man by the neck, flew into blind panic and ran off. 'Jesus Christ,' blurted Corr, as he took in the scene unfolding around him. The gunman then levelled his pistol at the heads of the two captives and pulled the trigger another couple of times. Billy Mitchell looked on, the only witness to what had unfolded. The gunman then handed the weapon to Corr for safekeeping.[8] Corr was later sentenced to two five-year jail terms for removing the gun from the scene and also burying the bodies of the two UDA men.[9]

East Antrim was one of the most ruthless units within the UVF in 1975. Most of its members lived in Rathcoole, Monkstown, Carrickfergus, and as far north-east as Islandmagee and the port town of Larne. Many of its members were employed, typically in unskilled, semi-skilled and, occasionally, skilled labouring roles. Norman Cooke joined the UVF in 1972 and was interned for his activities from October 1973 until May 1974. He had been arrested on 7 September 1972 along with Geordie Sloan and another prominent UVF man, twenty-nine-year-old Billy Greer, when police raided their social club at Jack's Lane, an old farm with outbuildings, which lay across a narrow footbridge over the Belfast to Londonderry railway line. Police discovered a veritable arsenal, including five rifles, three revolvers, a pistol, one sub-machine-gun, 14 magazines, 6,260 rounds of assorted ammunition, a blast bomb, two flares, 30lbs of explosives, detonators and fuse wire, as well as medical supplies. They also discovered a military training manual on guerrilla warfare.[10] After his release, Cooke became involved in the Welfare section of the East Antrim UVF. Like everyone else who joined the organisation at the time, regardless of whether they opted for an auxiliary role or not, Cooke was tasked with all sorts of activities in support of the group. He soon proved to be a dedicated volunteer. Other members of the unit had only been in the UVF a matter of months when the killings at the Gobbins took place. The Carrick commander, Geordie Anthony, had been involved for a longer period of time. Anthony was a stickler for administration, and kept meticulous records on every member of the unit; how much membership dues they had paid, and what their role was within the unit.

Most of the East Antrim UVF's training took place at Jack's Lane and in the Royal British Legion premises in Carrickfergus, effectively the group's headquarters. Like the Shankill UVF, which a decade earlier had met and trained in the Standard Bar, the East Antrim UVF chose these places on the basis of the rigid code of *omertá* it could enforce upon its members, their supporters and sympathisers, and also on the local people in their area. Another tool that the East Antrim UVF had in its armoury was the involvement of several serving UDR soldiers. Two of these men were imprisoned for giving UVF members training and instruction in how to use firearms in the British Legion.[11]

★★★

Houston Park, Lurgan, County Armagh, Evening, 27 July 1975

Forty-five-year-old Billy Hanna was returning home from a night out at the British Legion in Lurgan. Accompanying him was a close friend and comrade. As Hanna pulled up into his driveway, two men, Robin Jackson and Harris Boyle, took out their handguns and approached the vehicle on the driver's side. They had gone to Hanna's home with the express purpose of killing him. After parking the vehicle, Hanna climbed out to be greeted by Jackson, who casually walked up to him and pointed his pistol at the older man's temple. Without hesitating, he pulled the trigger. As Hanna dropped to the ground Jackson stood over him and fired another shot into his head to finish him off. A veteran of the Korean War, Hanna had subsequently joined the B-Specials and, in 1970, became a Permanent Staff Instructor with his local UDR battalion. The Security Forces suspected that he held dual membership of the UDR and the outlawed UVF and, as a result, had placed him under surveillance. This was strenuously denied at the time by the RUC and army.[12] Rumours persisted nonetheless, and he was believed to have been the leader of the Mid Ulster UVF from 1972 to his death.

The reason that Jackson assassinated Hanna was simple. He believed the rumours that the war veteran had been a high-level informer or agent working to put the Mid Ulster UVF out of business. What had apparently sealed Hanna's fate was the allegation that he had passed on specific information to British military intelligence implicating Jackson in the Dublin and Monaghan bombings. 'There was always the belief they were probably working for British Intelligence. Mid Ulster leaked. You were never sure who was British Intelligence. It leaked like a sieve,' one UVF leader later told journalists.[13] Consequently, Hanna was disowned by the UVF.[14] In a bid to stop loyalist paramilitary groups from carrying out further attacks, the British Army attempted to infiltrate the organisation. In doing so they were able to call upon former or serving soldiers who were explicitly tasked with joining illegal armed groups with the intention of preventing attacks.[15]

It would later be alleged that Jackson was at worst an agent, and at best an informer, working for the intelligence services.[16] It is impossible to say for certain whether Jackson was working for the state, simply because none of the intelligence agencies would ever confirm or deny this. The lack of a paper trail also leaves much to conjecture. What can be inferred from the killing of Billy Hanna is that, by eliminating his rival, Jackson was demonstrating to his UVF comrades that he could be ruthless and efficient when he needed to be. This would greatly aid his bid to assume overall command of the Mid Ulster UVF.[17] As a sign of the twisted nature of loyalist paramilitarism at the time, Jackson even turned up to Hanna's funeral to pay his respects to the dead man's wife, Ann, who had witnessed the murder of her husband. The man who had pulled the trigger took his place amongst the mourners.

★★★

Buskhill Road, A1, 11km north of Newry, 2:10 a.m., 31 July 1975

The Miami Showband were busy playing the Castle Ballroom in Banbridge. The dance finished at 1 a.m. and the band left in their light blue and cream Volkswagen van around 1:45 a.m. and headed south towards Newry on their way back home to Dublin. Five members of the band were on board. Twenty-nine-year-old Fran O'Toole, a married man with two children, twenty-three-year-old Anthony Geraghty, thirty-two-year-old Brian McCoy, twenty-four-year-old father-of-one Des McAlea and twenty-four-year-old Stephen Travers.[18] The van was stopped at Buskhill, Donaghmore, Newry on 31 July 1975 at 2:10 a.m. One of the survivors recalled what happened next:

> As we went along the second dual-carriageway we were stopped by what appeared to be an army patrol. They used a red light to stop us. As far as I can remember there was only one man on the road with the red light. When we stopped I saw two or three more men come out onto the road from the nearside hedge. They were all wearing combat gear and some were wearing green and some black berets. The man with the torch was carrying what appeared to be a sub-machine gun. He went to the driver's window and spoke to Brian. He asked Brian his name and also to produce his driving licence. I heard Brian give his name and tell the man with the torch that we were the Miami Showband. This same man then asked us all to get out of the minibus. We all got out and went to the rear of the bus. One of the men was Brian McCoy and he appeared to be dead. The other was [name redacted] and he was alive but could not speak as he was badly shot up. I then said to [name redacted] that I was going to get help and I got out over the hedge onto the road. I ran across the road to the opposite side of the dual carriageway where a lorry was stopped. I asked the driver for help as we had been shot but I don't think he

believed me and would not let me into the cab. I again begged him to take me to the police station and he eventually let me into the cab.[19]

The force of the explosion was so intense that one of the survivors was blown through a hedge by the roadside. The RUC's Senior Investigating Officer gradually pieced together what happened:

> They were stopped by what they believed to be an army road stop. It transpired that the persons operating this road stop were in fact terrorists. There were five members of the Showband in the minibus at the time. All were ordered out of the minibus and were told to stand along the side of the road, where they were asked to answer a number of questions relating to their identity. At this stage an explosion occurred, and it is surmised that this was as a result of a bomb being placed in the minibus by the terrorists. This was followed by a number of shots being fired by the terrorists at the Showband members. As a result of this attack there were three members of the Showband fatally injured. In relation to the other two bodies found at the scene i.e. the two previously mentioned as being badly mutilated – these persons were later claimed by the Ulster Volunteer Force as members of their organisation and were named as follows: (1) Harris Boyle, [address redacted] and (2) William Wesley Somerville, [address redacted].[20]

After the bomb exploded the other UVF men present opened fire on the surviving band members. Fran O'Toole was shot over twenty-two times in the head, neck and chest, and Brian McCoy had bullet wounds to the neck and lower body. Anthony Geraghty had bullet wounds to the head and body. The viciousness of the attack shocked the whole of Ireland.

A few days later, detectives raided the homes of Thomas Raymond Crozier and James Roderick Shane McDowell, both from Lurgan, who were subsequently arrested, charged and imprisoned for the murders. Pleading 'not guilty', Crozier told the court, 'I was taking the last name when there was a big bang. Then there was a lot of cracks which I knew was shooting. Someone shouted "Two of them got it".[21] The judge recommended that they serve no less than thirty-five years each. One of those who was later convicted of the Miami Showband attack and a host of other murders was John James Somerville, whose thirty-four-year-old brother Wesley had been killed in the attack. Both brothers were from Moygashel Park in Dungannon.

Also killed in the attack was Robin Jackson's close friend, twenty-four-year-old Harris Boyle. He was given a large paramilitary-style funeral.[22]

Across Mid Ulster, the UVF was becoming more effective in mounting attacks against Catholic civilians. Much of this was down to the group's ruthlessness and cunning, but it was also partly the by-product of individual members of the Security Forces joining forces with the terrorists. The full picture of this form of 'collusion' would not emerge until after the murder of thirty-nine-year-old shopkeeper William Strathearn in Ahoghill in 1977. Members of the so-called 'Glennane gang' called to his door at 2 a.m. on 19 April 1977, and lured him out on the pretence of helping an injured child. He was shot twice in cold blood. Those involved in William Strathearn's death included two members of the RUC's Special Patrol Group (SPG), Constable Billy McCaughey and Sergeant John Weir, who were both charged with the murder.[23] McCaughey later claimed that the murder was in retaliation to other murders carried out by IRA gunmen. The SPG were a paramilitary-style force that operated in tight-knit units, and drew some of the most bigoted police officers into their ranks. One senior NIO official would later explain how the SPG were 'normally deployed in periods of great tension to deal with potentially highly dangerous situations', but they were in 'no sense ... the "Bobby on the beat" patiently getting to know his flock, but rather people rushed into situations where their own nerves are near to breaking point. They may be unfamiliar with local personalities and in any case unable to give first priority to the niceties of police courtesies.'[24] The reluctance of police commanders to deploy the SPG in West Belfast in the late 1970s probably stemmed from the unit's reputation in other, more rural, parts of Northern Ireland.

★★★

Carrickfergus RUC Station, early September 1975

It was early September 1975 when a twenty-seven-year-old UVF officer walked into Carrickfergus RUC station and surrendered himself to the police. He had escaped the clutches of makeshift Court Martial proceedings in the British Legion in Carrickfergus, and had gone straight to the RUC. After several rounds of questioning by CID officers, he led detectives to a lonely road at the Gobbins, a small enclave near Islandmagee, along the County Antrim coast, where, he informed them, the UVF had buried the bodies of two UDA men, thirty-six-year-old Hugh McVeigh and twenty-year-old David Douglas, who had been abducted from a North Belfast street in April. The police officers hadn't been digging long before their shovels threw up a shoe. After clearing the top soil away, they discovered a shallow grave sliced into the heavy clay earth. What greeted them was an awful sight. Two bodies, one on top of the other, with their feet closest to the road. Both corpses were male. They had their hands tightly bound behind their backs with rope. The larger man's feet had been broken, and his shoes were missing. Large holes were visible on both skulls, indicating that they had been shot through the head.[25]

Dr Derek Carson, the Deputy State Pathologist for Northern Ireland, undertook the autopsies on both bodies. He was able to positively identify both men from dental records. He concluded that they had been kneeling when they were both shot through the back of the head, and that the two badly decomposed bodies had lain buried in the shallow grave for several months.[26]

By killing McVeigh and Douglas, the UVF were upping the ante in an ongoing feud with their arch rivals in the UDA. Both groups seemed impervious to the calls of politicians to seek a peaceful way out, and settle their differences by talking. Ironically, this feud had broken out right at the point when it seemed that loyalist paramilitaries were coming in from the cold. Their leaders had met regularly with government officials to talk about the prospects for peace. Hugh McVeigh had been on these delegations, as had Billy Mitchell, the UVF Brigade Staff officer now suspected by the UDA of ordering the abduction and execution of their men. As far as the UDA were concerned, Mitchell would be elevated to the top of the hit list. Joining him was another East Antrim UVF commander, Geordie Anthony.

After an exhaustive investigation of the McVeigh and Douglas murders, including an extensive de-briefing of the young UVF man turned informer, the Security Forces resolved to swoop on the suspects involved. Operation Jigsaw was launched on 6 October 1975, and involved 500 RUC officers and 1,000 troops. Geordie Anthony was one of a number of men rounded up. During his interrogations he became increasingly paranoid about the murders of McVeigh and Douglas.

'That's who I'm worried about, didn't youse put it out on the news that we were lifted for the killing of McVeigh and Douglas?'

'We didn't put anything out on the news. It was the BBC who did that,' replied the detective.

'Yes, but it was the police who give them the statement.'

'How did you know what was said in the news.'

'I heard it in here.'

'It's obvious. The wombles will be out to get every man who was lifted.'

'What do you mean?'

'Well, McVeigh and Douglas were UDA men, weren't they? Isn't it certain that they will be out to get the men that done that?'

'What was your part in that? Did you kill them?'

'No, I didn't kill them.'

'What was your part in it?'

Anthony remained silent. He told the detective that he couldn't confess. He feared for his life.

'I can't confess,' he protested. 'I can't say anything. I'm going away for thirty years and when I'm inside I'll have to watch my every move. It will be bad enough trying to watch the wombles, but if I confess to anything I'll not be accepted by the UVF either.'

'You will be safe in prison. You'll be guarded every minute of the day,' said the detective.

'What about the boys who have already been done in jail? The boys who were supposed to have committed suicide, hanging and cyanides. Those boys didn't commit suicide, you know, they were done in.'

'Don't you think you're being a bit dramatic, George? Things like that don't happen in prison.'

'Maybe they don't. I happen to know they do.'[27]

Anthony was right to be concerned. The UDA's Inner Council had just dispatched UFF member Kenny McClinton to track down Billy Mitchell. Just as McClinton was about to catch up with Mitchell, the UDA hierarchy pulled him off the job so that he could devote his energies to constructing parcel bombs to be mailed to IRA suspects in the post.[28]

Meanwhile, the UDA's Supreme Commander Andy Tyrie received a call from a senior UVF commander, who apparently wept as he spoke of the terrible mistake his organisation had made in murdering the two men. 'What was it for?' Tyrie asked him. 'You couldn't have picked two more innocent men,' he told the UVF leader.[29] The incident would continue to poison relations between the rival groupings for many years afterwards.

★★★

Billy Mitchell was a key link-man in the rejuvenation of the UVF in the 1960s. Like other members, he had joined the organisation in response to the dire warnings of Ian Paisley, who talked enthusiastically of collusion between Rome and republicanism. As a senior UVF commander, he had become well-versed in justifying the UVF's campaign in the pages of *Combat* throughout 1974 and 1975. It was only natural, therefore, that he would emerge from the shadows to speak to the press on St Patrick's Day in March 1975. He was one of two masked gunmen who appeared at an impromptu press conference to reiterate the UVF's objectives. They had talked to their rank and file, they had talked to the British, they had even talked to their republican enemies, but now they were addressing the people of Northern Ireland directly. Mitchell was eager to deny the 'black propaganda' that the organisation had surrendered. On St Patrick's Day, however, he spun a different story. The UVF statement he read out categorically denied that the organisation had any 'Communist or Official IRA ties'.[30] The masked men said that the UVF, in its most recent policy statement, made it 'quite clear that it deemed the Official IRA to be the most dangerous long-term enemy of the Ulster people'.[31]

While the UVF leadership had emerged from the shadows to communicate their organisation's policy, its rank-and-file membership remained hidden. Conservative estimates put the number of UVF volunteers at approximately 1,500 in the mid-1970s. It was by no means a mass organisation like the UDA. The man who had emerged from the shadows to brief the press, Billy Mitchell, explained its size and shape:

> Even up to about 1975, membership of the UVF was by invitation only, after which it was up to the local unit if you were accepted. The UVF did not swell its ranks until it was legalised in 1974, when Merlyn Rees tried to politicise the UVF by bringing into the political process the Volunteer Political Party. The UVF was not a massive organisation until the legalisation [was passed, which legalised it for a brief period in 1974–5].[32]

For Mitchell, the UVF saw itself as 'a military machine, there to defend the constitution'.[33] Everything it did was orientated towards implementing its own military policy. Like all armed groups its reputation was built on the ruthlessness of its core membership. But why then had it taken such extreme steps to eliminate its nearest loyalist rivals? His answer would prove illuminating:

Regimental loyalty was the key factor in competitiveness – not unlike the regular British Army – in many cases the focus was territory, there would not have been any philosophical disagreements between the two organisations – there would have been issues around personalities, feelings on both sides that 'we are the elite'. There was the UDA flirtation with independence.[34]

And so, in the mid-1970s, the UVF was prepared to gun down anyone who challenged its authority in its own areas. In going on the offensive, the organisation could also count on a cadre of dedicated volunteers.

One veteran UVF terrorist, 'Jake', a painter and decorator who worked in East Belfast, spoke liberally about how the UVF operated at this time. Both the UVF and UDA had 'bastards' and 'cunts' in their ranks from the outset. The UVF also had a stringent system of internal control. As a rank-and-file gunman in the organisation, Jake pulled no punches when describing the quality of the other volunteers around him. One man, 'Jamesy', had been sentenced to life imprisonment for his involvement in the murder of a young Catholic man. A man with a fearsome reputation, Jamesy had a rough chiselled face with deep lines carved into it. His normal expression was that of a grimace. He had a habit of keeping watch on everyone who crossed his path. He saw everything. A hard man with a long, pensive stare, he didn't suffer fools gladly. Jake hated his guts. He thought him 'a fucking prick', 'a two-faced bastard', who had been in charge of the organisation's Provost Marshal's section (the UVF's internal security branch) in East Antrim before his arrest and conviction in the late 1970s.

Tasked with investigating the theft from the UVF's coffers, Jake was accused by Jamesy of being 'up to his neck in it'. It later transpired that he had been fingered by another UVF volunteer, 'Clarkey', who had tried to chat up Jake's wife in 'The Farm', a UVF-run social club perched on the slopes of Carnmoney hill, a long extinct volcano that overlooked Rathcoole housing estate. Clarkey's disrespect was palpable, recalled Jake, and he intended to teach him a lesson by 'offering the fucker outside for a "fair dig"'. The fight was intended to settle the disrespect shown towards Jake's wife. Later, a fabricated story had been fed to the local leadership that Jake had been skimming off the top from the proceeds of a fundraising event in the club. Jamesy duly paid him a visit.

Jake was relieving himself in the farm's toilets when Jamesy burst in with a couple of other burly volunteers. He was caught off guard, struck by a 'sly dig' to the back of the head; his face shoved against the wall above the urinal. 'Take our money did ye, ye fucking bastard,' Jamesy barked, spit flying everywhere. 'How dare you fuck with me!' By now the man with the ingrained grimace was taking it personally. Before Jake could protest his innocence, he took out a Browning 9mm pistol, cocked it, releasing a round into the chamber, and thrust it violently against the base of Jake's neck. 'You'll not be stealing fuck all now, sure you won't,' Jamesy told the young UVF man through gritted teeth. 'I'm going to put a bullet in your brain, you fucking scumbag,' he snarled. That even hardened triggermen, like Jake, were policed by their own organisation, showed just how militaristic the UVF had become. Fighting back with all the willpower he could muster, it was only a jammed pistol that saved Jake from being 'nutted'. He had narrowly cheated death. Clearing the pistol for a second time Jamesy suffered a sudden change of heart. 'Fuck it lads; let the bastard go,' he snapped, before the men promptly left the toilets. And with a wry, drunken smirk Jamesy let Jake live. In return for this compassion, Jake was ordered to pay his respects and return the lost cash to the local leadership.[35]

Despite the frequent clash of personalities, the organisation's members were expected to adhere to a strict, albeit unwritten, code of conduct when it came to paying respects to the chain of command. The *omertà* was the lifeblood of the secretive sub-culture of paramilitary loyalism, and it had marked the UVF out from its rivals in the UDA. The quasi-military trappings of discipline reinforced the internal and external impression of the UVF as a centralised, coherent grouping, which ruled its membership according to strict rules and regulations.

For most UVF members, the spectre of competition with their rivals in the UDA was frequently at the forefront of their minds. There were those, like 'Bobby', a middle-aged man who had initially joined the UDA in South East Antrim and rose through its ranks before quickly gravitating towards the UVF, after becoming disillusioned with the broad-based vigilante movement. He diligently paid his 'dollar a week' into the UDA's coffers, only to see some of its commanders enjoy the high life on his hard-earned cash. Bobby was a machine operator in a local manufacturing firm. A working man, a tough guy, who was also a member of the Orange Order, he was a middle-aged man by the time the troubles broke out. Bobby was rumoured to have drank with Gusty Spence and the Shankill UVF team in the Tiger's Bay area of North Belfast in the mid-1960s.

Bobby recalled how, one Sunday afternoon at The Farm, a group of UVF volunteers resolved to take action against the UDA in the Alpha, a one-time cinema turned shebeen (illegal drinking club). The UDA had roughed up one of the team's members, leaving him badly shaken and thirsty for revenge. Bobby was told to mind the drinks. 'We'll be back once we sort these fuckers out.' And off they went, several burly men climbed into four London black cabs and made off down to the Alpha to 'teach the UDA a lesson'. Many of the men carried iron bars rolled up in newspaper. They assaulted the doorman and stormed into the bar. Pushing men to the floor, the ringleader got up on the stage. Waving a pistol in the air he made a direct threat to the UDA commander in the local area that they would not stand for the 'cowboy antics' of his grouping. They left, having turned the bar upside down.

Later on that day the UDA turned up at The Farm en masse. Surrounding the club, they called for the UVF commander who had led the raid to come outside. Bobby said that the Alpha crowd mustered hundreds of shock troops, many of whom had arrived in cars, taxis, buses and even a tractor. Outnumbered and outgunned, the UVF team reluctantly surrendered their man. He was beaten to within an inch of his life. The incident served to sour relations between the rival groups for years in Rathcoole and wider afield.[36] It also led to a shooting war that broke out in February 1975, and lingered on for much of the year. It was incidents like these that contributed to the continuation of deadly feuding within loyalist paramilitary organisations.

'Ray', a volunteer from the Shankill area of West Belfast, recalled how the UVF at this time 'was very secretive' and was modelled, in his view, around 'the idea of a family'.[37] UVF members were certainly known in their local communities but they rarely flaunted their stuff, unlike, I was often reminded, their rivals in the UDA. The UVF had a certain all-consuming quality about it, with its clandestine nature, rough characters and propensity for violence. Many UVF members were linked through blood, though the connections ran much deeper. At its heart, the organisation reverberated with what Ray called a deep 'sense of community'.[38] The organisation could rely upon support from people from a range of backgrounds, who would not have necessarily had the capability to become triggermen themselves but who nonetheless gave tacit encouragement to those who did take up the gun and bomb. Ray said that when the car he was using to transport weapons broke down, the only place close to him was his grandfather's home. In his mind, there was 'not a question of not being able to hide them in his outhouse'.[39]

Ray initially joined the UVF when he was eighteen. A tearaway at school, he had been approached to help set up the Young Citizens Volunteers (YCVs) in the Silverstream area of Belfast. As a sergeant in a platoon of YCVs, Ray was responsible for ferrying weapons, making petrol bombs and acting as a 'dicker' (lookout) for UVF men on operations. Indeed, most of his role models were working-class men who spent their days toiling away as painters, plasterers and shipyard workers, but who moonlighted as death dealers for the organisation. Like so many other young men at the time, Ray's father was also in the UVF, and had been extremely active in the early 1970s. Ray was eventually caught and convicted for 'terrorist offences'. He was convicted of planting a car bomb in the mid-1970s. As a 'lifer', he was designated 'high risk' and confined to a single cell in the newly constructed Maze Prison near Lisburn, made famous by its H Block design. Like his father, Ray was part of a military team, a volunteer who had no compunction in carrying out whatever the UVF asked of him. The UVF was fortunate in being able to call upon a hard core of people, like Ray, who were prepared to follow through with the organisation's brutal campaign of armed resistance.

UVF members in military teams were asked whether they would have been capable of close-quarter assassinations or planting bombs. From this, a pool of people became known in UVF ranks for their 'capabilities' to inflict damage on the organisation's enemies. In Ray's words, 'it was horses for courses', in so far as some people were clearly better suited to particular tasks and would be relied upon time and time again, until they were either killed or imprisoned. He also confirmed that the organisation drew heavily on the skills of its small numbers of volunteers. 'Those who did not have the "bottle" to kill were allocated other duties,' he said.[40] For those who did have the 'bottle' to kill, the UVF's violence was about to take a horrific new turn.

7

THE SHANKILL AND ITS BUTCHERS

'Unfortunately, it became increasingly clear during 1975 that a number of members of the UVF were deeply involved in sectarian violence and that the organisation was departing from the path of political argument ... Actions of this kind are crimes of the worst sort and are totally offensive to society ... I hope that the UVF will once again turn back to political argument.'

Merlyn Rees, Secretary of State for Northern Ireland,
4 November 1975[1]

Shankill Road, Belfast, Late November 1975

In the six months after he was released from prison, twenty-three-year-old Lenny Murphy helped establish a close-knit team that would operate independently from Billy Mitchell and the other members of the UVF Brigade Staff.[2] The Murphy team met in the Brown Bear Pub on the Shankill Road. Lenny Murphy's older brother, twenty-five-year-old John Murphy, was the mastermind behind the gang, with Lenny and his twenty-six-year-old friend Billy Moore providing the muscle. The group's second-in-command and quartermaster (i.e. the individual who equipped the gang with their weapons) was a twenty-six-year-old from the Shankill Road who will be referred to as Mr A. For legal reasons, this is the name given to him by journalist Martin Dillon as he is still alive and, at the time of writing, has never been arrested for his role in the gang's activities. It was said of Mr A that he was 'a cold, astute and ruthless character' who shared, with the other men, a deep hatred of the Catholic community.[3] Under the control of the Murphy brothers, the Brown Bear team embarked on one of the most ruthless and grotesque killing sprees Belfast had ever seen.

On the 24 November, Lenny Murphy called a meeting at the Brown Bear with three associates – Billy Moore, Archie Waller and Benjamin 'Pretty Boy' Edwards – all of whom decided they would take a drive into the city centre in Moore's Hackney black taxi to abduct a Catholic civilian. They believed that this would strike fear into the heart of the Catholic community. The gang had been motivated to seek out a victim in retaliation for the IRA's killing of four young soldiers in South Armagh two days earlier. As the four UVF men toured the city centre looking for a victim, they happened across Francis Crossan, a thirty-four-year-old Catholic civilian who was making his way home to Suffolk in South Belfast from an evening in the Holy Cross Bowling Club in Ardoyne, North Belfast. Francis had just crossed Library Street on his way towards Royal Avenue, the main thoroughfare in the city centre, when he was spotted by Moore at approximately 12:30 a.m. Murphy ordered Moore to pull up alongside their victim while he, Edwards and Waller jumped out to grab the man. As they walked towards Francis, who was inebriated from heavy drinking that evening, he had little time to react and was promptly hit over the head with a wheel brace by Murphy, who dragged him into the back of the cab. After driving to Wimbledon Street in the Shankill, they parked and carried Francis Crossan into an alleyway. Murphy took out a butcher's knife and stood above Francis, before running the blade across his neck, cutting his throat. He then proceeded to saw into Francis's neck until he had cut back to the spine. Covered in blood, Murphy boarded the taxi with the others and drove home. The victim's body was discovered hours later.[4] The *Belfast Telegraph* reported the murder on 26 November with the front-page headline 'Slaughter in Back Alley' and carried a photo of the body of Francis Crossan with a blanket over it. As the Murphy team had acted without UVF authority, they were not in a position to claim the murder.

A few days after the Crossan murder, on 29 November, Archie Waller was sat in his car outside the Loyalist Club in Rumford Street when he was approached and shot dead by two gunmen. The Medical Examiner found that the first bullet struck the left side of his head, a second hit him in the cheek, a third hit him on the outer side of his right arm and a fourth hit him in the groin. So violent were the effects on his body that Waller lost three pints of blood from a severed artery.[5] A lady sewing in a house nearby heard three shots, one after the other. It was a deliberate, planned assassination.

In retaliation, Lenny Murphy ordered William Moore and two other members of the Brown Bear team, Norman Waugh and David Bell, to lift three men he blamed for Waller's death – Noel 'Nogi' Shaw, Dessie Balmer Jnr and Roy Stewart – from the Windsor Bar.[6] When the men arrived at the bar, Moore stayed in the vehicle and sent the other two men to fetch Shaw. Shaw was quickly overpowered and taken the short distance to the Lawnbrooke Club, rather than the unit's headquarters at the Brown Bear Pub, where he was questioned about the Waller shooting. Shaw admitted that he had been present, but had not pulled the trigger. It didn't matter. The blood was up, and the men were busy working him over until Murphy arrived. After discussing Shaw's fate with Mr A, Murphy suggested that the members of the team present in the club should draw straws to decide who should kill Shaw. The young man selected for the task was quickly made a reluctant executioner.[7] He refused to kill Shaw. Losing little time, and in full view of his men and the punters gathered in the club, Murphy pulled out his pistol and shot Shaw in the head four times at point-blank range.[8] In a cruel twist, the UVF gang stuffed Shaw's body inside a wicker laundry basket and carried on drinking. A short time later they carried their victim's body out to a black taxi that they had earlier hijacked. They drove the vehicle to Urney Street, where it was abandoned with its engine still running.[9]

When he discovered what Murphy had done to Shaw and that he might be next, Dessie Balmer Jnr dispatched a team of his own to assassinate his nemesis. Before they could get to Murphy, Balmer was himself shot and wounded in the street, but managed to crawl into a house and escape the squad who had come to kill him. By now Murphy and his team were determined to eliminate anyone they perceived as a threat to them and their operations, including those close to the UVF leadership. This included people on the non-combatant, welfare wing of the organisation. Not satisfied with wounding Balmer, the son of a prominent UVF man, Murphy personally went in search of a close friend of the Balmer family, the UVF's political spokesman, Hughie Smyth.

Smyth had been elected to Belfast Corporation in 1972, the ill-fated Northern Ireland Assembly in 1973 and, most recently, to the Northern Ireland Constitutional Convention in May 1975. A close associate of Gusty Spence and members of the UVF Brigade Staff on the Shankill, Smyth was also part of a small network of friends which included Shankill UVF men Dessie Balmer Snr, Norman Sayers and Harry Stockman Snr, who spent a lot of time in each other's company. Smyth always accepted that he was a prime target for the Provisional IRA, which had attempted to murder him on two separate occasions, including a machine gun attack on his parents' home at 32 Ainsworth Drive, not long after his election to the Convention. What he didn't expect was for volunteers within the ranks of the UVF to seek him out for assassination. After casually knocking on the door of Smyth's flat on the West Circular Road, Lenny Murphy stood back and pulled out his pistol. Just before Smyth answered the door, Murphy cocked the weapon and took aim. As Smyth opened the door Murphy squeezed the trigger but nothing happened. The gun had jammed. Murphy quickly rushed the door but Smyth pushed against him, catching Murphy's arm in the door. Smyth believed that had he not managed to close the door there was every chance that he would have died that night.[10] Those close to Smyth believe Murphy targeted him for no other reason than he was close to the Balmers.[11]

★★★

Belfast City Centre, 7 February 1976

It was 7 p.m. when the deputy editor of the *Sunday News*, Jim Campbell, received a call to the newsroom. The man on the other end of the phone said he was 'Major Long of the Young Militants'.[12] 'The body of a militant republican can be found on the grass at Forthriver Way,' the caller barked down the line at the journalist. 'This is retaliation for the murder of the RUC Sergeant.'[13] Once he had noted the details of the statement, Campbell rang the information through to the RUC at Tennent Street on the Shankill Road. The Station Sergeant on duty then quickly organised a search and, an hour or two later, police officers found the body of Thomas Patrick Quinn, a fifty-five-year-old unemployed road-sweeper. Thomas was lying face down in a steep ditch one hundred yards from the Forthriver Road/Forthriver Way junction. It appeared that Quinn had been abducted and murdered the previous night, and that the person responsible had dragged his body from a vehicle, across a grass embankment and then disposed of it as if he had been fly-tipping rubbish.

The Scenes of Crime Officer (SOCO), who arrived at Forthriver Way in Glencairn, made his way down into the ditch to examine the area for forensics. What he saw shocked him:

> I was called to the scene of a murder at Forthriver Way from 8:30 p.m. to 8:55 p.m. on 7 February 1976. Lying on the bank near a stream was the body of a male person, aged approximately 55 years, dressed in an overcoat and no hat. The body was cold and rigor mortis was present

on all four limbs, the left forearm being flexed at the elbow joint and fixed. Examination of the body was difficult as the bank on which he was lying was slippy and wet, also steep. A large area 2" wide and 4" long of scalp was reflected backwards. Death had occurred as the result of having his throat cut very deeply right down to the backbone. There was no sign of tentative cuts on the neck and the depth of the wound and its direction ruled out suicide. Estimation of time of death was difficult due to the cold and damp conditions, but would appear to have occurred around lunchtime, on the same day. There was no evidence of robbery as there was about £15 present in his pockets.[14]

Another SOCO combing the area around the top of the grass bank discovered a gold fountain pen and a metal comb, which appeared to have fallen out of the victim's pocket as he was dragged into the ditch by his assailant.

When the body of Thomas Quinn was taken to Fosters Green morgue for examination by a Medical Examiner (ME) from Queen's University, it was further revealed that the man had a 'very large amount of alcohol' in his body, enough, in the opinion of the coroner, to 'have facilitated his capture by his assailants'. Injuries to his head, neck and chest revealed that he had been brutally assaulted. Blows to the man's jaw, perhaps with a fist, and another to the head with a blunt object like a metal rod or bar, together with a heavy blow to his left shoulder suggested he had little opportunity to defend himself when struck by his attackers. The overpowering of their victim, on this occasion, was swift, particularly in light of how inebriated he would have been from the alcohol in his system. The ME also found that:

> There were several incised wounds on the front and sides of the neck, caused by a sharp cutting object such as a knife. Some of the wounds were relatively superficial but one was very deep. Extending back to the spine. In its depths the windpipe had been divided, as had also the main artery and veins on the left hand side of the neck. This wound would have caused quite rapid death.[15]

The grisly nature of the murder of Thomas Quinn, a widower with two children, who had been living rough as a vagrant in the city, was truly shocking. In their inquiries, detectives quickly established that Thomas had been staggering drunk along Library Street in Belfast city centre, when he was hit over the head with a wheel brace and then bundled into a car. What was not known until later was that, after Thomas Quinn had been abducted, his kidnappers drove to the Shankill to collect a large butcher's knife before making the short uphill journey to Glencairn, where he was taken to the back of a community centre, severely beaten with a wooden baton and had his throat cut back to the spine. The killer's *modus operandi* was identical to that in the case of Francis Crossan.

In modern-day police investigations, officers are trained to analyse the location of a murder for clues that may reveal why the specific location where the body was dumped had been selected by the perpetrator, how the victim and/or offender got to the scene, how the offender may have made their escape, and whether the scene was familiar to either the victim or the offender. Other considerations factoring into the analysis of a crime scene usually include the proximity of the body to nearby pubs, clubs or housing estates. Investigators typically infer from the available evidence other deductions, including how the victim and offender may have encountered one another, and whether the killing and disposal of the body were pre-meditated. Finally, detectives are interested to know whether there is a relationship between the crime scene and the victim or the offender.[16]

Despite the obvious advance in policing techniques, we know from the work of journalist Martin Dillon that the murder squad based at Tennent Street would have asked these or similar questions when they discovered the bodies of Francis Crossan and Thomas Quinn. However, given the sheer volume of murders in Belfast in the mid-1970s, not to mention the Murphy gang's ability to abduct and murder victims in two separate policing districts, Charlie and Delta Divisions, it stands to reason that the RUC was not in the immediate position to connect the dots between the two deaths. In all there were 126 troubles-related murders in the C and D divisional areas in 1976.[17] D Division's headquarters was at North Queen Street RUC Station, a modern building opened in 1973, and its area of responsibility stretched from the southern edge of the New Lodge out to Greencastle along the Shore Road in North Belfast and beyond to Whiteabbey and Monkstown. D Division had responsibility for the major republican and loyalist strongholds of New Lodge, Unity Flats and Tigers' Bay out to Rathcoole and Glengormley. C Division was based in Tennent Street, and covered the Shankill, Woodvale and Falls areas. What hampered most Criminal Investigation Department (CID) investigations at the time was the very real lack of an inter-divisional information sharing system, effectively stove-piping the efforts of small teams of detectives. The failure to move quickly to apprehend those responsible for the murders would have serious repercussions as Lenny Murphy and his gang, imbued with a sense of confidence in their death-dealing methodology, continued on with their campaign of terror.

On 26 February 1976, twenty-six-year-old Francis Rice, an unemployed labourer, left his home on the Cliftonville Road at 7:30 p.m. to join a few friends in the city centre for a drink. After a few hours in the pub in Winetavern Street, near Royal Avenue, he left to make his way home at 2:30 a.m. As he made his way up to Millfield, along the bottom of the Shankill Road, he was abducted by a group of men who jumped out of a black taxi on Upper Donegal Street.[18] One of those involved in his murder, Billy Moore, later revealed how the attack unfolded:

> Sometime around the beginning of last year, I was out for a run in my taxi when we picked up another lad and done him in. Lenney [sic] Murphy, [name redacted]. I don't know his second name, Basher Bates and me were in the Long Bar drinking, it was a Saturday night. At about one o'clock on Sunday morning we all left the bar. Lenny was driving my taxi and the rest of us were in the back. There were two girls in the front of the taxi but I would rather not bring them into this. Lenny drove down the Shankill and stopped outside the *Telegraph* Office and I then took over the driving. Lenny got into the back and he told me to drive up Upper Donegal Street to look for a Taig. As I was driving along this street I saw a man walk out of Union Street and across Donegal Street in front of me. Murphy told me to stop the taxi and as I pulled up beside him Murphy jumped out of the back door and hit him across the head with a wheel brace. This man fell in the middle of the roadway as Murphy hit him. Basher Bates and [name redacted] got out and helped Murphy with this man into the taxi. This man was dressed in a black jacket and had long blondish hair. Murphy told me to drive on. I drove up Upper Donegal Street turned left into Upper Library Street across Upper Library Street and up the Shankill to [redacted] to Murphy's house. Murphy and Basher Bates got out. [Name redacted] was sitting on top of this man in the back seat and talking to him. [Name redacted] hammered him and told him he was going to be killed. Murphy and Basher got back in and I then drove back up the Shankill and to Mayo Street where Murphy told me to

stop opposite an entry which runs off Mayo Street to Esmond Street. Murphy, [name redacted] and Basher Bates pulled the injured man out of the back seat. Lenny Murphy had a knife with him, which he got from his own house. Murphy told me to turn the taxi and that they would be waiting on me when I came back up. The two girls were still with me in the taxi. I drove down Mayo Street turned left and left again up Esmond Street up to the entry which is only a few yards from the Shankill Road end. The three of them came running down and got into the back of the taxi. Murphy told me that he had cut his throat. I drove up to Glencairn and left [name redacted], Murphy and the two girls off in Forthriver. I then drove back down and left Basher Bates off at his house in West Circular Road. I then drove home.[19]

Francis Dominic Rice's body was found the next morning by a local resident. He was seated against a wall, his throat was cut and he was covered in blood. His eyes were wide open, fixed and dilated, as if he had been staring into space. The terror of the trauma he had gone through was obvious to those RUC officers and forensic scientists who first encountered the body. It was an image that would haunt them for the rest of their lives.

***

Antrim Road, North Belfast, 2:50 a.m., 2 March 1976

The car made slow but steady progress along the Antrim Road. Inside were two young women, twenty-five-year-old Mary Murray and her twenty-eight-year-old friend Margaret McCartney, who were on their way home from a dance in Ballymena. The girls had just dropped off another friend at 2:30 a.m., when they turned right up onto the Cliftonville Road. The street was poorly lit and so they were taken by surprise when a car drew up behind them at speed, flashing its lights and driving erratically. Thinking it was an army or police patrol, Mary slowed down. 'I recognised this car as a big Cortina but I was unable to see the colour, as I then heard shooting and the side windscreen shattered.' She was gripped by panic. 'I immediately realised I had been shot as I felt a burning pain in my right shoulder and right side. As the car passed I could see flashes coming from the car but I am not sure whether the shooting was coming from the front seat or the back left-hand seat. The car continued to travel up the Cliftonville Road. I am not able to identify anyone in this car. I never lost consciousness and I turned on the Cliftonville Road and drove back home with Margaret.' It was a remarkable feat of endurance for the young woman who was by now bleeding profusely from her shoulder and lower chest. Her determination to maintain control of the car as she drove through the streets of Belfast probably saved her life and the life of her friend. Once she gained some distance between her and her assailant, Mary began to pass out. The next thing she remembered was the flashing lights of an ambulance, then being transferred to the Royal Victoria Hospital.[20]

Meanwhile, a nearby army patrol from J Battery, 3 Royal Horse Artillery Regiment, had heard the shots and took off in high pursuit towards Ballysillan where they believed the gunmen were headed. The soldiers at the vehicle check-point on the Ballysillan Road saw the suspect vehicle, a bronze-coloured Cortina, which approached them before mounting the kerb to get around them. At this point, Lenny Murphy lent out of the car and fired two shots at the patrol. One soldier, Gunner Mallinson, took up position as the car passed the patrol, and fired an aimed shot. Another member of the patrol also fired a shot and hit the car, which lost control but then righted itself. Murphy ordered his driver to drive to Lowwood Park near the Shore Road, where he set fire to the Cortina and hid the pistol in a bush.

At 4:05 a.m. Murphy was travelling in a red Fiat along with Basher Bates and two other men, when the vehicle was stopped and Murphy was arrested by a soldier from the 1st Battalion, the Argyll and Sutherland Highlanders, who recognised him as a person of interest. He was taken to the Royal Military Police office at Hastings Street, who then handed him over to police at Tennent Street where he was swabbed for gunshot residue. At 8:30 a.m. soldiers searching the scene close to where the Cortina had been burnt out discovered an automatic pistol, which was handed over to the RUC. Meanwhile, with little to go on, Detective Inspector Jimmy Nesbitt from the Tennent Street murder squad had no other choice than to release Murphy. Believing that he was guilty of the offence, Nesbitt placed surveillance on the spot where the pistol had been discovered, deducing that Murphy would return to retrieve it.

At 8:15 a.m. the following day, Murphy did indeed return to the scene in a lorry, which he drove for his employer. He was observed by several witnesses searching for something in the garden of No. 27 Lowwood Park, but couldn't find what he was looking for. As he made off in the direction of the Antrim Road he was stopped by an RUC patrol and arrested. Forensics had since returned with a match for the bullets recovered from Mary Murray, and would soon be proven to match the handgun recovered from the Lowwood area.[21] Detectives then began questioning Murphy again about his suspected involvement in the attempted murder. In an interview with Detective Sergeant Wilson, Murphy denied any wrongdoing.

'You must be joking,' Murphy told him. 'I know nothing about any shooting. Chuck [Berry] invited me and Basher up to the Brown Bear for a drink.'

'Who do you work for?'

'Billy Smith, Ballygomartin Road.'

'What were you doing in the Antrim Road area?'

'I was going to the tip head to get tickets from the gateman for dumping rubbish.'

'What direction did you travel after leaving the yard with the lorry on the Ballygomartin Road?'

'I went along Twaddell Avenue onto Crumlin Road, and turned right onto Ballysillan Road and continued onto the Antrim Road.'

'Which way did you go on entering Antrim Road?'

'I turned left and then took a road off to my right. I don't know the name of the road. As I drove along this road I felt as if the back wheel of the lorry was punctured [*sic*] so I turned left at the bottom of this road and left again towards Antrim Road and left the lorry there.'

'Which wheel of the lorry was punctured?'

'I'm not sure but it was one of the back wheels.'

'Are you familiar with the area of the Antrim Road?'

'I know it fairly well but I couldn't tell you the name of the streets.'[22]

A Reserve Constable who was tasked with guarding Murphy recalls the Shankill man telling a forensic expert swabbing his hands for gunshot residue, 'I've washed my hands.' Murphy was then asked if he had been wearing the same coat all day. He said he had. As the forensic expert left the room Murphy turned to the Constable and said, 'That's the first mistake I've made.'

DI Nesbitt and the other detectives, who worked around the clock in the investigation into Murphy's activities, later charged him with the attempted murder of Mary Murray. Lenny Murphy was a proficient gunman, but his hubris would prove to be his downfall. The RUC detectives working on the attempted murder case were well aware of the threat he posed, and were eager to ensure that he was imprisoned before he could do any further damage. One of those on Nesbitt's team was Bill, a detective who, by then, had over ten years of experience in the CID:

> Our investigation finished him. Murphy came from a mixed background. When you talked to him he was intelligent. He explained how the IRA opened fire but loyalists couldn't. [We believed that] … the plan was hatched to abduct the target. There was no noise, no commotion. Later the victim would be reported missing. By then the gang would have taken him away, killed him, then burnt their clothes. Nothing sadistic – who better than a butcher. It was premeditated. Hold him for three days' suffering and then kill him – out of sight, out of mind.[23]

Despite some detectives suspecting Murphy of other offences, including the Crossan and Quinn murders, the only charge they could make stick, for now, was the attempted murder of Mary Murray. It took the jury in the Crumlin Road Court House less than six hours to find Murphy guilty. His personal involvement in the Brown Bear team's campaign of terror was over, for now, but that did not stop the other men involved in the gang from continuing with their murder spree.

With the removal of his close friend, Billy Moore found it hard to come to terms with the enormity of the tasks John Murphy was now handing down to him. The Murphy brothers had clearly seen potential in Moore, but the truth was that, without Lenny Murphy around to provide the controlled aggression necessary to counter-balance his tendency to engage in spontaneous violence, Moore's behaviour became more and more erratic. Moore's participation in the murders finally began to wear him down psychologically. One evening, after drinking for several hours in the Loyalist Club, he decided to rob an Indian takeaway on the Shankill. Pulling a pistol out of his waistband, Moore pointed the gun at a terrified young woman behind the counter. 'You packie bastard,' he snarled, as he reached over the counter and grabbed money from the till.[24] The robbery was impromptu, and demonstrated that Moore was becoming prone to risk-taking. For their part, the UVF Brigade Staff saw an opportunity to bring the group more firmly under its centralised command structure, especially with Lenny Murphy now behind bars. However, their attempts to tighten up internal discipline were about to hit unexpected turbulence with the removal of one of their most senior officers.

★★★

Woodburn Estate, Carrickfergus, 10 a.m., 29 March 1976

Billy Mitchell had been on the run for over six months. He had successfully escaped the clutches of the Security Forces since they made their first swoops on his men on 6 October 1975. In a major operation involving 1,000 troops, 500 uniformed RUC officers and 60 detectives, Castlereagh Interrogation Centre was cleared to make room for the UVF suspects, who were later placed on remand awaiting trial.[25] Word soon reached Mitchell from inside Long Kesh that the Security Forces were actively looking for him. He was told to 'get offside', something he decided to do when he claimed he was shown photographs of him by 'friends in the Police and Military'.[26] Although Mitchell left behind his wife and two young children to go on the run, he nevertheless felt safe in Carrickfergus amongst a growing number of UVF supporters and sympathisers. He even continued to openly socialise in the Royal British Legion in the town, which doubled as his headquarters. At the end of March, Mitchell made a bold decision to retrieve several files he kept stashed in a safe-house on the Woodburn estate. His counter-surveillance tradecraft was good. He rarely stayed in the same safe-house for more than a few nights, and had even gone to the trouble of dying his hair.

Mitchell's luck, however, was soon to run out. On the morning of 29 March 1976, he was sat in his light-blue-coloured Vauxhall Viva car, in a lay-by near the bottom of Pinewood Avenue next to Sunnylands Primary School in Woodburn, when he was spotted by a passing army patrol. It was an enthusiastic Lance Corporal from the Lifeguards who first saw Mitchell, whose name and photograph had been high on the routine 'suspect lists' issued by the police to their military colleagues. Realising that they had potentially one of the highest-ranking UVF officers on their patch, the commander of the Army Land Rover ordered the driver to turn the vehicle around and to intercept the suspect. Mitchell noticed that the patrol had turned, and in response pulled his vehicle out of the lay-by and drove up Pinewood Avenue before hanging a right along Oakwood Road. The soldiers followed suit, but lost him when they were forced in behind a passing coal lorry. A few hundred yards along the road they were surprised to see the suspect's car coming towards them, having made another quick U-turn at Burleigh Drive. The driver of the Land Rover quickly pulled his vehicle across the road to block Mitchell's path. In a desperate bid to escape, the UVF commander drove straight into the side of the Land Rover as he attempted to get around their vehicle.

Hoping to catch the soldiers off-guard, Mitchell immediately jumped out and asked them what was wrong. The patrol commander asked for his name and to produce documentation, which he did. The name he gave was 'Noel Gilmour' of Ballysillan Road, an alias Mitchell had been using for many months. Quickly recognising that the documentation did not match with the man stood in front of him, the soldier ordered his driver to search Mitchell's person and then to search his car. On the floor behind the passenger side seat was a green clip folder, a blue clip folder and a purple receipt book. All these documents clearly pointed to articles that were specific to a terrorist group, namely the UVF. The soldier immediately radioed Carrickfergus RUC station and was requested by the station sergeant to bring Mitchell in for questioning.[27]

At the station, Mitchell again gave the false name. He was charged under Section 10 of the Emergency Provisions Act, processed, relieved of his belongings and taken to a cell, where he was locked up until detectives could question him. At 3:15 p.m. he was visited by Detective Chief Inspector Hylands, who cautioned his prisoner, before informing him that he was investigating the murders of Hugh McVeigh and David Douglas.

Hylands had, by now, established the rough facts of the double murders. He informed Mitchell of how he suspected the senior loyalist had met with members of the East Antrim UVF in the Brown Trout Inn in Carrickfergus to arrange for the digging of a grave, and how he had himself been present when both men were taken to meet their deaths. Mitchell became nervous as DCI Hylands continued filling in the gaps. He denied being party to the killings. 'I am a law-abiding citizen and have always supported the forces of law and order,' he told the Senior Investigating Officer.

The interview terminated at 5:40 p.m. and Mitchell was returned to his cell. Later that evening, Hylands' deputies, Detective Inspector John Wilson and his Detective Sergeant, again interviewed Mitchell. DI Wilson was the first to speak:

'I believe you were present at the scene of that shooting when both men were murdered at Gobbins Road, Islandmagee. You do not have to say anything but it may harm your defence if you say something that can be used in a court of law.'

'I know nothing about it,' replied Mitchell. 'I have told Hylands everything I know.'

'I believe that this murder was committed by the UVF and that, at that time, you were a high-ranking member of the organisation.'

'No, I resigned from that in 1974.'

'When did you rejoin?'

'I am still out of it.'

'When you were arrested this morning, you had documents in your possession which indicates that you are still a high-ranking officer, and I suspect that you are their Intelligence Officer.'

'I know they look bad but I can explain it all.'

'From what I have read you will have difficulty putting an innocent explanation forward for possession of these documents. I will now go through each with you and your replies will be taken down to each.'

The detectives proceeded to question Mitchell for over an hour, painstakingly taking him through his alleged movements at the time of the murders, and the details contained in the folders found in the car that he was driving.

'We will now go through the documents that you had in the car. They were in your possession, weren't they?'

'I agree that they were in my possession, that is all I want to say about them.'

'It appears that you have collected the names of men in the OIRA and the PIRA. Why is that?' The detectives proceeded to show him a small piece of paper.

'I have no comment to make.'

Mitchell continued to deny that he had written any of the documents, or that he was compiling information on possible targets. By now, Mitchell felt under pressure by the line of questioning. He asked the officers if he could smoke. They consented, and threw him a box of matches across the table. Mitchell lit up his pipe and puffed on it furiously.

DI Wilson looked across at Mitchell. It was obvious that neither man was prepared to depart from their entrenched position; one man wishing to get to the truth of UVF violence, and the other tight-lipped about his role in that organisation's campaign of terror.

'I put it to you that Intelligence files would only be compiled and kept by an intelligence officer, and from what I have read it appears that you are an intelligence officer for the UVF. What do you say to that?'

'I am not a member of the UVF.'

The evidence now in police possession told a different story. It was damning. Mitchell had listed suspected PIRA haunts, and provided names and details of Catholic ex-servicemen. He had also listed members of Sinn Féin and many other people suspected of being sympathetic to the republican cause. Some of those on the lists were designated 'Provie activists', and they included ordinary civilians, such as GAA members, as well as training areas thought to have been used by the IRA in the Irish Republic. It was an incredibly detailed dossier. Some of the material, which included maps, had clearly been stolen from the military. The maps detailed areas where explosive devices had been found. Other lists related to SDLP members, defectors from the Irish Republican Social Party (IRSP), a breakaway faction of the Official IRA, as well as republican connections with international terrorists. The detectives were able to prove that all of these documents were meticulously produced by Mitchell on his own typewriter, which he kept at his home.

'It seems to point that you not only typed the papers, but had other intelligence in the same book, for some sinister use,' said the detective.

'There is nothing sinister in it, I just don't want to implicate myself anymore regarding the papers,' Mitchell responded.

When Mitchell was asked why he had the papers in his house, he claimed he was writing a book.

'From my reading of this book it appears that it is a complete dossier on republicanism and Roman Catholics in this country. Is that true?' The detective was now zeroing in on the facts of the matter.

'I don't equate the two,' Mitchell replied.[28]

The next evening, at 8:40 p.m., DI Wilson returned with another detective. They were eager to push him further in order to tell them the exact circumstances that led to the murders of McVeigh and Douglas. Mitchell refused to divulge any information regarding the specifics of the dark secret he and his subordinates shared. Instead, Mitchell changed tact and engaged the detectives in broader structural conditions that had given rise to loyalist paramilitarism a decade earlier. 'When loyalist paramilitary organisations first emerged,' Mitchell told the detectives. They had been 'well-meaning and led by moderate men, but other, more violent men had later taken over and the moderates were relegated to intelligence gathering and welfare and had no say over decisions made'. Mitchell was by now attempting to distance himself from his own role as one of these more violent men. It was a convenient façade, for there were moderates on the UVF Brigade Staff at the time – men like Jim McDonald, the UVF leader in charge of the Loyalist Prisoners' Welfare Association (LPWA) – but Mitchell wasn't one of them. Billy Mitchell was, in fact, the group's Director of Operations and

Intelligence Chief, a role he had more than likely assumed in the wake of the murder of Jim Hanna in April 1974. Mitchell suspected that the police were well-aware of this and so tried to remain calm and to keep his mouth shut. He resolved to put his faith in the *omertà* in the hope that the men below him hadn't implicated him in the murders of the two UDA men in that lonely and secluded part of Islandmagee.

At 10:05 p.m. on 31 March 1976, having refused to break his silence any further, Billy Mitchell was taken to Townhall Street in Belfast, where he was charged by DI Wilson with the murders of Hugh McVeigh and David Douglas. Mitchell replied 'definitely not guilty'. He was remanded in custody, pending his trial.

★★★

Chlorane Bar, Belfast City Centre, 10 p.m., 5 June 1976

It was a warm summer's night on 5 June 1976. Light was fading fast as men laughed and joked in the quiet comfort of the Chlorane Bar in Gresham Street. Samuel Corr, a fifty-three-year-old joiner and married man, was passing the evening in the company of sixty-four-year-old James Coyle, the landlord and a married man, Edward Farrell, a forty-five-year-old Merchant Seaman and married man, and Daniel McNeill, a forty-seven-year-old machinist and married man, were also in the bar at the time. John Martin, a fifty-eight-year-old bachelor and scaffolder by trade, was also enjoying passing the evening with a drink in the bar.

On the Shankill, the UVF leadership had hatched a plan to retaliate after an IRA attack on the Time Bar in North Belfast. Two teams, drawn from the Windsor Bar and Brown Bar, were tasked with carrying out the attack by the military commander of the UVF in West Belfast. As the UVF men clambered into a black taxi in Mansfield Street, they loaded and checked their weapons and then drove the short distance down the Shankill Road and over Peter's Hill into North Street before turning right into Gresham Street. The taxi pulled up outside the Chlorane Bar as the gunmen pulled on their masks and got out. Adrenaline ran high amongst the gunmen. Some of the men were drunk. Others, who hadn't taken nearly as much alcohol, started to get very nervous.

The jovial atmosphere inside the Chlorane Bar was quickly interrupted by a gunman, who came barging into the bar with a yellow cloth bag over his head. There were three holes cut out for his mouth and eyes, which made him look simultaneously ridiculous and yet menacing. 'Where's the prods and where's the Catholics? Is there any Prods here?' the man barked. Bitterness seeped through his every word. He was joined by other gunmen. 'I'm a Prod,' replied one man. 'I'm a Catholic,' replied another.[29] One of the patrons who had been sat at the other end of the bar realised what was happening, and promptly got up to make a move towards the toilet at the back of the bar, from which two men emerged. Seeing the gunmen at the front door, they quickly tried to turn back to the toilets. 'Come back here. Where youse going?' shouted the lead gunman. They refused, and continued walking, which elicited a swift response from the gunman, who fired at them. It was at this point that the other gunmen followed suit. 'Everyone started to fire, then,' recalled one of the gunmen, Robert 'Basher' Bates. His own gun jammed, but not before he shot the landlord, James Coyle. Realising that he had a stoppage, Bates cocked the working parts of the automatic back and pulled the trigger again. Nothing happened. He couldn't clear the round from the chamber. The volume of fire was continuous and unrelenting. The man who led the team was a commander in the Windsor Bar team, another one of Lenny Murphy's fiercest rivals.[30] The commander screamed 'That's it', and all the men ran back out to the taxi. By now the driver had turned the taxi around and was facing in the direction of North Street. As the men boarded to return to the Shankill Road, they were in high spirits. They had accomplished the job they had been set by the UVF hierarchy.

When they reached the safety of the Shankill, the driver parked the taxi up in Beresford Street, which ran between Albany Street and Agnes Street. The men inside got out and walked across to the Long Bar. Once inside, Bates informed the man who had led the attack and his second-in-command that his gun had jammed. When Bates walked outside he was greeted by another man, who told him to follow. Both men walked across to the back of the Windsor Bar, where he took the gun from Bates. After fiddling with the weapon for a few minutes, he pulled the working parts back several times to clear the stoppage and pulled the trigger. It fired. When Bates got back to the Long Bar, where he worked, another man set up a 40oz bottle of vodka for the man who led the attack on the Chlorane Bar and his deputy. 'It was their payment for doing this job,' Bates later told police.

Meanwhile, back at the scene of the crime, the UVF gunmen had left a trail of death and destruction. The result of their hail of bullets was devastating. Men had fallen where only moments earlier they had stood, quietly sipping their pints. Others slumped over onto their seats, the air knocked out of their lungs by the sustained crack and thump made by the bullets that had hurtled through the air, shattering everything in their wake. One eyewitness gave the following account of the events that had unfolded:

> I did not see any other gunmen behind me, but I was aware there was more than one. When the shooting started [name redacted] got down on the floor and shouted to me to get down. When the shooting stopped I got up and asked [name redacted] could he not get up, and he said 'No. I've been hit on the legs.' I looked around and saw the security man lying on the floor under the table. Mr McNeill was lying slumped over, and the fellow next to him was lying slumped over too. I saw other people lying about too. I told [name redacted] to be quiet and stay where he was and not to move, and went up to try and use the phone beside the bar. When I got up there I saw the barman Mr Coyle lying dead. I decided to go outside to get help. When I got to the door a girl shouted down the stairs: 'What's wrong.' I told her there were people lying around dead and she asked me about Mr Coyle, and I told her he was dead. [Name redacted] who was upstairs came down to help. [Name redacted] used the phone to call for help. I stayed with [name redacted] until the police and ambulance arrived. A policeman told me to go outside because I was shocked. The only description I can give of the gunman is he was about 6' tall, heavy built and wearing light-coloured trousers. He had a light-coloured hood on, with slits for his eyes and nose. I did not see any of the other gunmen. The gunman I saw had a small automatic gun, black [in] colour. I was not injured in the shooting, but on Sunday I found two bullet holes in the bottom of my right trouser leg and two bullet holes in my cap.[31]

It was around 10:06 p.m. when the RUC received a call to alert them that an armed robbery was in progress in the city centre. A few minutes after the attack, a police Special Patrol Group (SPG) unit from nearby Tennent Street arrived on the scene.

As the officers dismounted from their vehicle, they were greeted by scenes of utter carnage. The barmaid who had survived the attack reported that the gunmen had fled. The dead lay all around, motionless, while the injured wrestled with their bodies and cried out in pain. Other victims were unresponsive. Blood splatter was everywhere. 'Inside the bar I saw eleven people, eight of whom appeared to have been wounded. We all then attended to the wounded, dying and dead until the arrival of other police and ambulance,' recalled one of the RUC officers.[32] A civilian eyewitness told the SPG commander that 'there had been three raiders all of them dressed in dark clothes'. Some of the victims had been shot in the head, others in the chest and a few others in their legs, suggesting they had been hit by ricochets, or that at least two of the gunmen had deliberately aimed low.

'Basher' Bates would later explain to the police about the plan to launch the attack on the Chlorane Bar. He was keen to emphasise that it was carried out on the spur of the moment:

> When I was in [name redacted], I heard on the news that the Times Bar on York Road had been blown up and people had been killed. When I returned to the Long Bar to carry out work, I was approached by [name redacted] known as [name redacted]. He told me that I was to take part in a job in retaliation for the bombing of the Times Bar. He told me to stand by. [Name redacted] then left the bar, and a short time later, when he came back, I was standing along with [name redacted], [name redacted], [name redacted] and [name redacted]. [Name redacted], at that time the Battalion Commander in the UVF and [name redacted] who was the Provost Marshall in the UVF, were also along with us. [Name redacted], who was a Military Commander in the UVF, told us that we were to hit the Chlorane Bar in Smithfield. We all went over to the Windsor Bar. [Name redacted] arranged to get the masks. He handed me one. It was a yellow-coloured money bag with holes for the eyes in it. [Name redacted] arranged to get the guns. He arranged to get one from the Lawnbrook Club. This turned out to be a snub nosed .45 revolver. He got another .45 revolver from the Loyalist Club. [Name redacted] had his own 9mm pistol and a .22 pistol. [Name redacted] took the .22 pistol. There was [sic] two .38 revolvers in the Windsor Bar at the time, but they had no ammunition for them. I was given one of the snub nosed .45 revolvers. Somebody else in the Windsor Bar had ammunition, and they loaded both .45 revolvers.[33]

It would appear from Bates's statement that this attack was sanctioned from the very top of the UVF, unlike other operations carried out by the Brown Bear team whenever Lenny Murphy had been assisting in its leadership.

Bates's own personal motivations for engaging in the Chlorane Bar attack were more complicated than even he would admit under caution. After claiming that the Windsor Bar team were 'the most feared unit in the Shankill area', he said he was caught in a catch-22 scenario. 'This was another situation that was impossible for me to refuse to carry out orders. I had no choice but to do what I was told, as reprisals would have been taken against me or my family,' he added.[34] Yet, it seems that he was willing to go along, as his statement also indicated, because the UVF hierarchy's justification for the attack was directly attributable to the IRA's attack on a Protestant bar on the York Road. Like others, he sought to minimise his involvement and thereby shield himself from the legal categorisation of the attack as pre-meditated murder, while also distancing himself from the horror he had unleashed on the unsuspecting customers in Belfast city centre. 'The next morning I read in the *Sunday News* that some men had been killed in the bar. I'm not sure how many, I think it was four,' he said.[35]

It is accepted by some sociologists and psychologists that to kill another human being is difficult, especially when it comes to killing at close range. In *On Killing*, perhaps one of the most influential books on the subject of what motivates human beings to kill, how killing is done and what impact this has on perpetrators, Dave Grossman writes: 'At close range the resistance to killing an opponent is tremendous. When one looks an opponent in the eye, and knows that he is young or old, scared or angry, it is not possible to deny that the individual about to be killed is much like oneself.'[36] It stands to reason that without Murphy there to lead them, Moore, Bates and the others in the Brown Bear team were not as proficient in the act of killing as they were when he was present. In working-class areas at that time alcohol was the most readily available means of anaesthetising those individuals who were being forced by paramilitary groups to perpetrate murders they would not have normally carried out. Yet, when mixed with hatred, peer pressure and the UVF code of *omertá*, which bound the men in its ranks to a tight disciplinary structure, alcohol would prove a deadly intoxicator. Incredibly, even after engaging in the act of killing at close quarters, Moore and the other members of the Brown Bear team would return to the everyday pattern of working and socialising as if nothing had happened. It created a close bond between the killer gang – one that would prove difficult to break. An added dimension in all of this was the role of John Murphy, who instilled so rigid a loyalty in the men around him that they followed him as much in fear as in loathing.[37]

***

New Lodge Road, North Belfast, 11:45 p.m., 1 August 1976

Forty-eight-year-old Cornelius Neeson was making his way home from St Kevin's Hall in the New Lodge, not far from St Patrick's chapel in Little Donegal Street. Con was a well-liked man in the local community, and gave up his spare time to help out at the bingo nights. Upon making his way up the Cliftonville Road and arriving at the junction with Manor Street, he was savagely beaten to the ground by 'Big Sam' McAllister, a member of the Brown Bear team, who stood over six-foot tall and weighed over sixteen stone.[38] He had been brandishing a hatchet. The blows from the weapon that struck Con were so deep and severe that the blood clotted as it ran out of his motionless body and down a nearby sewage drain. Scattered next to the large pool of blood were freshly made lettuce and tomato sandwiches that Con had been carrying home. One eyewitness recalled driving up the Cliftonville Road from the direction of the Antrim Road. As he approached, a youth with long fair hair ran across the road. He also saw three other men standing over the body of Cornelius Neeson. Realising that something was out of place, he turned around and drove back the way he had come, where he found the body by the footpath.[39] The police and military arrived not long after the call went out of a serious assault. Soldiers attempted to apply first aid until the ambulance arrived. Con, however, had suffered a serious blow to the head and was unconscious. Despite the best efforts of medical staff at the RVH, Cornelius Neeson died on the operating table at 2:45 a.m.

8

'THAT BASTARD MURPHY'

'No society could get itself into such a mess without a majority of its population being involved – not through their deeds but through words and attitudes that create an atmosphere conducive to hatred, suspicion and revenge. It would be dishonest and ultimately unhelpful to ignore this harsh fact.'

Dervla Murphy, *A Place Apart* (1978)[1]

Loyalist Club, Rumford Street, 10 p.m., 31 January 1977

'I'm away down here kid. I'll see you about,' said thirty-year-old James Curtis Moorehead, a member of the Shankill Road UDA. Moorehead stood at 5'7" in height and was well-built, with dark curly hair and a moustache. That evening he was dressed in dark trousers with a fine stripe running down them. He wore a blue and white-striped shirt, over which he sported a waistcoat jacket and a shirt. Braces held up his trousers, under which he wore a pair of zipped-up platform boots.[2] He looked like a Bay City Roller. Moorehead stuck out that evening, not only because of the way he was dressed, but because of his dark, swarthy skin. He happened, also, to be despised by members of the Brown Bear team. 'There's your man, the nigger,' one man said to the other three standing beside him in the Loyalist Club. Moorehead passed them as he headed into the toilets. One of the men at the bar went after him. A commotion ensued – the man who had followed Moorehead into the gents grabbed and held him in a headlock. Moorehead struggled, but couldn't free himself. The other men soon joined their comrade. They were armed with a spanner and a knife. One of the men was told to wait outside the toilet as the other two went to work on their victim:

I saw Nigger [the derogatory way the members of the gang referred to Moorehead] lying on the floor and there was blood everywhere. He was lying on his stomach with his head a bit to the side. I was handed the big spanner and told to hit Nigger with it. I hit him one blow which I think hit him on the shoulder. Altogether four of us hit Nigger to make sure we were all in it. We all came out of the toilet and closed the door leaving Nigger on the floor. I knew he was dead at this time.[3]

The men ordered the bar to close and Moorehead's body was dragged outside. It was left there for several minutes before being taken outside to the backyard. 'Somebody told me that Nigger's real name was Moorehead, and that he lived in East Belfast,' one of the men involved later admitted. The orchestrator of the attack then ordered his men to take the body to Carlisle Circus and dump it in waste ground. Moorehead's body was discovered on 31 January in Adela Street. He had suffered a fractured skull and multiple lacerations to the head. The Brown Bear team had murdered Moorehead in an altercation that had nothing to do with politics or rivalry with the UDA, at least not directly. They then disposed of his body. Their blood was up, and they were anxious to find another victim.

***

Not long after the attack on Moorehead, the Brown Bear team were back in action. This time they were on the lookout for another Catholic, and so took their well-worn route down into the city centre. 'I'm originally from Carrick Hill,' 'Trevor' said, as he recalled an incident in which he was chased through the streets of Belfast by a black taxi. 'People there referred to Turf Lodge as "the reservation".' It was given the nickname because there was a feeling that it was 'out in the country', being situated outside inner city Belfast. 'It looked like something from hillbilly country.'[4] Even though it sat beyond what were fast becoming interface areas and was, consequently, relatively safe and self-contained, the people who lived there still had to occasionally venture out of the estate for recreational purposes, to socialise and shop in the city centre, and to work. Trevor grew up watching cowboy movies on TV. He imagined Turf Lodge to be what people said it was: a reservation, that is, a frontier nested on the western outskirts of Belfast. By the time he reached adolescence, he realised that it was just not other working-class Catholics who saw him differently, but also Protestants. 'Fuck me, I'm not the cowboy, I'm the Indian. That kind'a freaked me out,' he joked. 'It would have made you wary of going into Protestant areas. I was always wary of going in and around Protestant areas.' His friends often encouraged him to say that his name was 'Billy'.

Trevor had just turned seventeen when he started to venture down from Turf Lodge into the city centre to attend discos. Young Catholics, he said, were always very wary of being beaten up by Tartan gangs, who roamed the streets late at night looking for victims. 'You were experimenting and that's when it really got serious. You had to have your wits about you, because around about then – I mean, there was always assassinations and stuff like that – you were always wary of people driving cars. It was then that you recognised there was a serious atmosphere in the city, and that you had to be on guard all the time.' Given the city's sectarian geography, local people soon became intuitive about where they could and could not go. At night, though, nowhere was safe. Trevor recalled:

> Because we were underage we went to places where they didn't know us, and one of the places that we went to for a drink was the New Lodge. We used to have to get a black taxi into town and walk across – walk across Millfield, walk across Union Street. You couldn't walk across Millfield, so you would'a walked across Union Street out into Donegal Street, opposite the *Irish News* [offices], and then up Donegal Street and across North Queen Street, past the police station and into the New Lodge.[5]

By 1977 this route home was considered to be one of the most dangerous in the entire city, especially as news emerged of how the throat-cutting murderers had actually come into contact with their victims.

> You were avoiding the Shankill. So, if you were walking across Millfield, there was always the opportunity that a gang would come running out of Brown Square. So, at night, you avoided walking across Millfield, especially if you were on your own, because you would more than likely get jumped if you were on your own. So, there was always gangs of people hanging around, trying to pick up Catholics who were walking home on their own, because Catholics would be coming from Hamill Street, John Street, those areas ... Carrick Hill would have been the Catholic area ... You could have been coming from your mummy's or your granny's or your auntie's, you know that kind of 'networking routine' – so to avoid being seen you went in round and through

Gresham Street across into Union Street. And that would have been considered a more Catholic area, and the streets were all blocked off and they used to close the gates.[6]

Having this kind of local knowledge certainly helped young Catholic men and women navigate the city's 'political geography' in such a way as to avoid coming into contact with 'the other side' – yet it wasn't a full-proof guarantee of safety, especially at night.

That evening, as Trevor crossed another type of reservation, he was conscious of a black taxi following him as he walked along the street. As he crossed over, the taxi slowed down. The hairs on the back of his neck stood on end, as adrenalin was slowly released into his body. He became increasingly nervous. The taxi got closer, then stopped across the street. Several men jumped out. 'From my memory it would have been very, very spontaneous. It wouldn't have been "Right, we're going to get [Trevor] on Friday night at 7 o'clock." They would have known that that was the routes that Catholics would have used and that's why Union Street was a particular favourite place for them. Because a lot of Catholics there would have been drunk and staggering home at night. That's the way they would have come.' As more adrenalin was released into his body, he knew the situation was life-threatening and, rather than freeze, he took flight and ran away as fast as he could.

This was not the last time Trevor would encounter the Brown Bear UVF gang. On the afternoon of 10 April, as he walked along Beechmount Avenue to watch the annual Easter Rising commemorative parade, he was caught in an explosion that blew him off his feet. The smoke from the explosion added to the confusion as people fainted, screamed or other ran off in different directions. Trevor was thrown into a doorway by the force of the blast. He had not been far from the seat of the explosion, and was lucky to have been sheltered by the brickwork of the doorway. When he came around, he saw a young boy lying still in the middle of the road, dressed in a blue anorak and blue jumper with a little pattern of different colours around the bottom of it. The boy was also wearing a pair of blue trousers and brown shoes. The boy's name was Kevin McMenamin, and he was eight years old. One of Kevin's friends said that the boys had decided to visit a relative's house to collect Easter eggs:

The parades were on that day and I wanted to see the bands. We all walked along the street to the corner. I was passing the wee bakery shop that's now closed down. I heard a loud bang. I don't remember anything else, but that a man then came up to me and lifted me up off the ground and put me in the ambulance. He asked me my name and I gave it to him and also where I lived. I was taken to the big Royal Hospital. I had my right leg off from just under my knee. I'm wearing a pylon now and I'm waiting on my new limb. Some metal went into my tummy and I had to have some stitches – seven stitches. I was in hospital for six or seven weeks. I also had three stitches in my left hand, the top part. I had some cuts in my face too. My left leg was also burned and the District Nurse came round to see me after I left the hospital to dress my burns, for a couple of weeks. I also had a hole on the top part of my right thigh. I had to have two stitches in my bum. I went to the Musgrave Park Hospital after I came out of the Royal Hospital for a while for some treatment. I don't remember anything about the explosion except the bang that I heard.[7]

It was not long before the army arrived at the scene and carried out a controlled explosion on a suspect car. The army's Ammunition Technical Officer in charge of the scene saw a blue plastic bag on the rear seat, which had parts of a clock, a battery and gas cylinder inside. The device was attached to between three and five pounds of commercial explosive.[8]

It later transpired that the bomb attack had been proposed to the UVF's Brigade Staff by Mr A, who was subsequently given the green light to go ahead with the operation.[9] One of the Brown Bear team who participated in the attack explained how the attack arose:

The day before the Provisional IRA had their march from Beechmount Avenue I was approached by a man while I was drinking, and he told me to see him about 11 o'clock that night. He said there was a bombing job on for the next day, Easter Sunday. He said we were going to hit the Provos hard. I said alright. I met him and other people that night, but I don't want to say where. We went up to a place at the top of the Shankill. There was a green van there. After a while I saw two men putting a steel barrel with the bomb in it in the back of the van. They shut the doors then. I got into the front seat beside the driver and a boy got into the back and was holding the barrel steady. We went into Ainsworth Avenue well into the morning, but I'm not too sure of the time. There was a Cortina in front of us with two men in it. They were making sure there was nobody about. It stayed in front of us the whole way down. We turned left down the Springfield and turned down a street past Mackies. There was a chip shop on the corner. The car was in front of us. We went over three or four ramps. We went down a long street and the driver said 'This is it here'. The car was stopped about forty yards ahead. I got out and walked round and opened the back doors. I gave him a hand down with the barrel. We put it down beside other barrels. There was something like a big factory where we left it. I ran round and got into the van. The boy jumped in the back and closed the doors. We went down the street, and then on to the Falls and then up the Springfield. We went on up the Shankill and met a man. He said, 'was everything alright' and we said, 'Yes'. We left the van back. We had a couple of beers in somebody's house and I went home. I was in bed the next day when I heard a bang. It was about a quarter to three or three o'clock. I seen it in the news that night about the bomb. It was the Provisionals we were after.[10]

Panic ensued in the aftermath of the explosion, as the two wings of the IRA blamed each other for the bomb. Further along the parade at Milltown Cemetery, guns were produced by the two factions, and one man was killed in the gun battle that followed.

The UVF team responsible for the bombing, nevertheless, were safely back in the Shankill where they contemplated their next move.

$$\star\star\star$$

Antrim Road, North Belfast, Evening, 10 May 1977

Twenty-year-old labourer Gerard Arthur McLaverty was making his way along the Cliftonville Road to the Simon Community building on the Antrim Road, when he noticed a yellow Cortina that sat facing up the road. Two men were in the front. Two others standing nearby approached him. One of the men was about 6-foot tall and fat. 'Hello sir. I am a CID officer from Tennent Street. We would like you to accompany us to the station,' said the fat man, as he produced an ID card. Before Gerard could ask why he had been stopped, the fat man thrust a gun into his back and walked him over to the car. He was bundled into the back seat and held down. The driver did a U-turn in the street, took a right at the junction onto the

Antrim Road. A few minutes later they were at Carlisle Circus, where the driver took a right turn onto the Crumlin Road, passing the Mater Hospital and making his way along Cambria Street, before turning down onto the Shankill Road. No one spoke during the journey.

When the car came to a halt, Gerard was dragged out of the vehicle and into a derelict building. The room was dark. A light was switched on. The men lifted Gerard onto a chair in the middle of the threadbare room. Two electric heaters blew hot air into the room. He recalled what happened next:

> The fat man and the car driver went behind this counter, and came back each of them with a stick. The stick the fat man had had a nail driven through the end of it. Both of them started beating me around the head with the sticks. I put my hands up to protect my eyes, as I was afraid of the nail that was sticking through the fat man's stick piercing my eyes. The fat man said, 'Get your fucking hands down or we'll give you some more'. I started to squeal with fear and pain, and they stopped beating me. They had a teapot and kettle and the driver of the car went and made tea. The fat man asked me did I want tea, and I refused. I said I wanted to go home. The fat man said, 'You're not going home there's no way you're getting out of this'. They sat and drank their tea. I was sitting in the corner and they were sitting watching me. When they had finished their tea, they put their cups away and came back to me again. The driver punched me on the side of the face and eye and knocked me to the floor. He then took his heel and drove it into the side of my face. They sat me back up on the chair again, and the driver of the car took the lace out of my right boot. He gave it to the fat man and then he held my hands behind my back. The fat man went behind me and tied the lace loosely round my neck. Throughout all this, the other two men never touched me. They stayed at one of the two doors in the room. When the lace had been tied loosely round my neck those other two men who hadn't touched me left and locked the door from the outside. The fat man and the car driver had broken open the other door before the other two left. When I was alone with the fat man and the car driver, they took me out this door which led into an entry. The yellow Cortina car was in the street at the end of the entry. At this time the fat man had a knife. It was a large clasp knife. The driver started slashing my clothes with

the knife. With the tightening of the lace I lost consciousness. When I came to I was still lying in the entry. There was a crowd of people round me and an ambulance, and I was taken to the Royal Victoria Hospital. I saw that both my wrists were severely slashed and my neck was sore and swollen.[11]

Gerard McLaverty survived this brutal ordeal and was taken into protective custody. On 18 May he was given a disguise and taken by detectives along the Shankill Road, where he pointed out the men who had attacked him.

★★★

Castlereagh RUC Station, East Belfast, 19–23 May 1977

After the positive identification of McLaverty's assailants, detectives at Tennent Street put in place a plan to swoop on all members of the Brown Bear team. Police officers came for Billy Moore on 19 May 1977. In a dawn raid on his home, he was arrested under Section 12 of the new Prevention of Terrorism Act (1976), and taken to Castlereagh RUC Station. He was fingerprinted and processed, then locked in a cell before being brought out into an interview room for long hours of interrogation.

Like other members of his UVF unit rounded up by the RUC that day, Moore prefaced all his remarks to detectives by denying that he had played any role whatsoever in the murders he was accused of committing. When asked by Detective Sergeant William Stockdale about his suspected involvement in killings, Moore casually protested his innocence, stating curtly that he had 'nothing to do with them'. At one point he even went as far as to pin the blame for the murders on the UFF's C Company, which was based in the Lower Shankill at the time and boasted two experienced operators in its ranks, Kenny McClinton and John White. A founder member of C Company, White had engaged in throat cutting in the early 1970s, when he murdered thirty-nine-year-old Senator Paddy Wilson, an SDLP politician, and his twenty-nine-year-old friend Irene Andrews. Detectives considered then rejected the lead that he and other members of the UDA were involved. McClinton, a much more violent and calculating man, was still at large when Moore and his gang were arrested. The UFF commander was finally picked up on 27 August 1977, only showing a willingness to confess to the murder of two men that year, though he boasted his involvement in others. McClinton later gave his own cryptic insight into his past actions, telling detectives that he had once proposed to his boss in the UDA, James Pratt Craig, that the UFF 'should behead Catholics and impale their heads on the railings of Woodvale Park'.[12] Talk of beheading Catholics stayed at just that for McClinton, but not, as it would quickly emerge, for members of the Brown Bear team, which included Billy Moore.

DI Jimmy Nesbitt soon arrived at Castlereagh to interrogate Moore in more detail. It was not long before he got him to open up and admit his role in his team's actions.

'I was the driver when the man was done at the corner of Manor Street. I think his name was Neeson,' Moore told Nesbitt.

'Go on,' the seasoned detective urged.

'I drove over to the Cliftonville Road. I stopped the car in Manor Street and the two fellows with me got out and waited. They saw the man coming up and they knocked the ballacks out of him.'

'And then what did you do?' Nesbitt inquired further.

One night about the beginning of August last year – as far as I can remember it was a Sunday night – I was drinking with two fellows in the club. Later on, when the club was closed, we had a bit of a chat and decided to go out and get a Taig and give him a digging. It was decided I would go and get a black taxi and drive us to do the job. I went to someone I know and I asked him for the lend of his black taxi. I didn't tell him what it was for. The other fellows were with me when I got the taxi. They got in and I drove down the Crumlin Road and turned into Manor Street. It had been said that if someone was got walking on the Cliftonville Road he would be a Taig. I drove along Manor Street to the end at the Cliftonville Road. We saw a man walking up the Cliftonville Road. He was on his own, just dandering along. There was no one else about. The other two fellows got out of the taxi and stood on the corner of Manor Street, and waited until the man got up to them. They whaled him and knocked him down, and got stuck into him. They kicked the lights out of him. They kicked him for a couple of minutes. I swung the car round on the Cliftonville Road and faced back up Manor Street. The two fellows got back into the taxi and I drove back along Manor Street. I drove back up to the club and we got out of the taxi. The other two took it back to the man that owned it, and I got my own motor at the club and drove home.

The next morning I heard on the news on the wireless that the man we had done had been found at the corner of Manor Street and that he had died in the Mater Hospital. There was [*sic*] no guns or anything in this job. It was just a digging.[13]

Moore was lying. Moore always lied. He could not distinguish the truth from his lies anymore. His involvement in the Brown Bear team murders had eaten away at the last strips of moral fibre in his body. He asked for time to think things over. He was afraid of what John Murphy and others would do to him. The fear of breaking the UVF's *omertà* made his mind race.

On the third day of questioning, Moore sat motionless in the interrogation room in Castlereagh RUC Station as he recalled in detail his involvement in the murder of Thomas Quinn. He had again been cautioned by DI John Joseph Fitzsimmons that he 'did not have to say anything but it may harm your defence if you later rely on in court'. By now Moore was past caring. He had been broken down by the RUC's systematic approach to interrogation. His dishevelled appearance did little to bring out any semblance of humanity left in the man. He remained defiant. The murder squad would have to work hard to get him to confess on his own volition. By the early evening, DI Nesbitt had returned to question Moore further. He entered the interview room flanked by his sergeants. Fitzsimmons introduced his colleague, before Nesbitt launched straight into another line of questioning, informing Moore that he was also making enquiries into the murder of Francis Dominic Rice, whose body was found in an entry off Mayo Street on 22 February 1976. The policeman told Moore that the victim's throat had been cut. 'I had nothing to do with it,' replied Moore. He spoke abruptly, by now settling into a well-worn routine of denying his involvement. Nesbitt then told Moore that he was also investigating five other murders, all of which had the same *modus operandi*. Again, Moore denied any involvement. 'They're nothing to do with me. I've only seen them on TV. I've never discussed them with anyone else nor has anyone ever mentioned them to me,' he protested.

Realising that Moore was intent on remaining uncooperative, Nesbitt tried another angle.

'Are you employed as a butcher?' he asked Moore.

'When I worked at Woodvale Meats one of the men I worked with had shown me how to do the job and let me help him.'

'Have you any butchers' knives at home?'

'I've never had any knives at home.'

Nesbitt eyeballed his suspect, searching for any sign of weakness, before continuing.

'You've admitted involvement in the attack on Mr Gerard McLaverty, and that you were the driver in that incident. The circumstances of that crime are identical with the details of the murders we are questioning you about. All the men killed had been walking alone at night in the Cliftonville/ Antrim Road/Donegall Street/Millfield area. All had been abducted at the same time and were taken into a car and driven to a secluded area where they were killed,' said Nesbitt.

Nesbitt then put it to Moore that the RUC had carried out extensive enquiries into these murders and, as a direct result, that they had reason to believe he was intimately involved. Moore became agitated. 'Look,' he told Nesbitt, 'I was never involved in any jobs with a knife. I couldn't do that sort of thing.'

The policemen then switched tact again. 'Are you a member of the UVF?' he asked Moore.

'Not really, I just drive them wherever they want to go.'[14]

The interview terminated a short while after. Moore was returned to his cell. Less than twenty-four hours later, he was back in the interview room for questioning. Yet again, he protested his innocence.

After refusing a harsh line of questioning, Moore finally had a change of heart at lunchtime on 21 May 1977.

'Wait, I want to see you.'

'Why?'

'I can help you.'

[At this stage two detectives walk the suspect back to the interview room.]

'Well?'

'I know about the throat cuttings.'

'I would like to remind you that you're still under caution Mr Moore,' said Detective Sergeant John Scott. 'What do you know about them?'

'I don't know what to do. I'm scared. I want time to think this over.'

'You can have time to think it over,' replied the second detective.

'I'm scared. I don't know what to do. Will youse two see me again?'

'Yes, think it over in your cell and we will see you after tea.' Moore was returned to his cell at 1.30pm. At 7.35pm he was brought back into the interview room.

'Have you had plenty of time to think it over?' inquired Detective Sergeant Scott.

'Yes.'

'What do you want to tell us about the cut throat murders?'

'I am involved in them all.'

'Did you do any of the slashings yourself?' inquired Detective Constable John McCawl.

'Murphy done the first three and I done the rest,' replied Moore.

'Why did you do the rest?' Scott asked him.

'It was on Murphy's instructions, when Murphy was in jail.'

'What do you mean?'

'To take the suspicion off Murphy,' said Moore, as he broke down in tears. 'It was that bastard Murphy led me into all this,' he told the detectives. 'I had to carry on to take the pressure off him ... That bastard Murphy, that bastard Murphy, that bastard Murphy ... My heads away with it ...'[15]

Moore was visibly shaken as he spoke to the detectives about his involvement in a catalogue of grisly murders. At first it didn't appear that he had any intention of confessing to his involvement in the murder spree. Moore was, after all, a seasoned terrorist before the age of thirty. 'Do you think I'm wise?' he repeatedly asked detectives from the regional crime squad as they interrogated him over three long days at Castlereagh. It was clear from Moore's erratic behaviour during questioning that the UVF man had something weighing heavily on his mind. To the team of detectives who sat opposite him in the interview room, this was a secret that their prime suspect was not ready to reveal without putting up at least some resistance.

There was a lot troubling Billy Moore the day he broke during questioning by police. It might have been the shame of what he had done that finally nudged him towards confessing his part in one of the most notorious series of serial killings of the late twentieth century. Journalist Martin Dillon, who wrote the most comprehensive book on the so-called 'Shankill Butchers' gang, doubts whether Moore had a conscience at all.[16] He believes the Shankill man had something akin to a bloodlust, and enjoyed the thrill of the kill. There is considerable evidence to suggest that Moore was more concerned with the code of *omertà* that governed the UVF than the pang of guilt concerning what he and his team were involved in during the mid-1970s. Whatever the factor which gave rise to his eventual confession, Moore was clearly afraid of the consequences of revealing the names of his accomplices, particularly Mr A and John Murphy, the two men in control of the unit. Deep down, even in the darker recesses of his mind, Moore knew that he risked the wrath of the UVF being turned on his elderly mother once he entered the prison system. He had to resist the urge to fill in the details of who was actually responsible for these crimes, no matter what his conscience told him to do.

Up until the point at which he finally broke down, Moore showed no signs whatsoever of disclosing any information to detectives. Although there was little formal training in anti-interrogation techniques at the time, Moore's UVF unit were not prepared to willingly give up any information. As his interviews drew to a close, Moore would only go as far as to give the detectives short, cryptic answers when asked about specific details relating to the charges levelled against him. 'You'll be sending for me when I'm in prison,' he told detectives in his final interview. When asked why, all he would say was 'I just know', and left it at that.

At the conclusion of the interview, Moore was arrested by Nesbitt and charged with the murder of Francis Rice. Moore looked forlorn. 'I was there, I didn't kill him,' he told the detective.[17] He was returned to his cell.

The more time he spent in his cell, the more he reflected on what he had told detectives. On 23 May he asked to see DI Nesbitt. 'I just wanted to see you about a mistake I made the other night when I told you about the man Neeson that was killed,'[18] he told the RUC officers. Moore had come to change his statement, wishing to revise the number of people involved in the Neeson murder.

> I just wanted to see you to clear up a mistake about the murder I told you about on Thursday night, the man Neeson. It happened just much as I said, except that there was just two of us, me and Sam [McAllister]. I made a mistake when I said there was two other fellows with me. I didn't sit in the motor the way I said. I got out and gave the man a digging too. Sam hit him with the hatchet, I just kicked him. When Sam hit him over the head with the hatchet, I just kicked him. When Sam hit him over the head with the hatchet, he knocked him to the ground. When the man was lying there Sam hit him about two or three times, and I kicked him and gave him a doing. That's all, the rest of it about the motor and that was right.[19]

It is entirely plausible that Moore changed his story because he feared retribution by an accomplice he had inadvertently implicated in the murder. With Lenny Murphy inside, the killing of Mervyn Connor must have also weighed heavily on his mind, as it did the mind of Geordie Anthony when he refused to divulge the name of his accomplices in the McVeigh and Douglas murders some months earlier.

When he was initially questioned about his involvement in the murder, Sam McAllister denied that he was even there. He told Detective Constable Philip Boyd, 'It wasn't me.' Twenty-four hours later, having had time to mull it over in his cell, he made a full statement to DI Fitzsimmons and Detective Sergeant James Reid, admitting his guilt:

> One Sunday night, it was the 1st August last year, about half ten or a quarter to eleven or maybe later. I was out in a car with another fellow who I don't wish to say. We drove down Manor Street towards the Cliftonville Road. We were looking for a Taig for a kicking. We stopped the car in Manor Street near the Cliftonville Road. There was a hatchet in the car, and I took it with me and got out and stood round the corner on the Cliftonville Road on the same side as Manor Street. He walked past me across the mouth of Manor Street. I walked after him, I hit him on the back of the head with the wooden part of the hatchet and he went down. I then hit [him] with the hatchet. I hit him about twice when he was down. The other fellow with me came over but didn't hit him. We then ran to the car and drove away. We knew he was a Taig because he was walking up there. It was only meant to give him a digging. He was not meant to be killed. I don't wish to name the other fellow. I think drink was the biggest cause of this.[20]

Although journalist Martin Dillon has exposed how Moore, McAllister and Bates were well read on the law and used that knowledge to distance themselves from their crimes, these statements also reveal how the men were prepared to remain silent due to fear of retaliation if they talked. Above all else, however, these statements tell us something about the dynamics of the Murphy gang, in its demand for adhering to the code of *omertá*. This presaged the need for obedience to authority and loyalty, which, within the team itself, reflected a form of esoteric militarism engendered in the broader ranks of UVF at this time.[21]

Meanwhile, detectives were having trouble getting Bates to talk. Although DI Nesbitt had brought him up from his cell for questioning, Bates refused to admit his involvement in the Rice murder, or even his membership of the UVF. He also refused to divulge the names of anyone else involved for, he claimed, 'I would be afraid for my own life or my family's', although he did admit to the detectives that he had helped a 'fellow' 'lift him in to the taxi' and later 'helped the others to take the man out of the taxi and down the entry, between Mayo Street and Esmond Street'. Chillingly, Bates also told detectives, 'After the thing in Glencairn I knew he was going to be killed with the knife.'[22]

***

Jimmy Nesbitt was one of the RUC's most dedicated detectives. In his service with the RUC it was reported that he had solved 250 murder cases out of 311, and was awarded a record sixty-seven commendations, making him one of the most successful detectives in British policing history. He was good, but no matter how many eighteen-hour days he worked, his squad couldn't catch a break. The murder gang they were pursuing were good at stopping their close-knit community from speaking out.[23] As Nesbitt told journalist Martin Dillon, it was relaying news to families that really hit him hard, 'not simply seeing the bodies but witnessing the heartbreak and tragedy of the living and knowing that in those people it would remain'. Nesbitt had interrogated Murphy on several occasions. He found him a dedicated member of the UVF who was cool and calm under pressure, even during long hours of police interrogation. Often regarded as a psychopath, suggesting focused control over his actions and a lack of empathy, Murphy could indeed be ruthless, cunning and calculating. Some police officers who worked on the Shankill Butchers case saw Murphy as an accomplished terrorist. 'When you talked to him he was intelligent,' said one detective. 'There was nothing sadistic in the murders. They were carried out without fuss and in a cold, premeditated manner.'[24] Martin Dillon wrote, that despite the heinous nature of their crimes, 'the defendants were declared by a psychiatrist to be sane and not suffering from a diagnosable mental illness. I suspect the same analysis would have applied to Murphy had he ever been so tested'.[25]

Although the murder squad have since been criticised for the length of time it took to bring the killers to justice, this overlooks the severe constraints on police investigations at that time. The RUC was resilient but poorly equipped to deal with the sheer onslaught of murder and mayhem from all sides. In the two areas where the Brown Bear team were most active, West Belfast and North Belfast, there were 398 and 390 deaths linked to the troubles between 1969 and 1977.[26] We know, for example, that in the case of the Yorkshire Ripper, Peter Sutcliffe, who was found guilty in 1981 of murdering thirteen women, 304 detectives were involved in the investigation – in the case of the Butchers it fell to a squad of only eleven. Despite the heavy odds stacked against them, the RUC detectives eventually succeeded in securing the convictions of nineteen men, who were handed forty-two life sentences between them.

In their day-to-day policing operations the RUC faced unique problems in the divided communities across Belfast. Although Protestant areas were generally more amenable towards the Security Forces, the same was not true of Catholic areas. They varied from the apathetic to the outright antagonistic and dangerous. One of the detectives who investigated the Jean McConville abduction recalled how he could not venture into Catholic areas without military support.[27] Of the three resident regular battalions in Belfast, two companies of soldiers were needed to support police when they went into hostile areas like the Divis flats. Police officers were frequently greeted with cat-calls and abuse. 'It rained down piss pots, bricks and bottles,' recalled one detective. It led to nervousness amongst the police and soldiers. 'When we knocked on the doors we were told to "fuck off".' As these seasoned detectives recalled, this was 'not the place for Shire policing, which just didn't work. We faced more challenges. It was a nearly impossible task.'[28] As a consequence, there were frequently delays in going into areas to investigate crimes. Bodies sometimes lay for days as it was so dangerous a place for the Security Forces to maintain a presence. In the period between 1971 and 1976, the army were in the driving seat as far as the operational dimension of security policy was concerned and, occasionally, refused to put soldiers in to assist the RUC. In addition to this, it was difficult finding eyewitnesses to many crimes – people feared for reprisals if it ever got back to the paramilitaries.

By 1977 the military had handed responsibility for the operational end of Security Force operations over to the RUC. 'Police primacy', as the policy became known, was returned at the height of sectarian violence. Throughout the 1970s the army's knowledge and understanding of loyalist paramilitary violence had been minimal. In early 1976 the military hierarchy in Thiepval

Barracks, Lisburn, were telling the NIO that they 'fully recognise that the loyalist paramilitaries might indulge in a wide range of illegal activity as a challenge to the Government's authority', though the soldiers were continually perplexed by their reluctance to 'seek a confrontation with the SF [Security Forces]'.[29] The truth was that the army was blind to the dangers posed to Catholic civilians by loyalist paramilitaries and, instead, saw the Provisional IRA as the only real threat to security in Northern Ireland.

After a meeting with the army battalion based in the area, the 1st Battalion the Devonshire and Dorset Regiment (1 D&D), one NIO official reported that the 'sectarian violence has slackened off recently' but that there remained a view amongst the Security Forces that it could return. 'As we know only too well,' remarked the official, 'the terrorists select specific and not always obvious targets to attack, and the chances of a successful catch are small. However, the Security Forces have managed a few successes,' he added. The main focus of police and army patrols was, therefore, to continue to maintain a presence on the ground to 'deter and suppress' terrorist attacks as far as possible. In one single weekend, 1 D&D fielded forty-five separate mobile patrols. But operational intensity could not remain indefinitely, and was ineffective for as long as intelligence available to the military remained 'inadequate'.[30] To augment its lack of mobile patrols, however, the army did establish a network of observation posts, six of which were based around Ardoyne, and another six around New Lodge.

With the Brown Bear team behind bars, a resurgence in military reassurance patrols remained little more than a token gesture to allay the fears of the local Catholic population, who were in the firing line when it came to loyalist paramilitary activity. Nonetheless, as 1977 came to a close, another optimistic government official reported to the Secretary of State for Northern Ireland, Roy Mason, that police work in the division was 'geared, on the uniformed side, to maintaining a presence where there has been none for some time, such as in the Bawnmore estate and the Fortwilliam area, where a police station has recently been introduced. There is, of course, a backlog of crime to be cleared from previous years. But significant progress is being made in securing convictions'.[31] In D Division alone there were almost 350 full-time RUC and RUC (Reserve) officers to police an expansive area. Despite these moves in stabilising the security situation, the public perception was that the police were doing little to combat loyalist paramilitary organisations.

Taking up the issue with Roy Mason was the backbench Labour MP Kevin McNamara. In a conversation that he had with AA Pritchard at the

NIO, McNamara mentioned 'an impression widely held in London that the security forces' efforts were concentrated almost entirely on the minority population and that little if any success was being achieved against loyalist paramilitaries'.[32] Mason was moved to write to McNamara to disabuse him of what he regarded as a misperception, outlining how the 'charges brought against UDA/UVF members so far this year amount to nearly a third of the total charges for all terrorist offences', and to reassure him that 'the efforts of the Security Forces are not directed disproportionately against the minority community'.[33] Despite the belief inside the NIO that the Security Forces were pursuing 'even-handedness' in their security policy, the widespread perception amongst Labour backbenchers and many in the Catholic community nonetheless persisted.

★★★

Shankill Road, West Belfast, Late 1970s

'I can't sleep at night. I have to sleep during the day because of all the things I've done,' said John Murphy in conversation with a woman who claimed she let the gang use her house for meetings. The Shankill Butchers were alleged to have had three safe-houses – one in Wimbledon Street, a second in Matchett Street and a third in Snugville Street. 'I didn't know what they were up to,' she said emphatically. 'It's only years later that you find out. I do remember one of them talking about a dispute. "I'll cut his fucking throat," the fella said. That was the only time I heard anything like that. I would have sat here and had a drink with them,' she added. 'Moore was never in my house. I wouldn't have him anywhere near me. He gave me the creeps. Big Benny ['Pretty Boy' Edwards] was happily married – I think he just got caught up in it all. McAllister, Bates and Moore all had it in them, like. They seemed to be scared of John Murphy. He was the leader of the pack,' said the woman. 'They used to come and wrap me up [knock my door] in the early hours of the morning. They would stay and have a cup of tea. They were just ordinary guys. You would never think in a million years what they were up to, and you wouldn't have known to look at them.'[34] Did she believe Lenny Murphy was guilty of all of the crimes attributed to him by other members of his gang? 'As I say, they used to blame Lenny. They tried to say he gave the orders, but he was in jail most of the time. They were that frightened of John.' According to the woman, there is little doubt that John

Murphy played a key role in sustaining the Shankill Butchers' campaign of terror. 'He got his comeuppance when he hit a roundabout and went through the car windscreen. Some people are just evil. There's an evilness there,' she said.[35]

Murders linked to the Shankill Butchers gang

25 November 1975 – Murder of Francis Crossan (34)

30 November 1975 – Murder of Noel Shaw (19)

10 January 1976 – Murder of Edward McQuaid (25)

6 February 1976 – Murder of Thomas Quinn (55)

9 February 1976 – Murders of Archibald Hanna (51) and Raymond Carlisle (27)

5 June 1976 – Chlorane Bar Murders – James Coyle (64), Edward Farrell (45), Daniel McNeill (47), Samuel Corr (53), John Martin (59)

22 June 1976 – Murder of Francis Rice (26)

1 August 1976 – Murder of Cornelius Neeson (49)

30 October 1976 – Murder of Stephen McCann (21)

20 December 1976 – Murder of Thomas Easton (22)

31 January 1977 – Murder of James Moorehead (30)

3 February 1977 – Murder of Joseph Morrissey (52)

1–20 March 1977 – Conspiracy to murder Roman Catholics on the Falls Road

30 March 1977 – Murder of Francis Cassidy (43)

10 April 1977 – Murder of Kevin McMenamin (10)

10 May 1976 – Attempted murder of Gerard McLaverty

17 July 1982 – Murder of Norman Maxwell (33)

1 September 1982 – Murder of James Galway (34)

5 September 1982 – Murder of Brian Smyth (30)

30 September 1982 – Murder of John O'Neill (28)

24 October 1982 – Murder of Joseph Donegan (48)

9

A MILLION MILES FROM HOME

'If only "them" and "us" had the same ideas we'd get on like a house on fire, but they don't see eye to eye with us and we don't see eye to eye with them, so that's how it stands and how it will always stand.'

Alan Sillitoe, *The Loneliness of the Long Distance Runner* (1959)[1]

Long Kesh Prison, County Down, circa 1977

'Read that there. He's a republican. When you read that there defend him,' said Gusty Spence, the Commanding Officer of all UVF and RHC prisoners inside Long Kesh prison camp.[2] Billy Mitchell stared back at Spence, unsure how to respond. As he sat perched on the edge of his bunk leafing through the book Spence had just handed him, he was intrigued to see that, on first glance, it featured the personal struggle of legendary IRA man Liam Mellows. Mitchell saw some comparisons with his own predicament. A soldier imprisoned for underground guerrilla activity, he too had been politically motivated and ideologically driven to carry out certain actions, which his enemies had labelled criminal, terrorist acts.

Written by the influential communist writer and activist C. Desmond Greaves, the biography of Mellows struck a chord with Mitchell. Up to that point he wouldn't have dared even pick up a book on physical-force republicanism, let alone one written by a communist about a dedicated IRA man. He was flummoxed. The heretical thoughts of reading such books percolated in his mind, causing him some disquiet. It was a feeling he had not experienced since attending secret meetings a few years earlier with Provisional IRA men, Dáithí Ó Conaill, Seamus Twomey and a young Martin McGuinness. As a direct consequence of these meetings – and now his studies – Billy Mitchell was utterly convinced that he needed to comprehend his enemies; to get under their skin, and to see what made them tick. The enormity of the challenge both excited and worried him.

Although Mitchell had certainly read more than the average UVF man, he hadn't really studied Irish history, and certainly not the Irish republican version of history, in any great depth. The previous half dozen years outside prison were spent primarily as a man of action, not letters. After taking command of the East Antrim UVF and, more recently, since his appointment to the UVF's ruling Brigade Staff, Mitchell led a frugal existence as a senior officer in the upper echelons of the UVF. He was married, with two young children, though he spent more time between safe-houses than at the family table. His home was frequently raided, the police frustrated time and again when they discovered he had once again evaded capture. He was accustomed to being a man on the run, difficult to pin down, to understand where he was coming from and where he was headed to next.

In early 1974 Mitchell began to edit and publish *Combat* magazine, the UVF's principal propaganda organ. The motto in its masthead was 'Always on Target', though its articles sometimes fell wide of the mark, with some demonstrating a palpable mistrust of the English that bordered on xenophobia. This was curious, given that the UVF claimed to be dedicated to maintaining the link between Northern Ireland and Great Britain.[3] *Combat* served its purpose as a fanzine for the ordinary rank-and-file UVF volunteer, carrying stirring updates from the frontline of the organisation's military campaign. There were also articles on the pressing political issues of the day and a sprinkling of interesting pieces outlining how the UVF agitated on the socio-economic concerns of the Protestant working class.

Billy Mitchell and his commanders often met in the less than salubrious surroundings of their headquarters at the Royal British Legion Club in Carrickfergus. Their other haunt, the Brown Trout Inn, was located just outside the town. They kept many of their weapons at a disused farm at Jack's Lane in Monkstown. For much of this time, they were eager to expand the parameters of the debate on the finer details of their strategy to encompass a political as well as a military response to the conflict. Often, they were preoccupied with the idea of forming a community-based movement in East Antrim and West Belfast, which would come to be known as the Ulster Loyalist Front (ULF). The ULF would act as a catalyst for delivering the UVF's 'good works' in the community, for it was conceived as a grassroots movement, designed to articulate the concerns of working people by political and military means.[4]

Mitchell believed that the ULF idea had the potential to win considerable sympathy within the broader Protestant working-class community, even if it wasn't staffed by elected politicians. If nothing else, it would enable the UVF to put down firm roots in the surrounding loyalist hinterland, which stretched all the way from Rathcoole in the south-east up the County Antrim coast to the eastern port town of Larne.

The UVF's flirtation with electoral politics was to be short-lived. They all but died when Ken Gibson failed to get elected to Parliament in the organisation's West Belfast heartland, in the Westminster election of October 1974. Gibson's performance wasn't a complete disaster. In many respects, he maximised the pre-existing vote garnered by the NILP's Billy Boyd, who stood aside after the earlier poll in February, thereby giving the UVF's candidate an opportunity to tap into the wider Protestant working-class vote. This was significant, not only because he attracted more votes than the NILP on a lower turnout, but because it ate into the DUP's vote in the constituency.

Although some of the articles in *Combat*, such as those dealing with the ULF model, were highly sophisticated, *Combat's* function wasn't to pontificate about socio-economic or political matters. In this sense it was very unlike *An Phoblacht* (*Republican News*), the Provisional IRA's in-house journal. For Mitchell, *Combat's* primary function was to communicate the UVF's armed opposition to militant Provisional republicanism.[5] That didn't require an intimate understanding of Provo politics either, for much of what passed for politics in the republican movement was 'embryonic' and subordinated to the needs of what they termed the 'war' for most of the 1970s.

An Phoblacht reflected these oscillating political tendencies, articulating a left-wing internationalism while at the same time occupying a protectionist and nationalist position. Insofar as the Provisionals had an ideology, it was just as contradictory as anything the loyalists could muster, preferring to mix 'blood sacrifice' republicanism with separatism and radical Marxism.[6] Despite modest attempts by Mitchell and certain members of Brigade Staff, prior to the abortive leadership coup by younger members in 1975, the UVF wasn't much further along the political road either.

Many UVF volunteers saw themselves first and foremost as a dedicated vanguard for the defence of the Protestant community in Northern Ireland. Insofar as *Combat* dealt with political ideas, these were confined to welfare matters primarily aimed at alleviating the burden on the families of those volunteers who had entered the prison system as a consequence of what they came to call 'armed resistance'. In practical terms, this meant maintaining essential services for the organisation's core support base in places like the Shankill, Rathcoole, Monkstown, Carrickfergus, the Newtownards Road and Portadown, where the UVF drew men and (occasionally women) into its ranks in large numbers. When *Combat* did entertain a more thorough examination of the political situation in Northern Ireland, it concentrated on hardline loyalist positions that were not too dissimilar from those held by parties like the DUP. Political analysis, such as it was, was limited to esoteric pronouncements on the British constitution, rather than Irish history and politics. As its first editor, Billy Mitchell indulged his own narrow hardline cultural loyalist sentiments, all of which placed the blame for the current upheaval in Northern Ireland squarely on the shoulders of the republican enemy and the wider Catholic community. English politicians, whenever they warranted mention, were regarded as little more than perfidious midwives in the war process.[7]

By the time he entered Long Kesh, Billy Mitchell was transfixed by a cascade of contradictory political activities. His UVF work took him into meetings in Belfast and Dublin with the Official and Provisional wings of the IRA. He had met with British government officials, like James Allen, to discuss the potential for developing a UVF political wing in 1974–5.[8] In hindsight, Mitchell thought that the British were much more enthusiastic about UVF electoral prospects than the UVF itself. Yet, amidst all of this, he had always been extremely self-conscious of his own limitations. He knew that he couldn't move ahead of his followers. He had to tread carefully. 'The problem was if you try to lead too far from the front the people are that far behind you that you are not really leading at all, you're out on your own,' he would later say.[9] Lacking in concrete gains for the loyalist community, these open-ended and unstructured talks, particularly with republicans, inadvertently whet his appetite and left him hungry for more information on his enemy.

Gusty Spence was offering him the opportunity to do just that when he passed him the well-leafed book on Liam Mellows.

Gusty, who everyone called 'sir', even his twenty-two-year-old nephew Frankie Curry, who joined him in the compounds on a possession of weapons charge, was now forcing the volunteers under his command to see things from an alternative perspective. As Mitchell would later reveal, it was a process designed 'to see how conservatives thought, to see how socialists thought, to see how liberals thought. Read this, read that, read the other', he added. 'Through reading and then debating and then analysing what we were debating, and also debating with the Provos and the Stickies',[10] Mitchell and his fellow 'L Men'[11] had embarked on a personal and political transformation, even if they were uncertain about where it was likely to lead them.

★★★

After several months spent on remand in Crumlin Road prison (known to prisoners as 'the Crum'), Billy Mitchell finally entered the compound system in March 1977. At that time, the UVF's highly disciplined prison regime had been in place for four years. It was in early 1973 that Spence had begun to organise a tighter daily routine centred around strict discipline, a sense of regimental pride and political education. It was born more out of necessity than design. Depression amongst the prisoners soon set in due to the harsh conditions that greeted them. Food was typically served cold, there was only one handwash basin and one toilet for every thirty men, and the accommodation was in a poor state of repair.[12] In order to improve the men's morale, Spence initiated a system that saw them come to think of themselves as prisoners of war, not simply as the terrorists or criminals that the state and a hostile media had branded them following their conviction.

Although it was a conservative organisation, dedicated to maintaining the status quo, the UVF began to model itself, under Spence, along the lines of an underground army. Like the revolutionary Black Panthers in the United States, the UVF developed its own uniform. Clad from head to toe in a cap comforter similar to that worn by commandos in the Second World War, black shirts, black jumpers, black trousers and a black leather jacket, the men paraded in well-polished drill boots, which made a crunching sound as they marched around the compounds of Long Kesh. They also adopted the trappings of military organisations by drilling in sections and platoons, and wearing military insignia and adhering to a rank structure.

The UVF's restructuring on the outside had been in train ever since Gusty Spence was abducted by the organisation in the summer of 1972. He was on his way to his daughter Liz's wedding when a UVF unit took him into 'protective custody'.[13] Soon afterwards, black uniforms were being worn by units on the outside, most notably when Billy Mitchell's East Antrim Battalion made their first mass appearance at Sinclair Johnston's funeral in

September 1972. On the inside, though, Spence's military-based regime was accepted by the vast majority of the men who enjoyed the camaraderie it afforded them. Colin Crawford, a prison education officer at Long Kesh, reported to the prison authorities at the time that the compound system was well-liked by the prisoners and by those who guarded them. The 'screws' enjoyed good relationships with the prisoners and were on first name terms with them. As far as Crawford could ascertain, the UVF and Provisional IRA prisoners adhered to a strict chain of command – the UDA less so.[14]

As Commanding Officer of the UVF's prisoners, known colloquially at the time as the 'invisible battalion', Spence was a hard taskmaster and soon earned a robust reputation as a strict disciplinarian. The whole regime was designed to give the men purpose and bearing. In practical terms, it assisted them in dealing with the psychological challenges of incarceration. Spence was eager to impress upon them the position that they were not individuals undergoing the long years of incarceration alone. Their individual actions were part of an organisational and community response to the dangers posed by physical-force republicanism. If anything, these men were to come to see themselves as soldiers in a war. Spence lost little time in informing his subordinates that their self-proclaimed prisoner-of-war status distinguished them from common criminals.

In his memoir on a five-year spell in the compounds, Plum Smith recalled a briefing by Spence in which he told his men that 'prison would either make us or break us; that we would either emerge as bitter men or better men. He was determined that most of us would leave the camp as better men.' This was a challenge of 'Everest proportions',[15] Smith admitted, though it became an ultimately successful mechanism for disciplining the bodies and minds of those behind the wire. It made them more confident, more self-aware and more ideologically cohesive as a body of men.

The military-based compound structures came under threat in November 1975, when the Secretary of State for Northern Ireland Merlyn Rees announced a new plan to phase out Special Category Status from 1 March 1976.[16]

In time, the change in government policy was to prove a disaster, as the paramilitary prisoners coveted the political status extended to them by the previous Conservative Secretary of State for Northern Ireland William Whitelaw in 1972. Unsurprisingly, this led to a souring of the atmosphere inside the Crum and newly constructed H Blocks at Long Kesh, with republicans pledging to resist the changes; loyalists at first refused to wear prison clothes but could not generate enough support from within the wider unionist community to sustain their own concerted resistance. Like earlier attempts at hunger strikes in the Crum, most unionists 'could not understand why loyalists were on the blanket protest – they were seen as siding with republicans', some even without the support of their families.[17] Loyalists were not the only prisoners suffering from a blow to morale caused by Britain's new criminalisation policy. The republican 'blanket protest', begun in 1976, failed to generate a broader base of support. With 'nothing to show' for their meagre efforts to counter the new prison regime,[18] prisoners arriving after March 1977 were transferred directly from their spell on remand to the new H Blocks.

Billy Mitchell was one of the last L men to enter the compounds. He had only arrived in Long Kesh when Spence appointed him to what he called 'a position of influence'. Having been on the UVF Brigade Staff on the outside – with 'one foot in the Shankill and the other foot in East Antrim',[19] as one of his comrades put it – it was only natural that he would maintain his officer status when he entered the compounds. 'I was more or less seconded to interact with Hugh Feeney and Gerry Kelly,' he said.

> So we would have had eleven-aside football – they had fifteen aside for Gaelic so we demanded the same number. Among the extra people, my job was to engage in dialogue with them. We engaged in dialogue with the Stickies who were in the next compound to us. The whole idea was not so much to fraternise with the enemy but to understand where they were coming from. Was there any common ground? And it was about seeing the humanity of the other person. To understand the things they'd done.[20]

Spence also gave Mitchell the task of acting as the prisoners' Welfare Officer. His main job was to look after the men's well-being, to ensure that they had their fair share of visitations and that their personal mail was getting through, amongst other duties.

'You weren't sitting by yourself crying in your tea, or crying in your beer if you had it!' recalled Billy Mitchell. 'There was drill, PT, education; the whole thing was structured so that you didn't vegetate.'[21] The fitness regime was not really Mitchell's cup of tea. On one occasion he had gone for a visit and didn't come back for a while. Some of the men began to wonder what had happened to him. It later transpired that he had collapsed. 'Billy wasn't like the rest of us getting into our weight-lifting, running, football and all the rest of it,' said 'Jon'. 'Something he told me about a spasm in his back. Very painful. Passed out, I think he was taken to the hospital; nothing too bad and then he came back up'.[22] To compensate for his physical inactivity, Mitchell liked to take exercise by walking the wire with Spence, and sometimes on his own. He cut a solitary figure at times, more bookish and reflective than lonesome or isolated.

'When I arrived, Gusty was a powerful figure,' Jon remembered fondly. 'I was told by a friend to mention his name and that Gusty would look after me. Other prisoners thought I was not giving him the respect he deserved, and so I got a bollocking for calling him Gusty once.'[23] Jon admitted he was young and immature and didn't know any different, though he quickly got the hang of the disciplinary regime. He found a ready ally in Billy Mitchell. 'Billy was one of the older guys. It was said at one point that Northern Ireland had the youngest prison population in Northern Europe and at one time that had touched nineteen. I was nineteen when I went in ... The guy charged with me was sixteen when he went in. Mitchell was a very quiet, pleasant man. I liked talking to him, and over time we became friends. We had things in common.'[24]

Jon and Billy were committed readers. They even formed a book group with some of the other prisoners. The book group read widely and avidly,[25] though they liked to punctuate the long hours of reflection with physical exercise. At times Mitchell even showed a willingness to join in. 'So, the funny thing I remember about Billy is in the summer was that we would all be running around in shorts and Billy would come out with these big, wide khaki pants. I can only describe it in one way, the popular BBC World War II comedy show, *It Ain't Half Hot Mum*. And there would be these thin, spindly white legs sticking down from khaki shorts. And he had a very distinctive walk, which is more of a slouch. He really was a funny looking character. But, as I say, I met many personalities in there and he was definitely one of them.'[26]

Mitchell's real passion remained the education classes that Spence facilitated for the men. These covered topics as varied as the UVF's armed campaign, the National Health Service, socialism and the political deficiencies of the old Stormont regime.[27]

Another ranking officer in the compounds – and one of Spence's key lieutenants – was Billy Hutchinson. He explained where Spence was headed with the education programme. 'What he was basically pushing was his own brand of politics, which was basically working-class,' Hutchinson said. Their political outlook was closest to the NILP, though it was considered suspect by those young UVF and RHC men who believed the party was 'too republican or whatever', and inhibited their development of a more sophisticated ideology.[28] So, the socialism taken up by some of the prisoners, insofar as it was light pink rather than light green, took its inspiration from a long-established tradition that drew its strength from a close association with the British Labour Party, before it threw in its lot with the SDLP in the mid-1970s. The development of a class-based unionism would become increasingly important once the political thinking seeped out of the compounds, to those key people in the non-combatant ranks of the UVF.[29]

One of the principal preoccupations of the prisoners was the extent to which volunteers were invited to question and challenge what they were being told. 'Why are you here?' was Spence's routine Socratic question to those UVF members who wound up in the compounds. When they answered flippantly, like a young David Ervine did – 'Possession of explosives' – Spence immediately followed it up with the same question: 'No, no, no, no, no. *Why* are you here?' Ervine paused, before answering again. 'Arrogant bastard – for defending my people!'[30] Not only was Spence developing the men's political awareness, he was forcing them to soak up as much information as they could so that it could later be put to good use. 'If you looked at what was happening outside, you realised that it would be counter-productive if you were to go outside and start pushing new ideas too strongly,' Mitchell later recalled. 'I feel that if you are going to read something there has to be an outcome; you can't read for reading's sake. There's no point in reading if you're not going to learn, and there is no point learning if you don't use that learning. But you have to strike a balance when sharing your learning with others who have not yet shared the same journey.'[31]

UVF and RHC prisoners also began to look beyond Ireland's shores to what was happening around the globe. 'In Long Kesh, under the tuition of Gusty, people looked at the world. They didn't look at Northern Ireland. Northern Ireland was a very, very small part of the world ... And I can remember having a debate in 1975 on whether we should have a federated Europe, and what that would mean. And how that would lessen the republican struggle for a united Ireland in terms of having a federated Europe,' said Hutchinson, who remembered how the prisoners 'considered a federated Europe and the effect that would have on conflicts throughout Europe, and particularly our own.'[32]

While Hutchinson and other compound men were beginning to entertain the kind of sophisticated political ideas that might one day carry them beyond the high prison walls and back into their communities, they were also putting their backs into the construction of an escape tunnel. As the UVF's prison leadership adhered to British Army rules and regulations, they were convinced that, as prisoners of war, they had a duty to escape. In a bid to break out of the Colditz-type environment, the prisoners began to dig a tunnel. It took them longer than expected, for they had run out of places to hide the clay in Compound 18. 'As you would see in the movies and in the TV shows ... this stuff ... would come up to our compound and we would have to find out what to do with it.'[33] Unlike the men's commitment to wrestling with new ideas, the tunnel came up short. Not only were they a mile from the fence, but they had been digging in the wrong direction all along!

As other, mainly republican-based, narratives inform us, loyalists were also headed in the wrong direction in terms of their fixation on the maintenance of the union. 'None of us went into Long Kesh with an ideology, so it was in Long Kesh that we hammered it out,' Billy Mitchell would subsequently admit. For him, like so many other incarcerated volunteers, the risk of individuals sinking into a deep depression was an ongoing concern. For now, he spent his time contributing to the building of a sophisticated political outlook that was more class-based and connected to the working-class communities from where the men had come:

I think there was a consensus among some of us, certainly amongst Davy [Ervine], Billy [Hutchinson], Eddie [Kinner] and Martin Snoddon. There was a consensus among a lot of us. We maybe didn't articulate it in terms of socialism, as in Marxism. Davy used to use an awkward phrase 'working classism'. What we realised, I mean from the set up of the state – and we analysed the civil rights – we were saying 'but hold on, what they were asking for we should have been asking for?' We lived in a two-up, two-down with an outside toilet. A lot of us lived in fallen down [houses]. I was reared in a wooden hut on the Hightown Road. I mean, I've done an article 'the privileged Prod and the travelling tinker', where I compared my life to a group of tinkers that used to come every year to a field beside us. We suffered social and economic deprivation, but I'm not sure any of us ever read Marx or the academic books on socialism. It was coming from inside. We realised that we had suffered deprivation and poverty, the same as working-class Catholics.[34]

The Spence regime triggered an awakening of the political consciousness of those UVF and RHC men, who were now confronted with the harsh reality of their predicament. They were incarcerated volunteers in a war, where, on their own side at least, their leaders had departed the field of battle as soon as the first shots had been fired. Believing themselves to have been encouraged to take up arms, compound men began to question what had driven them to take the law into their own hands in the first place.

Loyalists would later develop a more sceptical understanding of their own contractual relationship with the British state via its proxy administrators in the old Stormont regime.[35] Unlike their rivals in the UDA, who favoured independence for Northern Ireland, Billy Mitchell and the other UVF and RHC members developed their thinking along the lines of redefining the union between Great Britain and Northern Ireland. As Mitchell explained:

And what we were, more or less, saying was that if we are going to fight for the union – and we want to be part of the United Kingdom – then we want equal citizenship … Supporting the union and being loyal to the Crown doesn't mean being loyal to a class of unionists who don't have our social and economic interests at heart. So, we began to explore all the issues around trade unionism and labour politics. And then, while we used the term 'socialist' loosely, none of us that I know of would be socialist in [the sense] of being Marxists or Trotskyites or anything like that … I would model my socialism on the Christian socialists; the likes of Keir Hardie … George Lansbury, RH Tawney. Just ordinary, old-fashioned labour politics. Most of the Northern Ireland Labour Party-type people were Methodist-type people. A lot of them were Christians. They weren't loony lefties. A socialism or a 'workingclassism' that gives respect to the working class. That helps the working classes to empower themselves, to take ownership of their own lives and their own communities.[36]

Mitchell held firm to his belief that the 'fur coat brigade' (middle-class unionists in loyalist parlance at the time) had abandoned the paramilitaries, after they had stepped forward to answer the call to arms. This was a view gaining some ground amongst grassroots UVF activists on the outside.

The key link-man between the UVF's 'invisible battalion' on the inside and the organisation on the outside was Hughie Smyth, the organisation's political spokesman. Along with Jim McDonald, Jackie Hewitt and another former NILP member, Davy Overend, Smyth had formed the Progressive Unionist Group in 1977, which was rebranded as the Progressive Unionist Party (PUP) in 1979.[37] In Smyth's mind, the main objectives of the party were, firstly, to promote working-class unionist issues through a campaign of lobbying and agitation; secondly, to support loyalist prisoners of war; thirdly, to support Old Age Pensioners by organising food parcels for those living in poverty, amongst other things; fourthly, to provide an advice centre for the people to visit and communicate their issues to government bodies and statutory agencies; fifthly, to establish a political direction for the UVF; sixthly, to provide a public relations front for the UVF and Red Hand and, finally, to fund raise.[38] Billy Hutchinson outlined how the process worked:

> I mean they always asked us for input, which was given by Gusty and others to those on the outside, in terms of policy formulation and things like that. So, it was always there. And the small group on the outside – people like Jim McDonald and Hugh Smyth and other people who have remained nameless until now – some of those people would have been members of the Northern Ireland Labour Party and former members of the Northern Ireland Labour Party. The Northern Ireland Labour Party was collapsed by then.[39]

Out of the NILP's collapse sprang the PUP, which presented a liberal, left-leaning and working-class alternative to mainstream unionism.[40] It was to represent grassroots loyalists in a way that gave a voice to the dissenting brand of working-class unionism, represented by Spence and the men under his tutelage.

In time, the PUP would contest elections and seek a mandate from the broader Protestant working-class community. In the late 1970s, though, it was in a very embryonic phase: its 'founding fathers' were still hard at work exchanging ideas with one another in the accommodation huts, classrooms and exercise yards of the Long Kesh compounds.[41]

★★★

Billy Mitchell paced up and down in his room. He was restive. He stretched his back, feeling a distant pang of the spasm that hit him weeks earlier. He heard the footsteps of visitors behind him. He turned around to find another UVF officer scrutinise the cleanliness of his bed space. 'My pit is fine,' he remonstrated with the officer who came to inspect it. A heated exchange soon developed. 'It's not a pit,' replied the other man. By now a row was in progress over Billy's use of what the man regarded as a derogatory term to describe his bed space. According to UVF regulations, volunteers were to take pride in keeping their lines 'squeaky clean'. The rigorous daily routine of fatigues and ablutions saw to that. Mitchell's room was always spic, span, Spartan. Where the rest of the men had pictures of footballers and boxers covering their walls, Mitchell's cubicle was quite plain. There was a monastic feel to it, in fact. 'I am referring to *cock*pit,' he told his brother officer sternly, as he tried to explain that he was using Royal Air Force terminology for his living quarters. He hated clutter and preferred the solitary confinement of being left alone in his pit to hammer out a steady stream of letters and articles. Writing helped to satisfy his creative urge, his need to grapple with the big issues of the day. Turning to the typewriter also helped him to get through the long days in the compounds. It became a ritual. Other men chose to exercise their bodies in the way that Mitchell did with his brain. As far as he was concerned, he was still engaged in an intellectual and political struggle, despite being incarcerated.

Like other prisoners, Billy Mitchell used to say he was 'only half a mile from freedom but a million miles from home'.[42] He needed to keep the connection with the outside world that his imagination guaranteed him.

Although Mitchell was well-respected, his unpredictable political posturing drew open mouths and expletives from some UVF prisoners. In one incident, during his left-leaning phase, a young volunteer from East Belfast took exception at the older man's suspected 'communism'. He detonated and launched himself at Mitchell. 'I'm not sure if there was actual fisticuffs but I really didn't like the idea of a younger fella hitting Billy, cos Billy wasn't really built for scrapping. He wasn't of that sort of ilk. But it was sorted out and all the rest of it.'[43] Robert Niblock was nearby at the time, and saw what happened. There was a brief scuffle, he said, as Mitchell was jumped in an unprovoked attack. 'When they were brought before a court martial, the fella attacked Billy again. There was no place for that. Anyone starting trouble was put out of the compound.'[44]

After the incident, Mitchell strolled back to his pit. He felt dejected by the whole experience. He looked around at a room without furniture. It was threadbare, but his mind burst with the creative energy caused by a cascade of new ideas. The bare walls, adorned with a single bookshelf, a desk, a chair and a typewriter, betrayed a more cerebral existence, full of wonder, depth and dedication to exploring the wider world beyond Long Kesh.

He sat back down, stretched his back slightly for a moment, and got back to work.

10

AN ATMOSPHERE OF PURE HISTORY

'The unemployed, particularly the young, can easily fall prey of the paramilitaries who provide excitement and meaning to otherwise drab lives.'

Briefing Note for the Secretary of State for
Northern Ireland (1978)[1]

Ministry of Defence Main Building, Whitehall, London, Summer 1977

Brigadier James Glover was busy in his office in the MoD's headquarters, finalising the covering note for a top-secret report his team had put together entitled *Future Terrorist Trends*. A veteran of counter-insurgency operations in Malaya and peacekeeping operations in Cyprus, he had commanded his regiment, the 3rd Battalion, Royal Green Jackets, in Northern Ireland in 1970, and was held in high esteem by his men as a competent commander, especially when he led them in their efforts to secure British Sovereign Base Areas after the Turkish invasion of Cyprus in July 1974.[2] At forty-eight, Glover was the British Army's most senior officer dealing with intelligence matters relating to Northern Ireland. For several months in 1977 he and his staff officers had been busy compiling their highly classified report on the Provisional IRA's strategy and tactics. That year was to herald a new departure for the IRA, following as it did in the wake of the disastrous ceasefire of 1975–6. The organisation had refined its military capability to such an extent that it could now carry out highly synchronised attacks on multiple targets across Northern Ireland and the British mainland. They were eager to try and forecast future trends in IRA violence now that Jimmy Drumm had announced the beginning of a 'long war' at the Provo's Easter Sunday parade in Bodenstown.[3] British military intelligence believed that IRA was shifting from a 'hit and run' guerrilla campaign to a longer-term terrorist campaign, which placed the wearing down of the London government's will to remain in Northern Ireland at the heart of its strategy:

> PIRA strategy is based on the premise that a campaign of attrition, with its attendant costs in both lives and money, will eventually persuade HMG to withdraw from Northern Ireland. The Provisionals probably aspire to raising the tempo of their operations to such a level that the normal processes of administration and government break down. But having failed to achieve this in the earlier part of the campaign, they probably realise that they now have little hope of success. Indeed, they may accept that to raise the level of their activity beyond a certain point would evoke such intense response [*sic*] from the Security Forces that their organisation during the next five years is likely to remain such that the leadership will wish to avoid action that could put large numbers of its men at risk. A further influencing factor is that the PIRA leadership appreciate that their campaign will be won or lost in Belfast. Although operations elsewhere are important, and in the border area easier to achieve, success in Belfast is critical.[4]

In fact, the Provisionals were moving towards a more ruthless approach altogether, as the next twelve months would prove.

The step-change in Provisional IRA strategy was prompted by the ascendency of Gerry Adams, allegedly to the role of chief of staff, an appointment that proved short-lived. According to Ed Moloney, Adams only directed IRA operations for a mere seventy-eight days, from late 1977 until his arrest in early 1978.[5] One of the major tenets in the IRA's revised strategy was its renewed assault on so-called 'soft targets', principally off-duty RUC and UDR personnel, which would complement the organisation's war of attrition against uniformed members of the Security Forces. The reinvigorated strategy began slowly. One of the first Protestants killed by the Provos in their new departure was fifty-six-year-old Cecil Grills, a married man with two children and an off-duty corporal belonging to a part-time company of the 3rd Battalion of the Ulster Defence Regiment (UDR). Grills was shot dead in Newry on 12 January 1978, as he made his way home from his civilian job at a timber and coal yard in the town. The IRA man who shot Grills had been armed with a high velocity rifle. His marksmanship proved deadly accurate, firing on a moving vehicle and hitting the UDR man in the cheek and in the back of the neck, killing him instantly.[6] Local

Protestants believed that the killing was motivated by sectarianism, but the IRA's statement claiming responsibility for the killing stated that Grills had been targeted because he was 'part of the British war machine'.[7]

Less than a month after the murder of Cecil Grills, the IRA struck again. This time killing two off-duty UDR men, John Eaglesham and William Gordon, in Pomeroy and Maghera respectively. Worse was to come on 17 February, when IRA volunteers detonated a huge incendiary bomb at the La Mon House Hotel in County Down, slaughtering twelve Protestant civilians, seven of them women, as they attended an Irish Collie Club dinner dance. The IRA had placed barrels of gasoline around the fire exits of the hotel and exploded them without warning, incinerating the men and women in one of the most nakedly sectarian acts ever perpetrated in the troubles.[8] La Mon was a departure from the concentration of force on off-duty soldiers, but nonetheless pointed to the organisation's ruthless pursuit of softer targets in the Protestant community. On 14 April, the Provisionals shot and killed off-duty UDR member James McKee, and an off-duty RUC officer John Moore a day later. The group then proceeded to kill another eight off-duty Security Force members in 1978, as it escalated its campaign of attrition even further.

Although the Provos had demonstrated their new-found effectiveness against soft targets, they were proving much less effective against mobile Security Force patrols. They did score some successes, like in their targeted assassination of undercover soldiers, like Lance Corporal Alan Swift from 14th Intelligence Company (known colloquially by soldiers as 'the Det'), who was shot by an IRA gunman as he sat in his unmarked car in Foyle Road, Londonderry, on 11 August 1978. A civilian who saw the attack said he watched the assailant dismount from a pick-up truck, casually walk across to Corporal Swift's car and fire twenty-five rounds from a machine-gun into the vehicle. The Provisionals had taken great care in mounting this operation, hijacking the truck used in the murder and taking its driver hostage until the gunman had safely escaped from the area.[9]

Most of the Provos' other attacks were much cruder – albeit equally effective – and consisted mainly of drive-by shootings of RUC and army personnel entering barracks or returning from patrols. These targets were easy to distinguish because they wore uniforms, and could be killed from a distance, either by way of the IRA's assortment of high velocity rifles or by way of its ready stock of command-wire IEDs. Like other guerrilla-based movements, IRA members preferred to operate at a safe distance from their targets, in terrain they knew intimately and with the aid of a vast network of safe houses, which offered them shelter from any follow-up Security Forces operations. Soldiers called the IRA's tactic 'shoot and scoot' and it would become the organisation's *modus operandi*, particularly in rural areas.

As the 1970s entered its final year, the Provisional IRA began to debate the future direction of its 'armed struggle'. The arrest and imprisonment of Gerry Adams on IRA membership charges cleared the way for a new Chief of Staff, the Derry republican Martin McGuinness. According to Moloney, McGuinness shifted from his role as the organisation's officer in charge of the Provo's Northern Command.[10] It was during McGuinness's tenure as their overall commander that the Provos increased their military pressure on the British by seeking out higher profile targets, which, they believed, would force a British withdrawal quicker than any number of assassinations of off-duty Security Forces personnel.

On August 1979, the IRA got its wish when it killed Lord Louis Mountbatten, a close relative of Queen Elizabeth II, in a bomb attack on his boat as he relaxed onboard with his family in Donegal. Later that day, IRA bombers struck again when they detonated two radio-controlled bombs on a passing military convoy returning to Newry from its patrol base in Warrenpoint. Eighteen soldiers were killed instantly, sixteen of whom were members of the 2nd Battalion, the Parachute Regiment.[11] Both of these attacks brought the Provisional IRA notoriety around the world. They had proven their ability to strike at the heart of the British establishment and inflict mass casualties on one of the British Army's toughest regiments in ways even members of the IRA Army Council could scarcely have dreamt possible just a few years earlier.

Ironically, the IRA's unit in Newry, which had helped carry out the attack, was considered one of the weakest links in the organisation's feared South Armagh brigade at that time. Up until August 1979 it was said that the unit's military record had been a 'demoralizing tale of incompetence and ineptitude'.[12] The Warrenpoint ambush demonstrated that local IRA men could plan and execute operations methodically. IRA volunteers were elated by the bombings. Their search for weakness, for patterns established by a clumsy enemy, was paying massive dividends. By completing a reassessment of the Provisional IRA's structure, strategy and intelligence, Brigadier Glover's report was designed to give the Security Forces a greater idea of what their enemy were doing and why. However, like most reports at the time, it was too little, too late, and, besides, its contents were to find their way into the public domain, courtesy of the lax personal security of one soldier who left it in open view in his car, and the ingenuity of a handful of republican propagandists.

★★★

Long Kesh Prison, County Down, November 1979

Although Billy Mitchell found great camaraderie inside the compounds, he had not yet discovered what he was looking for in life. As a consequence, he was prone to lurching from one seemingly contradictory political position to another, without any clear direction. His close comrade, 'Jon', felt that the older man was beginning to wrestle with his conscience in more profound ways. He was rediscovering his humanity and, more surprisingly, the humanity of those he had once considered mere targets for assassination:

> The thing that struck me was that he seemed to be searching for stuff, because at one time he seemed to be leaning towards extreme right-wing – and that would be [the] National Front, which sort of grew to prominence through the '80s in the UK. And then he would lurch the other way and be … taking on socialist, if not communist type leanings. So, I often wondered when I walked in and spoke to him, 'What is it today Billy?' you know. And then, out of the blue, came about this thing he was gonna be a Christian. One of the things in the compound was there was a small group of so-called born-again Christians, which is okay. I never joined that group but if that's the way people were then that was okay, so, I was a bit puzzled but I knew then that Billy was starting to study the Bible. And knowing Billy the way I did, whatever he would get into, he would get into in-depth. We had a few discussions around the whole thing about Biblical teaching, Christianity, what it means, Jesus, that sort of stuff. But he was never a 'tambourine type Christian'. Singing and all that sort of stuff. He was more a thoughtful – an intellectual – Christian, and [was more interested in] what it actually meant.[13]

In the closing months of 1979, Billy Mitchell received a visit from a Presbyterian minister. Although still antipathetic to the religious moralising he saw reflected in the mindset of well-meaning do-gooders, he was encumbered with a sense of spirituality that brought him closer to a tipping point. What the visiting cleric did was to force this thinking to a head. 'Do you repent for your past?' asked the clergyman. Mitchell paused for a moment. 'Did he mean my paramilitary past or did he mean general repentance? Was he being specific?' Mitchell believed he was. He felt anger wash over him before he answered. 'It is not me who needs to repent,' he told his shocked visitor. 'It is a society of bigots led by an elite of bigots who brought this war about and it is they, not me, who ought to repent. I am just the outward manifestation of their inner evil.'[14]

It was an abrupt meeting, and both men left the visitors' room disappointed at the acrimonious outcome. What the clergyman did not know at the time was that Mitchell had been trying hard to convince himself that he was not responsible for his actions leading up to his arrest and incarceration. It was society that was responsible, he believed, in moments of cognitive dissonance. Mitchell later reflected that the meeting was crucial, for it awoke in him a more introspective analysis of himself as a person and as a UVF leader:

I was the product of a Protestant-loyalist bigotry and the paramilitary monster of which I was a part was the creation of mad religio-political 'doctors'. In fact I often likened the relationship between the Protestant-unionist establishment and the loyalist paramilitaries as something akin to the relationship between Dr. Frankenstein and the creature in Mary Shelley's gothic novel and I have always, when reading Mrs Shelley's original, had a deep sense of sympathy for the unfortunate creature. It took a very long time even as a Christian, to come to terms with the past and to accept personal responsibility and guilt for my paramilitary activity. The fact that it was two years after my conversion before I relinquished my status as a 'special category' prisoner is evidence enough that I had a lengthy personal struggle with the issue of guilt and responsibility. This is not to say that the politicians and religious leaders who have kept alive the flames of sectarianism for so long are blameless, or that the Frankenstein-Monster/Loyalist Leader-Paramilitary analogy is not true; on the contrary, the political and religious leaders are guilty, the so-called 'Loyal' orders are guilty, and the mass of narrow-minded bigots who made up the population are guilty. There is such a thing as collective guilt. But notwithstanding all that, I and I alone am responsible for my own individual actions and

I, and I alone, must bear the guilt and shame for my personal support of, and involvement in, a terrorist organisation.[15]

In his reading of English literature, philosophy and Irish history, Billy Mitchell had undergone something akin to an intellectual metamorphosis. He had come to abandon his long-held belief that he had only taken part in violent acts as a direct result of some kind of spell he had been under thanks to the hate preached by loyalist cult figures like Ian Paisley. Now, he had reached a point in his life where he couldn't escape the simple intellectual and moral truism that he must also bear some responsibility for the acts he had personally sanctioned and perpetrated as a UVF commander.

The only problem was that he was still unsure of how to bridge the yawning gap between these two distinct positions.

Although Mitchell had not yet come to terms with the enormity of what he had been personally responsible for on the outside, he had moved further than any other UVF man at the time. As one of the most active members of Brigade Staff on the outside, he had more to atone for than younger UVF members like Hutchinson, Snoddon, Kinner and Ervine. They had undoubtedly been responsible for carrying out their actions on behalf of the organisation, but it was leaders like Mitchell who shouldered the burden of responsibility for sending these young men out to kill. He had been personally responsible for targeting a range of people with ruthless efficiency. Mitchell, more so than perhaps even Gusty Spence, was better placed to accept that he had helped create a monster that was entering a long war strategy of its own, which would come to mirror that pursued by the Provisionals, albeit on a level more limited in scope.

In the end, Billy Mitchell's guilt and sense of morality had come to weigh so heavily on his conscience that he felt he had no other option than to resign from the UVF, and leave the compound system entirely.

***

H Block 2, HMP Maze, County Down, 1980

By the late 1970s many more young, working-class Protestants had flocked to the UVF banner to replace those who had been taken out of circulation by death or incarceration. One of these young men was twenty-two-year-old William Stephen Wright. Known as Billy to his friends, he was born in Wolverhampton on 7 July 1960 to a mother and father from Northern Ireland. He was one of five children. The Wright family moved back to Portadown, his father David's birthplace, when Billy was four years old. Soon afterwards, the relationship between his parents broke down, and Wright was sent to live with a foster family in the small Protestant village of Mountnorris in South Armagh.[16]

Wright joined the UVF when he was fifteen. He hadn't been active in the organisation long when he was arrested in 1977 and sentenced to six and a half years for possession of illegal firearms. While in prison Wright became more and more militant, especially after learning the news that his uncle Jim Wright, a Reserve RUC officer in Portadown, had been killed in a car bomb placed by the INLA. The murder of Jim Wright on 27 July 1979 awoke an insatiable desire for revenge in the young Billy Wright, who had been fond of his uncle and looked upon him as a father figure, especially since Billy's own father had, in his words, 'taken to drink and fled the family home'.[17] Wright would later exact revenge on those he blamed for targeting his family.

A hardliner and a commander in the Young Paramilitary wing of H2, Wright drew his first opinions from that experience. 'I remember standing at the gates of an H Block. Where the blanket protest was taking place ... Standing beside me was a blanket protestor. He hadn't washed in a year. He was jaundiced. The stench of excrement filled the air. But there was an atmosphere of pure history,' Wright recalled a decade later. 'I stood in awe and said to myself what I'm seeing is pure history ... Here was a movement that could inflict violence on itself. What would it not inflict on human beings? It was a danger to my people.'[18] Scores of men went on hunger strike, the ultimate republican display of tenacity in their struggle against the British, with ten men starving themselves to death in the summer of 1981.[19]

After forty-two months in prison, Wright was released in 1980. As he walked through the gates of the Maze, his aunt and girlfriend looked on in 'total disbelief' as Wright turned to the British Army's observation post on the perimeter fence and shouted 'Up the UVF'.[20] Soldiers manning the tower looked on in mild amazement. Although eager to re-join the UVF's military team in Mid Ulster, he moved to Scotland where he found a job in the hospitality industry. In a matter of days, Special Branch officers from the Metropolitan Police were serving him an exclusion order, banning him from Great Britain. He promptly returned to Portadown and re-joined the ranks of the UVF.

Despite the weakness of the Provisional IRA in North Armagh, Wright came to see all of those who supported its armed struggle as a threat. Under his direction, the Mid Ulster UVF went on the offensive.

The group's first kill came on 17 November 1981. Twenty-year-old Peader Fagan was leaving his friend's house in Levin Road, Lurgan, when a car passed by with a number of men onboard. Wright is said to have sat calmly in the passenger side, armed with a pistol. Cocking the weapon, he casually wound down the window, pointed the gun at the young man and shot him at point-blank range. Fagan died instantly. It was later reported that Wright and his accomplice had entered the exclusively Catholic housing estate in Portadown looking for a particular target; when they couldn't find their man, they drove to Lurgan and shot Fagan instead, a popular GAA player in the town.[21] Wright and other men from Mid Ulster were arrested and charged for the murder and other terrorist offences on the word of twenty-three-year-old Clifford McKeown. Other men were implicated by McKeown,[22] all of whom remained on remand, despite McKeown having refused to sign his deposition that implicated them.[23]

***

Shankill Road, West Belfast, Summer 1982

The imprisonment of Wright and his team pointed to a new challenge for the UVF leadership in Belfast. Informants passing on occasional information to the police on a confidential basis began to threaten the internal cohesion of the organisation, which relied on its code of *omertá* to keep its activities secret.[24] The motivations of those inside the UVF who tipped off the RUC, British Army and intelligence services were mixed. Some did it for money, others because they had been aggrieved by paramilitaries in some way, or perhaps because they had been caught in the commission of a criminal act. However, it was to be another few years before the RUC managed to get a well-placed agent inside the UVF. In the meantime, the police had a new weapon in their armoury. In 1982 they offered some UVF suspects the opportunity to reduce their prospective sentence – and, in some cases, immunity from prosecution – if they were prepared to turn Queen's evidence in order to escape the harshest penalties courtesy of the criminal justice system.

Just as Wright had re-entered the prison system, the UVF was about to be reintroduced to one of its most proficient killers. Thirty-year-old Lenny

Murphy was finally released from prison in May 1982 after completing six years of a twelve-year sentence for possession of an illegal firearm. He had escaped the lesser charge of attempted murder because the evidence presented by the RUC in open court left reasonable doubt about whether he was the man who had carried out the drive-by shooting against two young Catholic women on the Antrim Road. Murphy was far from a model prisoner. He was unable to conform to the Spence regime during his internment in Long Kesh from April 1973 until October 1974. After a fight with Jim Irvine, the Officer Commanding Compound 12, he was expelled, only to be brought into Compound 11 by John McKeague. He struck up a friendship with a fellow loyalist internee, 'Geordie', who claimed that he was Murphy's 'muse', asking him how he might charm women he came into contact with. Geordie also said that Murphy had an annoying habit of playing songs by *The Carpenters* over and over again in the compound hut. 'You know who else had a penchant for *The Carpenters*?' asked Geordie. 'Jeffery Dahmer'.[25] He found Murphy 'creepy'. With a reputation for disrespect for authority and odd behaviour, Murphy struggled to serve out the remainder of his time and was transferred to Magilligan prison in County Londonderry after the Long Kesh fire of October 1974, from where he was released in April 1975.[26] One UVF man who brushed shoulders with him on remand in Crumlin Road prison insisted that, wherever he went, Murphy had an aura about him. 'One of the things we all had to do was go on hunger strike,' recalled Jon. 'And you could feel the mood, certainly within the loyalist prisoners, changing because he was there and everybody knew what he was.'[27] As Murphy counted down the days and weeks to his release from the H Blocks, working out more in the prison gym – he couldn't wait to get back out onto the streets. He was eager to help his brother John and Mr A form a new team and return to killing. By beating the greater charge of attempted murder, Murphy proved his worth as a skilled terrorist. He knew he had more to offer the UVF.

Within hours of his release, Murphy started to show his face around the Shankill. He frequented bars and clubs all over West Belfast. He was a young man in a hurry. One teenage boy who worked in the Rex Bar at the time remembers how Murphy had been drinking heavily on the premises one afternoon when he left his half-finished pint and crossed over to the Eagle for a meeting with the UVF leadership. 'I was in collecting LPs for our sales so this would have been the '82 period. I was around fourteen or fifteen years old. Comms [prison communications] then came out on loo roll. I can't actually recall, today, how I came to be sat reading it [the comm] but he basically snatched it off me and gave me a hiding and threatened that if I ever read "UVF business again" he'd shoot me.' The boy panicked, frozen in place, frightened at the prospect of Murphy's next move. 'Thon's a communiqué from the POWs, something none of these cunts would know anything about,' Murphy barked at him, as he hit the teenager another slap for good measure. The UVF leaders in the room sat still and said nothing. It was said that they were petrified of Murphy.[28]

✴✴✴

Shankill Road, afternoon/evening, 5 September 1982

Thirty-year-old Brian Smyth was in good spirits when he left his home near Donaghadee for a Sunday afternoon out with his friends on the Shankill Road. A former sailor in the Royal Navy, he had since acquired a garage on the Gransha Road in Bangor from which he sold second-hand cars. He was travelling to Belfast to collect the money for an Opel he had sold Lenny Murphy a few days earlier.[29] The men arrived at the Loyalist Club in the afternoon, where Smyth had a meeting with Murphy about the money. Smyth was told in no uncertain terms by Murphy that he couldn't expect to receive his money for another few days. Leaving the meeting empty-handed, Smyth and the others decided to head to the Liverpool Club further up the Shankill Road. Murphy followed suit. When Smyth and his friends left for the Loyalist Club Murphy was again hot on their heels. On a whim, Smyth decided to call into the Ohio Street Club, rather than return straight away to Rumford Street. The friends had only just ordered their drinks when Smyth took a swig of his Bacardi and coke and quickly spat it out, loudly asserting that someone had tried to poison him. He passed the drink to his friend Samuel to taste, and he too vomited.[30] Both men made for the toilet, but they didn't get far before throwing up again. After complaining to the barman, the atmosphere suddenly became tense, and they were made to feel unwelcome. They left for the Crusader's Social Club on the Shore Road, where they drank beer for another hour or so, before Brian realised that his coat was missing. After driving back to the Shankill at 9:30 p.m., Smyth and his two companions decided to stay on and continue drinking. It was a decision that would have profound repercussions for all of them.

After some time had passed, Brian and his friend Sam became violently ill from the effects of the spiked drink they had ingested earlier that evening. Trying desperately to sober up, they resolved to drive to the Mater Hospital on the nearby Crumlin Road to seek medical assistance. As the two friends made their way along the Shankill in their silver Saccio 1000 car, they saw the single headlamp of a motorbike approach their vehicle from the rear. Thinking it was the police, they turned into the junction of Crimea Street and Riga Street and slowed down. The pillion passenger then signalled for them to pull over. After stopping the car, the two men got out and milled around on the pavement. As soon as the cold air hit them they felt fully inebriated by the alcohol. 'All of a sudden there was a silhouette of a person amongst us, and then the shooting started,' Sam later told the police. He then heard Brian shout 'the fuckers have got me', before falling to the ground. Sam instinctively threw himself on top of his friend. 'You've killed him, you've killed him,' he shouted at the gunmen. After five or six shots, Sam heard the gun click. The fact that a revolver has been used rather than a semi-automatic pistol probably saved his life.

Murphy had killed Smyth because he believed he had short-changed him for the car. It had nothing to do with an 'internal feud', as later accounts would suggest. At 5'11" and weighing nearly fifteen stone, Brian Smyth was of muscular build and heavily tattooed. As a former serviceman, he had the look of a man who could handle himself in a fight. Realising that he could not hope to take on the former sailor and win, Murphy decided to poison him, before hunting him down and murdering him in cold blood. Drunk and vulnerable, Smyth had no chance. The bullets discharged from Murphy's pistol tore through Brian's body, leaving several small abrasions, each of which left behind large exit wounds on his chest.[31]

After he killed Smyth, Murphy entered a downward spiral. He became uncontrollable. His actions soon drew the attention of other loyalists who resented the heat that his score-settling was bringing down on their criminal operations in West Belfast. Although he didn't know it at the time, Murphy was on borrowed time. Journalist Martin Dillon claimed that 'the UVF leadership was terrified of having to cope with Murphy and at least one member of the UVF leadership was resigned to the fact that Murphy should be assassinated'.[32] The implication was that if another organisation moved against him, they would not stand in their way. It later emerged that RUC Special Branch had been watching Murphy since his release from prison. On 24 October, apparently after surveillance had been lifted on him, Murphy kidnapped and murdered forty-eight-year-old Catholic civilian, Joseph Donegan.[33] He had help on this occasion from eighteen-year-old Tommy Stewart, a young UVF member who would, some years later, become the organisation's commander in Ballysillan. Murphy, Stewart and two others abducted Donegan and took him to the former Murphy family home, which had since become derelict, where the men tortured their victim, a married man with seven children. After pulling out Joseph's teeth from their roots with a pair of pliers, Murphy dragged his victim out into the back yard and handed Stewart a shovel, telling him to 'finish off the taig'.[34]

Three weeks after the murder of Joe Donegan, Murphy himself was gunned down by the Provisional IRA as he left his girlfriend's house in Forthriver Park. There were two ironic twists to the story of Murphy's demise. The first happened on 10 October, when he returned from his uncle Jackie 'Nigger' Irvine's bail hearing to his girlfriend's home in Forthriver Park to receive an anonymous phone call. Murphy immediately rang the Head of CID at Tennent Street, Alan Simpson, to report the threat to his life. Simpson regarded Murphy as an 'arrogant and self-confident' individual, who was, worryingly, now gathering a new following of younger UVF members around him. Simpson couldn't believe Murphy's brazen attitude, for it was well-known, if difficult to prove, that he had been responsible for multiple murders. When Simpson asked him what the caller had said to Murphy, he simply said, 'we are coming to get you, Leonard.'[35] The second twist to Murphy's assassination was that he died yards from where Billy Moore and other members of the Shankill Butchers gang had dumped the body of their final murder victim, twenty-one-year-old student Stephen McCann. The blue Marina van used by the IRA in Murphy's assassination was driven at speed down a minor road behind some houses, and then abandoned. The gunmen made good their escape into Ligoniel via a small country lane next to where McCann's body had been discovered.

It would later transpire that the individual who was chiefly responsible for Murphy's death was not a leading Provisional, as initially thought, but the UDA's West Belfast commander James Pratt Craig. The UDA boss was rumoured to have personally engineered Murphy's demise and those of other loyalists, including outspoken loyalist councillor George Seawright. Craig's motivation was, apparently, simple. Murphy's 'killing sprees brought too much police attention into the Shankill area, and this threatened Craig's criminal activities'.[36] For one NIO official based at Stormont, the press speculation on collusion between loyalists and republicans, which is believed to have led to Murphy's death, was unhelpful. '[N]either we nor the RUC have any evidence to support this theory; and we have had no other reports suggesting contact between the UVF and PIRA or INLA for some considerable time,' reported the NIO official. He continued:

> There have been a number of RUC intelligence reports suggesting meetings between a leading UDA member and representatives of both PIRA and INLA, but discussion during such meetings is generally restricted to the topics of racketeering and tax evasion. It seems likely that if any contacts between loyalist paramilitaries and Republican terrorist groups exist they are at a low level and primarily concerned with criminal matters.

Even the NIO believed that the 'ad hoc links' established between loyalist and republican prisoners and the limited cooperation on the segregation campaign did not 'seem to reflect any outside co-ordination.'[37]

Eighty-seven separate death notices appeared in the *Belfast Telegraph* the day after Murphy was assassinated by the IRA. Some were from his closest comrades in the UVF, and others were received from the likes of leading UFF men John White and Kenny McClinton. As Murphy's coffin was brought out of his parents' home in Brookmount Street, six hooded men appeared alongside it wearing dark glasses and carrying guns. They fired three volleys over the coffin as a salute to their fallen comrade.[38] In a bid to prevent the press from taking photographs of the ritual, women stepped forward and opened their umbrellas. The message was clear – the press was as unwelcome as Murphy's local commander, who was apparently also shunned by the family.[39] As the funeral cortege made its way down the Shankill Road a lone piper played *Abide with Me* as hundreds of mourners joined in behind to pay their respects. After a short service, the cortege made its way out of the city towards Carnmoney Cemetery, where the piper played another lament and the coffin was lowered into the ground. One of the UVF's most ruthless killers was buried, ironically, yards from where his old unit's last murder victim, Stephen McCann, had been interred. Both men had died within yards of each other. Now they would be laid to rest almost the same distance from one another in the graveyard.

★★★

The late 1970s and early 1980s was a period of radical change in the mindsets of those UVF and RHC men who passed through the compound system. Not all of them came to renounce their actions like Billy Mitchell, nor had they begun to develop a political consciousness, as David Ervine, Billy Hutchinson and Eddie Kinner had done. Some, like Lenny Murphy, Billy Wright, Trevor King and Frankie Curry, were on a journey of self-discovery of their own, emerging from prison eager to re-enter the organisation's military teams so as to drive forward a renewed campaign of terror.[40] They believed that their careers as triggermen had been cut short, and that their work was not yet finished. Outside of the Spence regime, there was a fairly lax system for personal development. UVF prisoners were permitted to arrive at their own conclusions about why they were there. That is why, when they reached this fork in the road, some took a political path while others walked to a more military drumbeat, in a very different direction indeed.

Republicans, meanwhile, were undergoing a more collective shift towards what they would come to call their 'long war'. The 1981 hunger strikes generated huge sympathy for militant republicans and their political associates, and would lead to a mushrooming of electoral support for Sinn Féin within the nationalist community, though this was more a calculated exploitation of circumstances than a clear-sighted strategy. Loyalists were playing catch-up, but the intervention of the PUP in the 1981 local government elections (in which they polled 2,434 votes, returning Hugh Smyth but not David Overend) surprised even republicans, with their 1980 Ard Fheis deciding against contesting the polls. Loyalism, in reality, was not lagging that far behind at all.

11

AT THE BOTTOM OF THE WELL

'We are sinners. You know what a sinner is? A sinner is someone who goes against God'.

William Stephen Wright, *Testimony before God* (circa 1983)

Castlereagh RUC Station, East Belfast, Late May 1982

'He didn't look at me,' recalled Bobby Norris, as he explained how the RUC had brought him face-to-face with his accuser, thirty-six-year-old Joseph Bennett. Four to five burly police officers entered the interrogation room to prevent Norris from lunging at Bennett, up until that point the Commanding Officer of the UVF's South Belfast battalion and a former compound man. One detective read from a prepared list of questions. 'Well, what do you say to these allegations?' asked the policeman. Norris paused, then replied to the stern-looking officer, 'I've never had any dealings with that man in my life.' 'It was true,' Norris said. 'Bennett didn't know me from Adam.' During the interrogation, Norris told detectives that the information they were putting to him was 'complete lies'.[1]

On the morning Norris was arrested he had got up and left for work as normal. He was employed as a roofer at the gas works. Having completed the first half of his shift, he decided to take a stroll to a nearby pub for lunch. Before he even got inside, Norris was confronted by several police officers, who arrested him under Section 12 of the Prevention of Terrorism Act (1976). Still dressed in his work overalls, Norris found himself incarcerated at Castlereagh RUC station, along with fifteen other suspects. At Castlereagh, the men were held in single cells to prevent them from communicating with each other. Norris didn't know the other men in the cells. Only one or two of those on remand were 'on nodding terms'. Charged with a total of sixty-six offences, including murder, possession of guns and explosives as well as membership of a proscribed organisation, Norris and his co-accused appeared in Townhall Street on 1 June 1982, where they were placed on remand.

The round-up was in response to information supplied by Bennett, who had earlier been arrested after a botched armed robbery of the post office in Killinchy on 5 May 1982. It was a violent incident in which the postmistress, sixty-four-year-old Maureen McCann, a Protestant, was stabbed and shot by the UVF men. Bennett had since become what the RUC termed a 'converted terrorist', known to everyone else as a 'Supergrass', and was now placed in the awkward position of testifying against men he had known for years – and others he clearly didn't know at all – in exchange for immunity from prosecution for the murder of Mrs McCann. Consul for Bennett claimed the Belfast man had been prepared to engage in murder and illegal activities for the group, and had been willing 'to travel abroad to further the organisation's aims'.[2]

Little did the RUC know at the time, but Bennett was regarded as a 'spoofer' in UVF circles. One UVF life-sentence prisoner, Jon, who met him in Long Kesh in the late 1970s, recalled how Bennett spent an evening in the compounds regaling him and others with tales of a pub bombing he claimed he had carried out. Later, when Jon retired to his own bunk for the night, another prisoner whispered quietly over to him, 'That was us. Don't trust a word that comes out of that man's mouth.'[3] Desperate to cripple the UVF, RUC officers did listen to Joe Bennett, and were prepared to mount a less than watertight case against the UVF suspects on that basis.

The sixteen men being held had mounted a vigorous defence against the allegations put to them by police, especially when it emerged that some were denied legal counsel for several days after their arrest. That was not the only challenge facing the men. The introduction of the no-jury (or Diplock) court system in the 1970s was due to the threat posed to the lives of those who might have found themselves presiding over the fate of dangerous terrorists. In this case, it was a tool the British sought to use in order to secure convictions. Recognising the seriousness of the legal mechanisms now mounted against them – supergrasses combined with Diplock Courts – the UVF leadership sanctioned dialogue between the men on remand and republican prisoners facing similar charges. They were anxious to see if there was any common ground on which they could collaborate to fight the system.

In London, Conservative government ministers were giddy at the prospect of striking at the beating heart of loyalist and republican paramilitarism in Northern Ireland. Their security chiefs agreed that the scheme presented some problems, but that these paled into insignificance when the process promised to disrupt terrorist activity long term and, perhaps even, prevent further attacks altogether. Senior civil servants identified four clear benefits of using supergrasses which ranged from the gathering of intelligence against terrorist organisations; collecting information leading to the seizure of terrorist weapons and explosives; the ability to use statements by converted terrorists to prompt confessions by other terrorists and, finally, the opportunity to use converted terrorists as witnesses against other terrorists in open court.[4] For the British, the granting of immunity from prosecution to the supergrass was 'normally unconditional and irrevocable'.[5] It was essentially a Faustian Pact between the state and a well-placed terrorist that was not always guaranteed to work. 'It is not conditional on the witness giving evidence in court against his former accomplices,' read a report written for British ministers at the time. 'He retains his immunity, even if he retracts his evidence. The point here is that at the time he gives his evidence the witness should be under no pressure to give false evidence in court.'[6] In theory it was a brilliant, if unethical, use of the judicial system in a bid to decapitate the leadership of these armed groups and thereby ensure they couldn't operate with the same impunity that had driven them in the previous decade. And it had been used with vigour against dangerous criminals in England in a bid to take them out of circulation. One of those arrested on the word of Joe Bennett admitted that the process 'did quieten things down for a while' and 'caused havoc simply because people didn't trust each other'.[7]

One of the areas also acutely affected by the supergrass system was Mid Ulster, which, in the early 1980s, seemed to lack any proper paramilitary structures at all. This became evident when Clifford McKeown was arrested on a murder charge. After questioning him for several hours the RUC judged that McKeown knew much more about the Mid Ulster UVF in the region than they had first thought. Realising that they had the opportunity to dismantle one of the most ruthless units within the UVF, detectives offered McKeown the opportunity to reduce his sentence in exchange for turning supergrass. The deal secured the arrest of over twenty suspects on McKeown's evidence, all of whom were subsequently brought to trial. As he stood in the dock, McKeown was heckled by supporters of the defendants, who sat patiently through proceedings in the public gallery. Under the weight of intimidation and threats, McKeown broke and quickly recanted his evidence amidst angry scenes. Nine people were released immediately, though the others remained in custody.[8]

Eight months later, the RUC caught a lucky break in Crumlin Road Courthouse. The barrister defending the sixteen Belfast men caught up in the Bennett case was the influential unionist, Dessie Boal, considered, at this stage, to be one of the most effective QCs in Europe. In his summing up at the twenty-one-day supergrass trial, Boal made an impassioned plea to the court that all of the accused were of good character and innocent of the charges brought against them. 'It was all good theatre,' recalled Bobby Norris.[9] By the time the judge came to make his remarks, he was unimpressed by the defence counsel. Without much deliberation, he passed a guilty verdict on all of the defendants. The men in the dock were startled. Immediately they began to jostle with the prisoner warders. Supporters in the public gallery shouted 'no surrender' and 'there will be plenty more to take your place' when the ruling was made.[10] Police officers standing nearby held on tightly to their machine guns. There were worries that the UVF might attack the court, and so a contingency plan was drawn up. Should trouble break out, Mr Justice Murray (who wore a bulletproof vest throughout proceedings) could beat a hasty retreat from the courtroom, closely followed by Joe Bennett, and protected by a phalanx of eighty-six police and prison officers. There was no need to put the plan in operation, and the officers managed to restrain the men. The presiding judge handed down convictions to fourteen of the sixteen UVF suspects, including two life sentences and a 200-year prison sentence for the remaining men. Boal was apoplectic with rage. Shouting directly at the judge, he demanded to know how he could possibly have found in favour of the charges. Taking off his wig, Boal flung it on the table in front of the judge in disgust.

News soon spread across the Crumlin Road to the prison. Republicans facing similar charges reportedly 'burst out crying'.[11]

★★★

Almost a year had elapsed since the introduction of the supergrass scheme. Both loyalists and republicans remained contemptuous of the legal system. Amnesty International even challenged the process on the basis of its negative effect on the human rights of the accused, claiming it violated the liberal democratic norm of a right to a fair trial.[12] In the background, the scheme had other flaws, namely that it afforded the supergrass a high degree of protection that would cost the taxpayer millions of pounds in order to resettle them and their families. The RUC were unapologetic, and remained convinced it was a price, be it high, that was worth paying in order to defeat the terrorists. The Chief Constable at the time, Sir John Hermon, saw the scheme as a key tenet in his overarching counter-terrorism strategy:

> The complexities and sensitivities of using converted terrorists was enormous, as were the administrative procedures necessary when arresting and interviewing many hardened terrorists. Laborious though it was, a system of processing such cases developed during the early 1980s, and 'supergrasses' kept emerging. Many dramatic trials – each of long duration and vehemently contested by those accused – took place, with very positive results in terms of convictions and sentencing. From the beginning, I had recognised the benefits of the system of converted terrorists, and was eager to see it continue. I was satisfied that the proper procedures were followed, with all steps monitored and approved by the DPP.[13]

In the time period between November 1981 and December 1985, some twenty-seven supergrasses testified against 600 loyalist and republican suspects. Although the Bennett trial was one of the most prominent, it was not the first time UVF suspects found themselves in the dock. The first major trial involved 'Witness X', a member of the East Antrim UVF, which saw twenty-eight people charged and twenty-six convicted. The men were handed down sentences totalling 1,038 years in 1977.

As the months wore on, the use of supergrass came under more intense legal, political and diplomatic pressure. Some regarded them as little more than 'show trials' and 'paid perjury'. Even the great champion of legal abuses and judicial reform, Lord Longford, campaigned against the use of supergrasses, visiting John Bingham at his home and even staying overnight.[14] Amidst a barrage of criticism, government ministers in Whitehall, London, now moved to undertake a cost-benefit analysis of the entire supergrass scheme:

> At first blush, there have been damaging reversals in cases involving converted terrorists over the last two months. That impression is substantially misleading. On balance positive developments outweigh the negative. Clearly, problems connected with the grant of immunity remain and are likely to give the DPP pause for the future. Delays in bringing cases to trial impose strains on the converted terrorist as much

as on the defendants. Grimley's case [Jackie Grimley was an INLA supergrass] raises doubts about the wisdom of using the evidence of individuals who have previously been paid police informers. But the complexity of the judicial process and the variety of individual cases continues to present major difficulties for those who would wish to see changes in either law or practice.[15]

At a Security Policy Meeting on 23 January 1984, a forum which brought together the Secretary of State for Northern Ireland, the RUC Chief Constable and the British Army's General Officer Commanding, the continuing use of supergrasses was up for discussion. Secretary of State Jim Prior was deeply concerned that the convictions might be overturned in light of the recent decision in the McCormick case. In a briefing paper sent to Prior's Private Secretary, it was admitted that there was 'no indication as yet that the judgement in the McCormick case will have any effect on these outstanding appeals', but that the 'cases will no doubt raise a variety of legal difficulties, and we must have some qualms about the prospects for Bennett at any rate; he was a poor witness (of appalling character), and the judge's summing up may reveal weaknesses. But at present, there do not seem to be implications for policy.'[16]

The government's view was that 'impartial enforcement of the rule of law' must be the principal means by which terrorism and crime was detected and prevented in order to bring it to an end. Although now costing more in the short term, it was still thought that:

> Converted terrorists present a powerful threat to the structure and cohesion of terrorist organisations. These organisations have therefore sought to prevent their members from turning against them by actual or threatened murder, violence or the kidnap of relatives. In a few cases these tactics have been successful, but in several others they have failed and kidnap victims have been released.[17]

The jury was, quite literally, still out on whether the scheme actually went some way towards tackling the root cause of terrorism in Northern Ireland. Nonetheless, the government position remained that:

> The impact of converted terrorists has profoundly disconcerted some of the operations of terrorist organisations, and has encouraged

other members of the public to assist the police. As a result of the information gained, arms and explosives have been seized, acts of terrorism prevented and, without doubt, lives saved. The community has benefited immeasurably from this development.[18]

The use of supergrasses had a double-edged effect on the UVF. The man believed to be the organisation's second-in-command and Director of Operations was forced to keep a low profile, thereby almost grinding the group's activities to a halt. Intriguingly, he had sat through every court case and listened to every piece of evidence presented by the Crown.[19] Yet, it also led to the emergence of a more robust Provost Marshal structure, to weed out informers and to enforce a stricter code of *omertá* on the UVF's rank-and-file volunteers. Interestingly, the Provisional IRA now accelerated its process of cellularisation, and made it more difficult for the state's security agencies to penetrate the organisation. By the mid-1980s loyalists had begun to follow suit.[20] For the UVF, the public exposure of its members prized open a secretive world that enabled the IRA to more effectively target them.[21] For the UVF leadership, 'It was as if someone said to the police, "You can have use of this immoral instrument, but only for a wee while." Once you're done with it you have to give it back.'[22]

***

The collapse of the McKeown supergrass trial saw Billy Wright back on the streets. His spell in prison led him to question his beliefs, and drove him further into the arms of Christian fundamentalism. While in the Maze, Wright had converted to Christianity, facilitated by Kenny McClinton. During his religious testimony on 24 June 1983, Wright likened his own story to one he told of a 'bear trapped in the prison house':

> You know we are all born sinners. You know dear friend. You are in that prison house tonight. There is only one person. Dear friend you are in that prison house tonight. People say, 'What is wrong with one drink?' Go and ask the alcoholic. He will tell you … I was born in Wolverhampton. Dad took a drink and it ruined the home. They split up. We ended up in a welfare home. Eventually my mother took an overdose. [My sister] Connie is praising God. She's come through it rightly. I love youse with all your heart. Mum got up the next morning

and disappeared from our lives. This is God's word. God that made heaven and earth. God has told us all. Even as wee boys. We are sinners. You know what a sinner is? A sinner is someone who goes against God.[23]

McClinton would become one of Wright's closest confidants. 'He witnessed to me about the Lord Jesus Christ,' Wright told those gathered to hear his testimony before God:

> When I was in prison a young girl wrote to me. When I realised that I was going to hell. Used to say that there is someone else in this prison cell with me. 'What about the dances, the mates, the good times?' You need to be saved. But I have something inside me that motivates me. And it's a love for the Lord Jesus Christ. A deep-rooted love. You know, sometimes I'd go to bed and [when] God puts that desire inside you.[24]

When he was released, Wright did not return to his old ways, at least not immediately. Believing that he had been given a second chance, Wright walked away from the UVF in 1982 to become a preacher of the gospels. By the mid-1980s, he was still unsure what the future held for him. 'Now I was not sure what the Lord was telling me. Was I to be a preacher? Was I to be a saver of souls abroad as Billy Wright has often thought of doing, or did the Lord have other work for me ...'[25] He would soon return to the ranks of the UVF, finding the gravitational pull of that world unavoidable.

Elsewhere in Long Kesh, other UVF and RHC prisoners were on their own personal journey. They began to build a political education project centred around a form of socialist unionism. 'Globalisation was happening at that particular time,' Billy Hutchinson recalled. 'You had all sorts of political movements, like the New Right that started to come about in the mid-80s through Thatcher and Reagan. And all those things were threatening to ordinary people. These were power blocs that were getting together to decide how capital would be spent, whether there should be an arms race, whether there should be a "Star Wars" [the anti-ballistic missile Strategic Defence Initiative (SDI) announced by US President Ronald Reagan] and all of these things. And people around the world were dying of poverty. And they weren't focusing on how you dealt with somebody's problem in Belfast or Londonderry. Those were things we were beginning to question.'[26]

These 'L men' began to question more than the external socio-economic forces that were blowing through Northern Ireland. Winds of change of a very different and more intensely personal kind were swirling around inside Billy Mitchell's pit. He had reached an incredibly difficult decision that would affect his remaining years inside. He opted to resign from the UVF. Over the course of a few days he reflected on his decision. Once he had spoken with the UVF hierarchy inside and outside of the prison, he turned to one of his close friends, Jon:

> So, I was a bit sad and shocked when he said one day he was leaving for the H Blocks. To us that was tantamount to saying you were gonna cut a leg off. The H Blocks was hell. They went through their dirty protests, lots of fighting, hunger strikes, and very much where the prison staff, the screws, were on top. They were in charge. And there was a feeling that anybody who left Special Category Status – voluntarily gave it up – would be getting a hard time over there, cos the screws would be saying, 'We're in charge now.' While we were in the compounds, we were in charge. There was no doubt about that.[27]

Not all UVF volunteers were as sympathetic to Billy Mitchell's decision as Jon had been. Others derided him. 'Here's another leaning on the Bible to do his time. Just do your time,' a few of them said in hushed voices, away from prying ears. Jon explained that even though it was an intensely personal decision for Mitchell, it had a collective effect on the other men.

> So, it took quite a bit of strength for any of us to turn around and say, 'I'm leaving here.' You were giving up something that was precious and as soon as you left Special Category status you never came back. No one ever came back. So, because of the vast distance between Special Cat and the H Blocks, once someone left, unless there was a channel or means of communication, they effectively left your life.[28]

Not long after Mitchell left, the last of the compound 'L Men' were transferred to the new H Blocks. Long Kesh, which had once been the scene of black-clad UVF men parading in ranks, was consigned to the history books. The hidden battalion of the UVF continued in another form, albeit with less cohesion and corporate discipline than before, once the men entered individual cells.

★★★

Meanwhile, on the streets, the UVF was developing elaborate plans to grow its 'war chest' by extorting money from businesses. In March 1984, the RUC uncovered a plot by UVF members to poison food being sold in supermarket chain Dunnes Stores, unless a £500,000 ransom demand was paid by the company's CEO, Ben Dunne Snr. The company, which had twenty stores in Northern Ireland, reassured its customers by implementing security measures in consultation with the RUC and An Garda Siochána.[29] The plot was soon foiled when the RUC lured the extortionists to a cash drop in Dromore, County Down, where they were intercepted by police. This latest threat had come nearly three years after Ben Dunne Jnr had been kidnapped and held for six days for ransom by republicans. He was later released unharmed.[30] The mastermind of the Dunnes Stores poisoning plot was rumoured to have been Mid Ulster UVF commander Robin 'The Jackal' Jackson, who promptly went on the run after the plot failed fearing he'd be moved up the Provisional IRA's hit list.

One man who was not so lucky to have survived a UVF plot unscathed was thirty-six-year-old John Longstaff, an arms dealer from Leeds, who was found dead and locked in the toilet of a Boeing 737 on the runway of Heathrow airport in March 1984. His throat had been slashed. The flight had just touched down from Germany when cabin crew discovered his body. It was believed that Longstaff was involved in a major arms sting to intercept weapons on their way to the UVF at the time he died. This was not the first time Longstaff had been involved in arms smuggling. In 1972 police arrested two men, John Charles Baird and John McKee, who had arrived at his shop in Leeds to collect weapons. 'During that year, all sorts of things were said,' Longstaff later told reporters after the incident. 'They have the ultimate solution for the troubles of Northern Ireland. You would never believe it if I told you what they were planning. I do not know why the UVF chose me. I have no Irish connections. If anyone comes after me it will be members of the UVF or even the IRA.'[31] The police later said that Longstaff had committed suicide onboard the aircraft. His family were unconvinced. For one thing, he wore a beard and wouldn't have had a razor in his possession.[32]

Some months later, the UVF attempted to kill the *Sunday World's* Northern Editor, Jim Campbell, the reporter who had taken the call from the mysterious 'Major Long' of the UVF almost a decade earlier. Now members of another UVF had turned up at his family home to shoot him in May 1984. It was the first deliberate murder bid on a journalist in the troubles and it appears that Campbell's stories about Robin Jackson and the Mid Ulster UVF had infuriated some within the organisation. The attack was promptly condemned by the National Union of Journalists.[33] As a sign of defiance in the face of UVF threats, Campbell penned a feature article in the *Sunday World* entitled 'The Jackal', which he attributed to the newspaper's security correspondent 'Robin Jackson'. It alleged that the Jackal was being shielded by British Intelligence, and proceeded to link the Mid Ulster loyalist to a raid on a UDR barracks in Lurgan in October 1972, in which eighty rifles, two submachine guns and 1,000 rounds of ammunition were stolen.

The *Sunday World* also linked Jackson directly to the Miami Showband massacre, and two machine gun attacks on 28 October 1973, in which thirty-four-year-old trade unionist Patrick Campbell was killed, and in April 1975. According to the newspaper, Jackson and his right-hand man, Wesley Somerville, had pulled the triggers that evening. The reason for Jackson's decision to murder Campbell, a colleague of his at Down Shoes Ltd in Banbridge, emerged out of a minor dispute between the two men on a night out after work. This was said to be Jackson's first murder in a long litany that stretched over the next two decades.[34] The *Sunday World* also claimed that Jackson was one of the gunmen who had murdered thirty-nine-year-old shopkeeper William Strathearn, a married man with seven children, in the quiet village of Ahoghill in County Antrim on 19 April 1977.[35]

★★★

On the road to HMP Maze, Lisburn, late October 1984

Detective Constable Ben Forde was making his way to the Maze Prison to visit Billy Mitchell. 'The irony is,' Ben said as he turned to his partner, Sam, 'that most of these fellas start out with the best of intentions as sincere and loyal members of the community. It never occurs to them that, far from helping to solve a problem, they're just adding to it.' 'Aye,' replied Sam. 'We've seen it too many times. They become so frustrated, so desperate to wipe out the enemy, that they fail to see they're falling right into the trap. Before they can turn round they've become terrorists themselves.' Sam paused to reflect on what Ben was saying. 'But, I have to admit, I understand how it can happen. When the terror comes close a man can feel so threatened, so helpless. The instinctive reaction is to strike back.'[36] Forde disagreed with the actions taken by loyalist and republican paramilitaries, but he was driven by an insatiable desire to try and understand why they did what they did. He was a committed Christian, a regular church-goer and gospel singer, and, as such, believed strongly in the Biblical edict of forgiveness. He also had a strong urge to assist those who had sinned to find redemption in Christ, should they be so inclined. On the day he was making a visit to the Maze Prison, Ben Forde believed that he was going to meet a man who had turned his back on his paramilitary past, and was interested in throwing himself into non-violent solutions to the problems facing people in Northern Ireland.

Billy Mitchell had certainly embarked on a journey of seismic personal transformation. After his resignation from the UVF in 1982 and his move out of the Long Kesh compounds, Mitchell began to make plans for the future, amidst the prospect of another fifteen years in prison. Crucially, he now began to distance himself from his actions as a UVF commander:

Since my conversion to Christ [Nov 1979] and particularly since my subsequent development of a Christian world-view, I look back with genuine horror and regret at the terrible misery for which the UVF has been responsible and for which I, as one of its more prominent officers, must bear the guilt and shame. For quite some time, even after my conversion, I attempted to off-load some of the blame and responsibility by mainly looking for scapegoats. The politicians with their fiery rhetoric and hate-mongering attitudes, the religio-loyal orders with their perpetration of sacralism through their secret lodges and their combination of religion and politics, the hot gospel anti-popery preachers with their passion-rousing sermons and their 'Israel–Ulster' allegories, together with the failure of government policies in the face of militant republicanism – all these, and many more, were raised by me and floated as possible excuses for my past beliefs and behaviour.[37]

Mitchell came to hear about Ben Forde's work on 'criminal caring', a project that had grown out of the Thatcherite turn towards 'community caring' in

Great Britain, which sought to unburden the state's responsibility for those with mental health problems onto the wider community. It was something he strongly believed in, and was anxious to gain some traction for it in the prisons, where he felt he could do invaluable work.

The visits from Ben Forde at this time were a vital lifeline for Mitchell. He was finding it increasingly difficult to put in the long days behind bars. He spent most of his time writing letters, for he found that it calmed him and allowed him to think more freely. 'You have been created and redeemed by the Lord who has a definite plan and purpose for your life,' he wrote. 'Why then have you the audacity to question your value?' He was experiencing 'a nagging, persistent sense of moral unworthiness'. He grappled with the problem of objective self-condemnation. He doubted his worth as a human being. Those who committed crimes were 'unlovable and unloved', he would say. Feelings of depression, self-pity, introspection, defensiveness, bitterness, resentment and envy crept into his mind on a fairly regular basis. He tossed and turned in his bunk at night in the early years as he made the transition away from paramilitarism and towards something resembling a civilian identity. Like all prisoners incarcerated for many long years, he went through ups and downs. His conscience ate away at him. Constantly questioning his own past actions, he found it hard to take praise or encouragement from others. He risked retreating in on himself.

It was in these dark days that Billy Mitchell found comfort in prayer. He prayed every evening after dinner. He intellectualised his prison experience. 'Christian prisoners – that is, offenders who have been converted to Christ while in prison,' he wrote, 'often find themselves struggling with self-condemnation in spite of the fact that they have truly repented of their sins (and crimes) and have been forgiven for them, and have committed themselves to a life of Christian service,' he would confide in his meditations on 'criminal caring'. 'Hence, notwithstanding Romans 3:1, 33, 34, many Christian prisoners suffer greatly from feelings of self-condemnation which stem from their own distorted evaluation of themselves.' Mitchell considered how Christians and non-Christians might greet his turn towards Christ. He wrote furiously about how prison chaplains might minister more productively to a flock that faced many years of incarceration. 'Most secular counsellors – psychologists and social workers – simply look at the emotional problem itself and fail to penetrate any deeper, to get to the roots of our troubled human condition. A Christian perspective, on the other hand, cannot afford to ignore the moral dimensions of the problem.'[38]

'Our God was one who resided in Israel, not Ulster,' remembered Ben Forde. 'You cannot understand Billy Mitchell without understanding the faith that sustained him and carried him through the latter half of his life.'[39] For Mitchell, faith was a guiding thread that ran throughout his life. It was what made him the man he was, particularly in the last decades of his life. 'We shared these verses. They got us through difficult times. I was his friend as we faced the future,' recalled Forde. 'We were instruments through which God did his work. Billy worked to a higher design. He was a mere vessel doing the Lord's work. We have no say. If God wants to use you, he will use you. If he wants to take this policeman, this paramilitary chief and use us for a higher purpose, who are we to contradict God's will?'[40] Forde believed that he and Mitchell had laid the foundations of a strong and binding friendship and, perhaps, even the early cornerstone for Mitchell's own understanding of peace and what it might mean for loyalists and unionists.

Apart from receiving an initial visit from Forde, Mitchell had begun a long dialogue and correspondence with a Baptist pastor from Lurgan, Ian Major. 'Billy's conversion didn't come out of nowhere. He wasn't a heathen in the jungle,' Major recalled. 'Billy would have been familiar with the truth that he had learnt at his mother's knee. It wouldn't have been strange for him to return to that truth. But it requires God's intervention. In the reformed theology that Billy would have returned to he would have understood that well.' The prison system had wrought terrible harm on Mitchell's body, and it was now burrowing deep into his spirit. 'I mind him saying, as he reflected on the murders he had been imprisoned for, that he had come to a point of existential despair. Really, he was at the bottom of the well,' said Major.[41] By the closing months of 1984, Mitchell had come through the worst of the self-doubt and his new-found strength in faith became a ready substitute for the hole left by his decision to leave the UVF.

Now that he had drifted away from the UVF, Billy Mitchell liked to occupy his time more fully by keeping up to date with current developments in Northern Ireland and beyond. 'Billy would have reflected on what was going on on the outside. He had gotten beyond the point of gut reaction and to the bigger picture. There was a marked increase in the violence. He attributed that to politicians scheming and failing in their duties. He began to question if civil war was inevitable or whether another future was possible,' said Ian Major.[42] By now Billy Mitchell's plans for the future were beginning to accelerate. His thinking during that first decade of imprisonment led him to the outer rings of existential despair. He knew, however, that he possessed the inner strength needed to return to safety, if only he kept his faith.

Kenny McClinton, who got to know Mitchell when he moved across to the H Blocks, remembers a man who was intellectually impressive. 'He was someone who could explain complex concepts easily and with precision,' McClinton believed. Every morning the two men shared half an apple. They 'talked, and talked, and talked', and very quickly became a sounding board for one another as they delved into the Scriptures more intently. A firm friendship was soon built between both men. This was all the more remarkable, given that Mitchell had been directly responsible for the deaths of two UDA men a decade earlier. McClinton, coincidentally, had been the man tasked by the UDA to exact revenge upon the UVF commander responsible, which was, of course, Mitchell.[43] Now, all that was forgiven. The past lay behind both men as they sought to lay the foundations for their much longed for life outside of prison.

★★★

1984 was to prove to be the first time the UVF did not embark on a major killing spree. In the first six months of 1984, the organisation killed only two Catholic civilians and one RUC officer. In the remaining months of the year, they killed a further two Catholic civilians, including twenty-five-year-old youth worker William Robert McLaughlin, a married man with three young children and another baby on the way. He was shot by a UVF gunman as he walked along Mill Road to his home in Bawnmore, Newtownabbey in November 1984. The *modus operandi* followed by the gunman was astonishingly similar to an earlier murder on the Shore Road in December 1983, in which twenty-five-year-old Joe Craven, a member of the INLA, was killed. Both men lived in Bawnmore, and both had been signing on at the local social security office on the edge of Rathcoole at the time. Although both killings were claimed by the Protestant Action Force, a cover name for the UVF, the military team at The Farm on the Rathcoole estate side of Carnmoney Hill was probably responsible. By now, The Farm had become a hub of UVF activity, while the organisation's leading lights in other parts of Belfast languished in prison until the end of the year. Even after an appeal saw the judge throw out the fourteen convictions from the Bennett supergrass case, the military team in Rathcoole would continue to play a major role in UVF operations.

12

COMPROMISE OR CONFLICT

'So stand up every mother's son, lift up your sights upon your gun. Take aim against the rebel scum, for victory is now.'

Some Mother's Son, UVF song (circa 1989)

Belfast, November 1985

1985 brought new challenges for the UVF. There was a feeling among Brigade Staff officers that a revised strategy was required following the huge setbacks caused by the supergrass trials. Of all the UVF supergrass cases, the biggest was that involving twenty-three-year-old William 'Budgie' Allen, in which forty-five men were arrested and charged with offences including murder, causing explosions, kneecapping and possessing guns. When they were sent forward for prosecution in the summer of 1985, the judge released twenty of the men (five others had made full confessions, while another twenty were awaiting trial) on the basis that he found Allen's evidence 'unworthy of belief'.[1] Whether believable or not, the UVF was still reeling from the arrests, illustrated most notably by its ability to kill on only four occasions, twice in Belfast, once in Newtownabbey (under its PAF cover name) and once in Lurgan. In 1983, it had killed four Catholics and a Protestant. The body count may have been low, but the UVF was by no means completely diminished in its operational effectiveness. It limped on, throughout the remainder of the year, until it was thrown a life-line from the most unexpected of directions.

In her haste to find a solution to the threat posed by the Provisional IRA and its penchant for launching attacks from the safety of the Irish Republic, Prime Minister Margaret Thatcher initiated a new rapprochement with Taoiseach Garret FitzGerald, under the auspices of the Anglo-Irish Intergovernmental Council. Although regarded with deep scepticism by unionists and loyalists, who saw the council as a way to push Northern Ireland from the union and secure joint sovereignty, the resulting Anglo-Irish

Agreement following talks was principally aimed at securing British national security interests rather than accommodating nationalist aspirations for a united Ireland. Although a porous border had opened up in the face of vast numbers of troops and police at the outset of the troubles, the truth was that it had been in place since the partition of Ireland in the early 1920s. By the 1980s it remained an unchecked channel for the smuggling of illicit goods and people, including terrorists who used the Irish Republic as a safe haven due to the Security Forces' inability to pursue them across the international boundary.

For many unionists in Northern Ireland, however, the Anglo-Irish Agreement of 15 November 1985 posed an even greater danger than the porous border to their position within the United Kingdom. DUP politicians were soon lining up to denounce the Agreement, with the party's Deputy Leader Peter Robinson claiming that Mrs Thatcher had 'signed away the Union at Hillsborough Castle yesterday'. In his opinion, unionists were now 'on the window ledge of the Union'.[2]

Predictably, young men in UVF heartlands responded to such bombastic rhetoric with anger. Ethnic rage fused with adolescent angst brought thousands of these young men onto the streets to protest the Agreement. On 23 November, enormous crowds of over 100,000 people gathered outside Belfast City Hall to the sound of the medieval Lambeg drums. They had come from across the province to hear Ian Paisley denounce British government duplicity over the Agreement. 'I want to ask a question today,' Paisley boomed. 'And the question is simple. Where do the terrorists operate from? From the Irish Republic. That's where they come from. Where do the terrorists return to for sanctuary? To the Irish Republic. And yet Mrs Thatcher tells us that that Republic must have some say in our province. We say never, never, never, never.' The DUP leader's thunderous rhetoric was met by huge applause.[3]

Behind the scenes, the UVF was benefiting from the political fallout. The Brigade Staff now turned their attention to recruiting some of these disaffected young men into their ranks. One of the new recruits was 'Matthew'. He explained how Paisley's emphatic words had carried him into the ranks of the UVF's Woodvale-based B Company:

> The UVF was almost decimated by the supergrass trials. Really, its booster came in 1985. After the Anglo-Irish Agreement. After being near decimated, '85 was a big booster and it radicalised people. But

the problem was they didn't have enough guns. But you were running around getting sawn-off shotguns, the odd house break-in for pistols. It wasn't enough. You could have bounced in anywhere with one of them rattly boxes that people were making in the shipyard and Mackies and in their garages, and you could have emptied two magazines into a room and you might have been lucky if you killed somebody. You might have injured four or five people, but the calibre of the bullets weren't good.[4]

In the wake of the supergrass trials, the UVF leadership decided to make all of its members, especially those in military teams, undergo basic training to beat the RUC's interrogation system. The RUC had always placed great emphasis on securing a confession from loyalist suspects as quickly as possible. Sometimes, this even meant applying a certain amount of coercion to get the result they needed.[5] Countless UVF men had gone straight to prison on their own word, especially in the 1970s. They put up hardly any resistance at all. For the organisation to be more proficient at beating the charges, it needed to condition its members in resisting the tendency to 'fess up'.

Apart from tightening up discipline in its ranks, the UVF leadership also began to make contingency plans in the event of the imposition of joint sovereignty. In this, they claimed, they sought advice from several quarters, including from the influential barrister Desmond Boal, a close confidant of DUP leader Ian Paisley. While Paisley was busy making loud, bombastic speeches on an anti-Agreement platform, Boal was allegedly locked in deep political and strategic discussions with UVF leaders in his chambers at the Crumlin Road courthouse. He was eager to take soundings from them on what they thought about the prospects for joint sovereignty. 'He outlined several scenarios,' recalled one of the men who attended the meeting. 'What if this happened? What if that happened? In one of the scenarios, a doomsday scenario, Boal was emphatic and persuasive. We just sat there and looked at each another.' The conversation stalled, as the enormity of the prospect of a joint rule by London and Dublin sank in amongst the three men. 'What if that scenario happened,' one of the UVF leaders asked Boal. 'Well, if that happens, you two get on the boat,' replied the gregarious QC.[6]

Although prepared to think more strategically about how they should use force, the UVF was not about to abandon ship without attempting to fill the void left by the politicians with a military response. One of the group's most proficient commanders, John Bingham, who was now heading the group's 1st Belfast Battalion, was busy setting up a small network of new military teams that drew a steady stream of disaffected young men, who replenished UVF ranks as older men drifted away. By the summer of 1986 the *Irish Independent* newspaper was even reporting that the 'UVF had shrunken in size', a change which, ironically, enabled the organisation to carefully vet its existing members more closely and weed out informers.[7] Meanwhile, in the Maze Prison, the UVF's invisible battalion was becoming more restive. 'I got a letter from a friend just the other day, the guy who did the Miami Showband', Bingham told one reporter, 'and he was telling me how frustrated they all feel (in jail) about what's going on. I have never seen the tension run so high in this area. It's incredible, all the young lads are feeling the frustration, the anger', he added.[8] Bingham boasted that Ballysillan was now more hardline than the Shankill. 'The loyalist paramilitaries', he said, 'so far have harnessed the frustration of the young men. We don't want to bring anarchy but if you think of the harness as being held up by a number of buckles then the unbuckling could begin tomorrow (the 12th). We're changing … young guys letting go at the RUC with automatic rifles, that was the Provie's role for years.'[9] Although aggressive in his stance, Bingham was only one of several commanders eager to use newly radicalised younger members to begin the UVF's long-awaited offensive.

Despite a new-found energy for military activities, the UVF was also inviting its more politically minded prisoners and those volunteers from the welfare component of the organisation, not to mention their allies in the PUP, to come up with political contingency plans too. Billy Hutchinson was one of those key individuals closely involved in this process, which culminated in the drafting of a PUP document called *War or Peace? Conflict or Conference* (1986). 'The PUP were saying that the UVF now had an opportunity to compromise, which is about sitting down round the table with people who are then the republicans who are continuing with the violence.' Even though the UVF Brigade Staff were open to fresh political ideas being put to them – as demonstrated by the formulation of this policy document and in their meeting with Dessie Boal – but they were also under pressure from hardliners in their own ranks who wanted to strike at republicans. 'I think those policies were 20 years ahead of their time', Hutchinson said, 'and people weren't ready for that sort of compromise. It is an irony [though] that people who were involved in the conflict were coming up with constructive ways of actually dealing with the conflict.'[10]

In many respects, the violence had not yet run its course, with the UVF leadership opting to continue with their campaign of terror.

In practical terms, this would have deadly consequences for civilians who would bear the brunt of UVF violence in the summer of 1986. Under its PAF cover name, the UVF began to target Catholic taxi drivers. One journalist claimed that 'rogue elements' within the RUC Special Branch 'gave the go ahead' for the killing of Catholic civilians by the UVF. Without any hard evidence whatsoever, such assertions lack foundation. What is not in doubt, however, is that the supergrass trials had brought many prominent UVF members to the attention of the general public. By continuing to publicise the alleged activities of some of these men, the local tabloid media, in particular, was effectively handing republican paramilitaries a targeting list.

★★★

Ballysillan Crescent, North Belfast, shortly after 1 a.m., 14 September 1986

Three men climbed into a white Renault Deauville to make a short journey from Ardoyne to Ballysillan in North Belfast. They travelled up Alliance Avenue and along the Oldpark Road before reaching their destination just over a mile away. The journey took them less than ten minutes. The car pulled up outside the modest three-bedroom home in Ballysillan Crescent. An Ulster flag hung outside, just above the living room window. Two masked and armed men got out and ran to the doorway of a house. Both were of slim build. The taller man wore light-coloured denim jeans and a dark top. They were carrying a large axe, which they used to smash their way into the house. Bursting into the living room, the gunmen were greeted by Dora Bingham. They demanded to know where her husband was. 'He's not here,' she replied as the two men pointed their weapons at her and one of the couple's young children. As they moved back into the hallway, Dora shouted at the top of her voice to rouse her husband, thirty-three-year-old father of two John Dowey Bingham, from his sleep. Bingham had gone to bed around 11:30 p.m. He got up and made his way to the landing, where one of the gunmen fired three shots upstairs. Bingham managed to close the security door on the landing but the men fired three revolver shots into it. As Bingham made his way to the small bedroom with the intention of escaping through the window, the gunmen fired two more rifle shots as they moved upstairs. Cornering him in the room, they fired another seven shots. He was hit in the body and legs. They ran back down the stairs and out to a getaway car. One of the men shouted 'come on' to his accomplice who, one eyewitness said, cried out with a '"whoop" of joy'.[11]

Most of the Bingham's neighbours in Ballysillan Crescent had heard the commotion and some had even heard the shots. Over two dozen of them gave statements to the police, providing accurate descriptions of the car, gunmen and number of shots they had heard fired during the incident, demonstrating how well-known and liked Bingham had been in the area. One eyewitness who was sat in his living room watching television said that although he didn't see any guns, 'from the noise of the shots, it was an Armalite'.[12] The neighbour ran over to the house and up the stairs to find his neighbour, John Bingham, lying prostrate with wounds to his legs. He had been shot seven times. There was a profound smell of cordite hanging in the air. By now a crowd had gathered outside. Their lights began to flicker into life. At 1:29 a.m. paramedics were directed to a call regarding a shooting incident. They arrived at 1:35 a.m. Entering the property, they saw Bingham on his back with the wounds to his legs. He was still breathing, and they attempted to dress them as best they could.[13] Despite the efforts of the paramedics, they failed in their bid to resuscitate Bingham. He died at the scene.[14]

Forensic tests on the weapons used to kill Bingham revealed that the .223 FMC rifle had been used in two earlier attempted murders of RUC officers, while the .38 Special revolver had been used in two previous (undisclosed) incidents.[15] The getaway car was later found abandoned in Jamaica Court in Ardoyne at 4:45 a.m. Inside, police found a small radio transmitter on the back seat that had been used by the Provisional IRA gunmen to navigate their way through police and army patrols in North Belfast.[16] The follow-up police investigation also revealed details about IRA intelligence gathering on Bingham. One neighbour told detectives she had seen suspicious activity around the Bingham's home seven to eight weeks before the killing. The lady had been sweeping up leaves outside her home when she spotted a maroon-coloured car stopping outside the house. One of the occupants was a young man of seventeen to eighteen years of age, who had a small thin build. The man accompanying him was older, probably about thirty-eight years old. He was stockier in appearance, had a receding hairline and a bald spot, and wore glasses. 'Do you know a man called Bingham who lives in this area?'

the older man asked the woman. 'No,' she responded.[17] After the murder, two men fitting this description were arrested in Ardoyne and taken in for questioning. Despite the seizure of clothing and the arrests, the police did not release any further information regarding their inquiries. The truth of what, if anything, the suspects told police has never been made public. One thing that is certain is that no one was ever charged with Bingham's murder, and the inquest into his death returned an 'open verdict'.[18]

Although the IRA had been planning Bingham's assassination in detail for over two months, the truth was that he had been on their radar since he first addressed television cameras after his acquittal of charges in the supergrass trials of 1984. With reports of his activities now appearing in Sunday newspapers throughout 1986, the IRA had all the justification they needed to kill him. In its statement claiming the murder, the IRA's Belfast Brigade said they would 'avail of every opportunity to remove from the face of the earth those who callously gun down and murder our people'.[19] Although republicans could easily deduce who performed what function on the UVF's command structure in the area, what remains a mystery is exactly how they had obtained more detailed information about Bingham's movements on the weekend of his death. Only a small number of people knew that Bingham had returned home early from his caravan in Millisle to spend time with his family in Belfast.

For some loyalists at the time and since, the murder of John Bingham was part of a wider conspiracy by the British government to 'clip the wings' of those loyalists who were more militant than the men around them, and who might well have become inimical to any moves towards peace. One loyalist active in the period who was a friend of Bingham's claimed that violence was being 'wound up in order to wind it down'.[20] There is little, if any, evidence to support this view. What we do know is that John Bingham had been one of the UVF's most accomplished commanders. He planned operations with enthusiasm, and prided himself on paying attention to even the smallest of details. He could also be utterly ruthless in ensuring that those he commanded carried out his instructions to the letter. In a visit to Bingham's home, just prior to his assassination, journalist Martin Dillon recalled how the loyalist leader had stuck a gun in his mouth because he didn't like what Dillon had written about him. 'Next time, I'll blow yer fuckin' brains out,' he warned the journalist.[21]

According to one man who knew him well, John Bingham was 'one of the best. A super guy. As you peeled away the onion skin you found principles – integrity, a love for the Protestant people, and so on.'[22] He was one of the UVF's most dedicated volunteers, yet he was never convicted for his role in directing terrorism, a charge that would have been applied to him had he survived the 1980s.[23] Bingham's prosecution under the supergrass system in 1984 had been overturned after he spent two and half years in prison. Those close to him said that Bingham disagreed fundamentally with criminality, and would never have tolerated it amongst his underlings. 'There were no two sides to John Bingham,' they said.[24] Two weeks after his murder, the UVF Brigade Staff allegedly received a letter from a member of the Catholic community giving details of the men responsible for Bingham's murder. The letter was signed 'a friend in ligoniel'.[25]

There could be no doubt that the killing of John Bingham was a huge loss to the organisation, and removed one of its most proficient operators. His involvement in the UVF from the beginning of the troubles, together with his natural leadership abilities, meant that, by removing him, the Provisionals in Ardoyne had struck a huge blow against loyalist paramilitarism.

The assassinations of key UVF personnel continued into 1987. On 28 April, thirty-nine-year-old Billy 'Frenchie' Marchant, a married man with four children, was gunned down by the IRA as he stood outside the PUP's offices on the Shankill Road. He had been active in the UVF's West Belfast battalion. The coroner said the killing had all the hallmarks of 'Chicago in the 1920s'. The elimination of UVF members continued, with the IRA killing of thirty-five-year-old Charlie Watson, a former member of the UDR and the Prison Service, in Clough, County Down, on 22 May 1987. Later the same year, on 19 November, republican paramilitaries moved against thirty-six-year-old George Seawright, a firebrand politician and one of John Bingham's closest confidants. Originally from Scotland Seawright achieved notoriety in 1984 for saying that those who objected to the British national anthem were 'Fenian scum' and that they should be 'burned in an incinerator along with their priests'.[26] Seawright was shot by the Irish Peoples' Liberation Organisation (IPLO) as he sat in his parked taxi in Dundee Street, off the Shankill Road. He died from his wounds three weeks later. The day after Bingham's murder, Seawright had called for revenge for the killing of his friend, though it was not known until twenty years later that he was a member of the UVF. The UVF blamed his murder on Martin 'Rook' O'Prey. As with the Bingham and Marchant assassinations, however, the organisation remained suspicious over who set up Seawright.[27]

It was a tense time in Northern Ireland. Not only were O'Prey and his IPLO faction locked in a bitter internecine feud with their parent organisation, the INLA, but on 8 May 1987 the Provisional IRA suffered its worst operational disaster. At Loughgall in County Armagh, eight of its most experienced volunteers were eliminated by British Special Forces when they launched an attack on the RUC station in the tiny Protestant village. The killing of so many hardline loyalist and republican paramilitaries in 1986–7 raised concerns amongst some loyalists that they were being deliberately removed by British intelligence to create space for more moderate individuals to emerge.[28] Special Branch officers have since made the case that this 'hindsight bias' neglects the reality that 99.5 per cent of those targeted in covert police-led operations were captured, not killed. According to one former Head of RUC Special Branch, the organisation's priority was 'always tactical, dealing with the immediate and the short term, but nobody saw it that way at the time. We had no room to deal with anything else,' he maintained. 'That's the reality of it.'[29]

***

Orange Cross Social Club, Shankill Road, 16 February 1989

A group of friends were enjoying a pint after completing a shift on the voluntary ACE scheme, when three men burst into the club armed to the teeth. The lead gunman carried an UZI submachine gun, a light and compact Israeli-made weapon that held forty rounds of ammunition and, by adhering to careful marksmanship principles, could drill a small grouping of 9mm holes in a target at a range of fifty yards. Another man was armed with a Scorpion machine pistol, a less accurate but equally devastating weapon. The third gunman carried a 9mm pistol, regarded as the weapon of choice for those operating in small and confined spaces. They were members of the IPLO, a splinter group of the INLA.

'We were wearing white boiler suits. The lead gunman was Martin "Rook" O'Prey from the IPLO. He barked out "Youse three up against the wall",' recalled 'Sam', one of the five young men sat around the table. The men did as they were ordered, spread-eagled adjacent to the jukebox with their fingertips touching on the wall. Stevie McCrea placed himself behind Sam. The others lingered just off to his left-hand side. Rook O'Prey and the other gunmen were about four feet away from the friends. O'Prey nodded to his accomplices as the three IPLO gunmen slowly drew up their weapons. McCrea, who had experience of weapons as a shooter for the Red Hand Commando, knew instinctively what was coming next. In a split-second decision he pushed his young companion to the ground as the bullets started flying. 'It was like balloons popping,' Sam said. 'I could see chunks of wood fly'in out of the juke box. You could smell the cordite in the air.'[30] When the shooting stopped, O'Prey checked his weapon to discover that there were some rounds still left in the magazine. He shouted to his accomplices to leave the bar. As they scrambled out the door. O'Prey turned casually to a woman sat in a booth next to the door. 'You dare, you dare!' she shouted defiantly, as O'Prey laughed in her face before discharging the remaining rounds into her. Seconds later he was gone, disappearing into the street where a getaway car took him and his men to a safe-house.

The scene O'Prey and his accomplices left behind was one of carnage, with those who had survived the attack crying out in pain. Others were unconscious and bleeding profusely. Sam, who McCrea had pushed to the ground, felt warm blood seeping onto the back of his neck. He realised that his friend had been shot behind the ear and that his life was oozing from him through a gaping wound. The young man grabbed a bar towel and tried desperately to stem the flow of blood, but his friend was panic-stricken and fought back because of the shock. 'He was pulling at my face,' said Sam. 'The blood flying out was unreal. He just lay there in shock. He sacrificed his life for mine … I looked up at the door and saw a sterling machine gun poking "round the corner".' In blind panic, he thought the republican assassins had returned to finish the job. When he saw the uniforms, he relaxed slightly when the police officers strolled into the bar. 'You fuckin' black bastards. Where were you?' Sam shouted. 'The peeler turned 'round and said "Fuck up".'[31] Although the IPLO subsequently claimed that it was targeting the UVF Brigade Staff, this was not an excuse that washed with those who were in the club at the time.[32] The truth was that the UVF leadership were around the corner when the shooting started, and actually ran to the scene only after news of the attack began to filter through the Shankill.[33]

The attack on the Orange Cross Social Club was one of a number of 'wildcat attacks' on loyalist clubs and pubs as the IPLO opened up a second front on groups like the RHC and UVF.[34] As with previous attacks, the Red Hand and UVF felt compelled to seek revenge. Retaliation came on 10 March whenever a UVF team sprayed the Orient Bar on the Springfield Road with automatic gunfire, killing Jim McCartney, a local man who was working for the security team on the premises. In many ways, this was a soft target for the UVF, more in keeping with the casual nature of the tit-for-tat murders that were now, once again, becoming commonplace across the city. One of those responsible for the Orient Bar shooting was Davy Hamilton, believed to be one of the UVF's most active members on the Shankill at the time. Not wishing to let the killing of Jim McCartney go unanswered, the Provisional IRA entered the flat of UVF man Jackie 'Nigger' Irvine on Skegoneill Avenue six days later, and shot him fifteen times. He had been unmasked as a one-time senior UVF commander by the Supergrass trials and, like many others, such as Robert 'Squeak' Seymour, John Bingham and Frenchie Marchant, would find his way onto the IRA's hit list for engaging in loyalist paramilitary activity.[35] Irvine was the uncle of Lennie Murphy, who had met a similar fate at Provo hands seven years earlier. In reply, the UVF shot and killed another civilian, David Braniff, as he knelt to say his evening prayers at his home on Alliance Avenue on 18 March 1989. There could be no doubting the intensity of hatred now governing the decisions being taken by these rival paramilitary organisations.

***

As the 1980s drew to a close, the UVF was much stronger, better armed and more strategically aware than it had been at the beginning of the decade. It had ridden the crest of a wave of Protestant angst during the Anglo-Irish Agreement, though, notwithstanding the terror campaign of the Shankill Butchers gang, it had not yet reached its full killing potential. The assassination of John Bingham in September 1986 removed one of the UVF's most proficient operators, leaving a gaping hole in leadership terms in the Greater Shankill area. Elsewhere, in East Antrim, many of the 1970s triggermen had drifted away from frontline activities, while, in Mid Ulster, the leadership was growing older and more cautious. Its ability to trade on the reputation of its few hardliners was quickly diminishing. Even the indiscriminate Provisional IRA bomb that slaughtered eleven civilians at the war memorial in Enniskillen on Remembrance Sunday failed to replenish the UVF's ranks with new blood. For some members, it was left to a small core group of militants in the Shankill and Portadown to carry on the war.

In 1989, the UVF's Woodvale-based B Company numbered 200 members. About 150 of these individuals were in the welfare component, while the other fifty could have been loosely said to have made up the military teams.[36] Although there were larger company-level meetings and welfare meetings held on a regular basis, military meetings within a small cadre of gunmen took place weekly and had a variety of purposes. Out of the smaller number in the military team, an even smaller percentage – perhaps fewer than ten – were active in shootings and bombings at this time. UVF members estimate that these ten people, in turn, formed two ASUs which carried out the most serious of military operations. Few people would have known the actual detail of murders, and the hardcore militants were actively discouraged from 'talking shop' within their wider UVF unit. Instead, the UVF's 'military business' would only rarely be discussed in the open in pubs and clubs. Public parks, swimming baths and football matches were actually the preferred venues for UVF men to discuss targeting.[37] 'I don't know why I never went to jail,' one senior UVF officer admitted. 'Maybe I was just lucky, or careful. Maybe I trusted the right people. Who knows.'[38] The truth was that he knew exactly why he had evaded capture for so many years. Those in the ranks below him were governed by two major transformations in the organisation since the supergrass trials: a younger group of men in their late teens and early twenties who took their paramilitary obligations more seriously than their predecessors, and the UVF's own strict code of *omertà*, enforced by a re-energised Provost Marshal system. Without these mutually reinforcing mechanisms, the organisation simply couldn't have operated at a time when the RUC and British intelligence were becoming more adept at technological surveillance and human intelligence (HUMINT). The system was by no means infallible, as the UVF would come to realise before the end of the year.

✶✶✶

The UVF had come through the troubles having suffered considerable blows to its operational capability. In the 1970s, informers had brought down the entire leadership of East Antrim. In the early 1980s both Mid Ulster and Belfast were rocked by the supergrass trials, thereby exposing its leaders to the wider world. By the late 1980s that had begun to change. UVF military teams were tighter, operating according to a cell system similar to what the IRA had been following for many years.

The UVF's *modus operandi* had also changed. In Belfast, its military teams had become more close-knit. On a typical operation, cars or

Gusty Spence pictured inside Long Kesh in the late 1970s. A tough streetwise individual, Spence used his previous service in the British Army to mould the UVF into a military-based organisation. © Courtesy of Long Kesh Inside Out

An East Antrim-based loyalist, Billy Greer was one of the UVF's most respected area commanders who helped to sustain the group's campaign for forty years. © Private Collection

Lenny Murphy smiles for the camera during one of his spells inside HM Crumlin Road Prison. © Author's Collection

Representatives of the UVF's Belfast Brigade pictured inside Long Kesh in the late 1970s. From left to right – Frankie Curry, Joe Bennett, Trevor King, Jackie Mahood, Billy Hutchinson and Billy Mitchell. © Courtesy of The Billy Mitchell Legacy Project

Officers from the UVF's Belfast Brigade pictured in the front rank of the UVF's 'Invisible Battalion' during a formal parade. Their uniform was a cross between the British Army and the Black Panthers movement in the US. © Courtesy of The Billy Mitchell Legacy Project

Lenny Murphy, looking dapper, poses for a photograph in the inner courtyard of Belfast City Hall sometime in 1982. He is pictured beside his Austin Princess. © Author's Collection

John Bingham, the UVF's 1st Belfast Battalion Commander, was an energetic and enthusiastic leader who 'lived and breathed the UVF'. © Pacemaker Press International

Brian 'The Buck' Robinson, one of the most respected members of B Company's military team on the Shankill Road. © Pacemaker Press International

CLMC representatives pose for a photo after the announcement of the loyalist ceasefires at Fernhill House in West Belfast – from left to right, John White, Davy Adams, Jim McDonald, Gusty Spence, David Ervine, William 'Plum' Smith and Gary McMichael. © Pacemaker Press International

Mid Ulster UVF Commander Billy Wright relaxes in the home of one of his closest friends and comrades during Christmas 1992. He was a ruthless terrorist who planned his operations meticulously but also had a reputation as a family man and practical joker. © Author's Collection

Johnny Adair was the feared commander of the UFF's C Company on the Lower Shankill who formed a close partnership with Mid Ulster UVF commander Billy Wright in the 1990s. © Author's Collection

Billy Wright walks down Charles Street in Portadown alongside his second-in-command Swinger Fulton during the Drumcree stand-off in the summer of 1995. Next to Wright, wearing a beanie hat, is North Belfast UVF commander Tommy Stewart who was shot dead in disputed circumstances in October 1996. © Author's Collection

Hugh Smyth was the UVF's most promin[ent] political spokesmen who went on to form [the] PUP in the late 1970s. He was first elected [to] Belfast Corporation in 1972, serving as L[ord] Mayor in 1994–5, finally stepping down [due] to ill health in 2013. © Courtesy of Long K[esh] Inside Out

The front page of the UVF's journal *Combat* after the shooting of Brian Robinson on the Crumlin Road on 2 September 1989. Some of his closest comrades believe that an agent compromised the operation, which led to Robinson's death. © Private Collection

COMBAT

Date of Issue: 25th September 1989   Price 50[p]

SUMMARILY EXECUTED

AN ACT OF APPEASEMENT

Portadown District L.O.L. No. 1

Orange Hall
Carleton Street
Portadown

Dear Kenny,

May I first of all thank you for letter of the 16th. Secondly, and more importantly, could I congratulate you on your ordination and wish you Gods richest blessing in your ministry. I realise just how busy you must be and it was good and gracious of you to take the time to write. Could I also thank you for the kind remarks you have made about me, I honestly don't think I am worthy of all the praise I have received from so many kind and generous people, including your good self. I can assure you that I am the first to admit that without the support of my own District, the loyalist people of Portadown and the Brethren and loyalists from over Ulster, victory may not have been achieved. I am also well aware of the crucial role played by Billy Wright, whom I must confess I had never met, and his comrades, in the final outcome. I have by the way written to him to let him know how much I appreciated his support. When I first spoke to Billy at Drumcree he asked if I were going to carry my stand to the end. I assured him that I was totally committed to see this through, no matter how long it took and he assured me that he would support me all the way. We ill know he was true to his word. Can I also say that at our next District meeting no one will be left in any doubt of how much we owe to Billy and his friends.

Could I also thank you for bringing to my attention the part played by Robert Wallace and the two friends you mentioned. I was unaware that they had met with your group leaders, he certainly did not tell me. I will ask him at our next committee meeting and find out who his two friends were, because as you rightly state, they deserve recognition for their initiative and I will see they get it.

Once again Kenny may I take this opportunity to thank you for the part you played, I personally will never forget the joy of yourself and Billy along with thousands of loyalists when we eventually reached Park Road. We have all given our people something to be proud off. Lets hope and pray our efforts have not been in vain.

May God Bless you always

Your Friend,
Harold Gracey

In this letter, District Master of LOL 1 in Portadown Harold Gracey asks Kenny McClinton to pass on his regards to Billy Wright and 'his comrades' for their assistance at Drumcree. © Courtesy of Kenny McClinton

W. Wright A5970
C. wing H1.
Maze

Cheers Johnny!
thanks for the card
and kind words, its appreciated,
Life isn't to bad mate, bar-outside
if you get my meaning, still mate every dog has its day
I'll have mine be sure of that.
Swinger was saying he had a bit
of crack with you the other week, a cracker man, he
was letting me know your feelings. Always remember wee
man, they've done all they could, not only on you, but
your wee family — they are shite.
I sent a message to your big
mate outside (Did he get it)? Tell him Johnny to be
extra careful.
On a lighter note, I hear your in
brave shape, fair play to you. I'm trying to do like
wise. I seen big Stewy he's in right shape. outside
of that we started a degree, time is flying by
God willing I'll get a pint with
you, when your out, don't worry about Mid-Ulster
none of their dirt are slabbering stuck stuck, your well
respected, anyhow Johnny you'll enjoy being in the
company of real old fashion loyalists

The close working relationship between Billy Wright and Johnny Adair is captured in this letter from the Mid Ulster commander in 1997. © Private Collection

Billy Hutchinson pictured here with David Ervine after they were successfully elected to the Northern Ireland Assembly in 1998. Both men had served prison sentences for UVF activity and came to represent a progressive brand of working-class politics that placed pluralism, non-sectarianism and liberalism at its centre. Both men would go on to lead the UVF-linked PUP. © Pacemaker Press International

In retaliation for the killing of senior UDA member Tommy English, the UFF in Rathcoole shot dead UVF member Mark Quail, pictured here third drummer from the left inside HMP Maze in the 1990s. © Private Collection

Rab Warnock, pictured alongside Billy Greer near the Menin Gate in Ypres, was active from the 1970s until his death in 2012. He commanded the UVF's North Belfast and East Antrim Brigade for a decade. © Private Collection

Billy Greer commanded the East Antrim UVF from the 1970s until the mid-1990s when it merged with North Belfast. Although he was second in command to Rab Warnock, the two were inseparable. Greer was one of the UVF's most visible spokesmen. © Private Collection

A mural in homage to the late PUP leader David Ervine who died in January 2007. He was recognised as a pugnacious, articulate and visionary politician who became a key architect of the Northern Ireland peace process. © Author's Collection

Gary Haggarty, the self-professed commander of the UVF in North Belfast and East Antrim, replaced Rab Warnock in 2004. He was ousted in 2007 in the wake of the Police Ombudsman's report into the death of Raymond McCord Jnr. © Pacemaker Press International

PSNI officers struggle to cont[...] widespread civil disturbances [...] working-class Protestants, wh[...] followed in the wake of [...] removal of the Union Flag fr[...] the City Hall in early Decem[...] 2012. © Private Collection

A UVF mural in Ballyduff estate on the outskirts of North Belfast acknowledges how the UVF and its weapons have 'fallen silent' but 'if needed we will rise again'. The grouping has yet to complete its transition towards a fully civilianised role in post-ceasefire Northern Ireland. © Author's Collection

motorbikes would have been stolen, their plates changed and held in a lock-up until they got the go-ahead to move. When the operation was triggered, usually by the UVF military commander for an area following consultation with his boss on the Brigade Staff, the vehicles would have paired up. By the late 1980s, some former UVF members claimed, they were equipped with walkie-talkies and a police scanner to evade police or army VCPs. They disagreed with suggestions from nationalists that they were simply allowed through roadblocks. One man said that volunteers would often laugh when they listened to police scanners, hearing RUC officers haplessly trying to piece together suspect vehicle locations in the wake of an attack.[39]

The UVF was also proving much more skilled in intelligence gathering and the acquisition of weapons. One of the organisation's intelligence officers in Belfast explained how they compiled information on republicans:

> See by '89 [it] all changed. And the intelligence started swamping. The leakage from security forces was phenomenal. If republicans realised how much intelligence the UVF had on them, it would have scared the life out of them. So that became a perfect storm, almost. From the 1980s the IRA thought they could defeat [the British] – they did, they thought there was a military victory going to take place here. By the time loyalists had perfected their intelligence operation and had gained high-powered weaponry, that changed. You know, a lot of them ran over the border and hid. They were running [between] two and three houses. They were frightened.[40]

A key factor in ensuring the UVF did not suffer from the ability of its members in the 1970s to admit to all of their terrorist activity and to implicate others was the resistance to interrogation training it was now providing for its members.

> After the supergrass trials. The best thing the UVF leadership done [*sic*] – and they did do a good job – was that it was no longer you were just brought in and told, 'If you're lifted keep yer mouth shut.' They actually took people away and gave them interrogation training. So, you had probably four weeks of anti-interrogation training, anti-interrogation techniques. And you were actually taken away for two days and you were placed in a flat and the flat was done up. You were held in a wee room – there was actually the front room. You were held

in the bedroom like a cell and the front room of the flat would have been a police interrogation room. And two people played policemen. Now, that hardened loyalists. A lot of loyalists. It gave people an idea of what a police station was like, what you would suffer. And they also produced their own little booklets and things like that there on interrogation. That did change loyalists a lot because it give [sic] them a sense of what to expect. Because a lot of people who were arrested were threw in, and they were frightened and didn't know what to expect.[41]

At the beginning of the 1990s the UVF was becoming a more professional killing machine. In many respects, it was matching the Provisional IRA in terms of the calibre of its volunteers, and in the sophistication of how it conducted its operations.

Now finding it difficult to break UVF volunteers through the psychological advantage which Castlereagh gave them,[42] the Security Forces did not remain idle. In 1987–9, RUC Special Branch's *Threat Book* for the Greater Belfast area alone recorded 730 republican threats against individuals, with only 36 threats from loyalists against individuals. Republicans were responsible for 55 per cent of all murders, and loyalists for the other 45 per cent.[43] In total, it was believed that loyalists were behind 166 shooting incidents in that period, with republicans responsible for 185.[44] The UVF was particularly active, and Special Branch came to realise that they had to step up their operations against the organisation. One UVF volunteer in West Belfast got straight to the point. 'The best thing the security forces had was their ability to spread mistrust,' he said. 'It was almost better for the security forces, even if there wasn't [sic] any agents. See if people were arrested through surveillance or stupid talk on phones. Even a one-in-a million chance. It was always better that they put across that there were agents there so that doubt was always, always left.'[45]

The Security Forces now turned their attentions to penetrating the UVF at its highest levels so as to effect greater arrests like they had done at the beginning of the decade. At that time, intelligence operations were stepped up by MI5 and RUC Special Branch, which made great strides in 'nullifying' the terrorist threat emanating from the UDA. Evidence of this came when large consignments of weapons and explosives were seized from loyalists across Northern Ireland.[46]

As autumn approached, for some UVF members, British state attempts to frustrate the organisation in its operational effectiveness would, however, come in the most dramatic of ways.

✦✦✦

Ardoyne/Crumlin Road, Belfast, 10 a.m., 2 September 1989

Forty-three-year-old Paddy McKenna, a local man from Ardoyne who lived with his mother Catherine, was standing outside a fruit and veg shop, when a gunman dismounted from a motorbike, walked over and shot him eleven times.[47] He died instantly. This was not the first attempt on McKenna's life by the UVF. In the 1970s he was sent a St Valentine's package with a bomb inside by UVF man Trevor King in 1975,[48] who would later become the UVF's West Belfast commander. McKenna had opened the package, believing it to be from an admirer, which immediately blew up in his face. Some UVF members drew grim satisfaction from his disfigurement, even disparagingly referring to him as 'Paddy "yuck yuck" McKenna', but it was not enough for others who wished to dispatch him to an early grave. He was spoken about in the organisation's circles as 'that cunt McKenna'. Sometime in 1988, a decision was allegedly taken by King to kill McKenna.[49] The plan was to shoot the Ardoyne man as he sat in his car, either stationary outside his home, at traffic lights or at his place of work. As with several other killings at this time, the UVF's *modus operandi* would have been to reconnoitre the area around the target's home. Once the job was given the go-ahead a motorcycle would have been stolen and then hidden in a secure lock-up. The operation would also have been on a 'need-to-know' basis and the number of people aware of what was about to take place would have been extremely limited. The gunman chosen for the operation was twenty-six-year-old Brian Robinson, one of the most respected members of the B Company military team. The UVF's official roll of honour picks up the story:

> Upon completing an Active Service Assignment, Volunteer Robinson and a comrade were intercepted by undercover SAS troops on Belfast's Crumlin Road. The undercover soldiers rammed their vehicle into the ASU's motorcycle, forcing the driver to crash. As Brian lay on the roadside, unarmed, injured, stunned and helpless, a female SAS officer coldly riddled his body with gunfire, killing him instantly. The other member of the ASU was later apprehended and detained. The SAS had

every possible opportunity to take Volunteer Brian Robinson alive. They relinquished this option in favour of cold-blooded murder![50]

It was not long until the news of Robinson's death reached his elderly mother Margaret, who, upon hearing of her son's violent death, collapsed and died of a heart attack.

There is some dispute over whether Patrick McKenna had been a member of the Provisional IRA. UVF members remain convinced that he was still active in republican paramilitarism, even if he was not claimed by the organisation, but those closest to him deny that he was ever in the IRA. Paddy McKenna might have kept the company of men who were members, they said, but he certainly was not one himself at the time of his death. What is not in doubt, however, is that the UVF suffered a massive reversal of its fortunes in the wake of the killing of Brian Robinson. As one of his closest comrades, Matthew, revealed:

> Probably the UVF – and specifically the UVF in the Woodvale – nearly disintegrated after that. Nobody knew what was going on or what was happening … Reports were that the information had come from someone working for the army and others that it was someone working for the Branch. But what it did was … clear the way for [Colin] Crazy [Craig, a prominent member of the unit]. Those who had been in charge – there wasn't any suggestion that they were informers – they had just had enough. [The B Company commander at the time] took it that bad, he hit the drink. That made way for Crazy. Crazy then became 2IC … From 1989 until 1992, he was in charge of everything in that area. He was the commander … The strange thing was that there were probably ten operations. They never really succeeded in doing anything. There were people who were lifted here [and there as a result].[51]

The killing of Brian Robinson also raised suspicions within UVF ranks about how the British Army unit had known that Robinson and his accomplice, twenty-four-year-old Davy McCullough, would be making good their escape along the Crumlin Road from Ardoyne. The four shots that hit Robinson – one hit him in the wrist, another hit him in the back and the two shots to his head at close range, known by military firearms experts as the 'double-tap' – from the weapon fired by the undercover soldier, dealt a body blow to the UVF. Matthew, a close friend and comrade of both Robinson and McCullough, said that the killing devastated morale within the organisation. 'Where you would have had ten operations lined up and on the go [at the same time], once Brian was killed it never really succeeded [in regaining that tempo again].' The organisation 'nearly disintegrated after that', said Matthew. 'People stood themselves down. They took it that bad.'[52] Having survived the supergrass trials in the early half of the decade, the UVF benefited from the 'booster' given to it by the mobilisation of many young men in the wake of the Anglo-Irish Agreement protests. The killing of Brian Robinson left the organisation reeling. Some members of B Company believed the killing on the Crumlin Road was the British state's way of 'skelping the loyalists on the arse' because of their increased capacity in targeting republicans.[53]

The loss of Brian Robinson came at a time when the UVF had just taken possession of high-grade intelligence from disgruntled members of the Security Forces. One UVF Intelligence Officer said that the dossier allegedly detailed the movements of known IRA players, their girlfriends, wives, brothers, sisters, uncles, aunts and known associates. It was the most comprehensive picture yet of the intelligence product, and it was suggested that someone within the Security Forces community was deliberately leaking information to terrorist groupings. The truth is, as ever, more simple in scope than subsequent commentary has suggested. Those UVF activists involved in gathering intelligence on their republican enemies claim that they were able to glean information from a number of different sources. Some of the low-level information about republican players came from almost daily fraternisation with soldiers who patrolled West Belfast. Matthew was allegedly a former UVF intelligence officer in the area. He claimed that young loyalists would seek general information on 'republican players' by asking soldiers if 'such and such a person lived in a certain street'. Another way the UVF gathered intelligence was by recruiting sympathisers who worked in Security Forces' bases in Belfast to help identify republican 'players' homes marked out on wall maps in operations rooms.[54] It was a simple but effective method of infiltration by the UVF, but there is no way of proving when and where it happened. 'If they'd known how much we knew about them it would've scared the shite out of them,' Matthew said rather cryptically.[55]

The question of 'collusion' has nevertheless continued to bedevil discussion about loyalist paramilitary activity. According to the UVF's leadership, they did not work hand-in-glove with the Security Forces. 'David Ervine used to say, "Sure why wouldn't loyalists collude with security forces. We were all on the same side anyway", said the group's second-in-command when asked about collusion. 'I wouldn't say it was systematic,' he said. 'We were never controlled in the way republicans claim we were. Sure, there was collusion on all sides.'[56] By denying UVF members the autonomy of taking action without state control, republicans obfuscate the bitterness individual loyalists had towards those they considered their enemies. 'If the British government were colluding,' asked former loyalist prisoners when questioned about collusion, 'why was the UVF never armed properly?'[57]

Although the idea of systematic collusion is casually dismissed by the UVF, the same could not be said of the British State, which was moved to investigate the allegations in the late 1980s. The government appointed a senior English police officer to investigate. The announcement that Deputy Chief Constable for Cambridgeshire Constabulary Sir John Stevens would be conducting an inquiry into the leakage, incensed the UDA, whose members released a dossier they claimed revealed the names of suspected IRA members. Retaliating at the intrusiveness of the investigation, loyalists started to post photomontages of terrorist suspects on gable walls in North and West Belfast in early February 1990. UTV, the local independent television station, dispatched a reporter and camera crew to film an interaction between a loyalist dressed as an RUC officer and two masked men. The RUC dismissed it as 'street theatre.'[58]

In 2011, the Secretary of State for Northern Ireland appointed Sir Desmond de Silva QC to undertake an independent review into the allegation that the State had been involved in the murder of human rights lawyer Patrick Finucane. The inquiry would turn out to be one of the most comprehensive analyses of intelligence matters ever undertaken by a government-appointed official in Northern Ireland. It revealed what many suspected to be the case – that loyalist terrorist groups were significantly penetrated by the late 1980s, and their operations were mostly frustrated and disrupted as a consequence. However, that does not necessarily mean that these agents were working to systematically eliminate republicans. As Sir Desmond concluded in his report:

> Any attempt to crudely describe loyalist terrorists as simply 'State-sponsored forces' is, in my view, untenable and fundamentally at odds

with a substantial body of contemporary evidence and the historical context of the relationship between loyalists and the security forces during this period. The evidence of collusion between elements of the State and loyalist terrorists that I have uncovered during the course of this Review does, therefore, need to be positioned in the context of this chapter and the action that was being taken by the State to thwart loyalist paramilitaries.[59]

Evidence uncovered in interviews with loyalist paramilitaries for this book, as well as from other sources, broadly concurs with this conclusion. In the 1970s the UVF was ordering its volunteers to infiltrate the legitimate forces of the State in order to gain weapons training. By the 1980s the vast majority of these individuals had been thrown out of military ranks. Additionally, many soldiers and police officers had been intimidated out of loyalist areas. In the absence of traditional avenues for information on republicans, the UVF had to look at new ways of gaining access to intelligence.

★★★

By 1990 those teenagers who had joined the UVF in West Belfast in the wake of the Anglo-Irish Agreement were now being blooded into the military teams. One of those who had joined B Company said that he was ordered to carry out surveillance on Tom Hartley, a high-ranking member of Sinn Féin. Matthew recalled the specifics of the reconnaissance mission. 'I had to walk past his house ten times in a morning. I hadn't a gun. I was shitting myself. What the fuck was I meant to do if somebody came out? We were wee lads from the Shankill.' Other UVF sources claim that the organisation was actively targeting Martin McGuinness at that time too, one of the Provisional IRA's most senior commanders. They suggest that the UVF had put an elaborate plan into operation to target McGuinness as he drove out of Derry City along the Glenshane Pass where his vehicle would be specifically attacked by small arms and explosives.[60] For whatever reason the plan was never put into operation.

One of McGuinness's former associates, thirty-seven-year-old Roger Joseph Bradley, a recently-released Provisional IRA prisoner, was not so lucky. UVF sources claim he was a key member of the Provisional IRA team responsible for the Claudy atrocity on 31 July 1972. A few days after the Claudy attack, a farmhouse near Bradley's home in Craigavole, Swatragh, a small village in County Londonderry, was raided by the RUC and troops who discovered 200lb of homemade explosives, two 100lbs primed bombs, detonators and other bomb-making materials as well as a Thompson sub-machinegun, a .45 pistol, 400 rounds of ammunition and a crossbow. A car found at the scene, containing a combat jacket was one of two stolen from the Loop, Magherfelt. The other stolen car was one of three used in the Claudy bomb.[61] Bradley was later arrested along with two other men and charged with the attempted murder of soldiers in Kilrea. They were subsequently jailed by a special court sitting in Coleraine, along with another man who was charged with causing an explosion.[62] UVF sources further claim that Bradley was specifically targeted when it became known that he had been released from prison after his lengthy sentence. The UVF shot Bradley dead as he took a lunch-break while working on house renovations for the Housing Executive in Rathcoole estate on 4 April 1990.[63] A day after Roger Bradley's murder, the Provisionals news-sheet, *An Phoblacht*, issued a statement claiming that the victim was 'singled out because he was a Catholic by the two gunmen who shot him dead'.[64] Interestingly, the IRA's roll of honour does not carry Bradley's name, despite him serving a long sentence as a political prisoner.

Despite the Belfast UVF's success in targeting republicans, the same, however, could not be said of its teams in other parts of Northern Ireland. In Mid Ulster, Billy Wright, who had undergone a brief religious conversion in prison in the early 1980s, had become a key member of the Mid Ulster UVF command staff. His unit was busy planning a new offensive primarily aimed at Catholic civilians with no connection to physical force republicanism.

13

THE KITCHEN CABINET

'Reason tells us that revenge merely multiplies the murder and injustice that it reacts against; and reason, not rage, must be our guide ... In this democracy, no political purpose, whatever it may be, will be advanced by a single inch through the use or the threat of violence. No campaign, however horrible or protracted, will shift us from that determination ... In this democracy, it is only through dialogue – dialogue between those who unequivocally reject the use or threat of violence – that the foundation will in the end be found for a fair and hence a lasting peace'.

Sir Patrick Mayhew, Secretary of State for Northern Ireland, speaking at Westminster, 25 October 1993[1]

HMP Maghaberry, Lisburn, County Antrim, 1990

The day had come for Billy Mitchell to be released from HMP Maghaberry, after serving fourteen years of his prison sentence. He was a changed man, having become a born-again Christian in 1979 and then voluntarily relinquishing his Special Category Status when he resigned from the UVF in 1982. In doing so he had drifted away from the Spence contingent, preferring to arrive at his own conclusions about political violence. Indeed, it was the murder of a young Catholic schoolteacher, Mary Travers, shot in a Provisional IRA assassination bid on her father on 8 April 1984, that had the greatest effect on Mitchell. 'I can remember sitting in my cell, in H4,' he later told his biographer Kate Fearon. 'It was a turning point in terms of violence. It didn't push me over into absolute pacifism but it certainly had a massive impact when I thought of the futility and uselessness of it all.'[2] Mitchell thought about how he would feel if it were his own daughter who had been killed. It spurred him towards confronting his inner demons, which had haunted him since the first years of his incarceration.

Amidst these last, very difficult, six years, Mitchell began to turn to plans for how he could make a more positive contribution to society.

He had drifted from one extreme philosophical and political position to another, encompassing everything from Protestantism and loyalism to socialism and anarchism. Mitchell admitted to ending up 'the worst sort of existentialist', and by November 1979 complained that he was 'lost in a black sea of existential despair and had given up hope of ever finding meaning and purpose to life'.[3] After searching his mind, he found nourishment for his soul in Christianity or, more precisely, a form of Christian socialism that shared much in common with the founders of the British Labour tradition.[4] After a few setbacks, the sentencing review body accepted the views of a broad spectrum of people who had engaged with Mitchell in these years. It was accepted that he had turned a corner and would, when released, do everything he could to become a productive citizen. Privately, Billy Mitchell was determined to be a better father to his children and a better husband to the wife he had left behind in 1976. Beyond that, he resolved to champion the cause of the most marginalised and disadvantaged members of the wider community. In his last years inside, Mitchell had 'talked long into the evenings about what would become the LINC Project', recalled fellow prisoner and one-time close friend Kenny McClinton.[5]

Gusty Spence, David Ervine, Eddie Kinner, Tom Winstone and Billy Hutchinson had all been released before Mitchell and, in their own way, were committed to making a difference at the grass-roots level by throwing themselves into community development and community relations work. Recognising that these men had a positive contribution to make, the UVF leadership endorsed their attempts, and the attempts of others, including Christian community worker, Jackie Redpath, to put out feelers to the nationalist community to explore the grounds for dialogue aimed at bringing the conflict to an end. The UVF's long-serving Chief of Staff believed that 1989–90 was a crucial time for the organisation's Brigade Staff, in that they had now chosen to sanction an exploratory back-channel process.

Father Alec Reid, a Redemptionist priest at Clonard Monastery in the Falls Road area of Belfast, became a vital conduit in this initiative. At the centre of a parallel process with the Provisional IRA he had, in turn, met with Protestant clergy, who made contact with community representatives in loyalist areas. In doing so, he facilitated a form of shuttle diplomacy in which several 'what-if' scenarios were explored, initially by the Provisional IRA leadership, in which they floated the idea of 'what if we stopped killing you, would you stop killing us?'[6] The UVF rejected this out of hand. They saw it as an unacceptable trade-off. Having long regarded itself as a 'counter-terrorist outfit', the UVF always believed that it was simply responding to IRA attacks on Protestant civilians and members of the Security Forces. In the eyes of the UVF leadership, an attack on one was an attack on all, and they had a duty to 'respond in kind'.[7]

The UVF's retaliatory policy had long been in evidence, even back to the days of the Chlorane Bar murders, though it now formed an essential plank in its bargaining strategy with the Provisionals in these years. One example of how it was employed came at the beginning of March 1991 when a UVF team travelled to Boyles Bar in Cappagh, County Tyrone, to carry out an attack on IRA volunteers who were known to frequent the pub. Three IRA men, twenty-three-year-old John Quinn, seventeen-year-old Dwayne O'Donnell and twenty-year-old Malcolm Nugent, were all shot and killed, along with a fifty-year-old Catholic civilian, Thomas Armstrong. A few days later another UVF team from West Belfast carried out the murder of a taxi driver, Michael Lenaghan. Worse was to come at the end of the month, when Billy Wright's Mid Ulster UVF team committed a sectarian triple murder. As they stood talking inside a mobile sweet shop in Craigavon, a gunman boarded the shop and shot dead nineteen-year-old Eileen Duffy and sixteen-year-old Katrina Rennie. The gunman then dragged twenty-nine-year-old Brian Frizzell outside onto the road, where he forced him to lie down before shooting him dead. The attack drew condemnation from across the political spectrum. It also led to the Provisional IRA carrying out a reprisal attack in Tyrone, when it shot and killed thirty-one-year-old Derek Ferguson.

Amidst the killings, the government was eager to gauge the collective mood on talks aimed at ending the violence. Seeking to make itself relevant to the parameters of ongoing debate, the UVF, together with PUP leaders, formed a strategy group, known as the 'kitchen cabinet', which pulled together a number of former members of the organisation who were now engaged in community development. Its members included Gusty Spence, Billy Hutchinson, Plum Smith and David Ervine, as well as representatives from the UVF's Brigade Staff. Although some close observers of loyalism have since characterised the kitchen cabinet as representing a renewed appetite within the UVF for politics,[8] the fact is that it was still operating a military strategy, not a political one. The 'organisation was at its zenith militarily',[9] the UVF leadership argued, and so the kitchen cabinet acted primarily as a 'clearing house' in which Spence and the others could provide 'political analysis' to the Brigade Staff. The primary responsibility of the 'non-combatant' members of the kitchen cabinet was to scrutinise the information coming in from 'various sources' at that time, including the back-channel involving the Protestant clergy, Father Reid and the Provisional IRA leadership. 'A concern at the time was for progressive loyalists to make sure their analysis was sound, because they felt that it was always loyalists who were blamed for starting the conflict,' recalled 'The Pipe', the UVF's Chief of Staff. 'They therefore needed to be at the head of the game for finishing it.'[10] To that end, he argued:

> A series of discussions and consultations was initiated by the UVF leadership with its grassroots to debate the potential of calling for a unilateral ceasefire. In the absence of party politics connected to the UVF, Robin Eames was asked by the leadership to talk to the British Government – effectively, he was given the role of keeping his eye on the bigger picture. A unilateral ceasefire was announced in April 1991 to enhance the fortunes of the Brooke Talks, which had followed on from Peter Brooke's declaration in 1990 that Britain no longer had any 'selfish economic or strategic interest in Northern Ireland' – a statement seen as a key cue for the republican movement to engage in negotiations. The Brooke message (November 1990) in relation to no strategic self-interest was gauged by the UVF as a message to the IRA to stop the military campaign – and not about the prospect of a British withdrawal.[11]

As a key component of the Combined Loyalist Military Command (CLMC), the UVF believed that the ceasefire was a magnanimous gesture. Yet, it was ignored by the British, who remained firm on their public pronouncements not to negotiate with terrorists. 'We were aiming to create the space for dialogue,' recalled The Pipe. 'But it was slapped back.'[12] As the organisation's second-in-command, known subsequently by the codename 'The Craftsman', later reflected: 'A ceasefire requires more than one side to buy into it … If it was just one organisation it wouldn't have worked.'[13] Considerable doubt now stalked the UVF's heartlands. Was the ceasefire too much, too soon? The UVF Brigade Staff certainly thought so, resolving to return to their 'counter-terrorism' strategy.

While the UVF may not have been in a position to lobby for another ceasefire, its leadership continued to sanction the efforts of community activists in finding more creative ways for loyalists to have their voice heard. Billy Hutchinson advocated a grassroots approach to bringing about a ceasefire between republican and loyalist paramilitaries:

> I mean, before the ceasefires, when I worked in West [Belfast] ... I worked on a project which is now called Interaction ... Some of the work that we did was around 'What would happen if people called ceasefires?' And 'What would republicans do?' And all that sort of stuff. And some of that stuff we did at that particular time was amazing. I was talking to a guy the other day at that CFNI [Community Foundation for Northern Ireland, a non-governmental organisation] conference called Jim Auld [a former republican prisoner], who works for CRJ [Community Restorative Justice, a community-based organisation]. And he was on my management committee ... [who said] 'We did a lot of this in 1992 in a piece of work called *Life on the Interface*'. It was a pamphlet [produced after] a conference where people were being killed outside the door, and people in the room were going to kill each other. But what they decided to do at the end of that conference was to come back to discuss the major issues that came out of it.[14]

It would be another two years of hard work at grassroots level to keep this dialogue going before it would lead to a positive outcome. In the meantime, loyalist and republican paramilitaries remained locked in mortal combat on the streets of Northern Ireland. Peace seemed as far away as ever.

★★★

Corcraine Estate, Portadown, Christmas Day, 1992

Thirty-two-year-old Billy Wright lounged around at the home of one of his closest friends and comrades, 'Margaret'. He was well turned out for his Christmas lunch, dressed in the smart casuals of stonewash jeans turned up at the bottom, a freshly laundered white shirt with the cuffs rolled up, exposing his tattoos on both arms, and complete with duck egg grey waistcoat and black boots. At 6' 1", Wright was tall and slender, towering over most of the old men and women who stopped to talk to him in the streets around the estate. Apart from his sharp dress sense and height, Wright was easily distinguished by his closely cropped strawberry blonde hair, well-groomed moustache and pleasant manner. His reputation as a staunch loyalist in the close-knit community of Corcraine preceded him. Amongst his inner circle, where he could let his hair down, he has even a reputation as being something of a practical joker. While Margaret busily cooked Christmas dinner for a packed house of friends and family, Wright was restless, and wanted to keep an eye on her progress. He got up from his seat and sauntered into the kitchen of the neat working-class home to banter Margaret about the size and shape of the spuds she was cutting up. They laughed and joked like the close-knit family they had become over the years. Billy Wright felt safe in the company of these people.

A few nights earlier he been sitting on the sofa for over an hour with a plate of chicken curry in his hands, talking. He loved to talk. 'He would have talked the leg off a stool,' said Margaret. He talked incessantly about everyday things. About things that he had seen, about people he had met. The minutes turned into hours, as time marched on. Sometime after midnight, he returned from the kitchen with another cold can of lager in his hand and lifted a guitar for a sing-song. 'I would have driven him around the place,' recalled Margaret. 'I was working at the time, and so he would have come to me if he needed anything, like the lend of money or whatnot. He would have spent more time in my house than in his own flat.'[15] On Christmas Day 1992, Billy Wright was at home with the people he loved most, and who he trusted with his life. Drinks were served. More cans of lager were cracked open, and vodka and coke was shared around those gathered for the festivities. Children's toys littered the floor. Music blurred away in the background. Looking in through the window of this modest three-bedroom home, anyone would have been forgiven for thinking this was a normal family, like many others in the estate. Except that this wasn't a normal home, not really.

This was a family with a difference. They shared a dark secret that they couldn't tell anyone. For this was the nucleus of the UVF's Mid Ulster Brigade. In the UVF's long history, the militaristic language of battalions, companies and platoons is little more than stage-managed propaganda to give the impression that there is a huge organisation with several hundred robotic killers in its ranks. The reality is somewhat different. Out of the several hundred members of the UVF in Portadown, for instance, only four to six were active in killing.[16] A senior CID officer who would come to head the RUC's South Region, which covered Portadown and Lurgan, placed the number at about three.[17] The team was small. They kept things tight. Since the very formation of the UVF, the organisation prided itself on secrecy.

Few outside its military teams knew the details of operations until the last minute. This became especially important in the early 1990s when the UVF became more proficient at targeting republicans.

Billy Wright was always fascinated by the Shankill, and Margaret would have ferried him to meetings with the organisation's Brigade Staff in the early 1990s. She recalled how Wright and his predecessor, Robin Jackson, were 'good buddies', even if the relationship suffered as Wright climbed the ranks of the Portadown UVF and began to assert himself, in just the way that Jackson had done fifteen years earlier. Wright eventually took over from Jackson and, as a result, the Mid Ulster UVF became more calculating, more ruthless and more determined to pinpoint Provisional IRA members. As one of Wright's close associates revealed:

> In the 1970s, loyalists would have come into a bar or club and announced that they had 'slotted yer man'. By the mid to late 1980s, that had changed. There had been a transition towards a more professional operation. They could not have been so successful had it not been for the closeness of the unit. There was camaraderie there.[18]

By keeping a small praetorian guard of trusted people around him, Wright would never have asked them to do something that he was not prepared to do himself. They placed their complete trust in him and his targeting methodology, which they explained as follows:

> On an operation, we knew the QRF [Quick Reaction Force, a British Army unit ready to response to terrorist incidents] had fifteen minutes to respond. You had two minutes to get in, do the job, and get away. Within three more minutes you had changed cars – or from a car to a motorcycle – and you would have been away. On one occasion 'Swinger' [Mark Fulton, Billy Wright's right hand man] had gone to do a job, only his motorcycle ran out of petrol and he had to abandon it on the A3.[19]

The Portadown operation was run on less than a shoestring budget. On one operation, one individual allegedly had to 'borrow £20 off a wee women to fill two cars with petrol'.[20] That these individuals were prepared to kill, despite their lack of resources, proves that all the Mid Ulster UVF needed to fulfil their killing potential was a handful of willing volunteers, tight discipline and a good plan. With Wright, they had a leader who planned everything meticulously, from the moment they left on a 'job', until they returned safely to their homes. It was a deadly combination, and one that, ironically, the UVF Brigade Staff on the Shankill found difficult to control and the RUC in the South Region found difficult to stop.

For those officers in the RUC's Special Branch, Wright and his associates were diverting an enormous amount of their covert surveillance teams away from what they saw as their main effort against the Provisional IRA. At this time, Special Branch expended inordinate amounts of time and energy into trying to prevent loyalist attacks, particularly against softer targets, like Catholic civilians. But, as one former Branchman concluded, this was easier said than done. 'They were dragging us away from the "main enemy",' he said. 'They were so disorganised and *ad hoc*. They would get a lot of drink in them and decide to commit murder. The INLA were the same. They got high on drink and drugs and went out to kill a police officer. The Rah [IRA] planned things more meticulously. Even if you had a source within an ASU, they mixed things up a lot and moved quickly. You didn't always have time to respond.'[21] At one stage, Tasking and Coordination Group (TCG) South Region were mounting some ten covert surveillance operations, drawing on a wide array of Headquarters Mobile Support Units (HMSUs), military Close Observation Platoons (known in military parlance as COPs) and human sources every day but only getting a return of 1 or 2 per cent success. That amounted to one hundred ops every seven to ten days, with only a tiny number resulting in the recovery of weapons, the prevention or disruption of terrorist operations and, ultimately, what the RUC was aiming at: the saving of lives.[22]

Despite the RUC's best efforts, loyalist paramilitaries continued to crank up their terror campaign. In the period 1990–3, loyalist paramilitaries killed twenty-one republican paramilitaries or ex-paramilitaries and thirteen Sinn Féin activists. Only ten Sinn Féin activists had been killed by loyalists in the previous sixteen years. Two of the most active units carrying out these operations were Billy Wright's Mid Ulster UVF, based in Portadown, and Johnny Adair's C Company of the UFF, based on the Lower Shankill. For the first time ever, it can now be revealed that the two units forged a close working partnership, despite being from rival paramilitary organisations. It was a relationship that centred around the two charismatic figures of Wright and Adair. They first encountered each other sometime in the early 1990s:

I'll tell you what happened. When I got introduced to Billy, the main soul of his relationship with me was he respected what we were doing. He realised that we were very, very active. And he realised that every bit of help you could get was crucial. And, when I met him, that was the basis of our [relationship]. He says, 'Look, listen, I respect what youse are doing. You're doing a brilliant job, same as the boys in Mid Ulster.' He says ... 'I'm UVF, but I'm not like that.' He says, 'Johnny. It's the Red Hand of Ulster I'm interested in', he says. 'The letters don't mean much to me.' He says, 'We're all one. It's the Red Hand of Ulster' and ... Billy says, 'There'll come a time where we might be able to help you, in terms of cars or assistance, or whatever, and vice-versa', he says .... And that's what we done. We assisted each other. We had mutual respect for each other.[23]

Adair also revealed that Wright's unit did 'a lot of work' in Belfast at this time, which would indicate that they had a network of allies and sympathisers in other UVF brigade areas throughout Northern Ireland. Similarly, C Company had proven that they were prepared to venture outside Belfast if a targeting opportunity arose, perhaps best illustrated in their assassination of popular Sinn Féin councillor Eddie Fullerton in Buncrana, Donegal, on 25 May 1991.

Unsurprisingly, Adair began to emulate Wright's leadership style. He appreciated how committed his close associate was to the cause of loyalist paramilitarism:

From what I knew of Billy, Billy's life just revolved around loyalism. Now, obviously, he'd family, but I didn't know that side of him. I didn't really know his family that well, so I can't give an opinion. I know Billy was like myself. I know he was. He was just 24/7, when it was the UVF, and then when it was the LVF, it was just 24 hours at trying to bring the republicans to their knees. And that was what most of his life revolved around. I don't know what his private life was like. I don't know. Did he have hobbies? Did he have interests? Anytime I seen or dealt with Billy, it was business ... Did he come across to me as a wealthy person? No, he did not. You could just tell that money was not Billy's God.[24]

What surprised Adair most about Wright during these years of a 'working partnership' (or what Adair called 'the other CLMC') was the lengths that the UVF Brigade Staff appeared to go to curtail their Mid Ulster brigadier:

> I think Billy's problem was in Mid Ulster that they were short of weapons too and I know of instances where the UDA lent them weapons, etc. But that should have been the UVF's job ... I remember one specific meeting one day [on the Shankill] where they had asked them for the lend of a pistol, a Browning, and Big Kingo [Trevor King] says, "You're not getting it." And I was shocked. 'Billy Wright? They should be giving youse [whatever you were asking for]. Have you not got that type of weaponry down there?' I think they just played about with a couple of AKs, one or two handguns.[25]

It is likely that King and the Brigade Staff were wary of Wright for a number of reasons, particularly after Cappagh, when Wright's unit counter-balanced the UVF 'good-news story' of a 'hit' on what the Brigade Staff would have considered a 'legitimate target' with a nakedly sectarian attack a few days later. In all probability, the issue came down to the inherent tension between the UVF's centralised leadership and the autonomy it devolved to its local units.

Despite its internal logistical setbacks, the Mid Ulster UVF continued to work alongside C Company. Adair was philosophical about the challenges this secret alliance posed:

> But you've got to remember ... see, when you're operating like that, you'll get casualties. You'll lose men and you will lose weapons. 'Cos when you're operating the way Billy did and we did, see, it's the clean-up after an operation. The Branch, if ... you get away Scot free, they'll come down hard on you. They'll blatter houses. They'll try and turn up guns. I was at the top of it all ... But again, they couldn't stop me. They couldn't buy my soul. And even with using informers against me, they still failed. They were forced to introduce legislation to bring about a charge to get me done. And I believe, I don't take credit, it was the men of C Company. They were courageous and dedicated young men. And they were the men who took the war right into the heart of republican West Belfast, an area where loyalists hadn't ventured in almost 30 years of the troubles. Once we got a safe house in there, we were in there fucking every single day. The record speaks for

itself. Daring raids. Broad daylight. Fucking Connolly House. Rocket attacks. Sinn Féin offices and Sinn Féiner's homes. We had them on the run, like. We did.[26]

There is no disputing that the loyalist paramilitary kill-rate reached an extraordinary tempo at this time but they were also assassinating people who had absolutely no connection with republican paramilitaries. Such comments about 'daring raids' must, therefore, be juxtaposed with the horrific reality of loyalist gunmen, often armed with AK47 or VZ58 assault rifles, entering ordinary peoples' homes, workplaces, and places of recreation, and opening fire on them in enclosed spaces, their wounds too horrific to recount. Nevertheless, for the first time, loyalist gunmen were out-gunning the IRA. Adair was of the opinion that, without the leadership he and Wright provided, the terror campaigns would not have been as successful as they were in the early 1990s:

You see, loyalism, in my opinion, is all about leadership. You could have a hundred good men below you, right. But you could have a leader … and he has the first and last say. Now, if he's an agent, your hundred men below him are worthless because he will be controlling them. Now, see if the leader is not an agent and he's a hardliner, and he's got a hundred good men below him, he will make them good men. He will give them confidence, credit. That, in my opinion, is what loyalism is about. You were only as good as the men below you. But the men below them were only as good as the leader 'cos he said either 'go' or 'don't go', and when we were under Tommy Lyttle there were very, very few operations getting conducted. Maybe a couple a year. He was stopping them at the behest of the Special Branch. 'No, don't let them go. Let them go out and extort wee shops, but don't be killing. We want these killings to stop.' And that's why, under his leadership, there were very few killings. There were one or two operations carried out a year. But then when [other] people … came across. It was just like the IRA. 24/7. Boom, boom, boom, boom. If a target arose it was targeted. It wasn't like this here, 'Let's get drunk and wait another six months.' It was, 'Let's fight these bastards. Let's smoke them out. Let's keep doing it. We've got the men. We've got the weapons.' And for people like me, Billy was a shining light. It drew people into the ranks of the Ulster Young Militants.[27]

Inevitably, Adair and Wright became firm comrades. They respected each other, and enjoyed a warm friendship. For Adair, he believed he had much in common with Wright:

> Most of these UDA or UVF leaders have no personalities. They're grumpy looking old men. Look at me and Billy. We were happy go lucky. We went onto the ground with the men. Not only did we go onto the ground with the men, but we went into the battlefield with the men. Do you understand what I mean by that? I remember when I was on the [UDA Inner] Council, not one of them men had pulled a trigger. I remember saying 'I don't believe a man should be a brigadier till he's done the business or, not only done the business, but also been held for seven days and kept his mouth shut.' Right. All them'ums had never done that. They had failed miserably. Billy was like me, he had gone onto the ground with his men, even when he was a brigadier. I know for a fact that Billy wasn't an armchair general like the rest of them. And that's where you get a load of respect. And that's where, I believe, I got a lot of respect.[28]

By the autumn of 1993, there was little feeling in the ranks of these hardcore loyalist paramilitary units that an end to the violence was on the horizon. As far as they were concerned, their terror campaign would continue.

★★★

Carnmoney, Newtownabbey, Evening, 21 October 1993

A milkman from Rathcoole was collecting his weekly delivery money in the relatively quiet suburban neighbourhood of Carnvue in Carnmoney, when he stopped his young helper from calling to the door of one of his customers, John Gibson, because of 'something that happened the night before'. The young teenager was curious. As he stared down Mr Gibson's driveway he saw little yellow and green circles around what appeared to be the chalk outline of a body. Less than twenty-four hours earlier, John Gibson had arrived home from work to be greeted by a stranger as he climbed out of his car. The stranger trained the sights of a weapon on him before firing a number of shots at close range. He died instantly. The young man who pulled the trigger, twenty-one-year-old Robert Duffy,[29] then made off in a white Nissan Micra a short distance down the nearby Prince Charles Way, past Carnmoney cemetery and onto the O'Neill Road to the Valley Park with its vast playing fields. Duffy and his accomplice abandoned the vehicle, setting fire to it, before making off in the general direction of the predominantly nationalist Antrim Road.[30]

Fifty-one-year-old John Gibson, a father of one, was in a jovial mood before he arrived home to be murdered on his doorstep. He had just been informed that he was being nominated for an award for his charity work in raising awareness of the scourge of diabetes. The Provisional IRA subsequently claimed responsibility for his murder. The reason the IRA gave for murdering John Gibson, a man who, in his son's words, 'wouldn't have hurt a fly', was that he was a director for the construction firm Henry Brothers, who held a contract for rebuilding Security Force bases after the IRA had blown them up. Mr Gibson was the fifth director of the firm to be assassinated by republicans.

John Gibson's death puzzled local people. Why had this man – a church-going Christian, a pillar of the local community and a champion for charitable causes – been murdered on his own doorstep? What could he have done to deserve this?

John Gibson's neighbours, who had heard the fatal shots that wet and blustery evening, were caught in a state of shock for several days after the assassination. As the newspapers that carried word of his death circulated, and the television news reports were filled with information of his murder, working-class people in the local area knew instinctively why he had been targeted. In their eyes, John Gibson was killed because he was a Protestant, and the Provisional IRA knew no bounds when it came to slaughtering ordinary people from this community. The IRA's convoluted talk about 'legitimate targets' didn't wash with working-class Protestants in areas like this, where its people had borne the brunt of political violence for over two decades.

Terrorist groups in Northern Ireland always had a tendency to stretch the concept of 'legitimate target' to encompass everyone from bus drivers to builders to soldiers. The term 'legitimate target' was suggestive of a very wide spectrum indeed. In any other war – whether an interstate armed conflict or a non-international armed conflict – John Gibson would have been designated a non-combatant and, therefore, off-limits. But in Northern Ireland's grubby little war, he had fallen foul of the Provisional IRA's peculiar logic when it came to justifying the murder of innocent men, women and children. What made matters worse was that because the British State framed its own security response in terms of emergency legislation under the domestic Prevention of Terrorism Act (1974; 1989), concepts from international law just didn't apply. If they had, then John Gibson's death would have been designated by the United Nations, the International Committee of the Red Cross and other human rights organisations (as the custodians of international law) as a 'war crime'. As such, the international community of states would have been obligated to seek sanctions against the organisation that carried out the murder.

In many respects, the IRA's rebranding of John Gibson's pre-meditated murder as something politically inspired was viewed as a flag of convenience by the local unionist community, who regarded the IRA as having obfuscated its cold-blooded assassination of a civilian who played no direct role in hostilities. Of course, this was not something unique to republicanism. Loyalist paramilitaries stretched the label of 'legitimate target' to encompass everyone from ordinary Catholics (with no republican ties whatsoever) all the way along to Sinn Féin activists and IRA volunteers, at the other end of the spectrum. This found deadly expression in the twenty-four hours after John Gibson's death, when loyalists shot and wounded a Catholic taxi driver in nearby Glengormley, apparently in reprisal for the Provo's murder of the Henry Brothers Director.

At the time, John Gibson's killing sent out a signal to the wider Protestant community that, if they collaborated with the British, they would suffer the same fate.

The milkman and his young apprentice wondered if, by that perverse logic, that made them collaborators too, simply because they supplied Mr Gibson with milk for his cornflakes. And, by the same twisted logic, that meant that the local newsagent who supplied a newspaper to the Henry Brothers director put himself into the firing line, too. And his neighbours, who passed the time with Mr Gibson while he did his gardening – what of them? Were they 'legitimate targets' too? Local people believed they were all in the firing line. In killing John Gibson, the IRA sent out a message loud and clear that, in their armed campaign, no distinction whatsoever would be drawn between combatants and non-combatants.

One by-product of this and countless other killings in Newtownabbey was to keep young Protestants engaged in loyalist paramilitary activity. Recruitment in these groups remained healthy, as more and more young people decided that – in lieu of an effective Security Force response against the IRA – they would risk prison or death to protect themselves, their families and communities.

★★★

Shankill Road, Belfast, Lunchtime, Saturday, 23 October 1993

The Shankill Road was busy with shoppers going about their weekend chores. Men, women and children walked the bustling streets. Twenty-nine-year-old Sharon McBride, a married health worker with one child, was helping her father, sixty-three-year-old John Desmond Frizzell, at his fish and chip shop that day. After dropping off his wife, Sharon's husband, Alan, took their daughter on a short bicycle ride. When he returned, news began to filter through of an explosion. As he rounded the corner and saw the collapsed building, his heart sank. He knew that nobody was getting out of the rubble alive. Nine civilians died in the attack. John Frizzell and his daughter Sharon McBride, as well as sixty-three-year-old George Williamson and his forty-nine-year-old wife Gillian were also killed, along with twenty-seven-year-old Michael Morrison, his twenty-seven-year-old common-in-law wife Evelyn Baird and their seven-year-old daughter Michelle Baird. The family had gone in search of a wreath for Michael's father, who had just died. Other victims in the atrocity were thirteen-year-old schoolgirl Leanne Murray and thirty-eight-year-old mother of two Wilma McKee, who died of her injuries the next day.[31] Twenty-three-year-old Thomas Begley and his accomplice, twenty-one-year-old Sean Kelly, both IRA men, were planting the bomb in the shop when it detonated prematurely, killing Begley. Like many such attacks of this kind, the Provisional IRA statement said that the bomb was intended to remove the UDA's Inner Council, which it claimed was holding a meeting above the shop.

One of those who rushed to help dig people out of the rubble was Luke, a young member of the UVF's A Company in the Shankill, a unit known colloquially as 'Sweeneys'. 'I looked around at the carnage and the bodies of women and children being lifted out of the rubble and I said, "This has to stop – this just has to stop." It was a watershed moment for me.' Active as a UVF volunteer in the late 1980s and early 1990s, Luke recalls the UVF leadership broadly agreeing, in principle, with his position. The question was how to bring that about. 'You couldn't be seen to be adopting that position of calling for peace. All around, the up and coming ones were calling for war.' Luke was only a child when he saw his first troubles-related death. 'I was in between my parents when I saw my first murder – a man known to us. It was a black taxi driver, with his white shirt on and all these red blotches started to appear after two gunmen opened up on him at close range. No child should ever see that,' Luke recalled, during an interview, the tone and pitch of his voice changing suddenly. He became emotional at the thought of the killing and maiming he had witnessed first-hand. Like so many other young men, Luke had become involved with the UVF when he was in his late teens. He was in his early to mid-twenties by the time he entered the military teams in A Company. 'I'd be lying if I said people weren't talking about retaliation after the Shankill bombing. Wee Sharon was well-liked on the Shankill. The family were only out buying a wreath for Michael's father's funeral when they were caught in the bombing.'[32]

Within hours, B Company's rocket team were back out on the streets. An attempt to post a warhead into the door of a Sinn Féin office was aborted when the projectile failed to fire. Although they had no idea what had gone wrong with the weapon system, UVF men now believe that it had been 'jarked' by covert surveillance teams, on the nod of an informer. It would not be the only time that the Security Forces would move to 'clip the wings' of loyalist paramilitaries over the coming weeks and months as they sought to carry out reprisal attacks in the wake of the Shankill Bombing.

14

IN THE HANDS OF PHILISTINES

'And, as the IRA well know. The Ulster Volunteer Force have to be lucky only once. They have to be lucky all of the time.'

Combat, June 1994[1]

Teesport, England, Wednesday, 24 November 1993

The port was quiet. The freezing morning air was punctuated only by the breath of officials from Her Majesty's Customs and Excise, charged with leading the raid on a ship that had travelled from the Baltic Sea port of Gdynia, where the roll-on, roll-off 200-container ship Inowroclaw was making its weekly trip from Poland to the UK. Container ships like this passed through UK waters on a regular basis. Nothing appeared to be out of place until the cargo ship docked in Teesport and was boarded by customs officers acting on a tip-off from the Polish Secret Service, *Urzad Ochrony Panstwa* (UOP) and MI5, who were involved in a coordinated surveillance operation.[2] The haul, which included two tonnes of military-grade explosives, 320 AKM assault rifles, along with 60,000 rounds of ammunition, fifty-three Makarov P38 9mm pistols with 14,000 rounds, 500 F1 hand grenades, thousands of electric detonators and bayonets for rifles, had been concealed in crates of ceramic tiles. The container was to be unloaded in Teesport and driven to Stranraer in Scotland, where it was to be taken to its final destination in East Belfast, via the port of Larne.[3] It took customs officials six hours to unload the consignment of weapons and explosives. As soon as news broke of the seizure, the UVF middleman who had brokered the deal between the leadership in Belfast and the arms dealers in the Polish capital Warsaw reportedly went on the run from MI6, Interpol and the UVF.[4]

Something very curious had happened which had led to the seizure of the weapons. It emerged, from a subsequent investigation by the Polish liberal newspaper *Gazeta Wyborcza*, that the single container housing the contraband had actually passed through customs in Warsaw before being driven to Gdynia and loaded onto a ship on 19 November. Unusually, further checks were not completed before the ship set sail for England. The newspaper concluded that, 'it was not a case of an Irish buyer looking for a supplier, but an UOP agent looking for an Irish buyer'.[5] It appeared to be part of an international sting operation, designed to flush out middlemen and other arms dealers who had been capitalising on the flood of weapons into Western Europe and other parts of the world after the collapse of the Soviet Union two years earlier.[6] The newly appointed head of UOP, Colonel Gromoslaw Czempinski, initially defended his organisation when accusations were levelled at it in the press that the operation had been mounted without the requisite legal checks and balances being in place. This was important, especially in light of the ban on Polish secret service agents becoming involved in sting operations. Czempinski moved to robustly defend his officers, telling the press that 'all the relevant documents had been handed over to the Prosecutor's Office.' He concluded his statement by warning that if details of the operation were revealed, 'there'll be some corpses dropping on this side (in Poland) and on that side (in Britain)'.[7] This gave rise to speculation that an informer had been involved from the very moment the money changed hands between the UVF and the arms dealers in Eastern Europe.

In claiming responsibility for the arms seized in England, the UVF wished to 'make it clear to the people of Ulster that, whilst it is a logistical setback, it in no way diminishes our ability nor our determination to carry on the war against the IRA'. In typically bellicose language, it evoked imagery of the original UVF gunrunning Operation Lion, eighty years earlier. 'The spirit of "1912" and the "Clyde Valley" lives on,' read the statement. 'It is the heritage too proud to be cynically manipulated by political Quislings, nor brutally cowed by military means.' The UVF promised that for 'so long as we are in receipt of the support of the loyalist people, in whatever form, so we will continue to put at risk our volunteers to scour the world for arms to be used in their defence and for that of our country'.[8]

Although it could so easily have been dismissed as loyalist paranoia, there was now a widespread belief amongst unionists that the British Government had entered into secret talks with the Provisional IRA. The allegations seemed to be substantiated when an official at the heart of government in Whitehall leaked information to a DUP politician, the Reverend William McCrea MP. McCrea's colleague Peter Robinson, the

DUP's deputy leader, spoke for many in his party when he told the BBC that he believed loyalist paramilitaries were 'arming themselves in the event of the British and Irish governments doing a deal with the IRA'. In language redolent of that used by republican spokesmen at the time and since, he asked, rhetorically, whether other consignments had got through. 'The size and magnitude of this cargo was not to restock the depleted resources of a terrorist organisation,' Robinson concluded. 'This was to arm an army. This was preparation for war, much more than any terrorist campaign.'[9] The UVF agreed. 'Dialogue is the only answer,' it said in signing off its statement. 'But to enter into dialogue with murderers whilst they are still trying to enforce their will on us by the bomb and the bullet is wrong.'[10]

Those in the UVF leadership at the time put the seizure of weapons down to 'a number of variables'. Although allegations were subsequently made about where the authorities got their intelligence from, in reality, the UVF believed it could have come from any area within the organisation. 'It could have been a wee man mouthing off from a bar stool in East Belfast,' a former UVF Director of Operations admitted. 'At the end of the day, when you are dealing with arms dealers in Eastern Europe or the Middle East, or wherever, you are in the hands of Philistines. They don't care who they take their money from. It could be half a million pounds, for the sake of argument, but to them half a million is a drop in the ocean. They won't see you again so there's little incentive for them to remain true to their word.'[11] This admission suggests that internal discipline within the organisation was weak at the time, or that far too much faith had been placed in the UVF's *omertà*.

Writing around this time, BBC journalist Mark Urban believed that British Intelligence was becoming extremely worried about loyalist violence, particularly since they had managed to eliminate two dozen republicans in the previous three years. So concerned were they to prevent further attacks on republicans that the seizure of the UVF arms shipment made perfect strategic sense. Britain's political establishment could ill-afford loyalist paramilitaries killing the very people they were now sitting down with to engage in dialogue, for it would have undermined confidence-building measures already underway. In a world in which the Provisionals were considered to be a much more dangerous threat than loyalists, it was judged vital to national security that republicans were given as much breathing space to wind down their military campaign as possible.[12]

In late 1993, British intelligence was well ahead of the game, scoring a huge success by preventing the illicit cargo from Eastern Europe reaching the hands of the UVF's military teams back in Northern Ireland.

***

In the wake of the Shankill bombing, the UVF's Brigade Staff resolved to resist, by force of arms, any attempts to impose a deal on the unionist people. Yet, the grouping had also proven imaginative in being prepared to call a ceasefire in support of the Brooke initiative in 1991. Throughout 1993 it followed exactly the same twin-track strategy. Several months before the Teesport seizure, David Ervine, Gusty Spence and The Craftsman were meeting with Dublin-based trade unionist Chris Hudson, who acted as a go-between with representatives from the government in Dublin. Although these talks were little more than exploratory and, for the moment, their focus was on ensuring there was no return to the Anglo-Irish Agreement through the back door,[13] they did indicate that the UVF was, in wording that came later, 'prepared for peace, but ready for war'. Chris Hudson elaborated:

> It always struck me that there was clear agreement at the highest level within the UVF that myself and him [The Craftsman] were to talk to each other, and that he would be authorised to come down to Dublin in the earlier days, when things were more sensitive, and we were just developing the links. David Ervine would have come down with him a few times and David did most of the talking. But, as the thing moved on, David was always giving the political analysis but, from the military point of view, The Craftsman was the man who could make things happen. So, in other words, David could give the analysis both to us and to them, but then the logistics of making changes within the military wing [rested with] ... The Craftsman. And as he would even say to me, he didn't say anything to me that he didn't say to the average volunteer ... He maintained that he would have visited every section of the UVF to put across the point of view of where they were and the confirmation they had received from Dublin on a number of issues. For instance, the clear indicators were the Downing Street Declaration [15 December 1993]. That they saw some of their language was used in it, and then particularly the comment, at a later

stage, by Dick Spring when Dick Spring said that 'there can never be a United Ireland unless a majority of unionists want a United Ireland' ... Essentially, most of what we discussed was, 'How do we make this end up here?'[14]

That loyalist paramilitaries were prepared to engage in dialogue at this stage with the Irish Government, their sworn enemy, rather than the British Government, reinforced how serious the UVF was about seeking a peaceful resolution of the armed conflict.

Although a cycle of death-dealing had engulfed Northern Ireland in the aftermath of the Shankill Bombing, there were also signs that loyalist and republican paramilitaries were looking at ways to end the armed conflict. By the end of the year, republicans had killed thirty-eight people (a figure which included twenty-three Protestants and nine soldiers), while loyalists claimed responsibility for forty-eight (forty Catholics and eight Protestants), most of whom were civilians, who did not play any part in hostilities. The troubles were far from winding down, even if there was a serious effort now underway to bring an end to hostilities.

★★★

H Blocks, HMP Maze, New Year's Eve, December 1993

UVF prisoners in H Block 7 were in festive mood. They had participated in a short-lived protest at being 'locked up' in their cells but now the atmosphere had lightened, and the prisoners set about organising a fancy-dress party in the prison canteen. According to *Combat*, three volunteers, Hendy, Jackie and Noel, played a selection of tunes on their guitars, ranging from blues to country. 'It being old year's night,' *Combat* reported, 'the men were defiantly set to ring out the old and bring in the new, and we had no shortage of "volunteer" soloists, ready and eager to strut their stuff.' One prisoner, Baz, took to the challenge of karaoke singing with gusto, bursting into the Frank Sinatra classic *My Way*. The place erupted into spontaneous laughter, accompanied by loud cheers and applause. The beer flowed as UVF volunteers forgot for a moment where they were. Next up on the karaoke was a prisoner known as 'wee Tokyo Joe', who did his best to entertain the troops with a Kenny Rogers impression. He hadn't finished his set when Brian G took to the stage with a rendition of 'Deeply Dippy'. The penultimate act, 'Big Mervyn' and 'Chats', who had gone to the trouble of dressing up as the Blues Brothers, fronted up with high-pitched, badly off-tune lyrics. The evening ended with a rave, not with the traditional good-humoured rendition of 'Auld Lang Syne'.[15]

On the outside, the UVF's military teams were ratcheting up the tempo of operations by carrying out a string of murders and attempted murders. Under its section 'Counter-Terrorist Reports' in *Combat*, the organisation claimed to be targeting republicans in Moy, Portadown, Craigavon, Ballymena and Belfast. In one incident on 24 January, it admitted that a unit from its North Antrim Brigade 'entered the home of Cormac McDermott in Fisherwick Gardens in the town of Ballymena and executed him'. A spokesman for the UVF, in a coded message to the media, accused McDermott of being a recruiting officer for the Provisional IRA in the area. The message also stated that he had been responsible for organising attacks against the local population. For this 'crime', the group claimed, 'he had been made accountable'.[16]

It was around this time that there was a real risk of a new tit-for-tat shooting war breaking out between the UVF and republican paramilitaries in Belfast. One activist connected to the UVF in North Belfast believed that the Provisionals were attempting to kill and maim as many people in the Protestant community as they could. All signs on the ground, he said, pointed towards the UVF adopting a new offensive posture, rather than any attempt being made to decrease its kill-rate:

> Prior to the ceasefires. Honest opinion? Anyone that I was friendly with at that time was against it. Totally. Because they seen [sic] that, essentially, the general feeling, if you're talking about guys on the street (and that's who I'm talking about. I'm not talking about anybody holding any positions of power), they were against it because they'd seen that the military aspect of things was very much to the fore.[17]

Given that the UVF offensive had undergone a gear-change, grassroots supporters of the organisation believed that its continuing violence served to keep people together. Ironically, it also exposed that, of the new influx of younger members, few had truly patriotic reasons for joining up:

> There was an element that I felt then, that's just starting to come to the fore now, of guys who looked further on than just, you know,

what the military aspect of the thing was … Within any paramilitary organisation … there are different people that are there for different reasons. And you have to accept that there's people there to line their own pockets. There's people there to stop other people from beating them up. There's also people there who genuinely believe in what they're doing. And, there's people there who see a way of making a living out of it. And, unfortunately, that has, in my view, come right through to the political wing as well as from military wing. But that's a personal point of view.[18]

For many of those in the UVF's rank and file at the time, there were mixed feelings about whether the campaign would intensify.

For David, the impact of the Shankill bomb was to sow contradictory seeds of doubt in the minds of rank-and-file UVF volunteers across Belfast:

In the early 90s there was a, I'd nearly say, an optimism amongst the trenches. There was actually a very strong optimism. But the difference was – and this is the problem I've often found in loyalism in general and paramilitaries in particular, loyalist paramilitaries in particular – they never went the long war. Loyalists never had a long-war scenario. They always had [this belief that] a victory … this week was not a victory next week, because the Provos had done something again so, therefore, there had to be another victory the following week. That maybe sounds quite convoluted but it's maybe not me explaining myself right. Whereas the Provos seemed to have an ability of saying, 'Alright, well, we got beat this week, but, you know, in six years' time we'll do this, or five years' time we'll do this'. I'm not saying there wasn't forward planning within loyalism – far from it – but on the ground, there wasn't the belief that it was possible. Or maybe I'm wrong there. Maybe not that it wasn't possible, but that it wasn't the type of war they wanted to fight. That's maybe a better way of putting it.[19]

Just what type of war loyalist paramilitaries were fighting was never fully appreciated by the men on the ground carrying out the shootings and bombings. Those higher up the UVF's chain of command, however, were in two minds about their strategy. They continued to keep the channels of communication with the Dublin government and the Provisional IRA open, for now.

It was a time of great nervousness in Protestant working-class areas. The British Government had begrudgingly admitted to secret talks with the IRA, despite John Major telling the House of Commons that it would 'turn his stomach' to do so. The reality was that the IRA 'spectaculars' in Great Britain were draining the economic resources of the State, and this kind of damage couldn't be sustained forever. Something had to be done, and fast.

★★★

While violence continued across Northern Ireland, the small group of Protestant community activists who had been involved in dialogue with their opposite numbers across the peace line in Belfast came together to take stock of recent developments in a discussion group. They were exhausted from their efforts, and saw republicans making clear political gains because of their campaign of violence. 'We have a whole new generation queuing up to join the paramilitaries,' one man told the group. 'They haven't a notion how it all started, and most of them couldn't care less. Civil rights are ancient history to them. They just see a hated enemy out to destroy them, and they want to fight back. I agree with them – whatever those wrongs were, they don't justify all the IRA killings.'[20] Despite overtures by Sinn Féin, the truth was that the murder of Protestant civilians did little to endear that community to the kind of united Ireland advocated by the Provisionals, especially when they showed a willingness to kill whoever got in their way. Sharing his frustration at the violence, one community activist noted how:

> My father was murdered twenty-four years ago by the IRA. He was not a member of the security forces, nor did he work for them, nor was he in any paramilitary organisation. He was a labourer at the coal quay, whose only concern was to support his family – a wife, four children and a baby on the way. He was an ordinary Protestant, presumably one of those 'ordinary Protestants' Gerry Adams tells us have nothing to fear. Yet the IRA left him bleeding to death in the street. In destroying our family Sinn Féin/IRA taught me all I need to know about their 'peace process.'[21]

Importantly, it was sectarianism that kept the Northern Ireland conflict alive in the early months of 1994. This was one of the major obstacles to ending it. As one participant would write in the conclusion to the pamphlet published after the discussion group event: 'Only when sectarianism is brought to the surface and fully analysed can there be any hope of eradicating it. The entire Protestant working class must define what it is as a community, good aspects and bad. Only then can more positive labels begin to gain any credibility.'[22]

By the summer of 1994 loyalist paramilitaries were killing people in greater numbers than ever before. Their targeting of members of the IRA and Sinn Féin led some UVF volunteers to believe that the tide was finally beginning to turn on their enemies. 'They were running scared,' said one former member.[23] For the Brigade Staff, there was an even greater indication now that the Provisionals were close to calling a ceasefire. Nonetheless, they were taking few chances and issued a warning to their members to be careful.[24]

The UVF carried out a wave of attacks on Catholic civilians in May, with the particularly brutal sectarian murder of seventy-six-year-old Rose Mallon at her relative's home near Dungannon on 8 May. The attack was perpetrated by the Mid Ulster UVF. On 17 May the East Antrim UVF shot dead forty-two-year-old Eamon Fox and twenty-four-year-old Gary Convie. The next day the Mid Ulster UVF attacked a taxi depot in Lurgan, killing seventeen-year-old Gavin McShane and seventeen-year-old Shane McArdle. A few days later the UVF blew up a public house in Dublin it said was frequented by IRA members, killing thirty-five-year-old IRA member Martin Doherty. By exploding a bomb in Widow Scallan's Pub on Pearse Street, Dublin, the UVF was also keen to demonstrate that it had the audacity to cause chaos south of the border, while also signalling that it had overcome its early 'logistical setback' at Teesport.

On 4 June 1994, the Provos retaliated with an assassination attempt on Mid Ulster UVF commander Billy Wright. Wright had intended to move his car when, shortly after turning the key in the ignition, he drove off. A malfunction in the bomb gave him time to escape the vehicle. When the bomb exploded, it blew out the windows of twenty-five nearby homes. Wright was rushed to hospital while three police officers who were responding to a call regarding suspicious activity were blown from their feet. It seems that the Provisionals were seeking to kill the loyalist leader and anyone around him at the time, including a ten-year-old boy who had a lucky escape with only minor injuries. In an act of defiance, Wright waved to journalists who had turned up to report the incident.[25]

A few days later the UVF were out for revenge for the bid on Wright. A team from B Company set out on a mission to assassinate leading republican Sean 'Spike' Murray. The UVF had received intelligence that he was meeting with another high-profile republican in the same house every morning in West Belfast. On the morning that the UVF sent a team to carry out an attack on Murray, the two republicans simply didn't appear. 'He was getting his wings but the other member of the team didn't turn up. They were waiting at ten o'clock as planned. It came and went.'[26] It appeared that the man tasked with leading the attack was thirty-one-year-old Colin 'Crazy' Craig. Craig would later give the excuse that his jeep broke down. It was fortuitous for him because the UVF volunteers he had sent to assassinate the men had got as far as their safe-house when they were intercepted and arrested by the RUC's covert unit E4A. Craig's failure to show raised eyebrows amongst the UVF rank and file.

Interestingly, shortly after the murder bid on Murray, republicans sent a team of their own directly to Craig's house where they forced their way in, pulling his wife by the hair as they said, 'You tell your husband he's fuck'in dead.'[27] It would appear that the Provisionals were aware of loyalist targeting of republicans, and that they had the steely resolve to venture into a hardline loyalist area to send a message to the UVF directly. Had Craig been in the house at the time, it is likely he would have been killed by the IRA gang. It was around then that Craig dyed his hair blonde and started sporting a baseball cap, which he wore backwards. It had 'Hard to Kill' stencilled across the back of it. US martial arts expert and actor Steven Seagal had brought out a flutter of movies in the late 1980s and early 1990s, and Craig liked to imagine himself as some kind of tough guy.[28] In the lead-up to the failed assassination bid, Craig's men said they began to notice a change in their commander's behaviour. He was becoming more irritable and jumpy, occasionally threatening violence against his subordinates if they looked into his business. Not satisfied with his operational remit of assisting Trevor King in running West Belfast, Craig had become involved with other UVF teams around the province. 'Shortly after he became involved with a wee team in Cookstown,' recalled one member of B Company, 'they were wiped out.'[29]

Loyalist bomb attacks against republicans were on the increase and were becoming more audacious. On 14 June, the UVF detonated a 2lb bomb in Sevastopol Street near Clonard Monastery and yards from one of the first attacks that the group ever carried out. Sinn Féin President Gerry

Adams claimed that the attacks were clearly 'the first loyalist response to the heightened confidence of nationalists, as evidenced by the increased Sinn Féin and SDLP vote in the European elections'.[30]

★★★

It was a balmy afternoon on the Shankill Road on 16 June 1994 when several high-ranking members of the UVF stopped to talk to one another on the street corner. The West Belfast commander, forty-one-year-old Trevor King, was standing next to his second-in-command, Crazy Craig, forty-three-year-old UVF member Davy Hamilton and another man, when a pair of INLA gunmen ran up to the four men and shot them at point-blank range. Craig was killed outright, Hamilton died the next day and King succumbed to his wounds three weeks later.

King was born in 1953 in the Bone area of Ardoyne, originally a mixed community before the troubles began. 'Kingo', as he was known to his friends and comrades, joined the Young Citizens' Volunteers (YCVs), the UVF's youth wing, aged 18, and took part in the so-called 'Battle of Springmartin' estate in 1972. Charged with possessing a number of illegal weapons, he refused to recognise the court and was sentenced to a spell in prison. He later served another sentence when he was convicted of sending letter bombs in 1976.[31] By 1994 King was the UVF's military commander on the Shankill. His comrades lamented, in *Combat* magazine, how he was not prepared to 'stand idly by to allow defenceless people to face slaughter without reply'.[32]

Like King, Craig was valorised as a true 'soldier' of Ulster. A matter of hours after his murder, a UVF honour guard formed up at a gable end on the Shankill. Four men dressed from head to toe in black, complete with stable belts and balaclavas, carried the UVF's regimental colours into the centre, after which three other men, clasping pistols, extended their arms into the air and fired a volley of shots into the night's sky. They moved with military bearing as they formed their guard around Crazy Craig's coffin. At Craig's funeral he was again praised by a key member of the UVF's Brigade Staff, who gave a stirring oration at his graveside. Craig had an 'extensive, illustrious and greatly valued war record', said the man. 'He will have, forever, our undying respect for the soldier he was, the man he was, the son he was, the father he was and the friend and comrade he has been.' In concluding his address, the Brigade Staff member looked to the 'purveyors of our misery and that of our people' and assured them that their time would come.[33]

However, what the UVF did not reveal at the time was that some of its members were engaged in an internal investigation into how several of its activists could have been killed in broad daylight. The inquiry threw up some unexpected evidence, which included a litany of disrupted operations, such as that which led to the death of Brian Robinson on 2 September 1989. Other questions were also raised about the tampering of weapons. VZ58 assault rifles with busted springs, firing mechanisms on RPG-7 systems failing to activate and then, of course, the leak that led to the seizure of arms and munitions at Teesport. As the net closed further, one individual's name kept coming up, time and time again: Colin 'Crazy' Craig.

To the UVF in the summer of 1994, Crazy Craig was a soldier who embodied traits like dedication, compassion and bravery, as well as commitment, sacrifice and steadfastness. After his death, though, serious questions were raised about his, at times, erratic behaviour. He apparently joined a UVF team in Ardoyne in 1984, and was involved in armed robberies for the next two years, after which he announced that he and his wife had won a holiday in a competition. They were not seen again for several years. The fact that Craig had disappeared in the mid-1980s raised eyebrows amongst his comrades in B Company upon his return. They were later to discover that Craig had joined the British Army. As Kingo's driver in the late 1980s, Craig accompanied his boss everywhere and, according to some loyalists, in 1988 'pushed and pushed' to have Patrick McKenna murdered.[34] The UVF team who were tasked with the assassination watched their target for over three months before they were ordered to carry out their mission. That Craig was so anxious to set the wheels in motion for McKenna's murder was enough to raise suspicions amongst some of his close comrades.

A short time after his death in 1994, someone close to Craig allegedly walked into the UVF's headquarters on the Shankill and presented the Brigade Staff with evidence that showed that Craig had over £27,000 in his bank account. Those close to the investigation into Craig's activities believe that he had been meeting his handler in the carpark of the Tesco in Newtownards every Saturday, where he talked through the UVF's planned activities for the coming weeks and months ahead. The UVF leadership were at a loss to explain how he had effectively penetrated the organisation to rise so rapidly through their ranks. The same members of B Company who had vowed at Craig's graveside to take the fight to 'the hell from whence it came' in reprisal for their commander's assassination now vented their anger by returning to the same spot to smash up Craig's headstone. 'There are only three or four cases where I would say there was incontrovertible evidence that a UVF volunteer was an informer,' said one former UVF Director of Operations. 'Crazy Craig was one of those. There were several things that went wrong, and every time it could be traced back to him. I would hang my hat on that and say, without a doubt, that he was an informer. I will go to my grave believing that. There is no question.'[35]

In the intervening weeks, months and years, the controversy over the shooting of the prominent UVF members on the Shankill grew. Some alleged that a member of the UVF's Brigade Staff, who was nearby at the time, discovered an 'early warning system' attached to Colin Craig's neck. It was said that he removed the device to prevent his father from knowing the truth about his son's duplicity. 'People were saying it was one gunman who did the three of them [King, Craig and Hamilton],' recalled one former UVF member. 'I asked the wee man sat across the street if he saw that, and he says, "There was so much blood. It was everywhere. Nobody tuck a necklace off him. Nobody got near them", he told me.' One of those who administered first aid to the four men at the scene was Pastor Kenny McClinton. 'Crazy took his last breath from me as I applied CPR,' he said, as he recalled how an off-duty nurse, assisted him. 'There was a piece of his brain lying on the ground. The blood was everywhere,' McClinton recalled. Although he later fell foul of the UVF, McClinton was able to confirm that the member of Brigade Staff had indeed come along to see if he could help. 'It doesn't look good,' McClinton told him. The former UFF commander claimed he had personally seen Gino Gallagher, one of the two INLA gunmen, cruising the Shankill Road in a car twenty-four hours before the shootings, and had reported it to loyalists. McClinton said he recognised Gallagher because he had encountered him in prison.[36]

In the immediate aftermath of the INLA's assassination of the three UVF men on the Shankill, the organisation returned to its war-footing promising 'blood on the streets'. Retaliation was swift. On 17 June, the East Antrim UVF shot dead twenty-seven-year-old Gerald Brady in the Sunnylands area of Carrickfergus. On the same day, the group carried out a gun attack on a workers' hut in Rushpark, just opposite Rathcoole estate, killing two Protestants, thirty-year-old Cecil Dougherty and thirty-two-year-old William Corrigan. The UVF claimed afterwards that they had mistaken the men for Catholics. In a particularly indiscriminate attack on 18 June, two masked men from a UVF unit in South Down entered the Heights Bar in Loughinisland and indiscriminately opened fire with a VZ58 assault rifle. Thirty-four-year-old Adrian Rogan, fifty-three-year-old Malcolm Jenkinson, eighty-seven-year-old Barney Green, fifty-nine-year-old Daniel McCreanor, thirty-five-year-old Patrick O'Hare and thirty-nine-year-old Eamon Byrne were all killed instantly and another five wounded. They had been watching the World Cup match between Italy and the Republic of Ireland on television.[37]

In a statement issued on 1 July 1994, the UVF said that there would be no compromise with violent nationalism. 'No space, no plot of land, no hiding place can be allowed to exist for the perpetrators of brutal pain and injury,' read the UVF statement. 'The violent republican movement cannot and will not defeat our cause.'[38] Behind the scenes, however, there were actually moves afoot to wind down the organisation's armed campaign. The pressure to do so did not come from British intelligence or from the backchannel with Father Alec Reid, or even from overtures by British or Irish politicians, but from certain sections of the UVF's rank and file itself. 'Although I couldn't say it publicly, this had to stop,' recalled Luke, who was a member of A Company. 'There were no boundaries. Nothing was off-limits. The Provos proved that with the Shankill bombing. The cycle would continue unless we found a way to end it.' By the summer of 1994, Luke and a number of other front-line UVF volunteers were behind bars. 'They called us the 103 Club [because 103 men were arrested and placed on remand over the summer months]. We were removed so they could have their ceasefire. [Later], I thought long and hard about the ceasefire and I supported it,' he added.[39]

★★★

Billy Mitchell, who had been so integral to the UVF's campaign in the 1970s, re-emerged from his quiet, post-release life to make the case, as a community representative, that the time for ending the conflict was almost upon the armed groupings. After a conversation with Eddie Kinner, Mitchell joined the PUP and very quickly became what his former cellmate, Kenny McClinton, called 'the PUP's brain'. While David Ervine began to emerge from the shadows to make the case for a ceasefire, Billy Mitchell was working tirelessly behind the scenes to move things on. He joined forces with Liam Maskey, a community activist with close ties to Sinn Féin, to lobby key influencers across the political spectrum. This reflected work already being undertaken by Billy Hutchinson, Jim Auld and others at the Springfield Inter-Community Development Project, which was beginning to gain traction again within both communities. 'And that's what they did. And it led to both the UVF and the IRA actually having public consultations about the violence and the way forward,' recalled Hutchinson. Parallel to this initiative, Mitchell and Maskey had managed to engineer a one-to-one meeting between senior leaders in the UVF and Provisional IRA. 'And that didn't come from the UVF and IRA in that meeting,' Hutchinson explained. 'Where it came from was both communities who said, "We need to actually think about what's going to happen." But in parallel, the UVF and IRA were doing what they were going to do.'[40] Due to the increased coordination amongst the Security Forces at the time, the British military had an inkling that there was going to be an announcement. The leakage of information within the Provisionals was such that the British sometimes knew what was going on before IRA rank-and-file volunteers knew themselves.

By the end of August, the Provos were moving to take soundings within their own organisation about how a ceasefire might be greeted by the rank and file. Tommy Gorman, who was one of the most respected Provisionals at the time, explained that Gerry Adams called seasoned IRA veterans into a meeting at Conway Mill. They were asked what they thought of the prospect of a ceasefire. They dutifully discussed it, then left. In a deft piece of Machiavellian intrigue, Adams had used the discussion session as a springboard to lobby for a ceasefire.[41]

On 31 August 1994, the IRA called a unilateral ceasefire. In a message to its volunteers, it said that the organisation believed that 'an opportunity to secure a just and lasting settlement has been created'. The IRA also made clear that they desired 'to significantly contribute to the creation of a climate which will encourage this'. Signing off the statement, the IRA urged 'everyone to approach this new situation with energy, determination and patience'.[42] For Sinn Féin Publicity Director Danny Morrison, who was serving out a prison sentence in the Maze prison at the time,[43] the IRA ceasefire was genuine:

> What was the other alternative? The other alternative was to cash in the chips of the armed struggle to produce an interim political agreement that would allow you to argue for and to set in train a

process of social, economic, political harmonisation on both sides of the border, through whatever structures you were able to establish. And the structures were the all-Ireland bodies, the cross-border bodies … The thing is that the IRA did not drive the British Army into the sea, nor was it its intention to do that either … it was to break the will of the British Government, force the British Government to consider talking to republicans and force the British Government to concede to republicans. And that went as far as it could go.[44]

The IRA now shifted its focus to political talks aimed at securing political concessions. 'The trouble with guns,' wrote respected journalist Malachi O'Doherty, a cool observer of the Provisional IRA, 'is that there is such a limited number of things you can do with them.'[45] Having all the military means at your disposal does not guarantee that an armed organisation will be able to translate such strategic advantages into political capital.[46] This was a point well understood by the Provisional leadership at the time. For loyalists, it was not at all immediately apparent.

UVF members greeted the news of the IRA cessation with a healthy dose of scepticism. One close confidant of the leadership in North and West Belfast, 'David', believed that the IRA ceasefire was 'well-signposted' and that 'everybody knew it was coming', but that some kind of backroom deal had been done with the British Government to make it happen. 'Initially the first thing (and I remember the day well) … was said to me was "Aye, what have the bastards got?" Typical loyalist, Ulster Protestant paranoia you know,' he recalled. 'That … it's not a case of winning, the other side has to fucking lose and not just lose but has to be seen to be losing and preferably battered into the ground.' Loyalists were distinctly unimpressed, though 'there was that element that sort of went, "Hold on here, what's the deal that's been done?" Again, I think at the time, particularly the British government and the media didn't play a very straight game as regards producing any sort of even-handedness … There was a lot of that "nod and wink" stuff'. As a careful observer of the loyalist grassroots, David took a worm's eye view of events as they unfolded at the time. 'But, to be fair, outside of certain areas the loyalist command structure kept very, very intact. I think everybody was sort of looking at the "Young Turks" (as was then) in the [U]DA and maybe some other elements outside of the Greater Belfast area who weren't gonna toe the party line as such.'[47]

To attempt to provide some kind of united response in the face of the IRA ceasefire, the CLMC met in secret to discuss their response. Very quickly, they agreed on a joint statement. This document soon became known as the 'Six Principles' and, loyalists believed, 'if suitably addressed', would enable loyalist paramilitary groups to 'make a meaningful contribution towards peace':

1. We have yet to ascertain the bona-fides of the permanence of the IRA 'ceasefire'.
2. The intent of the INLA has yet to be established.
3. To be convinced that no secret deals have been concocted between HMG and the IRA.
4. That our constitutional position as a partner within the United Kingdom is assured.
5. To assess the implications of the joint governmental 'framework' as soon as possible.
6. It is incumbent upon the British Government to ensure that there is no 'change' or 'erosion' within Northern Ireland to facilitate the illusion of an IRA victory. Change, if any, can only be honourable after dialogue and agreement.[48]

At the time, the CLMC was determined to take a more positive view of the ceasefire than those in the DUP, who saw it as a sell-out.[49] Privately, the UVF faced an uphill struggle in the wake of the IRA ceasefire, as they made themselves 'busy lowering the temperature in their strongholds'.[50] In a world of contradictions and half-truths, Gusty Spence emerged as the best hope for the UVF to encourage each battalion area of the merits of calling a ceasefire.[51] In this he was to have considerable success.

Following the announcement of the IRA ceasefire, Plum Smith, a former RHC volunteer, turned PUP spokesman, appeared on TV to welcome the news. It was the beginning of a six-week consultation process across the UVF's entire membership. Reflecting back on the events leading up to the ceasefire, the UVF leadership said that everything was 'viewed and analysed in purely military terms by the UVF and CLMC'.[52] For the Brigade Staff of the organisation, a 'county first' attitude was adopted at events aimed at internal dialogue. It was a way of permitting local UVF units and the prisoners – a significant interest group within the organisation – to raise issues internally and to clarify policy so as to present a united front. Unlike the Provisional IRA, which appeared to operate according to a Soviet form of 'democratic centralism', the UVF leadership did not make promises it couldn't keep. For instance, it was not within the UVF's remit to give undertakings to their prisoners that they would be unilaterally released in the event of a ceasefire. A member of the organisation's Brigade Staff, Norman Sayers, visited the Maze, accompanied by one of the UVF's most respected area commanders, Billy Greer, who had led the East Antrim UVF, to emphasise to the rank-and-file volunteers that seasoned veterans were onboard the organisation's decision to call a ceasefire. Greer was regarded as the quintessential UVF man, and his support for the ceasefire and ensuing talks with the Irish and British governments would prove crucial.[53]

In some areas, including the UVF's own West Belfast heartland, consultations were not as exhaustive as they would become until after the October 1994 ceasefires were called.[54] In others, like East Antrim, veteran members were consulted and, in some cases, given considerable latitude in scrutinising emerging developments. Billy Greer was keen to keep his most ardent members and supporters in the loop. They were to be crucial link-men for the UVF as it moved to bed down its ceasefire in the organisation's hinterland. It was important to keep everyone informed of the moves towards peace. Six weeks later, this distributive leadership approach was to pay off.

***

Rex Bar, Shankill Road, Belfast, 13 October 1994

Men stood shoulder to shoulder along the right-hand side of the long, narrow bar. The Rex was a haunt for UVF members, young and old, in the mid-1990s. It's where the organisation's leadership typically went for a beer, after holding meetings across the road in their headquarters. Billy Wright and his trusted comrade Margaret had travelled up from Portadown for the announcement of the loyalist ceasefire, which he had lobbied hard for behind the scenes. The organisation's leadership had earlier gathered at Fernhill House in West Belfast to hear Gusty Spence announce to the world that loyalists were calling a ceasefire. 'In all sincerity,' Spence told the world's media 'we offer to the loved ones of all innocent victims over the past twenty years, abject and true remorse. No words of ours will ever compensate for the intolerable suffering they have undergone during the conflict.'[55] Wright was elated as news filtered into the Rex. He had tears in his eyes. 'He was quite happy with the ceasefire and the way things had gone, and his emotions got the better of him. He embraced – and we mean physically embraced – the leadership, the organisation's Brigade Staff later said in a statement.[56]

For Wright and the other area commanders, with the UVF's armed campaign now wound down, they could now look to a more peaceful future. In the Rex Bar, Wright regaled the UVF's Brigade Staff with his plans for the future. His words were laced with promise, and a nod towards a brighter future. He wanted to go to university, he told them, to win back time he had spent as a dedicated UVF volunteer. On their return journey to Portadown, Wright confided in Margaret about his plans for life after paramilitarism. For Wright, his war was over, for now.

As the peace process began to bed down, however, some of the organisation's area commanders were beginning to have doubts about the ceasefire. A few months later, Wright said he had been handed a leaked copy of the Framework Documents by a senior unionist politician, which demonstrated, what he saw, as British equivocation on Northern Ireland's constitutional position within the UK. A few weeks later he had adopted a more sceptical outlook on the 'peace process'. 'He championed the ceasefire. He was beating the doors down to get it called,' said Dawn Purvis, who was close to the PUP's Multi-Party talks team at the time. 'He was the first one out of the blocks. "Get the ceasefire called. This is the right thing to do. We need to do this. We need to do this."'[57] The Craftsman, who had effectively negotiated the terms of the ceasefire from the UVF Brigade Staff's perspective, said that Wright had visited him personally to lobby for a ceasefire. '18 months before the ceasefire was called, Billy Wright and Swinger Fulton came to my house to sue for peace. They wanted a ceasefire called. They walked with me around the green in front of my house. Now you might say that that was Wright wanting to save his life – to be fair to Billy, he knew there was a distinct possibility that he might end up dead by becoming involved in paramilitarism – but he did genuinely believe that the time had come to call off hostilities.' After he spoke with The Craftsman, Wright paid a follow-up visit to David Ervine. 'I think they went to Davy after me because they didn't think I'd be supportive of the idea,' said The Craftsman with a wry smile.[58] Dawn Purvis was emphatic that this did not last long. 'Months later, he was beating down peoples' doors to say, "This is going the wrong way. The ceasefire needs to go."'[59] Purvis and others, like Ervine, Spence and Billy Mitchell, believed that this was the best loyalists could hope to achieve, given the British Government's prior overtures to the republican movement. Wright remained unconvinced, and knew that he could only carry his hardline rural support base with him so far. People in Belfast found it impossible to understand those who lived outside the urban area. 'Areas were given a certain degree of autonomy in terms of targeting,' said The Craftsman. 'I didn't believe it should be the case that the final word should come from Belfast, but that was not a view shared by everyone. I thought it important to brief all units.'[60] It appeared that Wright took this local authority to push his own agenda centrally.

There could be little comparison in the predicament between urban and rural Protestants, especially since the latter really did live side by side with members of the Catholic community. Those in Belfast remained oblivious to the constraints under which the UVF in Mid Ulster operated. 'I mean, the CLMC had issued their Six Points and every one of them was achieved. Every one of them,' recalled Purvis. 'And he [Wright] was part of that process, but yet he was beating down the door for the ceasefire to be called off, for the ceasefire to be broken. And you could turn round and say it had something to do with his ego. Maybe he seen [*sic*] himself as bigger than the UVF, and this was all about him.'[61] Portadown was not the only UVF heartland to maintain a healthy scepticism towards the ceasefire, however. In North Belfast, feelings were also mixed. 'My own personal feelings were that I was glad to see it. I had my fears and my reservations. But, personally like, I was glad to see it,' said David.

> I was glad to see it and I think Gusty summed it up for a lot of people, and lot of people, particularly of his generation who had drifted away and become uninvolved. Maybe he wasn't talking for my generation, but definitely for his own when he said 'abject and true remorse'. That was heartfelt, that was genuine. I do believe that was genuine. And having spoken to him over the years, prior and since, I think that it was something they put out and was a genuine belief that 'this is what we have to do here.'[62]

An astute political analyst, David made the case that the UVF was right to take their time and prepare its grassroots for the eventuality of an end to the group's terror campaign.

> I think it was a better thought-out ceasefire than the Provo one, for want of a better term. I mean, 'thought-out' is maybe wrong. They

looked at the constituency that they were talking to, but it was a wider constituency. The Provos were talking to themselves, unlike loyalists, who didn't have the succour and, perhaps, community support within their own areas. They not only had to look within their own ranks but also look within their own community and their government. And that was mainly where the difference came from. There was a lot of people who maybe thought, 'Where do we go from here?' People said 'Right, good, I'm more than happy to hang up the six shooters and retire to Millisle.'[63]

Those UVF men who had served lengthy prison sentences for their activities during the preceding twenty-five years were more sanguine. Gusty Spence had inculcated a considerable amount of self-confidence in those men under his command in the 1970s. 'We always knew it would be an uphill struggle,' recalled Billy Hutchinson. 'But, in many ways, I think that we all knew that someday we would get to play a part in bringing about peace. In terms of whether we would form a government – whether we would have been part of that or not – we weren't actually sure but we'd always known we'd be part of the process of bringing about peace.'[64]

★★★

For the two top security officials in Northern Ireland, RUC Chief Constable Hugh Annesley and GOC Sir Roger Wheeler, there was an operational imperative to greet the jubilation of the paramilitary ceasefires with caution. No one could be quite sure if the Provisional IRA would return to war and if Sinn Féin President Gerry Adams would be unable to secure republican objectives peacefully. 'The first was that we were going quite quickly from a situation where the soldiers and policemen worked together, day in, day out, to a separation because they were in their police stations and we were in our various camps, and patrol bases and barracks and the like … We had joint exercises … in order to keep that jointness … at a tactical level,' said Wheeler. 'We had conferences and study days at Brigade Command and Commanding Officer level. And so there was a need to try and hang onto the very tight jointness that we had achieved by August '94.' Wheeler referred to this as the 'principle of irreversibility', which demonstrated more clearly that the Security Forces could return to the operational tempo they had sustained for many years, if the ceasefire broke down. For the meantime, the huge watchtowers and various permanent checkpoints remained in place. Intelligence gathering and surveillance would continue, even if the Security Forces' footprint was to be lightened. 'By Christmas time '94 there we were, either having regular desktop exercises, regular tactical exercises … We decided where we needed to stay and we had begun to get out of some of the places we didn't want to be in,' said Wheeler. 'But we kept our framework of fixed observation posts in tall buildings in Belfast. We kept the border control points, and we kept the towers in South Armagh. All really to monitor the ceasefire.'[65]

For its part, the UVF's journal *Combat* maintained its own 'watching brief' on the ceasefire, and did its best to reflect all shades of loyalist opinion on how the resulting peace process might unfold. A year on from the ceasefires, it reported how Billy Wright, 'for many years, has been an outspoken advocate against the enemies of Ulster. His refusal to be muffled is well known in the Mid Ulster area, he is now an advocate of the peace process, but with personal reservations, and his proclaiming of those reservations, against the Irish Government, resulted in him, for a time, being "put out of commission"'. His brief arrest was thought to be an attempt by the Security Forces, in consultation with informers inside the UVF, to apply pressure on him to toe the line. *Combat* remained sceptical. 'Could it be that he touched on a tender spot by his declaring that the Irish Government had broken promises made for their own purposes? Could it be that there are those in the British and Éire governments who know more than they are divulging, and Billy Wright touched a very tender nerve?'[66] Only time would tell.

15

THEIR ONLY CRIME WAS LOYALTY

'I knew that the word of God would teach tenderness, forgiveness, lov'in and understanding, but my passion and my ways weren't conducive to Christianity. And I fell on my knees on the stairs of my house, and I apologised to God. But I told him I couldn't live a lie. And I couldn't. I just could not bring myself to say words that I did not mean and pretend that I felt things that I didn't feel. I felt contempt for the British Government, hatred for the IRA and a longing for justice for the Northern Irish Protestant. And I still *passionately* feel the want of justice for our people … As to what it has cost me, only eternity will tell. *Only eternity will tell.*'

Billy Wright, Portadown, 1995.[1]

Drumcree Parish Church, Portadown, 11:30 a.m., Sunday, 9 July 1995

Serious trouble had been brewing in Portadown for most of the year. Concerns had been raised by the Garvaghy Road Residents' Group about the 'traditional route' Orangemen proposed to use to make the journey from Carleton Street Orange Hall, under the railway bridge and along Obins Street to Drumcree Parish Church and back down the Garvaghy Road in the town. Although it was a route they had walked every year since 1807, changing demographics meant that the Garvaghy Road in the town had become almost exclusively Catholic in religious composition. The Rector of Drumcree Church, Reverend John Pickering did not believe it was an unreasonable request. At 11:30 a.m., as Orange brethren gathered for their annual Sunday morning service at Drumcree, he was upbeat, hoping that cool heads would agree to the Orangemen's request. His sermon to the several hundred Orangemen who packed out his small church and parochial hall reflected this optimism. As men, women and some children stood respectfully listening to his reading from the Scriptures, Reverend

Pickering launched into a well-prepared sermon. 'Jesus Christ offered the only real hope for the world through personal trust in him,' he told his attentive congregation. 'That makes all the difference – Jesus is alive. This hope is what the Orange Order, the Reformation and Christianity is all about. The answer for Northern Ireland and its people is spiritual renewal.'[2]

After the reading of a lesson from the Bible and the singing of a hymn or two, the District Master of Portadown LOL No. 1, Harold Gracey, publicly thanked those in attendance for their support. It had not been an easy few days, as the chorus of criticism from Garvaghy Road residents carried far and wide, facilitated by Sinn Féin and amplified by a hostile media. Gracey's words echoed across Drumcree, relayed by speakers that had been set up so that others could hear what he had to say. Some of those listening to the service outside were members of the Mid Ulster UVF. Amongst them was the unit's commander, Billy Wright. Gracey's words of defiance chimed with his own feelings that morning.

As Orangemen began to make their way from Drumcree church to the Garvaghy Road, they were stopped by RUC Land Rovers. Meanwhile, residents left their homes to try and block the route. Kenny McClinton, a former loyalist paramilitary turned pastor from the Shankill now living in Portadown, was asked by police if he could calm the situation. He agreed and used a bullhorn to evacuate women and children from police lines.[3] Tensions heightened as deadlock ensued between the Orange Order and residents, with the RUC in the middle. Just after 7 p.m. on Monday evening, the simmering tensions quickly came to a boil between police and marchers. As Orangemen and their bands made their way towards police lines to register their protest, the atmosphere became fraught. Violence ensued. Police in riot gear responded by discharging scores of plastic bullets at the protestors. It was the most serious rioting seen in Portadown for a decade.

Never one to pass up an opportunity to capitalise on inter-community tensions, Ian Paisley made his way from Belfast to Portadown, where he made a thundering speech to the Orangemen. 'If we don't win this battle all is lost,' he told a jeering crowd. 'It is a matter of life or death. It is a matter of Ulster or the Republic of Ireland. It is a matter of freedom or slavery.'[4] He was soon joined by the local MP for Upper Bann, David Trimble, and both politicians made their way to police lines. More serious, perhaps, was the threat of the violence spilling out across the province as thousands of loyalist protestors took to the streets. Some even blocked the port of Larne, one of Northern Ireland's busiest transport hubs. Life across the province looked like it was about to grind to a halt until the dispute in Drumcree was resolved. Loyalist politicians from the PUP and the UDA-aligned Ulster Democratic Party faced a difficult task in convincing their hardliners that they should exchange violence for dialogue.

Although few loyalist protestors knew it at the time, the RUC was under serious pressure at Drumcree. With trouble brewing on the Ormeau Road ahead of an Orange Order march there, they simply didn't have the resources to deal with an escalation of violence in Portadown and other parts of the province. One officer, who was in the command meeting between the police and military at Drumcree, recalls how the RUC were unprepared to resist the tens of thousands of Orangemen and their supporters in the event of Wright and the Mid Ulster UVF forcing their way through Security Forces lines. 'We had several lines of defence,' the officer said. 'In the first line there were thirty police officers with baton guns on each end. Behind that there was a platoon of 30 soldiers all carrying baton guns. Behind them there were soldiers with rifles and behind them there were GPMG [General Purpose Machine Gun] gunners.'[5] It was a recipe for disaster. One senior RUC officer reportedly addressed his men and the soldiers who had responded to their aid by giving a stirring speech. 'This is the darkest hour, before dawn,' he told those gathered. To which a senior army officer retorted, 'Yes, but the coldest hour is always the one after dawn.'[6] For soldiers, what they call 'H Hour' is when the metal hits the road on military operations. It is when training kicks in and, invariably, when those in command positions expect to take casualties. The RUC officer who attended the command group said that the police knew they would lose the nationalist community by forcing the marchers down the Garvaghy Road, but the alternative to resist the Orangemen and their paramilitary supporters would have been much worse. 'In later Drumcrees we always had a Plan A and a Plan B. That year there was no Plan B,' he said. 'Had the march not gone ahead it would have been a bloodbath.'[7]

From the UVF perspective, one senior loyalist who had travelled from Belfast to Portadown to advise Wright recalled advocating a change in tactics, where the protestors would bring 5,000 men up to police lines and simply march forward. 'The idea originally came from India in 1947,' he said. 'They would have been overwhelmed. The good Protestant people would not have stood for loyalist paramilitaries shooting at the police. 'Those poor wee policemen and soldiers,' he chuckled, as he described how 'auld dolls' would have reacted to the news. 'But if we triggered a violent response from the security forces, that might have swung things in a different direction. They [the Mid Ulster UVF] never went for it.'[8]

What they did go for was to have the threat of armed force in reserve, should it be required. A series of crisis meetings were held between Wright and Orange Order representatives. Although preferring to move in the shadows, Wright now came to play a leading role in providing paramilitary muscle at Drumcree. A BBC journalist who interviewed him at the time observed how:

> Billy Wright well understood this cultural mindset. He also understood that the old certainties were disappearing as quickly as you could say the words 'Anglo-Irish Agreement'. Not only was that social cement of guaranteed work for the brethren evaporating from the loyalist spiritual mix but a wide rift was also developing between an increasingly secular Belfast UVF and the 'country' UVF; between the 'city' (Belfast) and the rest of Ulster; between an increasingly successful anti-Agreement DUP and sections of Ulster unionism which might be willing, or cajoled, into making a deal with the enemy.[9]

UFF commander Johnny Adair saw a lot of Wright before his own arrest and imprisonment on Directing Terrorism charges in September 1995. His view of Wright was that he was a grassroots loyalist who dedicated his every waking moment to advancing the loyalist cause any way he could:

> I can see the pictures of them at Drumcree. That was a recruiting ground for them too. Billy and wee Swinger, they were like chalk and cheese, and you knew that. Their only crime was loyalty. They were two dedicated, genuine loyalists, and not only that. He was like myself. I seen [sic] him a lot. Most of the times I would have seen him would have been in Crumlin Road jail. He was up visiting. He was up and down to that jail a couple of times a week. Again, in my time, our so-called 'leaders' – they wouldn't have gone near the fucking jail. 'We can't go up to the Maze Prison.' And that's where I bumped into Billy. Every other day him and Swinger travelled all the way up from Portadown. Like me, his prisoners always came first. 'Cos they were the men who had sacrificed their freedom. I admired him for that too, 'cos he was always up in the jail.[10]

By now Wright was keen to be seen leading from the front in public. Behind the scenes, it was said that he often participated in operations himself, but his real strength as a terrorist came in his management of the men and meagre resources at his disposal. He immersed himself in every detail surrounding the acts of violence his unit carried out. In this respect, it surprised very few of his closest comrades that he would step into the centre of the fast-flowing situation at Drumcree in July 1995. The more the RUC refused to back down and the more the Garvaghy Road residents disabused themselves of the notion of compromise, the more Wright found people looked to him for leadership. His involvement threatened to bring an explosive and increasingly toxic mix of jingoism, stubbornness and stoicism to proceedings. A solution had to be found, and quickly.

It soon dawned on the RUC that with Wright and the Mid Ulster UVF now backing the Orange Order a solution to the impasse had to be found. Although he did not like the course of action he was about to take, RUC Chief Constable Sir Hugh Annesley ordered his Gold Commander, Freddie Hall, to permit the Orange Order to complete their march along the Garvaghy Road. Loyalists were jubilant, Garvaghy Road residents were not. It left nationalist protestors frustrated and angry. Rubbing salt into their wounds, Ian Paisley and David Trimble accompanied the marchers along their route and even joined hands to dance a jig upon their arrival at Carleton Street. They behaved like conquering heroes. In the shadows Billy Wright looked on, pleased with the assistance he had provided. As far as he was concerned, the politicians might represent the power of the people at the ballot box, but he knew he represented the real power behind the throne.

In recognition of Wright's central role in the standoff, Harold Gracey wrote a letter to Kenny McClinton, asking him to pass on his personal thanks to the local UVF commander for his assistance:

> I can assure you that I am the first to admit that without the support of my own District, the loyalist people of Portadown and the Brethren and loyalists from over Ulster, victory may not have been achieved. I am also well aware of the crucial role played by Billy Wright, whom I must confess I had never met, and his comrades, in the final outcome. I have by the way written to him to let him know how much I appreciated his support. When I first spoke to Billy at Drumcree he asked if I were going to carry my stand to the end. I assured him that I was totally committed to see this through, no matter how long it

took and he assured me that he would support me all the way. We all know he was true to his word. Can I also say that at our next District meeting no one will be left in any doubt of how much we owe to Billy and his friends.[11]

On this occasion, the UVF had provided the Orange Order and unionist politicians with a strategic bargaining chip in the battle of wills with the British State and its Security Forces. Little did they know that the British State would respond in kind as the 'peace process' gathered further momentum.

***

Canary Wharf, London, 7:02 p.m., 9 February 1996

According to reports on the Irish state broadcaster RTE in Dublin this evening, the IRA has broken its ceasefire in Northern Ireland. The ceasefire has been in force since the 31st August 1994. RTE said the source of their information was the same person who first informed them of the ceasefire being declared. And within the last few minutes, the London Fire Brigade has confirmed that there has been an explosion in the East End Docklands area. Eyewitnesses said they heard a huge blast just after seven o'clock this evening. There's no confirmation, as yet, whether the explosion was caused by a bomb.[12]

As broadcaster Peter Sissons read out the news bulletin, the shockwaves of the attack were felt right across Britain and Ireland. The enormous explosion in London had lifted the entire façades off hundreds of buildings, obliterating windows, sending debris flying and crushing parked cars in the heart of the city's financial district. Two men were killed outright. The damage was estimated to be somewhere in the region of £1 billion. But there were much more serious repercussions for the fledgling 'peace process'. It was a classic terrorist spectacular, as some republicans would later admit, and a move designed to send a clear message to Downing Street that they would not stand for their political associates, Sinn Féin, being locked out of talks. Loyalists were outraged. The PUP met with the UVF leadership in crisis talks, hoping to use its influence to prevent the organisation from retaliating. They were successful.

Several hundred miles away from London, in Carleton Street Orange Hall in Portadown, a local flute band were busy playing a few renditions of well-known loyalist songs. Their instrumental lasted for twenty minutes. Twenty young men standing to attention were all smartly turned out in blue uniforms, with white belts and red hats with red plumes jutting out from the top. Four men in the front rank carried the colours, which consisted of two Union Flags in the middle and two other historic flags on either flank, representing the old UVF and YCV which had fought as part of the 36th (Ulster) Division at the Battle of the Somme on the Western Front in 1916. Behind them on the stage was a long table with a banner draped over the front, which read 'Mid Ulster' and was emblazoned with two large badges in red lettering reading 'For God and Ulster'. There were two Ulster flags on top of the table, and another one on the wall behind it. A poster could also be seen, calling for the release of twenty-eight-year-old UVF member, Lindsay Robb, a Mid Ulster delegate on the PUP's talks team, who had met with government ministers in June the previous year to talk peace. A few weeks after meeting British officials he was in Scotland buying arms for the UVF, preparing for war.[13] Kenny McClinton was on the stage chairing proceedings for the evening. To his left sat the forty-two-year-old DUP politician Sammy Wilson, a former Lord Mayor of Belfast, and on McClinton's right was Robb's father. McClinton informed the crowd that they were gathered in the Orange Hall that evening to protest at the framing of Lindsay Robb by MI5.

Making reference to Robb as 'one of those faithful working-class men who allied with the strong men of the Orange Order' in pushing for victory at Drumcree, McClinton reminded the audience, by now a couple of hundred strong, how that victory had come about in July 1995:

And a man sitting here tonight, whom I know doesn't want to be named, gathered a little band around him, and he told high-ranking police officers that if rent-a-crowd on the Garvaghy Road can stop an Orange parade then rent-a-crowd in Charles Street can put them back in the tunnel where they should have been in the first place.[14]

The crowd broke into applause. McClinton continued:

Let me confide in you dear friends, and I know I am not speaking out of school. One of those working-class men with the courage to do that was Lindsay Robb. The victory achieved at Drumcree is a great victory. We must now cry out for victory for this man who is now a political hostage in a Scottish prison, and … far from his loved ones.[15]

The crowd again broke into applause. Around the room were several notable personalities. Front and centre was Harold Gracey, the District Master of LOL No. 1 in Portadown. A few rows behind him, on his left-hand side, was Billy Wright. He was sat next to one of his closest friends who was like an older sister to him. A few rows behind Wright was Robin Jackson, Wright's predecessor as Mid Ulster UVF commander.

McClinton then moved to introduce Sammy Wilson, who had travelled down from East Belfast to lend his party's support to the event. It gave him 'great heart', Wilson said, to be amongst the good people of Portadown, and to celebrate with them the victory of Drumcree. 'People like Lindsay Robb played a part in that victory,' he said. 'All too often in our history. Some of them had given up their freedoms. Many had lost their livelihoods for the cause.' By now working the crowd into hysteria, the DUP politician concluded, starkly. 'And far too often, many of those who have benefited from those sacrifices, have turned their back on the people. I want to tell you that I am proud to be associated with the people who made the sacrifices.' His words of defiance were met with a vigorous round of applause. He went on to chastise the media, the SDLP and, finally, the British Government. 'I'm proud to be a Democratic Ulsterman,' he said. And it was the British Government that Wilson reserved most of the barrage of criticism for. 'The British Government,' he informed his audience, 'is culpable in this particular incident. They have blackened him.' Importantly, Wilson qualified his remarks. 'I am guessing that, because I don't know the full facts of the case.' What Wilson was certain about, however, was that the duplicity of the British Government had a long pedigree stretching back over the entire history of its once great empire. 'You know the sad thing, throughout our history. The one thing they can be certain of, is that they've always found other people who have been willing to play a role in blackening. They have always found willing accomplices.'[16]

Having sent the DUP's message directly to the British Government, Wilson promptly sat down. McClinton rounded off the evening by reading out sixteen reasons why Robb's conviction was unsound. He thanked people for coming. As he closed the event, the crowd all stood up and gave the speakers on the platform a standing ovation. Wilson – and the vast majority of the people who had come to hear the speeches – left the Orange Hall. There is absolutely no suggestion that any of these people knew what was about to happen long after they had gone.

Later that night – and much to the chagrin of the Orange Order – the Carleton Street hall was taken over by Wright and his supporters. Chairs were cleared from the dance floor, the bar was opened and a band began to set up. As they did so, a new flag appeared. This time it was the standard of the modern-day Mid Ulster UVF. It was a navy-blue Saltire with a gold UVF badge in the middle and two Kalashnikov assault rifles either side. Billy Wright took to the stage. He told those who remained and who were now waiting patiently for the music to start that the band, 'Platoon,' had travelled all the way from Belfast. 'We would like to reciprocate by showing that we can behave in a decent and ordinary fashion,' Wright quipped. No sooner had he left the stage that some men in the crowd began chanting, 'U-U-UVF.' No one who stayed on that evening was in any doubt that, with the formal speeches over and the pugnacious DUP politician and other dignitaries long gone, that they were attending a welfare fundraiser for Robb. The first of many of the tunes played by Platoon that evening was 'Simply the Best'. Their cover version of the Tina Turner hit, however, had deeper meaning for those who listened to it. In their alcohol-fuelled bravado, many of the young men present believed it reflected the Mid Ulster UVF. Their team was simply the best – of that they were convinced. The tunes continued, with such UVF classics as 'Daddy's Uniform' and 'Here Lies a Soldier'. But there was one tune that would carry a message far beyond that evening to the UVF leadership on the Shankill. It was a defiant song called, simply, 'Mid Ulster UVF'. And its chorus ran:

> So get up on your feet and follow me and join these men today,
> These men who'll do their duty and destroy the IRA,
> So come and join these brave young men,
> These men they are the best,
> They're the men who'll do the business, the Mid Ulster UVF

The song was both a recruiting pitch and a simple boast by Wright's unit. These were, after all, 'the men who'll do their duty and destroy the IRA'.

Within a matter of weeks, Wright was causing serious difficulties for the UVF's Brigade Staff. It was a leadership composed exclusively of Shankill Road men. It met in secret, and policy was agreed upon by its

Chief of Staff, Director of Operations (who was rumoured to be double-hatted as the group's Director of Intelligence and second-in-command), Provost Marshall, Adjutant and Welfare Organiser. Five men, all of whom ran the UVF's campaign of terrorism. The growth of the Mid Ulster UVF – and specifically Billy Wright's stature – after Drumcree, was perceived as a challenge to this Brigade Staff. Discussions were now happening on the fringes of the Shankill's leadership meetings about how Wright might be placated in such a way that the organisation could maintain a united front as far as its support for the peace process was concerned. The Provisional IRA's return to war was just the excuse Wright needed to push the UVF in a more militant direction. It was a tense time for all concerned.

★★★

By the mid-1990s, the Province Executive Committee had become the operational-level hub for all Security Force operations in Northern Ireland. It was chaired jointly by the Deputy Chief Constable, the British Army's Commander of Land Forces for Northern Ireland (until 1996, when that position was removed and replaced by a lower-ranked Chief of Staff), the NIO's Permanent Under Secretary and the Director of Intelligence who was drawn from the ranks of the Security Service, MI5. By the spring of 1996 MI5's primary function, other than collating intelligence, was to provide reliable assessments on the activities of loyalist and republican paramilitary groupings. MI5 in Belfast, like its officers stationed at the agency's headquarters in Thames House in London, worked to a variety of stakeholders, including the NIO and Joint Intelligence Committee. What worried them most in the wake of the IRA bombing of Canary Wharf was the strategy of loyalist groups like the UVF. What were they thinking? Had there been any sign that they would return to war too? How did they view the nascent peace process? In order to gather accurate and timely intelligence from groups like the UVF, MI5 relied heavily on informants and agents. Agents were usually well-placed individuals, several of whom held leadership roles within the terror groups. These high-level agents provided MI5 with strategic intelligence. This was vital for the government in London, as it set about establishing a peace process to end the violence. One MI5 analyst explained the distinction between strategic and operational intelligence in the following terms:

Strategic intelligence, from our point of view, is primarily focused on what the leaderships of the paramilitary groups are concerned with at the time, their strategy, perhaps with regard to ceasefires, breaking ceasefires, their involvement in the political peace process and their relationships with other Loyalist terrorist groups, or, indeed, their views on the Republican terrorist groups. That differed quite differently from what we would regard as operational tactical intelligence, which was very much lower level, regarding the plans of a specific group to carry out a specific attack, or their day-to-day decisions about memberships and movements, and so on.[17]

In order to process this huge quantity of intelligence, MI5 worked closely with RUC Special Branch, particularly the Branch's Assessments Unit, which provided analysis of the threat posed by armed groups at street level.

In operational terms, the RUC did manage to score major successes against loyalist groups, though this has not always been reflected well in the historical record. According to one former head of RUC Special Branch, in the entire period between 1983 and 1996, the RUC were having success in arresting and seeking the prosecution of loyalists on a 2:1 basis with republicans.[18] The situation, as it stood in 1996, was undoubtedly a sea-change from twenty years earlier, when state agencies had been slow to penetrate loyalist paramilitary groups.

Billy Wright was fast becoming a thorn in the side of the UVF Brigade Staff, principally because of his refusal to toe their policy line. The UVF, like British Intelligence, believed the Portadown-based loyalist was on the verge of forming a breakaway group inimical to the ceasefire. Having heard directly from a high-placed informer inside the UVF, MI5 reported that Wright was 'taking a very hardline stance against the peace process and against all the ceasefires, and he wanted – or encouraged others – to take a hard line, and wanted to retaliate for the republican atrocity on the mainland'. In one report, sent by someone in the upper echelons of the UVF almost two weeks before Canary Wharf, on 31 January 1996, the informer told MI5 that Wright's Mid Ulster unit was no longer under its direct control, and had effectively become an autonomous grouping.[19] A significant air-gap had now opened up between Belfast and Portadown. MI5 was particularly concerned about the effects this would have on the UVF's support for the ceasefires.

In a meeting of the Province Executive Committee on 19 March 1996, attended by the Deputy Chief Constable responsible for operations, the army's Chief of Staff, MI5's Head of Assessment Group (HAG), and his opposite number in RUC Special Branch, the RUC reported that Wright was, 'in fact, behind the threatened breakaway group, and that he has support from militant elements both within the UDA and UVF both in Belfast and Mid-Ulster'.[20] This was interpreted by the Security Forces as Wright being allowed to let off steam. Portadown had become something akin to a pressure cooker, and Wright was himself facing calls from within his ranks to respond with armed force to the renewed Provisional IRA campaign. The very fact that Wright was close to abandoning his support for the loyalist ceasefire went some way to proving that state agencies had failed to recruit him as an agent, which meant that they had little influence over his actions.

MI5's assessment of Wright at that time was that 'he was a very charismatic leader and had a degree of support around him'. The written assessment of Wright saw him as able to garner support, 'not only from Mid-Ulster UVF, but from others elsewhere, primarily in Belfast', who 'were starting to be sympathetic to his hardline stance and his sort of anti-ceasefire stance', which 'caused a great degree of attention with the leaderships of the UVF, UDA in Belfast'.[21] In a Northern Ireland Intelligence Report (NIIR) at the time, HAG painted a dangerous and volatile picture of the Brigade Staff's inability to hold the line in the event of a full-scale return to armed conflict by the Provisionals. In a NIIR dated 4 July 1996 and entitled 'UVF: Loyalists threaten to end ceasefire if Drumcree Orange March rerouted', was based on a specific intelligence report from a covert human intelligence source (CHIS) inside the organisation's Belfast leadership:

> The UVF discussed – I just mention there this was at a time of heightened tension between UVF leadership and Billy Wright and his supporters. They had three options that they had considered. One there was to kill Billy Wright outright; the second one was to try to negotiate with him to come back under their command and control and in some way or another to cooperate with each other; or a third view was that in actual fact that he would formally break away from the UVF and form his own group.[22]

By now Wright was joined in his 'dissent' by another loyalist leader, Alec Kerr, the UDA's brigadier in South Belfast.

At the time it was thought that the UVF was set on killing Wright for his transgressions. Interestingly, one senior UVF officer informed respected journalists Henry McDonald and Jim Cusack a few years later that it 'was the UDA that argued we should go all the way and expel Billy Wright from the UVF and sentence the two of them to death. It's ironic that they were the one baying for Wright and Kerr's blood, even though much later down the line some of them would be linking up with Billy's new organisation [the LVF]'.[23] On 28 August 1996, the CLMC did indeed take the course of action advocated by the UDA and expelled both men. The UVF's representative on the CLMC was The Craftsman. Twenty years on from Wright's expulsion, he was more sanguine. 'It was the UDA that pushed to have Wright expelled, which is ironic given what happened subsequently,' he said. 'If there had have been a way back for Billy we would have taken it. As it was, he cut himself off from us when he came under the spell of certain unionist politicians.'[24] These politicians were thought to have included members of the DUP.

After the UVF's first forays into talks with the Irish Government in 1993, The Craftsman continued to spend a lot of his time in the company of PUP spokesman David Ervine. They liked socialising together and enjoyed each other's company. They often confided in one another. According to The Craftsman, Ervine was much more suspicious than the UVF itself about who was pulling Wright's strings. Was Ervine paranoid? Dawn Purvis, who also spent a lot of time with him during the multi-party talks, believed he wasn't. 'David was always right about agents. He called it in relation to … [a prominent Mount Vernon loyalist] as early as 1996 and he was convinced that Wright was merely a tool of those, he believed, who did not want the loyalist ceasefires to hold. David was convinced that the British State wanted a ceasefire from the Provos, but not by loyalists.'[25] If Wright had been an agent, which will never be confirmed or denied regardless of the release of documents in the future, it seems plausible that his behaviour could be explained by a clash between national and local intelligence interests. It is much more likely that Wright was simply a hardliner acting on his own initiative, and had allowed his megalomania to go to his head. He saw himself as the only bulwark now left between the Protestant community and a united Ireland in which Sinn Féin and the IRA would have had significant control. His belligerent attitude would soon find support amongst a significant number of loyalists as the marching season got underway.

★★★

Drumcree Parish Church, Portadown, Sunday, 7 July 1996

Soldiers from the Royal Engineers were busy erecting razor wire in the field a few yards from Drumcree Parish Church. One former BBC journalist claimed that Billy Hutchinson went to Portadown to ferry a message to Wright from the UVF's Brigade Staff. When he arrived, it was alleged that Wright attacked Hutchinson whenever the PUP spokesman raised the matter of the Mid Ulster UVF's purported involvement in drug dealing. The journalist also claimed that RUC Special Branch intervened to save Hutchinson's life.[26] But did Hutchinson ferry a message to Wright in July or August 1996? The answer, according to Hutchinson, is no. He did not. Not only did he not go to Portadown with a message for Wright, but he was never physically attacked by Wright. Hutchinson, however, was at pains to make clear that he believed at the time that Wright was an agent, a view he says he shared with his party colleague, David Ervine. 'On the two occasions I met Wright I challenged him on his activities,' Hutchinson recalled. 'I asked him how he managed to get away from the cafe, and return safely from the operation in Scotland whenever Lindsay Robb had been caught in a sting. Wright's story simply didn't add up. Wright was an agent. Everyone knew it.'[27]

Not everyone accepts this version of events. There are those who claim that, unlike Ervine, Hutchinson was not immediately convinced of Wright's duplicity. The evidence, according to Hutchinson, however, was irrefutable. A former member of the UVF who Hutchinson met at a Leeds United match in England, claimed Wright had threatened to shoot him if he went to the UVF headquarters on the Shankill to report allegations of operations having been compromised. 'There were four other UVF men prepared to make similar allegations to the UVF,' Hutchinson said. As far as Wright's former comrades in the Mid Ulster UVF are concerned, nothing could be further from the truth – their beloved leader was 'in no way, shape or form an informer'.[28]

What we can say with a degree of certainty is that Wright was now beginning to come under the influence of Kenny McClinton more than the UVF's Brigade Staff on the Shankill. Shortly afterwards, Wright broke away from the leadership of the UVF over the issue of militancy around the Drumcree parading dispute, in which Sinn Féin-aligned residents' groups refused to allow Orangemen to walk up the Garvaghy Road in Portadown. The policing operation – where military forces were deployed to erect barbed wire fencing around the field outside the church – became a symbol of loyalist defiance in the face of a refusal by nationalists to back down and allow the parade through.

The decision to re-route the Orange Order march on the 12th of July created a storm of protests across the province. Lorries were hijacked, rioting against the police became a daily and nightly occurrence. 'Drumcree II' was a watchword for loyalist reaction against what they saw as the 'appeasement' of nationalists. Working-class men were so supportive of the Drumcree standoff that they risked their livelihoods for a cause few outside of these small communities would have understood. In loyalist pubs and clubs throughout Northern Ireland these men sang songs that had strange connotations with the First World War, that recalled gallant actions in far-off lands and regaled those who listened with tales of daring do. Inevitably some got caught up in the moment, imagining themselves knee-deep in muddy trenches with the crash and thud of artillery shells and the crunch of bones and the tearing of flesh. It triggered the same kind of esoteric militarism that sociologist Sarah Nelson had first detected in the UVF's ranks twenty years earlier.

Within days of an escalation of violent protest, the UVF leadership was believed to be meeting to authorise Wright's execution. In a NIIR sent from HAG in Belfast to the JIC in Downing Street on 19 July 1996, it was believed that the action was imminent:

> I think it was less to do with the stability of the ceasefire and more to do with the command and control of UVF members across the province. That was the UVF leadership's main concern, maintaining some sort of cohesion amongst the group. They didn't want their members to break ranks, essentially, and join Wright and his supporters in large numbers, because that would undermine their own authority and command.[29]

This was a serious situation for the organisation. They were being directly challenged by one of their brigadiers in a fashion that would not have been tolerated twenty years earlier. The organisation was not beyond murdering Mid Ulster Brigadiers, as they had proven whenever Robin Jackson shot dead Billy Hanna on his own doorstep in July 1975, or, for that matter, Shankill Road chiefs, whenever the UVF's Director of Operations, Jim Hanna, was executed a year earlier in 1974. In a sign of things to come, hardline UVF commander, thirty-two-year-old Tommy Stewart, a successor to John Bingham in Ballysillan, was shot dead, the UVF later claimed, by 'rogue loyalists' on 28 October 1996.[30] There may have been more to it than this, as Stewart, a former confidant of Lenny Murphy's, had formed a close working relationship with Billy Wright and Swinger Fulton. Regardless of who killed Stewart, his assassination served as a deterrent to others within the organisation who might have been thinking of jumping ship.

The UVF leadership is much more pragmatic about Wright's transgressions twenty years earlier. 'You see, sometimes you outlive your usefulness and I think that's what happened to Billy,' one senior leader said. 'There are two things that corrupt – power and money – and I think, in relation to the first, that may have been what happened in Billy's case.' So power is the ultimate aphrodisiac? 'Almost certainly, in this case. Billy and Mid Ulster would have got a lot of kudos for things that happened in their area. In reality, as a man used to say to me, "for every good operation in Mid Ulster, like Cappagh, there was one that went wrong, like an old woman being shot".' The UVF leadership at that time is adamant that Wright 'took a lot of credit for operations that went well, but the men who carried out Cappagh were not from Portadown. Nowhere near it.'[31] Regardless of whether Wright was directly responsible for UVF operations in his area, his media profile continued to grow independently now that he set himself against the fledgling peace process.

Although it is impossible to know for sure if peaceful rapprochement was attempted with Wright, one source outside the UVF and the Security Forces has suggested that it did happen. 'I sat with Billy Wright about a dozen times on a park bench [in Corcraine Estate, Portadown] trying to bring him in from the cold. I nearly had him, but the lure of right wing pastors was too powerful. When I saw him take the stage with Willie McCrea in Portadown I knew I'd lost him.'[32] The UVF Brigade Staff saw Wright's posturing in a slightly different way. 'He became disillusioned, and certain politicians preyed on that disillusionment,' said the leadership.[33] Asked if they believed that Wright had met a premature demise, one Brigade Staff member replied cryptically. 'I do believe that Wright was an obstacle that was removed.'[34]

16

AN INTENSE AND LOYAL FOLLOWING

'The UVF and UDA are mirror images of PIRA and are also fascist. The difference however is they are reactive and would probably cease their attacks if PIRA were to do the same. They do not have the same ideological commitment as PIRA and when peace comes will find it impossible to maintain the same levels of support within their own community. They will remain as a vicious mini-Mafia which will take patience and resources to stamp out.'

Richard Needham, Under-Secretary of
State for Northern Ireland, 1985–92[1]

'People felt safe in the Corcraine estate whenever Billy Wright was around,' one of his closest associates, Margaret, recalled. Wright apparently performed an invaluable community service on a number of fronts. 'Whenever there was a drug party in the estate, he went straight to the house, regardless of the hour of the night, to break it up. When young people saw him coming they hid in cupboards, under beds in rooms,' said Margaret. 'Billy would have lifted them out and told them to go home. He wanted to put a stop to these activities.'[2] Journalists, including the Northern Editor of the *Sunday Times*, Liam Clarke, saw Wright as being little more than a psychopath and a drug dealer.[3] At a time when the NIO were dedicating themselves to shoring up the peace process, Wright was elevated to public enemy number one. It suited all concerned for unsubstantiated allegations to surface in the media, since it effectively sapped any oxygen of positive publicity the dissident loyalist was gaining for his anti-talks stance.

The RUC tried everything they could to remove Wright, but they couldn't turn any of his close associates against him. Wright kept things tight. The men and women under his command trusted him. Even the man who had turned against Wright in the early 1980s, Clifford McKeown, was admitted back into the fold. He hero-worshipped Wright, and couldn't be persuaded to betray his friend a second time. The RUC Special Branch even tried to recruit Wright and his closest comrade, Swinger Fulton. They were unsuccessful. Their inability to turn senior loyalists was evident even in the case of the UDA leader Jim Pratt Craig. 'He was a criminal, he was motivated purely by his own greed,' recalled a former Branchman. 'Wright was different,' he said. 'Wright was a highly motivated and ruthless paramilitary leader who commanded an intense and loyal following from within the UVF and beyond.'4 As for Wright's lieutenants, 'People worshipped him. There was no fear. There was only love for Billy Wright in Portadown.' In March 1997, the Security Forces saw an opportunity to remove Wright from the streets when they got wind of an altercation that he had had outside a friend's home. In a heated argument with a local woman whose son had been involved in anti-social activity, Wright threatened her. 'If you don't take yourself off, I'll kill you,' Wright told the woman. The RUC arrested him and worked hard to get the woman to testify against the loyalist leader.

After a period on remand for threats against the local woman, Wright was allowed bail to sort out his affairs. He visited Margaret. 'The last thing he said to me was, "Once I go in here, I won't be getting out alive",' she said, shrugging. The tears welled up in her eyes as she spoke. To Wright and his close friends and family, there was a high probability that he would be killed inside prison. 'I would have driven him about the country. I drove them down to Monaghan where they exchanged artwork with the General and his people.5 I did not know it at the time because I never asked questions. My thinking was, if I didn't know anything, I couldn't tell anything. On the odd occasion that people did talk, they were warned to "Keep yer fucking mouth shut".'6 The military team in Mid Ulster was a tight-knit set-up, with Wright as the linchpin holding it all together. With him inside, the authorities believed the benefit to the peace process would be immense. As 1997 wore on, they were to be disappointed, for the main groups carrying out murders was not the LVF in Mid Ulster or North Belfast, but units from within the UDA and UVF, two organisations supposedly on ceasefire.

With Wright now in prison, the INLA was making plans to have him eliminated. On 24 April, MI5 logged a NIIR with RUC Special Branch, warning them that their plan was at an advanced stage. However, because they were having a new computerised registry installed at the time (known as MACER), they did not enter the threat against Wright into their system until May 1997. When they did, it was under the heading 'INLA: desire to murder Billy Wright.'7 The RUC had not, therefore, had time to act on the intelligence from MI5 when, on 28 April, two high-risk INLA prisoners,

Christopher 'Crip' McWilliams and John Kennaway, took a prison officer hostage in Foyle House at the maximum security HMP Maghaberry. They were armed with a .32 semi-automatic pistol and a .22 zip gun. Prison staff were of the opinion that the two men wished to eliminate a former comrade, Kevin McAlorum, who had reportedly shot and killed one of McWilliams' close associates, Gino Gallagher, outside a benefits office on the Falls Road in January 1996. The reality was that the INLA men were not plotting an attack on a fellow republican, but on Billy Wright. Unknown to the two gunmen, they were late. Their five-hour siege only ended when they realised that their intended target had been transferred to the Maze Prison. On the same day, one of the governors at HMP Maghaberry apparently met with senior members of the INLA at the Quaker meeting house near Queen's University in Belfast to discuss prisoner issues.[8]

As Wright served out his period on remand, awaiting trial for threats made to the woman in Portadown, he became more and more embittered by the PUP's involvement in talks with Sinn Féin. In a diary entry written sometime between June and September 1997, he confided his innermost thoughts on what he saw as a 'sell out':

But worry not Albert [Reynolds] and Rose [Nelson], for while Billy Hutcheson [sic] and co., may wish to make peace with your client, the loyalists of Mid Ulster have a different sort of peace for him, it's called an AK 47.

Duffy be sure of this, we will send you to a court of judgement were [sic] Rose's lips will hold no weight, for the LVF unlike the PUP shall always seek real justice for our people.

As news breaks of trouble throughout North Armagh and as republicans paint on their hard done by faces, spar[e] a thought at least for twelve Protestant families to whom Colin Duffy brought republican justice (Death).

Oh yes Rose! Your client has gunned down at least twelve human beings – but then Protestants as seen through Rose's eyes and indeed Albert Reynolds, are but mere problems.

Of course there'll be no television documentaries into these injustices, no foreign dignitaries to lament their violent deaths, just salt rubbed into Protestant wounds.

No doubt Albert's career would have ended even earlier had he identified himself with any well-known mass murderer in the South.

And as for you Rose, solicitor you may be by profession, but human being you are by birth, to acquiesce in murder is a very dangerous occupation.

No doubt Colin you'll cry your way out of this present charge, but worry not Duffy, for no matter what Billy Hutcheson [*sic*], Davy and Gusty say to your SF/IRA [Sinn Féin/ Irish Republican Army] friends real justice for you will come from the end of a loyalist Volunteer gun – God speed the day![9]

Back in Portadown, the LVF were busy planning to kill prominent republican Colin Duffy. He became their number-one target, as did the people who associated with him. That included a civilian, the solicitor Rosemary Nelson.[10]

In Belfast, the UVF leadership had tried to put the Wright business behind them by continuing to throw its weight behind the PUP's participation in the talks process. The Craftsman, who was given authority by the UVF to negotiate on their behalf, had joined the multi-party talks team, which also included David Ervine, Hugh Smyth and Billy Mitchell, as well as Billy Hutchinson, Billy Greer and Jim McDonald. Discussions and negotiations were chaired by the US Special Envoy Senator George Mitchell and his team. In the talks on the issue of decommissioning, the PUP insisted that the peace process should not be unduly delayed by preconditions of prior disarmament by the armed groups. In the Forum Elections held in the late 1990s, the PUP had stood for election on a platform putting the case for a pluralist, non-sectarian and liberal Northern Ireland. It was a political programme that no one expected to hear articulated by what the DUP and UUP referred to dismissively as 'gunmen' and 'bombers'. Yet, it was perhaps the most sophisticated thinking being advanced at the time beyond that offered by the likes of UUP leader David Trimble or United Kingdom Unionist Party leader Bob McCartney. And its key architect was former UVF Brigade Staff officer, turned PUP strategist, Billy Mitchell. He explained what this new form of progressive unionism brought to the table:

There were two strands of thought. One, there was a realisation that middle-class ... unionists hadn't served us well, in terms of social policy or economics. There was also a realisation that most of our political philosophy was summed up in clichés. 'Not an inch', 'no surrender', 'what we have we hold'. So, there were two strands of thought. One, we realised that we hadn't been served well and we needed to develop our own leadership, we needed to take ownership of our own communities. But we also needed to understand what unionism was about. Was unionism about beating the big drum? Was it about Protestant domination of Catholics? Or was it about a civic unionism? A unionism that was about citizenship within the United Kingdom. That it was about the unity of the British-speaking peoples? And it was linked to Great Britain [having] moved down from the Glorious Revolution [to] the development of a liberal democracy. Great Britain had become a pluralist society, where you have all forms of ethnic communities. So, Britain was becoming pluralist, and if we proclaimed to be unionists, we had to adopt that pluralist attitude.[11]

This was not an approach to politics that had been given much voice throughout the conflict. Its first real test came when the PUP ran a record sixty-one candidates in all eighteen constituencies (the only time it ever did so), polling 26,082 votes, which gave the party the seventh largest share of the vote and two seats for Hugh Smyth and David Ervine.[12] The PUP's inclusion in multi-party talks did not please everyone, with the DUP and UUP leading the chorus of criticism, which also came from within paramilitary loyalism. One of the PUP's most outspoken critics was, of course, Billy Wright.

***

H6, HMP Maze, 9 a.m., Saturday, 27 December 1997

Prisoner A5970, William Stephen Wright, was roused from his cell by news of a visit. He had been relaxing on his bunk that morning after a shave, shower and breakfast. Clean-shaven, with close-cropped hair and a goatee beard, Wright had blue piercing eyes. He sported two earrings, one slightly bigger than the other, and was dressed casually. A prison officer led him out of the wing and into the H Block courtyard, where he boarded a prison minibus to take him to the meeting room where his girlfriend and young son were both waiting on him. At the same time, three INLA prisoners were putting a well-timed plan in motion, with the express intention of killing Wright. It was the second time two of the three men had attempted to assassinate the loyalist leader in prison. The first time was earlier in the year when they botched a murder attempt in Maghaberry. Now they had learned from their mistakes, and were determined to see their plan through to completion. Two of the three men were armed when, at 9:55 a.m., they scaled a fence and jumped down into the courtyard. Rushing over to the rear of the minibus, the men opened the door and shot Wright at close range. Amidst the chaos, prison staff in the Central Control Suite locked down the prison and roused the governor. Accompanied by the RUC, a doctor reached H6 at 10:50 a.m., where he took Wright's pulse. None was detected. Wright was pronounced dead at the scene at 10:53 a.m.[13] He had been assassinated while in one of the world's most renowned maximum-security prisons.[14]

News of Wright's assassination spread like wildfire throughout the prison. In H4, UVF prisoners threw up a cheer when news filtered through to them that Wright had been killed. For one amongst their number, however, there was nothing to celebrate. The death of someone this UVF prisoner regarded as a 'living legend' was an unimaginable tragedy. 'There wasn't one of them could have laced his boots,' the Shankill Road man said. 'I just went back to my cell and cried.'[15] Johnny Adair, who was in another wing at the time, was relaxing on the bunk in his cell. 'I remember it plain as day,' he recalled. 'I was lying on the bed. Saturday morning. Stoner [Michael Stone] came in. "Billy Wright's been shot, Johnny." What. You're fucking joking me. And again my stomach [churned]. That feeling. I couldn't believe it. I was hoping it was a joke, a wind-up. Fuck me.' Adair also described the atmosphere as the news began to sink in:

> Them bastards were gloat'in. And I remember somebody saying to me, and they named the specific bastard … a UVF man from the Shankill. And I just gave the bastard a dirty look and he dipped his head. And prior to that he would have said 'alright Johnny'. But boys had told me he had been shouting 'We got the bastard'. Imagine shouting that. 'We got the bastard'. That's what the UVF on the Shankill was shouting. 'We got the bastard'. 'We'? The enemies of Ulster had killed Billy. One of the best leaders they ever had. 'We got the bastard'? I'll tell you what that was, that was just sheer fucking jealousy.[16]

Adair's close friendship with Wright had grown throughout the 1990s and was forged by the murderous partnership the UFF and Mid Ulster UVF had struck up before the ceasefires. The C Company commander held the Portadown loyalist in high esteem. And, by all accounts, he wasn't the only one.

I remember stories about Billy going up to the Orange Hall up the Shankill, to dances, and [The Pipe] introducing Billy, with that wee leather waistcoat on. Introduced him onto the stage. And the whole fucking place in uproar. Standing ovation. 'Yeoooo'. They all wanted to be Billy Wright. Billy Wright was a loyalist icon. And you see what happens. See when you become good. See republicans, they build their people up and they keep them there. See the Prods. They built them up, then the jealousy takes over, and they knock them fucking down. They either send them to jail or they set them up to be shot. And that, sadly, is what happens within loyalism. It's sheer jealousy.[17]

Beyond the confines of the Maze Prison, word of Wright's assassination spread like wildfire. Revellers in loyalist pubs and clubs across Northern Ireland fell silent. Elsewhere, in nationalist and republican areas, there was a chorus of approval. At solitude football ground in North Belfast, where home team Cliftonville were playing Glentoran, supporters from both teams gathered for the 3 p.m. Saturday kickoff. Trevor, who hailed from a republican part of West Belfast, picks up the story. 'It was at Christmas time. What were they signing? Everybody tee-heeing and laughing. "All the huns they were crying, when Billy Wright was a'dying. What a wonderful way to spend your day, watching Billy Wright pass away." They sang it to the tune of *Walking in a Winter Wonderland*. The Glentoran fans stood in silence. He was a fearsome figure for nationalists.'[18]

In Portadown that weekend, Wright's LVF comrades fell into deep shock. Some were inconsolable with grief. Others refused to believe the news. They thought it was disinformation. 'Nobody had ever known that Billy had a dah until his funeral in 1997,' recalled one of his close associates. When his body was released and brought back down to Portadown, the LVF formed an honour guard around the coffin. 'Billy held everything together. When he was murdered it all began to fall apart,' said Margaret.[19]

Wright was undoubtedly perceived by those close to him as a charismatic figurehead. His vision of a province free from what he perceived to be the threat from militant Irish republicanism was never realised. For many of his close confidants, people who spoke of loving him like a son or brother, Billy Wright lived and died a hero. Billy Wright, one of the most feared and, in certain parts of Northern Ireland, one of the most respected loyalist paramilitaries, was finally laid to rest in Seagoe Cemetery. 'His aunt rang me up and asked if we had a plot for Billy. She was worried that his grave would be desecrated. He was buried in a predominantly Protestant area to stop that from happening,'[20] Margaret said as she welled up at the thought of the loss of her close friend.

For those who had killed Wright, the rationale for doing so was straightforward: 'A decision was taken to eliminate Billy Wright solely because he was the man who had opted to direct a ruthless campaign of slaughter of innocent Catholics from inside the Maze Prison.'[21] According to some loyalists, the killing of Billy Wright was the culminating point of penetration of the INLA by British Intelligence. It proved that they had perfected the ability to direct paramilitary groups to do their bidding. The reality was that the responsibility for the murder of Billy Wright lay with those who pulled the triggers that crisp morning after Boxing Day. 'I want to emphasise that, as an individual, I took no personal satisfaction of playing my role in the elimination of Billy Wright,' Crip McWilliams told reporters. Some republicans believe that McWilliams was given redemption within the INLA for his earlier move into the ranks of the IPLO and subsequent cold-blooded murder of Catholic bar manager Colm Mahon at his place of work on 15 December 1991. McWilliams had shot Mahon out of 'annoyance' or 'anger' at being thrown out of the premises.[22] It had nothing to do with politics. While the INLA triggermen may not have taken any personal satisfaction at Wright's demise, a lot of ordinary Catholics did. They believed, more through perception than reality, that Wright was the man who had dispatched up to forty people to early graves, a point disputed by journalist Chris Anderson.[23]

One thing was certain, though, and that was that one of the RUC's TCGs has been running surveillance against the INLA at the time. They had its Chief of Staff, second-in-command and a senior Ard Chorlian member in the frame more generally. 'Operation Jaw', as the surveillance mission was codenamed, was a major investigation into the INLA at the time and proved capable at exploiting human and technical intelligence in a bid to constrain the group's activities.

★★★

The assassination of Billy Wright removed a serious obstacle in the path of the Northern Ireland peace process. A few days after his murder, the Secretary of State for Northern Ireland, Mo Mowlam, visited senior loyalist prisoners in the Maze. At the scene of a two-week old crime, Mowlam, had gone there to ensure the British Government could count on mainstream loyalist paramilitary support for the ongoing all-party talks. The British suspected that the LVF was determined to unleash a wave of retaliatory killings across Northern Ireland in response to Wright's death. Mowlam was there to urge restraint. She had been taking increasing flak from her political opponents about talks with Gerry Adams and Martin McGuinness. Now, against the advice of her senior advisors, she went to talk directly to the loyalist leaderships. UFF leaders Johnny Adair and Michael Stone were there to greet her.

It was now vital for the UVF and its political associates in the PUP to keep its members informed of developments in multi-party talks. 'If I heard being in the loop once I heard it a million times,' recalled Dawn Purvis. Purvis was close to those in the PUP negotiation team, like Billy Mitchell, David Ervine and Hugh Smyth, and recalled the crisis points in the talks. 'During that time there were weekly liaison meetings between the PUP and the UVF where everything was discussed, [from] what was happening in the talks [to] what was happening outside the talks … Very often there was a lot more happening outside than there was inside and that impacted greatly on what was happening inside.' Sometimes other parties made things difficult for loyalists in the UDP and PUP talks teams. 'I remember, for example, the Irish Government in 1997 releasing some IRA prisoners in the South as a confidence-building measure to the Shinners,' said Purvis. 'And, of course, loyalism went berserk at that. As we were saying you had to safeguard the process, and they had gone outside the process and did this unilaterally. Of course, they are a sovereign government and they are entitled to do what they want to within their borders, but they had no idea what this was going to do within loyalism.'[24]

> There were lots of times when you felt that State agents were conspiring against loyalism. In fact, David [Ervine] said nearly every time there was something that we were working towards – 'batten down the hatches' because you can rest assured the agents would be out there working against it. And he predicted it every time that something was going to happen. So, every time loyalism was headed in the right direction, every time it was making moves towards peace and democracy there would be something that would set loyalism apart so that people could turn round and say, 'You see, they're not serious about it.' Certainly, David and Billy Mitchell and Gusty and others in the

conversations I was privy to … felt that it was state-sanctioned policy to upset loyalism, constantly. I mean, when the PUP got two people elected to the [mult-party] talks and the UDP got two people elected to the talks, I think it was a shock for unionism – big-house unionism, certainly. David Trimble, the DUP, were astonished that fringe loyalist parties could get elected. But, yeah, all the conversations I was privy to there were agents within the UVF, there were agents within loyalism that worked to a different agenda and it wasn't to assist loyalism on the path to peace and democracy, it was to criminalise loyalism and it was to try and show loyalism in a completely different light, where that phrase would be proven – that 'the only thing that could sort loyalism out was the police'. So, for example, in 1996, the Drumcree crisis … manufactured, many believe, by Billy Wright and others to elevate his wing of the UVF and loyalism to that level, [and] also included John White and Johnny Adair. You'd 1997, [which included] the council elections, and you had a wing of the UVF in Mount Vernon [embark on] … a series of murders … beyond the control of the UVF leadership. And again, if you'd read the Police Ombudsman's [Operation] Ballast Report, it would conclude that there were a number of agents within that part of the UVF.[25]

By now the PUP's joint decision with the UVF–RHC leadership to continue along the path of peace was placed under severe pressure by what they saw as the disruptive tactics employed by the intelligence apparatus. However, the truth was a little more complicated than what Purvis outlined in her analysis. What it overlooked was the fact that not all loyalists bought into the PUP's narrative of the necessity of engaging in the peace process. Some of these hard-liners were opposed to any deal which involved the Provisional IRA. They were not prepared to accept what they called 'peace at any price' and they now sought refuge under the umbrella of the DUP's anti-talks stance.

The fragmentation of militant loyalism and the emergence of the LVF led directly to a catalogue of murders in the Mid Ulster area. Robert Hamill, Sean Brown, Bernadette Martin and her boyfriend James Morgan, Gerry Devlin and Seamus Dillon all died in a wave of sectarian killings in 1997. What is often forgotten is that the UVF's Mount Vernon team were also busy killing and maiming members of their own community that year too. On 24 March, they beat to death a Presbyterian Minister, forty-three-year-old

Reverend David Templeton. Two months later they murdered thirty-nine-year-old Protestant John Harbinson on 18 May and killed a member of their own gang, Raymond McCord Jnr, on 9 November. Meanwhile, the North Down UVF also murdered Brian O'Raw and Glenn Greer, while the UDA were responsible for the deaths of John Slane, Robert 'Basher' Bates, Brian Morton and Edmund Trainor. What had not been acknowledged before is that the RUC believed at the time that many of these murders were the work of the UVF and UDA who were meant to be observing a ceasefire.[26] The two governments felt that they were caught between a rock and a hard place. 'The paramilitary associated parties had to be warned that violence was incompatible with the talks process,' observed historian Thomas Hennessey. 'Yet, at the same time, the logic of the peace process was to draw paramilitaries in from the cold.' The governments now settled for a 'shot across the paramilitaries' bows', readmitting Sinn Féin and the UDP for the final rounds of negotiation after their 'sin-binning'.[27]

★★★

Castle Buildings, Stormont Estate, Belfast, 10 April 1998

A sense of euphoria swept over the delegates sat around the negotiating table. The leadership of the UVF had accompanied senior PUP delegates to the talks. They were in an adjoining room watching proceedings as they unfolded in front of the world's media. It was getting late. The media had descended like vultures, looking for a lead from anyone who knew if a deal was close to being clinched. Prime Minister Tony Blair flew in from London to see through the final stages of the Agreement. Then, in the early hours of the morning on 10 April 1998, the parties emerged to confirm a deal had been made.

In the elections to the Northern Ireland Assembly that followed the endorsement of the Belfast Agreement, the PUP polled well, gaining 20,634 votes, and winning two seats for David Ervine and Billy Hutchinson. As with the Forum Elections, they came seventh in the pecking order, just behind the UK Unionist Party. It was a remarkable result that appeared to endorse the PUP's pro-Agreement stance.[28]

Not all loyalists had been supportive of the Agreement, of course. Some who had been close to Billy Wright and his Mid Ulster faction condemned it. They believed what they were being told in the inflammatory speeches made by leading anti-Agreement politicians. By now they were busy trying to mobilise unionists against the referendum on the Agreement that was scheduled for 22 May 1998. Clifford Peeples, a twenty-eight-year-old loyalist from West Belfast, had once been a close associate of Gusty Spence and the PUP on the Shankill, but in the wake of the Drumcree dispute he had become a close confidant of Billy Wright and Kenny McClinton. In 1998, his skills as a political strategist and mobiliser were being utilised by the DUP. Reflecting on this period, he explained why he was so opposed to the Agreement:

> By early 1998, it was obvious that the analysis and conclusions of what was taking place under the Blair government's engagement with the IRA were correct. I received a constant flow of leaked documents that suggested an almost capitulation on behalf of the government. This was backed up by the daily telephone briefings from political figures and weekly meetings. A number of intel briefs [they shared] also favoured this. The soundings suggested that the scenario laid out by [Professor] Antony Alcock would be played out, albeit in a projected format: the RUC would go, the RIR [Royal Irish Regiment] would be wound up, and loyalists would be forced into an ever-more isolated corner, while the IRA would receive a place at the heart of government. This would have to take place in order to asphyxiate any widespread rebellion against government plans.[29]

It was little surprise that those prominent in anti-Agreement politics remained under close scrutiny at this time. Peeples's public comments were closely reported by the media, which, by now, was universally supportive of the Agreement and refused to give much 'oxygen of publicity' to the naysayers. As Peeples explained:

> Briefings by the NIO and RUC press offices became an almost daily occurrence. The press, greedy for scandal, were a willing tool in the NIO propaganda machine. Any who did not acquiesce in this [process] were branded JAPs [Journalists Against the Peace] and sidelined or openly shunned. Stories soon filled up pages of 'Demon Pastors' and army agents working in tandem, all planted by government sources. The ever-more lurid stories now form part of the public narrative that the NIO fought so hard to control. All alternative voices were to be discounted and defamed in order to keep in place the duplicitous peace.[30]

It appears that the derision suffered by Peeples and other anti-Agreement activists was designed to ensure that the DUP's hardline stance was denied political legitimacy within the wider unionist community. Despite the constant barrage of criticism from these circles, the unionist vote began to swing in favour of the Agreement.[31] The leadership shown by PUP members like Spence, Purvis, Mitchell, Ervine, Hutchinson and many others ensured that just over half of all unionists voted in favour of the Agreement.

Despite the euphoria generated by the Agreement, the UVF remained armed and dangerous. It showed no signs of jettisoning its 'military-first' policy and, instead, looked to the coming of the new century without much of an idea about how it might transition into a civilian organisation. For a lot of volunteers, the thought hadn't even crossed their minds about what kind of future the Agreement would give birth to. For those UVF members who were beginning to think more seriously in political terms, the PUP offered one avenue by which those volunteers who did not wish to play an active role in hostilities could channel their energies. However, the real power in working-class Protestant housing estates lay with loyalist paramilitary groups.

★★★

1999 ended on a high for David Ervine and The Craftsman, though it could have been so different. Frankie Curry, the nephew of Gusty Spence and a long-time gunman for the UVF, had been shot dead on St Patrick's Day as he walked to Gusty Spence's home in the Lower Shankill. Although it was suggested that Curry had become close to the LVF, the truth was that his killing was actually the result of a falling out over money.[32] It has since been alleged that two of Curry's former comrades were so incensed by his murder that they met in secret to prepare for a retaliation against those they held responsible. Importantly, these were gunmen from within the ranks of the UVF, not dissident loyalists. Word had reached them that 'David Ervine was rubbing his baldy head and tee-heeing in a bar in East Belfast', along with The Craftsman. Their plan was to arm themselves with a pair of AK47s and travel the short distance across Belfast, then spray the window of the club in East Belfast where Ervine and his companion were meeting for a drink. The only thing that saved their lives was the intervention of a former member of the West Belfast UVF, who said he did not wish to see a further escalation of tensions which would lead, in his considered view, to the destabilisation of paramilitary loyalism. The men unloaded their weapons, placed them back in the hide and went home.

Tensions continued to run high within paramilitary loyalism as the new millennium approached. Johnny Adair recalled being invited to a meeting with one UVF leader shortly after his release under the terms of the Good Friday Agreement.

> I remember … [a senior loyalist] phoned me up. '[The Pipe] wants to see you,' he said. And they knew I had a good friendship with the LVF. Billy had been murdered. So, seemingly, or apparently, or according to … [The Pipe] anyway, it really hurt me. This is what … [The Pipe] must have thought. We'll get a wee dig at Johnny. He did. He sickened me to the core. So, I goes up to the PUP offices. [The senior loyalist was there and … The Pipe came in.] 'I've something for you here Johnny that you might wanna see.' And he handed me a picture. The taigs were driving up and down the Shankill throwing them out. I looked at the picture and, fuck me, my stomach just turned. God forgive me. And I knew [The Pipe] was doing that through malice. That was one of his men. And I looked at it and there was Billy on a slab 'ballack naked', you know, on the mortuary slab, ballack naked with all the bullet holes. I was shak'in [with anger] and I just looked at it and I knew that bastard was doing it out of spite. 'Yeah, the taigs were throwing them', he said. And I just looked at it, looked at [The Pipe] and I said, '… you remember. That was one of the best leaders you ever had.' And he was scundered. It backfired on him, you see. But I didn't think that was a very nice thing to do. But that was him gloat'in, pretending he wasn't gloat'in but I knew that was the whole nature of his [demeanour]. 'Tell Johnny I want to see him, I've something to give him.' To pretend to me that the taigs were coming up the Shankill and threw that picture out of the window. They got the picture somewhere. Ah fuck, it was sad. Billy lying naked on the slab with bullet holes.[33]

Adair walked away from the meeting angry. His close working relationship with Billy Wright and his Mid Ulster grouping from the early 1990s was now a decade old. His insistence on maintaining the link years after Wright's assassination would have serious consequences for paramilitary loyalism more broadly as the year wore on.

In early August 2000, a flute band carrying LVF colours passed the UVF's headquarters on the Shankill Road. It was seen as an act of defiance by the dozens of UVF men standing outside the Rex Bar that day. Having been drinking heavily all day they were a little worse for wear and one man, in particular, ran across the road and attacked the band. In that one single act, the internecine feud between two rival organisations, which had been ongoing since the murder, on 10 January 2000, of the UVF's Mid Ulster commander, Richard Jamison, exploded. It also dragged the UFF into the mix. Within minutes Johnny Adair was rumoured to have been preparing his troops for a retaliatory attack on the Rex. One eyewitness, a photojournalist, said that he was stood across the road from a bar frequented by C Company. Adair allegedly had his men standing around him, all hanging on his every word like a basketball coach surrounded by his players. After informing them of his plan, the group suddenly jumped back and scarpered in different directions. Minutes later a man came out from an alleyway carrying an AK47 assault rifle. He threw it into the boot of a car and climbed in. The car sped off up the Shankill and stopped near the Rex. The man got out, ran around to the boot of the vehicle and pulled out the weapon.[34] He cocked it and ran up to the street corner before opening up on the Rex. The attack wounded seven men. It was the beginning of a feud that would see hundreds of people displaced from their homes, seven men lying dead within weeks of each other, and the heart ripped out of the loyalist community.[35]

The UVF believed it knew the cause of the recent feud. In a speech to several hundred people gathered at the annual Brian Robinson parade in Disraeli Street, just off the Shankill Road, a masked UVF commander condemned the recent attacks. 'The people of the Shankill Road could not stomach the destruction, pollution and deprivation being caused by the spread of the drugs trade by members of the UFF's C Company in the lower Shankill,' he said.[36] The crowd of UVF supporters were defiant. In their eyes they could see the need for maintaining arms for protection from their enemies, which now included other loyalists.

17

'YOU'RE EITHER WITH US OR AGAINST US'

So, since this ruptured country is my home,
it long has been my bitter luck to be
caught in the crossfire of their false campaign.

John Hewitt, *The Dilemma*

Ballyduff Estate, Newtownabbey, Halloween Night, October 2000

'Out of the fucking road Doreen,' shouted the burly man who brushed past the wee woman on her own doorstep. 'I was heart scared,' she later recalled. She tried in vain to push the door shut to prevent the men from pouring into her home. They were too powerful, and swatted her aside like a fly. The burly man's accomplices followed him through the hallway and into the living room. The first man was tall, over six foot, well-built, with pale skin, a full bottom lip and dimples. Doreen English had heard a rap at the back door and had innocently opened it, thinking it was a neighbour or relative. Unwittingly she had invited in the death-dealers who had come to shoot her husband as he lay relaxing and watching television.[1]

Tommy English was a high-ranking member of the UDA, the UVF's main organisational rival in Newtownabbey. Like many other UDA men in the surrounding estates, he had relatives in the UVF. One was even alleged to be the UVF's military commander for the North Belfast and East Antrim brigade area. He was furious when he heard that his men were responsible for the killing, but he was powerless to do anything about it for the organisation was under pressure from the UDA from all directions. Other members of the group's command staff were rumoured to have met without their military commander's knowledge and made the unilateral decision to kill Tommy English. It demonstrated how ruthless they could be. One individual close to the UVF in East Antrim went as far as to say that, 'once they decided you had to go, that was it. You were fucking gone.'[2]

The crew that visited the English home that night came from the Mount Vernon estate on the Shore Road in North Belfast, which lay on a main ulterior route into the city centre. Mount Vernon has always been a compact working-class estate. There are only two roads in and out, the main drive sits adjacent to some playing fields, close to the turn in the road that takes you up to the predominantly nationalist Antrim Road at Fortwilliam and close to the M2 motorway. Given its close proximity to Belfast Lough, seagulls are frequent visitors to the estate, squawking through the air as they pick their way through the council-run waste dump a few hundred yards away. Mount Vernon is well-known for the large UVF mural that adorns the gable end of the building housing the local Community Association. Emblazoned on the mural is a chilling warning to the world that the organisation is 'Prepared for peace, ready for war'. For much of the 1990s the Mount Vernon UVF ensured that the estate would be forever sealed in the minds of the local community as a notorious place where life was cheap and fear stalked the streets.[3]

The Mount Vernon crew's fearsome reputation was a well-deserved reflection on their leadership at the time, several of whom were alleged to have been working as Covert Human Intelligence Sources (CHISs) – individuals are known as a 'chizz' in current police parlance – since the 1990s.[4] A chizz is tasked with gathering intelligence that may feed into a wider operational picture police that security agencies try to build up about terrorist groups. The chizz is a much-maligned individual in Ireland. Commonly referred to as an 'informer' or a 'tout', the chizz works for the authorities for a range of reasons, including financial gain, marital problems, sexual proclivities – even a newfound patriotism. The chizz lives a secret double life, and is tasked with gathering information on other individuals in criminal or terrorist organisations. The lack of 'effective strategic management of these informants' inside RUC/PSNI Special Branch was later judged by a Police Ombudsman's investigation to have inadvertently 'consolidated and strengthened' the UVF in North Belfast and Newtownabbey during this time. This would have deadly consequences as the loyalist feud gathered momentum.[5]

***

Rathcoole, North Belfast, Night, 1 November 2000

Rumours revealed that eyewitnesses heard shouts of 'Up the T-Bay UDA' as the men scarpered through a thicket of trees, making good their escape up a narrow laneway to a waiting getaway car parked on the Abbeycentre end of Rathcoole estate.[6] In their wake, they left twenty-six-year-old UVF member Markie Quail lying dead in his living room, brutally shot to pieces in front of his girlfriend. Several bullets fired at point-blank range ended the young loyalist's life on Wednesday 1 November 2000. The men responsible disappeared into the night as quickly as they had called to his door.

Known as 'The Glen', the escape route the UDA gunmen took was infamous for kneecappings and other grisly punishments, which were regularly meted out to working-class Protestants by loyalist paramilitaries who accused them of anti-social behaviour. The idea that a common slight towards one UVF or UDA member in this estate, or any other for that matter, could very rapidly escalate into a shooting war was well-known by local people. A capacity for unbridled aggression, whenever the situation demanded it, underpinned the loyalist monopoly of force in these areas.[7] Few ordinary people were prepared to step out of line by protesting the clatter of guns outside their homes. The scope for dissent was limited. Anyone who dared to go against the grain was threatened, intimidated, even sent into a kind of internal exile. 'The boys' were spoken of in hushed tones of reverence, at hearths and around kitchen tables. There was a degree of sneaking regard for paramilitaries in certain quarters, especially since, for more than a few families, they were providing an invaluable community service in the absence of effective State authority.

In the aftermath of the murder of Markie Quail, the local shops were alive with news of the shooting. Some people said they had spotted Johnny Adair in the estate a few days earlier, mixing things up by appealing to John 'Grugg' Gregg to join forces with C Company in their feud with the UVF.[8] Had he succeeded, the UFF would have met little resistance from the UVF. At the time, the UVF was chronically short of weapons. One of the group's quartermasters claimed that the organisation relied on reactivated weapons to protect its members during the feud. He estimated that the organisation in East Antrim had only a couple of sten guns, an antique snub nose .38 special pistol, one VZ58 assault rifle and an UZI. The UZI didn't fire properly, and tended to jam. 'The UVF never had many weapons. It's a myth [that they did]. We never had enough weapons,' he said. 'I was everywhere trying to get weapons.' He claimed he even purchased bullets on a trip overseas, wrapped them in a towel and brought them back home aboard a flight. When a senior commander found out what he had done, he threatened his subordinate with a court martial.[9]

The killing of Quail was said to have been carried out in retaliation for the UVF's shooting of twenty-one-year-old David 'Candy' Greer, a UDA member. It has since been asserted by local loyalists that a UFF team in Rathcoole killed Quail, not a group from another part of North Belfast.[10] On Thursday 2 November, the UFF were stalking the streets again, searching for another victim. They found one in the form of sixty-three-year-old Bertie Rice, a former UVF prisoner. He had just returned from a shift at Billy Hutchinson's constituency office when he was chased down his street and into his home. The UDA gunmen shot him in the hall. Rice's wife, who was profoundly deaf, had no idea her husband had been callously gunned down, until she walked out into the hallway to find his body covered in blood. She couldn't give the police any details of what had happened, and no other witnesses saw what had happened. 'It was as if the body had fallen out of a plane,' remarked the PSNI's Senior Investigating Officer on the case.[11]

Without question the feud impacted negatively on the life of the Protestant working-class community across Belfast and East Antrim. People were genuinely scared of being caught up in attacks. For young people living in these areas, it had become too dangerous to hang around bars and clubs that were known to be the haunts of rival loyalist paramilitary groups. The only safe haven seemed to be Catholic-owned establishments, or those where they could watch cars approach from a distance to give them time to make a run for it out a side door once the bullets started flying. The fear of being shot in an indiscriminate gun attack was palpable, as working-class areas across Belfast became a battleground.

★★★

Newtownabbey was – and remains – relatively free of interfaces between Catholics and Protestants. The main interfaces, such as they are, are between Protestants, and run like fault lines through working-class estates where the UDA and UVF compete for influence, control of territory and a slice of illicit activities. Beneath all of this is the same esoteric camaraderie and regimental loyalty that was evident from the rebirth of paramilitarism in the 1970s. When these armed groups went to war with one another it was usually ordinary people who became the silent witnesses to evil deeds.[12] It was ordinary people, most of whom were uninvolved in terrorism, who cowered behind closed doors as rival armed groups brought their weapons out onto the streets. In these places, where the central authority of the state was considerably limited, the police did not properly enforce law and order – this was done by the paramilitaries.

The loyalist feud that erupted in the closing months of 2000 hadn't come out of the blue in Newtownabbey. Street violence between rival members of the UDA and UVF was particularly acute in the year running up to feud. On one occasion the orange glow of street lighting under a clear night sky gave people in East Way, Rathcoole, front-row seats to a fracas between the two groups. Quite apart from the testosterone fuelled aggro, threats were shouted like a standard ritual. 'U-U-UVF' was greeted with 'U-U-UDA', as rival gangs jostled and threatened each other in full view of the public. As with violence of this kind elsewhere, there was a point when words turned to actions. Golf clubs, sticks and knives were produced and the groups openly clashed on the street. Punches were thrown and the intensity of the hatred gave way to some serious violence. One young man was chased up the street with a golf club and badly beaten. His crumpled body lay motionless as his friends stood back, panicking that they might suffer the same fate. No police officers attended the scene of this horrific assault, which could have very easily escalated into a shooting war between the rival armed groups. The rest of the estate remained on tenterhooks. Would guns be brought out onto the streets again as one organisation sought to save face against another? Only time would tell.[13]

It was a rare thing for working-class people to enjoy an uninterrupted night's sleep with the kind of internecine warfare now underway on the streets outside their homes. Loyalist paramilitary groups roamed unmolested and, as such, violence could escalate quickly from a slap in the face to the breaking out of AK47s and Browning 9mm pistols from makeshift armouries secreted under floorboards, in outhouses and lockups.

As the years wore on after the signing of the 1998 Belfast Agreement, there appeared to be little appetite by the State to dismantle paramilitary structures that so obviously remained in control of these marginalised communities. Billy Mitchell wrote at the time about how he thought it imperative to view the continued existence of paramilitarism as being inextricably linked to social and economic deprivation in low-income estates like Rathcoole and the Shankill. These were the places where the much-anticipated 'peace dividend' failed to materialise. 'If the focus of so-called constitutional politicians remains fixed on one form of violence,' Mitchell argued, 'then those people who remain excluded from the mainstream of social and economic life and continue to suffer the debilitating effects of structural violence will have little confidence in a process that appears to be passing them by.'[14] Mitchell's words reflected the objective realities pertaining in working-class parts of Northern Ireland, but his viewpoint failed to find a sympathetic ear from mainstream unionists. As far as unionist politicians were concerned, loyalists needed to quit their internecine warfare, decommission their weapons and end their system of 'rough justice'.

Mitchell's words obscured the fact that not everybody in low-income areas supported or sympathised with paramilitaries. The vast majority of law-abiding citizens living in these estates, who had no truck with the armed groups in their midst, were voiceless, trampled under the feet of paramilitary foot soldiers.

On the surface, the writ of the British State didn't appear to run in housing estates like Rathcoole.

★★★

In these housing estates where paramilitary groups held huge sway, they were rarely challenged. They were particularly brutal towards their own members. 'Sam', a young UVF member from Rathcoole, was asleep when he was awoken by the sounds of his front door being smashed in. A UVF punishment team had come to pay him a visit. A few days earlier Sam was formed up as part of a UVF colour party, complete with black combat boots, trousers, shirt, Sam Browne belt and dark glasses. The colour party wore no rank insignia other than a silver UVF badge over the left eye of their rolled-up balaclavas. Sam was carrying a UVF flag and responded to military-style commands at a gable wall end as other men produced AK47s to triumphalist sounds of cheering from supporters. On this particular morning, however, Sam was about to be disciplined for his alleged involvement in drug dealing.

That morning, Sam's neighbours woke to the bloodcurdling screams of the young man next door pleading for his life, as armed men broke into his home and chased him out. He jumped from a first-floor window and scaled a fence. Men hidden in the garden below were not far behind, and caught up with him as he was felled by a single shot to the leg. He was badly beaten, and had another two shots discharged into his legs. The men ran off, leaving the young UVF member crying from his wounds in a pensioner's back garden. The old man who lived in the house knew from many years' experience not to open the door. His grandson, was awoken to the sight of muzzle flashes silhouetted against the window blinds as the rounds entered the victim's lower limbs.[15] After the gunmen left, the old pensioner came out to wrap the young man in a duvet until the emergency services arrived. Reassuring him that the ambulance was on its way, the police were not far behind either. Soon the sky lit up with a helicopter searchlight. Paramedics arrived and carted the young man off to hospital. The next morning the outhouse wall bore all the hallmarks of the young man's plight, as he had tried desperately to escape the gunmen. The grass, normally lush and green, had been turned a mucky dark brown. Blood and stones from the pebble-dashed wall covered the ground.[16]

Days later, the pensioner made a visit to the deputy commander of the North Belfast and East Antrim UVF, Billy Greer, to complain about the punishment attack in his back garden. A well-respected loyalist in the area, the old man had known Greer for many years. The UVF leader reacted furiously to the news. He lost no time in giving the punishment team a dressing down. If punishments had to happen, and the organisation believed they should, then they should be done away from residential areas and in places like the Glen. Greer offered the old man an apology, and told him it wouldn't happen again.

There was no such apology regarding the brutal actions meted out by UVF members to their victim that evening. The truth was that UVF volunteers like Sam were informed about what they were getting themselves into before taking the decision to join. The swearing in ceremony served as an opportunity for the UVF to warn prospective members that they risked death and imprisonment. Some of these volunteers might have thought twice about joining had they known that this risk came primarily from the organisation's own internal disciplinary process. Still, it didn't seem to put many of these young men off. If anything, it gave them an opportunity to add meaning to their lives. By joining a paramilitary organisation, young men believed they were taking a step to defend their community, proud, defiant and martial in their self-professed loyalty to the Crown.[17]

★★★

Rathcoole, Remembrance Sunday, November 2000

A long line of men and boys formed up along Derrycoole Way in Rathcoole early on Remembrance Day morning, the second most important annual fixture in the calendars of Ulster's Protestants. Their ranks seemed to stretch for around a mile. All of those who had turned up on parade were members of the UVF's North Belfast and East Antrim Brigade. They had come to pay their respects to fallen comrades at a mural commemorating the life of twenty-three-year-old Colin 'Colly' Caldwell, a young UVF member who had been killed alongside twenty-seven-year-old UDA member Robert Skey, when the Provisional IRA detonated a bomb in Crumlin Road prison on 24 November 1991.

But it was the deaths of other UVF members in more recent days that overshadowed the event, with the father of Markie Quail leading the wreath-layers. There was an extremely intense moment when the UDA turned up in force, led by their brigadier, John 'Grugg' Gregg. Grugg decided to pass alongside the UVF men in a deliberate attempt to up the ante. And it seemed to work, until the UVF members were snapped into line by a command from a former British Army soldier. The contrast between the two groups couldn't have been more obvious to onlookers. While UVF members were smartly turned out in dark suits and sporting UVF lapel badges, the UDA had turned up in tracksuits, smelling of drink and looking the worse for wear. The UDA contingent was also much, much bigger. Grugg had drafted in men from all over Belfast and County Antrim. He was determined to send a signal to his UVF rivals.

It was said that when word reached one Mount Vernon UVF leader about what Grugg had done, he was livid. 'He wanted a submachine gun to go and rake the command staff of the UFF in South East Antrim,' recalled one of his associates. 'He was denied access to the weapons by the local quartermaster. He rang Rab [Warnock] and pleaded his case. He was again knocked back.'[18] For now, the UVF was practicing restraint.

As their troops lined the road in their hundreds, a red estate car arrived. The driver jumped out and opened the boot, lifting out a microphone, stand and speaker, and placed them on the grass verge in front of the shops. Another man appeared. He was older, had grey hair and a weather-beaten face, wearing a sharp suit and tightly knotted tie with a long, formal black coat. He began by reading out a statement to mark the occasion. The man was the UVF's former Brigade Staff officer, turned PUP strategist, Billy Mitchell.

Mitchell's speech saw him equate the actions of the original UVF with those carried out by this much newer organisation, which he had done so much to bring into being. The speech emphasised what Mitchell saw as the hypocrisy of the unionist political establishment. 'So-called respectable unionism doesn't mind someone else doing their killing for them, as long as it's done within the law,' he said a few months after his oration. 'So, you can zap a thousand people in Vietnam, as long as it's done within the law, by a law enforcement agency or a legal army. It's ok. But if Joe Bloggs happens to zap half a dozen people with a car bomb, he's a scumbag. There's a sort of twisted form of morality there.'[19]

Throughout 2000, Mitchell was attempting to formulate his thinking on how those associated with the PUP and UVF-RHC could challenge mainstream unionism.[20] The guidance he drafted was entitled *The Principles of Loyalism*, and its main purpose was to provide political legitimacy for the UVF to base its decision to move beyond paramilitarism. Its underlying philosophy drew on the Ulster Solemn League and Covenant, which the former UVF leader saw as 'the birth certificate of Ulster, of modern Ulster'. Mitchell was now articulating a rationale for why the UVF had played such an important role in taking up arms. 'Although the Covenant didn't state clearly that they would take up arms,' he emphasised, 'there was a clause in it that said, "We will resist by all means necessary", which, clearly, was a ... threat of arms.'[21] In comparing the old and new UVFs, Mitchell understood that the conflict had taken on a different character, which reflected how the troubles had become more insidious in its violence. 'If people were getting blown to pieces in the street in the Shankill, in Ballymena, would the old UVF have just stood back and said, "We can't retaliate. We have to wait on the legal forces of law?"'[22] It was an interesting proposition. However, as Mitchell stood to attention to deliver his oration at the Colin Caldwell memorial mural on that cold November day, amidst another loyalist feud, it is likely that the futility of political violence once again crossed his mind. If it did, however, he didn't show it.

★★★

As cool heads began to prevail in the loyalist feud, the threat from the UDA towards their rivals in the UVF dissipated. However, it did not remove the challenge which still existed from within the LVF, many of whom had a deep-seated hatred for the UVF. The truth was that the LVF had long since stopped being a politically inspired paramilitary faction, and had descended into something more akin to a right-wing gang that had moved along the spectrum from terrorism towards criminality. Without the leadership provided by Billy Wright, the LVF became directionless. Perhaps the second biggest blow to its activities came when its leader, Swinger Fulton, was returned to prison. He had lasted less than ten months on the outside before being sucked back into the deadly feud with the UVF. Another six months later, on 10 June 2002, he was found dead in his cell with a belt wrapped around his neck in an apparent suicide.[23] With several of the LVF's leading lights now dead, incarcerated or under threat of death from the UVF, the group went into terminal decline. By now the centre of gravity in the LVF's activities had shifted from Mid Ulster to Belfast, where the group began to muscle in on territory previously controlled by either the UVF or UDA. The LVF team in Belfast were soon to come under the watchful eye of the UVF, which bided its time, collating intelligence on their opponents' activities, watching and waiting. The UVF's Shankill Road leadership were playing the long game. The time to move against the LVF would soon come, but, first, they had several problems to deal with that threatened to degrade their internal cohesion.

***

Beyond the internal fluctuations of loyalist paramilitarism, the wider political process was under severe pressure. It faced collapse. For the Provos, the move towards a token response was needed to ensure Sinn Féin's continuing participation in talks. It, therefore, took the important decision to decommission. The Provisional leadership took this 'unprecedented move' in order to 'save the peace process and to persuade others of our genuine intentions.'[24] For the UVF, there would be no immediate reciprocity. At this time PUP MLA Billy Hutchinson had been nominated as the interlocutor between the UVF and the Independent International Commission on Decommissioning. 'This was the point we tried to explain, but people thought it was a stalling tactic for decommissioning,' he said. 'The whole idea of decommissioning was that the decommissioning wouldn't happen before all of the institutions were in place and it was the right thing to do for the people of Northern Ireland.'[25] For Hutchinson and the UVF leadership, the issue of disarmament went much further. 'Anybody can decommission arms, but you need to do it for the people because if it wasn't done for the people of Northern Ireland then what was the point?' In his view, the language was important to get right. 'And they used this phrase "beyond use", and I had actually said to them, "What about beyond reach"? And they went, "What does beyond reach mean"? And I says, "Well, it could be a bunker in a bog, or whatever", I said, "so that it's beyond the reach of people. Like, if there was a fight in a pub on a Saturday night, somebody can't just go and grab it, right?" So, I'd said, "If we got to "beyond reach" we got to "beyond use".[26]

Hutchinson believed that the Provisionals had decommissioned for cynical reasons, as a means of keeping their ministers in government. 'I thought it was totally crazy, not on the basis that I didn't want to see them decommission weapons, but on the basis that they had, excuse the pun, "jumped the gun". Why they jumped the gun was that they were doing it to keep two people in government. They weren't doing it because it was right for Northern Ireland society.' Hutchinson came to see the real problem as being a psychological one. It was about 'decommissioning the mindsets', he argued.

> I had three other people who were working with me on this. They were the commissioners and I was the interlocutor. We had a number of meetings about this, and we were arguing with the Decommissioning Body, with the Irish Government, with a number of other people and the British Government. A gun and a bomb is only dangerous when it's in the hands of somebody, because it takes somebody to pull a trigger and it takes somebody to detonate a bomb. And that was our argument. Our argument was that, if the Provos decommissioned, there was other people there who were opposed to that decommissioning, or it was some sort of token [gesture], or people would pull the trigger or detonate the bomb. We've seen this. Dissidents have grown out of this, you know. Some of those weapons that were in the hands of the Provisionals have been moved over to them. Now, you know, that could happen in any organisation, including loyalist organisations … People might have some stashed away and then they give it to somebody else … And it was dismissed by a lot of people as a stalling tactic. It wasn't a stalling tactic at all. I mean … the whole point of it was, I sat for weeks in the Assembly when they were talking about whether a word should be 'shall', 'would', 'could', or something else. When you think that it took about six weeks to decide what word they would use … [27]

What made it more difficult for the UVF to decommission its weapons unilaterally was the continuing campaign being undertaken by dissident republicans, which had ramped up their activities after the lull caused by their indiscriminate bomb attack in Omagh back in August 1998 that killed twenty-nine people. Eighteen months later, dissident republicans were attacking police stations and army barracks with sophisticated mortars. They were also planning to bring their war to the mainland. An RPG was fired at the MI6 headquarters in London on 20 September 2000, while a bomb placed in a taxi exploded outside the BBC's news centre in March 2001. In May, a bomb exploded at a London post office and a car bomb in Ealing Broadway at the beginning of August injured seven people. A few weeks later, the dissident campaign was to be overshadowed by the Al Qaeda attacks on the United States on 11 September 2001 (later known as 9/11).

PUP MLA David Ervine watched the 9/11 attacks unfold on a small television wheeled into his office at Stormont. He was soon joined by Women's Coalition leader Monica McWilliams and a number of their staff, many of whom wept at what they were witnessing. One community activist who was in the room at the time said that Ervine was transfixed by the events across the Atlantic. 'Things have now changed, changed utterly,' Ervine was overheard saying, in words echoing the famous poem *Easter, 1916*, by William Butler Yeats.

> No old-fashioned armed group was going to exist. The Americans wouldn't stand for it. Me and another community activist talked about it in the car on the way home. That was a game-changer. [Militant] loyalism and republicanism died that day. You know that post-9/11 mantra of 'You're either with us or against us'. Ervine was well-tuned to what this meant for Northern Ireland.[28]

The truth was that the feud within loyalism had still not run its course and would break out again, first, within the UDA and then, second, between the LVF's Belfast-based team and the UVF.

***

Ballyboe Inn, Ballyclare, County Antrim, 1:05 a.m., 20 December 2002

Trevor Gowdy, a former Army boxing champion and doorman, was drinking in the Ballyboe Inn in Ballyclare when he got into a heated argument with several other men. The Ballyboe was a rough country pub with a reputation for violence and, as such, was often frequented by the 'hard men' of the town as well as loyalist paramilitaries. It had an upstairs open-plan loft-style bar, with seating overlooking the Rashee Road. That evening Gowdy's argument with the men escalated very quickly and led to a violent confrontation between them in which Gowdy chased the men with a pool cue, several of whom allegedly had connections with the UVF.[29] Most local people knew not to cross anyone associated with loyalist paramilitaries. Gowdy had no such fear, and soon after the men fronted up against him, he had little hesitation in defending himself.

Gowdy awoke late the next morning. He got up, had a shower and made some breakfast. It was sometime after midday that he caught a glimpse of the red Peugeot car outside his home. Two men got out and walked up to his door. Gowdy said he had known one of the men for over twenty years and saw him regularly in Ballyclare. They were let into his house. The man informed Gowdy that he was to attend a meeting at the Monkstown Social Club, some seven miles from Ballyclare. Gowdy felt unsure about the invitation, and sat passively, contemplating his next move. After some persuasion, he said he left the house with the men and climbed into his red Vauxhall Cavalier to make his way to Monkstown. According to Gowdy, the two men followed closely behind in another vehicle. He noted that one of the men was on his mobile phone during much of the journey. It was sometime between 1 p.m. and 1:30 p.m. when the two cars arrived at Monkstown Social Club in Cloyne Crescent. Gowdy drove into one of the car-parking spaces outside, switched off the engine and got out of the car. No sooner had he got out that he spotted two men walking towards him from a wall at the right-hand side of the club entrance.

Gowdy could see that one of the men was visibly angry. The man started shouting at him, demanding to know why he had hit the men the previous night. No sooner had Gowdy answered than one of the men drew a baton from his jacket and hit him across the forehead. In an attempt to defend himself, Gowdy punched the man, he later told police was thirty-two-year-old Mark Haddock, but it was a futile gesture. One of the other two men then came up behind him and one of them hit him over the head with a hatchet. 'If we had got you last night, you fucker, you'd be hanging from a tree,' one of the men barked at him, as Gowdy tried frantically to shield himself from the punches and kicks that now rained down on him. As Gowdy lay on the ground, one of the men lifted the car keys the Ballyclare man had dropped and walked casually over to his vehicle to open the boot. The others lifted Gowdy up and put him inside. At this stage Gowdy was still conscious. A heavy-set man, like most doormen, Gowdy could handle himself against one or two opponents – but not three. He was promptly thrown into the boot, and the car hastily accelerated away from the club.

While he lay badly beaten in the boot, Gowdy tried to use the mobile phone in his pocket to call a friend. His attempts to raise the alarm were futile, as he couldn't get a signal. By now panic had set in. His heart raced as he tried to wipe the blood from his face. It was at this point that he heard one of the men in the car say 'We'll leave him where we left McCord.'[30] No sooner had they uttered these words than they heard the beeping sound of Gowdy tapping on his phone. They stopped the car to take the phone off him, but Gowdy fought back in a desperate attempt to get out of the boot. He was hit again with a hatchet and a knife was produced and he was stabbed in the right knee, left torso and right thigh. It was a frenzied attack as red mist clouded his attacker's mind.

At this point Gowdy made one last attempt to break free from his captors and make a run for it. He discovered very quickly that his leg was broken and he fell to the ground. Gowdy was dragged over to a wall. 'You can die there, you fucker,' his attacker told him, as spit flew out of his mouth. The assailant then left in Gowdy's car. Although he was very seriously injured, Gowdy was still alive with severe hatchet marks to his head. He was dumped just yards from the front door of the social club.

When Billy Greer arrived back from a meeting in the Shankill, he spotted a man lying hunched over against a gable wall emblazoned with the words 'UVF – The People's Army'. He turned to one of his associates stood next to him and said, 'thon cunt looks like his dead', tasking the younger man to go across and check on the victim.[31] Greer and the others went inside the club. A few minutes later another man leaving the club called an ambulance who alerted the police. When Gowdy woke up, he found himself in a hospital bed. He told detectives that he recognised the main attacker, and that he had first met him at a party in Ballyclare.[32] Four years later Lord Justice Weatherup found Mark Haddock guilty of Grievous Bodily Harm and false imprisonment of Trevor Gowdy and also an arson attack on his car.[33] Haddock was sentenced to ten years in prison for the attack.[34] In an ironic twist, earlier in the summer, Haddock had been shot by fellow members of the UVF while he was out on bail and living at a house on the Doagh Road, close to the Monkstown estate where the attack on Gowdy took place.[35]

Violence like this had a huge effect, not only on the victims of such attacks but also in destabilising the UVF's political associates in the PUP, who were trying to represent the interests of marginalised communities at Stormont. Naturally it led to serious questions being asked across the political spectrum about just what was going on inside the organisation they were most closely connected to. 'The UVF conducted their own inquiries during this time, don't forget,' recalled one former senior PUP activist. 'They conducted their inquiry into the activities of Billy Wright, they conducted an inquiry into the activities of [a Mount Vernon based loyalist with a ferocious reputation] and what was happening in Mount Vernon.' David Ervine, said the activist, 'was absolutely convinced, particularly in both cases, that these people were agents of the State. And I remember him telling me about the inquiry into [the Mount Vernon loyalist] being halted by the leadership of the UVF. And it was his belief that they were getting too close [to unmasking informers and agents]'.[36] Events over the next few years would soon bear out Ervine's suspicions.

Murders linked to the Mount Vernon UVF

1. 24 February 1991 – Murder of Peter McTasney (25)
2. 17 January 1993 – Murder of Sharon McKenna (27)
3. 24 February 1994 – Murder of Sean McParland (55)
4. 17 May 1994 – Murders of Gary Convie (24), Eamon Fox (42)
5. 17 June 1994 – Murder of Gerald Brady (27)
6. 21 March 1996 – Murder of Thomas Sheppard (41)
7. 18 May 1997 – Murder of John Harbinson (39)
8. 9 November 1997 – Murder of Raymond McCord Junior (22)
9. 31 October 2000 – Murder of Thomas English (40)

18

FAMILY, IN A SICILIAN SENSE

'Knowledge of the enemy's dispositions can only be obtained from other men'

Sun Tzu, *The Art of War* (430BC)

Menin Gate, Ypres, Belgium, Evening, 30 June 2003

The bugler played the Last Post as young and old gathered at the Menin Gate to commemorate the sacrifice of huge armies that poured over sunken trenches to clash with one another on the bloody battlefields of the Western Front. The battlefields of France and Belgium hold a special place in the hearts of those from the UK and Ireland who make the trip across annually to pay homage to the memory of their fallen. This year was no exception.

Among the pilgrims that evening were members of the UVF's North Belfast and East Antrim brigade command staff, who had gone to the continent as part of a pilgrimage by the Monkstown Somme Association. Almost all of these men were firm friends. They had gone to school together, they lived on the same street as each other and they spent many evenings and weekends socialising together. Their kids even went to the same schools and their families occasionally intermarried, giving them an unbreakable bond. Like other UVF leaders, they saw themselves as a band of brothers, who came up through the organisation together, operated together and, for some at least, had even served prison sentences out together. It was a comradeship replicated across the organisation's ranks throughout Northern Ireland. Since its rebirth in the 1960s, this modern-day UVF drew its lineage and legitimacy from the past, to a time when their forefathers fought gallantly along the Western Front in the First World War.

As the second-in-command of the North Belfast and East Antrim UVF, Billy Greer was in Ypres at the end of June. He was conspicuous as he strolled down the old cobbled streets, dressed from head to toe in a full Glasgow Rangers Football Club away strip, one of the teams he had supported all his life. He wore a chunky gold chain and huge Colt 45 centrepiece around his neck. The gold rings on his fingers were stamped with the UVF badge. For years Greer ran Monkstown Social Club, a focal point for members of the community and patchwork quilt of surrounding housing estates. Monkstown bordered other hotbeds of loyalism, including Ballyduff, New Mossley, Rathfern and Rathcoole. An old-school loyalist, he had been arrested with a number of other UVF members in 1972 in the farm at Jack's Lane in Monkstown. Only UVF men were admitted to these 'club rooms'. It was where the organisation kept its guns and ammunition, its bombs and other war materiel.

Greer had been the founding member of the Monkstown Somme Association, and its first chairman. Visits to Thiepval for the commemorations on 1 July were the highlight of the group's annual calendar. It was an occasion that Billy Greer talked about with considerable pride. His own father had fought there, and he was part of a dynasty of Ulster loyalism stretching back a hundred years. At home, he had taken the bold step of ordering the removal of UVF paramilitary murals across the district, telling the local media that the new murals would 'attempt to ignite the flames of culture and historical awareness'. To that end the new wall paintings would commemorate only the old UVF and the 36th Ulster Division, the British Army unit which had absorbed the Ulster Volunteers into its ranks upon the outbreak of hostilities in 1914. In Greer's mind, the reinvention of this intimidating tribal street art would help 'enrich estates with history and culture' to help 'create a better living environment for people'.[1] The transition from long war to long peace had begun, and Greer wished to play his part in the process. It was a commitment to his community that had inspired him to join the UVF in the late 1960s and moulded him into a dedicated volunteer throughout the troubles.

In Ypres, Greer was joined by Rab Warnock, the overall brigadier for North Belfast and East Antrim. Warnock, one of the most gregarious loyalists inside the UVF, had been officer commanding of Compound 19 in Long Kesh in the mid-1970s. It was there that he and Greer struck up a close friendship that was to last the rest of their lives. After both men were released from prison and vacancies became available, Greer assumed command of the East Antrim UVF. After his election to Newtownabbey Borough Council in 1997, he stepped back from commanding the UVF in the area and Warnock came to the fore. As the two most senior members of the UVF in the area, everything that happened went through them directly. In later years, Warnock, who never wasted an opportunity to make people feel at ease, enjoyed a reputation as one of the toughest, most feared and respected UVF men in the organisation. That evening in Ypres, Greer and Warnock were in a fine mood as they walked the cobbled streets after the Last Post service. Joining them was PUP MLA Billy Hutchinson. Greer spoke in his typical blunt, matter-of-fact way to a young man from the local area who had come over to say hello. This was vintage Billy Greer. The sight of the loyalists wandering down the cobbled streets was one to behold. People enjoyed coffees and beers in cafes along the route as the men marched along the street with purpose and military bearing. They boarded their transport and headed off to their accommodation for the night an hour south of Ypres in the town of Arras.

The next morning, Greer, Warnock and the other men turned up in their smart green Somme Association golfing-style jackets. They gathered at the bottom of the carefully manicured garden in front of the Ulster Tower monument, taking their place amidst a huge fraternity of people who had crossed the English Channel to pay their respects to their war dead. The event at the Ulster Tower is traditionally tightly controlled by the British State and the Royal British Legion, though it is common to find an assortment of Orange Order, Apprentice Boys of Derry and loyalist paramilitary representatives there too. At the head of the official delegation that morning was the Secretary of State for Northern Ireland, Dr John Reid, and the senior commander of the Territorial Army in Northern Ireland, Brigadier David Keenan. Keenan was a Parachute Regiment officer with several tours of Operation Banner (the Army's codename for its military support to the RUC) under his belt. He had been the Adjutant of the 2nd Battalion, the Parachute Regiment, when that unit was ambushed by the Provisional IRA in Warrenpoint in August 1979. Now he was representing the British Army by laying a wreath on behalf of his brigade, 107 (Ulster), which had fought gallantly at the Battle of the Somme in July 1916.

After the official ceremony, Billy Greer and Rab Warnock led tributes by the new incarnation of the UVF.[2] It was a proud day for both men, who had family connections to the originals and had both been long-standing members of the present-day organisation. They had even brought the new UVF's colours out to the Somme and were pictured standing proudly in between them in the nearby Connaught Cemetery across the road from the Ulster Tower.

On their way back home to the UK, members of the Somme Association accompanying Greer and Warnock stopped overnight in the French town of Lille, close to the border with Belgium. The men were relaxing in a nightclub when they became embroiled in a bar brawl with some local men. It was later claimed that the loyalists were defending themselves against supporters of French right-wing politician Jean-Marie Le Pen. The locals, mistaking the Belfast men for English football hooligans, apparently started the fight. One of the three men arrested had suffered a broken nose, while another one was slashed across the face with the jagged edge of a smashed beer bottle. Billy Hutchinson, who was staying in the same hotel as the men, told the media afterwards that 'these men were in the wrong place at the wrong time' and called it 'an absolute nightmare'.[3] Five of the men were arrested and held while their comrades returned to Northern Ireland. Three of them were subsequently handed down six-month sentences. It was an inglorious end to what was intended to be a serious and respectful excursion to the battlefields of France and Belgium.

★★★

Although the Somme visit ended on a slight downbeat note, worse was to follow. It began when a member of the UDA allegedly came forward to the UVF Brigade Staff on the Shankill in the summer of 2003 to complain about harassment he had received from UVF members in East Antrim over money he owed for Class B drugs. The Shankill leadership couldn't act unless they had proof to substantiate the allegation, especially when it concerned some of the most respected members of their organisation. 'I asked if anyone else was prepared to come forward,' said The Craftsman, believed to be the group's second-in-command at the time. 'He said there was, and it turned out another six or seven men did. I initiated a series of internal investigations.' It wasn't long before Rab Warnock heard rumours of an investigation. He had got wind of it through a number of back channels, and, on the occasion of the funeral of UVF Brigade Staff member Norman Sayers, chose to confront The Craftsman about the matter. Warnock was furious. 'I asked him if he was dealing drugs. He said he was. "The UDA's doing it so, so are we", he snapped. He was very aggressive. I couldn't believe it. He said it like it was normal. There was zero tolerance policy for stuff like that there,' said The Craftsman. 'I think wee Billy [Greer] looked at it as if it wasn't a problem. If Rab had come along and thrown his hands up and said, "We've fucked up", then there would have been a way back for him. As it was, it was seen that the UVF was selling drugs, and we couldn't have that.'[4] It wasn't long before rumours began to emerge in the local media that some of the UVF-controlled shebeens in North Belfast were being used to sell drugs and hold all-night raves. The UVF Brigade Staff say they had no other choice but to act on the information they had received.

Warnock returned to Monkstown after Sayers' funeral, hoping that the matter would go away. He continued to direct the day-to-day running of his area. On 8 November, he authorised a punishment team to discipline thirty-one-year-old Jock Allen, apparently a close friend to Trevor Gowdy. Spotting men approaching his house with guns, Allen tried desperately to barricade his front door. Unable to gain access to the house, the UVF men shot at him through the door, wounding Allen. As he fell to the floor, they fired another shot, which hit him on the head. 'He was shot by accident', said one loyalist close to the local leadership at the time. 'He was throwing his weight around and a team went to put him back into line.'[5] Ironically, the Brigade Staff on the Shankill Road had just launched an 'internal consultation process' as a means of gauging the mood for disarmament amongst their rank and file.

While people privately wished UVF terrorism out of existence, publicly hectoring the group to disarm and 'go away' proved futile. Its volunteers simply ignored the pronouncements of the 'great and the good', as they disparagingly called them, for their opinions didn't count. Such external criticism didn't affect the way the organisation conducted its business. Outsiders who made their disdain for the UVF public were regarded as miscreants and rarely 'knew what the fuck they were bellyaching about'. 'Besides', grumbled an endless line of po-faced volunteers, 'opinions were like arseholes', 'everyone had one'. In the minds of most volunteers, no one understood the organisation outside of its own ranks, what it stood for and how its policy would only be decided internally, by its own membership.

Even 'The Professor', a nonagenarian and long-serving UVF veteran, found it difficult to believe the rumours which were now circulating about men he had long considered to be his closest friends and comrades. The Professor was a veteran loyalist who had joined the organisation in the late 1920s. He began his paramilitary career by ferrying guns round Belfast for legendary loyalist 'Buck Alec' Robinson and the Ulster Protestant Association (UPA), a small gang operating in North and East Belfast in the inter-war period. The UPA was an illegal, clandestine outfit, known to the

RUC for its predilection for stashing guns at Glentoran Football Club's pitch in East Belfast, and for inflicting severe punishments on its own members by strapping them to an upended round table and whipping them with a cat o' nine tails. It was a weird outfit, all pumped up on testosterone and machismo.[6] The UPA linked the old UVF, established under the centralised control of the Ulster Unionist Council in 1913 against the spectre of Home Rule for Ireland, with the rejuvenated UVF of the 1960s. These groups were made up of working-class Protestants who believed violent republicanism was about to re-emerge at any minute to smash the union between Great Britain and Northern Ireland.

The Professor was a tough character, having been chased out of Belgium by the Wehrmacht and subsequently evacuated from Dunkirk in 1940. He later returned to France when he landed at Arromanches on D-Day, 6 June 1944. The Professor was a Royal Engineer who was in charge of a section of the famous Mulberry Harbour, a floating contraption used as a disembarkation point for the huge Allied force that landed in Normandy to liberate France. Consequently, The Professor had become a legendary figure within the organisation, and had become re-engaged in UVF activities when the troubles broke out in the late 1960s. In his twilight years he had become something of a consigliere. 'I liked him a lot,' The Craftsman recalled, 'since before he came down here, when he lived in Highfield. He was an explosives expert.'[7] By 1974, The Professor was one of the key military men inside the East Antrim UVF. Part of his effectiveness was to play on his distinguished military career to tap soldiers living in Newtownabbey and beyond for any ammunition they might have been able to provide the organisation. Although The Professor was rebuffed on a number of occasions, he continued to instruct UVF men in the techniques he had learned over his many years in the British Army. It was not uncommon for The Professor to receive visits from British military intelligence, who were fond of presenting him with surveillance photographs they had taken of him in the company of well-known 'players' in the UVF. Much of his revered reputation was based on the fact that he could never be persuaded to betray his paramilitary comrades.[8]

In recognition of the connection between inter-war loyalist paramilitarism and the 'new UVF', the North Belfast and East Antrim brigade awarded The Professor a 'long service and good conduct' medal in 2002, ninety years after his birth, on behalf of the whole organisation. It was a symbolic gesture for a loyalist of his pedigree. Billy Greer had facilitated the award, and was proud that The Professor came to be associated with his UVF team from the early 1970s. This bond of loyalty between both men became important in 2004, when allegations began to surface about the internal investigation now underway. The Professor divulged little of what he had overheard about the trouble. For a man of his age, totally blind and partially deaf, he had kept his finger on the pulse.

It was for this reason that The Professor was one of the first people Greer had confided in after the UVF's Shankill leadership dispatched a Provost Marshal team to conduct an internal investigation into the allegations now surfacing. The Provost Marshals were the UVF's internal affairs department, charged with rooting out informers, scammers, drug dealers and those dabbling in other nefarious activities. They also had responsibility in each of the five brigade areas with enforcing discipline. Billy Greer was deeply shocked and embarrassed by how matters had developed. Whatever the compelling reasons for allowing him to remain at the helm of the local social club, the command group around him set themselves against Shankill Road policy.

After four decades in the organisation, Greer and Warnock were about to enter uncharted territory. The Craftsman, who had originally dispatched the investigation team to look into the allegations, met with The Pipe and other members of the Brigade Staff to discuss the matter. It was decided to gather all of the area leaders together for a showdown. 'I wasn't there, but I heard what happened. Rab said he wouldn't accept the investigation's findings. There was no way back.'[9] Ironically, The Craftsman had great respect for Warnock. They had come through a lot together, working up through the ranks to take on senior leadership positions. 'I even have a leather belt Rab gave me from his time in Long Kesh,' he said. 'It gave me no personal satisfaction to do this. Rab tried to go around me by appealing directly to [The Pipe]. [The Pipe] said if he wouldn't accept the authority of his 2IC then it was over.'[10] Shortly afterwards, the Brigade Staff recommended a discreet settlement to the whole affair. In a last-ditched effort to overturn the findings, Billy Greer drove to the Shankill where he met with The Pipe. After a short discussion, the Monkstown man tendered his resignation as one of the group's top commanders.[11] Greer, Warnock and two other men, were given a 'hangman's reprieve'.

It was said by some that men like Billy Greer and Rab Warnock had become corrupted by the power the UVF had bestowed on them over a long period of time. They remained committed loyalists who were politically motivated but they were not infallible, and were just as at risk of making bad decisions as the next man. In many ways, they merely reflected the tendency within the UVF and other loyalist and republican terrorist groups at the time to slide away from their founding policy.

Regardless of the reasons why Greer, Warnock and their team had been stood down, by pushing its old guard from its perch, rather than sanctioning them in another way, the UVF's Brigade Staff had little idea that they were creating an even bigger problem for themselves.

★★★

To ensure its operations ran smoothly, the UVF on the Shankill took the decision of imposing a new leadership on the area. Those close to a prominent Mount Vernon based loyalist with a ferocious reputation, who was widely believed to be in line to take over from Warnock, said this man saw an opportunity, and attempted to use the Brigade Staff's equivocation over Greer's resignation to lobby them to appoint him commander for the area. Much to his chagrin, the Mount Vernon loyalist was refused the request. The Shankill instead chose another man, thirty-two-year-old Gary Haggarty, in lieu of another close confidant Greer had hand-picked himself.[12] Haggarty was a surprising choice, to say the least. Having joined the UVF in 1991,[13] he was relatively unknown in Monkstown and the surrounding environs. It was rumoured that he had received a beating from the organisation some years earlier, and was even ostracised from the UVF wing inside Maghaberry Prison in the late 1990s.[14] Now, this innocuous figure was about to replace two of the best-known figureheads within the UVF.

Almost immediately, Haggarty came up against a tide of scepticism and suspicion. The general consensus amongst those in the UVF's ranks with a 'military record' was that this 'young fella' was little more than 'a trucilier, a ceasefire soldier, with no operational experience'.[15] Others were less critical. 'This here is the best brigadier the UVF has ever had,' one East Antrim UVF officer allegedly boasted at a social event a year or so after Haggarty was appointed. The man full of praise for his new commander had been only one of a handful of people to remain in favour with the 'old guard'. Yet, over the course of the year, he had been won over by Haggarty's charm. His words of praise rang hollow in the ears of other men who respected Greer's long years of service and remained intensely loyal to him, despite his fall from grace.[16] The removal of Warnock and Greer and the elevation of a 'Young Turk', however, was not all plain sailing for the UVF. Local supporters of the UVF in East Antrim balked at the changing of the guard. For them, the area should have continued to enjoy its own autonomy. They should pick who led them, they felt, not have an alien leadership imposed upon them by people with only the most tenuous links to the area. It was not long before the *Sunday World* was running stories referring to Haggarty by a long list of disparaging sobriquets, including 'The Beast' and 'Cowhead'.

Despite the scepticism in established UVF ranks, the change in leadership wasn't entirely negative. Senior members of the East Antrim PUP were beginning to notice changes in how the UVF was conducting its business. As the tenth anniversary of the loyalist ceasefires approached, Billy Mitchell believed it was an opportune moment to initiate a 'diagnostic check' on the health of the progressive loyalist strategy he had helped to devise.[17] Several decades of living in an abnormal society had conditioned the UVF to act with impunity. They had always been an extremely ruthless organisation but, for some of its membership, criminality had started to seep more and more into the frame. Former RHC leader 'Plum' Smith believed that the future of loyalism was 'probably greater criminality – there are leaders who only reinforce and give credence to this analysis – same is true in republican areas. Just look at Ardoyne', he told one researcher. 'Yes, the UDA went down that path first, with their internal feuds and squabbling, but they are not alone. The UVF is heading that way slowly to the point where you have a mixture of criminality and loyalism, which can't operate as one unit as it did during combat. For those willing to change in the UVF this is a difficult climate.'[18] The UVF faced a stark choice. It could either opt for disarmament and demobilisation, or play further into the hands of its criminal elements.

Changes in East Antrim allowed the UVF an opportunity to test-drive some of the ideas now being put forward by Billy Mitchell and others in the PUP regarding the way ahead. 'Karl', one of Mitchell's close associates in the PUP at that time, believed that a seismic shift was underway. There were grounds for optimism.

So, my guess'timation of what's going on in Newtownabbey or East Antrim is that there's a new leadership in from about November … And that new leadership – well, we'll take the optimistic view, the new leadership is younger, it's relatively untainted, it's anti-drugs and it's moved away from the 'Greer model', which is, if you're part of the movement, you're bought in. You drink in this club, you drink in that pub. You do this on a Friday night. You pay your dues. And you're family, in a Sicilian sense. And you don't move outside it. And, staying on the optimistic model, because we can talk about some of the drawbacks, if you like … what I'm getting is that people are free to move in any direction they want, free to drink when they want. Free to pretty much carry out any enterprise they want, with the usual caveats. They do pay their dues. They are 'on call'.[19]

Karl said that the impression he was getting was that the new leadership was of 'pro-community development'.

And the reason that's important is, as far as I know – and this is only based on a few examples in Carrick – there have been times when the PUP has said, 'Why don't we engage in political debate within the wider movement?' But the UVF has always said – and I only learned this recently – that UVF members cannot be members of the PUP, which confused me for a while and I didn't get it, but, from chipping away at a few blocks, what I've learned is that the UVF are busy trying to keep the PUP fairly pure in terms of its politics.[20]

Although this new dispensation stopped short of redefining the link between the party and the army entirely, it did nonetheless leave open the possibility that the PUP could escape politically unscathed from another UVF outrage, which had become a natural hazard in the run up to each election.

***

Haggarty faced an uphill struggle whenever he was put in charge of the East Antrim UVF. 'Things were a bit difficult for me and the team I brought in,' he said at the time. He believed that most people in his new Monkstown powerbase thought it was only going to be a short-term measure; that the old leadership would be back within a few months. 'There are issues around the club, with Billy still seen as running the club, a lot of people are not sure what way to take the new arrangements,' lamented Haggarty. 'Also, there are people thinking Rab [Warnock] is going to come back, or different elements of the previous leadership would be back,' he said with the hint of a wry smile. 'It will all take a while to settle down, to let people get used to the new way of doing things here.'[21]

Haggarty told his subordinate commanders that they would have to 'win the hearts and minds of the people' in the local areas throughout North Belfast and East Antrim. 'People are simply not going to trust us straightaway,' he said. He began to push the line that the UVF in the area had developed a bad reputation over the years and that he was, in some respects, its great white hope. Irony was not Haggarty's strong suit, for most of the activities he found abhorrent were actually perpetrated by members of his old unit, the Mount Vernon UVF, a team he helped to run along with another man who enjoyed a ferocious reputation.' It was just a matter of getting people round to our way of thinking,' Haggarty said at the time.

> We are ten to twelve years into the ceasefire, and there's people joining the UVF who should never have been in the UVF. We needed to change things, so we lowered recruiting – in fact it's almost non-existent here now. There had been a load of punishment beatings, but we didn't think they were necessary so we tried to address that – there were too many people punished before and it was unnecessary. The organisation needed to work out the best way of disciplining its own men.[22]

Publicly, Haggarty appeared a convert to the UVF Brigade Staff's drive to transform the organisation from a military-minded armed group into a politically astute 'old comrades' association'. Privately, Haggarty was well aware that he couldn't resist all of the calls by people in the local community who demanded severe punishments for those accused of being involved in anti-social behaviour. 'People were getting shot for the slightest of things – it became a badge of honour. People had "in" and "out" tattoos with the date they were shot. Years ago, there would have been a stigma when you were shot. You were shunned, but no longer, because it has been used too frequently. Now there have been so many people shot nobody really cares about it.'[23] Part of Haggarty's attempt to reduce so-called punishment beatings and shootings may well have come from his own personal experience at the hands of his own organisation some years earlier.[24]

★★★

For Gary Haggarty, being in charge of the North Belfast and East Antrim UVF was a full-time job. He had been entrusted with considerable responsibility. He was tasked with instilling confidence in one of its core support bases, while also taking it down the path of conflict transformation. 'Things have settled down over the year,' he confided in an interview he gave at the time. 'People no longer feel it's a temporary situation. Once I got the first of July over me – that was my first main event at the head of the event – after that I could see people's attitudes changing. Having said that, it doesn't feel like it's been a year, time has flown in,' he added.[25]

Haggarty's first major responsibility for the organisation came earlier in the year, in February 2005, when his team presided over the funeral of The Professor, one of the UVF's legendary figures. As a helicopter hovered above The Professor's small family home in Rathcoole estate one bitterly cold winter's morning, Haggarty and his top team formed an honour guard around the coffin. Little did they know that The Professor had always remained loyal to Billy Greer, who performed his own ritual over the coffin of his close friend and confidant. This was a friendship and comradeship that had been hard won throughout the troubles. Gary Haggarty had little in common with these men, other than the fact that he happened to belong to the same organisation.

Perhaps the one reason why Haggarty survived the bumpy ride he was now experiencing at the hands of the old guard and their supporters was the faith he had placed in him by the first commander of the East Antrim UVF, Billy Mitchell. Without that essential crutch, Haggarty would not have lasted five minutes in the position he now found himself occupying. Much of this faith came down to Haggarty's support for the PUP's important peacebuilding work throughout the area. The Mount Vernon man's public backing for the conflict transformation initiative – now being coordinated by Mitchell and a close team of grassroots party activists and critical friends – was crucial.

With the establishment of the East Antrim Conflict Transformation Initiative (EACTF), Billy Mitchell and those working alongside him demonstrated their commitment to addressing the legacy of the violent past in a way that would bring the paramilitaries 'out of the jungle'.[26] It was a contradictory process, for some of those in the local UVF brigade area who publicly supported the PUP's direction were also actively working against it. One of Haggarty's lieutenants, for instance, it was alleged, had been involved in criminality, despite the Brigade Staff's 'zero tolerance' on such illicit activities. On one occasion, Billy Mitchell even facilitated a meeting, in which one young community activist challenged Haggarty over allegations that were surfacing on a regular basis in Sunday newspapers. The UVF leader denied any involvement in criminality and gave an undertaking to address the matter.[27]

It would be unrealistic to side-step the effects of criminal activity on loyalist and republican paramilitarism. In December 2004, for instance, the Provisional IRA was rumoured to have pulled off one of the biggest heists in British and Irish criminal history, stealing £26.5 million from the Northern Bank headquarters in Belfast. The Chief Constable of the PSNI at the time, Sir Hugh Orde, believed that republicans had become 'organised criminals', while loyalists were not lagging that far behind, with their involvement in illicit activities, which careful analysts believed included drug trafficking, racist attacks, punishment beatings, killings and prostitution.

At a private briefing at PSNI headquarters in early March 2005, Orde said he thought that loyalists were 'more disorganised. They are disorganised criminals, I guess, rather than organised criminals'.[28] Unlike the Official IRA and Provisional IRA, loyalists were not as ambitious with their criminal enterprises. They didn't 'plan as well', he said. 'They are not sophisticated in their money laundering; they're not sophisticated in how they carry out their crimes; and they are far more infiltrated, so we know more about what they are doing.' A decade on from the ceasefires loyalists had moved away from terrorism towards gangsterism. Orde acknowledged that loyalists were 'far more infiltrated' by agents, but that he 'was surprised at how few we did arrest, and I said we will go after them in the same way – that is, we need to mirror the effort put into the republicanism side and we arrested quite a lot, quite quickly'.[29] The imbalance in arrests posed a dilemma for the PSNI, insofar as some of those individuals they were running as agents were also suspected of involvement in criminality, an assertion repeatedly made in public and in private by PUP leader David Ervine.

★★★

Rathfern, Newtownabbey, 10–12 September 2005

The first real test for Gary Haggarty's leadership came when the Parade's Commission banned the Orange Order from marching along the Springfield Road on the weekend of 10–12 September 2005. A massive riot ensued, and the violence marked a return to the dark old days of the troubles. Fifty police officers were injured and loyalists set up roadblocks in working-class areas across Belfast. In October 1969 Protestants took to the streets in a three-night 'Battle of the Shankill', in which they stretched the Security Forces to the limit. Police morale was hit so badly that the army had to be called in to quell the civil disturbances. Twenty-five years later, the trouble at Drumcree threw loyalists into a confrontation with the police. Now, a decade on from the first major Drumcree dispute, they were once again at loggerheads. Areas across the province were engulfed in flames. Loyalist paramilitaries returned to the streets. They hijacked cars and buses, burnt them out and attacked local business premises. Working-class people found themselves in the eye of the storm of protest action, as bus companies withdrew their services, hospitals warned of disruption to life-saving medical care and paramilitaries ran amok.[30]

Haggarty was now in an invidious position at the centre of the trouble, even though the extent of his control over the RHC, a UVF satellite grouping, was limited. With its own chain of command, the RHC had opted out of supporting Billy Mitchell's EACTF initiative.

'It was an expression of anger. We have seen our culture and our heritage eroded,' Haggarty argued at the time. 'Now relationships with the police in this area have been damaged as a result of the violence.' He regretted the fact that disruption was being caused to ordinary life in the surrounding communities, but explained the UVF's strategy at the time. 'The key to the violence in this area was that it was to draw the police out of Belfast, from the Whiterock, to stretch resources. It could have gone on for weeks. There were people behind the scenes mixing it as well – people letting on they were PSNI, going into the schools, telling them to close early because the roads were to be closed at four.'[31] In response to the drain in support now evident across working-class areas, the UVF began to urge restraint within its ranks.

★★★

Shankill Road, Lunchtime, Monday, 26 September 2005

The television advertisement flashed across the screen with news that a major announcement was expected by the former Canadian Chief of the Defence Staff, General John de Chastelain, at 2 p.m. The buzz of anticipation in the media clearly indicated that something momentous was on its way. Many people expected an announcement about IRA decommissioning. It had been in the pipeline for some time. A sprightly, well-groomed man in his fifties crossed the street towards the Rex Bar on the Shankill Road. Just as he got half-way over, the owner of the bar shouted to him to jump into the car. 'De Chastelain is coming on,' said the barman. 'I was actually going to go into the bar to watch TV', the other man replied. 'Sure the boys are watching the racing,' he answered with a wry smile. 'Typical,' thought the man. 'That sums up what it meant to my community.'[32] A few minutes elapsed, then the general spoke. 'We are satisfied that the arms decommissioned represent the totality of the IRA's arsenal,' he told those reporters gathered at the press conference. 'We have observed and verified events to put beyond use very large quantities of arms which we believe include all the arms in the IRA's possession.' It was a hugely significant day, for it signaled the end of the IRA's long war against the British State and Protestant unionist community.

The man eager to watch the televised statement was a member of the UVF's Brigade Staff. In The Craftsman, the UVF had one of its longest serving members. One of only a small handful of UVF men with a wide circle of acquaintances across the political divide, he was to paramilitary loyalism what Martin McGuinness was for the Provisional IRA. The Craftsman is believed to have joined the UVF on Easter Tuesday 1966, progressing through its ranks to become one of the organisation's senior leaders by the late 1970s. The Craftsman was the key point of contact between the UVF and Chris Hudson, a Dublin-based trade unionist who had been contacted by the organisation in early 1993 to act as a go-between for the UVF and the Irish Government. 'I quickly came to the conclusion that The Craftsman was also sincere about where he wanted to take the process. If David [Ervine] gave the analysis, then The Craftsman was the engineer of driving the process that would lead to a loyalist ceasefire, support for the GFA and, finally, the journey towards decommissioning,' recalled Hudson.[33] The Craftsman was the key architect now driving the organisation towards a mature response to the search for peace in Northern Ireland.

The Irish Government had been much more engaged in the process of taking the UVF out of the equation than the British Government. This was due to the fact that loyalist paramilitaries – and particularly the technically proficient UVF – posed a real threat to the national security of the Republic of Ireland in a way that the IRA did not, with its so-called 'Green Book', the IRA member's membership rules and regulations, forbidding attacks on twenty-six County State forces. While the IRA may have abstained from attacking the south – merely using the border areas as a training ground and, certainly in the 1970s, as a safe-haven from which to launch attacks, the reality was that the UVF had proven that it could send bombs south and bring carnage to southern Irish cities, like Dublin and Monaghan, with impunity in the 1970s and 1990s.[34] UVF attacks in the Republic cast a long shadow over Dublin's engagement with loyalists throughout the peace process, but the Irish Government nonetheless remained committed to assisting the organisation in its bid to formulate an effective Disarmament, Demobilisation and Reintegration strategy, first mooted under the EACTF initiative.

★★★

Monkstown, Newtownabbey, Evening, 4 October 2005

UVF members assembled in the large wood-panelled room in Monkstown Social Club. They sat according to their teams. New Mossley were perched over by the toilets, to the left of the long bar. Rathcoole were tucked away in the other side of the room, while Ballyclare, Ballyduff and Glengormley sat in different corners of the room. The Carrick and Larne teams also sent along representatives. The Monkstown crew were nestled beyond them on the far side of the big room, in a booth next to the dance floor. Chairs were laid out along the middle of the dance floor which showed significant wear and tear. In the centre of the room, in front of the invited guests, who included critical friends and PUP members, was a big projector screen. Men, for there were only four women in the room, waited in eager anticipation for the briefing to begin. They passed the time losing themselves in small talk. Laughter filled the room occasionally, as men made jokes at each others' expense. Most of those in attendance were relaxed, casually dressed, and some of the younger men were fashionably kitted out with the latest stylish jeans, T-shirts and polo shirts. A few of the older men sported chunky gold chains and rings. They had pensive looks on their faces. You could feel the testosterone in the room.

Close to the door into the hall, at the 'top table' where the organisation's main men usually sat, were two members of the UVF's Brigade Staff. One of the two, a man in his mid-fifties, with swept-back hair and sporting a fishing jacket and polo shirt, was The Craftsman. He chatted casually to a man with light-coloured hair sat on his right-hand side. Though few may have known him, this was allegedly The Pipe, the organisation's long-serving Chief of Staff.

Another man, in his mid-sixties, with greying hair stood upright a few feet away from them. Dressed in slacks, a neat polo shirt and a body warmer, was Billy Mitchell, the 'PUP's brain'. Next to him was Gary Haggarty. Three decades earlier Billy Mitchell had sat on the UVF's Brigade Staff after a spell in charge of East Antrim. The irony was not lost on those in the room with an understanding of the UVF's history. Mitchell looked across at the two men to his right, nodded, then began his briefing.

Those who met in Monkstown that evening were there to discuss the EACTF initiative. Between 2004 and 2006, regular meetings were held throughout the communities in East Antrim, from Rathcoole in the south east to Larne in the north east. It had garnered considerable public support, and involved representatives from statutory agencies, local schools and community groups. Even the PSNI attended its large standing conference at the Knockagh Lodge in Carrickfergus a few months later. Billy Mitchell now took the opportunity to outline his strategy for setting the conditions, by which the UVF could transform itself into an old comrades' association, should it choose to do so. Mitchell's PowerPoint presentation was interspersed with updates from those sitting on the dance floor of the club, which included a few handpicked 'critical friends'.

Once Mitchell had concluded his briefing, The Pipe stood up to address the packed room. He began by talking about how the UVF had arrived at its ceasefire statement in 1994. 'It was in this club that the CLMC statement was drafted,' he told those gathered. 'I was most impressed with the presentation delivered by Billy,' he added. 'Our group have been involved in our own transformation process for the last eighteen months – in fact, the early stages go as far back as three years ago.' At this stage, The Pipe took command of the room. Younger volunteers listened intently as the older man spoke. 'This presentation puts you in East Antrim ahead of the game,' he told his captive audience. 'This venue saw the formation of the CLMC and was central in the peace process negotiations. Indeed, the Roadshow started here,' he informed them. 'The volunteers need to engage with change. There is no help ahead from the government.' His words rested heavily on the minds of those who looked on respectfully as he spoke.

It was at this point that the man turned to the question on everyone's lips: what was the future for the UVF? 'Volunteers did it for the people,' he empathised to them. 'The question now is how do you bring those young volunteers who joined in the last ten years. How do you respond to the new Provo ceasefire? And their new role?' It was at this stage that he delved into more detail on the rationale for the so-called 'Roadshows', a drive by the UVF leadership to address groups as big as several hundred volunteers, such as the event that evening, to some as small as a couple of individuals over a cafe table in the middle of the Shankill. As far as The Pipe was concerned, it was imperative to encourage debate 'on every single issue about the conflict – [and that] questions, answers, concerns were raised in open forum'.[35]

Several of those invited along to the evening's proceedings included prominent PUP figures, such as Dawn Purvis and the chair of the group set up to look at conflict transformation, Dr John Kyle. Inviting questions from the floor, one local leader said he had been disgusted by the comments of David Ervine, who was not present, that they had been involved in a 'dirty, stinking, little war'. You could have heard a pin drop. It made for an uneasy moment or two as the 'critical friends' gathered looked at one another, no strangers to being in public meetings where someone says something that immediately seems as if it should have been left unsaid. The PUP politicians said they were committed to reconnecting with the UVF and with the wider community as a means of seeing through the conflict transformation process. The majority of volunteers in the room appeared to feel that the connection had haemorrhaged since the signing of the Good Friday Agreement in 1998. Another man then asked Billy Mitchell if the presentation could be relayed to the whole organisation. 'People here are representatives of the whole organisation,' said The Craftsman. 'And yes, it will be filtered down to grassroots level,' he assured them.

The next day The Craftsman was more sanguine. 'Anyone who knows paramilitaries will know that the worst approach is to try and force them to do something, this is when you get the most volatile reaction, that's when people dig their heels in. Much better to let things take their natural course,' he remarked.[36]

***

Monkstown, Newtownabbey, and York Road, North Belfast, July 2006

Billy Greer and his men returned home from a visit to the Somme battlefields in early July 2006, and had been enjoying the Twelfth of July celebrations when he was admitted to hospital complaining of chest pains. He died soon after, aged sixty-three, on 13 July. The epitaph on his grave is inscribed with their words 'Here lies a soldier', which sits above the UVF badge carefully etched in gold lettering on the headstone. Greer was a huge loss to the organisation. He died as he had lived, an unrepentant volunteer in an armed grouping that he had helped establish, in an area he had lived in all his life. It was widely believed by those close to Greer that his downfall had been engineered by British Intelligence, eager to replace him – and his close comrade Rab Warnock – with a more compliant leadership figure. Perhaps his removal was choreographed to bring the group closer into line with those 'multiple sources' apparently now operating within its ranks.[37] Whatever the real reason for his fall from grace, UVF members from across Northern Ireland gathered to pay their respects to one of their most respected volunteers.

Meanwhile, seven miles south in York Street on the edge of Belfast city centre, Billy Mitchell was busy at work in his office at LINC Resource Centre. His gaze flittered between the calendar on the wall and the window, which overlooked Yorkgate Train Station. It was a busy road junction, situated only yards from the local shopping centre and the Westlink dual carriageway, which carried cars from the north and east of the city to the M1 motorway south towards Lisburn, and beyond to Dublin. The office window overlooking the east of the city masked a painful reality for Mitchell. Half a mile away, just off the Limestone Road, was the junction of Newington Avenue and Atlantic Avenue, the site where Mitchell's men had kidnapped Hugh McVeigh and David Douglas on 7 April 1975. The murder and secret burial of the UDA men may have been an issue of 'regimental loyalty' for Mitchell, but it also symbolised the major schism within paramilitary loyalism, between those who wished to pursue an independent Ulster and those who saw their political, economic and social futures bound up more intimately with the United Kingdom. For Mitchell and several other UVF veterans, such death and destruction was a tragedy. Since before his release from prison in 1990, Mitchell had filled his time with thoughts and actions that would repay what they believed he had taken away from society. After sixteen years on the outside, Mitchell had decided to take it a little easier, and move into what he called 'semi-retirement' from community relations work. 'I'm down to 107 hours a week,' he joked with his close colleagues some weeks earlier.[38] Unfortunately, he never did get to enjoy his reduced work routine. He died on 20 July 2006.

Billy Mitchell's death robbed the EACTF initiative of its most respected, high-profile champion.[39] Six months later, in early January 2007, progressive loyalism was to be dealt another blow when its most recognisable politician, David Ervine, died from a stroke. His death attracted widespread media attention and even saw Gerry Adams, the long-serving President of Sinn Féin, attend Ervine's funeral in East Belfast. A few days after Ervine was buried the Police Ombudsman for Northern Ireland, Nuala O'Loan, published the findings of 'Operation Ballast', an investigation into the death of Raymond McCord Junior in November 1997 and other connected activities. The report was released despite lobbying from retired Special Branch officers, who believed the Ombudsman's Office was 'playing god' with its decision to publish the details of sources who had worked for the police. 'I remember saying at the time, "If you release this report, people will die"', recalled one retired officer. The Ombudsman's office dismissed the stark warning. 'That's your problem, not mine', the Special Branch officer was allegedly told when he registered his dissatisfaction.

The release of the report caused internal ructions within the UVF. Commanders in East Antrim panicked. Paranoia set in, then fear. Who exactly were these agents? Gary Haggarty allegedly arrived at the home of one of his associates carrying a thick file under his arm. Inside was a copy of the Ombudsman's report. It seemed that he had annotated it very carefully, colour-coding each page and underlining several paragraphs. Haggarty proceeded to offer a rebuttal of the allegations. 'See that person there, that's not me,' he told his startled associate. 'That there, that is me.' As he spoke, the individual listening couldn't believe what was happening. 'It was surreal,' he said.[40] Word soon reached the Shankill leadership about Haggarty's antics. They moved quickly to stand him down, along with several of his subordinate commanders across North Belfast and East Antrim.

The Operation Ballast report prompted yet another internal investigation within UVF ranks. Although Gary Haggarty vehemently denied being an informer, it would soon emerge that he had been passing on information to the police from 1993 until 2003 and again, after a short break, until this time.[41] The UVF investigation found him guilty but before the organisation could bring him to a kangaroo court, he went into hiding. Tried in absentia, he was sentenced to death for treason. In the months after he absconded, no one, least of all his wife, knew where he was. On 25 August 2009 Haggarty was arrested and charged by the PSNI for the murder of John Harbinson, a local man who was beaten to death by UVF members on 18 May 1997. On 13 January 2010, in order to seek immunity from prosecution, Haggarty became an assisting offender under the Serious and Organised Crime Police Act 2005 (SOCPA). He was spirited out of Northern Ireland to England and Wales for de-briefing by the PSNI, which took place between 13 January 2010 and 10 May 2011. Further interviews were conducted between 9 June 2011 and 7 December 2011. On 15 March 2011, Haggarty was charged with eight further offences, including directing terrorism, membership of the UVF, conspiracy to murder and various firearms and explosives charges.[42] In becoming an assisting offender, Gary Haggarty was to become the UVF's single most important supergrass since Joe Bennett in the early 1980s.

Another key individual outed by the report had been a taxi driver and middle-ranking member of the UVF in Rathcoole. Early one morning, a large white furniture removal van turned up outside his house. Driven by a police officer, all of the man's worldly possessions were lifted and carried to the van. He was never seen again. Rumours circulating at the time suggested that MI5 had moved him and his family into a witness protection scheme in England, far from the clutches of the UVF. 'The first I knew about it was when he told me the day before he left that he was moving to Scotland,' recalled one of his associates.[43]

As the findings of the Operation Ballast report were digested in UVF heartlands, a McCarthy style witch-hunt began, with some lower-ranking individuals suspended or summarily expelled. The UVF became more visible as it carried out this form of 'internal housekeeping'. Not since the supergrass trials of the 1980s had so many of its members been unmasked to the general public.

Also worrying for the UVF was the unmasking of so many deep penetration agents. According to some intelligence practitioners, the Ombudsman's report broke the cardinal rules of Human Intelligence (HUMINT) work. As one former Special Branch officer told reporters:

> A dead source is no use. A source who is incarcerated for his part in a crime which he dutifully reported on for our benefit is also of no use. A source who has become suspected by his terrorist comrades of 'touting' is no use. A source who is moving down through the ranks, out of contention and away from a position of access, is of less use than one who is on the rise.[44]

A direct casualty of the adverse media exposure that followed the release of the Police Ombudsman's report was the UVF's engagement in the conflict transformation process, which had been initiated by Billy Mitchell and others who wished to see paramilitaries 'leave the stage'. The EACTF initiative had been a test case for the UVF's decision to seek a way out of paramilitary activity, and its failure due to these destabilising factors would prove to have serious repercussions as the summer approached.

19

DECOMMISSIONING THE MINDSETS

'The past is important, so long as we use it as a guide to the future. We can't live in the past.'

Billy Mitchell, former UVF leader turned PUP strategist, 2001[1]

Fernhill House, West Belfast, 5 May 2007

Thirteen years after he had announced the loyalist paramilitary ceasefires, Gusty Spence, the 'Alpha and Omega' of militant loyalism, was back in Fernhill House to read out another important statement. 'Following a direct engagement with all the units and departments of our organisation,' the statement ran, 'the leadership of the Ulster Volunteer Force and Red Hand Commando today make public the outcome of our three-year consultation process.' It was a move many close to the process had been anticipating for many months. Both armed groups were now, Spence assured the assembled media, about to assume a 'non-military, civillianised, role' and move to end recruitment, cease military activities, including targeting, and render their intelligence 'obsolete'. Significantly, the leadership said it had de-activated its active service units. Disappointingly, the UVF and RHC did not confirm the disposal of their weapons, making an oblique reference to how they had placed their ordnance 'beyond reach'.[2]

Spence's decision to come out of retirement to preside over what he was led to believe would be the wind down of the UVF's campaign wasn't something he really wanted to do, but he was a man of principle. He believed it was right and proper that, as one of the first in a long line of modern-day paramilitaries, he should be the one to pull the final curtain down on their armed campaign. Spence had long since withdrawn from the front line of paramilitary-linked politics. Most of the time he lived a fairly innocuous life in Groomsport on the North Down coast. He had left Belfast following a UDA attack on his home in the Lower Shankill during the loyalist feud in 2000–1. He was often to be found in the Lock and Quay pub in Groomsport or in the Meadowbank Social and Recreation Club four miles along the North Down coast in Donaghadee. After the death of his wife Louie in 2002, Spence spent most of his Saturday afternoons in the company of close friends, enjoying a puff on his pipe and the sip of a few pints of Guinness. He liked to engage in long conversations with a diverse mix of people, mainly about his service in the British Army and his passion for military history, rather than his prior involvement in militant loyalism.[3] The Meadowbank was, coincidentally, just feet away from where the original UVF had landed some of its guns in 1914, a fact not lost on Spence. He would frequently sit up in the left-hand side of the club's main lounge, arms folded, sipping on his pint and staring across at the commemorative photograph of the original volunteers unloading Mauser rifles from a small shipping trawler in the tiny, picturesque harbour. Donaghadee was also the most easterly point between Northern Ireland and Great Britain and on a clear day Scotland can be seen by the naked eye. Prior to the expansion of Belfast in the late nineteenth century, Donaghadee was the principal port in Ulster through which all goods and people travelled to and from Great Britain.

In the years after the signing of the Good Friday Agreement, Spence barely saw Billy Mitchell or, for that matter, many of his other old comrades, though individuals did ferry messages of goodwill between the two men. This became important in the period 2003–6 as Mitchell set about devising and implementing his strategy for assisting the UVF along the road to disarmament and demobilisation. Both men maintained a healthy respect for each other in their twilight years. Spence even read and commented on pamphlets compiled by two community activists who Mitchell had charged with scrutinising the political strategy of what he called 'progressive loyalism'. In a clever use of semantics, Mitchell defined progressive loyalists as those people who aligned themselves with the UVF–RHC–PUP constituency.

Through his boundless energy and dynamism, his writings and his speeches, Mitchell began to use terms such as 'movement' and 'the people's army' as a means of binding together the disparate ranks of former gunmen and bombers, ceasefire soldiers, politicians and community activists. The ambitious goal he set for them all was to transcend the conditions that had given rise to paramilitarism in the first place. He led by example in his everyday work as a community relations worker in seeking to transform the conflict from violent competition within and between communities to peaceful, political and social engagement. He recognised, perhaps more than anyone else involved in this kind of work, that social injustice on both sides of the divide fuelled recruitment into paramilitary organisations.[4] In Billy Mitchell's mind, it was the disaffection that grew out of this inequality that politicians had always sought to exploit, ever since Ian Paisley arrived on the scene in the 1960s.

In the same way that he had helped Gusty Spence fashion an *esprit de corps* in the early 1970s – when UVF members, at least in public, began to dress in revolutionary black uniforms akin to the Black Panthers – Mitchell now spoke in profound terms of his desire 'to assist the UVF leadership to help bring their men out of the jungle'.[5] It was a turn of phrase that set Mitchell apart from other unionists and loyalists, as did his labelling of the DUP as 'Ulster's answer to the Taliban'. Mitchell sought to style progressive loyalism on those grassroots movements in Latin America, where 'former combatants' joined with ordinary people to enable them to play a more responsible role in generating positive change in societies seeking to emerge out of protracted conflict.[6] It was evidence of his extensive reading and reflection, perhaps, that Mitchell could look to the wider world for inspiration in constructing a strategy for helping to bring an end to paramilitary activity in Northern Ireland.

In one of his many engagements with those community activists working alongside Mitchell, Spence suggested that they seek out other Brigade Staff officers for their views on where they believed the organisation was headed.[7] He believed that this would help to drive the tenor of discussion. It was a point relayed back to Mitchell, who quickly arranged for an interview with The Craftsman. The Craftsman's analysis of the situation fed directly into a pamphlet on 'Progressive Loyalists and the Politics of Conflict Transformation', which was edited by Mitchell a year later in 2005. The pamphlet mapped out a course for the UVF, RHC and PUP, and its key recommendations were discussed in some detail at a closed PUP conference in October 2005 from which journalists were excluded. The party's leader, David Ervine, emerged from the meeting to comment on the 'hard decisions' taken inside, which included the PUP's decision to renew its link with the UVF, until such times as the conflict transformation process was complete. 'The UVF have a lot to talk about,' Ervine reported. 'The PUP is saying, yes, let's give them the space and secondly, let's sort it out.'[8] Spence's advice to those community activists on the fringes of the conference proved as careful and strategic as his re-organisation of the UVF three decades earlier. He remained convinced, through all of this, that the UVF should end its 'campaign of armed resistance'.[9]

In signaling an end to its forty-two-year-old military campaign, the UVF statement of May 2007 reflected much of Billy Mitchell's own thinking, despite his tragic death the previous July.[10] Nevertheless, in the run up to Spence's second appearance in front of the media in Fernhill House, some commentators had predicted that wider developments in the 'peace process' – specifically IRA decommissioning in 2005 – essentially removed the UVF's *raison d'être*. The truth was, however, that the UVF never saw itself as a purely reactive force and, in fact, its heritage was more readily situated in its rejuvenation as a political tool for right-wing unionism preying on the fears of working-class Protestants. That it was formed as a bargaining chip for those who wished to bring down the Northern Ireland Prime Minister Terence O'Neill – and not, primarily, as a blunt instrument to destroy the IRA – was a point lost on those who criticised the UVF's failure to disarm in the summer of 2007.

Although he hoped that the words he uttered in May 2007 would consign the UVF to history, an organisation he had become synonymous with for nearly half a century, Spence was a pragmatist. He knew, deep down, that other outstanding issues would have to be resolved before this could happen.

***

EPIC offices, Woodvale Road, Belfast, 17 July 2007

That the UVF failed to fully decommission in 2007 nevertheless remained a worrying development for nationalists and republicans. For those close to the UVF, like Tom Roberts, decommissioning was not a realistic possibility at that time. Roberts had looked on as Spence read out the statement at Fernhill House that balmy summer's day. 'That was our ultimate aim – to get as far-reaching a statement of intent as possible,' he said a couple of months later. When Spence read out the statement many loyalists were jubilant. Roberts judged it 'a very, very positive statement. People will be picking holes in it because it fell short of decommissioning, but decommissioning was never on our radar'. He was quick to remind doubters that, when the UVF and RHC began their internal consultation process, no group had fully decommissioned. 'So, for us to change … mid-stream and move it onto the agenda … probably would have negated everything we had achieved up to then. So, we just didn't do it … It wasn't a thing that was taken very seriously within the UVF because it was never one of the UVF's demands of the IRA to decommission.' To those, like Roberts, who provided advice to the organisation on how they might transition towards a more civilianised role, there was a feeling that the weapons weren't actually the problem. 'We always use the cliché of decommissioning mindsets. At the end of the day it wasn't guns or war materiel that was killing people. It was people that was killing people. You know, guns only give them the means to do that.'[11]

What mattered most to the UVF leadership was that they could make a unilateral statement that carried the bulk of their organisation along with them. Although the internal consultation process (the so-called 'roadshows') was directed by the UVF, it was Billy Mitchell's EACTF, which would be the model upon which the organisation's eventual move towards a 'non-military, civilianised role' would be predicated.

By early 2007, however, that process had floundered for two reasons, one internal and one external. The deaths of UVF-turned-PUP leaders Billy McCaughey, Billy Mitchell and David Ervine robbed the initiative of its greatest champions. The other factor was outside the UVF's hands, and came in the wake of the Operation Ballast report, which unmasked a network of PSNI informers and agents inside the organisation's North Belfast and East Antrim brigade. 'It was probably the [Police] Ombudsman's Report [which] had a big impact on the work that was going on down there,' Roberts admitted, 'making the positions of people in the UVF leadership in the area untenable.'[12] Eighteen months earlier, Billy Mitchell said that the initiative had only been made possible with the replacement of the leadership in East Antrim. The UVF's 'decision to replace that leadership gave the PUP the encouragement and inspiration to approach the new leadership with a new initiative', he said. 'The relationships now are vital.'[13] However, with the ousting of Gary Haggarty from his leadership position, those relationships were now in jeopardy. In hindsight, Billy Mitchell's trust in Haggarty may have been misplaced, but he was, nevertheless, restricted in that he could only deal with the new leadership the Brigade Staff had placed in charge of the area. The EACTF limped on for several months after Haggarty was stood down but the caretaker regime was no longer as committed to the initiative and it became emasculated.

The unmasking of Haggarty and others as police agents may have caused considerable upheaval and panic inside the UVF, but it also had an indirect effect of forcing the organisation and its political allies in the PUP to revisit the question of how they might respond to retrospective investigations into the group's role in the troubles. 'This drip-feed of information that is coming out about the past has the potential to destabilise anything that has been achieved to date,' Roberts said. 'So, you know, that's the reason why we are having serious debates about how we deal with the past in a constructive fashion.' Despite the very public pressure now being exerted on the progressive loyalist constituency, Roberts thought that a consensus was slowly being reached amongst the UVF's hierarchy. 'I would definitely say there has been a line drawn under that. Nothing has really changed in terms of the objectives, that is, to change the UVF and Red Hand into a more civilian-type force, more in keeping with the current situation as it exists.' In fact, the failure of the EACTF initiative meant that the UVF now lacked a discernible strategy to enable it to follow through on its assurances earlier in the summer that it would transition into a 'non-military, civilianised' role.

In a bid to plug the yawning gap between conflict and peace, the Action for Community Transformation (ACT) group was hastily established. It had a shopping list of objectives but, regrettably for those key activists who had supported the earlier EACTF initiative, no real strategy for achieving these. Roberts remained pragmatic. 'What I'm concerned about now is, with all the fanfare around the political developments here, we've been put on the back-burner in relation to government assisting us to go a bit further down the road here, you know, to progress to where we eventually want to get.'[14] It had become obvious some months earlier that the UVF was being given the cold shoulder by both governments and the local political parties. At a roadshow meeting in Monkstown in early October 2005, a week prior to the closed PUP conference, the UVF's Chief of Staff sounded the alarm bells, appealing for leadership to be shown from within mainstream unionism. This was ironic, particularly since the DUP had done so much to manipulate and then marginalise the same paramilitaries in the years immediately after the 1994 ceasefires.

Loyalist paramilitaries, like the Protestant working-class community of which they were part, returned time and again to the same leaders who had done so much to jeopardise their standing within the union. The DUP, in particular, had zero interest in improving the lot of those loyalists who suffered so much structural inequality in the wake of deindustrialisation across the United Kingdom. This was true of the early 1970s when Gusty Spence warned of '50 years of Unionist misrule' and it was certainly no different nearly four decades later.

By 2006, however, matters had moved on in the wake of the St Andrews Agreement, and the British and Irish governments were now looking to the DUP and Sinn Féin to lead the new dispensation. Even so, the deal agreed between Ian Paisley and Gerry Adams in May 2007 had little to say about paramilitary loyalism. 'I always found it easier to work with the sovereign government, be it the British Government or the Irish Government in terms of getting an understanding of where grassroots loyalism is at,' Tom Roberts said at the time. He was of the view that local political parties 'wouldn't want to increase the capacity of our constituency because they'd see that as a threat to themselves.'[15] Without any real incentives to do so, the UVF and RHC leaderships nonetheless pressed ahead with their unilateral decision to end their armed campaign.

★★★

In the days immediately following the UVF's May 2007 statement, some of its members began to ask their commanders whether they would still have to 'pay dues' in light of the group's decision to call a halt to paramilitary activity.[16] They were told that they were still members and that the subscriptions should continue. What would also continue would be the code of silence, the *omertá* that governed the UVF system. And that included preventing anyone from speaking out about their involvement in paramilitary activity. For Tom Roberts, the absence of a comprehensive process for 'dealing with the past', which included legal safeguards for those who were prepared to tell their story, mitigated against a corporate endorsement by the UVF for such disclosure. 'We had a modest look at the whole truth recovery debate a number of years ago,' he recalled. 'And there would be a deep suspicion within loyalism about the motivations for it all. It would be largely seen in unionist and loyalist circles to be a largely republican-driven agenda, you know. The view would be that republicans want to make everyone else accountable for the past, except for themselves, and more or less putting the British Government and the legitimate security forces in the dock, if you like.'[17]

Roberts had considerable insight into the wider debates around Northern Ireland's past because he sat as a representative on the Truth Recovery and Acknowledgement sub-group of Healing Through Remembering (HTR), a non-governmental organisation working to actively promote reconciliation. Legal experts had produced a report for HTR a few months earlier, which raised considerable doubt about the ability of eyewitnesses to recall the past with any kind of accuracy. 'It is indeed fair to say,' they argued, 'that time is of the essence where evidence of eyewitness testimony is concerned.'[18] In any case, it was a moot point. As a paramilitary grouping with rigid disciplinary structures, the UVF's *omertá* prevented its individual members from breaking ranks and seeking atonement for past acts of violence.

Serious doubt hung over the question of whether loyalists would respond to Sinn Féin's calls for a 'truth and reconciliation commission'. As a transitional justice model this process has been tried in societies where the state itself needed to be entirely reconstructed, such as in Chile and South Africa,[19] which were notable for their oppressive systems of government. In Northern Ireland, part of a wider liberal democracy, the state remained intact at the time of the peace deal in 1998. Its Security Forces were undefeated in the assyemmtric conflict of which they had been part since the Provisional IRA first fired a shot in anger in 1970. The reality was that the Provos had been beaten and, despite the introduction of the euphemism of 'stalemate' by republicans, it had taken its armed struggle as far as it could go.[20] For the British Government, the Northern Ireland troubles were essentially an ethno-national dispute, which required conflict management to return the two divided communities to a less antagonistic co-existence so they could administer rule on behalf of London.

It would later be revealed that the British State entered into a deal with the Provos in relation to their so-called On the Runs who were given assurances that they would not be actively sought out for terrorist offences. Although this was not known until several years later, there was little, if any, appetite amongst UVF and RHC members for a truth recovery process. Roberts repeated this view in his oral evidence to the Northern Ireland Select Committee at Westminster, there was 'a resistance to any sort of truth process because ... republicans are using this as a weapon to put the British Government and its surrogates in the dock if you like,' in order to 'make everybody else accountable for their role in the conflict except themselves'.[21] In addition, it was extremely unlikely that those volunteers who had moved on from their own involvement would willingly confess to their role in murders without a guarantee of an amnesty. 'See this notion of people going in and throwing their hands up thirty years later for something, I mean what benefit would that be to them or anybody else for that matter?'[22] Roberts asked. Although many people denied it at the time, there was a certain logic in this conundrum. Why would those who have since moved on with their lives wish to have their past 'involuntarily exposed' by coming forward and risking 'venom' if 'you didn't have to serve any time for throwing up your hands'? added Roberts.

★★★

East Belfast Mission Hall, 27 June 2009

The clock on the wall of the Mission Hall fast approached 10 a.m. when a stockily-built, middle-aged man with grey hair strolled out from the back room and took his place at a podium. Believed by some journalists to be a senior member of the UVF, he was there to issue a brief one-page statement. 'The leadership of the UVF and Red Hand Commando today confirms it has completed the process of rendering ordnance totally, and irreversibly, beyond use.'[23] Unlike the statement read out by Gusty Spence two years earlier, this one went much further. The UVF and RHC leadership didn't want to be seen as the final obstacle in the long road to peace, which had begun to bed down in the wake of the Paisley–Adams deal. For Dawn Purvis, now leader of the PUP, it was a 'truly momentous day in the history of progressive loyalism'. Flanked by her party colleagues Billy Hutchinson, Hugh Smyth and Brian Lacey as well as former loyalist prisoner Winston 'Winkie' Rea, she had come to deliver a vote of confidence in the steps now being taken by the UVF. 'The decommissioning of all weapons by the UVF and Red Hand Commando shows that peaceful, stable, inclusive democracy is the way forward for our country,' said Purvis.[24] An air of positivity greeted proceedings, especially in light of a simultaneous announcement by the UDA/UFF that they too had disarmed.

What practical steps had the UVF taken to facilitate the deactivation of its military mindset in the intervening twenty-four months? The truth was that most of the work in this regard had fallen to community activists associated with the PUP and, to a lesser extent, ACT, which now provided the only viable vehicle for many UVF and RHC members who were keen to play a positive role in the new political dispensation. With only one full-time worker, a post partly funded by an international humanitarian organisation, it could not hope to tackle all the root causes propelling young men into paramilitarism or in helping existing members out of the organisation. Even though money had been secured by circuitous routes from the British and Irish governments, loyalists lacked the necessary appetite to turn swords into ploughshares. Unsurprisingly, UVF membership now swelled in areas where the twin evils of high unemployment and low educational attainment acted as accelerants on disaffection. With the organisation lacking direction, it continued to do what it did best.

Gusty Spence, meanwhile, was becoming increasingly disillusioned by what he was seeing and hearing. The UVF was no further towards winding up than it had been when he read out the second UVF–RHC statement two years earlier.

As the months passed by since its major acts of decommissioning, the UVF continued to demonstrate an ability to control communities. Some of its members, claimed the Independent Monitoring Commission (IMC), were even engaged in a 'wide range of criminal activity throughout Northern Ireland for personal gain'.[25] Luckily, many of these activities stopped short of murder, though this would not remain the case for long.

In the UVF's West Belfast heartland, some of its former members were beginning to think and act 'out of turn' from the prevailing norm. As some individuals came into conflict with members of the UVF hierarchy, the Brigade Staff was beginning to grapple with the prospect of leaving the door open to further challenge from within its community support base further along the way. What its central leadership decided to do next would have profound consequences for the future of 'progressive loyalism'.

★★★

Donegal, Irish Republic, 29 May 2010

Dawn Purvis woke early after a night celebrating a friend's wedding in Donegal. Her phone had been switched to silent for much of the previous twenty-four hours, so as not to disturb the nuptials. Her attempts to find a signal in the remote venue in Donegal proved fruitless so she opted instead to slip it into her purse and quietly forgot about it. As an MLA for East Belfast, she rarely took time off. The weekend away across the border was an opportunity to relax in the company of close friends, far away from the hustle and bustle of Belfast. It was important to take time to enjoy the finer things in life, especially since her routine as a political leader was exacting on her time.

When Purvis switched her phone back on the next morning at breakfast, she was surprised to see that she had twenty-two missed calls. 'I knew that something was wrong,' she recalled. 'I just knew something was wrong.' The East Belfast MLA immediately sought out a friendly member of the hotel staff to ask where she could get a proper signal. She had only left the hotel lobby when the phone rang. 'Are you happy now you bastard,' the caller on the other end said in a threatening manner. She recognised the woman's voice immediately, having received several calls from her over the past couple of weeks. Before she could answer, the woman said it again. 'Are you happy now you bastard.' Purvis offered only a token reply before the woman hung up. The PUP leader was shocked. She had no idea what was going on, only that it must have been serious.

Purvis's phone rang again. This time it was a journalist who she knew well. He said that a forty-three-year-old man had been executed in cold blood on the Shankill Road. The name of the victim was Bobby Moffett, and he had served a thirteen-year prison sentence for armed robberies carried out on behalf of the UVF/RHC in 1991 and 1995.

The murder of Bobby Moffett had taken place in broad daylight on the corner of the Shankill Road and Conway Street at 1 p.m. on Friday 28 May. Two men wearing masks and high visibility jackets approached their victim from behind and shot him. As he lay on the ground they shot him a further two times. Both men made off on foot along Conway Street to a getaway vehicle. The murder was quickly labelled a 'public execution' by the media as it had taken place in full view of men, women and children from the local community. The cordite hadn't even evaporated into the still afternoon air when life on the Shankill began to ground to a halt. News spread like wildfire that someone had been shot dead on the Shankill Road. Rumours quickly circulated that the victim had been murdered by members of the UVF's B Company.[26]

Purvis drew breath, hurriedly reflected on what she should do next, then opted to speak to the media, 'from the heart', as her colleague David Ervine had always advised her to do. 'It was wrong. This man posed no threat to the peace process,' she told the journalist on the other end of the phone.

As soon as Purvis rang off, she immediately requested a face-to-face meeting with the UVF leadership, but was told the earliest they could see her was on Tuesday, a full three days away. She was angry. How could the leader of the PUP be kept waiting in line to see the UVF when a journalist had almost certainly met with them already? It irked her.

When Purvis arrived for her one-to-one with the UVF's Chief of Staff on the Shankill, he had brought along a chaperone. Purvis politely requested that the other man leave, which he did. 'I asked him if this had been sanctioned. He hummed and haa'd.' An answer wasn't forthcoming. 'When I asked if the perpetrators were caught by the PSNI and prosecuted, would they be rejected from the UVF wing? I was told "No."' There was an awkward silence as The Pipe shuffled in his seat. 'I had no other choice,' said Purvis. 'I told him I would be resigning.' The leading UVF man pleaded with her to stay. 'I said that all the good work done since the UVF met in Belgium in 2006 had been undone. When I asked the UVF leadership why Bobby Moffett had been shot, they said it was because he challenged the leadership of the UVF on the Shankill.' Purvis became visibly exasperated. She felt betrayed. 'You're not serious,' she said. 'You're not serious.' Her repetition was partly for effect, partly because she hoped it was actually some kind of perverse joke. The kind of black humour common in working-class areas. No answer came.[27] Moffett had reportedly vandalised the car of another senior UVF man. He had to be punished for his transgression, as far as the Brigade Staff were concerned.

The UVF felt it had no choice but to issue Moffett's death warrant in light of what they saw as disrespect. It was a face-saving exercise. They had to re-instil the kind of fear that stalked working-class communities in the Shankill and beyond. It was no longer a disagreement between two individuals. It was seen as a challenge to the entire organisation. It was believed by the leadership that the public execution would serve as a stark warning to other people not to underestimate the ability of this group to continue to rule the streets of West Belfast with fear. After Moffett's killing, the UVF issued another warning to local people to stay away from the funeral. It was ignored.[28]

Loyalist violence was fast losing its utility by the time the UVF passed its death sentence on Bobby Moffett. The bitter loyalist feuds of 1975, 1996–7, 2000–1 and 2004–5 alienated the very people who had begrudgingly accepted the existence of loyalist paramilitaries. By 2010, patience had run out amongst those who had periodically given the UVF the benefit of the doubt. One careful observer of paramilitary loyalism, Richard Reed, wrote that the 'enduring potency of the culture of violence' by which militant loyalists resorted to violence was 'a means of solving problems and confronting challenges'. It was the same instinct, argued Reed, that had 'governed the behaviour of the UVF leadership when it threatened Billy Wright with execution in 1997 and ruthlessly forced the LVF to disband in 2005'.[29] It also exposed how the UVF's structures, while moving towards civilianisation, were unprepared to tolerate any dissent in the ranks as they did so.

By handing down the task of policing dissent on this occasion to one of the most ruthless sub-units in West Belfast, the Brigade Staff were sending another message to their rank and file. The unit was said to be commanded by an individual whose methods of maintaining internal discipline were referred to by some former members of the UVF as 'Gestapo-like'. He was a figure that David Ervine had always been wary about. 'Who was this young fella wanting to take over an organisation in the process of going out of business?' Ervine had cause to ask on occasion.[30] 'If you're going to preside over beatings and shootings of people in your own community, you're hardly likely to be well-liked,' remarked one former UVF member, who knew the prominent leader in question.[31] It was the IMC's assessment that the UVF, 'when put under pressure, failed to throw off its violent propensities'.[32]

A year after the Moffett killing, tensions were still running high across working-class parts of Belfast. In the east of the city trouble broke out in June, which led to two nights of intense rioting. Such civil disobedience had deeper roots. Although violence has been seen primarily as a by-product of years of deprivation, poor education and life chances, it was given expression by forty years of a paramilitary sub-culture. For many young men (and women) their role models were more likely to be Johnny Adair or Billy Wright than they were Rory McIlroy or George Best.[33] At the time some commentators laid the blame for UVF involvement in such incidents at the door of the Shankill leadership, which was unwilling or unable to reign in local commanders in an organisation that was becoming increasingly balkanised. Ironically, statistics produced by official government sources showed that it was Catholic, and not Protestant neighbourhoods, that suffered most from poverty and deprivation between 2001 and 2011. When such statistics are carefully interrogated, especially in those interface areas where violence between Catholics and Protestants is acute. There are, of course, multiple deprivations detectable, which can explain disaffection.[34]

Therefore, there was evidence, if it was needed in 2011, that loyalism looked 'dangerously volatile', as the much-anticipated 'peace dividend' failed to reach those marginalised communities most in need of regeneration. For loyalists, the challenge was to 'break the downward spiral of despair by looking to the future with hope, not fixating upon the past'.[35] In this they were not best served by those in the DUP, who came to dominate political, social and economic life in the inner-city areas. Neighbourhoods like Cluan

Place and Pitt Park in East Belfast were rife with disaffection. The people who lived there were soon left behind as the 'peace process' advanced.

***

After a short illness, Gusty Spence died in hospital in September 2011, surrounded by his family. A few days later, mourners gathered outside St Michael's church in Mansfield Street, behind the old Loyalist Club, for his funeral service. As Spence's coffin was carried out it was greeted by an honour guard of veterans from the Royal Ulster Rifles, Spence's old regiment. That the founder and long-time figurehead of the UVF refused a paramilitary funeral spoke volumes to those who gathered to pay their respects. In death, as in life, Spence's legacy continued to exert a powerful gravitational pull over close observers of Ulster loyalism. On his deathbed he again denied shooting Peter Ward, maintaining that he had gone to his sister's house when the fatal shots were fired.[36] Spence died with two major regrets in his life. The first was that he never had the opportunity to clear his name and, second, that he never saw the end of loyalist paramilitarism.

In the fifteen months after his death, the frustration and disaffection that had been growing in Protestant working-class areas was to gather further momentum. Having been elected to the leadership of the PUP a few weeks after his old mentor's death, Billy Hutchinson was dividing his time between Mount Vernon and the PUP's headquarters on the Shankill Road. He was greeted every day by the sense of despair from within a community he had grown up in and served, in his view, as a paramilitary and now as a community organiser and politician. He started to gather an effective team of people around him. He anticipated long political battles ahead. What he didn't count on was a cynical attempt by mainstream unionists to goad loyalists into attacking liberal politicians who had always sought to steer a middle course between the two political extremes in Northern Ireland.

20

THE PRAETORIAN GUARD

'One of the things that I was taught while in Long Kesh was that people who fight wars, fight wars to bring peace, and the politicians, they make the decisions. Let me say this, politics is war without bloodshed, while war is politics with bloodshed. And what I want to see for future generations is that politics of war without the bloodshed ... People who decided to fight this war, whether they were in the security services or whether they were in the paramilitaries, they should now take up this political war. That political war is about defining the issues with which we need to deal.'

Billy Hutchinson speaking to the PUP annual conference on
13 October 2012[1]

Belfast City Hall, Night, 3 December 2012

It was a freezing cold evening at the beginning of December as people gathered at the front of Belfast City Hall to enjoy the annual continental Christmas market. Couples ate bratwurst and waffles dipped in chocolate, while young men in small knots enjoyed pints of German beer and bantered with each other incessantly about football results and women. There was a positive vibe about the place as the Christmas lights sparkled brightly, advertising a city transformed and open for business. Meanwhile, at the rear of the city hall, several Landrovers from the PSNI's Tactical Support Group (TSG) began to arrive. Officers clad in black boiler suits and PSNI baseball caps dismounted from their vehicles, weapons in hand. They exuded bearing and confidence as they eyeballed a small crowd of protesters now coalescing along the big black gates outside the city's most recognisable landmarks. The police officers had seen this sort of protest action before, and were expecting trouble. Police tactical commanders were now meeting to decide on a plan as to how best handle the escalating situation.

Inside, the building councilors were meeting to debate an Alliance Party motion to restrict the number of days the union flag was to be flown over the city hall building from 365 to 15. In the run-up to the vote, the DUP and UUP distributed 40,000 flyers in an attempt to whip up grassroots opposition to the Alliance Party's proposal. On the flyer, it asked, 'A Shared Future for Who?' and claimed, by way of statistics, that most people wanted the flag to remain all year round. The flyer used emotive language in calling upon people dissatisfied by the Alliance Party to 'Let them know'. 'We can't let them make Belfast a cold house for Unionists,'[2] it stated. Unsurprisingly, for many working-class Protestants across the city, this was interpreted as a call to arms to oppose what they saw as yet another sop to republicanism. The storm of anger and frustration which the two main unionist parties had whipped up was about to break in the most profound ways. When news began to filter out to the crowd that the council had voted by twenty-nine votes to twenty-one for designated days, the crowd surged forward and clashed with the police. Several officers and a press photographer were hurt when youths attacked them with metal barriers, golf balls and glass bottles.[3] The vote acted as a lightning rod for discontent and anger and would soon see civil disturbances break out across the city.

Liz Bingham was one of those loyalists who took to the streets to protest about the removal of the union flag from Belfast City Hall. She is also the daughter of the late UVF commander John Bingham. In her view, 'The flag issue was a tipping point for working-class Protestants', many of whom 'watched the erosion of our culture and our identity', during the long years of the 'peace process'. 'It was one more step closer in a direction we were not ready to go in,' she said. For Bingham, the removal of the flag was another concession to republicans. 'We had systematically watched our culture and our traditions being taken away from us,' she added. 'We had been losing marches and parades, our police force was totally scrapped and reinvented. We saw an increase in dissident republican terrorism, the glorification of IRA murderers, with parks named after them. We felt, crucially, that politicians and politics had left us behind.' As far as she was concerned, 'The flag being taken down was the straw to break the camel's back, so to speak.'[4]

That some loyalists were beginning to reappraise their unqualified support for the Good Friday Agreement and the 'peace process' after the city council vote demonstrated just how precarious they believed their position now was. Yet, this was curious, especially since the vanguard of loyalist paramilitarism repeatedly told their supporters that the union was 'safe' in 1994, and again in 2009, when loyalist groups finally ended their armed campaign and decommissioned their weapons. As Bingham explained, 'We were promised that the Good Friday Agreement would change things and make the union safer. Instead it has never been more unstable for the Protestant community.' Few outside working-class Protestant areas could understand why protest action was gaining such momentum. For Bingham and other flag protestors, the sacrifice they made for 'peace at any price' had not been worth it. 'There was no other way to vent our anger and [so] our feet were going to have to be on the street,' she said emphatically. 'Something would have to change and we were determined [that it would].'[5]

The widespread protests that followed were incredibly disruptive, and would go on to have a massive effect on the local economy, to say nothing of how they set community relations back by a decade. People across the world were soon asking themselves: 'Aren't the "troubles" in Northern Ireland over?' and 'Why did one section of a divided community feel so strongly about national identity in a society where division was thought to have ended with the signing of the Belfast Agreement?'[6] Amidst this turmoil, some in the political class in London wondered, exasperatedly, 'Why couldn't Protestants and Catholics just get along?' Although relatively inoffensive, such remarks completely missed the undercurrent of angst that animated the unionist community, with some well-informed commentators warning how people were, 'at their very lowest ebb socially, politically and economically' in the fifteen years since the signing of the Good Friday Agreement in 1998.[7]

It would be all too convenient to explain the street protests prompted by the removal of the union flag from Belfast City Hall as a final act in the petering out of ethnic antagonism in Northern Ireland, but it should not be forgotten that unionists and nationalists have always been divided. The flag dispute, initially a cynical move by mainstream unionist parties to damage middle-class unionist support for the cross-community Alliance Party, enticed politicians back into a blame game with one another. As the opprobrium rang out across Northern Ireland the same politicians desperately sought to regain their position by seeking to provide leadership to a section of the population that refused to be led. The real momentum for the protests came from a growing underclass, who felt themselves out of sorts, not only with politics in the city hall, but also in terms of the new political dispensation at Stormont. Follow-on protests that sprouted up outside the city hall and in the likes of Newtownabbey council offices were highly organised, giving rise to accusations by political, media and policing figures that loyalist paramilitaries were becoming involved.[8] Amidst an electric atmosphere, violence was inevitable.

A week after the city council vote, police were alerted to a petrol bomb attack on the offices of Naomi Long, the Alliance MP for East Belfast. As they investigated the incident, a young policewoman narrowly escaped death when someone in a mob milling around outside the offices threw a petrol bomb at a PSNI patrol car. At the time, Long said that the violence 'bore all the hallmarks of a pogrom'.[9] The next day, Alliance Party leader David Ford, who had responsibility for justice and policing at Stormont, interpreted the violence as being a 'contest between democracy and the rule of law on the one hand, and terrorism and fascism on the other hand. There can be no ifs, no buts and no qualifications in that debate', he told those in the Stormont debating chamber.[10] Just over three hours later, at Westminster, the Secretary of State for Northern Ireland, Theresa Villiers, also condemned the attack:

> Let us be very clear: no one can be in any doubt about the Government's support for the Union and its flag, but the people engaged in the kind of violence we have seen in the past few days are not defending the Union flag. There is nothing remotely British about what they are doing. They are dishonouring and shaming the flag of our country through their lawless and violent activities. They discredit the cause that they claim to support. They are also doing untold damage to hard-pressed traders in the run-up to Christmas, and they undermine those who are working tirelessly to promote Northern Ireland to bring about investment, jobs and prosperity.[11]

Those engaged in the violence, police believed, were part of a concerted campaign of civil disturbance, which soon involved loyalist paramilitaries from the UDA and UVF.[12]

By the New Year it was being alleged by local politicians and journalists that the East Belfast and North Down UVF were behind the violence. At Stormont, Deputy First Minister Martin McGuinness told the Assembly that it was 'also quite obvious that the Ulster Volunteer Force in East Belfast has played its part in the disturbances of the past couple of weeks', alleging that two of its leading members were the 'main instigators'.[13] Loyalist paramilitary involvement was merely the accelerant being poured onto an open fire of disaffection, sectarianism and violence. For the new leader of the PUP, Billy Hutchinson, violence was a direct result of 'people's frustrations that Sinn Féin are allowed to carry out a "Brits Out" campaign in Northern Ireland'.[14] The causes might have been academic to a plethora of commentators, but as Hutchinson was making clear, the consequences of the protests were disproportionately affecting the most marginalised communities across Northern Ireland. Those involved in the hospitality industry, for instance, amongst the lowest paid workers in the region, were handed radically reduced hours on zero contracts as hundreds of tourists cancelled their trips to Belfast. The nightly violence stretched police resources and endangered the lives of the most vulnerable who couldn't access the public services they needed.

★★★

In her defiance of such intimidation and threats, Naomi Long became an implacable enemy of the UVF in East Belfast. Her party had a long record of standing up to terrorist groups on both sides of the sectarian divide, and she was not about to break with that tradition now. However, the flag protests placed her in the eye of the storm. She refused to back down from her demand that loyalists end their demonstrations. It was a brave stance for an MP to take but it placed her in immediate physical danger. 'Well I suppose in terms of the party, it's kind of hard to measure because you don't know from one election to the next what's gonna impact on ya,' she said. 'But in terms of how we've been able to operate, in terms of the pressure that staff have been under, it has been immensely difficult to maintain some kind of normal service, which we have done over the kind of last two, two and a half years, but it has been at a lot of personal cost to myself and to my staff.'[15] Her courage under fire was undeniable. She would not allow paramilitary groups to dictate the terms of her position as an MP representing the interests of her constituents, the vast majority of whom did not support violence.

It was evident that the threats and intimidation deeply affected the East Belfast MP, but you would never have known that from her defiance. 'We've had to do things differently in order to connect with communities, because there have been two issues in terms of the direct threats to myself and my staff and colleagues in terms of how safe it is for us to do things and go to places,' she later revealed. 'In terms of even confirming where we're gonna be, it's often that we don't go to things or we can't confirm in advance because it's against police advice for us to do so.'[16] Local surgeries were affected. Constituents were often afraid to be seen entering the constituency offices. 'And the flip-side of that is that it has also been intimidating for our constituents who don't want to be seen necessarily to come into the office or attend a surgery or be seen to be working with Alliance on issues, even though they'd be happy privately to come to us for help. So, we've had to do things differently,' Long said. 'I'm not going to put those people in those neighbourhoods or the police or my staff at undue risk. So, it's about trying to find the balance between that.'[17]

Naomi Long would not be deterred. 'I am absolutely determined to not have any no-go areas. I have a responsibility to stand up to this,' she said. 'There are people who are afraid to speak out … I grew up in inner East Belfast and I know the score.' Mrs Long talked passionately about how she believed in facing down the threat posed by terrorist groups like the UVF. She recalled a story of a man who had been reprimanded by the organisation because he complained about a neighbour who had become an anti-social nuisance. The neighbour, the man told the MP, was dealing drugs for the UVF. 'So, people like that don't have a lot of options. But they are in communities afraid to speak and that is one reason why I am speaking out on their behalf,' said the East Belfast politician. Naomi Long also raised the interesting point of how the PSNI were now dealing with those who are known to be members of the UVF. 'Since 1998 it is still on the statute books, but it doesn't seem to be pursued as a crime.'[18]

The intimidation, threats and physical violence exerted on an elected MP shows how far paramilitary violence and control continued to influence the lives of many people in Northern Ireland. In line with police reluctance to venture into no-go areas in republican heartlands like north and south Armagh, parts of Belfast and Derry, loyalists were now establishing no-go areas years after the major armed conflict had subsided. Unlike the physical no-go areas that were smashed by the British Army in 1972 during Operation Motorman, these no-go areas are psychological, and managed by the continuing control exerted by paramilitary groups in marginalised areas. Disaffected young people who believe they have lost out in the peace process were providing ideal cannon fodder for more unscrupulous characters, while the State remained unwilling or unable to preside over the dismantling of the edifice of paramilitarism that ruled with an iron fist across parts of Northern Ireland in these years.

***

Internally, the upsurge in violence in 2010–12 created a dilemma for the UVF's Brigade Staff. By demonstrating that they were unable to grip their most active commanders, particularly in East Belfast, it revealed the parameters of the failure to create a robust model of conflict transformation. Through behind-the-scenes manoeuvring, however, the Shankill leadership was able to convince its East Belfast battalion to return to the fold. 'Would you rather we had another LVF on our hands?' one leading member remarked.[19] And he was right in many respects. The political parties exercising rule in Belfast on behalf of the British Government in London proved unable to normalise the situation. In the vacuum of moral compromises, malign groups emerged to fill the gap.

Meanwhile, the PSNI continued to seize slot machines and drugs in East Belfast, which seemed to constitute the main source of income for the UVF in that part of the city. Owners of shop units reportedly told police, 'Thank fuck you've taken that gear away. We didn't want it here in the first place.' According to some senior police officers, UVF members remained heavily involved in drug-dealing, extortion, threats and intimidation, but were doing so amidst the lack of political will to tackle the root causes of this activity. Ironically, the local government response to loyalist violence was crude. It sought to encourage loyalist paramilitary groups to align themselves more closely with political parties like the DUP, and to apply for funding which would ensconce paramilitary leaders with more authority than they had previously enjoyed. 'It is extortion on a strategic scale,' a senior PSNI officer admitted in private.[20] In the wake of the flag protests, however, it was the only real strategy for deterring a return to civil disturbances.

★★★

North and West Belfast, May 2015

The hatred of republicans still runs deep in loyalist areas. 'Young people are angry,' says 'Rob', a spokesman for the East Antrim UVF. But is there any need for paramilitary structures? 'Here's a question for you, mate,' Rob says, posing a rhetorical question 'What if the organisation wasn't there? What would happen?'[21] This is a familiar argument put across by loyalist paramilitary leaders. It is an argument parroted by the UVF Brigade Staff and several of its area commanders.

The Protestant working class is a diverse set of people. It is much broader than loyalism. When more militant elements from within this constituency mobilised in the 1960s, they did so against the tide of modernisation that was sweeping across Northern Ireland. They believed that it threatened their existence as a people. Some followed the leadership offered by rabble-rousing clergyman Ian Paisley and other independently minded unionist politicians who stood against Terence O'Neill's liberal regime. Comparisons were quickly made between the violent response by loyalists in 2012–13 and the actions taken almost half a century earlier. Yet, such comparisons were meaningless. Yes, educational underachievement, poverty and deprivation still existed nearly half a century on from the formation of the UVF and the appearance of Ian Paisley. Yes, grassroots Protestants felt that republicans were attacking their pro-British culture. But the protests were not only about this. The editor of the *Shankill Mirror*, John MacVicar, reminded his readers that the protests were 'not about the flag, they never were just about the flag. There is a deep-rooted disillusionment within PUL working-class communities that they have been left behind by those in power at Stormont'.[22] It was this disconnection between the two big unionist parties and their grassroots followers that ran like a golden thread through the essentially leaderless protests now underway.

Surprisingly, the challenges thrown up by the flag protests were actually addressed a decade earlier. In an article for *The Other View* magazine, entitled 'Nationalist Euphoria, Unionist Despondency', Billy Mitchell observed how:

> Personally speaking, I believe that Sinn Féin's preoccupation with flags and emblems has more to do with wanting to remove any visible sign of their failure to break the link with Britain than it has to do with republican ideals. Having lost the constitutional battle they have resorted to agitating for the removal of the symbols that remind them of their failure. British symbols are a stark reminder that after a sustained campaign to break the Union, Northern Ireland remains British and that is hard for nationalists to stomach. The removal of those symbols from certain public buildings may help alleviate the pain of failure but it is nothing for nationalists to be jubilant about or for unionists to be despondent about.[23]

Mitchell passionately believed that loyalists risked playing into republican hands if they over-reacted to 'hype' and 'symbolic battles' indulged in by their opponents. His position, simply stated, was that regardless of republican attempts to remove the union flag from government buildings, this did not necessarily make them any less British. Sinn Féin, Mitchell argued in 2002, 'has actually ended up helping to administer British rule in Northern Ireland'. No attempt by Sinn Féin to resolve that contradiction would succeed. He fully appreciated unionist attachment to symbols – and even advocated political resistance to Sinn Féin's 'programme of disculturation' – but the removal of a plaque or a flag didn't concern him. He remained what he called a 'confident unionist' and, had he lived to witness the flag protests, would have undoubtedly agreed with Billy Hutchinson's elucidation of 'confident unionism' in his address to the PUP's annual party conference in 2013. In this respect, at least, it is impossible to sidestep the conclusion that the same structural inequalities that drove many young men and (occasionally) women into the ranks of armed groups still existed at this time.

That the UVF remained active in 2015 was dramatically revealed in a PSNI and MI5 assessment of paramilitary groups in Northern Ireland. Published in October 2015 in the aftermath of the Provisional IRA killing of a former member of their organisation, it was based on an intelligence-led assessment. Not only did it reinforce a view held by Naomi Long and other political representatives opposed to paramilitarism but it also showed how little progress there had been in the UVF's 2007 claim to want to transition towards a 'non-military, civilianised role'.

> The UVF's leadership has attempted to steer its membership towards peaceful initiatives and to carve out a new constructive role in representing the loyalist community. A very small number of members have taken active roles in loyalist politics with the Progressive Unionist Party (PUP). However, a larger number of members, including some senior figures, are extensively involved in organised crime including drug dealing, extortion and smuggling. Members of the UVF are involved in conducting paramilitary-style assaults on those they accuse of anti-social behaviour. These activities have a significant impact on the local community.[24]

There could be little doubt that the lack of a comprehensive strategy for disarming, demobilising and reintegrating paramilitaries into society was a key factor in prolonging UVF and RHC activity.

★★★

Mount Vernon, North Belfast, Morning, 29 January 2016

'The loyalist community and the republican community are no different,' PUP leader Billy Hutchinson emphasises.

> If you take somewhere like here. People don't get up in the morning and look out to see if there's a union flag flying. People don't get up in the New Lodge and look out and see if a tricolour's flying, but the reality is that, if they don't have a job, they've educationally underachieved, they're in bad health, in bad housing, the flag becomes important because what identity do they have? The flag. Britishness. Irishness. And that becomes their identity ... They're not getting up and walking down the street with a briefcase to Queen's or anywhere else. They're not walking over to a job that's paying them £600 a week, you know, or £2,000 a month, or whatever ...[25]

For Hutchinson, the troubles have corroded the socio-economic fabric of the marginalised communities in which the violence was most acute. Hutchinson's instincts are grounded in democratic socialist principles but his outlook is solidly unionist. His father was a bookie and a socialist who voted for the old Northern Ireland Labour Party, which opposed the established Unionist Party.[26] In this he has been influenced by exactly the same factors in his upbringing as his late colleague, David Ervine.

'I am not suggesting for one minute that, you know, the troubles was down to jobs,' Hutchinson continued.

> But the areas it affected most were working-class communities. And I laugh all the time when I hear the Provos ... telling people that this was an 'economic war'. They drove bombs out of West Belfast, past shopping centres and past establishments to plant them in Bangor and Ballymena and Portadown, which are provincial towns that would have been seen as unionist ... Nobody can tell me that they didn't have to take them risks. They could have blew up West Belfast ... They had Delorean in West Belfast. They had Viseton. None of them were blown up. You know what I mean?[27]

This is a familiar analysis that could equally have been applied to the centre of Londonderry in the early 1970s, when the Provisional IRA's Derry Brigade bombed Protestant businesses out of the city and reversed much of the economic gains that could have brought wealth and prosperity to the northwest.

And it is that legacy which affects all parts of Northern Ireland. Today, the only ships that enter Belfast harbour are Singaporian-built cruise ships carrying tourists into the city. The light engineering industries, such as they are, depend disproportionately on economic migrants from across the world than they did in the 1800s. These skilled workers are brought in to backfill gaps left in the labour force by the decline in the ranks of home-grown workers. Shipbuilding and heavy engineering skills are now outsourced by workers from Gdansk, and airplane assemblers from the Philippines. These countries have maintained their distinguished industrial heritage, unlike Northern Ireland, which has been moving towards a service-based neo-liberal economy for decades.

Belfast, once one of the great industrial cities of the world, has declined. Its major employers are public and service sectors. It is banks, supermarkets, hotels, solicitors and call centres that are major providers of jobs, rather than the old staple industries. In the early 1970s this was all so very different. If you were a young man from working-class East Belfast, you followed in the footsteps of fathers, uncles, brothers and grandfathers who 'learned their trade' as shipwrights, boilermakers and riveters. The same could be said of working-class people in other parts of the city, who worked in a plethora of jobs based on a skilled, semi-skilled and unskilled labour.

The Northern Ireland 'peace process' may be touted as a model for conflict resolution elsewhere, but there is virtually no mention of the financial cost that is needed to keep paramilitary organisations from returning to violence. Since 1997 the amount of money ploughed into the peace process has surpassed the £3 billion, and the number of community workers has risen sharply to over 27,773 (with some 60 per cent being full-time employees) in the community sector. But has this investment been worth it? Has it addressed the causes of the conflict that continue to see paramilitary organisations recruit young people into their ranks? In short, has this helped Northern Ireland deal with the legacy of its violent past?

'We never dealt with the past,' says Billy Hutchinson, as he explores the dire socio-economic conditions that prevail in Northern Ireland. It is these conditions that prevent the UVF from completing the transition towards becoming a full, civilianised grouping. 'We never dealt with flags or parades. There was nothing in the "fresh start" that suggested they were going to do anything other than put things on the long finger ... I made this point back in 2012 before the flag protests ... These communities are more sectarian than they've ever been ... We haven't dealt with sectarianism. We were part of that architecture,' Hutchinson argued. To rethink the unequivocal support for the spirit of the agreement is to risk learning that it has not delivered for the people. As early as 2012 Hutchinson was proposing a complete overhaul of the institutional architecture at Stormont to ensure marginalised voices were heard. At the beginning of 2016, he was espousing the idea of radically rethinking the power-sharing mechanism set up in the late 1990s. 'We actually need to have an opposition. At the beginning, it was the right thing to do ... We need to deal with the past otherwise we will continue.'[28] His ideas would be taken up by centrist politicians in the UUP and SDLP many months later. Once again, an idea from a former UVF activist turned PUP strategist and leader was being implemented by mainstream political leaders who were distinctly out of touch with their grassroots followers.

While Hutchinson was unequivocal in his assertion of the founding principles of the PUP, he was mindful of the challenges which still existed, including the continuing existence of the UVF.

★★★

Belfast City Centre, Afternoon, 29 January 2016

'You see every Remembrance Sunday down in that Liverpool Club you have ones that sing "We are the boys from Company B, we fired at the Rah with an RPG". They were known as the UVF's rocket team. Not one of them has ever seen an RPG,' Matthew says. It is a common sight in loyalist areas as the rest of the nation gathers to commemorate wars far from Britain's shores. Meanwhile, in Northern Ireland, young men drunk on the power UVF membership affords them gather to commemorate what some older hands in the organisation call their 'war record'. Like in other areas, most of the UVF's gunmen on the Shankill Road have walked away from their paramilitary past. The numbers actually involved in the killings were low to begin with. It is puzzling for some of these former members to hear those left in the organisation's ranks described as 'combatants'.

The broadcast journalist Malachi O'Doherty has posed a similar question of republicans that follows from such a designation: what sort of combat is this when the majority of victims are unarmed civilians? Like the exaggerated stories of combat in conventional or irregular war, it seems that the roles of some people involved in this type of warfare grow in the telling. Few of the current crop of UVF members – sometimes referred to disparagingly by the older hands as 'ceasefire soldiers' – have actually 'done the business', Matthew is at pains to stress. 'You see after the Enniskillen bomb [in 1987], the call went out for men to join up. You know how many turned up at that club [on the Shankill] to operate? Four,' he says despondently. 'I went 'round the houses. Men were coming to the doors with babies in their arms. "She's at work mate", they said. "I can't come out."[29] And, so, they stayed at home. Their 'combat' limited merely to the role of cheerleader or sympathiser.

Matthew does not want to see things return to the way they were, though there is something inside him, a determinist view of Irish history that suggests otherwise. 'You know yourself,' he says. 'Irish history works in cycles. It may only be a matter of time. I'll be too old, but all those in the areas where they are strong, all them hundreds of men will run away and hide under their beds. What I call the "special few" will remain to do what needs to be done.'[30]

It is a grim thought. Hundreds of young men may like to think of themselves as being willing to join up and become active in paramilitary activity, yet the evidence suggests otherwise. When it comes down to it, when the chips are down, only a tiny number will be prepared to pull the trigger or plant a bomb. It is these few who will become the 'fourth generation of volunteers'. Preventing this seems to be an imperative for those current and former members of the UVF who wish to see things transition. Sadly, they seem to be in a minority. Disgruntlement amongst the UVF rank and file rarely manifests itself in public. What former members call a 'war record' is a rare commodity in the UVF these days. Only a handful of gunmen and bombers have remained in the ranks and even fewer are in leadership positions. The rest have walked away. It is left to the PUP and the ACT initiative to speak on behalf of a stunted membership with a groundswell of ceasefire soldiers in its ranks. Those men whose active period ran from the worst of the troubles in the 1970s to the 1990s are conspicuous in their absence.

★★★

Rathcoole, North Belfast, 5 April 2016

'It was agreed that we form a Praetorian Guard. I was one of those who walked away. My job description was fulfilled, as vague as it was. I said, "You've got my number if you ever need me." As far as I was concerned, I believed the words of the UVF statements,' The Craftsman says enthusiastically. 'I don't drive. I don't own my own house. I don't go on foreign holidays. I shop in Primark. I didn't do it for the money. I did it because I believed I was right at the time to do so,' he argues. 'We were just ordinary guys doing what we were doing because we were taking a stand and doing what we thought was right. You might criticise that today but that's how we saw it.'[31] The chances of needing to reactivate the UVF as a military-based organisation are now slim. For a man who was rumoured to have joined the UVF on Easter Tuesday 1966, it was a remarkable journey and one which, in many ways, was mirrored by so many other former UVF members in their own respective journeys from conflict to peace.

A few months before he died, Billy Mitchell was fond of saying that he played only a small role in the UVF's internal consultation process. Far from speaking on behalf of the UVF, he would be at pains to emphasise, his role was that of facilitator. 'I am not part of their inner circles. I am more of a "critical friend",' he claimed in his characteristically self-deprecating style. 'Those I interact with would be the progressive ones.'[32] It was the 'progressive ones', people like The Craftsman, who believed in moving Northern Ireland to a better place.

It is now left to the Praetorian Guard to oversee the full and unequivocal transition of the UVF towards full civilianisation. For that to happen it will require assistance from people beyond loyalist paramilitary ranks. That means the political descendants of the Unionist Party politicians who had a hand in rejuvenating the UVF in the mid-1960s should put their shoulder to the wheel as much as the community who sustained the UVF for many years. Every willing hand will be required to come together to assist the group in completing its process of transition. It will require legislation from the British and Irish governments to ensure that those who have moved away from their paramilitary pasts can be fully reintegrated and rehabilitated into society. And it will require victims and survivors of the troubles to work through the past to address the toxic legacy of politically inspired violence and to ensure that the mantra 'never again' becomes the watchword on everyone's lips. It is an ambitious goal, and one that may well be unobtainable. That at least some of those involved in transcending the conditions that gave rise to paramilitarism in the first place – while avoiding self-interested politicians preying on the vulnerabilities and fears of the poorest citizens in society – is cause for optimism. How realistic and achievable are the requirements for others to assist in the process of dismantling paramilitary structures, however, remains to be seen.

Epilogue

THE SEALED KNOT

'To make peace is to forget. To reconcile, it is necessary that memory be faulty and limited.'

Susan Sontag, *Regarding the Pain of Others* (2003)[1]

Belfast City Centre, Afternoon, 12 July 2014

The sound of flute bands echoes round the centre of town. The high-pitched whistle pierces the heavy thunder of the Lambeg drum as the loyalist party tunes carry far and wide across the city's streets. These are primordial sounds, channelled via the rattle and hum of cheap instruments. The ghosts of ancient enmities fall into awkward step with thousands of loyalist feet. This is the annual Twelfth of July celebration, commemorating the victory of the Protestant Dutchman William III over the Catholic Englishman James II in 1690. Although the battle was fought over 325 years ago, it is fresh in the minds of those who have been marching to the beat of a strong and unconscionable ethnic lineage all their lives.

Although the Orange Order has worked hard to make this a more inclusive occasion, only one community has turned out in force to watch the parade today. Everyday shoppers are conspicuous by their absence. A few can be seen scurrying into the odd pub that has opened its doors on what, for the other community at least, is an ordinary Saturday afternoon. Any familiar sounds have long since drained away as the everyday hustle and bustle gives way to patriotic Protestants who have turned out en masse to observe Ulster's sons (and a few of its daughters) return from 'the field'. Most shops, bars and restaurants are closed on this day. People with less than passing sympathy for loyalists are on a two-week holiday overseas. Only the faithful remain behind to discharge their tribal duty. This is a big deal for one side of a deeply divided society.

I made my way alongside the bands, dodging spectators and well-wishers lining the route of the parade. One district was making its way back to Clifton Street Orange Hall but had to pass its 'traditional route' past St Patrick's Catholic Church in Donegall Street. I pushed on through the temporarily erected police lines. I was anxious to put myself in the shoes of people who took a dim view of Orange parades. Had they turned out, as many Protestants seem to believe, with the express intention of being offended? It didn't seem so. I could see that most local people were already at Mass. I arrived at the church, just after it started. I could see that it was about half-full inside. Young people mingled with old. Everyone sat quietly listening intently to the sermon. The priest led his flock from the pulpit. Incense wafted freely through the air. This was no Presbyterian service, with its threadbare oak panel interior and lack of ritual. My wish for a speedy service is granted and I stand to leave. Not too quickly – I wouldn't want people to get wind of an uninvited guest in their midst. I feel distinctly uncomfortable, even with one or two friendly faces around me. I am from the other community; an undercover Prod here to observe proceedings from an alternative perspective for an hour or two.

Outside the weather is warm, sticky even, though a downpour had given the streets a slight sprinkling of rain, which glistens like a sea of light whenever the sun catches a fleeting glimpse of the land below. I mingled with an assortment of worshippers on the pavement, local nationalists and their supporters, the SDLP politician Alban McGuinness and a gaggle of 'independent' monitors strategically placed in Donegal Street. One middle-aged man, a republican commentator, offers up a waspish observation as the bandsmen pass us by, trying desperately to keep in step to the sombre, solitary beat of the drum. 'They look like a defeated army,' he groans at me, as he gloats at a steady stream of loyalist feet. 'Whoever said these guys were supremacist needs to see how they are deflated.' It was partially true. The band were certainly well turned out and dignified, but there was a sense in which, talking to them and their supporters earlier in the day, they had lost out. Their battleground, however, was not the blood-soaked streets of the troubles but the peace process that was designed by idealists to end armed conflict and reconcile two deeply divided communities. As each Twelfth of July passes, it does little except remind Protestants, unionists and loyalists of a historic moment when they were covered in glory, a feeling that eludes them today.

The irony is not lost on me that this part of Belfast was once the hunting ground of the Shankill Butchers. It was the scene of horrific cruelty, as UVF men struck down their victims with the swing of a hammer or butcher's knife, exploded a no-warning bomb that eviscerated their bodies or cut them down in a hail of bullets. This area I find myself standing in is, in many ways, the 'ground zero' of the UVF's terror campaign.

Less than twenty-five yards from where I'm standing, three Catholic men were abducted and had their throats slashed, another was beaten to death with a wheel brace and an axe. Another Catholic civilian, 'Trevor', a real survivor of that horrible little war, ran as fast as his teenage legs could carry him as William Moore and his henchmen chased him across Union Street and into New Lodge in their black taxi, a menacing machine that trawled the city and doubled as a mobile Catholic abattoir.

Two streets over is the site of the infamous Chlorane Bar massacre, where Robert Bates and others opened fire in a room full of vulnerable men and women, targeted on the off chance that they were Catholics. One street up from here is the rear of what is now Castlecourt shopping centre, where the UVF detonated a no-warning car bomb outside a long-gone pub, killing two young Catholic men socialising with their friends on a Saturday night. Halfway between these two sites is graffiti scrawled on shop shutters that reads 'RHC'. Even though the broken bodies have long since been interred, the debris of bombs cleared away, and the memories of such atrocities faded, there is little sign of the hate evaporating into the Belfast drizzle on this Twelfth of July afternoon.

★★★

It is eight months since I watched the loyalist bandsmen march past St Patricks as they made their way back to their respective orange halls in North and West Belfast. By now the weather has transitioned from summer, through a cold, blustery winter and into spring. I am in the place of my birth, Newtownabbey, on a visit home, when I receive a message from a man close to the local UVF, asking me what time I want to meet. He's eager to show me something. 'Can I call down a wee bit earlier Monkstown?' he inquires. I readily agree, as it's only a short stroll from where I'm staying. I make off towards the village. As I reach the rat-run into Monkstown from the Doagh Road, I shoot a glance across to the hockey pitches where there are several knots of men gathered, maybe 100 in total, all formed up and being drilled in smaller groups. I'm spotted by my contact, and called over. There is a sense of quiet aggression in the air. These are serious men, on a serious mission. They are clearly preparing for some kind of commemorative event. Young and old, drawn from working-class housing estates across East Antrim. I am puzzled. Whatever this is, it is no 'sealed knot', the organisation founded in the 1960s, which involved members recreating English Civil War battles. These are not middle-aged men, desperate to escape the reality of their humdrum lives by dressing up and playing soldiers. No. This is something altogether edgier, more purposeful, even. This seems to be the remnants of the modern-day East Antrim UVF on parade.

A year earlier, the Larne gunrunning parade had been the largest UVF commemorative event to be staged since the organisation first emerged from the shadows at the funeral of Sinclair Johnston in Larne in 1972. Then, it was a commander of the East Antrim UVF, Billy Mitchell, who had ordered that the men and women under his command parade in their revolutionary-style black uniforms, complete with masks, dark glasses and cap comforters. Nowadays, the men stand around in little squads, resting between being marched around the hockey pitches that double as a parade square. They were dressed casually, in jeans and jumpers. A few even wear tracksuits. That some were being drilled according to Vietnam-era American commands seems ludicrous to me. Here I was, witnessing the past being recreated without even a hint of irony or humour. Images of men parading around the compounds of Long Kesh or at gable ends on Remembrance Sundays flood my mind. These are men making an explicit connection with the past. In their ritualism they are, unwittingly perhaps, joining the original UVF with its most recent incarnation.

It was working-class areas like this that provided the cannon fodder for Britain's wars. One hundred years ago there had been no shortage of men willing to commit themselves to the colours, to march blindly into the enemy's guns on foreign battlefields. To give one's life for a cause greater than one's own did not matter as much as giving one's life for one's friend. It's a legacy that matters to some people, even today. But it is a memory tinged with irony. In these working-class communities there is a great feeling of having been abandoned by the state. Paramilitaries have been permitted to fill the gap, long after they should have departed the stage. In places where life hands its young people few opportunities, there is little alternative other than to get out or to stay and live under the writ of unelected paramilitarists. The sense of despair in places like this is palpable. Although they do not see it, or choose to ignore it, there is a disconnection between leaders and followers. In the haste to move the Northern Ireland 'problem' off the mainstream political agenda in London, power has been outsourced to a divided Northern Ireland Assembly and Executive that has done little to tackle sectarianism, disaffection or, even, to break the hold which paramilitary groups exert over these marginalised areas. It is conditions like these that have ensured the UVF remains in existence.

At that moment, I remember the words of the great American writer Mark Twain. 'History,' he wrote, 'does not repeat itself, but it does rhyme.' The trouble with Northern Ireland is that the past has a habit of repeating itself so frequently that it teeters on the brink of becoming farcical.

I am struck by the misguided sense of patriotism on display in Monkstown. I have seen it many times before. Ulster loyalism, high as a kite on nostalgia, sits willingly in a cul-de-sac, rather than at a crossroads. It is like other forms of nationalism. The Canadian-born liberal journalist and politician Michael Ignatieff was one of the first analysts of the post-Cold War era to bear witness to the bloody degeneration of places like Northern Ireland into ethnic civil war. 'With blithe lightness of mind,' he wrote, 'we assumed that the world was moving irrevocably beyond nationalism, beyond tribalism, beyond the provincial confines of the identities inscribed in our passport, towards a global market culture which was to be our new home.' This was part idealism, part fantasy, thought Ignatieff, for 'we were whistling in the dark. The repressed has returned, and its name is nationalism'.[2] Nowhere is this more readily apparent than in marginalised communities across Northern Ireland.

Despite the well-intentioned analysis advanced by (perhaps) well-meaning people, there is still a niggling feeling that Ulster loyalism, as a form of this repressed nationalism, had taken a perilous route years earlier. Now, no one was quite sure how to get back to where they started. As one prominent UVF member told me, 'the endgame' for his organisation 'should have been fifteen years ago'. That it hasn't wound up and that it is an organisation that includes rank upon rank of teenagers and young men, to say nothing of older men who should know better, demonstrates how far this particular section of a marginalised community has been marking time, destined to repeat the mistakes of the past, as the world around them marches onwards into a (hopefully) brighter future. That they were drilling with dummy rifles that day in Monkstown was an irony not lost on me. The futility of their martial choreography looks ridiculous. I might even say, unkindly, that it looks somewhat sinister to the uninitiated. The point, however, is that it percolates through the ranks of these men with a sincerity and sense of belonging that should not be underestimated.

A century on from the tumultuous events which saw the gun first introduced into Irish politics, and a generation after the paramilitary ceasefires and Belfast Agreement, Irish nationalists and Ulster unionists remain as bitterly divided as ever. Not only are they divided on issues like the flying of flags, commemorative parading, the legacy of the past and the constitutional future of Northern Ireland, but we find that there has not yet been a genuine attempt to facilitate a reconciliation process. The region is governed according to the logic of a 'peace process' that was designed by a British Government eager to placate the interests of two communities who choose, willingly, to live separate lives, while, importantly, keeping the British mainland insulated from the violent challenges posed by Irish republican terrorism. Elements of this peace process were imported from abroad, such as the belief that the best way to deal with diametrically opposed views is to formalise and entrench them in power-sharing structures. Consequently, this deep-freezing of ethnic conflict in society and politics has forestalled the development of an alternative political culture, based on a reimbursement of social justice and the bridging of a yawning gap between its people, which is surely the best way to stave off the prospect of future violence. As an organisation, the UVF is representative of a physical force tradition that has run through the Protestant community since the seventeenth century. It will continue to rear its ugly head whenever Protestants feel the union between Great Britain and Northern Ireland is under threat, whether that threat is real or imagined.

Yet, the more I see young men forming up under the banner of paramilitary organisations, the more I recall the rich personal memoirs of Professor Geoffrey Beattie, who wrote so movingly and attentively about growing up in the Protestant working-class community. In his illuminating narrative of returning to his home at the turn of the road near Ligoniel, perched high above Belfast City, Beattie reflected on those who he had known growing up who had joined the UVF. Their number had included men who have stalked the earlier pages of this book:

'Who will save Ulster?' was the question on everyone's lips at the time. I always assumed this was rhetorical. It's the same in any war. Who does the responsibility always fall on? Who pays the ultimate price? The answer is the kind of lads who hung around the corner. Who decides whether it is a war or not? And who makes the strategic decisions? And who makes the profit out of war? The answer is –

unknown individuals, but definitely not the lads from the corner. And so it turned out.[3]

Even now there are plenty of young men and women who remain supportive to the cause of loyalist militancy. They believe that the only way to stop the other side from getting what they want politically is to 'hit back'. It is regrettable that some senior loyalists believe the only safety valve that these young people have in their lives is the perpetuation of paramilitary organisations that prey on these fears and vulnerabilities.

★★★

'I have no regrets about my involvement,' a former UVF prisoner tells me. 'Those who got it deserved it. They got what was coming to them.'[4] For the past couple of hours, 'Thomas' has regaled me with tales of paramilitary activity that would make your hair stand on end. He relives his experiences and the experiences of others by driving me around the places that were formative in his life, and marking waypoints in his journey through the ranks of the UVF. We talk about members of the organisation, past and present. He throws nicknames at me that are plays on the surnames of a litany of men who have killed, maimed and gone to jail for the organisation. The body count keeps piling up. I'm numbed by the experience. 'One death a tragedy,' I think of the horrific quote attributed to Stalin, 'one million a statistic'. But all the perpetrators have names. He grew up with them. He knows them intimately. The victims, in turn, are nameless. They have been dehumanised. I remember their names. Who could ever forget the bloody tapestry of death and destruction unleashed on our streets by those who took the law into their own hands?

As Thomas talks, the death toll ticks over in my mind like the rolling digital display on the Iraq body count. Like US General Tommy Franks, the UVF doesn't do body counts, only when it's necessary to illustrate a point as to how effective they believe they've been. At what, I'm not quite sure. 'They were sent to bate that fella and ended up caving his head in,' he says, dismissive of the casual terror visited upon a man who subsequently died of his injuries. Some working-class Protestants involved in paramilitarism obviously take pride in their work, even when it is death-dealing. It turns out that one UVF leader in the local area suspected the man who died of being involved in something 'sexual'. UVF members were sent to rough him up, but ended up killing him. It was, apparently, a 'mistake'. Most of the UVF's murders seem to be casual errors, like when people pour the wrong type of fuel into their vehicle. It's an innocent mistake that can have huge implications, and may even be costly to rectify. When a UVF gang killed John Harbinson in May 1997, it was rumoured that the men who did it were punished by being 'hit a dig on the gub. Hardly fair punishment for taking a man's life, but there you go,' says Thomas.

Then he's off again. We take a right, then follow a narrow road until another sharp right and drive down into a lock-up area with garages on either side, and rubbish all around. Thomas pulls up outside the rear of a derelict building. It's a place of great significance to him. He wears his recollection of being arrested near here like a badge of honour. 'I was caught red-handed,' he says. I wonder if the red hand is a metaphor for his involvement in loyalist paramilitarism. He continues his story. I can see it's a cathartic experience for him to talk it all through, and to rationalise what he has borne witness to during his long years associated with the UVF.

He asks me what I'm interested in finding out about the organisation. 'You must have questions,' he inquires. 'I have questions, but I don't want to interrupt the flow of conversation,' I reply. I tell him I'm interested in the motivations of people like him. 'Why and how could you do what you did?' I ask. Like other loyalist paramilitaries, he distances himself from the action by talking me through how a UVF man he heard about on the 'grapevine' called to a house to kill a woman. As she turned to run he aimed his sawn-off shotgun at her back and pulled the trigger. She tried to drag herself to safety. 'He went over and grabbed her by the hair,' Thomas informs me, in a slightly sardonic way, 'then lifted her head up and shot her point-blank in the back of the head with the shotgun. Her fucking head came away from her body.' At this point I feel nauseous.

Thomas then talks about another man lured to his death on the pretence of a surprise birthday party. 'The fella then walked up to him, casual-like, and blew his fucking head off. He then tells me about the piece of brain, or whatever the fuck it was, flying out of the side of his head as the blood spattered all over the optics.' He laughs, nervously, unsure about how I'm going to react. I don't find it funny. He doesn't seem to either, really. But he assures me that the UVF member who told him the story said his 'stomach went at the sight of blood'. As if that makes his capacity for cruelty and barbarity more comprehensible. 'Funniest thing, isn't it,' he asks rhetorically as he drops me off. I get out and shut the door. He beeps his horn as he drives off, heading back to the crime scenes where he still lives, back into the depths of an estate, like so many others across Northern Ireland, that is unreconciled to the legacy of past violence, the intimacy of which only makes sense to a tiny number of people.

For me though, this ghost train has finally come to a halt. I get off willingly and head back inside. Another stark reminder, if one was needed, that the past has a habit of infecting the present like some kind of virulent disease, while corrupting the prospects for a more peaceful future.

★★★

In another part of the city I am back for a cup of coffee with Matthew. He likes to emphasise certain words when he talks. A native of the Shankill, his accentuated working-class vowels seep through when he is enjoying an in-joke with Luke, one of his comrades from their active period. We delve into a particularly uncomfortable conversation about a transgendered kid at Luke's son's school. 'The world has taken a turn for the worst these days,' he complains, 'whenever kids don't even know what they are.'[5] He leaves the observation hanging. I am more than a little reticent about parading my liberal credentials in front of two men for whom talk of a violent past, working with your hands and gauging the virility of the fella sat opposite them is more a right than simply a rite of passage in the community.

No matter how far Luke has moved in life, having left behind his paramilitary past for a bright future, he hasn't quite abandoned all of his prejudices. Who am I to change his mind? He and Matthew share some more in-jokes as I plough ahead with a soft-centred liberal response to defend people who are different from the men sitting in front of me. But it is of little use. As the conversation trails off, 'they' have been allocated the same status as those 'dishonest republicans' who have squandered peace for the sake of raw power and the steady flow of palm-pressing gratification on the world stage.

'How's that tune go,' Matthew blurts out, as he begins to hum the Leonard Cohen classic 'Everybody Knows'. It's not long before he breaks into the lyrics he's been rummaging through his mind to find. 'Everybody knows that the war is over,' he hums. 'Everybody knows that the good guys lost'. It's clear that despite both men having been part of the UVF's war, they took opposing views on the peace process. Matthew saw it as a sell-out, while Luke believed that the leadership was right to wind things down when it did. Both men wouldn't have done anything differently, though they are at pains to make clear to me that they don't wish to see other young people go to jail in the future. They have been there, done that and got the T-shirt. They know the awful consequences of a life of militancy.

★★★

A few weeks later Matthew rings me up. 'What was it all for,' he asks rhetorically. 'Twenty-two years on from the ceasefires, and there's not even a shop in this estate.' I think about asking him to go a step further, and outline for me how this might be rectified. How can loyalists make peace with the past so that they can move forward into the future as full citizens of the 'new Northern Ireland'? I stop short, for I fear I already know his answer.

'God bless,' he says, as he rings off.

My mind begins to drift back to Leonard Cohen's haunting lyrics. Did the good guys really lose? And who are the good guys anyway?

ENDNOTES

Preface

1   Bloch, Marc, *The Historian's Craft* (Manchester: Manchester University Press ([1954], 2012), p. 163.
2   Ignatieff, Michael, *The Warrior's Honor* (London: Vintage, 1999), p. 175.
3   I made this observation prior to one nationalist daily in Northern Ireland claiming that in Rathcoole, the working class housing estate where I am from, 90% of residents had 'connections' to loyalist paramilitaries. See Young, Connla 'Loyalist Connections for 90% of Rathcoole Estate', *Irish News*, 30 September 2015. Archived at: http://www.irishnews.com/news/2015/09/30/news/rathcoole-loyalist-connections-claim-277514/. Accessed: 30 September 2015.
4   This is a point made by David Miller in his first class analysis of Ulster loyalism and unionism, *Queen's Rebels* (Dublin: UCD Press, [1978], 2007), p. 150.
5   Very few commentators on the Northern Irish 'troubles' are prepared to make this case. Journalist Malachi O'Doherty is one of those. In his influential *The Trouble with Guns*, he summarised the challenge as follows: 'There is, however, a tendency to explain all violence in Northern Ireland as if it emerges simply from the unstable mix of intercommunal chemistry, without anyone actually being responsible. That is as simplistic and shallow an explanation as pure conspiracy theory', O'Doherty, Malachi, *The Trouble with Guns: Republican Strategy and the Provisional IRA* (Belfast: Blackstaff, 1998), p. 43.

Prologue

1   Santayana, George, *Soliloquies in England and Later Soliloquies* (London: Constable and Company, 1922), p. 102.
2   Greer's running mate was former UVF life-sentence prisoner Angus Knell, who was eliminated from the count and whose votes (85 of 134) transferred to Greer on the fifth count in the PR(STV) election saw him carried to victory. Greer would fall foul of the effective vote management system put in place by the dominant UUP and DUP parties in the 2001 local government elections, failing to be returned despite gaining 811 first-preference votes.
3   Statistics taken from McKittrick, David, Seamus Kelters, Brian Feeney and Chris Thornton *Lost Lives* (Edinburgh: Mainstream, 2001), p. 1495 and CAIN, http://cain.ulst.ac.uk/sutton/

Chapter 1

1   Hamilton, Lord Ernest W. *The Soul of Ulster* (London: Hurst and Blackett Ltd., 1917), p. 138.
2   Dudley Edwards, Ruth *The Faithful Tribe: An Intimate Portrait of the Loyal Institutions* (London: HarperCollins, 1999), p. 218.

3   Gibbon, Peter, *The Origins of Ulster Unionism: The Formation of Popular Protestant Politics and Ideology in Nineteenth Century Ireland* (Manchester: Manchester University Press, 1975), pp. 35–7; p. 39.

4   The modernisation project is usually associated with the Unionist Government led by Captain Terence O'Neill, who served as Northern Ireland Prime Minister between 1963 and 1969. For more on the modernisation programme see Mulholland, Marc, *Northern Ireland at the Crossroads: Ulster Unionism in the O'Neill Years, 1960-9* (Basingstoke: Macmillan, 2000).

5   Several excellent biographies of Ian Paisley have appeared over the years, including Moloney, Ed *Ian Paisley: From Demagogue to Democrat* (Dublin: Poolbeg, 2008) and Bruce, Steve *Paisley: Religion and Politics in Northern Ireland* (Oxford: Oxford University Press, 2009). Both books are updated studies conducted by both commentators in the 1980s.

6   According to some scholars, physical-force republicanism was down but by no means out. For more on the Paisley interventions see the excellent work of Simon Prince and Geoffrey Warner; Prince, Simon and Geoffrey Warner, *Belfast and Derry in Revolt: A New History of the Start of the Troubles* (Dublin: Irish Academic Press, 2011), pp. 66–7.

7   Dillon, Martin, *God and the Gun: The Church and Irish Terrorism* (London: Orion, 1997), p. 270.

8   Taylor, Peter, *Loyalists* (London: Bloomsbury, 1999), p. 34.

9   Garland, Roy, *Gusty Spence* (Belfast: Blackstaff, 2001), p. 48.

10   Dillon, *God and the Gun*, pp. 228–9.

11   Author interview with Billy Mitchell, 20 August 2002.

12   Public Record Office for Northern Ireland (hereafter PRONI), HA/32/2/8, Fiftieth Anniversary of the Easter Rising, Hon. Secretary to RWB McConnell, 9 October 1965.

13   Ibid., Top Secret Report on a meeting between the RUC and a deputation of loyalists, 15 March 1966.

14   Ibid.

15   Northern Ireland House of Commons Debates (Hansard), Vol. 64, Session 1965–6 (Belfast 1966), Col. 2280.

16   Taylor, Peter, *Provos: The IRA and Sinn Féin* (London: Bloomsbury, 1997), p. 25.

17   In reality the IRA had nowhere near that number of volunteers at its disposal. In the minutes of an IRA meeting held a year later in August 1967, the organisation's own leadership put the numbers at 614 volunteers on its books, only 274 were judged 'effective'. Only 212 of the total, a little over a third, were members of Sinn Féin. Furthermore, the Quarter Master estimated that the IRA had 'a very limited amount of arms and explosives', barely enough 'ammo for one good job'. See Hanley, Brian, *The IRA: A Documentary History, 1916-2005* (Dublin: Gill & Macmillan, 2010), p. 150.

18   PRONI, HA/32/2/8, Crime Special Report to the RUC Inspector General on Paisley's sermon 'The 1916 Rebellion – Should it be Celebrated in Northern Ireland', 3 April 1966.

19   In later years Paisley consistently denied any wrongdoing, or that he ever had any detailed knowledge of the clandestine attempts by his underlings to form an armed group. See Taylor, *Loyalists*, pp. 37–8. Journalist David Boulton, however, argued that, whether Paisley 'recognised or cared to admit it, the UVF was largely a product of his

own rhetoric and some of his closest associates were UVF men'. Boulton, David *The UVF 1966–73: An Anatomy of Loyalist Rebellion* (Dublin: Torc, 1973), pp. 51–2.

20 Boulton, *The UVF*, p. 31; p. 34.
21 PRONI, HA/32/2/8, Letter from Doherty to the Minister for Home Affairs, 6 April 1966.
22 PRONI, BELF/1/1/2/214/28, Statement of James F. Marshall, 27 June 1966.
23 'Reprisals Story in Court', *Belfast Telegraph*, 18 October 1966.
24 PRONI, BELF/1/1/2/215/7, Statement of Noel Doherty, 6 July 1966.
25 Taylor, *Loyalists*, p. 38.
26 PRONI, BELF/1/1/2/215/7, Statement of George Edward Bigger, 27 June 1966. Boulton reiterates the point Bigger made to police that he kept the gelignite and the gun at his home. Boulton, *The UVF*, p. 42. Interestingly, Boulton suggests that Bigger and Reid were members of the Shankill UVF, not the UPV.
27 PRONI, BELF/1/1/2/214/35, L.W. Smith to Leonard Fox, 15 October 1966.
28 PRONI, BELF/1/1/2/214/35, District Foreman to Fox Solicitors, 17 October 1966.
29 Boulton, *The UVF*, p. 42.
30 PRONI, BELF/1/1/2/214/35, Statement of Hugh Arnold McClean to Detective Constable Leo McBrien and Constable McMahon, 27 June 1966.
31 PRONI, BELF/1/1/2/215/7, Statement of George Edward Bigger, 27 June 1966.
32 PRONI, BELF/1/1/2/214/35, Statement of Hugh Arnold McClean to Detective Constable Leo McBrien and Constable McMahon, 27 June 1966.
33 PRONI, BELF/1/1/2/215/7, Statement of Noel Doherty, 6 July 1966.
34 Ibid.
35 Garland, Roy, *Seeking a Political Accommodation – The Ulster Volunteer Force: Negotiating History* (Belfast: Shankill Community Publication, 1997), p. 7.
36 Garland, *Gusty Spence*, p. 48.
37 Some of the oral history contributions collated for this book have been difficult to verify in the absence of written evidence, so it would be wrong to speculate. However, it appears that the archival record has been completely expunged of all mention of this suspected high-level conspiracy, which is suspicious for, even if it was an invention of the men subsequently arrested and prosecuted, it is reasonable to assume that the RUC would have had intelligence (in the absence of evidence) either proving or disproving its existence, yet no paper trail exists. For more on this point see Hugh Jordan's excellent book *Milestones in Murder: Defining Moments in Ulster's Terror War* (Edinburgh: Mainstream Publishing, 2002), pp. 50–1.
38 Harbinson, John F. *The Ulster Unionist Party, 1882–1973: Its Development and Organisation* (Belfast: Blackstaff Press, 1973), p. 182, p. 191.

Chapter 2

1 PRONI, BELF/1/1/2//215/3, Statement of James Doherty, 2 September 1966.
2 Private information, 2006.
3 Sociologists studying violence are of the opinion that killing is neither easy nor something that comes naturally to human beings. For more on this point see Collins, Randall, *Violence: A Micro-sociological Theory* (New Jersey: Princeton, 2008).

4   *Belfast Telegraph*, 21 May 1966.

5   Garland, *Gusty Spence*, p. 49.

6   Ibid., pp. 48–9.

7   PRONI, BELF/1/1/2/214/23, Statement of Harry Johnston, dated 21 August 1966.

8   Sociologist Sarah Nelson's research in the 1970s unveiled the Orange Order, as well as the workplace and recreational pursuits, to be an important catalyst for UVF recruitment. As one former UVF prisoner told her, 'After the Shankill meetings you'd get together and talk politics and discuss plans. I was very young then but I met a lot of UVF men and listened to them. They were my heroes in a way.' Nelson, Sarah *Ulster's Uncertain Defenders?* (Belfast: Appletree Press, 1984), p. 63.

9   Ibid., p. 65.

10   PRONI, BELF/1/1/2/214/35, Statement of George Edward Bigger, 27 June 1966.

11   PRONI, BELF/1/1/2/214/35, Statement of Leslie Thomas Porter, 27 June 1966.

12   PRONI, BELF/1/1/2/215/3, Statement of Alexander McClean, 2 September 1966.

13   McKittrick *et al*, *Lost Lives*, p. 26.

14   See Dillon, Martin, *The Shankill Butchers: A Case Study of Mass Murder* (London: Arrow Books, 1989), p. 14.

15   PRONI, BELF/1/1/2/214/23, Statement of Robert James Williamson, 29 June 1966.

16   Telephone interview with an eyewitness, 27 February 2016.

17   House of Commons Debates (Hansard), 28 June 1966, Vol. 730, Col. 1586.

18   Ibid.

19   Northern Ireland House of Commons Debates (Hansard), 28 June 1966, Vol. 64, Col. 652–653.

20   PRONI, BELF/1/1/215/3, Statement of Detective Sergeant Robert Agar, 2 September 1966.

21   'Ward Murder: Detective Denies IRA Remark', *Belfast Telegraph*, 5 October 1966.

22   This is an extremely important point noted by Steve Bruce in his book *God Save Ulster! The Religion and Politics of Paisleyism* (Oxford: Oxford University Press, 1986), p. 80. It points to the desperate nature of the RUC investigation and must leave open the possibility of a reappraisal of Spence's conviction.

23   PRONI, BELF/1/1/215/3, Statement of D/Constable George Thompson, 2 September 1966.

24   PRONI, BELF/1/1/2//215/3, Statement of Dr John Martin, Industrial Science and Forensic Laboratory, Verner Street, Belfast, 2 September 1966.

25   *Belfast Telegraph*, 8 October 1966.

26   Ibid.

27   Ibid.

28   PRONI, BELF/1/1/2/209/26, The Queen v. Augustus Andrew Spence.

29   PRONI, BELF/1/1/2/209/26, Deposition of Ronald Stone, 1 March 1965.

30   PRONI, BELF/1/1/2/209/26, Deposition of D/Constable Leonard V. McConaghy of Queen Street RUC Station.

31   *Belfast Telegraph*, 7 October 1966.

32   Anon, *A Special Category Book of Poem and Verse, compiled in Long Kesh by a Red Hand Commando–UVF Prisoner of War* (Belfast, 1973).

33   *The Round Table*, No. 224 (October 1966), p. 406.

34   Taylor, *Loyalists*, p. 43.

35   Author interview with Billy Mitchell, 20 August 2002.

36   Garland, *Seeking a Political Accommodation*, p. 10.

37   Taylor, *Loyalists*, p. 61.

38   O'Neill, Terence *The Autobiography of Terence O'Neill* (London: Hart-Davies, 1972), p. 87.

39   PRONI, D/4547, Ben Forde Collection, Billy Mitchell's Essay on Guilt: A Personal Testimony, dated 1985.

40   Ibid.

41   Ibid.

42   Author interview with Tommy Gorman, 23 June 2011.

43   O'Doherty, Malachi *The Trouble with Guns: Republican Strategy and the Provisional IRA* (Belfast: Blackstaff, 1998), pp. 55–6.

44   Hanley, Brian and Scott Millar *The Lost Revolution: The Story of the Official IRA and the Workers' Party* (Dublin: Penguin Ireland, 2009), p. 61.

45   Interview with Roy Garland, 20 May 2003. Garland would later come to reject what he viewed as 'close mindedness', preferring to expound a more progressive form of unionism.

46   *The Irish Times*, 9 March 1976.

47   Ibid.

48   Garland, *Seeking a Political Accommodation*, p. 11.

49   Private information, 2016.

Chapter 3

1   Ulster Volunteer Force Recruiting Circular (1971), cited in Carlton, Charles (ed.), *Bigotry and Blood Documents on the Ulster Troubles* (Chicago: Nelson-Hall 1977), p. 90.

2   You can read more about the trials and tribulations of this Ulster Labour tradition in the post-war period in Edwards, Aaron, *A History of the Northern Ireland Labour Party: Democratic Socialism and Sectarianism* (Manchester: Manchester University Press, 2009).

3   Devlin, Paddy, *Straight Left: An Autobiography* (Belfast: Blackstaff, 1993), p. 80.

4   O'Doherty, Malachi *The Trouble with Guns: Republican Strategy and the Provisional IRA* (Belfast: Blackstaff, 1998), p. 13.

5   The chaos sparked by intercommunal violence and its effects on the growth of Protestant paramilitary groupings is usefully explored by Gareth Mulvenna in his book *Tartan Gangs and Paramilitaries: The Loyalist Backlash* (Liverpool: Liverpool University Press, 2016), particularly within Chapter 4.

6   Campbell later said, 'That particular incident … sorry, I actually knew nothing about that, until half an hour before it took place.' McGurk, John 'McGurk's bar massacre victim confronts killer', *Belfast Telegraph*, 1 March 2011.

7   Details of the bombing can be found in the Police Ombudsman of Northern Ireland report, *Public Statement by the Police Ombudsman relating to the complaint by relatives of victims of the bombing of McGurk's Bar on 4 December 1971* (Belfast: PONI, 2011), pp. 40–1.

8   Garland, Roy, *Seeking a Political Accommodation – The Ulster Volunteer Force: Negotiating History* (Belfast: Shankill Community Publication, 1997), p. 9.

9   The people who died in the explosion were: James Cromie (13), Maria McGurk (14), Edward Kane (29), Robert Spotswood (35), Philomena McGurk (46), Thomas Kane (48), John Colton (49), David Milligan (53), Kathleen Irvine (53), Thomas McLaughlin (55), Sarah Keenan (58), James Smyth (58), Francis Bradley (63), Edward Keenan (69) and Phillip Garry (73). All of them were Catholic civilians from the local community.

10 The incident and its legacy are expertly analysed in Martin J. McCleery. See his *Operation Demetrius and its Aftermath: A New History of the Use of Internment without Trial in Northern Ireland, 1971–75* (Manchester: Manchester University Press, 2015), pp. 68–9.

11 McDonald, Henry and Jim Cusack *UDA: Inside the Heart of Loyalist Terror* (Dublin: Penguin Ireland, 2005), p. 22.

12 Devlin, *Straight Left*, p. 151.

13 McKittrick *et al*, *Lost Lives: The Stories of the Men, Women and Children who died as a result of the Northern Ireland troubles – Revised and Updated Edition* (Edinburgh: Mainstream Publishing, 2001), pp. 102–3, 105, 114–15.

14 Edwards, Aaron, 'Misapplying Lessons Learned? Analysing the Utility of British Counter-insurgency Strategy in Northern Ireland, 1971–76', *Small Wars & Insurgencies*, 21(2) (June 2010), p. 308. See also Sanders, Andrew, 'Operation Motorman (1972) and the search for a coherent British counterinsurgency strategy in Northern Ireland', *Small Wars & Insurgencies*, 24(3) (2013), p. 471. Much of the academic and popular understanding of internment has been revised by the excellent research undertaken by McCleery. See his *Operation Demetrius and its Aftermath*.

15 Edwards, Aaron, '"A whipping boy if ever there was one"? The British Army and the Politics of Civil–Military Relations in Northern Ireland, 1969–79', *Contemporary British History*, 28(2) (June 2014), pp. 166–89.

16 It used to be thought that Chief Superintendent Frank Lagan was excluded from this meeting. In fact, the Saville Inquiry discovered that he had been present. See The Bloody Sunday Inquiry Report. Archived at: http://webarchive.nationalarchives.gov.uk/20101103103930/http://report.bloody-sunday-inquiry.org/volume01/chapter009/. Accessed: 19 September 2016.

17 This was the conclusion reached by the Saville Inquiry. See Bloody Sunday Inquiry Report, Chapter 3. Archived at: http://webarchive.nationalarchives.gov.uk/20101103103930/http://report.bloody-sunday-inquiry.org/volume01/chapter003/. Accessed: 19 September 2016.

18 The National Archives, Kew, London (hereafter TNA), DEFE 25/295, The Defence Implications to Great Britain of a United Ireland, Letter from Nairne to Crawford, 22 February 1972.

19 TNA, DEFE 25/295, The Defence Implications to Great Britain of a United Ireland, dated 16 February 1972.

20 Devlin, *Straight Left*, pp. 163–4.

21 *Herald Scotland*, 29 November 1993.

22 For a more comprehensive treatment of British policy at this time, see Hennessey, Thomas, *The Evolution of the Troubles, 1970–72* (Dublin: Irish Academic Press 2007).

23 *Sunday Press*, 12 March 1972.

24 Bowyer Bell, J. *The Secret Army: A History of the IRA* (Cambridge, Massachusetts: MIT Press, 1974), p. 373.

25 Bodleian Library Special Collections, Oxford University (hereafter BLSC), Harold Wilson Papers, MS. Wilson, C. 908, Fol. 85, 'Dublin, March 13, 1972'.

26 McCleery, *Operation Demetrius and its Aftermath*, p. 40–1, p. 170.

27 BLSC, Wilson Papers, C. 908, Fol. 86, 'Dublin, March 13, 1972'.

28 TNA, PREM 15/1004, Secret and Personal letter on Northern Ireland from Alec Douglas-Home to Ted Heath, 13 March 1972.

29 *Lost Lives* attributes the killing to the UDA. However, the CAIN website states that the UVF was responsible. See McKittrick *et al*, *Lost Lives*, p. 165. For the CAIN entry see http://cain.ulst.ac.uk/sutton/chron/1972.html

30 McKittrick *et al*, *Lost Lives*, p. 1469.

31 Taylor, Peter, *Loyalists* (London: Bloomsbury, 1999), p. 96.

32 Fisk, Robert, 'Test of Vanguard power today', *The Times*, 27 March 1972.

33 McDonald and Cusack, *UDA*, p. 22.

34 Professor Steve Bruce makes the important point that 'What separated the UDA from the UVF was its ambition to be a mass social and political movement'. Both groups did not, however, enjoy the support from all classes in the Ulster Protestant community. As Bruce observed, in 1970, 'only the working classes were so stirred' by the threat posed by militant republicans. See Bruce, Steve, *The Edge of the Union: The Ulster Loyalist Political Vision* (Oxford: Oxford University Press, 1994), p. 5.

35 McDonald and Cusack, *UDA*, p. 24.

36 *The Times*, 15 November 1971.

37 Fisk, Robert, 'Mr Faulkner condemns advisory commission plan as undemocratic', *The Times*, 28 March 1972.

38 PRONI, GOV/3/3/129A, HQNI, Northern Ireland Operational Summary, 21–6 April 1972.

39 McKittrick *et al*, *Lost Lives*, p. 211.

40 Ibid., p. 239. My thanks to Dr Martin McCleery for his assistance with this section.

Chapter 4

1 United Kingdom House of Commons Debates (Hansard), 24 July 1972, Vol. 841, Col. 1351.

2 PRONI, BELF/6/1/1/38/30A, Deposition of Depot Manager, 15 February 1973.

3 Sinnerton, Henry, *David Ervine: Unchartered Waters* (Dingle: Brandon, 2002), p. 30.

4 Taylor, *Loyalists*, pp. 108–9.

5 Private information, July 2016.

6 Myers, Kevin, *Watching the Door: Cheating Death in 1970s Belfast* (London: Atlantic Books, 2006), p. 95.

7 Ibid. p. 96.

8   Mitchell, Billy, *The Principles of Loyalism: An Internal Discussion Paper* (Belfast, 2002), pp. 65–6.

9   Author interview with Billy Mitchell, 4 May 2001.

10   Mitchell, *The Principles of Loyalism*, pp. 65–6.

11   Author interview with Billy Mitchell, 27 September 2005.

12   PRONI, BELF/6/1/1/37/123A, Post-Mortem relating to the death of Ted Pavis, dated 29 September 1972.

13   PRONI BELF/6/1/1/37/123A, Statement taken by CID, 3 October 1972.

14   Ibid.

15   Dillon, Martin, *The Shankill Butchers: A Case-study in Mass Murder* (London: Arrow Books, 1990), p. 28.

16   PRONI, BELF/6/1/1/37/123A, Statement by Mervyn Connor, 16 January 1973. I have inserted Murphy's name into the statement because it is now well-established that he murdered Ted Pavis.

17   Author interview with a former member of C Company, West Belfast UVF, 5 April 2016.

18   PRONI, BELF/6/1/1/38/75A, Coroner's Inquest relating to the deaths of Patrick McKee and James Arthur Gillen, dated 12 April 1973. Reliable sources attributed the bombing to the UVF. McKittrick *et al*, *Lost Lives*, pp. 273–4.

19   Ibid.

20   Cadwallader, Anne, *Lethal Allies: British Collusion in Ireland* (Cork: Mercier Press, 2013), p. 26.

21   McKittrick *et al*, *Lost Lives*, p. 288.

22   PRONI, BELF/1/1/2/254/201A, Regina v Hugh Leonard Thompson Murphy & Ronald Waller – Forcibly Breaking out of a Cell, deposition of a witness, 15 November 1973.

23   PRONI, BELF/6/1/1/38/167A, Coroner's Inquest Relating to the death of Mervyn John Connor, deposition of doctor called to the scene.

24   McKittrick *et al*, *Lost Lives*, pp. 351–2.

25   Journalist Martin Dillon believes that 'Murphy was learning about the law, the nature of witness and forensic evidence, and when such evidence was ruled admissible or inadmissible. He sat and listened to the most complex legal arguments.' Dillon, *Shankill Butchers*, pp. 20–1.

26   McKittrick *et al*, *Lost Lives*, p. 270.

27   Author interview with Billy Hutchinson, 4 May 2001.

28   Author interview with a former UVF Director of Operations, 5 April 2016.

29   Interview with a former senior RUC officer, 7 April 2016.

30   For an analysis of the Sunningdale Agreement and its impact on unionism, see Patterson, Henry, *Ireland Since 1939: The Persistence of Conflict* (Dublin: Penguin Ireland, 2006), pp. 239–42.

31   Wood, Ian S. *Crimes of Loyalty: A History of the UDA* (Edinburgh: Edinburgh University Press, 2006), p. 37.

Chapter 5

1   PRONI, BELF/6/1/1/40/16A, Coroner's Inquest relating to the death of James Edward Francis Hanna, Deposition of Unnamed Bar Steward, February 1975.

2   PRONI, BELF/6/1/1/40/16A, Deposition of Jim Hanna's female friend, 13 February 1975.

3   PRONI, BELF/6/1/1/40/16A, Deposition of Unnamed Bar Steward, February 1975.

4   PRONI, BELF/6/1/1/40/16A, Verdict on Inquest, 13 February 1975.

5   PRONI, BELF/6/1/1/40/16A, Deposition of a Detective Chief Inspector, 15 June 1974.

6   Fisk, Robert, 'Leaders of illegal Ulster force meet IRA for secret talks', *The Times*, 21 February 1974.

7   Fisk, Robert, 'UVF held talks with the IRA North and South', *The Times*, 22 February 1974.

8   *Combat*, Vol. 1, No. 1, March 1974.

9   Author interview with Billy Mitchell, 27 September 2005.

10 Myers revealed Hanna's connection in his memoirs. See Myers, Kevin, *Watching the Door: Cheating Death in 1970s Belfast* (London: Atlantic Books, 2006), p. 168; p. 174. For more on the role of Hanna in behind-the-scenes talks with the IRA at the time see Cusack, Jim and Henry McDonald, *UVF: The Endgame* (Dublin: Poolbeg, 2008), pp. 144–5.

11 'UVF Chief may have been killed by other loyalists', *The Times*, 2 April 1974.

12 Myers, *Watching the Door*, p. 173.

13 Bew, Paul and Gordon Gillespie, *Northern Ireland: A Chronology of the Troubles, 1968–1999* (Dublin: Gill & Macmillan, 1999), p. 83.

14 Weir said in an RTÉ documentary in 2015 that 'everybody knows who was behind the Dublin and Monaghan bombs. But there were bigger men behind it. Security Services, Military Intelligence and Special Branch all had their own motives'. For further discussion on this point, see Cusack and McDonald, *UVF*, pp. 133–5; and Cadwallader, Anne *Lethal Allies: British Collusion in Ireland* (Cork: Mercier Press, 2013), pp. 213–42.

15 RTÉ, *Collusion* programme, aired 16 June 2015.

16 Mr Justice Barron's Statement to the Oireachtas Joint Committee, 10 December 2003. Archived at: http://www.oireachtas.ie/documents/committees29thdail/jcjedwr/InterimDubMon.pdf. Accessed: 1 January 2016.

17 Ibid.

18 Ibid. Author's emphasis.

19 Reed, Richard, *Paramilitary Loyalism: Identity and Change* (Manchester: Manchester University Press, 2015), p. 66.

20 At a press conference called by the UVF Brigade Staff in September 1972, UVF leaders claimed that 80% of UVF members were ex-servicemen and were organised into three battalions. They said they had 1,500 men in total, suggesting also that for every person accepted, they rejected another nine. In addition, the UVF leaders claimed to have 600 members of the Young Citizens Volunteers (YCVs), its youth wing, spread right

across Northern Ireland, 200 of whom were to be found in Belfast. *Belfast Newsletter*, 18 September 1972 and *Irish Independent*, 18 September 1972. By the beginning of 1973 the number of UVF members had grown to 2,000 men in Antrim, Belfast, Tyrone and Armagh. Myers, Kevin, 'My blind date with UVF leaders', *Observer*, 18 February 1973.

21   The UVF did not claim responsibility for the Dublin and Monaghan atrocities until 1993. Responding to media allegations that it had assistance from 'state agents', the UVF issued a statement denying it had any outside help. 'The UVF avails itself of this opportunity to state clearly and without reservation that the entire operation was from its conception to its successful conclusion, planned and carried out by our volunteers aided by no outside bodies', read the statement. Such an objective, they said, was 'well within our capabilities'. See CAIN, *Statement by the Ulster Volunteer Force (UVF), 15 July 1993*. Archived at: http://cain.ulst.ac.uk/othelem/organ/uvf/uvf150793.htm. Accessed: 3 October 2016.

22   Author interview with Geordie, October 2011.

23   So serious an issue was this infiltration in the 1970s, that the British intelligence community compiled a dossier on the matter. It estimated that between November 1972 and July 1973, seventy-three men had been discharged because of extremist views or because they were members of the UDA or other similar groups. Significantly, the majority of these cases were to be found in Belfast and East Antrim, where the UVF was particularly strong. See TNA, DEFE, 13/822, 'Subversion in the UDR, 1973'. Archived at: http://cain.ulst.ac.uk/publicrecords/1973/subversion_in_the_udr.pdf. Accessed: 3 October 2016.

24   Mitchell, Billy, 'Collusion or Infiltration', *The Other View*, Issue No. 13 (Summer 2003), p. 5.

25   *Combat*, No. 3, Vol. 1, 8 April 1974.

26   Author interview with Billy Mitchell, 27 September 2005.

27   *Combat*, No. 3, Vol. 1, 8 April 1974.

28   Author interview with Geordie, October 2011. On 2 October 1975, four UVF volunteers from Coleraine, David Swanson, Geoffrey Freeman, Aubrey Reid and Mark Dodds, were blown to pieces when the bomb they were loading into their car exploded. It was said that they were transporting the bomb to their target, a Catholic bar in the town, when it detonated prematurely, ripping through the car and killing all four men instantly. The scene which greeted a local RUC patrol arriving shortly afterwards was one of carnage. Scenes of Crime Officers managed to recover several handguns, but the bodies were barely intact.

29   Graham Spencer notes the contradictions inherent in UVF strategy throughout its history, arguing that the 'military focus of the UVF has therefore provided the organisation with a specificity of purpose and strategy presence which is different from the UDA' and that, at times, 'sectarian attacks have been integral to military strategy'. Spencer, Graham *The State of Loyalism in Northern Ireland* (Basingstoke: Palgrave Macmillan, 2008), pp. 63–4.

30   See Dillon, Martin, *The Shankill Butchers: A Case Study of Mass Murder* (London: Arrow Books, 1989), p. 14.

31 Young, Connla 'Sectarian Hightown killer wrote "Pope" nickname on road at crime scene', *The Irish News*, 13 October 2015. Archived at: http://www.irishnews.com/news/2015/10/13/news/sectarian-killer-left-sick-calling-card--292142/. Accessed: 25 January 2017.

32 My sincere thanks to the family of Ciaran Murphy for providing me with details of his life and murder.

33 Information gleaned from the HET Report on the Murder of Ciaran Gerard Murphy. My thanks to the family of Ciaran Murphy for permitting me access to the HET Report on Ciaran's murder.

34 Novosel, Tony *Northern Ireland's Lost Opportunity: The Frustrated Promise of Political Loyalism* (London: Pluto, 2013), p. 165.

35 Ibid., p. 166.

36 TNA, CJ 4/3734, JN Allan to Bourn, 'Loyalist Paramilitary Organisations: Meeting with NIO Officials on Monday 27 January', dated 27 January 1975.

Chapter 6

1 Author interview with Billy Mitchell, 27 September 2005.

2 PRONI, BELF/1/1/2/269/10A, Deposition of a Police Officer who discovered the van on 7 April 1975, dated 24 May 1976.

3 PRONI, ANT/6/1/1/23/143A, Inquest of Hugh McVeigh.

4 PRONI, BELF/1/1/2/269/10A, Statement of Norman Cooke, taken at Castlereagh RUC Station, 7 October 1975.

5 Anthony, Cooke, Sloan and Mitchell were all convicted of murder in March 1977. Corr was convicted for taking away the murder weapon and also burying the bodies. For more information on the murders see 'Jailed: the eight "ruthless" UVF men of east Antrim', *Belfast Telegraph*, 12 March 1977.

6 The name of this man has been redacted from the statements taken by police. It is likely that this was the same individual who later escaped from a UVF Court Martial and would become the first UVF supergrass. He received immunity from prosecution for his role in the murders of McVeigh and Douglas in exchange for his evidence against the other UVF men involved.

7 PRONI, BELF/1/1/2/269/10A, Statement by Sidney Corr, dated 6 October 1975.

8 PRONI, BELF/1/1/2/269/10A, The Queen v. George Watson Anthony, Norman Cooke, George Sloan, Sydney Corr, Jeremiah Stuart Kirkwood and William Irvine Mitchell, Statement of Sydney Corr, dated 24 May 1976. Corr was charged with concealing the revolver used in the murders. Jeremiah Kirkwood was acquitted of the charges because the Crown could not prove he was present at the graveside.

9 'Jailed: the eight "ruthless" UVF men of east Antrim', *Belfast Telegraph*, 12 March 1977.

10 '16 men in court after raid on Co. Antrim farm', *Belfast Telegraph*, 13 June 1973.

11 Both men would receive four-year sentences for their involvement in training members of the East Antrim UVF. 'Jailed: the eight "ruthless" UVF men of east Antrim', *Belfast Telegraph*, 12 March 1977. The judge at the trial said he 'could think of nothing worse than members of the UDR training members of the UVF'. One of the men, 38-year-

old John Gaw, would also be charged with the murder of Robert McCreight, one of the gang who had been accused of 'talking too much'. Gaw received a life sentence. He allegedly told another defendant that he was 'turned on by the sight of blood'. See Ryder, Chris, *The Ulster Defence Regiment: An Instrument of Peace?* (London: Methuen, 1991), pp. 156–7.

12   McKittrick *et al*, *Lost Lives*, p. 554.

13   Cusack, Jim and Henry McDonald *UVF: Endgame* (Dublin: Poolbeg, 2000), p. 134.

14   It would appear that suspected informers do not appear on the UVF's Roll of Honour, most recently published in 2006.

15   Author interview with a former soldier based at North Queen Street RUC station in 1975, July 2016. Also, Private Information, April 2016.

16   For more on this point see Cadwallader, *Lethal Allies*, p. 48. RUC sources suggest that Jackson was not an agent working for Special Branch but it is impossible to officially corroborate the validity of this viewpoint given that it is common practice for state intelligence agencies to neither confirm nor deny the names of agents.

17   Dillon, Martin, *The Dirty War* (London: Arrow Books, 1990), pp. 218–19.

18   For accurate accounts of what transpired in the attack, see McKittrick *et al*, *Lost Lives*, pp. 555–8; Travers, Stephen *The Miami Showband Massacre: New Edition* (Frontline Noir, 2017).

19   PRONI, DOW/6/1/1/54/2A, Fran O'Toole and others Inquest File, Deposition of a Witness, 1 February 1977.

20   PRONI, DOW/6/1/1/54/2A, Deposition of Detective Chief Inspector James Thompson Mitchell, 1 February 1977.

21   *Daily Express*, 1976.

22   See McKittrick *et al*, *Lost Lives*, pp. 557–8.

23   Ibid, pp. 716–18.

24   TNA, CJ 4/3960, Police in West Belfast, report by RA Nelson, Division 3, NIO, 27 March 1979.

25   PRONI, ANT/6/1/1/23/142A, Post Mortem Report, David Douglas, Opinion on the Autopsy Findings of David Douglas, 3 September 1975.

26   PRONI, ANT/6/1/1/23/143A, Post Mortem Report, Hugh McVeigh, Opinion on the Autopsy Findings of Hugh McVeigh, 3 September 1975.

27   PRONI, BELF/1/1/2/269/10A, Deposition of a Detective Sergeant who interviewed George Anthony on 8 October 1975, dated 26 May 1976.

28   Author interview with Kenny McClinton, 30 January 2016.

29   Private information, October 2016.

30   Murray, Alan 'UVF men say: We killed six', *Irish Press*, 18 March 1975.

31   'Open warfare feared after UVF threat', *Belfast Newsletter*, 18 March 1975.

32   · Author interview with Billy Mitchell, 27 September 2005.

33   Ibid.

34   Ibid.

35   Private information, June 2008. Sociologist Sarah Nelson was the first academic to witness how the UVF's 'mystique' carried in the everyday discourse of its members in public. Behind the scenes, there can be no question that the character of the UVF,

'with its atmosphere of secrecy and esoteric camaraderie' (p. 179) made it an extremely violent grouping indeed, which often meant keeping its membership in line through coercion, brute force and fear. For more on the UVF in the 1970s see Nelson, Sarah, *Ulster's Uncertain Defenders* (Belfast: Appletree Press, 1984).

36   Private information, 2004.

37   Author interview with Ray, 16 November 2010. Ray served a prison sentence between the late 1970s and early 1990s.

38   Ibid.

39   Ibid.

40   Ibid.

Chapter 7

1   House of Commons Debates (*Hansard*), 4 November 1975, Vol. 899, Col. 233–4.

2   Much of what we have come to know about Lenny Murphy and the Brown Bear UVF team is contained in the comprehensively researched book *The Shankill Butchers: A Case Study of Mass Murder* (London: Arrow Books, 1989), which was written by respected journalist Martin Dillon. Dillon had the full cooperation of the RUC at the time he wrote his book and, consequently, had access to many more files than have currently been released into the public domain over forty years since the so-called 'Shankill Butchers' gang committed its most heinous murders.

3   Dillon, *The Shankill Butchers*, p. 48.

4   The whole grotesque episode is recounted in Dillon, *The Shankill Butchers*, pp. 65–9.

5   PRONI, BELF/6/1/1/42/1A, Report of Autopsy on Archibald Waller, 30 November 1975.

6   Dillon, *The Shankill Butchers*, p. 98.

7   Ibid., p. 101.

8   When detectives later arrested Murphy's accomplice, William Moore, he confessed that Murphy had pulled the trigger, stating, 'Lennie Murphy. He did him for Archie Waller'. PRONI, BELF/1/1/2/281/109A, Regina v William Moore, Statement by JJ Fitzsimmons, 24 February 1978.

9   PRONI, BELF/1/1/2/281/109A, Regina v William Moore, Statement by William Moore, 19 May 1977.

10   Private information, September 2014.

11   Private information, January 2017.

12   Dillon, *Shankill Butchers*, pp. 120–1.

13   PRONI, BELF/1/1/2/281/110A, Statement of an RUC Constable, 15 July 1976.

14   PRONI, BELF/6/1/1/41/79A, Deposition of a Witness.

15   PRONI, BELF/1/1/2/281/110A, Opinion on the Autopsy Findings of Thomas Joseph Quinn.

16   ACPO, *Murder Investigation Manual 2006* (Wyboston, UK: National Centre for Policing Excellence, 2006).

17   Statistics taken from the Malcolm Sutton Index on the CAIN website. Archived at: http://cain.ulst.ac.uk/cgi-bin/tab2.pl. Accessed: 2 February 2017.

18 McKittrick *et al*, *Lost Lives*, p. 657.

19 PRONI, BELF/1/1/2/281/107A, Regina v William Moore and Robert William Bates, Statement by William Moore, 22 May 1977.

20 PRONI, BELF/1/1/2/270/49A, Hugh Leonard Thompson Murphy – Attempted murder (2 counts), Statement of Mary Murray, 9 October 1976.

21 Dillon, *Shankill Butchers*, pp. 143–4.

22 PRONI, BELF/1/1/2/270/49A, Hugh Leonard Thompson Murphy – Attempted murder (two counts), Statement of Constable David Pattison, 9 October 1976.

23 Author interview with three former RUC Detective Chief Superintendents, CID, 15 July 2015.

24 PRONI, BELF/1/1/2/282/43A, R v William Moore, Statement by Detective Constable Robert Turner, 28 March 1978.

25 Taylor, Peter, *Beating the Terrorists? Interrogation in Omagh, Gough and Castlereagh* (London: Penguin, 1980), p. 341.

26 PRONI, BELF/1/1/2/269/10A, Deposition of Detective Chief Inspector William Hylands, dated 27 May 1976.

27 PRONI, BELF/1/1/2/269/10A, Statement of Lance Corporal (Life Guards), dated 1 April 1976.

28 PRONI, BELF/1/1/2/269/10A, Statement of Witness, Detective Inspector John Douglas Wilson, from an interview with William Irvine Mitchell on 29 March 1976. This is an interesting source of evidence, which suggests that the UVF Brigade Staff were either in the process of compiling the dossier when Mitchell was arrested or that they deliberately chose to escalate their campaign on Catholic civilians in Northern Ireland and civilians south of the border. It might also suggest that the UVF was militarily incapable of deliberate targeting because of a lack of numbers, something that would increasingly come to hamper the group's campaign in the late 1980s and early 1990s.

29 PRONI, BELF/6/1/1/41/62A, Deposition by Survivor of the Chlorane Bar Attack, 23 May 1977.

30 Dillon, *The Shankill Butchers*, p. 162.

31 PRONI, BELF/6/1/1/41/62A, Deposition of an Eyewitness, 23 June 1977.

32 Ibid.

33 PRONI, BELF/6/1/1/41/62A, Statement of Robert William Bates, 26 July 1977.

34 Ibid.

35 Ibid., 24 May 1977.

36 Grossman, Lt. Col. Dave *On Killing: The Psychological Cost of Learning to Kill in War and Society* (New York: Little, Brown, 1995), p. 118.

37 Psychologist Max Taylor writes that, in fanaticism, the relationship between leader and follower is increasingly important. 'For example, some features of fanaticism may well lend themselves to use by the leader, and indeed because of the reciprocal relationships might draw both leader and follower towards more extreme positions.' See Taylor, Max, *The Fanatics: A Behavioural Approach to Political Violence* (London: Brassey's, 1991), p. 140.

38 Dillon, *The Shankill Butchers*, pp. 163–4.

39 PRONI, BELF/1/1/2/281/110A, Statement by a Witness, 28 March 1978.

Chapter 8

1 Murphy, Dervla *A Place Apart* (London: John Murray, 1978), p. 185.
2 PRONI, BELF/6/1/1/42/14A, Coroner's Inquest into the Death of James Curtis Banks Moorehead.
3 Ibid.
4 Author interview with Trevor, 4 June 2015.
5 Ibid.
6 Ibid.
7 PRONI, BELF/6/1/1/1/42/47A, Coroner's Inquest into the Death of Kevin McMenamin.
8 PRONI, BELF/6/1/1/1/42/47A, Statement of a Commissioned Officer in the Royal Army Ordnance Corps.
9 Dillon, *The Shankill Butchers*, p. 223, p. 225.
10 PRONI, BELF/6/1/1/1/42/47A, Statement with a twenty-five-year-old Welder at Castlereagh RUC Station on 8 June 1977.
11 PRONI, BELF/1/1/2/281/98A, Statement of Gerard Arthur McLaverty, 14 March 1978.
12 Dillon, Martin, *God and the Gun: The Church and Irish Terrorism* (London: Orion Books, 1997), p. 37.
13 PRONI, BELF/1/1/2/281/110A, Statement of William Moore, signed by Jimmy Nesbitt and witnessed by JJ Fitzsimmons. 19 May 1977.
14 PRONI, BELF/1/1/2/281/107A, Regina v William Moore and Robert William Bates, Statement of Detective Inspector JJ Fitzsimmons, 21 February 1978.
15 PRONI, BELF/1/1/2/281/104A, Regina v Robert S. McAllister, Benjamin Edwards, Edward McIlwaine, William Moore, William Bates, Edward Leckey, Norman Waugh, John Watt, William Townsley, Arthur McClay and David J. Bell, Robert William Bates, Statement of Detective Constable John McCawl, 28 February 1978 and Detective Sergeant John Scott, 10 March 1978.
16 Dillon, Martin *The Shankill Butchers: A Case Study of Mass Murder* (London: Arrow Books, 1989), p. 172.
17 PRONI, BELF/1/1/2/281/107A, Regina v William Moore and Robert William Bates, Statement of Detective Inspector Jimmy Nesbitt, 23 March 1978.
18 PRONI, BELF/1/1/2/281/110A, Statement by Detective Inspector Jimmy Nesbitt.
19 PRONI, BELF/1/1/2/281/110A, Statement of William Moore, signed by Jimmy Nesbitt and witnessed by D/Constable P Boyd, 23 May 1977.
20 PRONI, BELF/1/1/2/281/110A, Regina v Robert Samuel McAllister and William Moore, Statement by Robert Samuel McAllister, 21 May 1977.
21 The social psychologist Stanley Milgram undertook an experiment in the Department of Psychology at Yale University in 1960–3, where he tested the obedience of individuals ordered to carry out the wishes of an authority figure. Milgram found that the key to their actions lay primarily in their attitude to obedience. 'The key to the behaviour of subjects lies not in pent-up anger or aggression but in the nature of their relationship to authority. They have given themselves to the authority; they see themselves as instruments for the execution of his wishes; once so defined, they are unable to break free.' Milgram, Stanley, *Obedience to Authority: An Experimental View* (New York: Pinter and Martin, 2010), p. 168.

22   PRONI, BELF/1/1/2/281/107A, Regina v William Moore and Robert William Bates, Statement by Robert William Bates, 23 May 1977.

23   I interviewed Detective Superintendent Jimmy Nesbitt on 25 October 2010 and then, again, a year later and found the amount of detail he poured into our conversation about the Shankill Butchers case extraordinary. Nothing arose in my own interviews with Nesbitt that contradicts Martin Dillon's analysis of him or the RUC investigation in his book *The Shankill Butchers*.

24   Edwards, Aaron, 'Jimmy Nesbitt was a credit to the RUC', *Belfast Newsletter*, 24 September 2014. Archived at: http://www.newsletter.co.uk/news/opinion/aaron-edwards-jimmy-nesbitt-was-a-credit-to-the-ruc-1-6319223. Accessed: 30 September 2016.

25   Dillon, *The Shankill Butchers*, p. 332.

26   Statistics taken from the Malcolm Sutton Index on the CAIN website. Archived at: http://cain.ulst.ac.uk/cgi-bin/tab2.pl. Accessed: 2 February 2017.

27   Author interview with three former RUC Detective Chief Superintendents, CID, 15 July 2015.

28   Ibid.

29   TNA, CJ 4/4871, Brigadier CP Campbell, Chief of Staff, HQNI, to TC Barker, NIO, 4 March 1976.

30   TNA, CJ 4/2854, TJ Oyler to P Buxton, Visit to the 1st Battalion, the Devonshire and Dorset Regiment, 21 February 1977.

31   TNA, CJ 4/2854, PWJ Buxton Note on North Belfast, 16 December 1977.

32   TNA, CJ 4/4871, AA Pritchard to Paul Buxton, 23 November 1977.

33   Ibid.

34   In his ground-breaking work on perpetrators of the holocaust in Eastern Europe, Christopher Browning demonstrates how the men of Police Battalion 101, most of whom had never seen combat or fired a shot in anger in their lives, would often engage in social events after a day of slaughter in order to blot out their heinous acts. Many of these men may have been responsible for evil acts but they could not remain impervious to the everyday reality of their lives. Browning, Christopher R. *Ordinary Men: Reserve Police Battalion 101 and the Final Solution in Poland* (London: Penguin, 2005), p. 14.

35   Author interview with a loyalist source, 1 March 2016.

Chapter 9

1   Sillitoe, Alan *The Loneliness of the Long Distance Runner* (London: Grafton Books, [1959], 1985), pp. 7–8.

2   Author interview with Billy Mitchell, 4 May 2001.

3   An example of this kind of potent Ulster nationalism can be found in the front-page article 'What is a Nation?', *Combat*, Vol. 1, No. 2 (1 April 1974).

4   An important statement by the ULF is carried in the first issues of *Combat* in April and May 1974. The ULF is discussed by Tony Novosel in his book *Northern Ireland's Lost Opportunity: The Frustrated Promise of Political Loyalism* (London: Pluto, 2013), pp. 101–2.

5   Some academic experts, like Dr Sarah Nelson, who carried out the most difficult, dangerous and well-respected sociological analysis of Ulster Loyalism in the 1970s, have doubted that *Combat* was really an accurate reflection of wider UVF thinking. Nelson, Sarah *Ulster's Uncertain Defenders* (Belfast: Appletree Press, 1984), p. 176.

6   For more on this point see Murray, Gerard and Jonathan Tonge, *Sinn Féin and the SDLP: From Alienation to Participation* (Dublin: The O'Brien Press, 2005), pp. 75–7; pp. 82; pp. 100–1; and Bean, Kevin *The New Politics of Sinn Féin* (Liverpool: Liverpool University Press, 2007), p. 142.

7   Nelson pointed out that 'most politically minded UVF men were often surprisingly ignorant about the NF's [National Front's] philosophy; when this gradually sank in, they either felt hostile to it or saw no relevance to its rantings about black immigrants' (p. 173). It is also important to note that most UVF men would probably have been turned off by Mitchell's strict adherence to the word of the Scriptures. It is impossible to know for sure but while most UVF members would probably be God-fearing very few would be church-going Christians, which is ironic given that the UVF's motto is 'For God and Ulster'.

8   Author interview with Billy Mitchell, 27 September 2005.

9   Fearon, Kate, *The Conflict's Fifth Business: A Brief Biography of Billy Mitchell* (Belfast: LINC Resource Centre, 2002).

10 Author interview with Billy Mitchell, 4 May 2001.

11 'L Men' was a term used amongst loyalist prisoners to denote who was a Life Sentence Prisoner.

12 Green, Marion *The Prison Experience – A Loyalist Perspective* (Belfast: EPIC, 1998), p. 10.

13 Spence was to return several months later.

14 Crawford, Colin *Defenders or Criminals?* (Belfast: Blackstaff, 1999), p. 163.

15 Smith, William 'Plum' *Inside Man: Loyalists of Long Kesh – The Untold Story* (Newtownards: Colourpoint Books, 2014), p. 109.

16 Rees made the announcement of the, albeit, slow end of Special Category Status in a debate on Northern Ireland (Emergency Provisions in early November 1975. House of Commons Debate, 4 November 1975), Vol. 899, Col. 240.

17 Green, *The Prison Experience*, p. 24.

18 For more analysis on this formative period in Irish history, see the well-researched and highly respected work by F. Stuart Ross, *Smashing H-Block: The Rise and Fall of the Popular Campaign against Criminalization, 1976–1982* (Liverpool: Liverpool University Press, 2011), p. 61.

19 Author interview with Jon, 30 January 2016.

20 Author interview with Billy Mitchell, 4 May 2001. See also chapter 12 of Peter Taylor's book *Loyalists* (London: Bloomsbury, 1999) for an examination of the Spence regime.

21 Fearon, *The Conflict's Fifth Business*.

22 Author interview with Jon, 30 January 2016.

23 Ibid.

24 Ibid.

25 See Scott, Kirsty, 'Men of Letters, Men of Arms', *The Guardian*, 2 December 2000.

26   Author interview with Jon, 30 January 2016

27   Sinnerton, Henry *David Ervine: Unchartered Waters* (Dingle: Brandon, 2002), pp. 84–7.

28   Author interview with Billy Hutchinson, 4 May 2001.

29   Edwards, Aaron, 'Democratic Socialism and Sectarianism: The Northern Ireland Labour Party and Progressive Unionist Party Compared', *Politics*, 27(1), (February 2007), pp. 24–31.

30   Taylor, *Loyalists*, p. 142. The idea of 'Spence's Socratic gift to every hot-headed young man sent through to the gateway of his supervision' was coined by Connal Parr in his article 'Getting Beyond No', *Dublin Review of Books*, 6 March 2013. Archived at: http://www.drb.ie/essays/getting-beyond-no. Accessed: 23 November 2016.

31   Fearon, *The Conflict's Fifth Business*.

32   Author interview with Billy Hutchinson, 4 May 2001.

33   Author interview with Jon, 30 January 2016.

34   Author interview with Billy Mitchell, 4 May 2001.

35   Novosel, *Northern Ireland's Lost Opportunity*, pp. 65–8.

36   Author interview with Billy Mitchell, 4 May 2001.

37   Edwards, Aaron, 'The Progressive Unionist Party of Northern Ireland: A Left-Wing Voice in an Ethnically Divided Society', *British Journal of Politics and International Relations*, 12(4), (November 2010), p. 594; Novosel, *Northern Ireland's Lost Opportunity*, p. 181.

38   Correspondence with Glenn Bradley, the nephew of the late Hugh Smyth OBE, 7 October 2015. Smyth dictated these points to Bradley before he died.

39   Author interview with Billy Hutchinson, 4 May 2001.

40   For more on the influence of NILP members on the PUP see Edwards, Aaron, *A History of the Northern Ireland Labour Party: Democratic Socialism and Sectarianism* (Manchester: Manchester University Press, 2009), pp. 205–8.

41   I first analysed the intellectual genealogy of these radical ideas for an undergraduate thesis at the University of Ulster entitled *A Case for Class Politics? The Origins, History and Development of Political Thought within the Progressive Unionist Party* (Coleraine: University of Ulster, 2001). At that time, and since, major work on the PUP's ideas was completed by Professor James W. McAuley. See Ervine, David and McAuley, James W., *Redefining Loyalism: A Political Perspective, An Academic Perspective*, Working Papers in British-Irish Studies (4), (2001), pp. 1–31. Archived at: http://eprints.hud.ac.uk/8062/1/Redefing_Loyalism.pdf. Accessed: 26 September 2016.

42   This short vignette is based on the author's interview with Jon, 30 January 2016.

43   Author interview with Jon, 30 January 2016.

44   Author interview with Robert Niblock, 30 January 2016.

Chapter 10

1   TNA, CJ 4/3960, JA Daniel Briefing Paper for Secretary of State, 21 July 1978.

2   Kitson, Frank 'Glover, Sir James Malcolm (1929–2000)', *Oxford Dictionary of National Biography*, Oxford University Press, 2004; online edn, Oct 2008. Archived at: http://www.oxforddnb.com/view/article/74283. Accessed: 21 Jan 2017.

3   For more on the political significance of this announcement within the IRA see Patterson, Henry *The Politics of Illusion: The Political History of the IRA – Second Edition* (London: Serif, 1997), pp. 180–1.

4   MoD, *Northern Ireland: Future Terrorist Trends* (dated 15 December 1978), p. 9. This report was recovered from a vehicle in West Belfast and handed over to the IRA. It was authored by the then Director of Military Intelligence in Headquarters Northern Ireland, Brigadier James Glover. A copy of the document can be found in the Linenhall Library's Northern Ireland Political Collection.

5   For more on this point see Moloney, Ed, *A Secret History of the IRA: Second Edition* (London: Penguin, 2007), pp. 171–2.

6   PRONI, ARM/6/1/1/31/26A, RUC Police Report concerning death of Cecil Grills.

7   McKittrick, David, Seamus Kelters, Brian Feeney and Chris Thornton *Lost Lives: The Stories of the Men, Women and Children who Died as a Result of the Northern Ireland Troubles – Revised and Updated* (Edinburgh: Mainstream, 2001), p. 743.

8   The Provisional IRA murder of ten Protestant workmen in Kingsmills on 5 January 1976 was said to have been primarily motivated by the need to exact revenge on the Protestant community for the sectarian murders of the O'Dowd and Reavey families by members of the UVF. The attack on La Mon was attributable to the bloodlust of IRA men who were motivated primarily by sectarian hatred of Protestants.

9   TNA, CJ 4/4765, HQNI's Full Incident Report of Shooting of L/Cpl Swift in Londonderry, 14 August 1978.

10   Moloney, *A Secret History of the IRA*, p. 173.

11   For more on the Warrenpoint ambush see Edwards, Aaron, *The Northern Ireland Troubles: Operation Banner, 1969–2007* (Oxford: Osprey, 2011), pp. 65–6.

12   Collins, Eamon *Killing Rage* (London: Granta Books, 1997), p. 14.

13   Author interview with Jon, 30 January 2016.

14   PRONI, D/4547, Ben Forde Collection, Written Copy of Billy Mitchell's Essay 'Coping with Problems of Self-Condemnation', 10 October 1985. This section was censored and did not make it into the typed-up version. My thanks to Ben Forde for authorising access to his collection.

15   Ibid.

16   Anderson, Chris *The Billy Boy: The Life and Death of LVF Leader Billy Wright* (Edinburgh: Mainstream, 2002), p. 22.

17   Billy Wright's Religious Testimony (n.d. circa 1982). Copy in author's possession.

18   Interview conducted with Billy Wright in the 1990s. In author's possession.

19   For a detailed insider's view of the Hunger Strikes see O'Rawe, Richard, *Blanketmen: An untold Story of the H-Block Hunger Strike* (Dublin: New Island Books, 2005). Loyalist prisoners also went 'on the blanket' and some, like Gusty Spence, went on hunger strike in the 1970s, though this has been poorly reflected in the literature on the troubles.

20   Anderson, *The Billy Boy*, p. 28.

21   McKittrick *et al*, *Lost Lives*, p. 888.

22   *The Times*, 28 August 1982.

23   'McKeown freed but 26 others sent for trial', *The Irish News* and *Belfast Morning News*, 2 August 1982.

24 Former RUC Special Branch detectives made a clear distinction between informants, agents and others offering up information about terrorist groups during the troubles. For more on the methodology of intelligence operations against loyalist and republican groups during this period see Matchett, William, *Secret Victory: The Intelligence War that Beat the IRA* (Lisburn: Hiskey Ltd, 2016), pp. 98–112.

25 Author interview with Geordie, October 2011.

26 My thanks to Robert Niblock for his assistance in piecing together Murphy's prison record.

27 Author interview with Jon, 30 January 2016.

28 Author interview with an eyewitness, 11 September 2014.

29 PRONI, BELF/6/1/1/48/51A, Coroner's Inquest of Brian William Smyth, Deposition of a Witness, 23 November 1983.

30 The incidents leading up to Brian Smyth's death were detailed in a report by the *Belfast Telegraph* on 24 November 1983.

31 PRONI, BELF/6/1/1/48/51A, Post Mortem Report, Brian William Smyth.

32 Dillon, Martin, *The Dirty War* (London: Arrow Books, 1990), p. 449.

33 Holland, Jack and Susan Phoenix *Phoenix: Policing the Shadows* (London: Hodder and Stoughton, 1996), p. 107. Curiously, Martin Dillon reported that DI Jimmy Nesbitt and his team of detectives in C Division 'could not monitor his movements', though he does not say why, other than, implicitly, resource constraints. Dillon, Martin, *The Shankill Butchers: A Case Study of Mass Murder* (London: Arrow Books, 1990), p. 315. The RUC issued a statement after Murphy's assassination stating that 'while of interest to the police, was not under any surveillance before the attack'. *Belfast Telegraph*, 18 November 1982.

34 Dillon, *The Shankill Butchers*, p. 299.

35 Simpson, Alan *Murder Madness: True Crimes of the Troubles* (Dublin: Gill & Macmillan, 1999), p. 192.

36 Dillon, *The Dirty War*, p. 449.

37 TNA, CJ 4/4871, Cooperation between UVF and PIRA/INLA, dated 17 February 1983.

38 *Belfast Telegraph*, 19 November 1982.

39 Author interview with a former member of C Company, West Belfast UVF, 5 April 2016.

40 Edwards, Aaron, 'Militant Loyalism and the Hunger Strikes', *The Irish Times*, 5 July 2016. Archived at: http://www.irishtimes.com/culture/books/militant-loyalism-and-the-hunger-strikes-1.2706740. Accessed: 4 August 2016.

Chapter 11

1 Author interview with Bobby Norris, 14 October 2014.

2 Ford, Richard 'Informer the Key to UVF Trial', *The Times*, 17 February 1983.

3 Author interview with Jon, 30 January 2016.

4 TNA, CJ 4/4151, Memo by RUC Chief Constable Sir John Hermon to Philip Woodfield, Permanent Under Secretary at the NIO, 31 August 1982.

5 TNA, CJ 4/4625, 'Northern Ireland: Converted Terrorists', FCO/NIO Briefing Paper, dated November 1983.

6 Ibid.

7 Author interview with a loyalist source, October 2014.

8 Ford, Richard 'Uproar in court as RUC informer denies evidence', *The Times*, 16 September 1982. Clifford McKeown would later be permitted to return to the ranks of the UVF.

9 Author interview with Bobby Norris, 14 October 2014.

10 Ford, Richard 'Fourteen "loyalists" jailed for terror offences on "supergrass" evidence', *The Times*, 12 April 1983.

11 Author interview with a loyalist source, October 2014.

12 TNA, CJ 4/4625, Jim Prior to Thomas Hammerberg, 21 November 1983.

13 Hermon, Sir John *Holding the Line: An Autobiography* (Dublin: Gill & Macmillan, 1997), p. 202.

14 Private information, 2015.

15 TNA, CJ 4/4625, Minute on 'Converted Terrorists: Overview of Developments', dated 1 December 1983.

16 TNA, CJ 4/4625, Briefing paper on Converted Terrorists prepared for PS/Secretary of State, 9 February 1984,

17 TNA, CJ 4/4625, 'Northern Ireland: Converted Terrorists', FCO/NIO Briefing Paper, dated November 1983.

18 Ibid.

19 Author interview with a former UVF Director of Operations, 5 April 2016.

20 Author interview with a former senior CID officer, 4 April 2016.

21 My thanks to Dr Rachel Monaghan at Ulster University for clarifying my thinking on this matter. Dr Monaghan gave an important paper on the link between the supergrass trials and republican targeting of loyalists entitled 'On the word of a supergrass: An unlikely source of intelligence' at the annual International Studies Conference in Atlanta, Georgia, in March 2016.

22 Author interview with a former UVF Director of Operations, 5 April 2016.

23 Religious testimony of Billy Wright (n.d. 1982), In Author's Possession.

24 Ibid.

25 Ibid.

26 Author interview with Billy Hutchinson, 4 May 2001.

27 Author interview with Jon, 30 January 2016

28 Ibid.

29 *Belfast Telegraph*, 9 March 1984.

30 *Irish Independent*, 10 March 1984.

31 *Irish Independent*, 23 March 1984.

32 *The Irish News*, 23 March 1984.

33 *The Irish Times*, 19 May 1984.

34 McKittrick *et al*, *Lost Lives*, pp. 397–8.

35 *Sunday World*, 27 May 1984. See also McKittrick *et al*, *Lost Lives*, pp. 716–18.

36 Forde, Ben *The Long Victory* (Newtownards: Drumcree House, 1991), pp. 132–3.

37 PRONI, D/4547, Ben Forde Collection, Mitchell, Billy, 'Essay on Coping with the Problem of Self-Condemnation' (nd).

38   Ibid.
39   Author interview with Ben Forde, 11 December 2015.
40   Ibid.
41   Author interview with Ian Major, 6 April 2016.
42   Ibid.
43   Author interview with Kenny McClinton, 30 January 2016.

Chapter 12

1   Jones, Tim 'Loyalists freed in informer trial', *The Times*, 6 July 1985.
2   Bew, Paul and Gordon Gillespie *Northern Ireland: A Chronology of the Troubles, 1968–1993* (Dublin: Gill & Macmillan, 1993), p. 157.
3   Archive footage of this famous Paisley speech can be found via: 'Ian Paisley Speech Ulster Says No Rally Belfast City Hall November 1985', uploaded to YouTube, 4 January 2009. Accessible at: https://www.youtube.com/watch?v=8zSWlAHD29M
4   Author interview with Matthew, July 2015.
5   The use of coercive interrogation techniques by the RUC is detailed in two chapters in Ian Cobain's book *Cruel Britannia: A Secret History of Torture* (London: Portobello Books, 2013), Chapters 5 and 6.
6   Author interview with a former UVF Director of Operations, 5 April 2016.
7   *Irish Independent*, 16 July 1986.
8   O'Reilly, Emily 'Feeling the fear grow on the streets', *Sunday Tribune*, 13 July 1986. This broadsheet newspaper did not name Bingham at the time, nor give a concrete description of him. However, that did not stop the *Sunday World*, an Irish tabloid, from disseminating further details about the UVF commander.
9   Ibid.
10   Author interview with Billy Hutchinson, 4 May 2001.
11   PRONI BELF/6/1/1/53/2A, Coroner's Inquest relating to the death of John Dowey Bingham, Statement of a Witness, 14 September 1986.
12   PRONI BELF/6/1/1/53/2A, Bingham Inquest, Statement of a Witness, 25 February 1988.
13   PRONI BELF/6/1/1/53/2A, Bingham Inquest, Statement of the Ambulance Driver/ Attendant, 15 September 1986.
14   John Bingham's family allege that the RUC's Special Branch prevented paramedics from gaining access to save the UVF commander's life by ordering the military to block their route. They are adamant that an army patrol did so and would never have taken such action without orders coming from further up the Security Forces' chain of command. Attempts to track down records for the military unit in the area at the time proved fruitless. However, statements given by the ambulance driver to the RUC confirm that the paramedics received the call at 1:29 a.m. and arrived six minutes later at 1:35 a.m. Today, the journey would take between five–eight minutes from the ambulance station on the Crumlin Road to Bingham's former home.
15   PRONI BELF/6/1/1/53/2A, Bingham Inquest, RUC Report on Weapons Used in Bingham Murder, dated 17 June 1987.
16   PRONI BELF/6/1/1/53/2A, Bingham Inquest, Verdict, dated 25 February 1988.

17   PRONI BELF/6/1/1/53/2A, Bingham Inquest, Statement of a Witness, 14 September 1986.

18   PRONI BELF/6/1/1/53/2A, Bingham Inquest, Verdict, dated 25 February 1988.

19   *The Irish News*, 15 September 1986.

20   Author interview with John, 30 July 2015.

21   Dillon, Martin, *The Trigger Men* (Edinburgh: Mainstream, 2003), p. 278.

22   Author interview with John, 30 July 2015.

23   Author interview with a close relative of John Bingham, 13 November 2015.

24   Ibid.

25   Confidential information from a loyalist source, 30 January 2017.

26   Phoenix, Eamon 'Loyalist "nutcase" George Seawright posed dilemma for British', *The Irish Times*, 29 December 2014.

27   UVF, *The Fallen and the Brave: In Memory of Family, Friends and Comrades* (Belfast: UVF Regimental Association, 2006). See also McKittrick *et al*, *Lost Lives*, p. 1076.

28   Conversation with a former loyalist paramilitary, July 2015.

29   Cited in Matchett, William *Secret Victory: The Intelligence War that Beat the IRA* (Lisburn: Hiskey Ltd, 2016), pp. 218–19.

30   Author interview with a former loyalist prisoner, July 2015.

31   Ibid.

32   McDonald, Henry and Jim Cusack, *UVF* (Dublin: Poolbeg, 2002), pp. 256–7.

33   Private information, July 2015.

34   Cusack and McDonald, *UVF*, pp. 258–9.

35   McKittrick *et al*, *Lost Lives*, p. 1166

36   There are some excellent analyses of the UVF's structure, organisation and leadership. One of the best academic studies of the UVF – and loyalist paramilitarism generally – remains Bruce, Steve *The Red Hand: Protestant Paramilitaries in Northern Ireland* (Oxford: Oxford University Press, 1992), particularly Chapters 5 and 11. However, this study and many others do not appear to be aware that the UVF sub-divided into 'military teams' and 'welfare' units, the latter included a sizeable number of non-combatants or auxiliaries.

37   Author interview with former UVF members, 11 October 2015.

38   Author interview with a former UVF Director of Operations, 5 April 2016.

39   The scrambling of police frequencies is said to have taken place in 1992.

40   Author interview with Matthew, July 2015.

41   Ibid.

42   This was a point admitted in conversation with former RUC Special Branch officers, November 2015.

43   HMG, *The Report of the Patrick Finucane Review: The Rt Hon Sir Desmond de Silva QC Volume I* (London: 12 December 2012), p. 10.

44   Calculation made from a PSNI Freedom of Information Request, F-2010-00696, Figures for Terrorist Crimes, 1987–1993. Archived at: http://www.psni.police.uk/terrorist_crimes.pdf. Accessed: 25 October 2015.

45   Interview with a former UVF Volunteer, July 2015.

46   TSO, *Patrick Finucane Review*, p. 97.

47   Details of the murder of Patrick McKenna, including recollections by his family, can be found in Ardoyne Commemoration Project, *Ardoyne: The Untold Truth* (Belfast: Beyond the Pale, 2002), pp. 451–3.

48   '"Valentine" Bomb Men Jailed for 10 Years', *Belfast Telegraph*, 27 February 1976.

49   Private information, July 2016.

50   UVF, *The Fallen and the Brave*.

51   Author interview with Matthew, 11 July 2015.

52   Ibid.

53   Author interview with Mark, July 2015.

54   Author interview with a former UVF volunteer, 28 January 2016.

55   Author interview with Matthew, 11 July 2015.

56   Author interview with a former UVF Director of Operations, 5 April 2016.

57   Author interview with former UVF prisoners, July 2015.

58   Gorman, Edward 'Police attack "dossier handover" as a pathetic publicity stunt', *The Times*, 7 February 1990.

59   TSO, *Patrick Finucane Review*, p. 97.

60   Private information, March 2017.

61   *Northern Constitution*, 12 August 1972.

62   Ibid.

63   *The Irish News*, 5 April 1990.

64   *An Phoblacht*, 5 April 1990.

Chapter 13

1   House of Commons Debates (Hansard), 25 October 1993, Vol. 230, Col. 577–8.

2   Fearon, Kate, *The Conflict's Fifth Business: A Brief Biography of Billy Mitchell* (Belfast: LINC, 2002).

3   PRONI, D/4547, Ben Forde Collection, Letter from Billy Mitchell to Ian Major, 22 January 1986.

4   For more on this point see Edwards, 'Democratic Socialism and Sectarianism: The Northern Ireland Labour Party and Progressive Unionist Party Compared'.

5   Author interview with Kenny McClinton, 26 January 2016.

6   An interview with the UVF's Chief of Staff, reflecting on this process, is contained in Edwards, Aaron and Stephen Bloomer, *A Watching Brief: The Political Strategy of Progressive Loyalism since 1994* (Belfast: LINC Resource Centre, 2004), p. 12. Archived at: http://cain.ulst.ac.uk/issues/politics/docs/edwardsbloomer04.pdf. Accessed: 29 September 2016.

7   For more on the strategic logic of the UVF's campaign of 'armed resistance' see Edwards, Aaron, 'Abandoning Armed Resistance? The Ulster Volunteer Force as a case study of Strategic Terrorism in Northern Ireland', *Studies in Conflict and Terrorism*, 32(2), (February 2009), pp. 146–66.

8   Reed, *Paramilitary Loyalism*, p. 94.

9   Statement issued to the author by the UVF leadership, 28 January 2016.

10   Interview with the UVF Chief of Staff cited in Edwards, Aaron and Stephen Bloomer, *A Watching Brief? The Political Strategy of Progressive Loyalism since 1994* (Belfast: LINC Resource Centre), pp. 12–15. An electronic copy of the pamphlet can be found here: http://cain.ulst.ac.uk/issues/politics/docs/edwardsbloomer04.pdf. My sincere thanks to Stephen Bloomer for permitting me to cite from the interviews we conducted for our pamphlet.

11   Ibid.

12   Ibid.

13   Author interview with the The Craftsman, 5 April 2016.

14   Author interview with Billy Hutchinson, 14 December 2007.

15   Author interview with Margaret, 30 July 2015.

16   Following the mobile shop murders in Lurgan, the RUC told reporters that it believed no more than twenty members of the Mid Ulster UVF were involved in the killings throughout Armagh and Tyrone. The group was further sub-divided 'into tightly knit smaller groups' that were 'similar to the IRA'. 'Protestant gunmen using IRA tactics', *The Times*, 30 March 1991.

17   Author interview with the former head of CID South Region, 4 April 2016.

18   Author interview with a close associate of Billy Wright, Portadown, 30 July 2015.

19   Ibid.

20   Author interview with Margaret, 30 July 2015.

21   Author interview with a former RUC Special Branch Officer, 7 September 2015.

22   Ibid.

23   Author interview with Johnny Adair, 17 January 2016.

24   Ibid.

25   Ibid.

26   Ibid.

27   Ibid.

28   Ibid.

29   Robert Duffy was later released on licence under the terms of the Good Friday Agreement. He was involved in an altercation with a man, apparently wounding him with a shotgun. See McDonald, Henry, 'Son of IRA victim seeks fresh justice', *The Observer*, 6 April 2008.

30   McKittrick *et al*, *Lost Lives*, p. 1329.

31   Ibid., pp. 1328–33.

32   Author interview with Luke, 7 November 2015.

Chapter 14

1   *Combat*, June 1994.

2   Gillespie, Gordon *The Polish Connection: The Curious Case of the Inowroclaw* (Belfast: 1997), p. 2. My thanks to Dr Gillespie for pointing me in the direction of his research paper, a copy of which can be found in the Northern Ireland Political Collection of the Linenhall Library.

3   *The Times*, 25 November 1993.
4   *The Sunday World*, 28 November 1993.
5   Gillespie, *The Polish Connection*, p. 4.
6   Ibid.
7   *The Guardian*, 2 December 1993.
8   *Combat*, January 1994.
9   *Herald Scotland*, 25 November 1993.
10   *Combat*, January 1994.
11   Interview with a former UVF Director of Operations, 5 April 2016.
12   This is a point made in Mark Urban's excellent book *UK Eyes Alpha* (London: Faber, 1995).
13   For further context on the talks between the UVF and Dublin government see Cusack, Jim and Henry McDonald, *UVF: The Endgame - Fully Revised and Updated* (Dublin: Poolbeg, 2008), pp. 295–8.
14   Author interview with Chris Hudson, 6 February 2007.
15   *Combat*, March 1994.
16   Ibid.
17   Author interview with David, September 2004.
18   Ibid.
19   Ibid.
20   Hall, Michael (ed.), *Ulster's Protestant Working Class: A Community Exploration* (Newtownabbey: Island Pamphlets, 1994), p. 17.
21   Ibid.
22   Ibid.
23   Author interview with Matthew, 30 July 2015.
24   Interview with the UVF's Chief of Staff, cited in Edwards, Aaron and Stephen Bloomer, *A Watching Brief: The Political Strategy of Progressive Loyalism since 1994* (Belfast: LINC Resource Centre, 2004), pp. 12–15. Archived at: http://cain.ulst.ac.uk/issues/politics/docs/edwardsbloomer04.pdf. Accessed: 29 September 2016.
25   'Wave from loyalist after bomb escape', *The Irish News*, 6 June 1994.
26   Author interview with former members of the UVF's B Company, July 2015.
27   Ibid.
28   Ibid.
29   Author interview with Mark, 11 October 2015.
30   'Loyalists in bomb attack on press centre', *The Irish News*, 15 June 1994.
31   '"Valentine" bomb men jailed for 10 years', *Belfast Telegraph*, 27 February 1976.
32   Oration at the graveside of Trevor King in Roselawn, cited in *Combat*, September 1994.
33   Ibid.
34   Private information, July 2015.
35   Author interview with a former UVF Director of Operations, 5 April 2016.
36   Author interview with Kenny McClinton, 26 January 2016.
37   A subsequent Police Ombudsman's Report found that RUC Special Branch had 'failed to pass on intelligence into the activities of loyalist paramilitaries thereby protecting these individuals'. For more detail on the incident see PONI, *Statutory Report on the*

Murders at the Heights Bar, Loughinisland, 18 June 1994 (Belfast: PONI, 9 June 2016). Archived at: https://policeombudsman.org/PONI/files/17/17aea3d1-c4c6-4f02-8ebc-4eb39af9b168.pdf. Accessed: 21 March 2017.

38   *Combat*, July 1994.

39   Author interview with Luke, 7 November 2015.

40   Author interview with Billy Hutchinson, 14 December 2007.

41   Author interview with Tommy Gorman, 23 June 2011.

42   CAIN, Irish Republican Army (IRA) Ceasefire Statement, 31 August 1994. Archived at: http://cain.ulst.ac.uk/events/peace/docs/ira31894.htm. Accessed: 30 September 2016.

43   The conviction against Mr Morrison was later quashed.

44   Author interview with Danny Morrison, 23 November 2010.

45   O'Doherty, Malachi *The Trouble with Guns: Republican Strategy and the Provisional IRA* (Belfast: Blackstaff, 1998), p. 156.

46   For more on the strategic use of military force in securing political objectives in armed conflict, see Edwards, Aaron, *War: A Beginner's Guide* (London: Oneworld, 2017), pp. 32–47.

47   Interview with David, September 2004.

48   *Combat*, September 1994.

49   For an upbeat analysis of the political talks see Reed, *Paramilitary Loyalism*, p. 96. Reed makes the interesting point that, in contrast with talks with the Irish government since 1993, loyalists had not actually made contact with the British Government until shortly before the ceasefires. The British Government, he suggests, never really took loyalists seriously.

50   Cusack and McDonald, *UVF*, p. 312.

51   Ibid., p. 316.

52   Ibid.

53   Author conversation with a close associate of Billy Greer, 6 April 2016.

54   Author interview with Matthew, 26 July 2015. In many ways, this tallies with what some Provisional IRA volunteers have said in relation to their own ceasefire.

55   CLMC Ceasefire Statement, 13 October 1994. Archived at: http://cain.ulst.ac.uk/events/peace/docs/clmc131094.htm. Accessed: 29 August 2016. According to Plum Smith, Spence insisted on the word 'remorse' being included in the statement.

56   Statement issued to the author by the UVF leadership, 28 January 2016.

57   Author interview with Dawn Purvis, 28 February 2016.

58   Author interview with The Craftsman, 5 April 2016.

59   Author interview with Dawn Purvis, 28 February 2016.

60   Author interview with The Craftsman, 5 April 2016.

61   Author interview with Dawn Purvis, 28 February 2016.

62   Author interview with David, September 2004.

63   Ibid.

64   Author interview with Billy Hutchinson, 4 May 2001.

65   Author interview with General Sir Roger Wheeler, 28 January 2011.

66   *Combat*, September 1995.

Chapter 15

1   Interview with Billy Wright, circa 1995. Copy in author's possession.

2   Pickering, John A., *Drumcree* (Belfast: Ambassador Publications, 2009), p. 45.

3   Author interview with Kenny McClinton, 30 January 2016.

4   Watt, Nicholas, 'Ulster police battle with loyalist mob', *The Times*, 11 July 1995.

5   Author interview with a former RUC officer, 23 December 2015.

6   Ibid.

7   Ibid.

8   Author interview with a senior loyalist involved in the Drumcree protests, 28 January 2016.

9   Larkin, Paul, *A Very British Jihad: Collusion, Conspiracy and Cover-up in Northern Ireland* (Belfast: Beyond the Pale, 2004), p. 170.

10   Author interview with Johnny Adair, 17 January 2016.

11   Correspondence between Harold Gracey and Kenny McClinton, 22 August 1995. My thanks to Kenny McClinton for passing on a copy of this letter.

12   IRA bombs Canary Wharf, London (1996). Footage uploaded onto YouTube on 21 December 2009. Archived at: https://www.youtube.com/watch?v=6vtOV6HPz90. Accessed: 19 March 2017.

13   'Loyalist leader in court', *The Times*, 9 August 1995. Robb and two other men were eventually found guilty at Glasgow High Court in December 1995. Robb was released in 1999 under the terms of the Good Friday Agreement. He was stabbed to death in Glasgow in 2006 as a result of a row over a drug deal gone bad.

14   Video footage of the Lindsay Robb rally in Portadown Orange Hall (n.d.), in author's possession. Sammy Wilson would be elected to the Northern Ireland Forum a few months later and go on to serve as a Member of the Northern Ireland Assembly and as a Member of Parliament for East Antrim. As indicated in the text, he played no role in the event that took place afterwards, nor in the Drumcree dispute itself.

15   Ibid.

16   Ibid.

17   Billy Wright Inquiry, The Billy Wright Inquiry Oral Hearings, Hearing: 28 January 2008, day 24, Evidence from DO1, a member of MI5's Assessments Group. Archived at: http://webarchive.nationalarchives.gov.uk/20101210142120/http://www.billywrightinquiry.org/transcripts/date/20080128/. Accessed: 30 September 2016.

18   Author's notes, from a talk given by a former Head of RUC Special Branch, November 2015.

19   This section is based on oral evidence given to the Billy Wright Inquiry by an MI5 officer on 28 January 2008. For the full transcript, see Billy Wright Inquiry, The Billy Wright Inquiry Oral Hearings, Hearing: 28 January 2008, day 24, Evidence from DO1, a member of MI5's Assessments Group. Archived at: http://webarchive.nationalarchives.gov.uk/20101210142120/http://www.billywrightinquiry.org/transcripts/date/20080128/. Accessed: 30 September 2016.

20   Ibid.

21   Ibid.

22   Ibid.

23 McDonald, Henry and Jim Cusack, *UDA: Inside the Heart of Loyalist Terror* (Dublin: Penguin Ireland, 2004), p. 282.
24 Author interview with The Craftsman, 5 April 2016.
25 Author interview with Dawn Purvis, 28 February 2016.
26 Larkin, *A Very British Jihad*, p. 216.
27 Author interview with Billy Hutchinson, 29 July 2015.
28 Interview with former associates of Billy Wright, 30 July 2015.
29 Billy Wright Inquiry, Evidence from DO1, a member of MI5's Assessments Group.
30 *UVF, The Fallen and the Brave: In Memory of Family, Friends and Comrades* (Belfast: UVF Regimental Association, 2006).
31 Author interview with The Craftsman, 5 April 2016.
32 Private information, January 2016.
33 Statement issued to the author by the UVF leadership, 28 January 2016.
34 Author interview with the UVF's former second-in-command, 5 April 2016.

Chapter 16

1 Needham, Richard *Battling for Peace: Northern Ireland's Longest-Serving British Minister* (Belfast: Blackstaff, 1998), p. 320.
2 Author interview with Margaret, 30 July 2015.
3 Clarke, Liam 'Billy Wright – a helpful kind of psychopath', *Sunday Times*, 21 September 2010.
4 Author conversation with a former RUC Special Branch officer, 7 September 2015.
5 Martin Cahill, a Dublin-based gangster known as 'The General', reportedly stole seventeen paintings, including works by Goya, Velazquez and Vermeer, from the County Wicklow home of South African billionaire Sir Alfred Beit in 1986. Four volunteers from the Mid Ulster UVF, including Wright, acted as intermediaries for the General in an attempt to sell the paintings in Turkey. It appears that Cahill loaned them one of the paintings, 'The Letter Writer' by seventeenth-century Dutch artist Gabriel Metsu. The UVF were hoping that the 'commission' could be used to buy arms from the Middle East. See Gorman, Edwards and Sarah Jane Checkland, 'Loyalist group is linked to art theft', *The Times*, 8 March 1990.
6 Author interview with Margaret, 30 July 2015.
7 Billy Wright Inquiry, Evidence taken from an RUC Special Branch Officer, 4 March 2008, Day 42. Archived at: http://webarchive.nationalarchives.gov.uk/20101210142120/http://www.billywrightinquiry.org/transcripts/hearing-day/42/. Accessed: 31 December 2015.
8 The Billy Wright Inquiry – Report, presented to Parliament pursuant to Section 26 of the Inquiries Act 2005 Ordered by the House of Commons (HMSO, 14 September 2010), p. 391. The governor later claimed that he could not recall the subject of the meeting, a claim the Inquiry found to be 'extraordinary'.
9 Cory, Peter, *Collusion Inquiry Report: Rosemary Nelson* (London: HMSO, delivered 7 October 2003; published 1 April 2004), p. 156.
10 Rosemary Nelson, a married mother with three children, was subsequently assassinated on 15 March 1999 when an Under-Vehicle-Improvised Explosive Device (UVIED) was

triggered beneath her vehicle. The Red Hand Defenders, a cover name for loyalists drawn from within the ranks of the UVF and UDA, claimed responsibility for her murder. See McKittrick *et al, Lost Lives*, p. 1467.

11 Author interview with Billy Mitchell, 4 May 2001.

12 Statistics from the Forum Elections can be located on the ARK website. Archived at: http://www.ark.ac.uk/elections/ff96.htm. Accessed: 2 February 2017.

13 ECR Incident Report, 27 December 1997. Archived at: http://webarchive.nationalarchives.gov.uk/20101210142120/http://www.billywrightinquiry.org/filestore/documents/evidence/NP41-0005-0008.pdf. Accessed: 31 December 2015.

14 Controversy surrounding Wright's killing persists to this day. Several of his closest associates allege that one prison officer had twice been ordered to leave his post on the morning Wright was shot. The British Government inquiry set up to investigate alleged collusion between the prison authorities and the INLA gunmen later concluded that, while there had been negligence on behalf of the prison service, there had been no collusion between the state authorities and Wright's killers.

15 Author interview with a former UVF prisoner, July 2015.

16 Author interview with Johnny Adair, 17 January 2016.

17 Ibid.

18 Author interview with Trevor, 4 June 2015.

19 Author interview with Margaret, 30 July 2015.

20 Ibid.

21 *The Times*, 21 October 2000.

22 McKittrick *et al, Lost Lives*, p. 1262.

23 See Anderson, Chris, *The Billy Boy: The Life and Death of LVF Leader Billy Wright* (Edinburgh: Mainstream, 2002).

24 Author interview with Dawn Purvis, 28 February 2016.

25 Ibid.

26 See RUC Chief Constable Ronnie Flanagan's evidence to the Billy Wright Inquiry, 26 March 2009. Archived at: http://webarchive.nationalarchives.gov.uk/20101210142120/http://www.billywrightinquiry.org/transcripts/date/20090326/

27 Hennessey, Thomas *The Northern Ireland Peace Process: Ending the Troubles* (Dublin: Gill & Macmillan, 2000), p. 158.

28 A year later, at the 1999 European elections, David Ervine polled an impressive 22,494 votes, some 2,211 votes more than UK Unionist Party leader Bob McCartney.

29 Author interview with Clifford Peeples, 28 November 2016.

30 See the following articles: McDonald, Henry, 'Demon Pastors are Humbled', *The Observer*, 31 October 1999. Archived at: https://www.theguardian.com/uk/1999/oct/31/northernireland.theobserver. Accessed: 3 February 2017. McDonald, Henry 'Files Leaked to Loyalists by Army', *The Observer*, 5 December 1999. Archived at: https://www.theguardian.com/uk/1999/dec/05/northernireland.henrymcdonald1. In his 5 December 1999 article, McDonald claims that Peeples 'had security clearance at RAF Aldergrove'. According to Peeples, he never had clearance for the base. McDonald was, however, closer to the mark in his 31 October 1999 article when he said that Peeples' arrest for terrorist-related offences on 26 October 1999 was indeed 'highly

embarrassing for the anti-Good Friday Agreement unionists, and in particular Ian Paisley's Democratic Unionist Party'. Peeples had shared a platform with leading DUP figures in denouncing the Agreement on 24 April 1998. He would later serve a prison sentence for possession of munitions. Despite some commentators, like the academic Steve Bruce, suggesting that Peeples was '[t]he man who led the Orange Volunteers in 1998–99', Peeples says he 'never belonged to the group and have condemned them'. Author interview with Clifford Peeples, 28 November 2016. For the paper by Steve Bruce see 'Religion and Violence: The Case of Paisley and Ulster Evangelicals', The Irish Association Website, October 2003. Archived at: http://www.irish-association. org/papers/stevebruce11_oct03.asp. Accessed: 3 February 2017. Professor Bruce also attributes an unreferenced quote to Peeples, which Peeples claims he never gave.

31   For more on the New Labour government's strategy at this time see Powell, Jonathan, *Great Hatred, Little Room: Making Peace in Northern Ireland* (London: The Bodley Head, 2008), Chapter 5.

32   Author interview with Matthew, 30 July 2015.

33   Author interview with Johnny Adair, 17 January 2016.

34   Private information, 2016.

35   Conversation with a former member of the UFF's C Company, August 2016.

36   Ellis, Walter 'Loyalist says feud is part of drugs war', *The Independent*, 2 September 2000. Archived at: http://www.independent.co.uk/news/uk/this-britain/loyalist-says-feud-is-part-of-drugs-war-697891.html. Accessed: 29 September 2016.

Chapter 17

1   The description of the murder of Tommy English is taken from the Court Transcript of a trial of several men in 2011–12, which relied on evidence given by two 'assisting offenders' or 'supergrasses'. Both men were considered unreliable witnesses and the presiding judge subsequently threw out the case. Therefore, the description of the assailants must be treated with care. Archived at: https://www.courtsni.gov.uk/en-GB/Judicial%20Decisions/PublishedByYear/Documents/2012/[2012]%20NICC%205/j_j_GIL8293Final2.htm. Accessed: 28 November 2015.

2   Author interview with a former associate of the East Antrim UVF, 3 April 2016.

3   Even one of the UVF's harshest critics, Raymond McCord, admitted in his memoir *Justice for Raymond*, that there were still 'good people' in Mount Vernon, including some of his extended family, and not all of them 'feared' the UVF. McCord, Raymond *Justice for Raymond* (Dublin: Gill & Macmillan, 2008), p. 103.

4   *Belfast Telegraph*, 20 June 2014.

5   Police Ombudsman's Office for Northern Ireland, Statement by the Police Ombudsman for Northern Ireland on her investigation into the circumstances surrounding the death of Raymond McCord Junior and related matters (Belfast: PONI, 22 January 2007), p. 141.

6   Private information, 2000.

7   Professor Andrew Silke has analysed the sources of power of terrorist groups in Northern Ireland and concludes, 'Because of their organization and weaponry, terrorist

groups directly control physical power. Normally this is applied in a direct fashion in relation to the group's aims. So, for example, physical power is used to attack security forces and government bodies; it is also used to acquire money and other resources, and to punish traitors and informers. These are all directly related to the group's purpose and survival, but as an exercise in power they can have a surprisingly limited impact on the population.' Silke, Andrew 'Beating the Water: The Terrorist Search for Power, Control and Authority', *Terrorism and Political Violence*, 12(2), (2000), p. 84. In the case of loyalist paramilitaries, they rely upon core supporters and sympathisers to police the fringes of community dissent, to turn a blind eye by fear or favour.

8   When asked, Adair said he didn't remember the visit. He was at pains to suggest to the author that Grugg did not need any excuse to hate the UVF. He apparently spent almost every UDA Inner Council meeting attacking other loyalists, particularly the UVF. Adair claims that he was opposed to this attitude. Author interview with Johnny Adair, 17 January 2016.

9   Author interview with a former loyalist paramilitary, 3 April 2016.

10   Author interview with a former loyalist paramilitary, 2 March 2017.

11   Author interview with the CID's Senior Investigating Officer on the loyalist feud, 4 April 2016.

12   Andrew Silke informs us that 'allowing members of a local community to publicly express dissent or openly act contrary to the group's wishes is extremely dangerous. It can reduce dramatically the level of control it can exert over previously obedient witnesses to the dissent. Terrorists seem very much aware of this phenomenon and certainly the Irish groups can go to great lengths to eliminate expressions of dissent'. Silke, 'Beating the Water', p. 90. See previous chapters for examples of how this dissent was dealt with by physical violence, threats and intimidation.

13   I witnessed this incident first-hand. The potential for a shooting war developed quickly and when the 'loyalist feud' broke out shortly afterwards golf clubs and pool cues were exchanged for pistols, AK47s and bombs.

14   Mitchell, Billy, 'Building Confidence in the Peace Process', *PUP website*, 14 February 2001. This article first appeared in the *North Belfast News* (date unknown) and was subsequently published online via the PUP's old website. The PUP were one of the first political parties in Northern Ireland to utilise the Internet, though its website did not last. Original link: http://www.pup-ni.org.uk/articles/bm/confidence.htm. Accessed: 14 February 2001. Link no longer active.

15   Private information, October 2016.

16   Private information, 1999.

17   It is important to also acknowledge that there was a certain allure to paramilitarism in these marginalised communities. In Andrew Silke's words, 'Support is not simply the result of an active decision made by the people. It is also the result of the terrorist group's ability to use various power sources to increase its influence and authority.' At the end of the day we are talking about a very human activity and we must acknowledge the individual and community dynamics that inform it. See Silke, 'Beating the Water', p. 92.

18   Author interview with a former associate of the East Antrim UVF, 3 April 2016.

19   Author interview with Billy Mitchell, 4 May 2001.

20 Billy Mitchell subsequently published the pamphlet as *The Principles of Loyalism: An Internal Discussion Paper* (Belfast, 2002). I was one of the first people to read and comment on its early drafts.

21 Author interview with Billy Mitchell, 4 May 2001.

22 Ibid.

23 *The Irish Times*, 11 June 2002.

24 CAIN, IRA Statement on Decommissioning, 23 October 2001. Archived at: http://cain. ulst.ac.uk/events/peace/docs/ira231001.htm. Accessed: 29 January 2016.

25 Author interview with Billy Hutchinson, 29 January 2016.

26 Ibid.

27 Ibid.

28 Author interview with a former PUP member and community activist, 5 April 2016.

29 The Queen vs. Mark Haddock and Others, Judgement by Lord Justice Weatherup on 29 September 2006. Archived at: http://www.courtsni.gov.uk/en-gb/judicial%20decisions/ publishedbyyear/documents/2006/2006%20nicc%2021/j_j_weac5471.htm. Accessed: 29 January 2017.

30 Ibid.

31 Private information, 2 March 2017.

32 Several years later, Rab Warnock and three other men were found not guilty of charges of trying to intimidate Trevor Gowdy between August and September 2003. They were released by a judge on the grounds that much of the evidence rested on that presented by two loyalist supergrasses, which was judged by the court to be 'flawed' and 'unreliable'. For more on the case, see 'UVF charges over Trevor Gowdy attack dropped against four', BBC News, 2 March 2012. Archived at: http://www.bbc.co.uk/ news/uk-northern-ireland-17234073. Accessed: 31 March 2017.

33 The Queen vs. Mark Haddock and Others, Judgement by Lord Justice Weatherup on 29 September 2006.

34 'Senior loyalist gets 10 years for assault', *The Irish Times*, 20 November 2006. Archived at: http://www.irishtimes.com/news/senior-loyalist-gets-10-years-for-assault-1.799618. Accessed: 31 March 2017.

35 Ibid.

36 Author interview with a former senior PUP member, February 2016.

Chapter 18

1 McCambridge, Jonathan 'UVF pledges to replace paramilitary murals', *Belfast Telegraph*, 4 April 2003.

2 The renowned commentator on Ulster Loyalism identity and culture, Professor James W. McAuley, reminds us of the connection many loyalists feel there is between the old and new UVFs, which has meant that the modern UVF 'has often claimed direct lineage to the original organization' because of the similarities modern members feel towards those who engaged in 'militant and sometimes violent forms of political opposition, which marked the beginning of organized loyalist resistance'. See McAuley, James W., 'Climbing over Dead Brambles? Politics and Memory within Ulster Loyalism'

in Smyth, Jim (ed.), *Remembering the Troubles: Contesting the Recent Past in Northern Ireland* (Notre Dame, IA: University of Notre Dame Press, 2017), p. 109.

3   *Irish Times*, 8 July 2003.

4   Author interview with The Craftsman, 5 April 2016.

5   Interview with a loyalist source, April 2016.

6   For more on Buck Alec see O'Connell, Sean, 'Violence and Social Memory in Twentieth-Century Belfast: Stories of Buck Alec Robinson', *Journal of British Studies*, 53 (2014), pp. 734–56.

7   Author interview with The Craftsman, 5 April 2016.

8   Private information, 2004.

9   Author interview with The Craftsman, 5 April 2016

10   Ibid. Graham Spencer argues that by adopting the policy of sectarianism, the UVF opened its doors to others motivated 'to pursue criminal activity at personal gain'. However, the latest academic research on the 'terror-crime nexus' globally makes the case that, sometime in the 1990s, terrorist groups began to slide more towards the other side of the spectrum and into criminal activities, while criminal gangs, like the Italian Cosa Nostra and Mexican cartels, took on increasingly political roles as they sought to expand their criminal empires. The tendency in much of the academic literature and popular media to see paramilitary activity as being either terrorist or criminal is far too binary and betrays the nuances of the global phenomenon of organised violence, whether political or criminal in complexion.

11   Despite having a code of *omertá* governing its membership, the UVF sometimes leaked like a sieve. Much of what went on was reported in the pages of the *Sunday World*, even though the newspaper had a habit of embellishing stories from unnamed 'sources'. One story that proved closer to the mark revealed the difficulties now facing Billy Greer and Rab Warnock. See Cassidy, John, 'Top UVF men are ousted after theft', *Sunday World*, 21 March 2004, p. 5.

12   Author interview with a former loyalist prisoner, April 2016.

13   For more detail on Haggarty's involvement with the UVF see Barnes, Ciaran, 'Loyalist supergrass Gary Haggarty reveals UVF plotted to raid PSNI station for weapons', *Sunday Life*, 15 November 2016.

14   Author conversation with a former UVF prisoner, July 2015.

15   Private information, 2004.

16   Author interview with a former loyalist prisoner, April 2016.

17   One thousand or so copies of the pamphlet were printed and circulated around all of the UVF brigade areas. The document itself was launched at the PUP's annual conference at the Park Avenue Hotel in East Belfast in October 2004. The pamphlets distributed in Monkstown sat in a back office gathering dust. Billy Greer clearly had other things on his mind.

18   Edwards, Aaron and Stephen Bloomer, *A Watching Brief: The Political Strategy of Progressive Loyalism since 1994* (Belfast: LINC Resource Centre, 2004), p. 35. Archived at: http://cain.ulst.ac.uk/issues/politics/docs/edwardsbloomer04.pdf. Accessed: 29 September 2016.

19   Author interview with Karl, October 2005.

20 Ibid.
21 Interview with Gary Haggarty, 28 September 2005. Transcript in author's possession.
22 Ibid.
23 Ibid.
24 There is nothing unusual about terrorist groups enforcing rigid discipline on its own members during periods of ceasefire. As Malachi O'Doherty would write in 1998 in his penetrating analysis of the Provisional IRA, 'a ceasefire requires military discipline and this, in turn, requires military men to police it'.
25 Interview with Gary Haggarty, 28 September 2005. Transcript in author's possession.
26 Edwards, Aaron and Stephen Bloomer, *Democratising the Peace in Northern Ireland: Progressive Loyalists and the Politics of Conflict Transformation*, Conflict Transformation Papers, Vol. 12 (Belfast: LINC Resource Centre, 2005). Archived at: http://cain.ulst. ac.uk/issues/politics/docs/edwardsbloomer04.pdf. Accessed: 29 September 2016. This second pamphlet was also commissioned and edited by Billy Mitchell.
27 Private information, 2004.
28 Author interview with Sir Hugh Orde, 3 March 2005.
29 Ibid.
30 For coverage of the events see '50 police officers injured in Belfast riots', *The Guardian*, 12 September 2005. Archived at: https://www.theguardian.com/uk/2005/sep/12/ northernireland. Accessed: 31 March 2017.
31 Interview with Gary Haggarty, 28 September 2005. Transcript in author's possession.
32 Interview with The Craftsman, 6 November 2005, which was completed for Edwards and Bloomer, *Democratising the Peace in Northern Ireland*.
33 Author interview with Chris Hudson, 6 February 2007.
34 See the important analysis offered by Brian Rowan: 'Loyalists claim Dublin bomb could have wiped out SF', *Belfast Telegraph*, 31 August 2006. UVF leaders claimed that they planted a bomb in 1981, which, had it gone off, would have killed the Sinn Féin leadership.
35 Author's notes from a meeting held in Monkstown, 5 October 2005. I later reflected on the meeting a decade on. See Edwards, Aaron, 'We all have a role to play if loyalist leopard is to change its spots', *Belfast Telegraph*, 16 October 2015. Accessible at: http:// www.belfasttelegraph.co.uk/opinion/debateni/we-all-have-role-to-play-if-loyalist-leopard-is-to-truly-change-its-spots-34113635.html
36 Edwards and Bloomer, *Democratising the Peace in Northern Ireland*, pp. 47–8.
37 Some respected Intelligence Studies scholars believe that the return of policing and justice powers to Stormont twelve months later, together with MI5 assuming the lead on agent handling, effectively heralded the eclipse of the PSNI C Department (formerly RUC Special Branch) as the preeminent intelligence department in Northern Ireland. The focus now was on shoring up the peace process. However, what this meant in terms of the state's security strategy for dealing with loyalism remains unclear. For more on this point see Moran, Jon, 'Evaluating Special Branch and the Use of Informant Intelligence in Northern Ireland', *Intelligence and National Security*, 25(1), (February 2010), pp. 1–23.
38 Mitchell made the comment to me in a meeting in Monkstown shortly before his death.

39   I wrote about the effect that Billy's death had on this and other peace-building work he was involved in in *The Other View* magazine, a publication he had established together with former republican prisoner, Tommy McKearney, in 2000.

40   Conversation with Rob, 2015.

41   Private information, 2015.

42   Court dismisses application by Gary Haggarty for tapes of police interviews, summary of Judgement, 9 March 2012. Archived at: https://www.courtsni.gov.uk/en-GB/Judicial%20Decisions/SummaryJudgments/Documents/Summary%20of%20judgment%20-%20In%20re%20Gary%20Haggarty/j_sj_In-re-Gary-Haggarty_090312.html. Accessed: 31 March 2017. At the time of going to press, Gary Haggarty was facing an unprecedented 202 charges, including five murders, five attempted murders and sixty-six firearms offences, linked to UVF activity in the 1990s and 200s. See McDonald, Ashleigh, 'Case against "Loyalist supergrass" Gary Haggarty postponed', *Belfast Telegraph*, 9 December 2016. Archived at: http://www.belfasttelegraph.co.uk/news/northern-ireland/case-against-loyalist-supergrass-gary-haggarty-postponed-35281591.html. Accessed: 31 March 2017.

43   Author interview with Thomas, 3 April 2016.

44   'Ex-Special Branch officer: Why we did what we did with informers', *Belfast Newsletter*, 17 June 2016. Archived at: http://www.newsletter.co.uk/news/ex-special-branch-officer-why-we-did-what-we-did-with-informers-1-7435668. Accessed: 20 September 2016.

Chapter 19

1   Author interview with Billy Mitchell, 4 May 2001.

2   The full text of the UVF's statement can be found here: http://news.bbc.co.uk/1/hi/northern_ireland/6618365.stm. Accessed: 3 April 2016.

3   I was fortunate enough to spend many of these afternoons in his company and wrote about some of my observations in two separate articles. See Edwards, Aaron, 'The passing of former UVF leader Gusty Spence may give loyalists time to think about their efforts in making peace with the past, writes Aaron Edwards', *Belfast Newsletter*, 30 September 2011 and Edwards, Aaron, 'Spence, Augustus Andrew [Gusty] (1933–2011)', *Oxford Dictionary of National Biography*, first published Jan 2015. Available at: http://www.oxforddnb.com/index/104/101104169/. Accessed: 28 September 2016.

4   This was evident in Billy Mitchell's contribution to the PUP's *Rebuttal of the First Report of the International Monitoring Commission* (April 2004). Copy in author's possession. I also reflected on his strategy shortly after his death in Edwards, Aaron, 'The East Antrim Conflict Transformation Forum: A Vision for the Future', *The Other View*, Vol. 2 (Winter 2006), pp. 8–9.

5   Edwards and Bloomer, *A Watching Brief*, p. 36.

6   A useful resource for explaining the global, regional and national dynamics of Disarmament, Demobilisation and Reintegration strategies see Berdal, Mats and David H. Ucko (eds), *Reintegrating Armed Groups After Conflict: Politics, Violence and Transition* (London: Routledge, 2009). The most sophisticated analysis of loyalist attempts to construct a DDR strategy is provided by Dr Sean Brennan, based on

his extensive and original doctoral research. See Brennan, Sean, *Ulster's Uncertain Menders? The Challenge of Reintegration and Reconciliation for Ulster Loyalists in a Post Ceasefire Society* (Queen's University Belfast: PhD Thesis, 2017). My thanks to Dr Brennan for discussing his original findings from his important work.

7 I was the principal author on the pamphlet who engaged Spence in many conversations regarding the direction the UVF-RHC-PUP should take a decade on from the paramilitary ceasefires. I found Spence imaginative, direct and supportive in all my dealings with him and this was reflected in the two pamphlets I compiled with Stephen Bloomer in 2004 and 2005. See Edwards and Bloomer, *A Watching Brief* and Edwards and Bloomer, *Democratising the Peace in Northern Ireland*. Both pamphlets were edited by Billy Mitchell.

8 McAdam, Noel 'SDLP slates PUP for keeping UVF link', *Belfast Telegraph*, 17 October 2005.

9 This was an argument I made at the time, though I noted the disruption in the process that had led to this point, Edwards, Aaron, 'The UVF Abandons its Campaign of Terror', *Fortnight*, No. 452, May 2007, pp. 12–13. I later reflected on these developments in Edwards, 'We all have a role to play if loyalist leopard is to change its spots'.

10 The full text of the UVF's statement can be found here: http://news.bbc.co.uk/1/hi/northern_ireland/6618365.stm. Accessed: 3 April 2016.

11 Author interview with Tom Roberts, 17 July 2007.

12 Ibid.

13 Author interview with Billy Mitchell, 27 September 2005.

14 Author interview with Tom Roberts, 17 July 2007.

15 Ibid.

16 Private information, 2007.

17 Author interview with Tom Roberts, 17 July 2007.

18 Boyd, Denis and Sean Doran *The Viability of Prosecution Based on Historical Enquiry: Observations of Counsel on Potential Evidential Difficulties* (Belfast: Healing Through Remembering, 2006), p. 1.

19 In the South African case, the vast majority of those who confessed to their role in violent crimes, including murder and torture, were imprisoned. As the United States Institute of Peace confirms, the Truth and Reconciliation Commission, which ran between 1995 and 2002, recorded the testimonies of 21,000 people, including 2,000 in public hearings. Of the 7,112 amnesty applications received, amnesty was granted in only 849 cases and refused in 5,392 cases. Other applications were subsequently withdrawn. This was something that Sinn Féin have failed to explain to their own members, assuming we do not include those republicans who benefited from the On the Run (OTR) letters, one of the biggest scandals to emerge from the 'peace process' in more recent years. For more on the South African TRC see USIP, Truth Commission: South Africa. Archived at: http://www.usip.org/publications/truth-commission-south-africa. Accessed: 25 November 2016.

20 For more on this point see, Edwards, Aaron, 'Deterrence, Coercion and Brute Force in Asymmetric Conflict: The Role of the Military Instrument in Resolving the Northern Ireland "Troubles"', *Dynamics of Asymmetric Conflict*, 4(3), (December 2011), pp. 226–41.

21 House of Commons Northern Ireland Affairs Committee, *Ways of Dealing with Northern Irelandfairsst: Interim Report – Victims and Survivors, Vol. 2*, dated 6 April 2005 (London: TSO, 14 April 2005). Evidence of Tom Roberts and William Smith, Ev 7.

22 Author interview with Tom Roberts, 17 July 2007.

23 McDonald, Henry 'After 40 years, the terrorists turn to politics', *The Observer*, 28 June 2009.

24 Rowan, Brian 'Arms body confirms "major decommissioning by UVF"', *Belfast Telegraph*, 29 June 2009.

25 Independent Monitoring Commission (IMC). See the *Twenty-Second Report of the Independent Monitoring Commission* (HC 1085), (London: The Stationary Office, 4 November 2009), p. 20. Archived at: http://cain.ulst.ac.uk/issues/politics/docs/imc/imc041109.pdf. Accessed: 21 March 2017.

26 A well-informed analysis of the murder of Bobby Moffett and the rationale behind it was published by the IMC. See the *Twenty-Fourth Report of the Independent Monitoring Commission* (HC 443), (London: The Stationary Office, 15 September 2010). Archived at: http://cain.ulst.ac.uk/issues/politics/docs/imc/imcreports.htm. Accessed: 25 November 2016.

27 Author interview with Dawn Purvis, 28 February 2016.

28 In an academic article published in 2009, I made the case that the UVF was fast losing legitimacy amongst its grassroots supporters in the absence of a concerted threat from physical force republicanism. 'At a time when the stated political objectives of loyalist paramilitaries have largely been met – that is, the defeat of the IRA and the safeguarding of the union – there is less than residual support for the continuation of illegal extortion rackets, drug trafficking, and intra-communal violence in Protestant working-class areas.' In the wake of the Moffett murder, and since, this has come to pass. See Edwards, 'Abandoning Armed Resistance?', pp. 146–66.

29 Reed, Richard, *Paramilitary Loyalism: Identity and Change* (Manchester: Manchester University Press, 2015), p. 152. Based on empirical evidence, Reed (p. 153) concurs with the conclusions reached in the ad hoc IMC report published in the wake of the Moffett murder.

30 Private information, February 2016.

31 Author interview with a former UVF member, 3 April 2016.

32 IMC, *Twenty-Fourth Report of the Independent Monitoring Commission*, p. 6.

33 This was a point made by me and Richard Reed in an article for *Fortnight Magazine* at the time. See Reed, Richard and Aaron Edwards, 'Loyalist paramilitaries and the peace process', *Fortnight*, No. 477 (July/August, 2011), pp. 6–7.

34 This is a particular problem in relation to education. When she was an MLA for East Belfast, Dawn Purvis undertook research into the causes and consequences of this is a particular problem in relation to education. See Purvis, Dawn, Peter Shirlow and Mark Langhammer, *Educational Underachievement and the Protestant Working Class: A Summary of Research, for Consultation* (Belfast: Dawn Purvis MLA Office, 2011). For more on educational underachievement amongst working-class Protestants, see McManus, Cathal, '"Bound in darkness and idolatry"? Protestant working-class underachievement and unionist hegemony', *Irish Studies Review*, 23(1), (2015), 48–67.

35   Reed and Edwards, 'Loyalist paramilitaries and the peace process', p. 7.
36   Young, Connla 'Gusty Spence's family continue campaign over Peter Ward murder', *The Irish News*, 30 June 2016. Archived at: http://www.irishnews.com/news/ northernirelandnews/2016/06/30/news/spence-family-continue-campaign-to-clear-his-name-584891/. Accessed: 28 September 2016. See also Rowan, Brian, 'New information may clear Gusty Spence of 1966 gun killing', *Belfast Telegraph*, 24 January 2011. Archived at: http://www.belfasttelegraph.co.uk/news/northern-ireland/new-information-may-clear-gusty-spence-of-1966-gun-killing-28583694.html. Accessed: 28 September 2016.

Chapter 20

1   Cited in Edwards, Aaron, 'Rediscovering the Principles of Loyalism for a new generation', *EamonnMallie.com*, 3 December 2012. Accessible at: http://eamonnmallie. com/2012/12/rediscovering-the-principles-of-loyalism-for-a-new-generation/. Accessed: 21 March 2017.
2   For a comprehensive examination of the factors which gave rise to the protests see Nolan, Paul, Dominic Bryan, Clare Dwyer, Katy Hayward, Katy Radford and Peter Shirlow, *The Flag Dispute: Anatomy of a Protest* (Belfast: Queen's University Belfast, 2014). For a reproduction of the leaflet see page 36.
3   BBC, Violence in Belfast after council votes to change Union flag policy, BBC News, 3 December 2012. Available at: http://www.bbc.co.uk/news/uk-northern-ireland-20587538
4   Author interview with Liz Bingham, 27 November 2016.
5   Ibid.
6   See, for example, Gibson, Megan, 'Belfast's Flag Protests Stir Up Troubles Old and New', *Time Magazine*, 18 January 2013. Available at: http://world.time.com/2013/01/18/ belfasts-flag-protests-stir-up-troubles-old-and-new/
7   Mulvenna, Gareth 'Belfast's union flag debate kicks loyalist communities while they're down', *The Guardian*, 5 December 2012. Archived at: https://www.theguardian.com/ commentisfree/2012/dec/05/belfast-union-flag-loyalists. Accessed: 28 September 2016.
8   Nolan *et al*, *The Flags Protest*, pp. 47–8.
9   McDonald, Henry 'MP's office attacked in Northern Ireland', *The Guardian*, 10 December 2012.
10   Northern Ireland Assembly Official Report (Hansard), Vol. 80, No. 4, 11 December 2012. Archived at: http://www.niassembly.gov.uk/globalassets/documents/official-reports/plenary/2012-13/microsoft-word---aims-hansard-20130114213749334-2.pdf. Accessed: 4 February 2017.
11   House of Commons Debates (Hansard), Vol. 555, Col. 177, 11 December 2012. Archived at: http://hansard.parliament.uk/Commons/2012-12-11/debates/12121156000004/Nor thernIreland#contribution-12121156000411. Accessed: 25 September 2016.
12   Author interview with a senior PSNI officer in Belfast, 7 February 2013.
13   Northern Ireland Assembly Official Report (Hansard), Vol. 80, No. 5, 14 January 2013. Archived at: http://www.niassembly.gov.uk/globalassets/documents/official-

reports/plenary/2012-13/microsoft-word---aims-hansard-20130114213749334-2.pdf. Accessed: 4 February 2017.

14   Cited in Edwards, Aaron, 'Establishing trust is essential for moving beyond protests and violence', *EamonnMallie.com*, 16 January 2013. Accessible at: http://eamonnmallie. com/2013/01/establishing-trust-is-necessary-for-moving-beyond-protests-and-violence/. Accessed: 21 March 2017.

15   Author interview with Naomi Long, 9 February 2015. My thanks to the Head of Communications for the Alliance Party for facilitating this interview and to Mrs Long for taking the time to speak to me.

16   Ibid.

17   Ibid.

18   Ibid.

19   Conversation with a senior UVF commander, 2015.

20   Ibid.

21   Author conversation with a spokesman for the East Antrim UVF, May 2015.

22   MacVicar, John, 'So where to now?', *Shankill Mirror*, Edition 191, January 2013.

23   Mitchell, Billy, 'Nationalist Euphoria, Unionist Despondency: The Way I See It', *The Other View*, No. 9 (Summer 2002), p. 11.

24   NIO, Paramilitary Groups in Northern Ireland: An assessment commissioned by the Secretary of State for Northern Ireland on the structure, role and purpose of paramilitary groups focusing on those which declared ceasefires in order to support and facilitate the political process, dated 19 October 2015. Archived: https://www.gov. uk/government/uploads/system/uploads/attachment_data/file/469548/Paramilitary_ Groups_in_Northern_Ireland_-_20_Oct_2015.pdf. Accessed: 31 March 2017.

25   Author interview with Billy Hutchinson, 29 January 2016.

26   Stevenson, Jonathan *We Wrecked the Place: Contemplating an End to the Northern Irish Troubles* (New York: The Free Press, 1996), p. 67.

27   Author interview with Billy Hutchinson, 29 January 2016.

28   Ibid.

29   Author interview with Matthew, 28 January 2016.

30   Ibid.

31   Author interview with The Craftsman, 5 April 2016.

32   Author interview with Billy Mitchell, 27 September 2005.

Epilogue

1   Sontag, Susan *Regarding the Pain of Others* (London: Penguin, 2003), p. 103.

2   Ignatieff, Michael *Blood and Belonging: Journeys into the New Nationalism* (London: Vintage, 2001), p. 2.

3   Beattie, Geoffrey *We are the People: Journeys Through the Heart of Protestant Ulster* (London: Heinemann, 1992), pp. 27–8.

4   Author interview with Thomas, 3 April 2016.

5   Author interview with former loyalist prisoners, November 2015.

ABBREVIATIONS

AIA	Anglo-Irish Agreement
ASU	Active Service Unit
CID	Criminal Investigation Department
CLMC	Combined Loyalist Military Command
DCI	Detective Chief Inspector
DI	Detective Inspector
DUP	Democratic Unionist Party
EACTF	East Antrim Conflict Transformation Forum
EPIC	Ex-Prisoners Interpretive Centre
GAA	Gaelic Athletic Association
GB	Great Britain
GOC	General Officer Commanding
HAG	Head of Assessments Group
HMG	Her Majesty's Government
HMP	Her Majesty's Prison
HMSU	Headquarters Mobile Support Unit
IED	Improvised Explosive Device
IICD	Independent International Commission on Decommissioning
INLA	Irish National Liberation Army
IPLO	Irish People's Liberation Organisation
IRSP	Irish Republican Socialist Party
IRA	Irish Republican Army
JIC	Joint Intelligence Committee
LAW	Loyalist Association of Workers

LINC	Local Initiatives for Needy Communities
LVF	Loyalist Volunteer Force
MI5	British Security Service
MLA	Member of the Legislative Assembly
MoD	Ministry of Defence
MP	Member of Parliament
NICRA	Northern Ireland Civil Rights Association
NIIR	Northern Ireland Intelligence Report
NILP	Northern Ireland Labour Party
NIO	Northern Ireland Office
OIRA	Official IRA
PAF	Protestant Action Force
PIRA	Provisional Irish Republican Army
PRONI	Public Record Office of Northern Ireland, Belfast
PSNI	Police Service of Northern Ireland
PUP	Progressive Unionist Party
QC	Queen's Counsel
RHC	Red Hand Commando
RHD	Red Hand Defenders
RIR	Royal Irish Regiment
RUC	Royal Ulster Constabulary
SAS	Special Air Service
SB	Special Branch
SDLP	Social Democratic and Labour Party
SLR	Self-Loading Rifle
SMG	Sub-Machine Gun
SPG	Special Patrol Group

TAVR	Territorial Army Volunteer Reserve
TCG	Tasking and Coordination Group
TD	*Teacta Dála* (Member of the Lower House of the Irish Parliament)
TNA	The National Archives, London
UDA	Ulster Defence Association
UDP	Ulster Democratic Party
UDR	Ulster Defence Regiment
UFF	Ulster Freedom Fighters
ULF	Ulster Loyalist Front
UPV	Ulster Protestant Volunteers
USC	Ulster Special Constabulary
USSC	Ulster Special Service Corps
UUP	Ulster Unionist Party
UVF	Ulster Volunteer Force
UWC	Ulster Workers' Council
VPP	Vanguard Political Party
VUPP	Vanguard Unionist Progressive Party

UVF Organisational Chart

UVF Structure

Brigade Staff Officers
- Chief of Staff
- Director of Operations/ Overall Military Commander
- Adjutant
- Provost Marshal
- Welfare Organiser

Brigade Command Staff

RHC (Red Hand Commando)

The RHC is separate but linked to the UVF. It has its own command structure replicated across UVF Brigade Areas and it is often referred to as a 'satelite grouping'

Scottish and English Brigades
→ Battalions in Glasgow, Liverpool & London

Londonderry and North West Brigade
→ 1st & 2nd Battalions

North Antrim Brigade
→ 1st & 2nd Battalions

Mid Ulster Brigade
→ 1st & 2nd Battalions

East Antrim Brigade
→ 1st & 2nd Battalions

Belfast Brigade
→ 1st, 2nd, 3rd & East Belfast Battalions
Command groups included 'Brigadier', 2IC, quartermaster, welfare organiser, intelligence officer and military commander

Companies (i.e. in East Antrim)
Monkstown   Carrickfergus
Rathcoole   Larne
Ballyduff   Ballyclare
Glengormley   Whitehead

Military teams based in bars and clubs – known as 'pool teams'

Welfare component for prisoner-related issues, fundraising, recreation and other support functions

UVF Battalions i.e. Belfast

1st Battalion – West Belfast – centred on the Shankill area – stretched from the Shankill Road to Ballysillan in the north of the city (1st Battalion Intelligence Officer also served as the UVF's overall Intelligence Officer).

2nd Battalion – South Belfast – took in the Village and Donegal Pass areas.

3rd Battalion – North Belfast – primarily centred on the Shore Road and included areas like Tiger's Bay and Mount Vernon out to Rathcoole – this area was later merged with East Antrim, becoming the North Belfast and East Antrim Brigade of the UVF in the 1990s.

East Belfast Battalion – although coming under the control of the Shankill Road leadership, the East Belfast UVF had its own autonomous command structure. Combined with a high number of members, estimates put it at a battalion+ in size.

Battalions were further subdivided into lettered companies, i.e. A, B, C and D or according to geographical areas, which were usually based in bars and clubs. Sometimes other groups, i.e. Sweeney's, were referred to as platoons (usually numbering up to 30) but were actually large enough (where they had upwards of 100–200 members) to be classed as sub-units in their own right. In terms of size, battalions could number 200–1,000 personnel, a small number of whom were involved with the military teams.

Scottish and English Brigades of the UVF

Scottish and English 'Brigades' or 'Battalions' acted as support networks for the UVF and RHC in Great Britain. They mainly carried out fundraising activities, provided safe houses for UVF members 'on the run', and sometimes acted as conduits for the passage of information, weapons and explosives.

Protestant Action Force (PAF)

The PAF was a non-existent grouping, which was used as a flag of convenience by UVF and RHC members when they wished to claim sectarian murders.

The Red Hand Commando (RHC) is one of the smallest paramilitary groups in Northern Ireland. Closely aligned to the UVF, and formed 1970–2, it is headed by a 'Brigadier' and has a command staff similar to the UVF.

CHRONOLOGY

1912	The Ulster Solemn League and Covenant is signed
1913	Formation of the Ulster Volunteer Force
1914	The First World War begins; the UVF is subsumed into the ranks of the British Army
1 July 1916	Battle of the Somme begins
1918	End of the First World War
1920	Government of Ireland Act partitions Ireland
1921	The UVF is disbanded. Many of its members enter the ranks of the Ulster Special Constabulary
1922	The 'troubles' break out in Northern Ireland, leading to the deaths of approximately 500 people. The Ulster Protestant Association, involving some members of the UVF and USC, carries out a series of attacks
11 Dec. 1956	IRA launches border campaign 'Operation Harvest'
1958	Formation of Ulster Protestant Action
1963	Terence O'Neill becomes Prime Minister of Northern Ireland
Oct./Nov. 1965	The UVF is 'stood to' by members of the Ulster Unionist Party, and Gusty Spence and others are sworn into its ranks
1966	First attacks by the UVF across Belfast and East Antrim, including the murder of Peter Ward in June 1966. UVF declared illegal
Oct. 1966	Trial of Gusty Spence and others
1968	First Civil Rights march
April 1969	Terence O'Neill resigns as Prime Minister
Aug. 1969	Intercommunal violence breaks out in Belfast
Dec. 1969	IRA splits into Official and Provisional wings
1 April 1970	Formation of the Ulster Defence Regiment
3 July 1970	Falls Road curfew imposed, which lasts three days
4 Dec. 1971	McGurk's Bar massacre – UVF kills 15 civilians in retaliation for Provisional IRA bomb attack on the Shankill Road

30 Jan. 1972	'Bloody Sunday' – 1st Battalion, the Parachute Regiment, shoots dead 13 unarmed protestors, another man dies later
2 July 1972	Gusty Spence abducted by UVF
21 July 1972	'Bloody Friday' – Provisional IRA detonates bombs across Belfast, killing 11 people
16 Sept. 1972	Security forces shoot dead UVF member Sinclair Johnston in Larne
4 Nov. 1972	Spence captured by Parachute Regiment and taken back to Long Kesh
1 Dec. 1972	UVF explodes two no-warning car bombs in Dublin, killing two and injuring over 100
28 Dec. 1972	UVF carries out three bombings in highly synchronised attacks in Belturbet, County Cavan, killing two young girls, another in Clones, County Monaghan, and a third in Pettigo, County Donegal
Jan. 1973	UVF detonates a bomb in Dublin, killing one man and injuring 14 others
1974	Talks between the UVF and Official and Provisional wings of the IRA
17 May 1974	The UVF bomb Dublin and Monaghan, killing 33 people
Jan.–June 1975	UVF–UDA Feud
9 Feb. 1975	IRA declares truce
Oct. 1975	A major RUC and Army operation sees the rounding up of leading UVF members in North Belfast and East Antrim; Billy Mitchell goes 'on the run'
23 Jan. 1976	IRA ends truce
29 March 1976	Billy Mitchell is arrested by the British Army
12 March 1977	After a 77-day trial, the second-longest in British criminal history until that point, eight members of the East Antrim UVF, including Billy Mitchell of the UVF Brigade Staff, are convicted of various crimes
17 Feb. 1978	Provisional IRA murder twelve Protestant civilians in La Mon hotel, Belfast
27 Aug. 1978	Murder of Lord Louis Mountbatten, former Chief of the Defence Staff, and also murder of 18 British soldiers at Warrenpoint, County Down

1 Jan. 1980	John Hermon becomes Chief Constable of the RUC
1981	Republican hunger strikes
1984	Supergrass trials
15 Nov. 1985	Anglo-Irish Agreement
14 Sept. 1986	John Bingham shot dead at his home by the Provisional IRA
3 April 1987	Provisional IRA leader Larry Marley shot dead at his home by the UVF
28 April 1987	Leading UVF member Frenchie Marchant shot dead outside the PUP offices on the Shankill Road
3 Dec. 1987	George Seawright, a Belfast city councillor and a member of the UVF, shot dead as he sat in his car off the Shankill Road
11 Jan. 1988	John Hume begins talks with Gerry Adams
15 June 1988	East Belfast UVF member Robert Seymour shot dead
30 Aug. 1988	Hume–Adams talks end
16 March 1989	John 'Jackie' Irvine shot dead by the Provisional IRA at his home. He was the last leading UVF member to be killed in the 1980s as a direct result of having been unmasked by the supergrass trials earlier in the decade
9 Nov. 1989	Peter Brooke, Secretary of State for Northern Ireland, makes a speech in which he says that the IRA cannot be militarily defeated
April 1991	Brooke–Mayhew talks begin
17 April 1991	CLMC ceasefire announces a 'universal suspension of aggressive operational hostilities'
3 March 1991	Three Provisional IRA members and a civilian killed in the UVF attack on a bar in Cappagh, County Tyrone
1991	UVF rumoured to have mounted an attempt to kill Martin McGuinness near Londonderry
April 1992	Patrick Mayhew replaces Peter Brooke
Nov. 1992	Brooke–Mayhew talks process ends
April–Sept. 1993	Second Hume–Adams talks process
June 1994	UVF and Provisional IRA tit-for-tat assassination bids
16 June 1994	Trevor King, Colin Craig and David Hamilton shot on the Shankill Road

18 June 1994	UVF kills six civilians at the Heights Bar in Loughinisland
31 Aug. 1994	Provisional IRA announce a ceasefire
13 Oct. 1994	CLMC ceasefire announced by Gusty Spence in Fernhill House
July 1995	First Drumcree dispute
July 1996	Second Drumcree dispute. Billy Wright and the Mid Ulster UVF defy UVF Brigade Staff orders and lead protests
1997	David Ervine and Hugh Smyth elected to the Northern Ireland Forum to Multi-Party Talks process
10 April 1998	The Good Friday Agreement is signed in Belfast
1999	David Ervine and Billy Hutchinson, two former UVF prisoners, are elected to the Northern Ireland Assembly
2000–1	The 'loyalist feud' breaks out between the UDA and UVF
2002–3	Intra-UDA–UFF feud
2004	The UVF enters into another deadly feud with the LVF
2005	The IRA completes decommissioning and ends it 'armed struggle'
2007	The UVF calls a cessation of hostilities and agree to put their weapons 'beyond reach'
2009	The UVF says it has decommissioned its weapons
2010	The UVF kills former RHC member Bobby Moffett on the Shankill Road
2012	UVF members and supporters march in Belfast to commemorate the signing of the Ulster Solemn League and Covenant
3 Dec. 2012	Flags protests break out; UVF says it is not involved
2013	Flag protests spread. Individual loyalists come to the forefront
2014	UVF members participate in huge parade in Larne to commemorate the gun-running a century earlier
2016	UVF decides to form a 'Praetorian Guard' to oversee the remaining transformation of the organisation, 100 years after the Battle of the Somme

BIBLIOGRAPHY

Manuscripts, Archives

Bodleian Library Special Collections, University of Oxford – Harold Wilson Papers, London School of Economics Special Collections, Lord Merlyn Rees Papers

Northern Ireland Political Collection, Linenhall Library, Belfast – NIO Cuttings Files on the UVF, *Combat, Fortnight, The Other View, The Purple Standard*, Multi-Party Talks bound volumes, PUP documents, UVF related documents

Public Record Office of Northern Ireland – Cabinet Files, Ministry of Home Affairs Files, Inquest Files, Court Files, Ben Forde Collection

The National Archives, Kew, London – Records of the Foreign and Commonwealth Office, Home Office, Ministry of Defence, Northern Ireland Office, Prime Minister's Office

Newspapers

An Phoblacht/Republican News, Belfast Newsletter, Belfast Telegraph, The Daily Telegraph, The Guardian, Herald Scotland, The Irish News, Irish Press, North Belfast News, The Observer, Sunday Life, Sunday News, The Sunday Telegraph, Sunday Press, The Sunday Times, Sunday Tribune, Sunday World, The Times

Reports

Barron, Henry, *The Report of the Independent Commission of Inquiry into the Dublin and Monaghan Bombings* (Dublin: Department of the Taoiseach, presented to an Taoiseach, Bertie Ahern, on 29 October 2003; published 10 December 2003).

Cory, Peter, *Collusion Inquiry Report: Patrick Finucane* (London: HMSO, delivered 7 October 2003; published 1 April 2004).

—, *Cory Collusion Inquiry Report: Rosemary Nelson* (London: HMSO, delivered 7 October 2003; published 1 April 2004).

—, *Cory Collusion Inquiry Report: Billy Wright* (London: HMSO, delivered 7 October 2003; published 1 April 2004).

De Silva, Rt. Hon. Sir Desmond, *The Report of the Pat Finucane Review: Volumes I & 2* (London: TSO, 12 December 2012).

Morland, Michael, Valerie Strachan and Anthony Burden, Anthony, *The Rosemary Nelson Inquiry Report* (HC 947), (London: TSO, 23 May 2011).

MacLean, Lord, Andrew Coyle and John Oliver, *The Billy Wright Inquiry – Report* (HC 431), (London: TSO, 14 September 2010).

Police Ombudsman for Northern Ireland, *Investigative Report: Statement by the Police Ombudsman for Northern Ireland on her investigation into the circumstances surrounding the death of Raymond McCord Junior and related matters* (Operation Ballast), (Belfast: PONI, Monday 22 January 2007).

Books and Articles

Anderson, Chris, *The Billy Boy: The Life and Death of LVF Leader Billy Wright* (Edinburgh: Mainstream, 2002).

Aughey, Arthur, *Under Siege: Ulster Unionism and the Anglo-Irish Agreement* (London: Hurst, 1989).

Baron-Cohen, Simon, *The Science of Evil: On Empathy and the Origins of Cruelty* (New York: Basic Books, 2012).

Beattie, Geoffrey, *We are the People: Journeys Through the Heart of Protestant Ulster* (London: Mandarin, 1993).

—, *Corner Boys* (London: Orion, 1998).

—, *Protestant Boy* (London: Granta Books, 2004).

Bew, Paul and Gordon Gillespie, *Northern Ireland: A Chronology of the Troubles, 1968–1999* (Dublin: Gill & Macmillan, 1999).

—, Peter Gibbon and Henry Patterson, *Northern Ireland 1921–2001: Political Forces and Social Classes* (London: Serif, 2002).

—, *Ireland: The Politics of Enmity, 1789–2006* (Oxford: Oxford University Press, 2007).

Boulton, David, *The UVF 1966–1973: An Anatomy of Loyalist Rebellion* (Dublin: Gill & Macmillan, 1973).

Bowman, Timothy, *Carson's Army: The Ulster Volunteer Force, 1910–1920* (Manchester: Manchester, 2012).

Bowyer Bell, J., *The Secret Army: A History of the IRA* (Cambridge, Massachusetts: MIT Press, 1974).

Brown, Johnston, *Into the Dark: 30 Years in the RUC* (Dublin: Gill & Macmillan, 2005).

Brown, Kris, "'Our Father Organization": The Cult of the Somme and the Unionist "Golden Age" in Modern Ulster Loyalist Commemoration', *The Round Table – The Commonwealth Journal of International Affairs*, 96(393), (2007), pp. 707–23.

Bruce, Steve, *The Red Hand: Protestant Paramilitaries in Northern Ireland* (Oxford: Oxford University Press, 1992).

—, *The Edge of the Union: The Ulster Loyalist Political Vision* (Oxford: Oxford University Press, 1994).

—, 'Terrorists and Politics: The Case of Northern Ireland's Loyalist Paramilitaries', *Terrorism and Political Violence*, 13(2), (2001), pp. 27–48.

—, 'Turf War and Peace: Loyalist Paramilitaries since 1994', *Terrorism and Political Violence*, 16(3), (2004), pp. 501–21.

—, *Paisley: Religion and Politics in Northern Ireland* (Oxford: Oxford University Press, 2009).

Cadwallader, Anne, *Lethal Allies: British Collusion in Ireland* (Cork: Mercier Press, 2013).

Coakley, John (ed.), *Changing Shades of Orange and Green: Redefining the Union and Nation in Contemporary Ireland* (Dublin: University College Dublin Press, 2002).

Cobain, Ian, *Cruel Britannia: A Secret History of Torture* (London: Portabello Books, 2012).

—, *The History Thieves: Secrets, Lies and the Shaping of a Modern Nation* (London: Portobello Books, 2016).

Collins, Eamon, with Mick McGovern, *Killing Rage* (London: Granta, 1997).

Collins, Randall, *Violence: A Micro-Sociological Theory* (New Jersey: Princeton, 2008).

Cooke, Dennis, *Persecuting Zeal: A Portrait of Ian Paisley* (Dingle: Brandon, 1997).

Craig, Tony, 'Laneside, Then Left a Bit? Britain's Secret Political Talks with Loyalist Paramilitaries in Northern Ireland, 1973–1976', *Irish Political Studies*, 29(2), (2014), pp. 298–317.

Crawford, Colin, *Defenders or Criminals?* (Belfast: Blackstaff, 1999).

—, *Inside the UDA: Volunteers and Violence* (London: Pluto, 2004).

Cusack, Jim and Henry McDonald, *UVF: The Endgame* (Dublin: Poolbeg, 2000).

Darby, John and Roger MacGinty, *Contemporary Peacemaking: Conflict, Violence and Peace Processes* (Basingstoke: Palgrave, 2003).

Devlin, Paddy, *Straight Left: An Autobiography* (Belfast: Blackstaff, 1993).

Dillon, Martin and Denis Lehane, *Political Murder in Northern Ireland* (London: Penguin, 1973).

Dillon, Martin, *The Shankill Butchers: A Case Study of Mass Murder* (London: Arrow Books, 1989).

—, *The Dirty War* (London: Arrow Books, 1990).

—, *God and the Gun: The Church and Irish Terrorism* (London: Orion, 1997).

—, *The Trigger Men* (Edinburgh: Mainstream, 2003).

Drake, C.J.M., 'The Phenomenon of Conservative Terrorism', *Terrorism and Political Violence*, 8(3), (1996), pp. 29–43.

Dudley Edwards, Ruth, *The Faithful Tribe: An intimate Portrait of the Loyal Institutions* (London: HarperCollins, 1999).

Edwards, Aaron, 'Democratic Socialism and Sectarianism: The Northern Ireland Labour Party and Progressive Unionist Party Compared', *Politics*, 27(1), (February 2007), pp. 24–31.

— and Stephen Bloomer, *Transforming the Peace Process in Northern Ireland: From Terrorism to Democratic Politics* (Dublin: Irish Academic Press, 2008).

—, *A History of the Northern Ireland Labour Party: Democratic Socialism and Sectarianism* (Manchester: Manchester University Press, 2009).

—, 'Abandoning Armed Resistance? The Ulster Volunteer Force as a case study of Strategic Terrorism in Northern Ireland', *Studies in Conflict and Terrorism*, 32(2), (February 2009), pp. 146–66.

—, 'The Progressive Unionist Party of Northern Ireland: A Left-wing Voice in an Ethnically Divided Society', *British Journal of Politics and International Relations*, 12(4), (November 2010), pp. 590–614.

— and Cillian McGrattan, *The Northern Ireland Conflict: A Beginner's Guide* (London: Oneworld, 2010).

—, *The Northern Ireland Troubles: Operation Banner, 1969–2007* (Oxford: Osprey, 2011).

—, 'Deterrence, Coercion and Brute Force in Asymmetric Conflict: The Role of the Military Instrument in Resolving the Northern Ireland 'Troubles'', *Dynamics of Asymmetric Conflict*, 4(3), (December 2011), pp. 226–41.

—, *Defending the Realm? The Politics of Britain's Small Wars since 1945* (Manchester: Manchester University Press, 2012).

—, '"A whipping boy if ever there was one"? The British Army and the Politics of Civil-Military Relations in Northern Ireland, 1969–79', *Contemporary British History*, 28(2), (June 2014), pp. 166–89.

—, *War: A Beginner's Guide* (London: Oneworld, 2017).

—, *Strategy in War and Peace: A Critical Introduction* (Edinburgh: Edinburgh University Press, 2017).

English, Richard, *Armed Struggle: A History of the IRA* (London: Pan Macmillan, 2003).

—, *Terrorism: How to Respond* (Oxford: Oxford University Press, 2009).

—, *Does Terrorism Work? A History* (Oxford: Oxford University Press, 2016).

Ervine, David and McAuley, James W., *Redefining Loyalism: A Political Perspective, An Academic Perspective*, Working Papers in British-Irish Studies, 4 (2001), pp. 1–31.

Falls, Cyril, *The History of the 36th (Ulster) Division* (London: Constable, 1998).

Farrington, Christopher, *Ulster Unionism and the Peace Process* (Basingstoke: Palgrave Macmillan, 2006).

Foster, Roy, *Modern Ireland, 1600–1972* (London: Penguin, 1990).

Gallaher, Carolyn, *After the Peace: Loyalist Paramilitaries in Post-Accord Northern Ireland* (New York: Cornell University Press, 2007).

Garland, Roy, *The Ulster Volunteer Force: Negotiating History* (Belfast: A Shankill Community Publication, 1997).

—, *Gusty Spence* (Belfast: Blackstaff Press, 2001).

Gibbon, Peter, *The Origins of Ulster Unionism: The Formation of Popular Protestant Politics and Ideology in Nineteenth Century Ireland* (Manchester: Manchester University Press, 1975).

Gillespie, Gordon, *The Polish Connection: The Curious Case of the Inowroclaw* (Belfast: 1997).

Graham, Brian, 'The Past in the Present: The Shaping of Identity in Loyalist Ulster', *Terrorism and Political Violence*, 16(3), (2004), pp. 483–500.

Grossman, Lt. Col. Dave, *On Killing: The Psychological Cost of Learning to Kill in War and Society* (New York: Little, Brown, 1995).

Hanley, Brian and Scott Millar, *The Lost Revolution: The Story of the Official IRA and the Workers' Party* (Dublin: Penguin Ireland, 2009).

Harnden, Toby, *Bandit Country: The Provisional IRA and South Armagh* (London: Hodder, 2000).

Harris, Lyndsey, 'Introducing the Strategic Approach: An Examination of Loyalist Paramilitaries in Northern Ireland', *British Journal of Politics and International Relations*, 8(4), (2006), pp. 539–49.

Hennessey, Thomas, *A History of Northern Ireland, 1920–1996* (Basingstoke: Palgrave Macmillan, 1997).

—, *The Northern Ireland Peace Process: Ending the Troubles?* (Dublin: Gill & Macmillan, 1999).

—, *Northern Ireland: The Origins of the Troubles* (Dublin: Gill & Macmillan, 2005).

—, *The Evolution of the Troubles, 1970–72* (Dublin: Irish Academic Press 2007).

—, *Hunger Strike: Margaret Thatcher's Battle with the IRA, 1980–1981* (Dublin: Irish Academic Press, 2014).

Horgan, John, *The Psychology of Terrorism* (Abington: Routledge, 2005).

Jordan, Hugh and Ian Lister, *Mad Dog: The Rise and Fall of Johnny Adair and 'C' Company* (Edinburgh: Mainstream, 2004).

—, *Milestones to Murder: Defining Moments in Ulster's Terror War* (Edinburgh: Mainstream, 2002).

Kerr, Alistair, *Betrayal: The Murder of Robert Nairac GC* (Cambridge: Cambridge Academic, 2015).

McAuley, James W., *The Politics of Identity: Protestant Working Class Politics and Culture in Belfast* (Aldershot: Avebury, 1994).

—, 'Just Fighting to Survive': Loyalist Paramilitary Politics and the Progressive Unionist Party', *Terrorism and Political Violence*, 16(3), (2004), pp. 522–43.

—, 'Whither New Loyalism? Changing Loyalist Politics after the Belfast Agreement', *Irish Political Studies*, 20(3), (2005), pp. 323–340.

—, *Ulster's Last Stand? Reconstructing Unionism after the Peace Process* (Dublin: Irish Academic Press, 2010).

— and Graham Spencer, *Ulster Loyalism after Good Friday Agreement: History, Identity and Change* (Basingstoke: Palgrave Macmillan, 2011).

—, *Very British Rebels? The Culture and Politics of Ulster Loyalism* (London: Bloomsbury Academic, 2016).

—, 'Memory and Belonging in Ulster Loyalist Identity', *Irish Political Studies*, 31(1), (2016), pp. 122–38.

McCleery, Martin J., *Operation Demetrius and its Aftermath: A New History of the Use of Internment without Trial in Northern Ireland, 1971–75* (Manchester: Manchester University Press, 2015).

McCord, Raymond, *Justice for Raymond* (Dublin: Gill & Macmillan, 2008).

McDonald, Henry and Jim Cusack, *UDA: Inside the Heart of Loyalist Terror* (Dublin: Penguin, 2005).

McEvoy, Sandra, 'Loyalist Women Paramilitaries in Northern Ireland: Beginning a Feminist Conversation about Conflict Resolution', *Security Studies*, 18(2), (2009), pp. 262–86.

McGarry, J. and B. O'Leary, *Explaining Northern Ireland* (Oxford: Blackwell, 1995).

McIntyre, Anthony, *Good Friday: The Death of Irish Republicanism* (New York: Ausubo, 2008).

McKay, Susan, *Northern Protestants: An Unsettled People* (Belfast: Blackstaff, 2000).

—, *Bear in Mind These Dead* (London: Faber, 2008).

McKittrick, David, Seamus Kelters, Brian Feeney and Chris Thornton, *Lost Lives: The Stories of the Men, Women and Children who Died as a Result of the Northern Ireland Troubles* (Edinburgh: Mainstream, 2001).

McMichael, Gary, *An Ulster Voice* (Boulder, CA: Roberts Rineharts Publishers, 1999).

Matchett, William, *Secret Victory: The Intelligence War that Beat the IRA* (Lisburn: Hiskey Ltd, 2016).

Miller, David, *Queen's Rebels: Ulster Loyalism in Historical Perspective* (Dublin: UCD Press, 2007).

Milgram, Stanley, *Obedience to Authority: An Experimental View* (New York: Pinter and Martin, 2010).

Mitchell, Claire, 'The Limits of Legitimacy: Former Loyalist Combatants and Peace-Building in Northern Ireland', *Irish Political Studies*, 23(1), (2008), pp. 1–19.

Moloney, Ed, *A Secret History of the IRA: Revised and Updated Edition* (London: Penguin, 2007).

—, *Ian Paisley: From Demagogue to Democrat* (Dublin: Poolbeg, 2008).

—, *Voices from the Grave: Two Men's War in Ireland* (London: Faber, 2010).

Moran, Jon, 'Paramilitaries, "Ordinary Decent Criminals" and the Development of Organised Crime Following the Belfast Agreement', *International Journal of the Sociology of Law*, 32(3), (2004), pp. 263–78.

—, 'Evaluating Special Branch and the Use of Informant Intelligence in Northern Ireland', *Intelligence and National Security*, 25(1), (February 2010), pp. 1–23.

Mulholland, Marc, *Northern Ireland at the Crossroads: Ulster Unionism in the O'Neill Years, 1960-9* (Basingstoke: Macmillan, 2000).

Mulvenna, Gareth, *Tartan Gangs and Paramilitaries: The Loyalist Backlash* (Liverpool: Liverpool University Press, 2016).

Myers, Kevin, *Watching the Door: Cheating Death in 1970s Belfast* (London: Atlantic Books, 2006).

Nelson, Sarah, *Ulster's Uncertain Defenders: Protestant Political, Paramilitary, and Community Groups and the Northern Ireland Conflict* (Belfast: Appletree, 1984).

Nolan, Paul, Dominic Bryan, Clare Dwyer, Katy Hayward, Katy Radford and Peter Shirlow, *The Flag Dispute: Anatomy of a Protest* (Belfast: Queen's University Belfast, 2014).

Novosel, Tony *Northern Ireland's Lost Opportunity: The Frustrated Promise of Political Loyalism* (London: Pluto, 2013).

O'Callaghan, Margaret and Catherine O'Donnell, 'The Northern Ireland Government, the 'Paisleyite Movement' and Ulster Unionism in 1966', *Irish Political Studies*, 21(2) (2006), pp. 203–22.

O'Doherty, Malachi, *The Trouble with Guns: Republican Strategy and the Provisional IRA* (Belfast: Blackstaff, 1998).

—, *Belfast 1972: The Telling Year* (Dublin: Gill & Macmillan, 2007).

—, *Gerry Adams: An Unauthorised Biography* (London: Faber, 2017).

O'Neill, Terence, *The Autobiography of Terence O'Neill* (London: Hart-Davies, 1972).

Parr, Connal, 'Managing His Aspirations: The Labour and Republican Politics of Paddy Devlin', *Irish Political Studies*, 27(1), (2012), pp. 111–38.

—, *Inventing the Myth: Political Passions and the Ulster Protestant Imagination* (Oxford: Oxford University Press, 2017).

Patterson, Henry, *The Politics of Illusion: A Political History of the IRA* (London: Serif, 1997).

—, *Ireland Since 1939: The Persistence of Conflict* (Dublin: Penguin Ireland, 2006).

Porter, Norman, *Rethinking Unionism: An Alternative Vision for Northern Ireland* (Belfast: Blackstaff Press, 1996).

Powell, Jonathan, *Great Hatred, Little Room: Making Peace in Northern Ireland* (London: The Bodley Head, 2007).

Prince, Simon and Geoffrey Warner, *Belfast and Derry in Revolt: A New History of the Start of the Troubles* (Dublin: Irish Academic Press, 2012).

Reed, Richard, 'Blood, Thunder and Rosettes: The Multiple Personalities of Paramilitary Loyalism between 1971 and 1988', *Irish Political Studies*, 26(1), (2011), pp. 45–71.

—, *Paramilitary Loyalism: Identity and Change* (Manchester: Manchester University Press, 2015).

Richardson, Louise, *What Terrorists Want* (London: John Murray, 2006).

Ross, F. Stuart, *Smashing H-Block: The Rise and Fall of the Popular Campaign against Criminalization, 1976–1982* (Liverpool: Liverpool University Press, 2011).

Rowan, Brian, *Behind the Lines: The Story of the IRA and Loyalist Ceasefires* (Belfast: Blackstaff Press, 1995).

—, *An Armed Peace: Life and Death after the Ceasefires* (Edinburgh: Mainstream, 2003).

Ryder, Chris, *The Ulster Defence Regiment: An Instrument of Peace?* (London: Metheun, 1991).

Sanders, Andrew, 'Operation Motorman (1972) and the search for a coherent British counterinsurgency strategy in Northern Ireland', *Small Wars & Insurgencies*, 24(3), (2013), pp. 465–92.

— and Ian S. Wood, *Times of Troubles: Britain's War in Northern Ireland* (Edinburgh: Edinburgh University Press, 2012).

Shirlow, Peter and Brendan Murtagh, *Belfast: Segregation, Violence and the City* (London: Pluto, 2006).

— and Kieran McEvoy, *Beyond the Wire: Former Prisoners and Conflict Transformation in Northern Ireland* (London: Pluto Press, 2008).

—, *The End of Ulster Loyalism?* (Manchester: Manchester University Press, 2012).

Silke, Andrew, 'Beating the Water: The Terrorist Search for Power, Control and Authority', *Terrorism and Political Violence*, 12(2), (2000), pp. 76–96.

Simpson, Alan, *Murder Madness: True Crimes of the Troubles* (Dublin: Gill & Macmillan, 1999).

Sinnerton, Henry, *David Ervine: Unchartered Waters* (Dingle: Brandon, 2002).

Smith, William 'Plum', *Inside Man: Loyalists of Long Kesh – The Untold Story* (Newtownards: Colourpoint Books, 2014).

Smyth, Jim (ed.), *Remembering the Troubles: Contesting the Recent Past in Northern Ireland* (Notre Dame, IA: University of Notre Dame Press, 2017).

Spencer, Graham, *The State of Loyalism in Northern Ireland* (Basingstoke: Palgrave Macmillan, 2008).

Stewart, A.T.Q., *The Narrow Ground: Aspects of Ulster, 1609–1969* (Belfast: Blackstaff Press, 1977).

Taylor, Max, *The Fanatics: A Behavioural Approach to Political Violence* (London: Brassey's, 1991).

Taylor, Peter, *Beating the Terrorists? Interrogation in Omagh, Gough and Castlereagh* (London: Penguin, 1980).

—, *Provos: The IRA and Sinn Fein* (London: Bloomsbury, 1998).

—, *Loyalists* (London: Bloomsbury, 1999).

—, *Brits: The War Against the IRA* (London: Bloomsbury, 2001).

Todd, Jennifer, 'Two Traditions in Unionist Political Culture', *Irish Political Studies*, 2(1), (1987), pp. 1–26.

Tonge, Jonathan, Peter Shirlow and James W. McAuley, 'So Why Did the Guns Fall Silent? How Interplay, not Stalemate, Explains the Northern Ireland Peace Process', *Irish Political Studies*, 26(1), (2011), pp. 1–18.

—, Máire Braniff, Thomas Hennessey, James W. McAuley, and Sophie Whiting, *The Democratic Unionist Party: From Protest to Power* (Oxford: Oxford University, 2014).

Travers, Stephen, *The Miami Showband Massacre: New Edition* (Frontline Noir, 2017).

Urban, Mark, *Big Boys Rules: The SAS and the Secret Struggle against the IRA* (London: Faber, 1992).

—, *UK Eyes Alpha: The Inside Story of British Intelligence* (London: Faber, 1996).

Walker, Graham, *A History of the Ulster Unionist Party: Protest, Pragmatism and Pessimism* (Manchester: Manchester University Press, 2004).

Whyte, John H., *Interpreting Northern Ireland* (Oxford: Oxford University Press, 1991).

Wood, Ian S., *Gods, Guns and Ulster: A History of Loyalist Paramilitaries* (London: Caxton, 2003).

—, *Crimes of Loyalty: A History of the UDA* (Edinburgh: Edinburgh University Press, 2006).

Wright, Frank, *Northern Ireland: A Comparative Analysis* (Dublin: Gill & Macmillan, 1992).

INDEX

Abercorn Restaurant bomb attack, the, 53
accidents from bomb-making, 53, 76
acquisition of explosives, the, 16–20
ACT (Action for Community Transformation), 312, 315, 333
Adair, Johnny, 208–12, 242, 260, 263, 264, 268, 269, 319
Adams, Gerry, 152, 154, 224, 226–7, 231, 237, 263, 304, 313
Agar, Robert, 32
agents engaging in criminality, 297
Al Qaeda, 281
alcohol as an anaesthetist before perpetrating murder, 25, 30, 112, 116, 162, 208
Allan, James, 81, 140
allegations of collusion between Loyalist paramilitaries and the Security Forces, 73, 197–9
allegations of police violence, 32
Allen, Jock, 289
Allen, William 'Budgie', 181
Alliance, Party, the, 321–2, 323, 324
Alpha, the, 95
amnesty for political prisoners, 48, 49, 314–15
Amnesty International, 169
Anderson, Chris, 262
Anderson, Jim, 52
Andrews, Alexander, 44
Andrews, David, 54
Andrews, Irene, 125
Anglo-Irish Agreement, the, 181–2
Anglo-Irish Intergovernmental Council,the, 181

Annesley, Chief Constable Hugh, 237, 243
Anthony, George (Geordie), 83, 85, 90–1, 131
anti-interrogation training, 130, 183, 193–4
areas to avoid for Catholics in Belfast, 120–1
arms dumps, 85, 199–200, 286
arms importations, 48, 175, 308
arms seizure at Teesport, November 1993, 217–18, 219, 220, 228
arms supplies, 62, 272
Armstrong, Thomas, 203
arrest of Billy Mitchell in March 1976, 6
assassination of Jim Hanna at the Loyalist Club, 69–70, 71–2
assassinations of key UVF figures, 185–8; of Billy Wright, 256–7, 259–62, 268; of Lenny Murphy, 163–4, 191
Auld, Jim, 231

B-Specials (USC), the, 13, 14, 17, 20, 35, 86
Baird, Evelyn, 215
Baird, John Charles, 175
Baird, Michelle, 215
Ballysillan, North Belfast, 184
Balmer, Dessie, Snr, 27
Balmer, Dessie Jnr, 98–9
Balmoral Furniture Company bombing, 45
Barr, Glen, 68
Bates, Ernest, 44

Bates, Robert 'Basher', 103–4, 105, 113, 115–16, 131, 132, 135, 265, 337
'Battle of Springmartin' estate, the, 227
Battle of the Boyne, the, 18
'Battle of the Shankill' riots over a banned march, 297–8
Beattie, Prof. Geoffrey, 340–1
Begley, Thomas, 215
Belfast (Good Friday) Agreement, the, 265–6, 274, 302, 322–3
Belfast and industrial decline, 40–1, 331
Belfast Telegraph (newspaper), 34, 98, 164
Bell, David, 98–9
Bennett, Joe, 305
Bennett, Joseph, 166, 167, 168, 169, 171
Bigger, Geordie, 17–20, 28–9
Billy Greer funeral, the, 1–2, 3–4
Bingham, John, 77, 170, 184, 254, 322; assassination of, 185–8, 191
Bingham, Liz, 322, 323
Blakely, William, 19, 28–9
blanket protest, the, 143, 158
Bloody Friday bombings, Belfast, 55–7
Bloody Sunday, January 1972, 45–6, 49
Boal, Desmond, 21–2, 169, 183
'Bobby', (UDA volunteer), 94–5
bomb-making capabilities of the IRA, 53, 74
bomb-making skills of the UVF, 74, 76
Boyd, Billy, 139
Boyd, DC Philip, 131
Boyle, Harris, 86, 88, 89
Boyles Bar killings, Cappagh, March 1991, 203, 210, 254

Bradley, Roger Joseph, 199–200
Brady, Gerald, 229, 284
Braniff, David, 191
British Army, the, 45–6, 49, 105, 122, 133–4, 154, 248, 287; and Army Intelligence, 151, 154, 231; as experience for Loyalist paramilitaries, 74, 75; focus of patrolling, 108–9, 134; infiltration of Loyalist paramilitaries, 44, 86; and Operation Motorman, 57–8, 326; QRF (Quick Reaction Force), the, 207
British contingency plans for a united Ireland, 46
British Embassy burning, the, 46
British policy to discredit loyalism to further the peace process, 263–4
British responses to IRA violence, 57–8
British support for a united Ireland, 49–50
Brooke, Peter, 204
Brooke talks, the, 204
Brown, Jonty, 80
Brown, Sean, 264
Brown Bear Pub, the, 97, 99 (*see also* Shankill Butchers, the)
Brown Trout Inn, the, 138
Burton, Hugh, 76
Byrne, Eamon, 230

C Division, RUC, 102
Cahill, Joe, 47, 48
Caldwell, Colin 'Colly', 277
Campaign for Social Justice, the, 35
Campbell, Jim, 100, 176
Campbell, Patrick, 176
Campbell, Robert James, 42, 43
Canary Wharf bombing, the, 244–5
Carleton Street Orange Hall, 245–7

Carnmoney Hill, 93, 180
Carpenters, The (band), 160
Carrickfergus (Carrick) and Ulster
  Protestantism, 18
Carson, Dr Derek, 90
Carson, Sir Edward, 22
Castlereagh Interrogation Centre,
  108, 126–32, 166, 194
Catholic civilians as targets, 58–61,
  78–80, 87–9, 93, 117, 159, 180,
  222, 225, 230; and the Chlorane
  Bar massacre, 112–15, 337;
  Dublin and Monaghan bombings,
  the, 7, 72–4, 300; and Gusty
  Spence's dictum, 30, 77; and Peter
  Ward, 30, 31, 33, 34; and the
  Shankill Butchers, 97–8, 102,
  103–5, 119–22, 123–5, 133,
  136, 163, 336–7; targeting of
  taxi drivers, 185, 203, 225; and
  Thomas Patrick Quinn, 100–2,
  107, 127
'ceasefire soldiers' of the UVF, 332–3
CFNI (Community Foundation for
  Northern Ireland), 205
Charles, Prince, 1
Chichester-Clark, James, 38
CHISs (Covert Human Intelligence
  Sources), 271
Chlorane Bar massacre, June 1976,
  112–15, 337
CID (Criminal Investigation
  Department), the, 102–3, 107,
  163, 206
Civil Authorities (Special Powers)
  (Northern Ireland) Act (1922),
  the, 31
civil rights marches, 35, 38, 45–6
Clarke, Liam, 255
'Clarkey' (UVF volunteer), 93
Claudy atrocity, July 1972, 199

Cliftonville v Glentoran football
  match, 261
CLMC (Combined Loyalist Military
  Command), 204, 233, 236, 251,
  301
'Co-Op mix,' the, 53, 74
code of *omertá* on members, the, 85,
  94, 112, 127, 129, 131, 159, 172,
  192, 219, 313, 314
Cohen, Leonard, 343
Combat (magazine), 71, 75–6, 92,
  138, 139–40, 221, 222, 227, 238
Conlon's Bar bombing, the, 61–2
Connor, John Mervyn, 60–1, 63–5,
  131
Connor, Mervyn, 131
conspiracy to defend Ulster by force,
  16–20, 32–3
consultations and dialogue with the
  nationalist community on the
  potential of a ceasefire, 204, 219,
  220–1, 223, 224, 231, 299
conundrum of confessing to past
  murders without guarantee of an
  amnesty, 314–15
converted terrorists and the
  supergrass system, 171–2
Convie, Gary, 225, 284
Cooke, Norman, 82–3, 85
Cooper, Stephen, 56
COPs (Close Observation Platoons),
  208
Corr, Samuel, 112
Corr, Sydney, 83, 84
Corrigan, William, 229
Coyle, James, 112, 113, 114
Craftsman, The, 5, 6, 299, 300–1, 302,
  309, 333–4
'Craftsman, The' (codename), 204, 220,
  235–6, 251, 258, 267, 288–9, 290
Craig, Bill, 14, 15, 48, 51, 52, 68

Craig, Colin 'Crazy', 196, 226, 227–9
Craig, James Pratt, 126, 163, 256
Craven, Joe, 180
Crawford, Colin, 142
Crawford, Sir Stewart, 46
Crime Special Department, the, 14, 15, 21 (*see also* Special Branch (RUC), the)
criminal activity, 175, 293, 296–7, 316, 327, 329
'criminal caring' and the mental health of prisoners, 177–8
CRJ (Community Restorative Justice), 205
Crockett, Robert, 32
Crossan, Francis, 98, 102, 107
Crothers, Billy, 55–6
Crozier, Thomas Raymond, 88
Crumlin Road prison, 32, 33, 61, 62–5, 141, 143, 160, 242, 277
Currie, Austin, 13
Curry, Cassie, 29, 30
Curry, Frank, 29
Curry, Frankie, 50, 165, 267
Cusack, Jim, 251
Czempinski, Col. Gromoslaw, 218

D Division, RUC, 102, 134
Dahmer, Jeffery, 160
de Chastelain, Gen. John, 298–9
de-proscribing of the UVF, the, 92
de Silva, Sir Desmond, 198–9
decommissioning issue, the, 258, 279–80, 298–9, 310; for the UVF, 315–16
Devlin, Gerry, 264
Devlin, Paddy, 41, 44, 47
Diamond, Harry, 31
Dillon, Martin, 97, 102, 129, 131, 132, 162, 187
Dillon, Seamus, 264

Diplock no-jury court system, the, 167
Direct Rule on Northern Ireland, 49–50, 67–8
disinformation by the government, 44
dissident republicanism, 280–1
distrust of liberal Unionist and British politicians, 15–16, 27, 52, 57–8, 67, 147–8, 235, 246, 274–5, 308–9; and the DUP, 312, 319–20; and the PUP to represent working-class Protestants, 147–8, 258–9, 278; suspicion of secret deals with the IRA, 51, 71; of Terence O'Neill, 22, 35 (*see also* Loyalist doubts about the peace process and ceasefire)
Divis Flats, the, 133
divisions within Unionist politics after the Sunningdale Agreement, 67–8
Doherty, James, 24–5
Doherty, Martin, 225
Doherty, Noel, 15–16, 17, 18, 20
Donegan, Joseph, 163
dossier of UVF targets found on Billy Mitchell, 110–11
doubts that a conflict would break out, 34–5, 41
Dougherty, Cecil, 229
Douglas, David, 84, 90–1, 109, 111, 112, 303
Douglas-Home, Alec, 49–50
Downing Street Declaration, the, 220
Drumcree stand-offs, the, 239–42, 243, 245–6, 252–3, 264, 298
Drumm, Jimmy, 151
dual membership of the British Army forces and the UVF, 75, 89
Dublin and Monaghan bombings, the, 7, 72–4, 86, 300

Duffy, Colin, 257, 258
Duffy, Eileen, 203
Duffy, Robert, 212–13
Dunne, Ben, Jnr, 175
Dunne, Ben, Snr, 175
Dunnes Stores, 175
DUP (Democratic Unionist Party), the, 57, 139, 140, 182, 266, 309, 312, 319, 322; and the Belfast Agreement, 233, 242; on the PUP, 258, 259, 264 (*see also* Paisley, Rev. Ian)

EACTF (East Antrim Conflict Transformation Initiative), the, 296, 298, 300, 301–2, 304, 306, 311, 312
Eagllesham, John, 153
Eames, Robin, Archbishop, 204
East and Mid Tyrone Unionist Association, the, 13
East Antrim UVF, the, 170, 191, 225, 229, 286, 290, 293–4, 296, 327, 338; and Billy Greer, 4, 5, 234; and Billy Mitchell, 57, 82–5, 109, 141–2
Easter 1916 anniversary celebrations, the, 11, 13, 15, 33–4, 121–2
economic legacy of the Troubles, 330–1
Edwards, Benjamin 'Pretty Boy', 97–8, 135
efforts to wean the UVF towards politics, 57
Emergency Provisions Act, the, 109
English, Thomas, 270–1, 284
EOKA, 21
Ervine, David, 1, 56, 57, 145, 157, 198, 203, 267, 281, 302, 319, 330; death of, 304, 311; development of political outlook, 146, 165;

electoral performance of, 259, 265; and exploratory talks for a ceasefire, 220, 230, 235, 236–7; and the peace process, 251, 258, 263, 267; and the PUP, 203, 309; suspicion of state agents in the UVF, 252, 284, 297
escape attempt from Crumlin Road prison, 62–3
escape attempt from Long Kesh, 146
Europa Hotel, the, 70–1
eyewitness testimony into past events, 313–14
E4A covert unit, 226

Fagan, Peadar, 159
'Farm, The,' 93, 95, 180
Farrell, Edward, 112
Faulkner, Brian, 67, 68
Fearon, Kate, 201
feelers for dialogue with the nationalist community, 202–5, 221
Feeney, Hugh, 143
Ferguson, Derek, 203
Fiddler's House Bar bombing, the, 44
Fisk, Robert, 51, 71
Fitt, Gerry, 31, 47
Fitzgerald, Garret, 181
Fitzsimmons, DI John Joseph, 127, 131
flags and emblems, 328–9, 330
Ford, David, 324
Forde, DC Ben, 176–7, 178, 179
forensic examinations, 32, 100–1, 104, 105–6
Forum elections, the, 258, 265
Fox, Eamon, 225, 284
Free Presbyterian Church, the, 10, 14–15
Frizzell, Brian, 203
Frizzell, John Desmond, 215

Frizzell's shop bombing, October 1993, 215–16, 223
Fullerton, Eddie, 209
Fulton, Mark 'Swinger', 207, 235, 242, 254, 256, 279

Gallagher, Gino, 229, 257
Garland, Roy, 38, 39
Garvaghy Road Residents' Group, 239, 243
Gazeta Wyborcza (newspaper), 217
general election (1974), 139
Geraghty, Anthony, 87
Gibney, Jim, 41
Gibson, John, 212, 213, 214
Gibson, Ken, 68, 81, 139
Gillen, Jimmy, 61–2
'Glennane Gang', the, 73, 89
Glentoran Football Club, 261, 290
Glover, Brig. James, 151, 154
Gordon, William, 153
Gorman, Tommy, 37–8, 231
Gowdy, Trevor, 281–3, 289
Gracey, Harold, 240, 243–4, 246
Greaves, C. Desmond, 137
Green, Barney, 230
'Green Book', the, 299–300
Greer, Billy, 3–4, 85, 258, 276, 283, 291–2; death and funeral of, 1–2, 302–3; as East Antrim UVF commander, 4, 5, 234; relations with The Professor, 290–1, 296; and the Somme Association, 285–8
Greer, David 'Candy', 273
Greer, Glenn, 265
Gregg, John 'Grugg', 272, 277
Grills, Cecil, 152
Grimley, Jackie, 171
Grivas, Col. George, 21
Grossman, Dave, 116

Grosvenor Homing Pigeon Society, 43

H Blocks at Long Kesh, the, 142, 143, 158, 174, 221–2
Haddock, Mark, 282, 283
HAG (Head of Assessment Group) of MI5, 250, 253
Haggarty, Gary, 4, 292, 294–7, 298, 301, 304–5, 311
Haines, Joe, 47
Hamill, Robert, 264
Hamilton, Davy, 191, 227
Hamilton, Lord Ernest, 9
Hanna, Billy, 85–7, 253
Hanna, Jim, 6, 69–70, 71–2, 112, 253
Harbinson, John, 265, 284, 305, 342
Hardie, Keir, 147
Harding-Smith, Charles, 52
Hartley, Tom, 199
Heath, Ted, 46, 47, 49
Hennessey, Thomas, 265
Hermon, Sir John, 170
Herron, Tommy, 52
Hewitt, Jackie, 148
Hewitt, John, 270
HMSUs (Headquarters Mobile Support Units), 208
HTR (Healing Through Remembering), 313–14
Hudson, Chris, 220, 299
HUMINT (technological surveillance and human intelligence), 192, 305
hunger strikes, the, 165
Hutchinson, Billy, 66, 157, 184, 203, 265, 287, 288; and Billy Wright, 252, 258; on decommissioning, 279–80, 315; and the peace process, 237, 257, 267; political awakening of, 144–6, 165, 173; as PUP leader, 320, 321, 325, 329,

330–2; and search for a ceasefire, 205, 231

Hylands, D.C.I., 109

Ignatieff, Michael, 339
IMC (Independent Monitoring Commission), the, 316, 319
imprisonment of UVF leaders, 32–3, 35
incidents at checkpoints, 66–7
independent review into the murder of Patrick Finucane, 198
infiltration of the British Army, 75
informers, 86, 89–90, 159, 192, 216, 218, 228–9, 248, 271, 284, 304–5, 311
INLA (Irish National Liberation Army), the, 158, 164, 189, 208, 227, 229, 233, 256–7, 259–60, 262
inquiry into the Dublin and Monaghan bombings, 73–4
intelligence, 44, 86, 193, 206, 238, 262, 329; British Army intelligence on Protestant paramilitary groups, 44, 52–3, 219–20, 303; British Army intelligence on the Provisional IRA, 151–2, 231; and HUMINT surveillance system, 192, 305; and surveillance, 208, 216, 217, 238, 262, 290; by the UVF on the IRA, 110, 193, 197, 199 (*see also* MI5; Special Branch (RUC), the)
intercommunal peace and the labour force, 40–1
internal inquiry within the UVF into Colin Craig, 228–9
internment, 45, 49, 85
interrogations by the RUC, 90–1, 106 (*see also* Castlereagh Interrogation Centre)

IPLO (Irish People's Liberation Organisation), the, 188, 189–90, 262
IRA, the, 11, 14, 17, 25, 26, 33, 35, 37–8 (*see also* Provisional IRA, the)
Irish government, the, 11, 73, 219, 221, 238, 251, 263, 280, 299–300, 313, 334
IRSP (Irish Republican Socialist party), the, 111
Irvine, Billy, 55–6
Irvine, Jackie 'Nigger', 81, 163, 191
It Ain't Half Hot Mum (TV show), 144

Jackson, Robin, 86–7, 175, 176, 207, 246, 253
'Jake' (UVF volunteer), 93–4
James II, King, 18
'Jamesy' (UVF volunteer), 93–4
Jamison, Richard, 269
Jean McConville abduction, the, 133
Jenkinson, Malcolm, 230
Johnston, Harry, 26
Johnston, Sinclair, 58, 141–2, 338
Johnston, William, 26

Kearns, Eddy, 81
Keenan, Brig. David, 287
Kelly, Gerry, 143
Kelly, John, 47
Kelly, Sean, 215
Kennaway, John, 257
Kennedy, Sir Albert, 14
Kerr, Alec, 250
Kerr, James 'Jiffy', 62
Kilfedder, James, 21–2
killings, 2, 3, 24, 25, 161–3, 176, 181, 190–1, 195–6, 256, 264–5, 341–2; abduction and execution of UDA

men, 82–4, 89–91, 109, 111, 112, 303 (*see also* Catholic civilians as targets; sectarian reprisals)
Killops, Tommy, 55
King, Trevor, 165, 210, 227, 228
Kinner, Eddie, 146, 157, 165, 230
'kitchen cabinet' strategy group, the, 203–4
Kyle, Dr John, 302

La Mon House Hotel bombing, the, 153
Labour Party (British), the, 68, 135, 145
Lacey, Brian, 315
Lansbury, George, 147
larceny charges against Gusty Spence, 33
Larne gunrunning parade, the, 338
Le Pen, Jean-Marie, 288
'legitimate targets' and international law, 213–14
Lemass, Seán, 10
Lenaghan, Michael, 203
liberal Unionism, 10, 15–16, 22, 34 (*see also* distrust of liberal Unionist and British politicians)
LINC Project, the, 202
Londonderry and civil disorder, 45–6
Long, Naomi, 324, 325–6, 329
Long Kesh, 141–2, 160, 286; and conversions to Christianity, 172–3, 174; and political thinking by prisoners, 81, 137–8, 140–1, 143, 144–7, 155–6, 173–4
Longford, Lord, 170
Longstaff, John, 175
Loughgall deaths of Provisional IRA volunteers, 189
Lower Donegal St car bombing, 51

Loyalist Club, the, 69–70, 107, 115, 118–19, 161, 320
loyalist doubts about the peace process and ceasefire, 235–6, 238, 250, 264, 280
loyalist paramilitary feuds, 268–75, 278, 281, 303, 307, 318; between the UVF and UDA, 90, 91, 93, 94–5, 118–19, 270–1, 272, 273, 274 (*see also* abduction and execution of UDA men, the)
loyalist reaction to the Belfast (Good Friday) Agreement, 265–7; and reappraisal of and sense of betrayal, 322–3, 328, 338, 343–4
loyalist reluctance for a truth and reconciliation process, 314–15
loyalist-republican collusion, 164, 167
loyalist thinking of the union with Great Britain, 147–8
LPWA (Loyalist Prisoners' Welfare Association), 111
LVF (Loyalist Volunteer Force), the, 251, 256, 258, 261, 267, 268, 269, 278–9
Lyttle, Tommy, 211

MacDermott, Lord Chief Justice, 33
MacLellan, Pat, 46
MacStiofain, Sean, 48
MacVicar, John, 328
Mahon, Colm, 262
Major, Ian, 179
Major, John, 224
Malvern Street shootings, June 1966, 29–32
Marchant, Billy 'Frenchie', 72, 188, 191
marches and parades, 335–6, 337, 338
Marshall, James Frederick, 16–17, 18, 19
Martin, Bernadette, 264

Martin, John, 112
Martin, Leo, 30
Maskey, Liam, 231
Mason, Roy, 134, 135
Maxwell, Winifred, 44
Mayhew, Sir Patrick, 201
Maze Prison, the, 96
McAfee, William, 54
McAlea, Des, 87
McAllister, Sam, 117, 130, 131, 135
McAlorum, Kevin, 257
McArdle, Shane, 225
McBride, Alan, 215
McBride, Sharon, 215, 216
McBrien, Leo, 32
McCann, Maureen, 167
McCann, Stephen, 163, 164
McCartney, Bob, 258
McCartney, Jim, 190–1
McCartney, Margaret, 104–5
McCaughey, Billy, 89, 311
McCawl, DC John, 129
McChrystal, John, 24–5
McClean, Alexander, 29
McClean, Hugh, 18, 19, 25, 28, 29, 32, 34
McClelland, Samuel 'Bo', 39
McClinton, Kenny, 91, 125, 126, 164, 172, 173, 229, 252, 266; and the Drumcree stand-offs, 240, 243, 245–6; relations with Billy Mitchell, 180, 202, 230
McCloskey, Con and Patricia, 35
McConnell, Brian, 13
McCord, Raymond, Jnr, 265, 283, 284, 304
McCorkindale, 'Big Sam', 75
McCoy, Brian, 87
McCrea, Rev William, 218, 254
McCrea, Stevie, 62, 189, 190
McCreanor, Daniel, 230

McCrory, Patrick, 50–1
McCullough, Davy, 196
McCullough, Eddie, 26
McCullough, Geordie, 33
McDermott, Cormac, 222
McDonald, Henry, 251
McDonald, Jim, 27, 57, 81, 111, 148, 258
McDowell, James Roderick Shane, 88
McDowell, Thomas, 36
McGrath, William, 37
McGuinness, Alban, 336
McGuinness, Martin, 137, 154, 199, 263, 299, 324
McGurk, John, 53
McGurk's Bar massacre, the, 42–4, 53
McGurran, Malachy, 48
McKeague, John, 160
McKee, James, 153
McKee, John, 175
McKee, Patrick, 61
McKee, Wilma, 215
McKenna, Paddy, 195–6, 228
McKenna, Sharon, 284
McKeown, Clifford, 159, 168, 255
McKittrick, David, 39
McLaughlin, William Robert, 180
McLaverty, Gerard Arthur, 123–5, 128
McMenamin, Kevin, 121
McMillan, Liam, 10, 11
McNamara, Kevin, 134–5
McNeill, Daniel, 112, 114
McParland, Sean, 284
McQuade, Johnny, 15, 21
McShane, Gavin, 225
McTasney, Peter, 284
McVeigh, Hugh, 81, 90–1, 109, 111, 112, 303
McWilliams, Christopher 'Crip', 257, 262

McWilliams, Monica, 281
media and the peace process, the, 266
meetings between Loyalist paramilitaries and the British government, 81–2
Mellows, Liam, 137, 140
Miami Showband massacre, the, 87–8, 176
Mid Ulster UVF, the, 86, 168, 191, 206, 210, 225, 240, 245, 252; under Billy Wright, 159, 200, 203, 207–8, 247–8, 252, 254, 256; and divisions with Shankill Road leadership, 236, 247–8, 249
Millar, Billy, 33
Millar, Harry, 26
Mitchell, Billy, 17–18, 39, 58, 71, 97, 108–12, 143–4, 303–4, 307, 328–9, 334; conversion to Christianity, 177–80, 201–2; death of, 303–4; and the EACTF initiative, 296–7, 298, 301, 306, 311; as East Antrim UVF commander, 5–7, 57, 75, 76, 82–5, 92–3, 109, 141–2, 338; and feud with the UDA, 81, 90, 91; influence of Ian Paisley and religious fundamentalism, 34–5, 36–7, 92, 157; and inter-community dialogue for a ceasefire, 230–1; life after prison, 201–2; and the peace process, 258, 274–5; political awakening of, 137–8, 140–1, 146–8, 149–50, 155–7, 165, 174, 308; and progressive loyalism and distrust of mainstream Unionists, 277–8, 308–10; and the PUP, 263, 293, 301, 302; resignation from the UVF, 179, 201
Mitchell, George, 258

MI5, 194, 217, 245, 248–9, 256, 305, 329; and HAG (Head of Assessment Group), 250, 253
modern crime scene investigation analysis, 102
Moffett, Bobby, 317–18
Moloney, Ed, 152, 154
Monkstown Social Club, 286, 300–1
Monkstown Somme Association, the, 285, 287, 288
Moore, Billy, 97, 98–9, 103, 107, 116, 125, 126–31, 135, 163, 337
Moore, John, 153
Moorehead, James Curtis, 118–19
Morgan, James, 264
Morrison, Danny, 231–2
Morrison, Michael, 215
Morton, Brian, 265
Mount Vernon estate, North Belfast, 271
Mount Vernon UVF, the, 284, 292, 295
Mountbatten, Lord Louis, 154
Mowlam, Mo, 262–3
'Mr A', 97, 99, 122, 130, 160
Mulberry Harbour, 290
Mulholland, Patrick, 78
murals, 3, 4, 271, 286
Murdock, Jim, 16, 17
Murphy, Ciaran, 78–80
Murphy, Dervla, 118
Murphy, John, 97, 107, 116–17, 127, 129, 130, 132, 135–6, 160
Murphy, Lenny (Hugh Leonard), 62–3, 64, 113, 116, 131, 159–63, 165; death of, 163–4, 191; and the murder of Ted Pavis, 60–1, 65; and the Shankill Butchers, 97, 98, 99, 100, 103–4, 105–7, 115, 135
Murphy, Patrick, 79–80
Murray, Harry, 68

Murray, Leanne, 215
Murray, Mary, 104–5, 106, 107
Murray, Sean 'Spike', 226
Myers, Kevin, 56

Nairne, Pat, 46
National Front, the, 155
National Union of Journalists, the, 176
Needham, Richard, 255
Neeson, Cornelius, 117, 130
Nelson, Rose, 257, 258
Nelson, Sarah, 253
Nesbitt, DI Jimmy, 105, 106, 126, 127–9, 130, 132
Niblock, Robert, 149
NICRA (Northern Ireland Civil Rights Association), the, 35, 38
NIIRs (Northern Ireland Intelligence Report), 250, 253, 256
NILP (Northern Ireland Labour Party), 27, 139, 145, 147, 148, 330
NIO (Northern Ireland Office), the, 89, 134, 135, 163–4, 248, 255, 266
Norris, Bobby, 166–7, 169
North Belfast UVF, the, 4, 295, 296
North Queen Street RUC Station, 102
Northern Bank robbery, the, 297
Northern Ireland Assembly elections(1998), 265
Northern Ireland Select Committee, the, 314
Nugent, Malcolm, 203

Ó Conaill, Dáithí, 47, 49, 137
oath for UVF recruits, 25–6
objectives of, 75–6, 82, 92–3
O'Connell, Dr John, 47, 49
O'Doherty, Malachi, 232, 332

O'Donnell, Dwayne, 203
Official IRA, the, 70, 71, 92, 110, 111, 123, 297
O'Hanlon, John Patrick, 53
O'Hare, Patrick, 230
O'Loan, Nuala, 304
Omagh bombing, the, 281
Ombudsman's report into the death of Raymond McCord Junior, 304, 305, 306, 311
On Killing (book), 116
On the Run IRA members and a possible amnesty, 314
O'Neill, Ann, 72
O'Neill, Edward, 72
O'Neill, Terence, 10, 22, 34, 35, 36, 38, 310, 328
Operation Ballast (see Ombudsman's report into the killing of Raymond McCord Junior)
Operation Jigsaw, 90–1
Operation Motorman, 57–8, 326
O'Prey, Martin 'Rook', 188, 189–90
Orange Cross Social Club killings, February 1989, 189–91
Orange Order, the, 9–10, 13–14, 17, 26–7, 287, 297–8, 335; and the Drumcree stand-offs, 239–42, 243, 244, 245–6, 252–3
O'Raw, Brian, 265
Orde, Sir Hugh, 297
ordinary people caught up in paramilitary feuds, 273–4
Ormeau rally by Vanguard, 51, 52
Other View, The (magazine), 328–9
O'Toole, Fran, 87
outbreak of the Troubles, the, 38–9, 41
Overend, David, 148, 165
Oxford Street Bus Station bombings, 55–6

PAF (Protestant Action Force), the, xii, 180, 181, 185

Paisley, Rev. Ian, 17, 27–8, 55, 182, 183, 240, 243, 313, 328; religious fundamentalism of, 6, 14–15, 34–5, 38, 157; sectarianism of, 10–12, 92

Parachute Regiment of the British Army, the, 46, 154, 287

paranoia of Loyalist Protestants, the, 25, 34, 51, 218, 232

parliamentary debate on Unionist extremism, 31

Pavis, Ted, 58–61, 63, 65

'peace dividend,' the, 274–5, 319

peace process, the, 235, 244, 248, 256, 258, 259, 262–3, 265–6, 279–80, 319–20, 331, 336, 340

Peeples, Clifford, 266, 267

Phoblacht (Republican News), An (newspaper), 139, 200

Pickering, Rev John, 239–40

Pipe, The (codename), 291, 301, 302, 318

Place Apart, A (book), 118

poisoning of food in Dunnes Stores, 175

'police primacy' and Security Force policy, 133–4

policing in Catholic areas, 133

political issues in the mainland UK, 68

Pomeroy and Protestant militancy, 9, 10

Porter, Leslie, 28, 29, 32

Portora Royal School, Enniskillen, 21–2

power-sharing executive at Stormont, the, 66, 67

Press, Dr John, 70

Prevention of Terrorism Act (1976), the, 125, 166, 214

Principles of Loyalism, The (pamphlet), 278

Prior, Jim, 171

prison conditions, 141–4, 149–50, 158, 160, 174, 221–2

prisoner protests for political status, 142–3, 174

Pritchard, AA, 134–5

Professor, The, 289–91, 296

progressive loyalism, 308, 309

Progressive Loyalists and the Politics of Conflict Transformation (pamphlet), 309

Progressive Unionist Group, the, 148

proscription of the UVF, 31, 33

Protestant militancy and thinking, 9, 10, 13–14, 36–7

Protestant sectarianism, 11–12

Protestant working class and republicanism, the, 327–9

protests over the removal of the union flag on Belfast City Hall, 322–5, 328, 329

Province Executive Committee, the, 248, 249–50

Provisional IRA, the, 2–3, 5, 99, 122, 123, 175, 189, 196, 202, 248, 297, 299–300, 314, 330–1; and the assassination of key UVF members, 163, 164, 185–7, 188, 191, 329; attacks on buildings and infrastucture, 55–7, 244; attacks on the British Army, 98, 154, 287; bomb-making capabilities, 53, 74; British Army and UVF intelligence on, 110, 151–2, 193, 197, 199, 231; calls a unilateral ceasefire, 231–2; and changes in strategy, 152–4, 165, 172, 232; and decommissioning, 279–80, 298–9,

310, 311; and 'legitimate targets', 213–14; and secret talks with the UVF, 71, 137; and sectarian attacks, 44–5, 51, 54, 112, 215, 222; and talks with the British government, 47–50, 67, 218–19, 224

Provost Marshal section of the UVF, 93, 172, 192, 291

PSNI, the, 273, 297–8, 304–5, 311, 321–2, 326, 327, 329 (*see also* RUC, the)

psychological motive to kill a human being, the, 116

punishment beatings, 275–6, 289, 290, 295, 329

PUP (Progressive Unionist Party), 1, 148, 184, 203, 241, 244, 284, 311–12, 315, 333; and ceasefire talks, 4, 230, 235; electoral performances of, 2, 165, 258–9, 265; leadership of Billy Hutchinson, 320, 321, 325, 329, 330–2; and the peace process, 257, 258, 259, 263, 264, 265, 267; strategy after the Belfast Agreement, 293, 294, 296 (*see also* Mitchell, Billy)

Purvis, Dawn, 235, 236, 251, 263, 302, 315, 316–18

Quail, Markie, 272, 273, 277

Quinn, John, 203

Quinn, Thomas Patrick, 100–2, 107, 127

Rathcoole estate, North Belfast, 41, 93, 180, 200, 271–2, 274, 275

'Ray' (UVF volunteer), 95–6

Rea, Winston 'Winkie', 62, 315

reaction to the IRA ceasefire, 232–3

Reagan, Ronald, 173

reasons for the continued existence of loyalist paramilitaries, 339

reconciliation across a divided community, 7

Red Lion Pub bombing, 45

Redpath, Jackie, 202

Reed, Richard, 318

Rees, Merlyn, 47, 48, 49, 72, 92, 97, 142

regimental loyalty in the UVF, 92–3

Reid, Dessie, 18–19, 28, 32

Reid, Dr John, 287

Reid, DS James, 131

Reid, Fr. Alec, 202, 204, 230

religious fundamentalism and Protestant militarism, 36–7, 39 (*see also* Paisley, Rev. Ian)

Remembrance Sunday atrocity, Enniskillen, 191

reminiscences by former UVF prisoners, 341–4

Rennie, Katrina, 203

Republican concerns of a Protestant backlash, 48

residential segregation, 41–2

resources available to the RUC, 133

Rex bar shootings, the, 269

Reynolds, Albert, 257

RHC (Red Hand Commando), the, 50, 62, 68, 81, 145, 147, 148, 165, 190, 293, 298, 312, 313, 315

Rice, Bertie, 273

Rice, Francis, 103–4, 127, 130

RIR (Royal Irish Regiment), the, 266

Robb, Lindsay, 245–6, 252

robberies for weapons, 62, 75

Roberts, Tom, 310, 311, 312, 313, 314–15

Robinson, Brian, 195–7, 228, 269

Robinson, 'Buck Alec', 289

Robinson, Margaret, 196

Robinson, Peter, 182, 218–19
Robinson, Sammy, 26
Rooney, John, 62
Royal Black Preceptory, the, 27
Royal British Legion, the, 85, 89, 108, 138, 287
Royal Ulster Rifles, the, 21
RUC, the, 11, 13, 14, 86, 88, 114, 169–70, 189, 198, 265, 266, 290; combatting of loyalist paramilitary organisations, 25, 32–4, 66–7, 134–5, 208, 216, 249, 255; discovery of arms dumps, 85, 199–200; and the Drumcree stand-off, 240, 241; and forensics, 32, 80, 100–1, 104, 105–6; and the 'Glennane gang', 73, 89; infiltration of the UVF, 159, 167, 194–5, 198, 271; and intelligence, 44, 192; and interrogations, 90–1, 106, 108, 126–32, 166, 183, 194; and Lennie Murphy, 60, 65, 102–3, 105–7; reaction to the IRA/UVF ceasefires, 237–8; resources of, 102, 133, 134; responsibility for security policy with the British Army, 45–6, 133–5 (see also Special Branch (RUC), the)
rural/urban divide within the UVF, 242, 247–8

sabotage of weapons, 228
Sands, Bobby, 41
Sandy Row pub bombings, 44
SAS, the, 195–6
Sayers, Jack, 34
Sayers, Norman, 27, 99, 234, 288
Scappaticci, Freddie, 41
Scotland Yard, 38
Scott, DS John, 128–9
Scullion, John Patrick, 23–4, 33

SDLP, the, 47, 67, 145, 332
Seagal, Steve, 226
Seawright, George, 163, 188
secret meeting between the UVF and the Provisional IRA, 71, 137
secret meetings between the British government and the IRA, 47–50, 218–19, 224
secret societies, 9
sectarian divide since the peace process, the, 331–2, 340
sectarian reprisals, 44–5, 53, 62, 189–91, 203, 214, 216, 222, 225–6, 229–30; and the Chlorane Bar massacre, 112–15, 337; perceived as defensive retaliation, 37, 76
Security Forces assessment of Protestant resentment, 52–3
Security Policy Meeting, january 1984, 171
sense of deflation in the Protestant community, 336
September 11 terrorst attacks, the, 281
Seymour, Robert 'Squeak', 191
Shankill Butchers, the, 97–100, 102, 103–5, 107, 116, 117–25, 133, 134, 135–6, 163, 191, 336–7; interrogation at Castlereagh, 126–32
Shankill Mirror (newspaper), 328
Shankill Road UVF, the, 26–7, 66, 94, 99
Shaw, Noel 'Nogi', 98–9
Sheppard, Thomas, 284
shooting at shop in Crimea Street, 28–9
Simpson, Alan, 163
Sinn Féin, 165, 208, 224, 240, 244, 257, 279, 314, 325, 328, 329
Sissons, Peter, 244

'Six Principles', the, 233, 236
Slane, John, 265
Sloan, Geordie, 83, 84, 85
Smith, William 'Plum', 62, 81, 142, 203, 233, 293
Smyth, Brian, 161–2
Smyth, Hugh, 27, 76, 99–100, 148, 165, 258, 259, 263, 315
Smyth, Jimmy, 27
Snoddon, Martin, 146, 157
social issues for working-class Unionists, 147–8
SOCO (Scenes of Crime Officer) examinations, 100–1
SOCPA (Serious and Organised Crime Police Act (2005), 305
soft-targeting by the Provisional IRA, 152–4
Somerville, John James, 88
Somerville, William Wesley, 88, 176
Special Branch (RUC), the, 38, 45, 162–3, 164, 185, 189, 194, 208, 249, 252, 255–6, 271, 305
Special Category Status of prisoners, 142–3, 156, 174, 201
Special Powers Act, the, 65
Spence, Augustus Andrew 'Gusty', 28, 29, 34, 43, 65, 94, 157, 203, 220, 266, 307–8, 312, 315, 316; death of, 320; dictum on targeting republicans, 30, 77; and the future role of the UVF, 309, 310; joins the UVF, 21, 22; and the murder of Peter Ward, 30, 32, 33, 320; oath and initiation for new recruits commander, 25–6; and the PUP, 148, 203, 267; and regime of discipline in Long Kesh, 137, 140, 141–2, 143, 144–5, 147, 237; and the UVF ceasefire, 233, 234, 235, 307

Spence, Billy, 21
SPG (Special Patrol Group) of the RUC, 89, 114–15
Spring, Dick, 221
Springfield Inter-Community Development Project, the, 231
St Andrews Agreement, the, 313
Standard Bar, Shankill Road, 26, 28, 85
Stewart, Leonard, 79
Stewart, Rev John, 57
Stewart, Roy, 98–9
Stewart, Tommy, 163, 254
Stockdale, William, 125
Stockman, Harry, Snr, 27, 99
Stone, Michael, 260, 263
Storey, Bobby, 4
Strathearn, William, 89, 176
Sunday Times, The (newspaper), 255
Sunday World (newspaper), 176, 293
Sunningdale Agreement, the, 68
supergrass system, the, 167–72, 180, 181, 185, 188
surveillance, 208, 216, 217, 238, 262, 290
suspension of Stormont, the, 49, 51, 54
Sutcliffe, Peter, 133
Swift, Alan, 153

TA (Territorial Army), 75, 287
TARA, 37, 38, 39
targeting of off-duty RUC and UDR personnel, 152–3
Tawney, RH, 147
Templeton, Rev David, 265
Thatcher, Margaret, 181, 182
Thompson, George, 32
three demands of the Provisional IRA, 48, 49
Times, The (newspaper), 51, 71

training, 85
Trainor, Edmund, 265
Travers, Mary, 201
Travers, Stephen, 87
Trimble, David, 240, 243, 258, 264
Troubles, the, 2–3, 224–5, 314
Turf Lodge, West Belfast, 119
Twain, Mark, 339
Twomey, Seamus, 137
Tyrie, Andy, 68, 81, 91

UCDC (Ulster Constitution Defence
    Committee), the, 15, 16–17
UDA, the, 80, 125–6, 163, 164, 198,
    210, 215, 277, 281, 288, 293, 324;
    abduction and murder of Douglas
    and McVeigh, 82–4, 89–91, 109,
    111, 112, 180, 303; and Andy
    Tyrie, 68, 81; and Billy Wright
    and the LVF, 250, 251, 256, 278,
    279; feud with the UVF, 90, 91,
    93, 94–5, 118–19, 270–2, 273,
    274, 278, 307; nature of, 52, 212,
    255; and sectarian reprisals, 44–5,
    53, 54, 265
UDR (Ulster Defence Regiment), the,
    62, 73, 75, 85, 152–3
UFF (Ulster Freedom Fighters), the,
    125, 126, 208, 210, 260, 269, 272,
    273, 277
UK Unionist Party, 258, 265
ULF (Ulster Loyalist Front), the,
    138–9
Ulster Democratic Party, the, 241
Ulster Solemn League and Covenant,
    the, 278
Ulster TAVR, the, 46
Ulster Tower monument, Ypres, 287
unilateral ceasefire, April 1991, 204
union flag on Belfast City Hall,
    321–2

Unionists goading loyalists to attack
    liberal politicians, 321
United Irishmen, the, 9–10
UOP (*Urzad Ochrony Panstwa*), 217,
    218
UPA (Ulster Protestant Action), 10
UPA (Ulster Protestant Association),
    the, 289–90
UPV (Ulster Protestant Volunteers),
    the, 16, 17–18, 35–6
Urban, Mark, 219
UUP (Ulster Unionist Party), the, 12,
    27, 67, 258, 259, 332
UVF, the, 7, 31, 34, 39, 50, 58, 111–
    12, 115, 116, 176, 191, 202, 218,
    242, 244, 260, 324, 326–7, 336–7;
    adopts non-military civilian role,
    307, 309–10, 312, 313, 331, 334;
    attacks, 29, 35–6, 42–4, 45; B
    Company, Woodvale, 191–2, 195–
    6, 199, 226, 229; bomb-making
    skills, 74, 76; chances of an return
    to militarism, 334; characteristics
    and initiation of recruits, 21,
    25–6, 27, 28–9, 43, 74, 77, 84–5,
    92–3, 95–6; and criminality, 175,
    252, 293, 296–7, 316, 327, 329;
    decommissions its weapons,
    315–16; differences with the
    Mid Ulster UVF, 250, 251, 252,
    253–4; and the EACTF, 301–2;
    and the failure to decommission
    arms, 310–11; feigned attacks,
    15; feud with the LVF and UFF,
    269, 277, 279, 318; feud with
    the UDA, 90, 91, 93, 94–5,
    118–19, 270–1, 272, 273, 274,
    278, 307; growth of, 35, 62, 92;
    impact on from the loss of Brian
    Robinson, 196–7; infiltration of,
    264, 305, 311; and intelligence

gathering, 193, 197, 199; and internal discipline, 85, 93–4, 95, 107, 116, 131, 159, 162, 172, 183, 219, 234, 249, 275–6, 295, 313, 314, 317–19; internal feuds, 98–100, 253–4, 267–8, 281–4; internal investigations into drug dealing and informers, 288–9, 291–2, 304–5; and mistrust of the English, 138; and moves towards a ceasefire, 230, 231, 233, 234–5, 236–7; operational planning and strategy, 77, 93, 96–8, 183–4, 187, 192–3, 194, 195, 200–1, 204–5, 206–8, 223, 267, 292, 293–5, 298; and political awakening, 57, 66, 71, 72, 138–40, 144–7, 173–4, 184, 203–4; and prison regime, 141, 142–4, 149, 165, 174–5, 184, 221–2, 260, 286; reasons for its continued existence, 338, 339, 340; reasons for joining, 4–5, 6, 37, 39, 56, 67, 75, 92, 182–3, 214–15, 216, 222–3, 224, 276, 286, 316, 332–3, 340–1; strategy to deter a return to violence, 327, 329, 334; structure of, xi-xii, 65–6, 141–2, 168, 191–3, 210, 233–4, 236, 292–3, 318–19; support for PUP talks in the peace process, 258, 265, 280; targeting of IRA members, 199–200, 202–3, 207, 208, 210–11, 225, 226–7; as a threat to the South, 299–300

UWC (Ulster Workers' Council), the, 68

Vanguard movement, the, 48, 51, 52
Villiers, Theresa, 324
violence and its roots in the paramilitary sub-culture, 319

violence since the 1994 ceasefire, 2
volunteer groups across Ulster, 20
VUPP (Vanguard Unionist Progressive Party),the, 57

Waller, Archie, 97, 98
Waller, Ronald, 62–3
War or Peace? Conflict or Conference? (UVF document), 184
Ward, Peter, 30, 31, 33, 34, 320
Warnock, Rab, 4, 277, 286–9, 291–2, 294, 303
Warrenpoint bombings of the British Army Parachute Regiment, 154, 287
Watson, Charlie, 188
Waugh, Norman, 98–9
weapons and explosives knowledge of UVF members, 74–5, 290
Weir, John, 73, 89
Wheeler, Sir Roger, 237
White, John, 125, 164
Whitelaw, William, 67, 142
Whiterock parade, the, 29–30
William of Orange, 18, 335
Williamson, George, 215
Williamson, Gillian, 215
Williamson, Robert, 30–1
Wilson, DI John, 109–11, 112
Wilson, Harold, 31, 47, 48, 49
Wilson, Paddy, 125
Wilson, Sammy, 245, 246–7
World War I commemorations, 277, 285–6, 332
Wright, Billy, 157–9, 165, 246, 249–51, 254–6, 257–8, 266, 319; assassination attempts on, 225, 256–7; assassination by the INLA, 259–62, 268; conversion to Christianity, 166, 172–3, 200, 239; differences the UVF

leadership, 249–51; imprisonment of, 158, 159, 172; influence at the Drumcree stand-offs, 240, 241–4, 264; Johnny Adair on, 208–12, 242; and the Mid Ulster UVF, 159, 200, 203, 206–10, 247–8, 252, 254, 256; relations with Billy Hutchinson, 252, 258; status as local figure in Portadown, 205–6, 255; UVF ceasefire and the peace process, 234–6, 238 (*see also* LVF (Loyalist Volunteer Force), the)

Wright, Jim, 158

YCVs (Young Citizens Volunteers), 96, 227, 245

Yeats, William Butler, 281

36th Ulster Division, the, 286

103 Club, the, 230